THE DEVELOPMENT
OF COGNITION

Steve Croker

※ CENGAGE
Learning·

Australia • Brazil • Japan • Korea • Mexico • Singapore • Spain • United Kingdom • United States

The Development of Cognition

Steve Croker

Publishing Director: Linden Harris

Publisher: Brendan George

Development Editor: Annabel Ainscow

Editorial Assistant: Lauren Darby

Production Editor: Lucy Arthy

Production Controller: Eyvett Davis

Typesetter: Cenveo Publisher Services

Cover design: Adam Renvoize

For product information and technology assistance, contact **emea.info@cengage.com**.

For permission to use material from this text or product, and for permission queries, email **emea.permissions@cengage.com**.

British Library Cataloguing-in-Publication Data
A catalogue record for this book is available from the British Library.

ISBN: 978-1-4080-0777-8

Cengage Learning EMEA
Cheriton House, North Way, Andover, Hampshire, SP10 5BE United Kingdom

Cengage Learning products are represented in Canada by Nelson Education Ltd.

For your lifelong learning solutions, visit **www.cengage.co.uk**

Purchase your next print book, e-book or e-chapter at **www.cengagebrain.com**

Printed in China by RR Donnelley
1 2 3 4 5 6 7 8 9 10 – 14 13 12

Brief **contents**

Contents

About the Author

Steve Croker is Assistant Professor of Psychology at Illinois State University. After a childhood and adolescence spent in Reading, he moved to Nottingham to attend Nottingham Trent University, where he received a BSc in Communication Studies. He then pursued an MSc in Intelligent Systems and a PhD in Psychology at the University of Nottingham. Dr. Croker held the positions of Senior Lecturer and Assistant Head of Psychology at the University of Derby before relocating to the USA in 2009. Over the last decade he has taught courses in many different areas of psychology, including psychology skills, introductory psychology, educational psychology, cognitive science and cognitive development. Dr. Croker's research interests focus on cognitive and developmental psychology. In particular, he is interested the development of scientific thinking and reasoning in adults and children, and the interaction between domain-general reasoning processes and domain-specific knowledge.

To Corinne

Acknowledgements

I started writing this book in the UK, whilst I was working at the University of Derby. I finished writing it in the US, at Illinois State University. I would like to thank my colleagues at both institutions for making life fun and intellectually stimulating. Special thanks go to my friends and collaborators who I have worked with on cognitive developmental research: Heather Buchanan, Rebecca Knibb, Frankie Maratos, Miles Richardson and Corinne Zimmerman. I would also like to thank the many students I have taught and worked with over the last decade. Many thanks go to the reviewers who provided excellent feedback on draft versions of this book, and to all the people at Cengage Learning who have been involved in this project. Extra special thanks go to Sally Mortimore, without whose persistence this book would never have been written. I would like to thank my family for their role in my own cognitive development. Finally, I thank Corinne for her limitless help, patience and support throughout the writing of this book.

Preface

My aim in writing this book was to provide a textbook that can be used as the main text for post-introductory cognitive development courses. Whilst there are many developmental psychology books on the market, the majority are aimed at introductory courses. Although there are a few excellent books with a focus on cognitive development aimed at students taking advanced undergraduate or graduate classes, I was never satisfied with any one book as a main text for the third year Developmental Cognition course I taught at the University of Derby for many years. This was not due to the level or quality of the available books, but rather because none of them covered all the topics I wanted to see present in such a book. For example, I have found that students are keen to learn about atypical cognitive development (autism in particular), yet this is generally not covered in cognitive development textbooks, even though this subject's popularity has been clearly reflected in journal articles and conference presentations over recent years. This textbook also includes a chapter on the computational modeling, a key technique within cognitive science that has seen increasing use within developmental psychology, but is almost always entirely neglected in textbooks.

This book is structured thematically such that the chapters can easily map onto a lecture series. This could be a 10-12 week course, commonly found in European universities, but instructors could also base longer or shorter courses around the book, either by omitting some topics or by devoting two weeks to selected topics. As well as providing a structure for such courses, my aims include assisting lecturers with course preparation by providing extra pedagogic features such as downloadable presentations, and assisting students in identifying and interpreting relevant primary sources. For example, each chapter opens with a discussion of a classic study in cognitive development, including figures or tables illustrating the design and/or results. I have also provided a selective reading list at the end of each chapter, including a few books, book chapters and journal articles. Some of the readings on these lists were chosen because they offer an accessible overview of the topic at hand, some were chosen because they are classic empirical papers and some were chosen for a more contemporary analysis of relevant issues. The discussion questions presented at the end of each chapter can be used by lecturers as formative or summative essay questions, or to frame in-class discussions. Alternatively, the questions could be used by students as a review guide to check their understanding of the material.

In writing this book, I undertook a very enjoyable expedition through the last few decades of cognitive developmental theory and research. In doing so, I came across many new ideas, and came to appreciate some older ideas more fully. I hope you learn at least as much as I have!

Steve Croker
Normal, Illinois
September 2011

Walk Through Tour

Chapter 1

Introduction: Cognitive development, themes and theories

Learning Outcomes

At the end of this chapter you should be able to:

- Understand what cognitive development is and why we study it.
- Describe some of the important issues and themes in cognitive developmental psychology.
- Discuss different theories of cognitive development.

Learning Outcomes appear at the start of each chapter to help you monitor your understanding and progress through each chapter.

Questions appear helpfully throughout every chapter to encourage knowledge retention.

Box features appear in every chapter, providing a focus on key issues in cognitive development.

Glossary definitions appear in the margins throughout, with the according key words emboldened in the text.

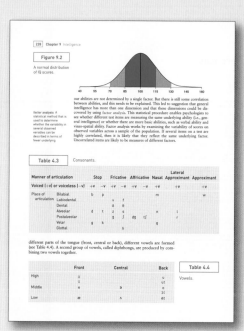

Figures and Tables appear throughout the chapters, providing invaluable visual aids to learning.

Summary each chapter ends with a comprehensive summary that provides a thorough recap of the issues in each chapter, helping you to assess your understanding and revise key content.

Discussion Questions at the end of each chapter can be used by lecturers as formative or summative essay questions, or to frame in-class discussions.

Further Reading a selective and very useful reading list is included at the end of each chapter, including a few books, book chapters and journal articles.

Accommodation One of two aspects of Piaget's concept of adaptation. Accommodation is the process by which cognitive structures are modified or created as a result of new experiences which do not fit into current structures.

Adaptation The process, described by Piaget, by which children meet environmental demands through the modification of cognitive structures by assimilation or accommodation.

Affordances Features of the environment that provide opportunities for a particular action.

Analogical reasoning A type of reasoning that involves finding correspondences between new and old problems in order to transfer knowledge from the old problem to the new one.

Aphasia A disorder in which language comprehension and/or production are affected as a result of brain damage.

Appearance-reality task Task in which an item has an appearance which conflicts with what it really is (e.g., a sponge that looks like a rock or a candle that looks like an apple). The aim of the task is to see whether children can hold two different representations of the same object.

Assimilation One of two aspect of Piaget's concept of adaptation. Assimilation is the process by which new experiences are incorporated into existing conceptual structures.

Attention deficit hyperactivity disorder (ADHD) A disorder characterized by hyperactive-impulsive and/or inattentive behaviour.

Autism A developmental disorder characterized by a triad of impairments in socialization, communication and imaginative or symbolic play.

Autobiographical memory Memory for episodes from one's personal life.

Cardinal number A number that refers to the quantity of items in a set.

Cognitive/computational model A simulation of cognitive processes instantiated in a computer program.

Cohort design A research design in which two or more groups of children who were born in different years are compared at the same age.

Conditioned head rotation A procedure in which responses in the form of orientation towards stimuli are reinforced.

Connectionist models Also known as neural networks. A cognitive model in which knowledge is stored as a pattern of connection weights between two or more layers of units.

Conservation The ability to understand that a quantity remains the same after a physical transformation.

Constructivist A theoretical position in which it is argued that meaning, in the form of mental representations, is constructed through interactions with the environment.

Control of variables strategy A domain-general strategy in which unconfounded experiments are designed such that valid causal inferences can be made. For example, designing a series of experiments in which only one variable is manipulated at a time enables one to determine which variables have an effect on the outcome.

Critical period hypothesis The idea that there is a window of time in the first few years of life in which exposure to language is necessary for normal linguistic development to occur.

Cross-sectional design A research design in which two or more groups of children of different ages are compared.

Deceptive box task Task in which the contents of a box differ from what would be expected to be in it. Children are asked what someone else will think is in the box in order to determine whether they can (a) understand that another person can hold a false belief and (b) understand their own initial false belief.

Declarative memory Conscious memory for facts (semantic memory) and events (episodic memory).

Deductive reasoning Reasoning in which a specific, logically valid, conclusion can be drawn from more general premises.

346

Abell, F., Krams, M., Ashburner, J., Passingham, R., Friston, K. J., Frackowiak, R., Happé, F., Frith, C. D. and Frith, U. (1999). The neuroanatomy of autism: A voxel-based whole brain analysis of structural MRI scans in high functioning individuals. *NeuroReport, 10*, 1647–1651.

Adams, M. (1990). *Beginning to read: Thinking and learning about print.* Cambridge, MA: MIT Press.

Adams, M. J., Treiman, R. and Pressley, M. (1998). Reading, writing, and literacy. In I. Sigel and A. Renninger (Eds), *Handbook of child psychology, Volume 4: Child psychology in practice* (pp. 275–355). New York: Wiley.

Adams, R. J. and Courage, M. L. (1995). Development of chromatic discrimination in early infancy. *Behavioural Brain Research, 67*, 99–101.

Addis, D. R., Pan, L., Vu, M. A., Laiser, N. and Schacter, D. L. (2009). Constructive episodic simulation of the future and the past: Distinct subsystems of a core brain network mediate imagining and remembering. *Neuropsychologia, 47*, 2222–2238.

Addis, D. R., Wong, A. T. and Schacter, D. L. (2007). Remembering the past and imagining the future: common and distinct neural substrates during event construction and elaboration. *Neuropsychologia, 45*, 1363–1377.

Adrian, J. A., Alegria, J. and Morais, J. (1995). Metaphonological abilities of Spanish illiterate adults. *International Journal of Psychology, 30*(3), 329–353.

Aguiar, A. and Baillargeon, R. (1998). 8.5-month-old infants' reasoning about containment events. *Child Development, 69*, 636–653.

Aguiar, A. and Baillargeon, R. (1999). 2.5-month-old infants' reasoning about when objects should and should not be occluded. *Cognitive Psychology, 39*, 116–157.

Aguiar, A. and Baillargeon, R. (2003). Perseverative responding in a violation-of-expectation task in 6.5-month-old infants. *Cognition, 88*(3), 277–316.

Aitchison, J. (2008). *The articulate mammal: An introduction to psycholinguistics.* Abingdon: Routledge.

Alcock, K. L., Ngorosho, D., Deus, C. and Jukes, M. C. H. (2010). We don't have language at our house: Disentangling the relationship between phonological awareness, schooling, and literacy. *British Journal of Educational Psychology, 80*, 55–76.

American Psychiatric Association. (1987). *Diagnostic and statistical manual of mental disorders* (3rd ed., revised). Washington, DC: American Psychiatric Association.

American Psychiatric Association. (2000). *Diagnostic and statistical manual of mental disorders* (4th ed., text revision). Washington, DC: American Psychiatric Association.

Amsel, E. and Brock, S. (1996). The development of evidence evaluation skills. *Cognitive Development, 11*(4), 523–550.

Anderson, J. E. (1939). The limitations of infant and preschool tests in the measurement of intelligence. *Journal of Psychology, 8*, 351–379.

Anderson, M. (1992). *Intelligence and development: A cognitive theory.* Oxford: Blackwell.

Anderson, M. (1999). Project development – the shape of things to come. In M. Anderson (Ed.), *The development of intelligence* (pp. 3–15). Hove: Psychology Press.

Anderson, M. (2005). Marrying intelligence and cognition: A developmental view. In R. J. Sternberg and J. E. Pretz (Eds), *Cognition and intelligence: Identifying the mechanisms of the mind* (pp. 268–287). New York: Cambridge University Press.

Apperly, I. A., Samson, D. and Humphreys, G. W. (2005). Domain-specificity and theory of mind: evaluating neuropsychological evidence. *Trends in Cognitive Sciences, 9*(12), 572–577.

Apperly, I. A., Samson, D., Chiavarino, C. and Humphreys, G. W. (2004). Frontal and temporo-parietal lobe contribution to theory of mind: Neuropsychological evidence from a false belief task with reduced language and executive demands. *Journal of Cognitive Neuroscience, 16*(10), 1773–1784.

Aristotle. (2007). *Prior analytica* (A. J. Jenkinson, Trans.). Adelaide, Australia: eBooks@Adelaide. Retrieved from http://ebooks.adelaide.edu.au/a/aristotle/a8/pra/index.html (Original work published approx. 350 BCE).

Arterberry, M. E. (2008). Infants' sensitivity to the depth cue of height-in-the-picture plane. *Infancy, 13*, 544–555.

Arterberry, M. E., Yonas, A. and Bensen, A. (1989). Self-produced locomotion and the development of responsiveness to linear perspective and texture gradients. *Developmental Psychology, 25*, 976–982.

Ashcraft, M. H. (1995). Cognitive psychology and simple arithmetic: A review and summary of new directions. *Mathematical Cognition, 1*, 3–34.

Aslin, R. N. (1981). Development of smooth pursuit in human infants. In D. F. Fisher, R. A. Monty and J. W. Senders (Eds), *Eye movements: Cognition and visual*

312

Glossary a complete glossary is helpfully compiled at the back of the book.

References extremely comprehensive references are included at the back of the book.

DIGITAL SUPPORT RESOURCES

Dedicated Instructor Website

To discover the dedicated digital support resources accompanying this textbook please register here for access: **http://login.cengage.com**

Resources include:

- Instructor's Manual
- ExamView Testbank
- PowerPoint Slides

Cengage Learning's CourseMate™ brings course concepts to life with interactive learning, study, and exam preparation tools that support the printed textbook. Make the most of your study time by accessing everything you need to succeed in one place. With CourseMate™ you can read your textbook, take notes, review flashcards, and take practice quizzes. CourseMate™ goes beyond the book to deliver what you need!

Interactive Teaching and Learning Tools

CourseMate™ offers a range of interactive learning tools tailored to *The Development of Cognition*, including:

- Quizzes
- Flashcards
- Videos
- Games
- Links to useful websites
- And much more . . .

Interactive eBook

In addition to interactive learning tools, CourseMate™ also includes an interactive eBook. You can take notes, highlight, search and interact with embedded media specific to your book.

Engagement Tracker (Lecturer access only)

Lecturers can use the integrated Engagement Tracker in CourseMate™ to assess students' preparation and engagement. The tracking tool can be used to monitor progress of the class as a whole or for individual students.

Accessing CourseMate™

- Students can access CourseMate™ using the unique personal access card included in the front of the book.
- Instructors can access CourseMate™ by registering at **http://login.cengage.com** or by speaking to their local Cengage Learning representative.
- A CourseMate™ demo is available at: **www.cengage.com/coursemate**

© Losevsky Pavel/Shutterstock

Chapter 1

Introduction: Cognitive development, themes and theories

Learning Outcomes

At the end of this chapter you should be able to:

- Understand what cognitive development is and why we study it.

- Describe some of the important issues and themes in cognitive developmental psychology.

- Discuss different theories of cognitive development.

In one of the most famous studies on the development of children's thought, Jean Piaget (1952a) demonstrated that, prior to the age of 7 or 8, children think in an intuitive rather than a logical, or rational, manner. In one task, children aged from 4 to 7 years were presented with two identical glasses of orangeade (glass A1 and glass A2) and asked whether there was the same amount of drink in each glass. All the children replied that the two glasses held the same amount of drink. The contents of one of the two glasses was then poured into one or more glasses that differed in size from the original glasses, such as two smaller glasses (B1 and B2) or one thinner glass (C). The children were then asked which of the glasses contained the most drink. In some cases this meant making a comparison between glass A1 and glasses B1 and B2, in others the comparison was between A and C. Most children under the age of 7 stated the drinks were no longer equal once the second drink had been poured out of glass A2. One of the children discussed by Piaget, when comparing A1 with B1 and B2, argued that there was more drink in A1. Another child answered that there was more in B1 and B2 than in A1. Later on, when shown a different comparison, the same child stated that there was more in C (the thin glass) than in A1 (the wide glass).

> Q. Why do you think the children thought there was more or less drink after the drink had been poured from A2 to B1 and B2? What about when it was poured from A2 to C?

Children aged 7 and older were less likely to make these mistakes. They knew that the amount of liquid remained the same, regardless of the number of glasses, or shape of the glasses, containing it. They also knew that if one glass started off with more liquid, there would continue to be more when it was poured into different glasses. When the younger children were asked to compare glass A1 with glasses B1 and B2, they made two errors. They either claimed that there was less in B1 and B2 because the level of the liquid was lower than in A1, or they claimed there was more drink in B1 and B2, because there were more glasses. When asked to compare A1 with C, they made the mistake of thinking that C had more liquid because the level was higher.

> Q. What is the difference between the younger children and the older children?

The older children were capable of seeing that the level of the liquid alone does not indicate the quantity of water. They could also tell that if a wide glass and a thin glass both had the same level of liquid there was less in the thin glass. The younger children relied on simple perceptual clues as to the quantity of liquid. A glass with a higher level *looks* as though it contains more liquid, if that is the only dimension that is taken into account. According to Piaget, the difference between younger and older children is not just that the older children make more sophisticated perceptual judgements. The older children come to know that, logically, the glasses cannot contain different quantities. Nothing has been added to the quantity, nor taken away from the quantity; it has merely been transformed into a new shape. Piaget (1968) referred to this new concept as **conservation**, which he defined as 'the invariance of a characteristic despite *transformations* of the object or of a collection of objects possessing this characteristic' (p. 978). Piaget claimed that the ability to conserve develops during the third stage of cognitive development, the concrete operations stage, which occurs between the ages of 7 and 11 years. Prior to this, children are in the pre-operational stage (2 to 7 years), and do not yet think logically.

conservation The ability to understand that a quantity remains the same after a physical transformation.

As well as studying the development of conservation of liquid, or continuous quantity, Piaget (1952a; Piaget and Inhelder, 1974) also studied conservation of number, mass (or substance), weight and volume. Figure 1.1 illustrates the conservation of number, mass and liquid tasks. In each case, children are asked whether the two items are the same or if there is more of one than the other. Once they have confirmed that the two rows of buttons, balls of clay, or glasses of liquid are the same, one of the pair is transformed to make it appear longer/taller. The children are then asked whether the two items are the same or different. The children Piaget studied developed conservation of liquid, number and mass at around 7 to 8 years of age, but he found that children do not discover conservation of weight until 9 or 10 years, and it is not until 11 or 12 years that they develop conservation of volume, which Piaget assessed by using tasks in which objects are put in water so as to displace some of the liquid, thus making the level higher.

Figure 1.1

Three conservation tasks.

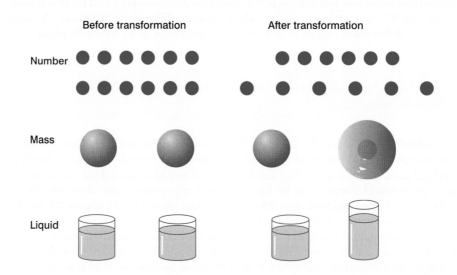

Following on from Piaget's studies, research by other psychologists has demonstrated that children in the pre-operational stage *are* able to pass conservation tasks when modifications are made to the experiments. Winer (1974) found that 4-year-olds could conserve numbers when presented with rows of just two or three items, although they did not do so well on larger sets. Rose and Blank (1974) hypothesized that the reason children usually say there is more on the second trial of the number conservation task (after one of the rows has been spread out) is because, having already given the answer that both rows are the same, they take the second question as a cue that they should change their answer. To test this hypothesis, they gave some participants a version of the task in which they saw the original, equal, arrangement of two rows and then watched the transformation *before* they were asked to make a judgement. Rose and Blank found that 6-year-olds were less likely to make errors on the modified task than when given the standard version of the task. McGarrigle and Donaldson (1974) came up with a very clever way of assessing whether the deliberate alteration of one of the rows by the experimenter cued children into the assumption that a change in number had occurred. They presented 4- to 6-year-olds with the standard version of the task, in which the experimenter requests a judgement, spreads out one of the rows, and then asks for a second judgement, and also with a modified version of the task in which the transformation of one of the rows occurred 'accidentally'. In the accidental condition, a naughty teddy bear (introduced to the participants at the beginning of the experiment) was moved towards the rows of counters while the experimenter said 'It's naughty teddy! Oh! Look out, he's going to spoil the game'. The teddy was then moved so that he disarranged one of the rows. McGarrigle and Donaldson found that children made the correct judgement that the rows contained the same number of counters more often in the accidental condition than in the standard version of the task.

I have picked the topic of conservation as an introduction to this book as it illustrates many of the issues that cognitive developmental psychologists are interested in, such as what children know and don't know, what their intellectual abilities are and how their knowledge and rational ability changes over time. The researchers who followed Piaget were interested in clarifying the results of the original studies, by examining the conditions under which children pass and fail conservation tasks. Some of these studies also demonstrated that how psychological research is done can be important. They showed that factors such as the setting in which children's knowledge is assessed, and the cues that may be given by an experimenter, can have an effect on how children respond. In this introductory chapter, I will outline some of the themes raised by the research of conservation, for example why we may be interested in studying the development of cognition and how we go about studying it. I will introduce some of the issues that are prominent in the field, such as whether there are distinct stages in development, and some of the theoretical perspectives taken by cognitive developmentalists.

What is cognitive development and why should you study it?

The study of cognitive development is the study of the development of cognitive processes such as thinking, reasoning, memory, perception, theory of mind and language. It is also about the investigation of the acquisition of knowledge, mainly in children. In studying cognitive development, we are interested in the content of a knowledge domain. By a domain, we mean an area of cognitive knowledge, such as perception or language. Many researchers focus on just one or two domains, although some – Piaget, for example – have studied many different domains. One of the basic questions we attempt to answer is: What do children know at different ages? For example, many studies have demonstrated that children can perceive depth by the time they are 5 or 6 months old; we will cover this in Chapter 2. Psychologists have also found that at about 4 years of age, children come to 'know' that other people have thoughts or knowledge that can differ from their own; this is known as having a **theory of mind**, and will be covered in Chapter 5. Piaget's research led him to conclude that children are not able to conserve quantities until they are around 7. These facts are, of course, interesting in and of themselves. However, understanding what children know, and what skills they have at different ages, doesn't tell us how they think or how they acquire knowledge. So we need to investigate two other things: the structure of children's knowledge and the processes by which knowledge and skills are acquired.

theory of mind An understanding that people have minds and, via the attribution of mental states such as thinking, knowing and believing, that others may have mental states that differ to our own.

The structure and acquisition of knowledge

By the structure of children's knowledge, we mean how knowledge is represented in the mind, and how these representations change over time. One of the main issues concerns whether the structure of knowledge changes *qualitatively* over time. Are there stages of development, as suggested by Piaget, in which the nature of children's knowledge is transformed quite radically from one stage to the next? Or is development better characterized by a sequence of small changes, by which our knowledge gradually changes, as argued by information-processing theorists? If we take conservation as an example, what is the difference in children's knowledge between the age at which they do not see that the quantities are the same, and the age at which they pass the task? Is there a qualitative change in the way knowledge is structured in the child's mind, or is the difference a result of the gradual acquisition of new knowledge about the world? We need answers to these questions in order for us to build a picture of how children think and how their cognition develops. With respect to the acquisition of knowledge, there are several further questions we can ask.

- How do children gain knowledge from the environment?
- How do they store and organize knowledge?
- How do they reorganize knowledge to generate new knowledge and regulate their actions?
- How does new knowledge change prior knowledge?
- How does acquisition affect development?

To continue with the example of conservation, we need to find out what processes have occurred which have added to children's knowledge. Do they, for instance, acquire knowledge about mass, number and liquid separately, or do they acquire a more general concept of conservation? Do they learn from experience with the physical world, or do they use a growing ability to reason logically? Does the acquisition of conservation depend on advances in general intelligence? This is where theory comes in. We can carry out an experiment and use the results to describe the behaviour of children. We can then make assumptions about children's knowledge, but we need a theory to investigate the processes of knowledge acquisition and structure of knowledge. Without a theory, we are just fumbling amongst experimental data, we cannot ascertain how or why children produce the behaviours they do.

Why do we study cognitive development?

There are a number of reasons why we might be interested in cognitive development. First, there are theoretical reasons. We might be interested in epistemology – the study of knowledge. We might want to know what knowledge is and where it comes from. This is a philosophical question, but it can be addressed by looking at development. We might be interested in evolution because we are interested in how human cognition evolved. It may be that by examining the development of the individual, we can gain some insight into the development of cognition within the human species. Or, we may want to enrich our understanding of adult cognition by looking at how cognitive processes develop. Perhaps we choose to study cognitive development simply because we want to. Studying any topic for its own sake is a perfectly good reason!

Second, there are practical reasons. We may want to apply the results of research to facilitating children's mental growth. To this end we may be interested in evaluating the impact of television, books and computer games on cognitive development. We may want to inform educational practice, or we may be interested in the diagnosis and treatment of childhood disorders. However, in applying the results of research, we must tread with caution. There are often a number of possible interpretations of child data and there may be disagreement as to whether a study supports a particular theory of development. This is why critical evaluation of both theory and research is important.

How do we study cognitive development?

You may already be knowledgeable about various research designs, but the study of development can be different as we are interested in how things change over time. Generally speaking, most developmental studies use a variation of one of the following methods:

Observational research. An observational study is one in which children are studied in a naturalistic setting, such as the home or at school. This may be an individual case study or a study of a group of children either cross-sectionally or longitudinally. Examples of observational research include video or audio recordings of children, checklists of behaviours and questionnaires for parents to fill in. The main advantage of this type of research is that children behave naturally, in a way they may not behave in an experimental setting. The disadvantages are that interfering factors cannot be controlled for and that there may be a subjective interpretation of children's behaviour by observers.

Experimental designs. In a cross-sectional design, two or more groups of children of different ages are tested. For example, if we were studying some aspect of the development of theory of mind, which is usually taken to emerge at around the age of 4, we could conduct an experiment in which the participants are a group of 3-year-olds and a group of 5-year-olds. The advantage of this type of design is that the research is quick and easy to carry out, as both groups can be tested in a short period of time. The disadvantage is that we cannot discover much about the process of change. If there *is* a difference between 3-year-olds and 5-year-olds, how does this change occur?

In a longitudinal design, the same group of children are tested repeatedly over a period of time. Collecting data in this way may enable us to capture the process of development, but it can be quite time-consuming. Also, if the interval between testing is too long, we may miss something. Another potential problem is that in carrying out a longitudinal study, it is not always practical to have large groups of participants, which may mean that the sample is not representative of the population. If, for example, we want to capture the development of memory over the first five years of school in the UK, the population of interest is all UK schoolchildren. Without a lot of funding and many investigators, it is likely that a study may be limited to following children from just a few schools and, over time, some of those children may move to a new area, or miss testing dates.

In a cohort design, different cohorts (samples born in different years) are compared at the same ages. This enables us to look at historical, social and cultural differences. We can ask questions such as: Are children who were born in the 1980s different to children born in the 2000s? This is, however, *very* time-consuming and, again, tells us little about processes of development.

The type of design used in a study depends on the nature of the research. If we cannot manipulate the variable we are interested in, perhaps as a result of ethical considerations, we can carry out an observational study. If we want to describe children at different points in time, then a cross-sectional design is appropriate. If we want to capture the process of change, we may use a longitudinal design. Finally, if we are interested in the impact of culture, then a cohort design will be best.

cross-sectional design A research design in which two or more groups of children of different ages are compared.

longitudinal design A research design in which the same group of children are tested repeatedly over a period of time.

cohort design A research design in which two or more groups of children who were born in different years are compared at the same age.

Themes in cognitive development

There are many themes or issues common to much of the research and theory in cognitive development. The themes identified here are by no means an exhaustive list, and not every study addresses one of these themes, but they have been, and continue to be, important concepts that have guided the field.

The nature–nurture debate

For hundreds of years, there has been argument as to whether we are born with innate knowledge (nature) or whether we learn everything we need to know through our interactions with our environment (nurture). This is a long-running debate, going back to the ancient Greeks, and was a prominent topic of discussion among seventeenth-and eighteenth-century philosophers, such as Kant and Locke; see Chapter 2 for a brief overview of the history of this topic. Aristotle and Locke both favoured the position that a child is born as a 'blank slate', and that experience will dictate what comes to be written on that slate. This concept was reflected in the behaviourist ideas of Watson (1926) and Skinner (1974), both of whom believed that children developed through a system of stimulus, response and reinforcement. The opposing point of view, that of innate properties, stems back to Plato, and – in the eighteenth century – to Rousseau, who believed that children develop through a set of predictable stages that are guided by an innate timetable. The idea of a set of predictable stages is present in Piaget's theory, whilst the notion of innate knowledge survives in modern nativist theories, such as Chomsky's theory of language acquisition (see Chapter 4).

Over the last few decades, the debate has moved away from the simplistic dichotomy of whether development progresses according to one or the other extreme; few psychologists would dispute that both nature and nurture play vital roles in cognitive development. Instead, the focus is on the more complex, but much more interesting, question of how nature and nurture interact. This involves investigating what innate abilities or knowledge children have, how the environment and children's experiences impact upon development, and how the interaction between the two produces development.

One important line of evidence comes from cross-cultural research. By conducting a study on participants from different cultures, we can learn something about the universality of cognitive development. This can tell us whether a particular aspect of cognitive development develops in the same way for everyone, whether it develops in a culturally-specific way. Certain aspects of development, such as Piaget's formal operational thinking, are now understood to be a product of Western educational systems. Other cultures have other cognitive developmental milestones, which suggests that the development of formal operational thought isn't an inevitable end to an innately driven maturational developmental course. It is important to note that even if everyone does share a particular developmental milestone this doesn't necessarily mean it is innate. It may be that they all share similar learning environments, despite cultural differences. However, what we can say is that if children's development *differs* from culture to culture, it means that the environment *is* having an effect.

Are there stages of development?

Another theme in the study of cognitive development, mentioned above, is the question of the course (or 'shape') of development. The most common debate regarding the course of development is whether development, be it in a single domain of knowledge or cognition in general, proceeds in stages, or whether skills and knowledge structures change in a continuous way. According to stage theorists, such as Piaget, there are qualitative 'jumps' in development, whereby abilities or knowledge change very rapidly over a short period of time, and then show little change for a longer period of time. However, there are many possible 'shapes' of development. Four examples are illustrated in Figure 1.2.

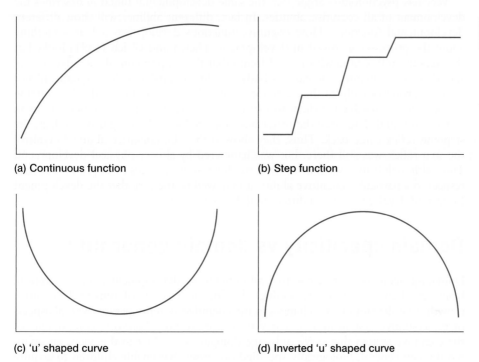

(a) Continuous function

(b) Step function

(c) 'u' shaped curve

(d) Inverted 'u' shaped curve

Figure 1.2

Four patterns of development. The x axis of each graph represents time, and the y axis represents level of ability.

Some theorists, such as information-processing theorists, consider development to proceed, not in stages, but in a continuous manner. The continuous function describes a course of acquisition in which the child slowly develops over time. An example of this is physical weight gain. Children grow quite quickly at first, putting on a bit more weight every day. As they get older, weight gain decreases, so although they are getting heavier, they are getting heavier more slowly until weight stabilizes during adolescence. It may be the case that cognition develops in this way, such that children's cognitive abilities gradually improve over time.

Other theories argue that development occurs in stages. This is also referred to as the discontinuous or step function. There will be a long period of no development, followed by a sudden developmental leap. An example of this is children's physical mobility. Infants are (obviously) immobile to begin with. Around 6 to 9 months, they quickly learn to crawl. At about 12 to 18 months they start walking. Each of these achievements can be seen as a developmental milestone, a relatively sudden change from one state to another. Some cognitive developmentalists, such as Piaget, believe that cognitive development occurs in this way; sudden changes from one stage to another with little happening in between.

A third pattern is the 'U' shaped curve. This is when abilities are present early on, disappear for a time and then re-emerge. For example, babies are born with a step reflex. If supported, newborns display a coordinated step reflex, as if they are walking. This disappears only to re-emerge when they begin to stand and walk at about 12 months. Finally, there is the inverted 'U' shaped curve, a shape found more often in lifespan psychology. Visual acuity is a good example of this. Our visual acuity (how clearly we see) gets better and better in childhood, stays constant for a while in adulthood, then starts to diminish in old age. This shape can also be found in the development of speech. Babbling emerges at about 6 months of age then disappears when the child starts to learn to talk.

Very few psychologists argue that the same developmental function describes the development of all cognitive abilities. In fact, different abilities will show different developmental functions. How cognitive functions develop can tell us something about the processes involved in development. Thelen and Ulrich (1991) looked at the stepping reflex in newborns and found that the suppression of the effect corresponded to the infants' increase in body weight. Infants' muscle strength did not increase proportionally so they surmised that older infants did not do the stepping reflex as it was harder for them to lift their now heavier legs. They put infants in water and found that, once the water buoyancy reduced the weight of the legs, the stepping reflex came back. Thus, they showed that the cognitive ability to control the step reflex was still there, but was hampered by slower physical development. Thus, although it may seem as if there are, for instance, stages of development with respect to a particular cognitive ability, it may well be the case that the development (or lack of development) of a different ability is masking it.

Domain specificity vs domain generality

domain-general
Referring to abilities or processes that operate across multiple domains of development.

domain-specific
Referring to abilities or processes that operate over just one domain of development.

Domain-general theorists argue that all domains of development (e.g., perception, language, theory of mind, reasoning) develop as a result of universal cognitive growth; that developmental changes in the cognitive system operate over all aspects of the cognitive system in a similar way. There are not, therefore, components of the cognitive system that serve only one domain. According to this view, an infant has domain-general, biologically specified processes that enable children to acquire knowledge in all domains of development. Domain-specific theorists, however, argue that different domains develop at different rates. Nativist researchers, who often place an emphasis on innate knowledge, are usually domain-specific theorists. According to this view, there are components of the cognitive system that operate on a restricted set of information. Thus there may be a language acquisition module that is pre-programmed to pay attention to and interpret language, and a visual perception module that is pre-programmed to make sense of visual information. Knowledge gained by the visual perception module impacts very little on the language domain and vice versa. One of the issues facing cognitive developmentalists is ascertaining whether a particular skill, ability or knowledge structure develops as the result of domain-specific knowledge, or a domain-general learning procedure. In Chapter 10, we will see that children with autism seem to have an impaired theory of mind, but children with Down's syndrome do not. If the development of theory of mind relies on domain-general processes, we might expect that children with autism and children with Down's syndrome would both have impaired theory of mind. However, as there is evidence that this is not the case, does this mean that the development of theory of mind depends on a specific cognitive module? Is theory of mind a result of the maturation of part of the brain that is impaired in autism but not in Down's syndrome? Does the fact that Down's syndrome children tend to have a more domain-general deficit mean they have impaired general learning mechanisms or impairment in lots of domains?

Theoretical approaches

The importance of theories

A theory is a frame of reference for examining behaviour. A good theory must be able to do three things: *describe*, *explain* and *predict* behaviour. A theory of cognitive development *describes* changes over time in one or several aspects of behaviour or psychological activity. For example, a theory of perception describes what the perceptual abilities of children are and how they change over time; a theory of language development describes what children's language abilities are and how they change over time. Some theories attempt to describe development in lots of domains of cognitive development but most concentrate on one or two domains. To use one example, Piaget's theory describes how children's cognitive ability should change over time, from the sensorimotor period in which children can only perceive and feel, rather than think, to the formal operations stage, during adolescence, when children are capable of rational, logical thought.

A theory of cognitive development *explains* why children develop the way they do, and how change occurs. Piaget's theory explains cognitive development in terms of the interactions between the maturation of cognitive structures and environmental influences. His theory explains the process by which the development observed in children comes about. As well as describing observed behaviours (and changes in behaviour) and explaining these behaviours and changes in terms of cognitive processes, a theory must be capable of making predictions. Descriptions and explanations are necessary, but we need to be able to test theories in order to determine whether the descriptions and explanations bear some resemblance to what is occurring in the mind. Because we cannot open a child's head and see mental processes or changing cognitive schemas, we need some other, indirect, way of making observations. This, of course, is why psychology exists as a field of inquiry, and is not just a specialized subdiscipline of biology.

A theory is often designed to explain certain cognitive achievements, but in order for the theory to be tested it has to make novel predictions that can then be tested against the data. If the predictions are upheld, the theory is supported, if not it has to be discounted or modified. As we saw at the beginning of the chapter, Piaget made the prediction that children younger than about 7 years of age, who have therefore not entered the concrete operational stage, should not be able to conserve. Other researchers designed studies so as to be able to test this prediction. The results suggested that children under the age of 7 *can* pass conservation tasks. What does this mean for Piaget's theory? It could mean several things. For example, it could mean that everything he claimed was wrong. However, the studies discussed above did not test every aspect of the theory, just the ability of young children to give the correct answers on tests of conservation. The findings could, then, mean that Piaget was wrong about the age at which children enter the concrete operations stage. Or, that there are not distinct stages, but rather a more gradual process of development, which may vary from child to child. Hypotheses such as these need, in turn, to be tested to see which is the best explanation. In order to do this, we need to make more predictions. If children enter the concrete operations stage earlier, we could design experiments to test other aspects of concrete operational thinking in order to see whether younger children can pass these tests as well. If we think that there are no stages of development, we could design experiments or observational studies in which we follow children over time, to see if there are sharp changes in cognitive ability, or whether there are gradual changes, and whether there is a large amount of variation across children with respect to the timing of these changes. To summarize, testing the predictions derived from a theory allows us to evaluate the theory.

This all sounds like rather hard work! Perhaps, instead of constructing and testing theories, we could simply observe children and see what they can and can't do at different ages. Although such an approach would give us some insight into cognitive development, it would be a very limited view. Without theories, we cannot say what the ability (or lack of ability) to carry out a particular task *means*. What, for example, is the meaning of young children's inability to see that the amount of water does not change when it is poured from a short, wide glass to a tall, thin glass. Does it mean that they have a fundamental misconception about the nature of matter? Or do they think that water becomes less dense in a thinner glass? Perhaps they suspect some sleight of hand on the part of the researcher? Maybe they are lying! Without theories there would be no way to make sense of the data that researchers collect. Piaget's theory enables us to make sense of the observed behaviour. According to the theory, pre-operational-stage children focus on a dominant aspect of the appearance of the glasses (height) and make judgements based on this one dimension. Not only does a theory allow us to make sense of the data, it drives the development of new studies. Without Piaget's theory, would anyone have thought to see whether children have an appreciation of the fact that quantities stay the same when they are transformed in such a manner? Theories, therefore, tell us what new research to carry out in order to further investigate behaviours.

Piaget

Piagetian and neo-Piagetian theories are more likely than other theoretical approaches to consider cognitive development as a whole, rather than attempting to explain specific domains of development. This results from an endorsement of domain-general learning, the idea that general cognitive development will affect all aspects of cognition, including mathematical ability, language and so forth. The proponents of such theories are interested in investigating general cognitive abilities to a greater extent than domain-specific achievements.

Piaget's (1962a, 1970; Piaget and Inhelder, 1969) theory is the most influential developmental theory of cognitive development. Many modern theories take elements of Piaget's theory and incorporate them into new theories, or they present accounts of development that run contrary to Piaget's theory, but few theorists ignore it. I will not cover Piaget's theory in any great depth in this book, as it has been extensively covered in many papers, monographs and textbooks. There are also many empirical studies and theoretical treatises refuting many of the main tenets of the theory, spanning the last four decades. Whilst the theory is often presented in a simplistic form, it is actually very complex.

One of the fundamental aspects of Piaget's theory is that it is a stage theory of development. He argued that children go through different stages of development and at each stage their thought is qualitatively differently to that of the previous stages. Older children are capable of thoughts that are simply beyond younger children. It is as if older children have a different kind of brain than that possessed by younger children. Although I (together with most other authors of textbooks) emphasize this aspect of the theory, it is important to note that in his later years, Piaget (1985) came to view development as less like a step function, with a greater period of transition between different degrees of cognitive ability.

Piaget was interested in epistemology – the study of knowledge. He was interested in how we come to know things. He wanted to know whether objective knowledge is possible or whether all our knowledge is influenced by our own nature. He also wanted to find the degree to which knowledge is innate or acquired. These are the general questions of **genetic epistemology**, which Piaget attempted to answer by studying the development of cognition. He studied developmental changes in the process of knowledge acquisition and in the organization of knowledge. He studied the basic categories of thought, which are time, space, causality and quantity. He argued that knowledge is a process rather than a state, that it is a relationship between the knower and the knowledge. In other words, people *construct* knowledge. This is why his theory is known as a **constructivist** theory. In order to do this we actively seek and interpret information from the environment. Children's knowledge of the world changes as they themselves develop. As changes in the cognitive system take place, the nature of the child's knowledge changes. This means that an infant's view of the world is significantly different to that of an older child or an adult.

Piaget took a biological approach to development, focusing on the general processes by which living organisms adapt to the world. He argued that children's development was simply a way of adapting to the world in order to live in it more successfully. He argued that the processes of **adaptation (assimilation and accommodation)**, by which animals and plants adapt to the natural world, were active in children as they developed. Piaget also argued that a small set of mental operations underlies a wide variety of developments, which is why his theory is a domain-general theory. The nature of these mental operations, or structures, changes through development, through maturation and adaptation, as the structures themselves develop. According to Piaget, the cognitive structure of an infant is very different to that of a 5-year-old, in contrast with the information-processing and behaviourist approaches that argue that the nature of children's mental structures remains the same but the capacity and ability of these structures grow.

An analogy that may clarify the difference between Piaget and information-processing theorists, is physical growth. Growing taller doesn't change our bodies qualitatively. We are still the same shape but a bit taller every day, whereas puberty changes us qualitatively; our body shape and functions are different after puberty than they were beforehand. Piaget saw the development of cognitive functions as a series of steps that change our minds to the same radical extent that puberty changes our bodies. Information-processing theorists, on the other hand, argue that development only changes our minds in the same way that getting taller changes our bodies.

According to Piaget, changes occur in cognitive structures as a result of maturation (biologically predetermined changes) and adaptation to new experiences. These changes enable children to perform more successfully in the environment in which they find themselves. There are two processes that enable children to adapt to their environment. The first of these is called assimilation. By this Piaget means that we assimilate new information into existing thought processes or cognitive structures. We take in information and process it in a way that is compatible with our current view of the world and with our current cognitive structure. For example, when presented with the liquid conservation task, a child may use an existing cognitive structure, based on a comparison of height, to determine that the glass of orangeade with the highest level has the most liquid. The second process is accommodation, in which the child notices discrepancies between information coming in and the thought processes or cognitive structures she already has and changes her thought processes and cognitive structures as a result. If the child realizes that the two glasses cannot be accurately compared on the basis of height alone, she may modify the cognitive structure used for comparison to include an integration of both height and width information.

genetic epistemology The study of the origins of knowledge.

constructivist A theoretical position in which it is argued that meaning, in the form of mental representations, is constructed through interactions with the environment.

adaptation The process, described by Piaget, by which children meet environmental demands through the modification of cognitive structures by assimilation or accommodation.

assimilation One of two aspects of Piaget's concept of adaptation. Assimilation is the process by which new experiences are incorporated into existing conceptual structures.

accommodation One of two aspects of Piaget's concept of adaptation. Accommodation is the process by which cognitive structures are modified or created as a result of new experiences which do not fit into current structures.

equilibration The process by which assimilation and accommodation are balanced to create stability.

Assimilation and accommodation are balanced by another process, **equilibration**. The motive for cognitive development is the desire to maintain a state of equilibrium. When a child encounters a new experience that does not fit in with her existing mental structures, she is in a state of disequilibrium. By a process of assimilation or accommodation, the child's cognitive schemes can be stretched or changed in order to understand the new experience, and equilibrium is achieved. However, assimilation will only lead to temporary equilibrium by forcing a new experience into an existing mental schema. By modifying these mental schemas, the new experience is not distorted, and a longer-lasting equilibrium can be achieved. Once the child understands that a transformation of the shape of a liquid does not affect the quantity, and realizes that this can be accounted for by integrating the two dimensions of height and width, she is in a state of equilibrium. Although equilibration happens on a daily basis for young children, as they encounter new aspects of the world, it is this same process that accounts for the stages of development that Piaget proposed. A child enters the concrete operations stage once her pre-operational cognitive structures are in equilibrium.

There are four stages of development in Piaget's theory:

Stage 1: Sensorimotor stage (0 to 2 years)
Stage 2: Pre-operational stage (2 to 7 years)
Stage 3: Concrete operational stage (7 to 11 years)
Stage 4: Formal operational stage (11+ years)

At birth, children's cognitive systems are limited to reflexes. During the course of the sensorimotor stage, children come to use their reflex actions in increasingly more complex ways, but they do not *think* in the sense of using mental representations. By the end of this stage, however, they start to use mental symbols. That is, they possess internal mental representations of objects and actions. This ability to think symbolically develops through the pre-operational stage, and is demonstrated in the use of language and drawings. Both words and pictures are symbols in the sense that they represent something else. The ability to mentally represent objects means that young children can think about objects when they are not physically present. However, this stage is characterized by many limitations. Pre-operational children's thought is restricted to an egocentric point of view, meaning they cannot take another person's perspective. They also lack the ability to carry out mental transformations, which means they cannot mentally manipulate the representation of a glass of water or a row of counters, as in conservation tasks. As we have seen, the transition to the concrete operations stage is marked by the ability to pass conservation tasks. This means that children in this stage can manipulate objects mentally, which includes reversing actions on objects. Concrete operational stage children can thus imagine pouring the liquid from the tall, thin glass back into the short, wide glass. Children in this stage can also adopt other people's points of view, and adopt multiple perspectives. Nonetheless, children's thinking is still limited to concrete phenomena. They cannot reason about abstract concepts, or think hypothetically; they do not yet possess full logical competence. During the formal operations stage, children develop logical thought and are no longer tied to concrete objects or events. They can consider abstract concepts, make and test hypotheses, and solve complex problems.

The sensorimotor stage of Piaget's theory will be discussed further in Chapters 2 and 3, on perception and memory. We will return to the later stages in Chapters 6, 7, and 8, and consider Piaget's ideas with respect to reasoning, scientific thinking and numeracy.

Information processing

Information processing is both a theoretical approach and a framework for conducting research. At the centre of the idea is the analogy of the mind as similar to a computer: both are seen as information-processing systems. This is not to say that information-processing theorists think that the mind is exactly the same as a computer. Rather, the ideas that have been inspired by work with computers can be applied to human cognition. Both minds and computers receive information (input), perform certain operations on the input, store it in memory and produce an output. Because of the computer metaphor, the language used in information-processing psychology is the language of cognitive scientists and cognitive modellers, in which the computing terms mentioned above (*input*, *storage*, *output*), along with *capacity*, *processing* and so on, are used to refer to aspects of cognition.

Different psychologists use the computer metaphor to different extents. Many cognitive psychologists accept most of the assumptions and concepts of information processing, but do not use computer simulations to model thought. Instead, they usually use more traditional experimental methods. Others not only use the language of the computer metaphor, but also build computer simulations, which are known as **cognitive or computational models**. We will examine some of these in Chapter 11. Proponents of the latter method assume that the processes at work within the computer simulation are comparable to the processes at work in human cognition and that, by building such models, we can understand something about the nature of cognition. An advantage of computational models is that all aspects of the cognitive process or system being modelled have to be specified precisely; one cannot be vague about how much information can be stored in working memory, for example.

cognitive/ computational model A simulation of cognitive processes instantiated in a computer program.

Computational models have become more and more popular in cognitive developmental psychology in recent years, as theorists have come to use such models as a tool with which theories can be tested. However, the use of a computer simulation does not necessarily make the psychologist using it an information-processing theorist. We can distinguish between those who see computers as an experimental tool, to be used in the same way as an experiment or an observational study, and those who adhere to the assumptions of the information-processing approach.

When studying cognitive development, information-processing theorists ask the question: 'What would an information-processing system require in order to exhibit the same behaviour as the child?' (Klahr and Wallace, 1976, p. 5). In order to answer this question, we need to think about what happens in a child's head when he/she is carrying out a cognitive task. Let us return to the conservation of liquid task. The child must listen to the instructions given by the researcher and look at the two glasses. Later on, there are more instructions to listen to and a further glass to see. We can think of these auditory and visual stimuli as the input received by the cognitive system. We need to think about how this information is perceived. The information is then stored in memory. We need to consider what this information might look like when it enters the memory system. For example, are the glasses encoded as a mental image? In order to make sense of the instructions, the glasses and the task, the child needs to organize and manipulate the new information with respect to the information she already has about glasses, orangeade, the meaning of spoken words, and so forth. Having interpreted the objects in the visual array, and understood the instructions, the child must formulate responses to the questions that the researcher is asking her. She must, therefore, retrieve some information from memory, and we must ask how this is done. She then needs to produce an output in the form of a spoken phrase, such as 'they are both the same'. Again, we need to explain how the various pieces of information in memory (some of which may have been in visual rather than verbal form) have given rise to some new information that is encoded into a speech format. In summary, information-processing theorists are concerned with how information is perceived (input), stored, organized and manipulated, retrieved and output.

Obviously, *developmental* psychologists are interested in how these systems for encoding, storing and retrieving information develop. The information-processing view is that development occurs as the child learns to process information more efficiently. Developmental changes occur in three main areas. First, our cognitive control processes develop. These are the processes that organize and store information and govern all cognitive activity. Second, our **metacognitive** ability – our ability to consciously understand our own mental activity – improves. An example of metacognitive ability is when we know that in order to remember a phone number (in the absence of a mobile phone, or writing implements such as a pen, lipstick, etc.), we must repeat it over and over until it is learnt. In other words our understanding of how to make the most of our cognitive abilities improves. Third, as we get older, the amount of knowledge we possess increases.

An important aspect of the developmental process is the idea that we develop through a process of self-modification and self-correction. In other words, we can act on our own cognitive system. We can reject procedures that turn out not to be useful, such as trying to remember a phone number by adding all the digits together. We can organize and reorganize our knowledge by, for example, encoding the phone number as a two or three sets of smaller numbers, and associating some of these smaller numbers with things that are meaningful to us, such as a year. We can also increase or decrease the number of situations in which we use a particular strategy, depending on how useful it is, and whether better strategies are available to us. By reorganizing our own system time and time again, we develop. This idea is not new; Piaget argued we organize our own cognitive system as we develop. However, this idea has been given impetus by computer models that can learn by self-modifying.

At the centre of this approach is the idea that we must look in detail at the behaviours used by children when doing a task. Most studies concentrate on just one task (e.g., conservation, addition) and there are sometimes hundreds of articles written about one small task. This may seem odd but each task differs in the cognitive skills needed to perform it, therefore each task needs to be analyzed differently. Information-processing experimenters focus on the unique demands of each task, work out what needs to be done to complete it, and then look at what children are doing and how they solve the task. Thus, theories often start out as theories of how children perform just one task. The idea is to extend theories so they fit other tasks as well. This is an ideal rather than a reality as most of the time as it is often very difficult to understand how to relate one task to another. However, computer simulations are allowing us to do this more effectively. A computer can first be programmed to learn one task the way a child learns it and to produce similar behaviour. It can then be tested on a different task to see how it behaves.

So how can we analyze children's behaviour on a task? There are a number of different ways. We can use timing information; the more cognitive activity there is, the longer the task will take to complete. We can look at errors; the types of errors children produce can tell us what rules they are using to do the task. Eye-movement data tells us what children look at. The order in which they look at stimuli tells us what they are attending to and encoding. By employing **microgenetic studies**, in which children are given the same task repeatedly in sessions spread over weeks or months, rather than years, we can observe small changes in performance that can give us an indication of where the big developmental changes come from.

---

metacognitive/ metacognition
Cognition about cognition. The ability to treat one's own thought processes as objects of thought.

microgenetic studies
Studies which look at change over a brief period of time (often days or weeks).

We will return to the information-processing approach in Chapter 3, when we will look at memory, as most explanations of how memory works adopt this perspective. Information-processing theories of scientific thinking, mathematics and reading, and intelligence will be discussed in Chapters 7, 8 and 9, respectively. Chapter 11 contains a more detailed account of how cognitive models have been used to examine development.

Neo-Piagetian theory

Neo-Piagetian theories can differ tremendously from one theory to another but they tend to share a few characteristics. They are all based on at least one aspect of Piaget's work, usually the ideas that children actively construct their own knowledge and that there are stages of development. They also include non-Piagetian ideas. Many include aspects of the information-processing approach, such as the idea that restrictions on memory capacity have an impact on development. They tend to take more account of domain-specific constructs rather than relying solely on changes in underlying domain-general mental competence. There are lots of neo-Piagetian theories, such as those of Fischer (1980), Halford (1993), or Karmiloff-Smith (1992), but we will not go into them all. However, we will briefly consider Case's (1985) theory as a good example of a neo-Piagetian theory.

Case is one of the most influential neo-Piagetians. His theory is a mix of information-processing theory and Piagetian theory. For Case, development is the result of increased efficiency and neurological maturation. Practice with a skill makes it more automatic and therefore more efficient. Increasing the speed of processing (efficiency) means that more capacity can be used for other cognitive activities. If counting is automatic, we can free up memory capacity, which allows us to carry out more operations (e.g., adding two numbers, then multiplying the sum by three). According to Case (1992), neurological maturation also increases available mental capacity.

As with Piaget's theory, Case's theory is a stage theory of development. He proposes four stages that result from structural changes in our cognitive mechanisms. These stages are very similar to Piaget's. Each stage is characterized by very different thought processes. As with Piaget's stages, the child thinks in fundamentally different ways depending on which stage she is in. In sum, the theory explains development by arguing that changes in mental capacity interact with neurological and maturational changes in cognitive structure to create development.

Some of the constructivist accounts of language discussed in Chapter 4 can be viewed as neo-Piagetian, as can the 'representational mind' theory of mind, which we will look at in Chapter 5. Stage theories of children's conceptual understanding of health and illness, and the development of reading will be covered in Chapters 7 and 8.

Nativism

It seems we are frequently hearing about evidence that very young children, or even babies, can count, recognize faces and imitate facial expressions. It has been argued that these point to evidence of innate knowledge in children (Bartrip, Morton and de Schonen, 2001; Meltzoff and Moore, 1977; Wynn, 1998). The linchpin of nativism is the idea that children are born with innately specified knowledge that enables them to understand the world and their own cognitive system, and to make sense of the behaviours around them. Nativism is based on three main concepts: innate knowledge, domain-specificity and a minimal role for the environment.

Chomsky, a linguist, first introduced the idea that children possess an innate system of language learning (Chomsky, 1957). Originally called the language acquisition device, and now called universal grammar, this system predisposes children to notice and search out the general grammatical properties of any language. Chomsky's theory of the acquisition of grammar has been very influential, and Chomskyan ideas have been applied to other aspects of development. Nativist developmentalists thus claim that knowledge is innate and, therefore, does not need to be learnt. This may seem to be an obvious idea, in that if we don't subscribe to behaviourism (where everything is learnt), then we must believe something is innate. Does this not mean we all are nativists? This is, however, a misconception. There is one main thing that separates nativists from other modern developmentalists: the nature of what is innate.

It is easy to get the impression that nativists argue for innate ability, an argument that is so self-evident that it seems strange that only nativists adhere to this view. But, arguing that we have innate *abilities* does not make one a nativist. The fact that we are born with innate ability is not disputed. I doubt you can find anyone who will claim that people are not innately better than, say, cats at learning language, using symbols to represent numbers, solving logic puzzles, and so on. What distinguishes nativism is that it is concerned with innate *knowledge* rather than innate ability. Some nativist psychologists have argued that children have innate knowledge of maths (Wynn, 1998), language (Pinker, 1989) and theory of mind (Leslie, 1988). The reason that children do not always demonstrate this knowledge is, according to nativists, due to other factors such as information-processing limitations (Fodor, 1992; Marcus *et al.*, 1992). The difference between nativists and other theorists is that nativists argue that we are born with domain-specific knowledge, which means that less has to develop than would otherwise be the case, whereas others argue that we are born with domain-general skills that enable us to develop. It is a subtle distinction but a very important one.

Nativist theorists are more likely than Piagetian theorists to concentrate on just one domain of development. You are unlikely to come across nativist theories that describe and explain lots of domains. This is because nativist accounts tend to explain development in terms of domain-specific knowledge. Children's abilities, knowledge and development in one domain (e.g., language) do not transfer to other domains (e.g., perception). This stems from Fodor's (1983) idea of the modularity of the mind. Fodor suggested that the mind is made up of discrete modules that interact only minimally. Domain-specificity doesn't necessarily mean the same as modularity. However, the idea is that since children have innately specified knowledge, this knowledge applies only to one domain and thus can influence development in only one domain. This is in contrast with the Piagetian view (and, to an extent, the information-processing view) that general changes in cognitive ability affect at least several, if not all, domains of development.

Because nativists posit some innate knowledge, there is a lesser role for the environment than for some other theoretical approaches. This is not to say that culture and social interaction are not essential. Nobody argues that children can, for example, learn to use language if they are not exposed to it. However, because it is argued that much of development occurs without learning, there is a limited role for cultural differences. Although one can find cultural differences in some aspects of cognition, such as the common finding that children from south-east Asian cultures tend to be ahead of their Western counterparts in mathematics (e.g., Fuson, 1992), this does not invalidate the idea of an innate number sense. Differences between cultures tend to be small compared with the enormity of the fact that all children follow broadly the same course of development and all become adults, who all tend to have the same fundamental cognitive skills and knowledge.

Nativist theorists will be discussed further in later chapters. In Chapters 2 and 4, we will look at nativist theories of perception and language acquisition. A modular theory of theory of mind is discussed in Chapter 5, and evidence for a nativist account of numeracy will be covered in Chapter 8.

Sociocultural theory

Vygotsky was a Russian psychologist who was born in 1896 – the same year as Piaget – and died in 1934 of tuberculosis. Although he was a contemporary of Piaget's, his work remained unknown until the latter half of the twentieth century. This was largely due to the ban placed on his work by Stalin's Communist party. Whereas Piaget thought that cognitive development occurred regardless of cultural and environmental differences, Vygotsky (1978) took a very different view. He argued that the environment has a very important role to play in development, that different contexts can determine different developmental pathways. According to Vygotsky, the main impact of culture occurs through social interaction, especially with knowledgeable others such as peers, parents and teachers. Development occurs as we take on board shared knowledge given to us through social interactions with the others who share our culture. How we develop, what we come to know, and how we think is, therefore, a product of our culture.

Piaget thought that children had to discover the world themselves, but Vygotsky thought that, within limits, children could be taught to do more than what they could do on their own. One of the central themes of Vygotsky's work is the zone of proximal development, which is a conceptual space containing a child's *potential* development. It is the difference between what a child can do on his own and what a child can do with help. If instruction takes place within this zone (and does not push children beyond their potential development), children can reach their full potential. An example of the zone of proximal development is given in Box 1.1.

zone of proximal development A conceptual space that describes the range of ability between what a child can do with and without support.

Box 1.1 An example of the zone of proximal development

Parent: Here are four books for you and the same for your brother.

Child: The same? (*He investigates his brother's pile of books.*) No, he has more (*spoken with annoyance*).

Parent: No, really, they're the same. Take another look.

Child: He does have more.

Parent: Try laying his out in a row. Then lay yours out too. Then compare.

Child: (*Does as suggested*) One two three four. One two three four. The same! (*He looks satisfied.*)

(Seifert, Hoffnung and Hoffnung, 1997)

In this example, the parent is providing the child with the framework in order for the child to solve the problem himself. The parent is not telling the child the answer but is helping him work it out for himself. The parent is providing the child with help within the child's zone of proximal development. Without help, the child would not have solved the problem. With help, he can do it. Instruction is most effective if it builds on previous knowledge. In this example, the child already knows how to count. The parent adds the new information that you can use counting as a way of making comparisons.

For Piaget, language was just another representational system; a symbol system like mathematics, a way of representing the world in our heads. Piaget thought that, prior to the concrete operations stage, children cannot use language to communicate successfully because they are egocentric, meaning that they cannot take another person's point of view. However, Vygotsky saw the role of language as central to development. Not only did he consider it to be necessary for social interaction, and therefore for the child to learn from others, but he argued that language and thought are closely interrelated and that the development of language was central for the development of thought. He observed that when children solve problems they often talk to themselves, giving themselves instructions, such as 'let's try that there. No, that doesn't work, what about there?' Vygotsky suggested that this *private speech* (speaking to oneself) was a stage in the development of thought. He suggested that young children were using instructions given to them by parents or other knowledgeable adults and using them to direct their own behaviour – a sort of internalized social interaction between a child and herself rather than between the child and a knowledgeable other. Later in development, this private speech develops into thought processes or *silent statements*. Children no longer need to talk out loud to themselves but talk internally to themselves. Once private speech has become internalized, children use this to plan and organize behaviour in the same way that adults do. In other words, speech has become thought. It is in this way, according to Vygotsky, that children develop.

Bruner (1966) and Bruner and Haste (1987) combined some of the ideas of Piaget and Vygotsky. Responsible for introducing Vygotsky's work to the non-Soviet world, Bruner developed a stage theory of development that emphasizes the role of social interaction in the learning process. Because Bruner's theory combines Piagetian stages with a role for social interaction, it is sometimes called a socio-cognitive theory of development. The first of Bruner's stages is the *enactive* mode or stage, which is similar to Piaget's sensorimotor stage. In this stage, infants represent the world through their actions, and their knowledge is based on their own physical actions and responses. The second stage is the *iconic* mode, in which children begin to rely on mental representations, as in Piaget's pre-operational and concrete operational stages. Children no longer have to physically act upon something in order to represent it. They can represent things as icons, which are mental pictures and images. However, as in Piaget's pre-operational and concrete operational stages, this is an inflexible type of representation. Children need to have experienced something in order to represent it; they have no hypothetical thought. The third and final stage is the *symbolic* mode. As in Piaget's formal operational stage, children develop symbolic representations and can symbolize the contents of their thoughts as words. This system is flexible in that children can adapt and rearrange information, think about hypothetical situations, and think in the abstract. Therefore, for Bruner, like Piaget, abstract thought develops out of concrete thinking.

However, unlike Piaget, Bruner emphasized the role of social interaction and interpersonal communication in development. Like Vygotsky, he claimed that the active intervention of expert others was necessary for development. He furthered Vygotsky's ideas of the role of instruction. Like Vygotsky, Bruner suggested that what children have the potential to achieve with help is greater than what they can actually do without help. Bruner furthered Vygotsky's ideas, stating that the method of instruction was important for development. He introduced the idea of scaffolding, the idea that expert others need to continually adjust their level of help in response to the child's level of performance. For example, if the child is successful the instructor can back off, if not he should provide more help. This continual adjustment within the zone of proximal development is what is necessary for the child to reach her optimum level of development.

The impact of socio-cultural factors on the development of cognition will be discussed in Chapters 8 and 9, when we look at the development of numeracy and literacy, and definitions of intelligence.

Summary

What is cognitive development and why should you study it? Cognitive development refers to the development of cognitive processes such as thinking, reasoning, memory, perception, theory of mind and language. In studying cognitive development, we are interested in the content of a knowledge domain. One of the basic questions we attempt to answer is: What do children know at different ages? However, understanding what children know, and what skills they have at different ages, doesn't tell us how they think or how they acquire knowledge. We also need to investigate the structure of children's knowledge and the processes by which knowledge and skills are acquired. There are several reasons why people are interested in cognitive development, including a desire to know about the origins of knowledge, a desire to enrich our understanding of adult cognition by looking at how cognitive processes develop and a desire to facilitate children's mental growth. Cognitive developmental psychologists use a variety of research methods including observation and different experimental designs.

Themes in cognitive development. There are many themes in cognitive development. Three of them are the nature–nurture debate, the question of whether development is stage-like or continuous and the issue of domain-general vs domain-specific knowledge or abilities. The argument of whether we are born with innate knowledge (nature) or whether we learn everything we need to know through our interactions with our environment (nurture) has been pursued for over 2000 years. More recently, the debate has moved away from the simplistic dichotomy of whether development progresses according to one or the other extreme, and turned to the question of how nature and nurture interact. The second theme regards the course of development. Does development proceed in stages, or do our skills and knowledge structures develop in a more gradual, continuous fashion? According to stage theorists, such as Piaget, there are qualitative 'jumps' in development, whereby abilities or knowledge change very rapidly over a short period of time, and then show little change for a longer period of time. However, other theorists, including many information-processing theorists, consider development to proceed, not in stages, but in a continuous manner. Domain-general theorists argue that all domains of development develop as a result of universal cognitive growth. According to this view, an infant has domain-general, biologically specified processes that enable children to acquire knowledge in all domains of development. Domain-specific theorists, however, argue that different domains develop at different rates. According to this view, there are components of the cognitive system that operate on a restricted set of information.

Theoretical approaches. A theory is a frame of reference for examining behaviour. A good theory must be able to do three things: describe, explain and predict behaviour. Piaget's theory is a domain-general, stage theory of development. It is also a constructivist theory, in that Piaget argued that people *construct* knowledge by interacting with the environment. Piaget also argued that a small set of mental operations underlies a wide variety of developments, which is why his theory is a domain-general theory. Changes occur in cognitive structures as a result of maturation (biologically predetermined changes) and adaptation to new experiences. There are two processes that enable children to adapt to their environment. Assimilation is the process by which we integrate new information into existing cognitive structures. Accommodation is the process by which cognitive structures are changed in order to fit the new information. Cognitive development is driven by equilibration, as a result of a need to avoid the state of disequilibrium. There are four stages of development in Piaget's theory. In the sensorimotor stage, children build on basic reflexes, but do not use mental representations. The ability to think symbolically develops through the pre-operational stage, and is demonstrated in the use of language and drawings. Pre-operational children's thought is restricted to an egocentric point of view, and they also lack the ability to carry out mental transformations. In the concrete operations stage, children can manipulate objects mentally and can adopt other people's points of view, but their thinking is limited to concrete phenomena. During the formal operations stage, children develop logical thought and are no longer tied to concrete objects or events. They can consider abstract concepts, make and test hypotheses, and solve complex problems. Neo-Piagetian theories are based on at least one aspect of Piaget's work, such as the notion of stages of development. They also include non-Piagetian ideas, often aspects of the information-processing approach. Information processing is based on the metaphor of the mind as a computer. When studying cognitive development, information-processing theorists think about the processes that happen in a child's head in computational terms. They are concerned with how information is perceived (input), stored, organized and manipulated, retrieved and output. They are also interested in how these systems develop. The information-processing view is that development occurs as the child learns to process information more efficiently. In order to study cognition, researchers look in detail at the behaviours used by children when doing a task. They focus on the unique demands of each task, work out what needs to be done to complete it and then look at what children are doing and how they solve the task. Computer simulations are often used as a way of testing theories. A computer can be programmed to learn a task the way a child learns it and to produce similar behaviour. In contrast to Piagetians and information-processing theorists, who tend to favour learning over innate knowledge, nativist theories argue that we are born with domain-specific knowledge or modules. It is important to distinguish between innate ability, without which it would be hard for any development to take place, and innate knowledge. Nativist theories include accounts of language, number and theory of mind. Because nativists posit some innate knowledge, there is a lesser role for the environment than for some other theoretical approaches, particularly sociocultural theories. Sociocultural theorists argue that the environment has a very important role to play in development, and that the main impact of culture occurs through social interaction, especially with knowledgeable others such as peers, parents and teachers. Development occurs as we take on board shared knowledge given to us through social interactions with the others who share our culture. How we develop, what we come to know and how we think is, therefore, seen as a product of our culture.

Overview of the book

I have organized the rest of the book in a somewhat chronological order, whereby the earlier chapters are concerned with domains that develop early in life, and the chapters in the middle of the book focus on domains where much of the research is on middle childhood. The topics of the final chapters, however, do not centre on a particular age range.

Chapter 2 addresses a domain in which most of the interesting development occurs early in infancy: perception. In this chapter, we return to the theme of nature vs nurture and consider the sensorimotor stage of Piaget's theory. You will also be introduced to the methods used in cognitive neuroscience. Chapter 3 is concerned with memory, and the theoretical focus is information-processing. Chapter 4 is about the acquisition of language, and nativist and constructivist theories are discussed. As with perception, this is a domain of development in which the nature?nurture issue is prominent. In Chapter 5, we turn to the development of theory of mind. One of the key issues with respect to this topic is the issue of whether there are stages of development or whether theory of mind is an ability that develops continuously.

Chapter 6 is about reasoning, and whether Piaget's theory offers a good account of the development of children's logical abilities. Chapter 7 focuses on scientific thinking, and a distinction is made between the development of children's conceptual understanding in scientific domains and their ability to reason scientifically. With respect to the former, the issue of whether knowledge is domain-general or domain-specific is discussed. With respect to the latter, Piaget's theory is contrasted with information-processing accounts of development. In Chapter 8, we turn to two other academic subjects: numeracy and literacy. Piagetian theory, information processing and nativism will be discussed, as well as cultural factors.

Chapter 9 is concerned with intelligence. The key issues are whether there is continuity across the lifespan, the extent to which intelligence is a result of heredity or environmental influences, and cultural differences in our conceptions of intelligence. Chapter 10 is about developmental disorders, and we will look at some ideas of why and how children with disorders such as autism, ADHD, dyslexia and dyscalculia differ from typically-developing children. Chapter 11 is concerned with how cognitive models can inform our understanding of development and help us to test competing theories. Finally, Chapter 12 presents a summary of the main themes discussed in this book.

Discussion questions

1   What do you think is the most interesting reason to study cognitive development?

2   Apart from conservation, what other predictions can you make about the differences between pre-operational and concrete operational stage children? How might you test these?

3   Choose a domain of development you are interested in. Do you think that children's abilities in this domain develop continuously or in stages?

4   What are the main differences between Piaget's theory, information processing and nativism?

Further Reading

Books and chapters

Miller, P. H. (2002). *Theories of developmental psychology*. New York: Worth.

Patricia Miller gives a very thorough account of a range of developmental theories. This is an excellent book if you want a detailed discussion of theories.

Piaget, J. and Inhelder, B. (1969). *The psychology of the child*. New York: Basic Books.

Jean Piaget and Barbel Inhelder present an overview of Piaget's theory and experiments. Although some of Piaget's work can be hard to read, I think this is one of the easier books.

Smith, L. (2002). Piaget's model. In U. Goswami (Ed.), *Blackwell handbook of childhood cognitive development*. Oxford: Blackwell.

Rowe, S. M. and Wertsch, J. V. (2000). Vygotsky's model of cognitive development. In U. Goswami (Ed.), *Blackwell handbook of childhood cognitive development*. Oxford: Blackwell.

Halford, G. S. (2000). Information-processing models of cognitive development. In U. Goswami (Ed.), *Blackwell handbook of childhood cognitive development*. Oxford: Blackwell.

These three chapters, all in the same edited volume, cover some of the most important theoretical perspectives in cognitive development.

Articles

Gopnik, A. (1996a). The post-Piaget era. *Psychological Science*, 7(4), 221–225.

This paper is Alison Gopnik's contribution to a special edition of the journal *Psychological Science*, celebrating the 100th anniversary of Piaget's birth. Gopnik presents a summary of several contemporary theoretical approaches to cognitive development.

McGarrigle, J. and Donaldson, M. (1974). Conservation accidents. *Cognition*, 3, 341–350.

A classic paper in which James McGarrigle and Margaret Donaldson demonstrate that 4- and 5-year-old children can pass conservation tasks if the transformation appears to occur by accident.

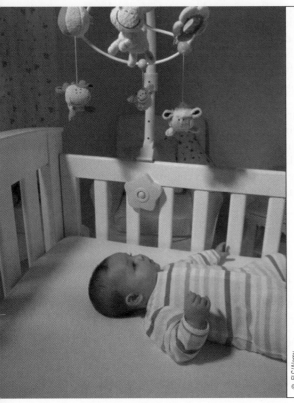

© ELC/Alamy

Chapter 2

Perception and cognition in infancy

Learning Outcomes

At the end of this chapter you should be able to:

- Describe the nature–nurture debate.
- Discuss and evaluate different theories of perceptual development.
- Describe research on basic perceptual abilities.
- Discuss the extent to which infants of different ages can interpret their perceptual experiences.

Renée Baillargeon, Elizabeth Spelke and Stanley Wasserman (1985) conducted a study to test Piaget's (1954) ideas concerning object permanence in infants – the idea that until the age of 9 months, infants do not conceive of objects existing continuously in time and space. The researchers wanted to see how young infants would react when faced with an 'impossible' event – a solid object that could pass through another solid object. They presented twenty-one 4- and 5-month-old infants with a 'drawbridge' that could rotate forwards and backwards through 180°. First, the infants were habituated to the drawbridge; this means they were repeatedly presented with the drawbridge rotating back and forwards until they were familiar with it. At this point, a yellow box was placed to the rear of the drawbridge. Infants were then given three pairs of test trials. In one of each pair of trials, the infants saw a 'possible' event; the drawbridge rotated backwards through 120° and was stopped by the box. In the other trials the infants were shown an 'impossible' event: the drawbridge rotated backwards through 180°, straight through the location of the box. Figure 2.1 shows what the infants saw in the habituation and test conditions. The dependent variable was the amount of time the infants spent looking at each event.

> Q. Do you think the infants looked longer at the 'possible' event or the 'impossible' event? Why?

Of course, given that objects can't pass through one another, the researchers had to come up with clever experimental apparatus in order to show the infants the 'impossible' event. This consisted of a wooden box containing two alleys, each with a drawbridge inside, with a one-way mirror placed diagonally between the two alleys (see Figure 2.2). If the front alley was lit and the side alley was dark, the infants could see through the mirror into the front alley. If the side alley was lit and the front alley was dark, the infants would see the side alley reflected in the mirror. The box used in the test conditions was placed in the front alley. The 'possible' test event was produced just by using the front alley. An experimenter rotated the drawbridge backwards, by means of a pulley, until it came into contact with the box, and then rotated it forwards again. For the 'impossible' test event, both alleys were needed. At first the front alley was lit and an experimenter rotated the drawbridge backwards through 120° until it was up against the box. At this point, the experimenter flipped the lights so that the side alley was lit up and the front alley was made dark. A second experimenter, who already had the drawbridge in the 120° position in the side alley could then rotate the visible side alley drawbridge back from 120° to 180°, and then forwards to 120°. At this point, the first experimenter flipped the lights again, making the front alley visible, and rotated the front alley drawbridge back to its initial position.

Another interesting aspect of this study is the way in which confounding variables were controlled for. The idea of the study was to see if infants would look longer at the impossible event than the possible event. However, there were two differences between the two test events. As well as the obvious difference of the drawbridge either passing through the box or not, there was a difference in how far the drawbridges rotated. In the possible event it always rotated back 120° and in the impossible event it always went all the way to 180°. This means that any differences in gaze duration may be due to a preference for the 180° rotation over the 120° rotation rather than the apparent impossibility of the event.

Habituation event

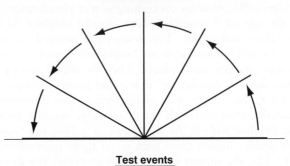

Test events

Impossible event

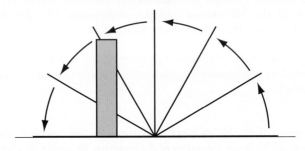

Possible event

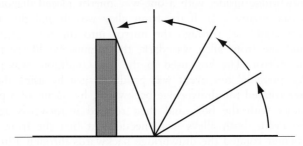

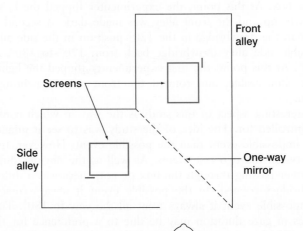

To get around this problem, Baillargeon and her colleagues also conducted a control experiment with a further twenty-two infants aged 4 to 5 months in which the only difference between conditions was the degree of rotation; the box was placed to the side of the drawbridge so that the drawbridge wouldn't come into contact with, or pass through, the box in either condition. The results, illustrated in Figure 2.3, show that the infants in the control experiment had no overall preference for the 120° or 180° rotations. However, the infants in the main experiment looked longer at the 'impossible' event than the 'possible' event, suggesting they were puzzled by the spatial impossibility. Baillargeon *et al.* concluded that 5-month-olds understand that objects continue to exist even when they can't see them.

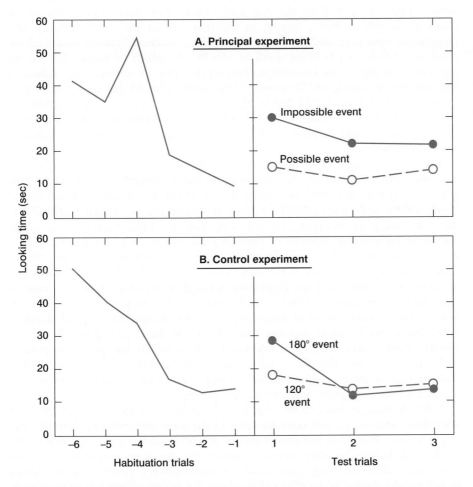

Figure 2.3

Results from Baillargeon *et al.*'s study.

Source: Reprinted from Cognition, 20, Baillargeon, R., Spelke, E. S., & Wasserman, S., Object permanence in 5-month-old infants, 191–208, Copyright (1985), with permission from Elsevier.

Q. What skills, abilities or knowledge do infants need to have in order to show surprise at the 'impossible' event?

Blank slate vs innate knowledge

The study described above demonstrates that infants of just 5 months of age understand two things. First, that objects exist independently of our perception of them, and second, that objects cannot pass through other objects. On the one hand, this may not seem very surprising as these concepts are obvious to anyone who isn't a young infant. On the other hand, we could ask of the 5-month-olds 'How do you know? Where did these concepts come from? Who told you? Or did you figure it out yourself?' Unfortunately, young infants possess neither the linguistic skills nor the cognitive skills to answer these questions. Even if they did, they would not have any insight into the nature of their mental structures. Some of the biggest questions in cognitive developmental psychology are questions of epistemology: 'How do we know what we know? What is the origin of knowledge?' These are the questions that started Piaget on the path to becoming a developmental psychologist. They also date back at least 2300 years, to the time of the Greek philosophers. Plato, writing in the first half of the fourth century BC, thought we were born with fundamental concepts, whereas Aristotle described the mind as a *tabula rasa* (a blank slate) in 350 BC, by which he meant that we are not born with any innate knowledge. This set the stage for the enduring debate of nativism versus empiricism. Descartes (1596–1650) believed that we are born with knowledge, and Kant (1724–1804) claimed that the origins of perception are innate. Locke (1632–1704), on the other hand, argued that all knowledge comes from experience, and Berkeley (1685–1753) reasoned that all perception derives from experience.

The nativist–empiricist, or nature–nurture, debate has been present in psychology since the inception of the discipline in the nineteenth century. Helmholtz (1821–1894) was an empiricist, Hering (1834–1918) was a nativist (Gordon and Slater, 1998), and James (1890) famously described the perceptual world of the infant as 'one great blooming, buzzing confusion' (p. 488). Although this debate can be found in many domains of psychological enquiry, perceptual development is one of two areas (along with language acquisition) in which it is most prominent. If we are to determine if the mind comes equipped with innate knowledge, or whether we have to learn everything through experience, it makes sense to study infants' knowledge, or lack of it. As understanding of perceptual experiences is the earliest manifestation of knowledge, we need to study perceptual development. Some psychologists conduct research on the basic perceptual abilities of infants, whereas others are more interested in how infants interpret their perceptual experiences and what they understand about the world. Although it is clear that the first of these programmes of research focuses on perception, the second represents both perception and cognition.

Before looking at research on what infants can perceive and how they interpret what they perceive, we will consider some of the most influential modern theories of perception. Piaget's constructivist theory is descended from the empiricists, and Spelke and Baillargeon offer nativist accounts, but this is an area where you may come across different categorizations of theories. Gibson's theory is often referred to as a nativist theory, as she claims that infants can perceive basic information without experience. However, Gibson and Pick (2000) place Gibson's theory at the other end of the theoretical continuum from both nativism and constructivism, arguing that the latter both require infants to build up an internal mental representation of the world, whereas the ecological view focuses on learning to detect information that is present in the environment.

Theories of perceptual development

Piagetian theory

As we saw in Chapter 1, Piaget adopted a constructivist perspective, in which an organism interacts with the environment to create or *construct* meaning. With respect to perception, Piaget (1954, 1969) argued that early perceptual abilities are based on action and experience. Newborn babies receive information from their senses but they cannot make sense of it without the mental structures to interpret it. As infants mature and gain greater experience, they modify and create mental structures through the processes of assimilation and accommodation. Interaction with the environment enables infants to learn to make sense of the sensory information they receive. In other words, they learn to perceive. According to Piaget, the development of perceptual abilities is a result of the development of general cognitive processes which enables infants to mentally represent objects. The starting point is not a blank slate, but an ensemble of reflexes, such as sucking, grasping and orienting towards stimuli. These reflexes may not seem to have much in common with the mental structures necessary for an understanding of depth perception or object permanence, but they are the building blocks upon which more sophisticated concepts can be constructed.

object permanence The concept that objects exist independently of being directly perceived.

The first of Piaget's four stages of development is the sensorimotor stage, occurring from birth to 2 years of age. Piaget posited six substages, during which infants develop from possessing a few basic reflexes through to creating mental representations of objects and events. At first, newborn babies' actions are reflexive, but over the first few weeks of life these reflexes are applied adaptively so that a baby will apply an action differentially to different types of object. It is here that the earliest use of accommodation can be seen. For example, newborns will initially suck equally on any object that comes into contact with their mouth, but they modify their sucking behaviour depending on the object. They will suck harder on a nipple than on an object which doesn't deliver milk; they have adapted their reflexes as a result of interactions with the environment. This first substage, which occurs during the first month of life, is concerned with the modification of reflexes. From 1 to 4 months, infants direct their actions more deliberately and will repeat actions if they produce an interesting effect. At this point, they will only reproduce actions that have an effect on their body. For example, if sucking a thumb is pleasurable, they will repeat the behaviour. In the third substage, from 4 to 8 months, infants become more interested in the world beyond their own bodies, and will repeat actions that have effects on objects in the world, such as striking a rattle to make it produce a sound. It is not until the fourth substage, from 8 to 12 months, that Piaget thought infants have any real understanding of the physical world. In this stage, infants coordinate their actions in order to achieve goals, such as moving an obstacle out of the way then reaching for a toy. This demonstrates an understanding of cause and effect. At the same time, Piaget observed that infants will search for objects they cannot see, suggesting they have – in the absence of the real object – created a rudimentary internal mental representation of the object. This representation is basic and lacks flexibility; infants will search for an object in the location they last found it, even if they have seen it moved to a new location. In the fifth substage (12 to 18 months) infants repeat their actions in a much more flexible way, searching for new ways to interact with objects. An example noted by Piaget (1962b) is dropping a series of objects whilst holding an arm out in different positions. The final substage of the sensorimotor stage (18 to 24 months) marks the transition from action to representation as infants start to create internal mental representations that are flexible and persist over time.

Piaget's account of the first two years of life demonstrates how, with just the simple motor reflexes of birth to begin with, infants build mental structures which enable them to act on different objects in different ways, coordinate their actions and put them into the service of exploring the behaviours of a range of objects. Without acting on the environment and experiencing the outcomes of these actions, infants would not be able to construct an understanding of the world.

> Q. If infants' interpretation of the world is based on action and experience, would we expect to find very early perceptual abilities?

According to Piaget's theory, we should not expect to find any sophisticated perceptual abilities early on. However, Baillargeon's experiments, using the violation of expectations method, show that infants perceive objects in an adult-like way much earlier than Piaget suggested.

Ecological theory

Eleanor Gibson's (1969) ecological theory is based on the perceptual theory of her husband James Gibson (1950, 1966). Whereas Piaget believed that we needed to carry out actions on objects in order to create perceptual knowledge (Gratch, 1975), Gibson argued that perceptions are direct. Gibson's position is that the world contains structure independently of our observations of it and that our sensory systems have evolved such that they are tuned for the types of information available in the world. Survival for animals and humans alike depends on accurate perception of objects and events, so the organisms that survived were the ones with more accurate perception. For Gibson, perception is therefore the process of making sense of, or 'picking up' the cues in the world without the need for mental representations to mediate between sensation and perception. Examples of the information necessary for an infant to make sense of the world include linear perspective, relative and familiar size, height in the visual field, surface texture, shading, shadows and motion. Another example is texture gradient, where the density of a uniformly textured surface increases with distance. Think of a pebbled beach. The observer can see a collection of pebbles, but as he looks into the distance, the pebbles appear to become smaller and more tightly packed. According to Gibson, texture gradients cue visual depth directly and the perceptual systems of newborns are capable of perceiving them. This means that young infants are therefore capable of perceiving visual depth to some extent. Features such as texture gradient are invariant, meaning they do not change, and give us important clues as to the nature of objects. Alongside this direct perception, another important concept in Gibson's theory is the idea of affordances. Affordances are qualities of objects, made available to us through their invariant features, which provide us with ways to interact with them. A handle affords grasping by virtue of its shape, for example, and a flat surface affords resting objects (or oneself) upon it. Some surfaces afford walking whereas others, such as stairs, afford crawling for an infant. These affordances are perceptible by infants without requiring that they develop concepts or mental representations.

This is not to say, however, that we are born with fully developed perceptual skills. There is plenty of room for perceptual learning in Gibson's theory.

direct perception
Picking up information from the environment without the mediation of mental representations.

affordances Features of the environment that provide opportunities for a particular action.

We develop by getting better at perceiving the information in the environment, with respect to both individual stimuli and the relationships between objects. We become more efficient at perceiving things and are also able to perceive more detail as our visual system becomes capable of finer discrimination. We also develop individual differences in our perception of affordances. Gibson and Pick (2000) give the example of rock climbers developing an appreciation of affordances present in surfaces which are not apparent to people who are not rock climbers. Gibson's view of the development of perception involves both biological and experiential components. We are born with perceptual abilities but we need experience of the process of perceiving to develop our abilities.

> Q. If Gibson's theory is correct, what perceptual abilities would we expect to find in newborn babies, and what abilities would we expect to develop later?

Later on in this chapter, we will look at how early in life infants are able to display perceptual abilities. We will also examine which abilities take time to develop, and the role of experience in these changes.

Core knowledge theory

Whereas Piaget thought that infants cannot perceive objects until they have had experience with them, and Gibson argued that they can perceive objects via the information inherent in them, Spelke (1994, 1998, 2000; Kinzler and Spelke 2007; Spelke and Kinzler, 2007) argues that the abilities of infants are best explained by positing a system of core knowledge. This core knowledge consists of sets of domain-specific principles that are used to construct representations and as a set of foundations on which new cognitive skills can be built. Initially, Spelke (1994) proposed four domains of core knowledge: physics, psychology, number and geometry. In more recent work she refers to these systems as relating to objects, agents/actions, numbers and places, and added a fifth system of knowledge: social partners (Kinzler and Spelke 2007; Spelke and Kinzler, 2007). With respect to objects, she proposes three principles young infants appear to make use of: cohesion, continuity and contact. Respectively, these principles are (i) objects are connected and bounded – they do not split or merge; (ii) objects trace a single path through time and space – they do not disappear and reappear elsewhere, nor can they pass through one another; and (iii) objects can only affect one another by touching – there is no action at a distance. According to Spelke, these principles guide infants' perceptual development with respect to physical objects, but they do not guide our understanding of the other domains of psychology, number or geometry. These principles are not, of course, the sum of an adults' knowledge of physics. We come to learn other principles, for example, inertia and gravity, over time. Spelke has marshalled a great deal of evidence in support of her position. This includes research demonstrating that animals possess constraints on their object representations consistent with the principles of continuity and contact (Santos, 2004), and research showing that human object knowledge is universal, regardless of other differences in language and cognition (Everett, 2005), as well as a huge body of work in developmental psychology (e.g., Aguiar and Baillargeon, 1999; Spelke, 1990).

Baillargeon (1994) initially disagreed with Spelke's idea that the evidence shows innate perceptual knowledge, arguing that we have innate mechanisms rather than innate knowledge. Baillargeon claimed that infants are not born with substantive beliefs about objects but with highly constrained mechanisms that guide the development of their understanding about objects and experiences. This account was based on the observation that infants often follow the same pattern of discovery each time they learn about a new physical phenomenon. For example, if infants possess the continuity principle, they understand that objects cannot pass through one another. If Spelke is correct, infants should be able to apply this principle to all relevant phenomena. They should not only understand that an object cannot pass through a solid barrier, but also that a large object cannot pass through a small opening. However, Baillargeon found that infants' expectations of the behaviours of different objects develop at different rates for different objects and actions. She proposed that for each type of event (e.g., collision of objects, occlusion of objects, or the barrier behind the drawbridge discussed at the beginning of this chapter), infants first form a preliminary 'all or none' concept that captures the essence of the phenomenon, then elaborate upon this concept. For example, if an object is placed on top of another, but only a small fraction of the surface is supported, then an 'all or none' concept would lead infants to expect that the object on top will not fall. With greater experience, they come to understand that whether the object falls depends on the proportion of it that is supported by the lower object (Baillargeon, Needham and DeVos, 1992). More recently, Baillargeon (2008; Baillargeon *et al.*, 2009) has proposed a core knowledge account, in which she replaces Spelke's principles of continuity and cohesion with a single principle of persistence, whereby infants possess the core knowledge that objects do not change their properties as they move through time and space. According to this account, the reason why infants fail to note violations of persistence in some tasks but not others, is because they have not included information about the key variable, such as the height or width of an object, in their representations of the event. As they get older, they become more adept at representing the important variables and no longer fail to be surprised by impossible events.

Research methodologies

In order to attempt to answer questions about what infants can perceive, psychologists have had to develop appropriate research methodologies. These largely focus on allowing us to discern whether an infant can detect a perceptual stimulus or not and whether they can discriminate between two stimuli. As infants lack the communicative skills to directly tell us what they can perceive, perception research relies on inferences from behaviours.

Fantz (1958, 1961) argued that measuring infants' preference for one visual stimulus over another is a useful way to examine their perceptual abilities. In order to determine their preferences he developed the preferential looking technique. In this technique, infants are presented with two stimuli. The amount of time they spend looking at each stimulus is measured. If the infant looks at one stimulus more than the other, we can conclude that they can discriminate between the two. However, if an infant does not exhibit a preference for one stimulus over another, it cannot be taken as evidence that he cannot discriminate between the two.

In the habituation procedure, a stimulus is presented to the infant, who will usually attend to it if there are no other changes to the environment. Over time, the infant's attention will decrease as he becomes familiar with it, which is called habituation to the stimulus. After the infant has become habituated to a stimulus, a new

preferential looking A technique in which the relative amounts of time spent looking at two stimuli are compared in order to determine which stimulus is preferred.

habituation A decrease in response to a stimulus after repeated exposure to it.

stimulus can be presented. If the infant can discriminate between the old stimulus and the new one, he will attend to the new stimulus, a process referred to as dishabituation.

The **conditioned head rotation** procedure was devised to assess auditory perception and can be used with infants aged 6 months and older (Werker *et al.*, 1998). A speaker is placed to the side of the infant. When a sound is played through the speaker, the infant will orient towards the sound. This head rotation behaviour can then be conditioned by reinforcing the response with the presentation of a toy or a cartoon. Once infants are conditioned, it is possible to play sounds in order to determine whether infants can detect them or to change between different sounds to investigate whether infants can discriminate between them.

The **high amplitude sucking** procedure makes use of habituation and conditioning. The infant is given a dummy to suck and presented with a 'reward' such as an image or a sound if he increases his sucking rate. When he loses interest in the stimulus, his sucking rate will decrease. The experimenter can then present the infant with a new stimulus. If the infant dishabituates and increases his sucking rate again, it can be inferred that the infant can discriminate between the two stimuli and is treating the new stimulus as novel. If there is no dishabituation, then it can be inferred that the infant cannot tell the difference between the two stimuli.

conditioned head rotation A procedure in which responses in the form of orientation towards stimuli are reinforced.

high amplitude sucking A rate of sucking above the baseline rate.

Basic perceptual abilities

Visual perception

Research has shown us that newborns' visual acuity is around one-twentieth that of an adult. Visual acuity is usually measured using the Snellen system, whereby normal vision is defined as discriminating a pattern separated by a visual angle of one minute at a distance of 20 feet. Visual angle refers to the width of the object in the visual field. One minute is one-sixtieth of a degree. If you have had an eye test in which you had to look at a chart consisting of various letters, with the largest at the top and smallest at the bottom, then your eyesight has been tested using this method. A person is said to have '20/20' vision if he can discriminate the one minute pattern at a distance of 20 feet. If the smallest line he can read is one in which the letters are twice as big, he has 20/40 vision. Newborn infants, therefore, have 20/400 vision. This means that an object 20 feet away from an infant would be as clear to them as it would be to you (assuming you have 20/20 vision) at a distance of 400 feet!

Fantz, Ordy and Udelf (1962) measured an involuntary response to a repetitive moving pattern, consisting of slow tracking of some part of the pattern followed by a saccade to another, succeeding part of the pattern, which is then slowly tracked, and so on. This response is called optokinetic nystagmus (OKN). They presented 46 infants aged from 4 days to 6 months with a large moving field of stripes, gradually reducing the width of the stripes. When the stripes are too thin for an infant to discriminate, the pattern appears as uniform grey and OKN ceases. They found that OKN was present in infants aged 0 to 3 months for stripes with a visual angle of 20 minutes. A stripe one-sixteenth of an inch wide, viewed from a distance of 10 inches, has a visual angle of 20 minutes. Infants aged 3 to 5 months responded to stripes with a width of 10 minutes, and the oldest group, 5- to 6-month-olds, could see stripes just 5 minutes in width. Figure 2.4 shows examples of stripes of these three different widths.

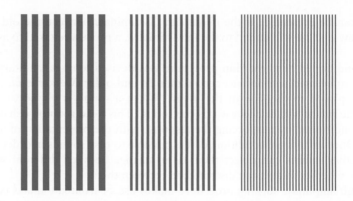

Figure 2.4

Stripes of 1/16th, 1/32nd and 1/64th inch in width. At a distance of 10 inches these have respective visual angles of 20, 10 and 5 minutes.

Fantz *et al.* (1962) used the preferential looking method as well as the OKN method. They presented 37 infants aged 1 to 22 weeks with one plain grey 'pattern' and one stripy pattern and systematically varied the width of the stripes. They found that the minimum width of stripes that could be reliably discerned by infants aged up to 2 months was 40 minutes of visual angle. Infants aged 2 to 4 months could discern stripes with a visual angle of 20 minutes, and infants aged 4 to 5 months could see thinner stripes with a width of 10 minutes. The findings are consistent with the results from the OKN experiment. Fantz *et al.*'s findings roughly correspond to 20/400 vision for infants aged below 2 months, 20/200 for 2- to 4-month-olds and 20/100 for 4- to 6-month-olds. However, other studies have shown even poorer visual acuity of 20/670 in newborns (Gorman, Cogan and Gellis, 1957, 1959). Visual acuity improves throughout infancy and early childhood, reaching adult levels at around 5 years of age (Mayer and Dobson, 1982).

Young infants prefer stimuli with moderate levels of intensity and complexity. A study in which they were shown checkerboard patterns with different numbers of squares shows this. At three weeks old, infants looked longest at boards with just four squares (a 2 × 2 array), 8-week-olds preferred an 8 × 8 board and 14-week-olds preferred a 24 × 24 board (Brennan, Ames and Moore, 1966). They also prefer curved or circular patterns to straight lines (Fantz and Miranda, 1975). Colour perception is limited at birth but develops throughout the first year of life (Kellman and Arterberry, 2006; Okamura, Kanazawa and Yamaguchi, 2007). Infants can discriminate between red and green when they are 1 month old and they can discriminate between green and yellow at 2 months, but they cannot discriminate red from yellow until 3 months (Adams and Courage, 1995). Newborns seem to prefer to look at moving objects rather than stationary objects (Nelson and Horowitz, 1987; Slater *et al.*, 1985), but they have difficulties in tracking them as their eye movements are jerky. It is not until 2 to 3 months of age that infants' tracking becomes smoother and more adultlike and even then they can only track slow moving objects (Aslin, 1981). A related behaviour is scanning, in which the eye traces a path across a visual stimulus. The eye cannot see all of one image at once so it makes small rapid movements to move from one point of focus to the next. One-month-old infants scan small localized bits of an object – usually around the edges, whereas 2-month-olds spend more time scanning finer details, especially facial features such as eyes nose and mouth (Maurer and Salapatek, 1976). Figure 2.5 shows typical scanning patterns for 1- and 2-month-old infants.

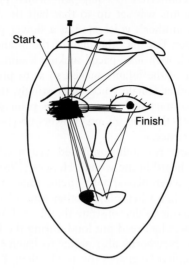

Figure 2.5

Typical face scanning patterns of 1- and 2-month-olds.

Source: Salapatek. P., Pattern perception in early infancy. In L.B. Cohen P. Salapatek (Eds.), *Infant perception: From Sensation to Cognition Vol. 1: Basic visual processes* (pp. 144–248). Copyright Elsevier (1988).

Auditory perception

Basic auditory abilities can be tested with the conditioned head rotation procedure, change in heart rate or the blink response. If a child hears a sudden, loud sound they will blink and their heart rate will increase. There are two basic aspects of sensitivity to sound: volume and pitch. Schulman-Galambos and Galambos (1979) found that the quietest sounds newborns could hear were around 20 dB; adults can usually hear sounds as quiet as 0–5 dB. However, people of all ages demonstrate a differential sensitivity to sounds, depending on pitch. Adults are more sensitive to middle-frequency sounds (around 2 to 4 KHz) than to low frequency (below 1 KHz) or high frequency (10 to 20 KHz) sounds (Schneider *et al.*, 1986). For reference, middle C is 261.6 Hz. Although infants are not as sensitive to any pitch as adults, the discrepancy is highest at the low end of the spectrum (200 to 400 Hz); 6-month-olds cannot detect these sounds as levels below 30 dB (about the volume of a whisper), whereas adults can usually detect them at 10 dB. Six-month-olds can hear high frequency sounds (10 KHz) at levels of 20 dB (Trehub, Schneider and Endman, 1980), compared to 5 dB for adults. Interestingly, by the time we get up to 19 KHz (6 octaves above middle C), infants' and adults' sensitivity is closer: 30 db for adults and 40 dB for infants (Schneider, Trehub and Bull, 1980). Over the first five years of life, children's sensitivity to volume across the frequency spectrum improves. By this point, sensitivity to 10 KHz sounds is at adult levels. It takes another three years to reach adult levels of sensitivity to middle frequencies and another two years to fully develop sensitivity to low frequencies (Trehub *et al.*, 1988).

Auditory perception may be limited at birth, but newborns still display some impressive abilities, such as recognizing the sound of their mother's voice. DeCasper and Fifer (1980) demonstrated that newborns prefer their mother's voice to the voices of other females within the first three days of birth. They demonstrated this using the high amplitude sucking technique with ten infants. First, the researchers made audio recordings of the infants' mothers reading a Dr Seuss story.

The infants wore headphones and were given a false nipple to suck. The nipple was connected to equipment which played sounds through the headphones. The apparatus was set up so that half the infants had to suck in rapid bursts to elicit their mother's voice, and at a slower pace to hear the voice of a different infant's mother. For the other half of the infants, the experiment was set up the other way round, with slow-paced sucking leading to the presentation of their mother's voice. Eight of the infants sucked so as to produce their mother's voice more often than the other female voice. Interestingly, the infants in this study had had 12 hours or less contact with their mothers prior to testing, which led DeCasper and Fifer to suggest that the infants' powers of voice recognition may be affected by pre-natal experience.

Later research confirmed that newborns exhibit a preference for sounds they have heard in the womb. Hepper (1988) found that 2- to 4-day-olds reacted differently when played a TV theme tune that their mothers had listened to whilst pregnant, than when played other tunes. DeCasper and Spence (1986) used the sucking technique to demonstrate that 2- and 3-day-olds preferred hearing a story that their mothers had read out loud during the last six weeks of pregnancy, to an unfamiliar story. Newborns also prefer to listen to the language spoken by their mothers to unfamiliar languages (Byers-Heinlein, Burns and Werker, 2010).

Tactile, olfactory and taste perception

Although there is relatively little research on these three modalities compared to the body of work on vision and hearing, the evidence indicates that infants can interpret tactile sensations, smells and tastes from birth. Newborns are highly sensitive to touch and can distinguish between hard and soft objects. They make different kinds of hand and mouth movements when their hand or mouth is in contact with a hard or soft object (Rochat, 1987). They can feel a puff of air on the cheek or forearm, although they show a stronger response to the facial stimulation (Muir, Humphrey and Humphrey, 1994), and are sensitive to temperature (Hernandez-Reif *et al.*, 2003).

It is possible to measure infants' reactions to smells and tastes using a variety of measures such as heart rate, respiration or event related potentials (see Box 2.1), but a simpler method is to look at their facial expressions as they will make a face in response to unpleasant odours and turn away from them. Engen, Lipsitt and Kaye (1963) found that newborns could differentiate between vinegar, licorice and alcohol, and Goubet *et al.* (2002) demonstrated they could discriminate between vanilla and anethole (a compound found in anise, fennel and liquorice). Infants who have been breast-fed prefer odours from their mothers to odours from other women, but bottle-fed babies do not recognize maternal odours (Cernoch and Porter, 1985). Bottle-fed female infants are, however, attracted to the smell of a lactating female with whom they are unfamiliar (Makin and Porter, 1989). The former result suggests that preference for the smell of the mother develops quickly, in the first few days of life, but the latter suggests that there may be an innate preference for smells associated with lactation.

Turning to taste, the pictures in Figure 2.6 are from Rosenstein and Oster's (1988) study in which they gave twelve 2-hour-old infants substances that were sweet (sucrose), sour (citric acid), salty (sodium chloride) and bitter (quinine hydrochloride). The newborns' responses demonstrate different reactions to the different tastes and, therefore, the ability to perceive them.

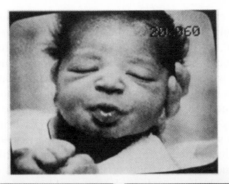

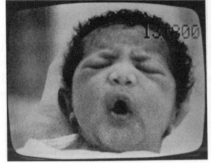 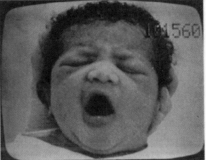

Figure 2.6

Reactions to different tastes: Sweet (top), sour (bottom left), and bitter (bottom right)

Source: Reprinted from Rosenstein, D., & Oster, H. (1988). Differential facial responses to four basic taste- sin newborns. *Child Development*, 59(6), 1555–1568, with permission from Wiley.

It is clear that newborns respond in different ways to sweet, sour, salt and bitter. They prefer sweet to salt (Crook, 1978), and can also detect levels of sweetness and differences between different sweet tastes. Desor, Maller and Turner (1973) gave 1- to 4-day old infants solutions of sucrose, glucose, fructose and lactose, each with four different concentration levels (0.05, 0.10, 0.20 and 0.30 moles per litre). The infants ingested a greater quantity of the solutions with higher concentrations of sugar, suggesting they preferred the sweeter solutions. They preferred sucrose and fructose more than glucose and lactose, suggesting they could discriminate between them.

Intermodal perception

Intermodal perception refers to the coordination of sensory information from different modalities, such as detecting the audio-visual synchrony of someone playing a musical instrument. This is the ability to understand that information received by one sense organ can relate to the information received by another sense organ. Gibson (1969) argues that the perception system is unified at birth, and is capable of detecting amodal relations. Rather than coordinating all their senses, infants do not differentiate between visual and auditory stimuli, for example, so if they hear a sound they will orientate all receptors to it. So in a sense intermodal perceptual development may not depend on coordinating different senses but on recognizing which sense is being stimulated. An opposing view is the integrationist position, consistent with Piaget (1954), which is that we start out with separate senses and need experience to coordinate them (Birch and Lefford, 1963).

The evidence points to very early competence. Sight and sound coordination seems to be achieved by infants of about 4 months old. There are lots of types of experiments. In one example, infants were shown two films concurrently, one depicting a woman hiding her face with her hands and uncovering it while saying 'Hello baby, peekaboo', the other showing a hand using a stick to rhythmically strike a wooden block. Although both films were presented at the same time, only one of the two soundtracks was played for the duration of the films. The aim of this experiment was to see whether infants would spend more time looking at the film that matched the soundtrack than the one that didn't. Spelke (1976) carried this study out with twenty-four infants aged 3–4 months. Each infant saw the films twice, once with each soundtrack. All but one of the participants spent more time looking at the film that matched the soundtrack than the film that didn't. She presents two explanations for this finding: Either the infants already knew what kind of images went with the sound, or they were able to perceive the similarities between the visual and auditory stimuli. Either way, it is clear that the ability to coordinate sight and sound is present by 4 months of age. Bahrick, Walker and Neisser (1981) carried out a series of experiments with the aim of determining the extent to which the soundtrack directed visual attention to one of the films. In one of these experiments, two films (one displaying rhythmic handclapping, the other showing a pair of hands manipulating a slinky toy) were initially superimposed along with either the sound of handclapping or the slinky toy. After 20 seconds, the sound ceased and the films moved so as to appear side-by-side. Thirteen of 16 participating 4-month-olds looked first at the film that did not match the soundtrack in the majority of the trials. Bahrick *et al.* interpret this as evidence that the non-soundtrack film appeared to be novel to the participants and that they had therefore not attended to it during the superimposition phase of the experiment. This supports the idea that visual attention was guided by the similarities between the visual and auditory stimuli.

Further research by Morrongiello, Fenwick and Chance (1998) investigated whether infants could learn arbitrary correspondences between visual and auditory stimuli. In this study, thirty-six infants aged 38 to 42 weeks old were presented with *Sesame Street* toys and a rattle sound. In one condition, infants were shown two toys, one on their left and one on their right, both of which were near loudspeakers. In the habituation trials, the toys were sometimes presented with Toy A on the left and Toy B on the right, and sometimes the other way round. In all cases the rattle sound came from the speaker near Toy A. Once the infants were habituated, the sound would come from the speaker near Toy B. The researchers were interested in whether the infants would look longer in the test trials, displaying renewed interest, which would suggest that they did not expect the new toy-sound pairing and had therefore learnt the original toy-sound pairing. In a second condition, the experimental procedure was the same except only one toy was presented, so that in the test trials the sound was played in a location where there was no toy. In the final, control condition there was again only one toy, but this time both toy and sound were always presented to one side of the infants during habituation, then moved to the other side for the test trials. If the infants have learned the toy-sound pairing, and know that an object and its sound does not depend on where they are located, they should not show surprise at the change of location. The results showed increased-looking times in the test trials for the first two conditions, but not for the control condition. Morrongiello *et al.* concluded that the infants were capable of crossmodal learning and that this finding supports Spelke's ideas about innate core principles. Evidence for even earlier intermodal perception comes from research conducted on 1-month-olds. Meltzoff and Borton (1979) gave 32 infants one of two different dummies to suck (see Figure 2.7). Importantly, the infants were not able to see the dummy they had sucked. The infants were then

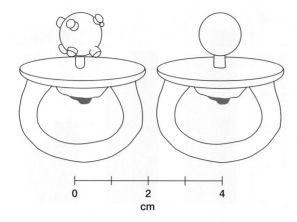

Figure 2.7

Dummies used by
Meltzoff and Borton.

Source: Reprinted by permission from Macmillan Publishers Ltd: Nature, 28: 403–404, © 1979.

shown the two dummies. Three-quarters of the infants looked more at the one they hadn't sucked.

Over time, infants' ability to integrate information from the different senses improves. Infants develop the ability to match faces to voices at 6 months of age (Bahrick, Hernandez-Reif and Flom, 2005) and there is a marked improvement in audio-visual integration at 8 to 10 months (Neil *et al.*, 2006). In addition to an increasing ability to integrate information across modalities, there is a large body of evidence that demonstrates an increase in the specificity of the types of information that are integrated, from global synchrony e.g., an object hits another object at the same time as a sound is made, to arbitrary relations e.g., the relationship between the pitch of a sound and the colour of an object (Bahrick, 2000). Lewkowicz and Ghazanfar (2009) argue that a process of 'perceptual narrowing' takes place during the first year of life. Perceptual narrowing refers to a decreasing sensitivity to stimuli that are not commonly present in infants' environments, such that they lose the ability to match crossmodal stimuli if, for example, the visual component is a non-human face (Lewkowicz and Ghazanfar, 2006) or the audio component is not a native speech sound (Pons *et al.*, 2009). Lewkowicz and Ghazanfar suggest that this may be due to selective elaboration of synapses; new synaptic connections are formed on the basis of experience and therefore infants become 'tuned' to stimuli they have a lot of experience with.

Making sense of the world

Face perception

As we saw earlier, newborn babies have very low visual acuity. We also saw that they prefer moderately complex stimuli and curved patterns, and that they start to attend to the middle of faces, rather than the edges, by the age of 2 months. Using the preferential-looking method, Fantz (1961) presented infants aged 1 to 6 months with a series of six flat disks with a diameter of six inches. These were a schematic face, a patch of print, a bulls-eye and three plain circles coloured red, white and yellow. He found that even infants who were less than a week old could discriminate between these different patterns. He found that a clear preference for the face stimulus was apparent at 2 to 3 months, and that that this preference increased after 3 months.

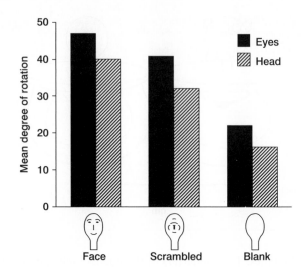

Figure 2.8

Results from Johnson *et al.* (1991).

Source: Reprinted from Cognition, 40, Johnson, M. H., Dziurawiec, S., Ellis, H., & Morton, J., Newborns' preferential tracking of face-like stimuli and its subsequent decline, 1–19, Copyright (1991), with permission from Elsevier.

Three decades later, Johnson *et al.* (1991) demonstrated that newborn infants display a preferential response to schematic faces over scrambled faces and blank head outlines (shown at the bottom of Figure 2.8). They showed the three head-size shapes to 24 infants, who were less than an hour old. Initially, each head shape was held directly above the infants' faces. Once the infants fixated on the shape, the experimenter moved the shape slowly to one side, then the other. The infants were videotaped and the angles of head-turn and eye-turn when tracking the stimuli were measured. Figure 2.8 shows the results: The infants turned both head and eyes significantly more for the face than the scrambled face, and significantly more for the scrambled face than the blank outline. Although this seems to indicate a clear preference for faces from birth, findings from another study conducted by the same team paint a less straightforward picture. Johnson *et al.* (1992) presented three groups of infants, aged 1 month, 10 weeks and 5 months, with four schematic head shapes projected on a screen. One shape was very face-like; the second had the configuration of eyes, nose and mouth, but without the actual features; the third had face-like features in a linear configuration; and the fourth had scrambled elements of face-like features (see Figure 2.9). In this experiment the images were not moved, and the amount of time the infants looked at each image before turning away was recorded. Johnson *et al.* found no significant differences in looking times for the four stimuli for the 1-month-olds, but they did find that the 10-week-olds looked longer at the face-like image than the others. There was also a difference in the 5-month-olds, but in the opposite direction; they spent *less* time looking at the face-like image than the other images. Johnson *et al.* thought that this surprising result may have been due to the fact that older infants have a more sophisticated understanding of what a face is like and expect the features to move, so they carried out a second experiment in which the features were made to move slightly. This time, they found that looking time duration was greater for the moving face than for the other stimuli in 5-month-olds.

Taken together, the findings from these studies show that newborns prefer schematic faces to less face-like stimuli, and also that it is not until 2 to 3 months that infants prefer faces. How can this contradiction be explained? Morton and Johnson (1991) propose the idea that there are two separate mechanisms at work. The first,

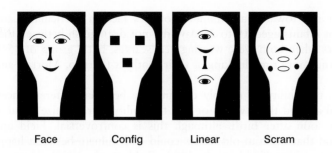

Face   Config   Linear   Scram

Figure 2.9

The stimuli used by Johnson *et al.* (1992).

Source: Copyright © 1991 by the American Psychological Association. Reproduced with permission. The official citation that should be used in referencing this material is Morton, J., & Johnson, M. H. (1991). CONSPEC and CONLERN: A two-process theory of infant face recognition. *Psychological Review*, 98(2), 164–181. The use of APA information does not imply endorsement by APA.

which they call CONSPEC, contains innate knowledge of the visual structure of the faces of conspecifics (members of the same species). The second mechanism is called CONLERN, and is used to learn about the visual features of conspecifics. According to Morton and Johnson, CONSPEC guides infants' attention towards faces, which is why newborns show a face preference in Johnson *et al.*'s (1991) study. Over the next two months, the subcorticol pathways utilized by CONSPEC are inhibited, whilst CONLERN guides the infant's acquisition of knowledge about human faces. This explains why 10-week-olds, but not infants, demonstrated a face preference in Johnson *et al.*'s (1992) study. Finally, the reason why 5-month-olds did not show a preference for a static face, but did prefer a face with moving features, is that by this age CONLERN has learned enough that simple static schematic faces are no longer interesting.

Alongside the preference for faces, infants develop the ability to distinguish familiar from unfamiliar faces early in life. A number of studies in the 1970s and 1980s provided evidence that 1-month-olds (Carpenter, 1974; Maurer and Salapatek, 1976), and even infants in their first week of life (Field *et al.* 1984; Bushnell, Sai and Mullen, 1989) can discriminate between their mother's face and that of a female stranger. In order to control for inadvertent cues, such as change of expression from the mother, Walton, Bower and Bower (1992) showed twelve 12- to 36-hour-old infants a still image of their mother on a computer screen. This was paired with an image of a stranger with the same eye colour, complexion, hair colour and hair style. Walton *et al.* used a sucking technique, whereby infants could control which image appeared on the screen by varying the rate at which they sucked on a dummy. A high sucking rate maintained the current image, whereas a delay of one second between sucks caused the other image to appear. The infants sucked significantly more in response to their mother's face than to the stranger's face. Taken together, the results of these studies suggest that very little exposure to their mothers is needed for newborns to recognize them. Does this offer support for Morton and Johnson's (1991) CONSPEC mechanism? Pascalis *et al.* (1995) designed a study to test this question. As the hypothesized CONSPEC mechanism must rely on configural information about facial features, rather than variable peripheral characteristics such as hair outline, infants should be able to recognize their mother when only these internal facial features are visible if they possess this innate knowledge. The researchers showed twenty 3- to 7-day-old infants an image of their mother and an image of a female stranger, both wearing pale pink headscarves attached under the chin. The infants did not look any longer at their mothers than the strangers, leading Pascalis *et al.* to conclude that the hairline and head contour are necessary for facial identification. Therefore, if there is a CONSPEC mechanism, it can direct attention to faces in general, but not towards an infant's mother's face in particular. Later research revealed that infants aged 19 to 25 days did not distinguish between their mothers and strangers when both were wearing headscarves, but a group of 35- to 40-day-olds did spend more time looking at their mothers (Bartrip, Morton and de Schonen, 2001).

Although the ability to reliably discriminate between different faces does not emerge until around three weeks of age, the ability to recognize facial expressions may appear soon after birth, although this is controversial. Field and her colleagues found that 36-hour-old babies could discriminate between happy, sad and surprised expressions (Field *et al.*, 1982; Field *et al.*, 1983). However, a more rigorously controlled replication study conducted a few years later failed to find the same effects (Kaitz *et al.*, 1988). More recently, Farroni *et al.* (2007) found no preference between fearful and neutral expressions in newborns, but did find a preference for happy faces over fearful ones. Older infants have been shown to discriminate between a wide range of pairs of expressions, including happy and angry at 3 months (Barrera and Maurer, 1981), sad and fearful at 5 months (Schwartz, Izard and Ansul, 1985), and happy and fearful at 7 months (Nelson and Dolgin, 1985). Infants can also discriminate between different intensities of a single expression. Kuchuk, Vibbert and Bornstein (1986) found that 3-month-olds spent more time looking at intense smiling faces than faces with only a mild smile.

Evidence from cognitive neuroscience. If there are specialized neural mechanisms that process information about faces, then one way of shedding light on their existence is to conduct studies using the methods of cognitive neuroscience. Some of the techniques that are available are described in Box 2.1. De Haan, Pascalis and Johnson (2002) examined event related potentials (ERPs) to see if there is a specific electrical response to faces in the infant cortex. It is known that an area of the fusiform gyrus, known as the fusiform face area, becomes active in adults when looking at faces (Kanwisher, McDermott and Chun, 1997), and that a negative ERP with a 170 ms delay (N170) is produced in response to face stimuli (Bentin *et al.*, 1996). De Haan *et al.* looked at the ERPs of thirty-four 6-month-olds infants when presented with human and monkey faces. Although they did find a negative potential that seems to correspond with the adult N170, it occurred later in infants (260–336 ms) and had a smaller amplitude. The infant 'N170' (which is now known as the N290) was larger for human faces than monkey faces, suggesting that the infants treated the monkey faces more like objects than faces. In addition to the negative ERP, de Haan *et al.* found a later positive potential, the P400, which they argue may be involved in processes which are integrated into the N170 by adulthood. De Haan *et al.* conclude that six months' experience is not sufficient for adult-like specialized face processing to develop. This means that, even if there are specialized neural circuits for face processing, they need time to develop. ERPs have also been used to study infants' processing of facial expressions. Rigato, Farroni and Johnson (2010) studied the ERPs of adults and 4-month-old infants who were watching pictures of happy and fearful faces. In adults, they found that N170 and P1 (a positive potential at around 120 ms) were affected by facial expression; the peaks of the responses were earlier for happy faces than for fearful faces. In the infants, both facial expressions elicited P1, N290 and P400 responses. The N290 and P400 peaked earlier for happy faces, suggesting that infant and adult processing of emotions is similar, as both the N170 in adults and the N290/P400 in infants reflect face encoding processes.

Box 2.1 Cognitive neuroscience methods

Developmental cognitive neuroscience is a field which has been growing rapidly over the last 20 years. This growth is partly due to the rise in use of cognitive neuroscientific tools and methods, and partly by a greater need for psychologists to test their ideas concerning development by attempting to map neural activity onto mental events and behaviours. The techniques used by developmental psychologists include:

Functional magnetic resonance imaging (fMRI) is used to measure changes in blood flow that result from neural activity. Active neurons increase oxygen consumption, leading to increased blood flow in the regions of activity. Oxygenated and deoxygenated blood have different magnetic fields, and it is these differences which are measured by placing the participant's head in a powerful magnetic coil. Prior to the invention of fMRI, blood flow had to be measured using positron emission tomography (PET), which involves injecting radioactive substances into the blood and using radiation detectors to measure where the blood concentration is highest. fMRI has the advantage of being non-invasive (unlike PET), and also has good spatial resolution (1 mm), but the temporal resolution is in seconds. fMRI can be used with children, but it does not lend itself to the study of infants as the procedure requires the participants to lie very still inside a very noisy cylinder.

Event-related potentials (ERPs) are electrical responses measured using electroencephalography (EEG). This is achieved by placing a net of electrodes on the scalp and measuring voltage changes. These can be either positive or negative changes and different responses occur at different times after a stimulus is presented. The responses are usually referred to by the directionality of the change and the delay between stimulus and response. Thus, an N170 is a negative voltage change occurring around 170 ms after stimulus onset, and a P300 is a positive voltage change with around a 300 ms delay. ERP recording is the most widely used method in psychology for studying brain activity as it is inexpensive, non-invasive, does not require the participant to be placed in a scanner and has high temporal resolution which means that the timing of electrical potentials can be recorded accurately (at the level of milliseconds). All of the above factors also make this method the most suitable for use with young infants. The one drawback is that there is very poor spatial resolution, making it hard to localize the response.

Magnetoencephalography (MEG) is the magnetic counterpart to EEG. Instead of measuring voltage changes, MEG is used to measure changes in the magnetic field. Whereas fMRI measures blood flow, MEG measures the magnetic fields generated by neuron activity directly. Another advantage over fMRI is that MEG does not require participants to lie in a noisy scanner; instead, they sit in a chair with the top and rear of the head inside a helmet containing the sensors, which are cooled to $-269°C$ with liquid helium. MEG has the same high temporal resolution as EEG, but much better spatial resolution, so can localize responses to within millimetres and milliseconds.

Near infrared spectroscopy (NIRS) is the most recent development in brain imaging. As with fMRI, it makes use of the changing blood flows as a result of brain activity. These changes of blood concentration can be revealed by examining the absorption of light in the near infrared range of the electromagnetic spectrum, just below the visible range. NIRS may provide an excellent way of measuring brain activity in newborns and infants as the light emitters and detectors can be worn as a cap and the technique does not require the infant to be completely still. Spatial and temporal resolution are not as good as fMRI and EEG, respectively, but NIRS can be combined with these techniques to get an improved overall spatiotemporal resolution than either one alone.

Figure 2.10

Imitation of tongue protrusion, mouth opening and lip protrusion.

Source: From Meltzoff, A. N. & Moore, M. K. (1977). Imitation of facial and manual gestures by human neonates. *Science*, 198, 75–8. Reprinted with permission from AAAS.

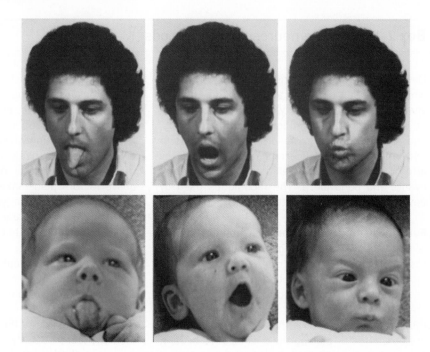

Imitation

It would seem that certain perceptual and cognitive skills are necessary for imitation. If you consider what is involved in imitating a facial expression, we need to see the expression, perceive and understand it, and determine what motor commands we need to send to our facial muscles in order to reproduce the expression. Piaget (1962b) thought newborns could not imitate as they lacked the necessary cognitive skills. He thought that infants' ability to imitate started at about 8 to 9 months of age. However, Meltzoff and Moore (1977) studied infants of between 12 and 21 *days* old and found they could match tongue protrusion, lip protrusion, mouth opening and hand opening and closing (see Figure 2.10).

These findings were replicated in 25 different studies in the 20 years following this initial study (Meltzoff and Moore, 1997). How can such early ability be explained? Meltzoff and Moore ruled out reinforcement on the part of the experimenters and parents as an explanation for this early ability. They hypothesize that early imitation is based on an innate ability to perceive the equivalences between vision and action – a type of intermodal perception. Infants compare the feedback they get from proprioception with the visual target and modify their actions if they do not match. This is not to say that newborns have adult-like concepts, but rather that they have rudimentary mental structures (Meltzoff and Moore, 1997, 1999). This explanation is a type of minimalist nativism, in which the minimum quantity of innate knowledge necessary to explain the behaviours observed is posited. It could, of course, be argued that even in the first two weeks of life, infants have learned something about perception and imitation. However Meltzoff and Moore (1983) found imitation of mouth opening and tongue protrusion in a sample of infants aged from just 42 minutes to 3 days old. In addition, Field *et al.* (1982) found that at just 36 hours of age infants could imitate more complex facial expressions such as happiness, sadness and surprise.

proprioception
Awareness of the position of one's body, derived from receptors in muscles, joints, tendons and the inner ear.

Some of our early ability may be explained by 'mirror neurons'. Rizzolati *et al.* (1996) discovered neurons in monkeys' premotor cortex which fired both when monkeys observed an action being performed, and when they performed it themselves. Mirror neurons are not just involved in the cross-modal association of vision and action, they are also activated for sound-action pairs (Kohler *et al.*, 2002). Until recently, there were no studies offering direct evidence of mirror neurons in humans as it is generally not possible to carry out the same single-cell recordings that have been done with monkeys. However, Mukamel *et al.* (2010) were able to test for the presence of mirror neurons by recruiting patients with epilepsy who had electrodes implanted in their brains to identify the location of their seizures. Mukamel *et al.* found neurons in the supplementary motor cortex and hippocampus that responded to both observing and executing actions. There is also supporting evidence that a more complex system, involving several brain regions, with properties similar to monkey mirror neurons is present in humans (Iacoboni *et al.*, 1999; Rizzolatti and Craighero, 2004). In this system, cortical activity is similar when observing an action carried out and when imitating the action. This may, therefore, provide a neural basis for the direct copying of actions.

Depth perception

Infants start to crawl at around 6 to 9 months. This gives them the ability to direct their own exploration of their environment for the first time. When infants start to crawl they frequently fall off objects such as beds and chairs unless their caregivers are constantly alert or erect a system of barricades to impede the infant. This behaviour suggests that they do not possess a conception of depth, or at least that they do not realize that a fall can be harmful. Depth perception is not just useful for avoiding falls; we use this ability constantly in order to gauge how far away objects are and to navigate through the world, avoiding collisions. Although they sometimes do not behave as if they perceive depth when crawling, infants possess size constancy from birth, which implies they can tell that two apparently different sized objects are identical, but that one is further away than the other. The question of when infants are able to perceive depth is one that has kept psychologists busy for decades. Gibson and Walk (1960) investigated depth perception with a classic experiment known as the visual cliff. The apparatus consists of a central platform with a drop on either side. On one side there is a very shallow drop and on the other side there is a deep drop. Both 'drops' are covered by a glass sheet at the same level as the central platform, and the floor on each side is covered with a patterned cloth (see Figure 2.11). An infant is placed on the central platform and her mother stands at one end beckoning to the child. Gibson and Walk tested 36 infants ranging from 6 to 14 months of age. They found that 27 of the infants crawled to their mothers over the shallow side, but only three crawled over the deep side. A series of follow-up experiments (Walk, 1966) led to similar results. Gibson and Walk concluded that the infants possessed depth perception, as they could discriminate between the two sides. When the patterned cloth was replaced with a homogeneous grey background, 52 per cent of infants aged 7 to 9 months and 29 per cent of 10- to 12-month-olds crossed the deep side. Similarly, a cloth patterned with quarter-inch checks led to 49 per cent of 7- to 9-month-olds and 20 per cent of 10- to 12-month-olds crossing the deep side. This is probably because the small check pattern was seen as a solid colour owing to relatively poor visual acuity. From this it is clear that a large pattern on the floor provides infants with depth cues they can interpret.

Figure 2.11

The visual cliff.

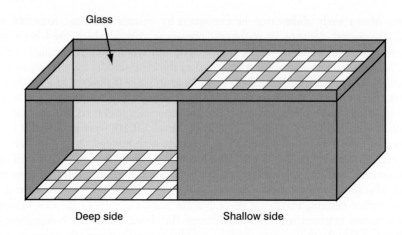

One could conclude from these studies that depth perception is innate. However, in order to conduct a study such as this, it is necessary for the participants to be able to crawl. It could be the case that depth perception is learnt through experience with the world, and crawling babies have lots of opportunities to explore the world and learn about it. In order to examine whether depth perception is a result of experience, Campos, Langer and Krowitz (1970) tested 1½ to 3½-month-old infants by monitoring their heart rates. They laid the babies face down on the apparatus and then suddenly exposed them either to the deep or the shallow drop. Babies exposed to the deep side showed heart rate changes that they did not show when exposed to the shallow side. Campos and Langer (1971) carried out another study on 2-month-olds and found the same distinction between the deep and shallow sides. Importantly, this heart rate change was a decrease, which indicates increased attention, rather than the increase one would expect if the babies were showing fear. This suggests that infants can perceive depth at 2 months, long before they start to move around, but have not yet learnt to be afraid of a drop. Subsequent studies showed that the heart rates of 5-month-olds also decreased when exposed to the visual cliff, but that 9-month-olds' heart rates increased (Schwartz, Campos and Baisel, 1973), and that infants who have been crawling longer are more likely to show fear (Campos *et al.*, 1978).

Another line of research has been conducted on objects that 'loom' at infants and how infants respond to these approaching objects. If we see an object moving towards us on a 'hit path' we will take a defensive reaction to avoid the impending collision. If infants show a reaction, this means they have interpreted the evidence of their senses as meaning an impending collision. There has been a lot of research on this, with some contradictory results. Bower, Broughton and Moore (1970) found that when they presented infants aged 6 to 20 days old with a cube that appeared to move towards them, the infants would raise their heads and arms. Bower *et al.* interpreted this as a defensive reaction. Ball and Tronick (1971) replicated this finding with infants aged 2 to 11 weeks and also demonstrated that infants would not show the defensive reaction if the object was not on a hit trajectory. However, there is more than one interpretation of this behaviour. As an object comes towards you, you have to move your head backwards to track the upper contour. So it may be that all the babies were doing was tracking the object, not showing a true defensive reaction. Yonas *et al.* (1977, 1979) carried out experiments in which an object 'loomed', but on a trajectory such that the top edge remained at the same height in the visual field. In these cases, babies less than 4 months old failed to show a defensive reaction. They concluded that head raising before this age is simply tracking upper contours of objects. They also found that arm raising occurred for all stimuli until about eight months of age. This suggests that a true defensive response, and therefore depth perception, is learnt. However, Náñez (1988) carried out further experiments and found that 3- to 6-week-olds blinked when faced with an apparent collision. Furthermore, he found that when these young infants raised their heads, they were focusing on the centre of the display – not the upper contour. A large body of research demonstrates that by 5 to 7 months of age, infants are sensitive to a variety of depth cues such as shadows (Yonas and Granrud, 2006), height of stimuli in the visual field (Arterberry, 2008), surface contour (Sen, Yonas and Knill, 2001), linear perspective and texture gradients (Arterberry, Yonas and Bensen, 1989), relative size (Yonas, Granrud and Pettersen, 1985) and familiar size (Yonas, Pettersen and Granrud, 1982).

Research on depth perception could, therefore, be interpreted as providing support for Gibson's ecological theory; the infants in these studies may be directly responding to perceptual cues in the objects, with an increase in response strength over time. On the other hand, it could be argued that experience is needed in order for infants to interpret these visual stimuli, and that the Piagetian view is correct. A confounding factor is the development of binocular vision. In order to see depth we need to coordinate both eyes; each eye provides one image and the disparity between them indicates depth to our visual system – this is known as stereopsis. This ability emerges in infants somewhere between three and six months of age and then rapidly develops over the next few months (Fox *et al.*, 1980; Shea *et al.*, 1980). Does this mean that we cannot have depth perception before this? Not necessarily. We can also make use of motion parallax to determine the distance of objects, without the requirement of binocular vision. If you move your head from left to right, you can detect differences in the relative motion of objects depending on how far away they are. Objects that are further away than the fixation point move more quickly across the field of vision than objects that are nearer. Further objects also appear to move in the same direction as the observer's head, whereas objects closer to the observer than the fixation point move in the opposite direction to the observer. Therefore, by moving our heads, we can tell whether objects are nearer or further than a fixation point by observing their apparent motion. In a longitudinal study following infants from 11 to 29 weeks, Nawrot, Mayo and Nawrot (2009) found that infants develop a sensitivity to motion parallax at around 14 to 16 weeks of age. This is within the same period that binocular vision develops, so depth perception may require a sequence of abilities before it is fully developed. It may well be that depth perception is to some extent innate but we are unable to use it until our visual system matures.

Object perception

A vast number of studies have been carried out on object perception in an attempt to discover how children learn to perceive objects in the way that adults perceive them. Piaget (1954) thought that infants younger than about eight or nine months of age are unaware that objects exist independently in time and space; that they exist independently of the child's own perception of the object. He demonstrated this with his object permanence experiments in which children failed to search for a hidden object. Piaget assumed that the failure to search for the object was because they did not realize the object still existed when they couldn't see it. He argued that it is only through repeated experience with objects that infants would come to perceive the true nature of objects, and that this does not occur until the fourth

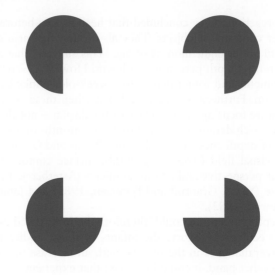

Figure 2.12

A square with
illusory contours.

substage of the sensorimotor stage of development. According to ecological and core knowledge theories, however, infants should be able to perceive objects as independent without the need for experience. There is a lot of evidence showing that newborns are capable of basic form perception (Slater, Morison and Rose, 1983). Both size constancy and shape constancy appear to be present at birth. Size constancy is the ability to perceive a familiar object as the same object regardless of whether it is nearer, and takes up more of the visual field, or further away, taking up less of the visual field (Slater, Mattock and Brown, 1990). Shape constancy is the ability to perceive an object as the same object even if seen from different angles (Slater and Morison, 1985).

Although newborns are sensitive to size and shape despite apparent changes to objects, higher-level visual functions which involve the integration of information about related objects emerge over the next few months. For example, it is not until 7 months of age that infants can perceive illusory contours such as Kanisza squares (see Figure 2.12), although 5-month-olds were able to discriminate the square after repeated exposure (Bertenthal, Campos and Haith, 1980).

Although lots of experiments on object perception have been carried out using stationary objects or pictures, young infants are actually better at perceiving moving objects. By three or four months they can perceive moving objects as whole units and they are able to recognize that an object is the same even if it is making different types of movement. For example, if an infant is habituated to a ball bouncing, she will not dishabituate (show more interest) if she is presented with the same ball rolling (Gibson *et al.*, 1979). By 4 months, infants can use movement cues to inform them that objects are solid and thus take up space. Baillargeon's experiments, based on the study described at the beginning of the chapter, also show that infants perceive objects in an adult-like way much earlier than Piaget suggested. Baillargeon (1987a) followed up on her 1985 study with a series of experiments in which she tested even younger infants. She found that 4½-month-old infants would look longer at the impossible event than the possible one, suggesting that, as with the 5-month-olds in the previous study, they could detect the spatial impossibility of the drawbridge passing through the box. Furthermore, some 3½-month-olds displayed the same preference for the impossible event. The difference between these youngest infants who looked longer at the impossible event and those who didn't was the speed with which they habituated to the initial presentations of the rotating drawbridge. Those who habituated faster at the beginning of the experiment looked at the impossible event for longer.

Baillargeon and colleagues have carried out many studies in which impossible events are presented to infants. This procedure is generally referred to as the 'violation of expectations' method. They have studied several different types of event, such as covering a tall object with a shorter object (Hespos and Baillargeon, 2006; Wang and Baillargeon, 2005), hiding a wide object behind a narrow one (Wang, Baillargeon and Brueckner, 2004), and passing a wide object through a narrow opening (Aguiar and Baillargeon, 1998, 2003), as well as further studies using the drawbridge apparatus (Baillargeon, 1987b). Their results have generally been taken as evidence that children much younger than the 8 to 9 months suggested by Piaget have an object concept. There are a range of experiments that show infants actually have quite sophisticated knowledge of the properties of objects very early on. Piaget was almost certainly wrong regarding the age at which infants' knowledge of objects develops, but does this mean that there is necessarily some innate knowledge? Baillargeon (1987a) suggested two explanations for this early understanding of object permanence: Either we are born with innate knowledge of the properties of objects, as Spelke (1985, 1994, 1998) proposed, or we are born with a learning mechanism that enables us to construct the concept of object permanence based on observations of objects.

Categorical speech perception

Although it takes many years for children to produce adult-like speech (see Chapter 4), they start to perceive speech very early on, even though they do not understand the meanings of the words. The auditory stimuli that we hear as speech are long streams of sounds. In order to make sense of these streams of sounds, we need to break them down into their constituent parts. The smallest units of speech are phonemes, which vary between languages such that phonemes present in one language may not be present in another, and vice versa. This is why it is sometimes hard to make yourself understood when speaking a new language; you are trying to make sounds that are not part of your native language. Even within a single language, some phonemes sound very similar to one another, such as *b* and *p* in English. Phonemes can vary in what is called their voicing or voice onset time, which is the period during which the vocal cords begin to vibrate relative to the release of air by the vocal apparatus. *B* and *p* differ in that the period between vibration of vocal chords and release of air is different. *B* has zero or negative voice onset time; the vocal cords vibrate either before or at the same time as the air is released (this is also true of *d* and *g*). *P* has positive voice onset time; the vocal cords vibrate after the air is released (it is the same for *t* and *k*). There is actually a continuum of possible variations in that the voice onset time for *b* could be −1 ms, −2 ms, −5 ms and so on. By gradually shifting the onset time later and later, the sound will shift from a *b* to a *p*. Although there is a huge range of possible variations with respect to onset time, adults hear the sound as belonging to one of two categories: *b* or *p*; we do not detect small changes in voice onset time. Because we only hear sounds as belonging to one category of phoneme, this is referred to as categorical

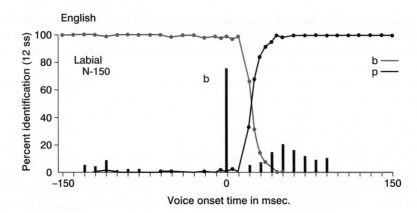

Figure 2.13

Voice onset time.

Source: Reproduced with permission of Lawrence Erlbaum Associates, from Jusczyk, P. W. (1985). On characterizing the development of speech perception. In J. Mehler & R. Fox (Eds.), *Neonate cognition* (pp. 199–229); permission conveyed through Copyright Clearance Center, Inc.

perception. Figure 2.13 shows where this category boundary lies for *b* and *p* in English speakers – at around 20 ms.

Using the high amplitude sucking technique, Eimas *et al.* (1971) found that infants of just 1 month of age perceived the same distinction between the two sounds as adults. This could be interpreted as evidence for innate categorical perception, but the participating infants had been raised in English-speaking homes and had therefore been exposed to many examples of distinct *p* and *b* sounds in everyday language. Subsequent research supported the idea of innate perception as it was found that infants are capable of making distinctions that are not part of their native language (Streeter, 1976; Trehub, 1976). Kuhl and Miller (1978) found that chinchillas were also capable of categorical perception and Kuhl and Padden (1982) found the same ability in macaque monkeys. So, although the ability may be innate, it cannot be interpreted as specific to language. Jusczyk (1985) suggests that this ability results from general auditory processing mechanisms. This does not mean there is no role for experience. The ability to make a distinction atrophies if that phoneme distinction is not present in the child's native language. Werker and Lalonde (1988) used a conditioned head turn procedure to investigate the development of phoneme perception. They showed that 6- to 8-month-old infants brought up in an English speaking environment could distinguish phonemes that are used in Hindi but are not present in English, but this ability declined in 11- to 13-month-olds. Werker and Desjardins (1995) report a series of studies in which various languages and phoneme pairs were used. All the results point to the loss of the ability to perceive non-native contrasts some time between 6 and 12 months of age. Werker and Tees (2002) compared English-speaking infants of different ages to Hindi- and Salish-speaking infants on a test of discriminating Hindi and Salish phoneme contrasts. Their results are illustrated in Figure 2.14. As you can see, the 6- to 8-month-old English infants performed almost as well as the native Hindi and Salish speakers, but performance declines over the next few months. Rivera-Gaxiola, Silva-Pereyra and Kuhl (2005) examined infant ERPs responses to English and Spanish phonemes. They found that the neural responses at 7 months of age showed a discrimination of both native and non-native contrasts, but that the neural responses of 11-month-olds only showed a discrimination of native contrasts. It seems that we become 'tuned' to hear sounds that are present in our environment, which assists with the task of learning language.

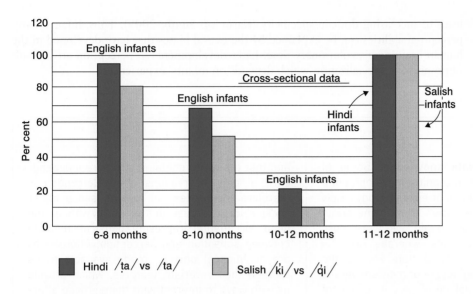

Figure 2.14

Proportion of infant subjects from three ages and various backgrounds reaching criterion on Hindi and Salish contrasts.

Source: Reprinted from *Infant Behavior and Development*, 25, Werker, J. F. & Tees, R. C., Cross-language speech perception: Evidence for perceptual reorganization during the first year of life, 121–133, Copyright (2002), with permission from Elsevier.

Concluding comments

There is clearly a lot of evidence demonstrating that infants have very early perceptual abilities. In some cases, these abilities are present at birth (e.g., recognition of mother's voice), others develop in the first year of life (e.g., depth perception). Does this mean that nativist accounts of perception are correct, or that children make use of environmental cues, as Gibson suggests? It is clear that Piaget underestimated children's abilities, but this may be because his studies of perception also required infants to perform coordinated actions (Baillargeon, 1987a). As a result, a constructivist explanation cannot be ruled out, particularly as it seems that experience with acting upon the world is necessary to develop the more sophisticated perceptual skills involved in interpreting the information available to infants, such as facial expressions and the behaviour of objects.

We have seen evidence for a process of perceptual narrowing that occurs throughout infancy across different perceptual modalities. Recent evidence indicates that infants lose the ability to match cross-modal stimuli (Lewkowicz and Ghazanfar, 2009), to discriminate non-native speech sounds (Werker and Lalonde, 1988; Rivera-Gaxiola, Silva-Pereyra and Kuhl, 2005), and to discriminate between faces that are not a constant part of the environment, such as the faces of individual monkeys (Pascalis, de Haan and Nelson, 2002). Scott, Pascalis and Nelson (2007) argue that perceptual narrowing is a domain-general principle, possibly achieved by the 'pruning' of disused synaptic connections.

The phenomenon of perceptual narrowing is consistent with the relatively new theoretical approach of neuroconstructivism (Mareschal *et al.*, 2007). According to this view, the infant mind is not a blank slate or a collection of core knowledge modules. Rather, we are born with a flexible ability to learn, coupled with a set of minimal biases, which are distinct from nativist ideas of core knowledge, that place constraints on how we process incoming information. These biases are a result of differences between networks in the brain, such as types and density of neurons, that lead to some networks being more adept at processing particular types of stimuli than other networks. Over time, these networks become more specialized, which leads to increasing domain-specificity (Karmiloff-Smith, 2009). Thus, infants' early perceptual abilities can be explained by the neural biases that have developed in the human brain over evolutionary time. Later developments in perception are a result of progressive specialization which depends on infants' experiences.

Summary

Blank slate vs innate knowledge. Some of the biggest questions in cognitive developmental psychology are questions of epistemology: 'How do we know what we know? What is the origin of knowledge?' Plato thought we were born with fundamental concepts, whereas Aristotle described the mind as a blank slate. This set the stage for the enduring debate of nativism versus empiricism. Perceptual development is one of two areas (together with language acquisition) in which this debate is most prominent. If we are to determine if the mind comes equipped with innate knowledge, or whether we have to learn everything through experience, it makes sense to study infants' knowledge.

Theories of perceptual development. Piaget adopted a **constructivist** perspective, in which an organism interacts with the environment to create or *construct* meaning; he argued that early perceptual abilities are based on action and experience. As infants mature and gain greater experience, they modify and create mental structures through the processes of assimilation and accommodation. Interaction with the environment enables infants to learn to make sense of the sensory information they receive. The starting point is not a blank slate, but an ensemble of reflexes, such as sucking, grasping and orienting towards stimuli. These reflexes are the building blocks upon which more sophisticated concepts can be constructed. During the sensorimotor stage infants develop from possessing a few basic reflexes through to creating mental representations of objects and events. Without acting on the environment and experiencing the outcomes of these actions, infants would not be able to construct an understanding of the world. An alternative to Piaget's constructivism is Gibson's ecological theory, which is based on the idea that perceptions are direct

and that the world contains structure independently of our observations of it. Perception is therefore the process of making sense of, or 'picking up' the cues in the world without the need for mental representations to mediate between sensation and perception. Affordances are qualities of objects, made available to us through their invariant features, which provide us with ways to interact with them. These affordances are perceptible by infants without requiring that they develop concepts or mental representations. Infants develop by getting better at perceiving the information in the environment, with respect to both individual stimuli and the relationships between objects. Gibson's view of the development of perception involves both biological and experiential components. We are born with perceptual abilities but we need experience of the process of perceiving to develop our abilities. A third theoretical approach is nativism. Spelke posits a system of core knowledge consisting of sets of domain-specific principles that are used to construct representations. With respect to objects, young infants appear to make use of the principles of cohesion, continuity and contact. Other principles, such as inertia and gravity, develop over time. Baillargeon has proposed a core knowledge account, in which she replaces Spelke's principles of continuity and cohesion with a single principle of persistence.

Research methodologies. In order to attempt to answer questions about what infants can perceive, psychologists have had to develop appropriate research methodologies. These focus on determining whether infants can detect a perceptual stimulus or not, and whether they can discriminate between two stimuli. As infants lack the communicative skills to directly tell us what they can perceive, perception research relies on inferences from behaviours. These methods include the preferential looking technique, habituation, conditioned head rotation and high amplitude sucking.

Basic perceptual abilities. Newborns' visual acuity is around one-twentieth that of an adult. Visual acuity improves throughout infancy and early childhood, reaching adult levels at around 5 years of age. Young infants prefer stimuli with moderate levels of intensity and complexity and they prefer curved or circular patterns to straight lines. Newborns seem to prefer to look at moving objects rather than stationary objects, but it is not until 2 to 3 months of age that infants' tracking becomes adult-like. One-month-old infants scan small localized bits of an object, whereas 2-month-olds spend more time scanning finer details, especially facial features such as eyes, nose and mouth.

Newborns can recognize the sound of their mother's voice and exhibit a preference for sounds they have heard in the womb. They can also interpret tactile sensations, smells and tastes. Sight and sound coordination seems to be achieved by infants of about 4 months old, and 1-month-olds show evidence of sight and touch integration. Infants' ability to integrate information from the different senses improves over time, but there is a decreasing sensitivity to stimuli that are not commonly present in infants' environments.

Making sense of the world. Newborns prefer schematic faces to less face-like stimuli, but it is not until 2 to 3 months that infants prefer faces. One explanation for this is that there are two separate mechanisms at work. The first, CONSPEC, contains innate knowledge of the visual structure of the faces of conspecifics (members of the same species). The second, CONLERN, is used to learn about the visual features of conspecifics. Infants develop the ability to distinguish familiar from unfamiliar faces in their first month. Over the first 7 months they start to discriminate between different facial expressions, however they can imitate simple expressions at just 2 to 3 weeks. Depth perception may be present by 2 months of age, but it is not until around 6 months that infants demonstrate a fearful response to depths, which suggests that experience in needed in order for infants to interpret what they see. Piaget argued that experience is also necessary for object perception and that infants younger than about 8 or 9 months of age are unaware that objects exist independently of the child's perception of the object. According to ecological and core knowledge theories, however, infants should be able to perceive objects as independent without the need for experience. Baillargeon's experiments, using the violation of expectations method, show that infants perceive objects in an adult-like way much earlier than Piaget suggested. Infants can discriminate speech sounds at just 1 month of age, but their ability to make these distinctions atrophies if the sounds are not present in the child's native language. By the time they are 12 months old they become 'tuned' to hear sounds that are present in their environment, which assists with the task of learning language.

Discussion questions

1 To what extent is each of the perceptual modalities innate?

2 Why do some perceptual abilities take longer to develop than others?

3 What is the role of knowledge in perception?

4 How important is experience of the environment for the development of perception?

5 How have psychologists worked round the constraints of using infants as participants? How do the methods used in infancy research differ from methods used with older children and adults?

Further Reading

Books and chapters

Gibson, E. J. and Pick, A. D. (2000). *An ecological approach to perceptual learning and development*. Oxford: Oxford University Press.

Eleanor Gibson and Anne Pick present the ecological theory and survey a range of evidence in support of this account of perception.

Meltzoff, A. N. and Moore, M. K. (1999). Imitation of facial and manual gestures by human neonates. In A. Slater and D. Muir (Eds), *The Blackwell reader in developmental psychology* (pp. 143–150). Oxford: Blackwell. (Originally published in *Science*, 198 (1977), 75–78.)

Meltzoff, A. N. and Moore, M. K. (1999). Resolving the debate about early imitation. In A. Slater and D. Muir (Eds), *The Blackwell reader in developmental psychology* (pp. 151–155). Oxford: Blackwell.

Andrew Meltzoff and M. Keith Moore's original 1977 paper on imitation is reprinted alongside an update article in which they present an explanation for their classic finding.

Slater, A. (Ed). (1998). *Perceptual development: Visual, auditory and speech perception in infancy*. Hove: Psychology Press.

In this edited volume, Alan Slater brings together a selection of chapters on many aspects of perceptual development, authored by some of the key researchers in the field.

Articles

Baillargeon, R. (2008). Innate ideas revisited: For a principle of persistence in infants' physical reasoning. *Perspectives on Psychological Science*, 3, 2–13.

Renée Baillargeon gives an overview of her research and explains how this provides evidence in support of core knowledge.

Morton, J. and Johnson, M. H. (1991). CONSPEC and CONLERN: A two-process theory of infant face recognition. *Psychological Review*, 98(2), 164–181.

An overview of their theory of neural mechanisms for face processing and the studies that support it by John Morton and Mark Johnson.

Spelke, E. S. and Kinzler, K. D. (2007). Core knowledge. *Developmental Science*, 10, 89–96.

In this paper, Elizabeth Spelke and Katherine Kinzler offer an overview of the evidence in support of core knowledge domains.

Werker, J. F. and Desjardins, R. N. (1995). Listening to speech in the first year of life: Experiential influences on phoneme perception. *Current Directions in Psychological Sciences*, 4(3), 76–81.

Janet Werker and Renée Desjardins discuss research on the development of phonemic perception.

Chapter 3

Memory

Learning Outcomes

At the end of this chapter you should be able to:

- Define the different types of memory studied by psychologists.
- Describe the information-processing approach to memory.
- Discuss research on memory in infancy.
- Discuss research on episodic memory in early childhood.
- Describe and evaluate research on the development of memory.
- Discuss the impact of memory research on eyewitness testimony.

Chapter 3

Memory

Learning Outcomes

At the end of this chapter you should be able to:

- Define the different types of memory studied by psychologists.

- Describe the information-processing approach to memory.

- Discuss research on memory in infancy.

- Discuss research on episodic memory in early childhood.

- Describe and evaluate research on the development of memory.

- Discuss the impact of memory research on eyewitness testimony.

Michelene Chi (1978) reported a study in which she looked at children's and adults' memory. The participants were six children, with a mean age of 10½ years, and six adults, who were graduate students and research assistants. All the participants were asked to remember two different sets of items. One of these was some lists of numbers; the other was a series of positions from chess games. In the number task, participants were shown a list of 10 digits for 10 seconds. As soon as the numbers were hidden, the participants had to write down as many as they could remember. In the chess task, participants were shown a board from a game of chess for 10 seconds. The boards had, on average, 22 pieces. As soon as the board was hidden, the participants had to take a blank board and arrange the pieces from memory. Each participant completed four trials of each of the two tasks. Unsurprisingly, the adults were able to recall more numbers than the children. However, the children remembered, on average, 3.4 more chess positions than the adults (see Figure 3.1). This rather interesting result can be explained by looking at one of the characteristics of the participants: their knowledge of chess. The children who took part in the study were recruited at a chess tournament and had a good knowledge of the game. The adults could all play chess, but did not have the same knowledge as the children.

Q. What does this finding tell us about memory?

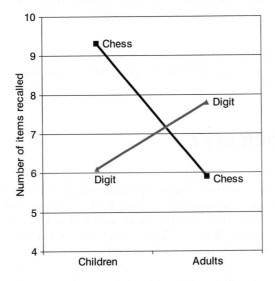

Figure 3.1

Results from Chi's (1978) study: The numbers of items recalled by children and adults for chess and digit stimuli.

Chase and Simon (1973) had already shown that knowledge of chess plays a role in how much chess-related information can be remembered by adults, with higher-ranking players demonstrating superior memory for positions than lower-ranked players. It can be concluded that memory is improved by a greater amount of knowledge. As a result of this finding, one could hypothesize that the reason memory improves with age is because as we get older, we acquire more knowledge. The point of Chi's study was to see if children's performance on a memory task would be better if they had greater knowledge. Her results show that children's memory was better than adults' in a domain in which the children had more knowledge than the adults. The scores on the digit recall task show that the children's performance was not a result of any general memory superiority. If, for some reason, this group of children had better general memory than the adults, the children would have out-performed the adults on the digit task as well. You might be thinking that, by this age, the children should have a good knowledge of numbers, and that they should do just as well on a test of memory for numbers as for chess positions. However, a key distinction between the chess task and the digit task is that the numbers were presented as random lists; they were not presented in a meaningful way. Chess positions, on the other hand, do have meaning for people who have good chess knowledge. A mid-game chess board contains relationships between pieces, such as one piece is poised to attack a second piece, while a third piece is protected by a fourth, and so on. In Chase and Simon's study, participants were also asked to recall random positions. In this condition, the arrangements of pieces were not taken from an actual chess game, but placed randomly on the board. The differences in recall between the players with different levels of expertise that were displayed for game positions disappeared for the random positions. This tells us that previous knowledge can only facilitate remembering new information if the new information has meaningful *structure*. The general improvements in memory over time, from infancy to adulthood, may thus be a result of the amount and structure of knowledge we possess as we get older. Knowledge is just one of the factors that may be important in understanding the development of memory.

> Q. What other factors do you think might contribute to the development of memory?

Later in the chapter, we will look at the role played by language, processing speed and strategies for remembering things, as well as examining the role of knowledge in more detail.

What is memory?

Over the years, there have been many different metaphors for memory. Most of these have been comparisons to ways in which objects are stored, for example, a house, a gramophone or tape recorder, a leaky bucket, a library and a computer program (Roediger, 1980). These metaphors all suggest that we think of memory as a receptacle for knowledge. If we use these metaphors to think about cognitive development, what are the implications for how memory changes over time? An obvious suggestion is that, as we progress through childhood, our receptacle (house, tape, bucket, hard drive) gets bigger. One of the topics of this chapter is whether the 're-ceptacle' of memory really does get bigger, or whether the reason that memory improves with age is a result of how we store memories, what we know about the way in which memory works, or what the existing contents of memory are (as illustrated in Chi's study). Regardless of which of these ideas is correct, it is clear that memory is not one big, undifferentiated mass of items that are stored haphazardly.

short-term memory
Limited capacity, limited duration store of information.

long-term memory
Permanent or semi-permanent store of episodic, semantic and procedural memories.

Memory can be divided into short-term memory and long-term memory. Short-term memory contains information that is currently active or in consciousness. Items can be held in short-term memory for short durations of up to 20 seconds. Long-term memory, in contrast, is our permanent or semi-permanent store of information. Items in long-term memory can be forgotten, but they can also remain with us for a lifetime. We can divide long-term memory into different types, or systems of information (Tulving, 1983). Some of your memories refer to facts and ideas that you have been taught or have read, but do not reflect personal experiences. Examples might include remembering that the distance from the Earth to the Moon is around 239 000 miles (on average), or that a hydrogen atom has one electron, or that Piaget is best known for his theory of cognitive development. These facts are stored in semantic memory. You also have other memories that are more personal in nature and reflect events that you experienced. Memories of your eighteenth birthday, a camping holiday, or taking a driving test are examples of episodic memory. If you think about the first CD (or record, or tape, depending on your age) you bought, it is likely that you are retrieving both semantic and episodic memories. 'The first CD I bought was x' is a fact from semantic memory, but remembering buying it from a specific shop, taking it home and listening to it in your bedroom, is an episodic memory. Both semantic and episodic memory are also referred to as declarative memory or explicit memory. A third type of memory, procedural memory or implicit memory, contains knowledge of how to do things, and includes procedures for perceptual (e.g., recognizing faces), motor (e.g., playing a musical instrument) and cognitive (e.g., playing chess) activities.

semantic memory
Memory for facts and general knowledge.

episodic memory
Memory for events.

declarative memory
Conscious memory for facts (semantic memory) and events (episodic memory).

explicit memory See declarative memory.

procedural memory
Non-conscious memory of how to do things; skills and procedures.

implicit memory See procedural memory.

Theories of memory development

Some topics in cognitive development (e.g., perception, language, theory of mind) have several broad theories that can be applied across the topic. Much of the theorizing in the memory development literature, on the other hand, is an attempt to explain a specific set of phenomena within memory, such as why we cannot remember our infancy, why children's recall of events improves with time and why young children do not use strategies as effectively or as often as older children. Accounts of these aspects of memory will be discussed at appropriate points later in the chapter. Almost all of these theories of the development of specific memory phenomena adopt an information processing approach, so rather than contrast competing theories of how memory develops, I will outline the information processing as a general perspective on memory and its development.

The information processing approach

One of the earliest information processing accounts of cognition was Atkinson and Shiffrin's (1968) model in which they attempted to explain cognitive processing in terms of the organization and structure of memory. In addition to components for short-term and long-term storage of memory, they also hypothesized a sensory register, a response generator and a set of control processes (see Figure 3.2). Their emphasis was on the way in which information flows through this system. First, input (such as sights and sounds) hits the sensory register. The sensory register has high capacity but extremely short duration, meaning that all the information that is sensed is stored here, but for less than a second. A subset of the information that gets into sensory memory will be processed further in short-term memory. Which information gets through is determined by processes of attention and perception.

The short-term store has very limited capacity and a duration of up to 20 seconds. Information can be kept active in the short-term store, and subsequently transferred to the long-term store by control processes such as rehearsal. Information in long-term memory can be retrieved back to the short-term store for use as and when necessary. Atkinson and Shiffrin conceived of both the short-term and

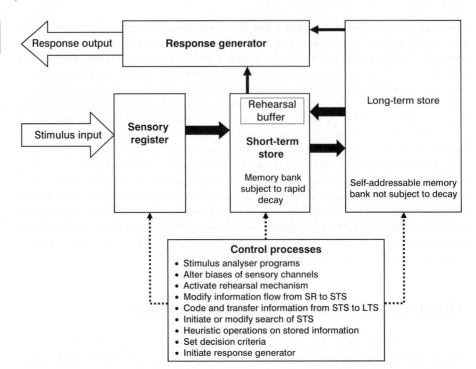

Figure 3.2

Shiffrin and Atkinson's model of the memory system.

Source: Copyright © 1969 by the American Psychological Association. Adapted with permission. The official citation that should be used in referencing this material is Shiffrin, R. M. & Atkinson, R. C. (1969) Storage and retrieval processes in long-term memory. *Psychological Review*, 76(2), 179–193. The use of APA information does not imply endorsement by APA.

long-term stores as unitary. In other words, each of these stores works in the same way, regardless of the nature and modality of the information. This means that rehearsing a list of similar items, presented as visual images, such as colour swatches (e.g., red, orange, yellow, green, blue, indigo, violet) should be no different to rehearsing a list of completely unrelated items presented as sounds (e.g., bucket, marshmallow, insomnia, Nottingham, relentless, beard, laser). Both lists should be equally forgettable. The key constraint on the short-term store was seen as capacity, and the increase of capacity throughout childhood was the explanation for improvements in performance on memory tasks over time. However, there was soon evidence that auditory and visual information are treated differentially, and that meaningful stimuli are easier to remember than random or abstract stimuli (Shallice and Warrington, 1974; Warrington and Shallice, 1972).

The working memory model. Shiffrin and Atkinson's limited conception of how the short-term store worked led Baddeley and Hitch (1974) and Baddeley (1986) to propose a more sophisticated account of short-term memory called the **working memory** model. Like Atkinson and Shiffrin's model, the working memory model was based on the findings that short-term memory is limited in capacity and that rehearsal can help us to remember information for longer. In addition, the model takes into account the differences between auditory and visual stimuli. The fine details of the model have been developed over several decades; the most recent version (Baddeley, 2000) is illustrated in Figure 3.3.

The central executive is the main component of the system. It directs attention, coordinates the different components of the system and allocates resources to them. The phonological loop is a short-term store for verbal and acoustic information, and has an articulatory rehearsal system. The visuospatial sketchpad is a store for, unsurprisingly, visual and spatial information. The most recent addition is the

working memory
Temporary storage area in which information is processed, monitored and manipulated.

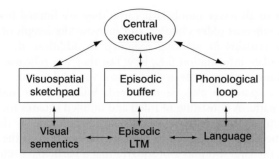

Figure 3.3

The updated working memory model.

Source: The updated working memory model (Baddeley, 2000) Reprinted from Trends in Cognitive Sciences, 4, Baddeley, A., The episodic buffer: a new component of working memory?, 417–423, Copyright (2000), with permission from Elsevier.

episodic buffer, a short-term store for episodic memory that is not limited to visual or auditory information, but combines them into multimodal codes.

According to Baddeley (2000) and Gathercole (1999), components of the working memory model have neural correlates in the adult brain. The central executive is associated with the dorsolateral prefrontal cortex, the phonological loop is represented in the left hemisphere (posterior parietal cortex, Broca's area, and the premotor cortex), and the visuospatial sketchpad is associated with activity in the right hemisphere (premotor cortex, posterior parietal lobe, anterior occipital lobe and inferior prefrontal lobe) (see Figure 3.4). Klingberg, Forssberg and Westerberg (2002) reported that the frontal and parietal areas are also active in children aged 9 to 18 on a visuospatial working memory task, with the older children showing greater activity than the younger children in these regions.

Although the working memory model was devised in order to explain adult memory, it has also proved to be useful for examining the development of memory. Take the digit span task, for example. This is a very simple measure of short-term memory, in which lists of digits are read out to participants who then have to repeat what they heard. The maximum list length that a participant can recall without error is his digit span. Adults typically have a digit span of around seven items, whereas 9-year-olds have a span of around six, 7-year-olds have a span of around five, 5-year-olds' spans are a little above four and 2-year-olds' spans are below two-and-a-half (Dempster, 1981). This developmental progression can be explained with respect to the phonological loop. According to Gathercole (1998), preschool and younger school-age children do not use subvocal rehearsal to keep items active in the phonological loop, and without rehearsal, information decays after two seconds.

Figure 3.4

Brain regions associated with working memory.

Source: Adapted from Trends in Cognitive Sciences, 3, Gathercole, S. E., Cognitive approaches to the development of short-term memory, 410–418, Copyright (1999), with permission from Elsevier.

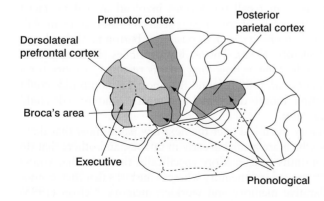

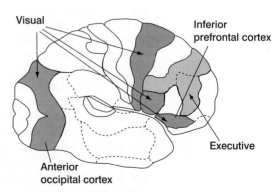

Left hemisphere   Right hemisphere

Younger children recall fewer numbers because they are limited by the short duration of the loop, whereas older children can increase the length of time that auditory information remains in working memory. In addition, the speed at which children can articulate information (i.e., how fast they can rehearse a list) increases, so we see continuing improvement in digit span across childhood.

Visual memory span can also be measured. Wilson, Scott and Power (1987) showed children patterns consisting of filled and unfilled squares for brief durations. After each pattern, another pattern was displayed with one of the filled squares missing, and participants were asked to indicate the position of the missing square. The pattern with the largest number of squares that a participant reliably remembers is his/her visual span. The results showed an increase in visual span from four items at age 5 to fourteen items at age 11, which is the same as adults. Note that the visual span is larger than the phonological span, which indicates that these are two separate aspects of working memory. Although it is tempting to suggest that these differences are solely due an increase in capacity of the visuospatial sketchpad, it is likely that children begin to use non-visual strategies that aid visual memory as they get older. Wilson *et al.* found that if they asked participants to count (forwards for younger children, backwards for older children) after presenting a pattern, performance on the visual task was impaired. Counting involves the phonological loop and the central executive, but not the visuospatial sketchpad, so this suggests that children were using one or both of these other components to help remember items on the visual task. The degree of impairment rose with age, suggesting that the increase in visual span over time reflects greater use of other working memory components.

Memory in infancy

We are capable of some degree of memorization even before birth. In Chapter 2 we saw that newborns prefer hearing a story that their mothers had read to them whilst pregnant to an unfamiliar story (DeCasper and Spence, 1986), indicating they have at least minimal recognition memory. Some of the other methods described in the previous chapter also rely on basic recognition memory. Habituation, for example, relies on an infant's recognition of the stimulus as staying the same over time; dishabituation is the result of not recognizing a stimulus.

In Chapter 2, we also saw how newborns were capable of imitating facial expressions. By 6 weeks of age, infants can imitate these facial expressions 24 hours after observing them (Meltzoff and Moore, 1994). This is called deferred, or delayed, imitation, and implies that they can recall the actions involved in making facial expressions from memory. By 9 months of age, infants start to demonstrate an ability to imitate actions performed on objects, such as pushing a button to elicit a beep, after a delay of 24 hours (Meltzoff, 1988). This ability continues to develop over the coming months. In a study looking at how long infants retained memory for a sequence of three actions, Bauer *et al.* (2000) found that most 13-month-olds could imitate the sequence after a three-month delay, and that most 20-month-olds could still perform the actions a year later.

The studies on infant memory discussed over the next few pages show that there are some aspects of memory which are available early in infancy, and others that do not develop until about 12 months of age. More specifically, the tasks that young infants can do involve implicit procedural memory whereas the tasks that they cannot yet do involve explicit declarative memory and working memory. Nelson (1995) argues that earlier memory abilities are based on neurological structures that develop early, including the hippocampus and the cerebellum, and that later developing memory abilities depend on later-developing structures, such as the amygdala and some regions of the inferior temporal cortex and prefrontal cortex. There is some debate regarding exactly when infants shift from a reliance on implicit memory alone to an ability to use explicit memory structures, but it is probably around 6 months of age (Barr, Rovee-Collier and Campanella, 2005; Bauer *et al.*, 2006).

Infantile amnesia

What is the earliest thing in your life you can remember? When you think about it, you will probably find that it is something that occurred when you were 3 or 4 years old. Although we saw evidence of the presence of aspects of memory in the preceding section, none of these abilities involve episodic memory in the form of explicit recollections about personally experienced events. This lack of **autobiographical memory** from the first few years of life has been termed 'infantile amnesia'. Freud (1905/2000) claimed that infantile amnesia was the result of the suppression of traumatic events experienced in childhood. Another explanation for our lack of memories of infancy is that we were not capable of encoding and storing memories at that age (Pillemer and White, 1989). Although this may seem plausible, research into infants' memories shows that they *are* capable of remembering early events.

Rovee-Collier and her colleagues (1980, 1994) have carried out a number of studies using the 'mobile conjugate reinforcement' procedure, in which they used operant conditioning principles to reinforce a behaviour. Young infants will naturally kick their legs, and this behaviour was reinforced by giving them a reward, which was that a colourful mobile hung over the crib would move. The infants learned that their kicking behaviour would result in the movement of the mobile. This was achieved by tying a ribbon between the mobile and the infant's leg. Rovee-Collier *et al.* (1980) gave infants two training sessions, with a 24-hour gap between them. Each training session consisted of a 9-minute reinforcement phase, in which the infant's leg was connected to the mobile, sandwiched between two 3-minute non-reinforcement phases, in which the mobile was still visible but no longer attached to the infant's leg. A third session, the same as the first two, took place two weeks later. One day prior to this third session, half the infants were given a 'reactivation treatment', which was 3 minutes of seeing the mobile move as a result of an experimenter tugging on the ribbon without the ribbon being connected to the infant's leg. The idea behind the reactivation treatment was that exposure to the mobile would prime the infant's memory, increasing the likelihood that they would be able to remember the learned relationship between leg-kicking and movement of the mobile. The infants who had received the reactivation treatment kicked just as much in the third session as they had during the second training session, whereas the no-reactivation group returned to the baseline kicking levels of the first session. In a second experiment, Rovee-Collier *et al.* increased the interval between the second and third sessions to four weeks and found that the reactivation group kicked more than the non-reactivation group. These findings demonstrate that a learned behaviour will be forgotten within two weeks if the event is not experienced again, but that infants can retrieve the memory if it is appropriately cued. In a later study, Rovee-Collier, Hartshorn and DiRubbo (1999) trained infants who were just 8 weeks old on the mobile task. Without any reminders, 8-week-olds will forget about the task after a day or two, but the researchers gave the infants reminders to reactivate their memories every three weeks. After 5 months most of the participants retained memory for the task. Therefore, infants' apparently poor memories may not be a result of deficits in encoding or storing memories, but rather they may reflect limitations on the retrieval process.

autobiographical memory Memory for episodes from one's personal life.

The above demonstrates that infants' memories decay very quickly. They are also fragile in several other ways. Rovee-Collier, Adler and Borza (1994) found that 3-month-olds who were trained to move a mobile by kicking, and were then exposed to a different mobile, would forget the original mobile after a few days. This shows that memory for the new mobile very quickly interfered with memory for the original mobile. Also, the context in which the memory is formed is important. Hayne, Rovee-Collier and Borza (1991) trained 3-month-olds to move a mobile by kicking in the way described above. When the experimenters exposed the infants to the mobile two weeks later, in the same location, the infants remembered how to move the mobile. But, if the mobile was placed in a new location, the infants did not kick. It seems that information about where an event was experienced is encoded as part of the memory for the event, and that the memory cannot be recalled if the location is changed. Although these studies do demonstrate that infants possess some memory ability, these are implicit procedural memories, not explicit autobiographical memories.

According to Fivush and Nelson (2004), the reason that autobiographical memories from the first few years of life are not available to us is due to a range of developmental and sociocultural factors beyond the development of memory, such as language and understanding of the self. They argue that language is not just used as a way of expressing existing memories, but is an important part of the way in which memories for events are initially stored. Simcock and Hayne (2002) studied the ability of 2- to 3-year-old children to recall an event six and twelve months after the event. Twenty-seven 27-month-olds, twenty-six 33-month-olds and twenty-seven 39-month-olds were introduced to a 'magic shrinking machine' which appeared to shrink a toy (in reality, a large toy entered the machine and a smaller, yet otherwise identical, toy emerged). Approximately half the participants were visited again after 6 months, and the other half were visited after one year. During the follow-up visit, the children were first asked to describe what they could remember about the game. They were then shown photographs of the toys that had been shrunk in the machine, along with distracter items, and asked to identify the toys they had seen being placed into the machine. The machine was then brought into the room and the participants were asked to demonstrate how it worked.

Across all three measures (verbal, photograph, re-enactment) there was a main effect of age, with the youngest group recalling less than the older groups, and an effect of delay between event and test, with the 6-month group recalling more than the 1-year group. The most interesting finding, however, was that there were differences between the three measures: the participants performed worse on the verbal measure than the photograph measure, and worse on the photograph measure than the re-enactment measure (see Figure 3.5). Furthermore, by examining the participants' language during both parts of the experiment, Simcock and Hayne showed that, during the second visit, none of the children used words to describe the shrinking machine event that were not in their vocabulary at the time of the event. The photograph and re-enactment tasks demonstrate that the children could recall more about the event than they could verbalize, but it seems that these memories could not be translated into the language they had acquired since the event. This has two closely related implications with respect to 'infantile amnesia'. First, children do have memories for early events, and these memories can be expressed non-verbally. Second, the reason we may not be able to remember events early in our lives is that we did not have the language skills and knowledge to encode these events.

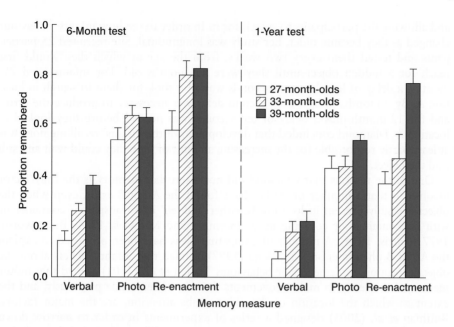

Figure 3.5

Results from Simcock and Hayne's experiment.

Source: Simcock, G., & Hayne, H., *Psychological Science*, 13(3), pp. 225–231, copyright © 2002 by Association for Psychological Science. Reprinted by Permission of SAGE Publications.

A-not-B error

Piaget's theory, as with just about every topic in cognitive development, contained an account of the development of memory. Like all aspects of cognition, Piaget thought that memory depends on intelligence. He distinguished between recognition and recall, arguing that recognition is essentially a product of perception whereas recall relies on symbolic representations (Piaget and Inhelder, 1973). Because recognition relies on perception, it is – according to Piaget – present in early infancy, but the ability to recall information can not develop until infants start to construct internal representations of their experiences, at around one year of age.

The idea of absence of memory in infancy is evidenced by the A-not-B task, which is conducted as follows. Over several trials, an infant watches while an object is hidden under a cloth, or behind a curtain, in location A. The infants will then search for the object in this location. Having done this several times, the experimenter then hides the object in a new location, location B. Piaget (1954) described how infants between about 8 and 10 months of age, would, at this point, continue to search for the object in location A. Piaget did not attribute this error directly to memory, arguing that infants had not yet developed an understanding of object permanence (see Chapter 2), and might think that the location of the object was dependent on where they looked, rather than where it was hidden, illustrating an egocentric conception of the world.

Diamond (1985) argued that the A-not-B error is partly due to an inability to inhibit the previous searching actions, but also to a memory deficit. Harris (1973) had already shown that infants were likely to make the error if they were allowed to search for the object straight away. He suggested that there was interference between the memory for the object at location A and the memory for the object at location B, and that unless the infant could search immediately, the stronger memory for the initial location would predominate over the more recent memory for the new location. In order to examine the role of memory, Diamond conducted a study in which she varied the delay time between hiding the object (a toy) in location B and allowing the participants to search for it. In order to see how infants' behaviour changed as they became older, her study was longitudinal. She recruited 25 participants and tested them every two weeks, from the age at which they would first reach for a hidden object until they were 12 months old. For infants aged 7½ months, a delay of less than two seconds was all it took for them to search in location A. By 9 months of age, a six second delay was necessary to produce the error, and for 12-month-olds a delay of ten seconds was needed before they looked in location A. Diamond concluded that development of the infants' recall memory was at least partly responsible for the increasing amount of time they could wait and still find the object.

One of the reasons that Diamond did not claim that memory is the only factor involved is that a number of studies have found the A-not-B error, even when the object is visibly present in location B, either 'hidden' in a transparent container or with no container or covering at all (Bremner and Knowles, 1984; Butterworth, 1977; Harris, 1974). A number of competing ideas have been proposed to explain the A-not B phenomenon. Munakata (1997) claimed that infants' beliefs about the object's location explained their behaviour. Thelen *et al.* (2001) argued that motor memory, a tendency to make movements that have been made previously, and the extent to which the location of the object grabs attention, are the major factors. Ruffman *et al.* (2005) designed a series of experiments in order to narrow down which of these proposed mechanisms was responsible. They concluded that belief of the object location (which depends on memory) is important, but that in some cases, motor memory, inhibition and attention can cause the error.

Topal *et al.* (2008) argued that the error may, in fact, be due to the communicative cues given to infants by experimenters. These cues, such as eye contact, speech, pointing and looking, could lead infants to interpret the actions of the experimenter as conveying general information about objects and locations, such as that toys are generally kept in container A. To test this, they placed 42 infants aged 10 months into one of three conditions: ostensive-communicative, in which the experimenter used standard eye contact, speech and looking behaviours; non-communicative, in which the experimenter looked away from the infants and did not speak; and non-social, in which the experimenter was hidden behind a curtain and the infants could only see the motions of the object. The results showed that 12 of 14 infants made the standard A-not-B error in the ostensive-communicative condition, but the infants in the other two conditions made far fewer errors: only 6 of 14 infants in the non-communicative condition and 5 of 14 infants in the non-social condition repeatedly looked in the wrong location. What this study demonstrates is that infants are not necessarily as bad at this task as previous studies have indicated, which means that the A-not-B error is not compelling evidence for a lack of memory in infancy. However, almost 40 per cent of the infants in the non-communicative and non-social conditions did still make errors, which means that there may still be some role for memory skills in explaining performance on this task.

Episodic memory

Earlier, we saw that infants are capable, to some degree, of memory for events, but it is in the preschool years that this ability emerges in a form powerful enough to ensure that we can remember some of these events years later. Children as young as 2 are able to talk about events that happened in the past (Fivush and Hamond, 1990; Nelson, 1984; Nelson and Ross, 1980), but require a lot of prompting from adults. By 3 or 4 years of age, children can answer questions with fewer prompts (Hamond and Fivush, 1991). This progression has led some psychologists to suggest that episodic memory develops gradually through the preschool years (Bauer, 2007; Nelson and Fivush, 2004), whereas others have argued that memory for events in children younger than 4 or 5 is actually semantic memory rather than episodic memory. Children younger than this can describe an event but their memories consist of knowledge of the event, rather than a recollection of personal experience (Perner and Ruffman, 1995; Wheeler, 2000).

This ability to remember events in general terms can be explained in terms of scripts (Schank and Abelson, 1977), a type of knowledge structure containing information about the typical way in which an event happens. The classic example given in journal articles and textbooks alike is the going-to-a-restaurant script. A restaurant script might include such elements as entering the building, waiting for a seat, being seated, looking at a menu, ordering from the menu, receiving some food, eating the food, paying and leaving.

scripts Mental structure containing a typical sequence of events.

> Q. Think of an occasion (such as a birthday) on which you went to a restaurant. Did you pay for your food? Can you actually remember paying for it?

I hope that the answer to the first question is 'yes', but it is likely that your answer to the second question is 'no' (unless the event was very recent). You may not have a specific memory of paying a particular restaurant employee a particular amount of money (Did you leave a tip? How much?), but you know that – in general – you always pay for your food.

Scripts can be a useful way of organizing information and helping to retrieve it for children and adults alike. However, the use of stereotypical event structures can lead to distorted recall of events if an aspect of the event does not match the standard script. There is evidence that effects of distortion are more common in younger children (Hudson and Fivush, 1983), perhaps because adults are better able to represent deviations from a script. If a child's recall of an event matches a typical instance of that event more than the specific event he is attempting to recall, this could be taken as evidence of script use, and therefore semantic, rather than episodic, memory. For example, a typical script for catching a bus may include paying the driver straight away, but there are other cases in which payment is collected during the journey by a conductor. If a child describes a bus journey in which it is known that the conductor was paid, but claims that the driver was paid upon entering the bus, then it can be inferred that he is using his general knowledge of bus journeys, rather than recalling a specific episode. Hudson and Nelson (1983) told children a story about a birthday party, but placed some of the elements in the wrong order. When children recalled the story, they would omit or correct the misordered items. Hudson (1988) told children stories about common events such as grocery shopping and a trip to McDonalds. She then presented the participants with sentences that either had or had not been in the story and asked them which sentences they had heard before. The children reported that they recognized sentences that were not in the story if the sentences conformed to the relevant script.

A further study by Hudson and Nelson (1986) illustrates the point that preschool children rely on scripts and semantic memory to describe events. They asked 3- and 5-year-olds questions about two events: a snack at camp and dinner at home. Some of the questions were phrased in a general way so as to elicit a script, such as 'what *happens* when you have a snack at camp?', whereas others were more specific: 'what *happened* when you had a snack at camp yesterday?' Both the 3- and 5-year-olds found it easier to answer in more general terms, which implies that they were making use of scripts rather than episodic memories. More recently, Quon and Atance (2010) carried out a comparison of semantic and episodic memory with children aged 3 to 5 years old. The participants were asked questions about eight different events, including having breakfast, playtime, going shopping for groceries and going to the park. For one group of participants, questions were phrased in the past tense, with the intention of eliciting episodic memories. For another group, the questions were phrased in the present tense in order to provoke script-based answers. A third group was presented with questions about the future in order to compare episodic future thinking with episodic memory. The children's answers were scored for specificity, accuracy and use of words that indicated that the participants were using scripts. These included present-tense verbs, and words that implied a typical event was being described, such as 'usually' and 'sometimes'. Although there were no effects of age or experimental condition on response specificity, the group who were asked questions in the present tense or questions about the future gave more accurate answers for some of the events than the past-tense group. This implies that semantic memory is more highly developed earlier on than episodic memory. What is interesting is that the events for which the children in the semantic and future conditions gave more accurate responses were those over which children have less control (e.g., grocery shopping). There were no differences between the children in the episodic and semantic conditions for events over which children have more control (e.g., playtime). This finding is quite hard to interpret, as it does not allow a simple comparison between semantic and episodic memory to be made. It does, however, suggest that the episodic memory develops gradually over a number of years, rather than abruptly at age four or five, and is more sensitive to the type of event being recalled than semantic memory.

Evidence from cognitive neuroscience

We have known that the hippocampus plays a role in memory formation for over 50 years, as a result of studies on patients who developed amnesia after surgery involving removal of this part of the brain (Milner, Corkin and Teuber, 1968; Scott and Milner, 1957), but other brain regions are involved as well. One of the interesting findings from Quon and Atance's study is that there were few differences between episodic memory for the past and episodic thinking about the future. A similarity between these two aspects of episodic cognition has also been found in recent neuroscientific, neuropsychological and clinical research (Szpunar, 2010). In an fMRI study on 16 adults, Addis, Wong and Schachter (2007) found that the left hippocampus and posterior visuospatial regions (right inferior parietal lobule, left superior occipital gyrus and right middle occipital gyrus) were involved in episodic memory for both past and future when participants were asked to call an event to mind. All the regions that were involved in past thinking were also involved in future thinking, although future thinking engaged other regions (right frontopolar cortex and right hippocampus) as well. Addis *et al.* (2009) suggest the reason that future thinking engages extra regions is because these are used for imagining novel events. Szpunar, Watson and McDermott (2007) also found shared regions for past and future thinking. They used a word-cueing task to get participants to think about personal memories and future events (e.g., using the word 'birthday'). Results from fMRI scans showed that regions of the medial prefrontal cortex, posteriomedial parietal cortex and medial temporal lobes were involved in thinking about both past and future events. Addis *et al*. (2007) also found that these same regions were engaged when they asked participants to elaborate on the events they had thought of by retrieving or generating more detail.

Further evidence for a shared neural basis of past and future thinking comes from a study of brain damaged patients. Hassabis *et al*. (2007) found that patients with hippocampus damage could not remember personal experiences or imagine future events, but retained semantic memory. This suggests that the hippocampus is more important for personal memories than for factual knowledge, and that these two aspects of explicit long-term memory are distinct in their neural realization. A study of children with hippocampal brain damage has confirmed this semantic–episodic distinction. Vargha-Khadem *et al*. (1997) studied three adolescents who were unable to recall many details of their personal lives. One child had suffered damage to her hippocampus at birth, another was 4 years old when he sustained brain damage and the third had drug-induced seizures which caused amnesia when she was 9. Although all three had impaired episodic memory and very small hippocampi, they had relatively normal semantic memory.

How does memory develop?

It is clear that our memory abilities improve as we progress through childhood, but what exactly is it that develops? It could be that there is an increase in capacity of working memory. This would enable us not only to remember more in the short term, but would allow us to encode and store more in long-term memory. Alternatively, it may be that we develop more efficient strategies for getting information into memory. A third possibility is that our memory improves as a result of our metacognitive understanding of memory, which leads to better allocation of resources and choice of strategies. Finally, our increasing body of knowledge may assist with memorizing new information and experiences.

Capacity and speed

Earlier in the chapter, we saw that the number of items that children can recall on the digit span task increases from around two-and-a-half at age 2, to seven in adulthood, and that visual span increases from four items at age 5, to fourteen by age 11. Children and adults alike can recall fewer letters than digits, but letter span also increases throughout childhood (Dempster, 1981). Measures such as these have been devised to assess the capacity of short-term memory, whereas long-term memory is considered to be infinite. We do not know that it *is* infinite, but there is no way of measuring how much information can be held in long-term storage.

Although postulating an increase in size, or capacity, of short-term memory may be a simple and appealing explanation for developmental changes, evidence from research reveals a more complex story. According to proponents of the working memory model, the *duration* of the phonological loop is a key constraint of how much information can be remembered. If this is true, then the speed with which we can process items should be as critical as the number of items we have to remember. Several studies have found that the speed with which words can be identified or articulated increases with age, and that these speed increases correspond to memory span increases (Case, Kurland and Goldberg, 1982; Hulme *et al*., 1984). Kail (1991a) analyzed data from 72 studies in which both adults and children were given speeded tasks (i.e., tasks in which participants are asked to make a response as quickly as possible). Data were obtained for a variety of tasks, including classification, identification, mental rotation, reading and visual search. He found that processing speed increases with age, and that the rate of increase is greater in younger children than in older children. Several explanations for this general increase in processing speed have been proposed, such as more efficient use of strategies, greater familiarity with the items being processed or biological maturation. At present, the evidence seems to favour a general age-related increase, which may be the result of faster neural communication (Kail, 2000)

Strategies

It is clear that in order to be able to recognize or recall facts, skills and experiences, we need to be able to retain information over time, and we need to be able to access, or retrieve it, when appropriate. But first, we have to encode information and get it into memory. Young children seem to be less efficient at encoding information than older children and adults because they seem less effective at using encoding strategies, such as rehearsal, organization and elaboration.

Rehearsal. Rehearsal refers to consciously repeating information over and over again to ensure it stays in memory. An example of this is repeating a phone number to yourself until you get a chance to write it down. Very young children tend not to rehearse, but children's use of rehearsal increases with age. Flavell, Beach and Chinski (1966) gave 5-, 7- and 10-year-old children the task of remembering the sequence in which sets of two, three, four or five pictures had been pointed to. Prior to the experiment, one of the experimenters had trained himself to be able to read lips for the names of the pictures used in the task. During the experiment he looked to see if the participants were subvocalizing the names of the pictures in order to remember them. Flavell *et al.* found that 10 per cent of the 5-year-olds, 60 per cent of the 7-year-olds and 85 per cent of the 10-year-olds rehearsed the names of the items they had to remember. An interesting additional finding was that the 7-year-olds who rehearsed were able to recall the sequence of items better than the 7-year-olds who didn't rehearse. This comparison could only be made for this middle group as almost none of the 5-year-olds, and almost all of the 10-year-olds used rehearsal.

Although Flavell *et al.*'s study suggests that using a strategy leads to better recall, later research showed that just using rehearsal is not always enough. Ornstein, Naus and Liberty (1975) studied the effects of different rehearsal strategies on recall of items in a list. They assigned 8-, 11- and 13-year-olds to one of two conditions: overt and covert. Participants in the covert condition were told to remember as many words in the list as possible, while those in the overt condition were instructed to rehearse aloud. The list items were presented at a slow rate of one item every five seconds, in order to facilitate rehearsal. The overt group actually recalled fewer items than the covert group, but there was a main effect of age for the overt group, with older children recalling more items. There were no age-related differences in frequency of rehearsal, so it is not the case that older children recalled more items because they rehearsed each item more often. When Ornstein *et al.* looked at which words the children had rehearsed, they found that older children were more likely to rehearse a greater number of different words between item presentations. The 11- and 13-year-olds rehearsed four to four-and-a-half items from the list together at most points during presentation of the items, whereas the 8-year-olds only rehearsed around two-and-a-half items at a time. The difference between older and younger children's recall is not, therefore, a result of increased strategy use, but of how the strategy is used, with older children rehearsing items in a greater variety of contexts.

Naus, Ornstein and Aivano (1977) compared groups of 8- and 12-year-olds who were either told to rehearse in the way that they usually would, or were instructed to rehearse the most recent item along with two other words from the list. There was no effect of rehearsal strategy on number of items recalled for the 12-year-olds, which is not surprising given that the older children in Ornstein *et al.*'s study spontaneously rehearsed more than three items at a time. The younger group, on the other hand, benefited from the instruction to rehearse a greater variety of items. From these studies, we can conclude that older children spontaneously use an effective rehearsal strategy, whereas younger children do not. Younger children are, however, capable of using this strategy and can be taught to use it. The developmental difference, therefore, is not in ability, but in knowing how to make best use of rehearsal strategies – a metacognitive skill.

Organization. A second strategy that we use for encoding information is organizing the items we want to remember into meaningful categories. If I asked you to remember the names of your classmates (pick one of your smaller classes!), you might construct a number of categories to aid you in this task: males and females, where people typically sit, groups of friends, people who work together and so on.

As with rehearsal, use of organization increases with age. Preschool children tend not to use the strategy. In the early school years, children do not spontaneously use the strategy, but they can be taught it and benefit from using it. By the ages of 10 or 11, children use the strategy spontaneously (Frankel and Rollins, 1985; Furth and Milgram, 1973; Hasselhorn, 1992). The differences in spontaneous strategy use are illustrated by a study by Schneider (1986). In this experiment, he gave 7- and 10-year-olds sets of pictures and instructed the participants to do whatever they wanted in order to remember the items. About 60 per cent of the older group spontaneously grouped the items into categories, whereas only 10 per cent of the younger children did. Another feature of this study was that there were two types of list: one in which the items could be easily categorized (e.g., table, chair, desk) and one in which the items were not so closely related (e.g., stool, bookcase, refrigerator). The 10-year-olds grouped the latter items into a 'furniture' category but the 7-year-olds did not. The younger children needed there to be an obvious similarity between items before they used the grouping strategy. Although the developmental trajectory was traditionally conceived of as a gradual progression, Schlagmüller and Schneider (2002), in a microgenetic study of 9- to 11-year-olds, found that there is a fairly abrupt transition from not using the strategy to using it.

However, organization can be facilitated by varying the nature of the task. Sodian, Schneider and Perlmutter (1986) tested the ability of 4- and 6-year-old children to sort sixteen toys into categories such as animals and furniture. One group of children were placed in a 'play and remember' condition, in which they were instructed to play with the toys for a while. They were then told that the toys would be hidden and that they would have to remember as many of them as they could. A second group were placed in a 'sort and remember' condition. They were told that the game involved sorting the toys into categories, the toys would then be hidden, and they would have to remember as many of the toys as possible. Sodian *et al.* found that 4-year-olds remembered more of the toys in the 'sort and remember' condition than in the 'play and remember' condition. The children who had been explicitly instructed to use the sorting strategy were able to recall more items.

However, this effect was not found for the 6-year-olds, suggesting that they used sorting as an aid to memory without the need for explicit instruction. This demonstrates that, as with rehearsal, younger children are capable of using organization as an encoding strategy, but tend not to do so without training.

Elaboration. Although rehearsal and organization can be useful strategies, they work best when items only have to be remembered for a brief period of time. For longer-term remembering, elaboration can be a more effective strategy. Elaboration involves generating relations between pairs of items so that memory for the items can be constructed in a meaningful way. This relation can be visual or verbal and often takes the form of an event that links the two items. If, for example, I asked you to remember 'guitar' and 'horse', you might imagine a horse playing a guitar or generate the sentence 'the horse played the guitar'. Unlike rehearsal and organization, elaboration is not spontaneously used as a memory strategy until adolescence, and even then it is not common (Beuhring and Kee, 1987; Pressley and Levin, 1977). Younger children can be taught to use elaboration (Pressley, 1982), suggesting once again that children's strategy use is not restricted by their capabilities, but they do not get the same benefits with respect to increased recall as older children (Reese, 1977).

Why don't young children use strategies? There is evidence that all of the strategies discussed above can be learned by young children, but are not spontaneously utilized until later, so why aren't they using these strategies? Two proposals have been put forward. One idea is that young children have a *mediation deficiency* (Reese, 1962), meaning that they do not have the ability to use strategies (or mediators). A competing explanation is that they have a *production deficiency* (Flavell 1970); it is not the case that the strategies would fail to produce a benefit, or that children lack the competence to use a particular strategy, but rather that the children just do not produce the strategy. The fact that children who do not yet use a strategy can be trained to use it implies that they have a production deficiency. Several researchers have attempted to induce spontaneous strategy use in young children by offering incentives for good performance on a memory task (Kunzinger and Witryol, 1984; O'Sullivan, 1993) with the general finding that incentives lead to greater attempts to memorize items and, in school-age children, to better performance on memory tasks.

The mediation deficiency and production deficiency accounts both attempt to explain why a potentially beneficial strategy is not used, but sometimes the opposite occurs: children will use a strategy that does not lead to any immediate increases in recall. This has been termed *utilization deficiency* (Miller, 1994) because although the strategy is being produced, demonstrating both competence and inclination to use it, their use of it is not immediately beneficial. Over time, use of the strategy does pay off, leading to improved memory, but at first it may even lead to a decrease in performance. If this is correct – and Miller and Seier (1994) cite dozens of studies in which such a deficiency was found – there are important implications for training children in strategy use. Just teaching children to use a strategy will not automatically lead to improved memory. Despite the vast number of studies demonstrating a period of utilization deficiency, there has been debate over whether this is a necessary step in the development of memory strategies (Waters, 2000). Also, many (but not all) of the studies demonstrating utilization deficiency are cross-sectional, rather than microgenetic or longitudinal.

In order to examine the course of strategy development, Kron-Sperl, Schneider and Hasselhorn (2008) conducted a longitudinal study, in which they followed

102 children from age 6 to 10, and an additional 86 children from age 8 to 10. The participants were given several verbal memory tasks every six months, and their use of the sorting strategy was measured. The researchers found that when children started using a strategy, they were more likely to see immediate performance benefits than to go through a period with no improvement. Only 14 children were found to be utilization deficient during the study. How, then, can these contradictory findings be explained? Kron-Sperl *et al.* suggest that the utilization deficiency phenomenon results, at least in part, from the very act of participating in a study on memory strategies. When children take part in such a study, they repeatedly practise strategies, which leads to an increase in reported strategy use without a corresponding increase in performance. One explanation of differences across studies, therefore, is that when children are not intensively training, their use of the strategy unfolds more gradually, and does not outpace the benefits of using the strategy.

The role of knowledge

Chi's (1978) study, discussed at the beginning of this chapter, provides an excellent example of the role of prior knowledge in encoding new information into memory. For the children with chess expertise, an assortment of shaped pieces on a chequered board was not a random array of objects, but a meaningful situation encompassing multiple relationships between the pieces. This effect of expertise is not limited to chess. Chi and Koeske (1983) examined the knowledge of a 4½-year-old boy who was an expert on dinosaurs (for his age!). Two lists of 20 dinosaurs that he had greater and lesser knowledge of were generated from interactions with the child, an examination of his books and judgements made by his mother. When given memory recall tasks, his performance was significantly better for the list of dinosaurs with which he was more familiar. But Chi and Koeske were not just concerned with quantity of knowledge, they wanted to know about the structural, or organizational, differences between the two categories of dinosaur. To this end, they structured their interactions with the child in order to elicit his knowledge of dinosaurs from which they could make inferences about the structure of his knowledge. First, he was asked to generate the names of all the dinosaurs he could think of. Second, the experimenters played a 'clue game' in which they described two or three properties, such as 'plant-eating', and the participant had to name a dinosaur that possessed those properties. From these responses, Chi and Koeske constructed a semantic network containing nodes that represent the names and properties of dinosaurs, with connections between properties and the names of dinosaurs that the participant linked them with. Dinosaurs who share a number of known similarities (e.g., lives on land, eats plants, walk on four legs) were therefore closely connected to one another. Dinosaurs about which the participant knew little had fewer links and were not closely connected to one another. Making an explicit representation of knowledge in this way demonstrates that greater knowledge of items leads to a more cohesive and integrated structure of knowledge, with densely inter-related items. As there was only one participant, it is highly unlikely that strategy or capacity variation explains the differences in recall for the two groups. His greater recall of familiar dinosaurs is therefore a result of the structure of his knowledge about them.

Gobbo and Chi (1986) conducted another study based around dinosaur knowledge, this time with ten children, five of whom had expert knowledge of dinosaurs, and five of whom were novices. Each child was presented with pictures of 20 dinosaurs, one at a time, and asked to tell the experimenter everything he/she could about each dinosaur. The children's descriptions were coded as a set of explicit and implicit propositions. Explicit propositions were pieces of information that could be observed from the stimulus pictures alone (e.g., 'it has spikes all down the back'). Implicit propositions were statements that could not be derived from the pictures (e.g., 'they travel in small groups'). Both the expert and novice groups produced a similar number of explicit propositions, but the expert group produced four times as many implicit propositions. In addition to coding for the types of information produced, the experimenters also analyzed the syntactic connectives between propositions (use of words like 'because' and 'if'); the number of characteristics such as habitat, diet and social activity that were mentioned; frequency with which comparisons between dinosaurs were made; and class membership (meat eater vs plant eater). The analysis of all these data led Gobbo and Chi to conclude that novices and experts differ in several ways. The experts produced more implicit propositions, their knowledge was more highly structured, and their structured knowledge led to a more sophisticated use of the knowledge, such as drawing inferences based on similarities. So how does this knowledge base affect memory? The idea is that the interconnected, detailed items of knowledge lead to faster processing of information. Individual items can be recalled from long-term memory quickly. This frees up mental resources which can be used on memory strategies (Bjorklund, Muir-Broaddus and Schneider, 1990).

It is clear that highly structured knowledge can lead to greater recall of information related to the knowledge domain, but is knowledge the only important factor that affects memory? If you were to listen to a story and had to remember the details, do you think that your knowledge of the domain would be important? What if the topic was something you know nothing about? Perhaps you consider yourself to be quite intelligent and think that your domain-general verbal reasoning and comprehension skills would overcome any lack of specialist knowledge. Schneider, Korkel and Weinert (1989) wanted to answer these questions, and did so by conducting a study on children's memory for a story about football (soccer to those outside the UK!). As well as dividing the participants into groups of novices and experts, Schneider *et al.* also gave them a cognitive ability test consisting of vocabulary, sentence completion and word classification tasks. On the basis of the scores from the test, participants were split into high and low aptitude groups, giving four groups (expert/high aptitude, expert/low aptitude, novice/high aptitude and novice/low aptitude) within each of three age groups (8-, 10- and 12-year-olds). An audio-recorded story about a young footballer that included an account of an important match was played to the participants, and they could read along at the same time. After a 15-minute break, they were given a questionnaire that tested their memory for details, ability to draw inferences and ability to detect contradictions. The results were surprising: Experts performed better than novices on all three measures, regardless of aptitude. There were no differences between high- and low-aptitude experts, and no differences between high- and low-aptitude novices. For all the measures, regardless of age, low-aptitude experts scored higher than high-aptitude novices. These findings are consistent with other studies on memory for baseball stories (Recht and Leslie, 1988; Walker 1987).

Metamemory

metamemory
Knowledge of the contents and processes of memory.

Another key aspect of effective use of memory is our metacognitive knowledge about the contents and processes of memory, or metamemory. Flavell and Wellman (1977) distinguished two categories of metamemory: sensitivity and variables.

Sensitivity refers to knowledge about when it is necessary to use memory strategies, and can therefore also be described as knowledge of procedural memory. Meta-memory for variables is our knowledge of declarative memory. This includes, for example, our knowledge that performance on a memory task can be influenced by different factors. These factors are person knowledge, task knowledge and strategy knowledge. Since Flavell and Wellman described these components of metamemory, other components have been added to the list. Schneider and Lockl (2002; Schneider, 2008) mapped out a taxonomy of metacognition that includes the ideas of Kuhn (1999, 2000); Flavell and Wellman; and Nelson and Narens (1990, 1994) (see Figure 3.6). Schneider and Lockl (2002) point out that this is not an exhaustive list of aspects of metamemory. Aspects of metacognition that are not displayed include conditional metacognitive knowledge, which refers to our knowledge of why we make decisions to use particular strategies under certain circumstances (Paris and Lindauer, 1982; Paris and Oka, 1986). An executive component that selects which strategies to use, monitors their use and modifies them if necessary, has also been proposed (Brown, 1978; Brown *et al.*, 1983).

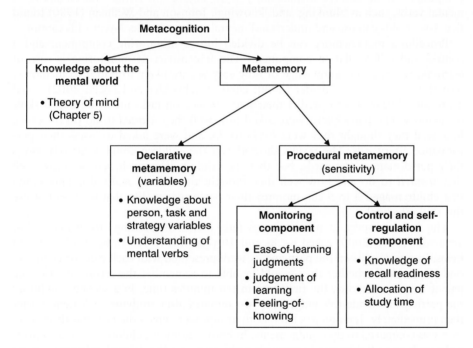

Figure 3.6

Schneider and Lockl's taxonomy of metacognition.

Source: After Schneider W. & Lockl, K. (2002). The development of metacognitive knowledge in children and adolescents. In T. J. Perfect & B. L. Schwartz (Eds.), *Applied metacognition* (pp. 224–257). Cambridge: Cambridge University Press.

With respect to declarative metamemory, a number of studies were conducted in the 1970s and 1980s with the aim of examining how the different aspects develop. In a study on person knowledge, which is knowledge about the memory strengths and limitations that people have, Wellman (1977b) asked 3- to 5-year-olds to rate the importance of four different factors on how good someone would be at remembering. Three of the factors were irrelevant (e.g., hair colour, clothing, weight) and the fourth was the relevant factor of age. Most of the participants rated two of the three irrelevant factors as unimportant, but only half of them indicated that age is an important factor. Kreutzer, Leonard and Flavell (1975) found that it is not until about 9 years of age that children understand the potential for memory variation both within and between individuals. More recently, Jaswal and Dodson (2009) conducted a study looking at 5- and 6-year-olds' understanding of other people's mistakes on memory tasks. Although 5-year-olds could not reliably distinguish between a mistake resulting from a guess and one resulting from a false memory, 6-years-old did make this distinction, suggesting that they have developed a sensitivity to the fact that memory is fallible. Kreutzer *et al.* (1975) also studied children's task knowledge, which is knowledge about what makes a memory task easier or harder. For example, knowing that a list with fewer items is easier to remember than a list with many items. They found that 70 per cent of 6-year-olds did not realize that pairs of words that were opposites would be easier to remember than pairs of unrelated words, whereas all the 11-year-olds in the study understood this.

The third type of declarative metamemory is knowledge of strategy. The development of strategy knowledge means children gain a greater understanding of what strategies are available to them, how they can be used and when they will provide a benefit. Justice (1986) and Schneider (1986) have demonstrated a developmental progression from 4 to 12 years of age. Younger children view all strategies on memory tasks as equally effective, whereas 8- to 10-year-olds start to discriminate between strategies, and 12-year-olds know which strategies work best. The final component of declarative metamemory from Figure 3.6 is the understanding of mental verbs, such as 'thinking' and 'knowing'. Johnson and Wellman (1980) found that 4-year-olds can use and understand mental verbs, whereas 3-year-olds cannot.

Procedural metamemory can be divided into a monitoring component and a control and self-regulation component. The first aspect of monitoring is ease of learning, which is our knowledge of how easy we are likely to find it to memorize something. Visé and Schneider (2000; cited in Schneider and Lockl, 2002) asked 4-, 6- and 9-year-olds to predict their performance on tasks involving motor skills or memory. The participants were asked how well they *wanted* to do on the tasks, how well they thought they were *likely* to do, and were asked to assess their performance afterwards. The results showed that the children could accurately assess their performance afterwards, but that they didn't distinguish between how well they *wanted* to do and how well they thought they would *really* do. This shows that children aged 4 to 9 can monitor their performance, but that they do not use this skill effectively.

The second aspect of monitoring is judgements of learning. To examine this, Schneider *et al.* (2000) asked 6-, 8- and 10-year-olds to remember lists of paired items. In one condition, the participants were presented with each pair for eight seconds then asked whether they would be able to remember the second item of the pair if they were shown the first item in ten minutes time. In a second condition, the participants made this judgement two minutes after studying each item, rather than immediately. Ten minutes later, both groups were given the task and their accuracy was compared to their judgements. In both conditions, children tended to overestimate how well they would remember the pairs, but the delayed judgements were more accurate than the immediate judgements. This finding is consistent with adult performance on a similar task (Nelson and Dunlosky, 1991), so it seems that even 6-year-olds have monitoring skills that are comparable to that of adults. The development of procedural metamemory may not, therefore, be a result of improved monitoring, but is likely to be an interaction between both aspects of procedural metamemory – monitoring and self-regulation.

Feeling of knowing is the final aspect of monitoring and refers to the degree to which we believe we know things. Wellman (1977a) asked children aged 6 to 9 years if they would recognize names of items that they could not recall the names of. The youngest children performed little better than chance, whereas the oldest group were very accurate in their predictions. Cultice, Somerville and Wellman

(1983) gave a variant of this task, with pictures of children who were very familiar, less familiar or unfamiliar, to 4- and 5-year-olds and found they were highly accurate in their judgements. This demonstrates that even preschool children can monitor their memories when the task involves meaningful material.

The second main component of procedural metamemory is self-regulation, which is our ability to plan, direct and evaluate our behaviour. One of the key ways in which we can make use of our metamemory is in allocating our time according to the demands of the task. An obvious example of this is something with which you may be familiar – the allocation of study time. Dufresne and Kobasigawa (1989) investigated this by giving 6- to 12-year-old children lists of pairs of items that were either related (and therefore easier to memorize) or unrelated (and therefore harder to memorize). The 6- and 8-year-olds spent a similar amount of time studying each type of list, whereas 10- and 12-year-olds allocated more time to studying the unrelated pairs. This finding was confirmed by Lockl and Schneider (2002; cited in Schneider and Lockl, 2002). Both studies found that although the younger children did not allocate time differentially, they did know the difference between easy and hard pairs.

The self-regulation component of procedural metamemory appears to develop gradually throughout childhood, but it is harder to present a simple picture of the developmental trajectory of the monitoring component. We have seen that 4- to 9-year-olds cannot make accurate judgements of how well they will do on a memory task, but that 6- to 10-year-olds are good at making judgements of learning after a delay. Also, 9-year-olds, but not 6-year-olds, are good at feeling of knowledge tasks, unless the material is highly salient, in which case 4-year-olds perform well. How do we go about explaining this differential ability? It may be that studies in neuroscience and neuropsychology can help.

Evidence from neuroscience. Chua, Schachter and Sperling (2009) used fMRI to look at the neural correlates of two metamemory tasks in adults. The first of these was a feeling of knowing task, similar to the ones described above. Participants were shown a series of faces that they had already studied and were asked to press a button to indicate whether they knew the name that went with the face, or, if they could not recall it, whether they had high or low confidence that they would recognize the name later. The second task was a retrospective confidence task, in which participants were again presented with a series of faces, this time with three names presented under each one. First, they had to choose which of the three names went with the face, then they had to rate whether they had high or low confidence that they had chosen correctly. Retrospective confidence judgements are similar to, but distinct from, feeling of knowing judgements as the former require monitoring past performance whereas the latter require prospective monitoring. The results showed that a large area, including the temporo-parietal junction, superior frontal gyrus and right inferior parietal lobule, were engaged during both tasks. These regions are associated with internally-directed (as opposed to externally-directed) cognition (Raichle *et al.*, 2001) which suggests that, during metamemory tasks, the participants were examining internal representations rather than external stimuli. There were, however, differences between the two tasks, including greater hippocampal activity for the feeling of knowing task, which may indicate that participants were accessing semantic information about the faces when making prospective judgements. Retrospective confidence judgements may also rely more heavily on the frontal lobes than feeling of knowing. Pannu, Kaszniak and Rapcsak (2005) gave

Box 3.1 Eyewitness testimony

Research into children's memory is not just of interest to cognitive and developmental psychologists. What we know about the factors that can affect memory has obvious implications for the classroom, and also for the courtroom. In cases where children have witnessed serious crimes, or been victims of abuse, it is important to know how reliable their testimony is. Failure to believe in a child's accurate testimony could lead to the failure to deal with dangerous criminals, the consequences of which may be the subsequent physical abuse, sexual abuse, or murders of more children. Alternatively, believing in a child's inaccurate report of events could have serious, damaging results for an innocent person. Even if the accused is never actually convicted, an allegation of child abuse is likely to have long-lasting, severe effects.

It has long been known that adults' eyewitness reports can be unreliable (Loftus, 1975; Loftus and Palmer, 1974), but what about children? When asked to provide a free-recall account of an event, young children tend to recall fewer details than older children (Roebers and Schneider, 2002), but what they do recall tends to be accurate (Cassel and Bjorklund, 1995). If children are asked generic questions in alleged abuse cases, they tend to give generic answers, whereas specific, episodic questions yield episodic answers (Schneider *et al.*, 2010). Recall can also be affected by IQ levels (Roebers and Schneider, 2001), and incentives can lead to more accurate recall (Roebers, Moga and Schneider, 2001). On the other hand, when given cues, such as 'tell me what the girl looked like', children of all ages often remember details that were not there (Bjorklund *et al.*, 1998). Children's accuracy of recall is more likely to decrease over time than adults, with adults showing greater accuracy after a five-month delay than 6-year-olds (Flin *et al.*, 1992).

Another important issue is the extent to which children are suggestible. That is, whether they can be made to recount events that didn't happen through the wording of questions and the way in which interviews are conducted. Research into this issue has found that preschoolers are more suggestible than older children and adults (Ceci and Bruck, 1993), but there is mixed evidence with respect to the susceptibility of children aged 4–11 (Bruck *et al.*, 1995; Lindberg, 1991; Saywitz and Snyder, 1993). It may be that these mixed findings result from the existence of a range of factors that can influence children's performance, so in studies that report conflicting results, participants may not be carrying out comparable tasks. Bruck and Melnyk (2004) reviewed 69 studies examining the relationships between children's suggestibility and demographic, cognitive and psycho-social factors. They found that although language ability was fairly consistently related to suggestibility in preschoolers, and creativity was associated with suggestibility in 5- to 8-year-olds, there is no strong evidence that any single demographic, cognitive or psycho-social factor predicts individual differences in suggestibility.

Lindberg (1991) identified three sets of factors that can have an impact on children's performance in studies of eyewitness testimony, only one of which is about memory. The other two categories are the focus of the study and characteristics of the participant. The set of factors that can affect memory processes can be subdivided into those that impact on encoding, storage and retrieval. With respect to encoding, the information that children receive prior to an event can have an effect on how the event is represented. Storage can be affected by information given after the event, including suggestive (or leading) questions. This subsequent information combines with the information from the original event to create a new representation of what happened. Factors that affect retrieval include the methods used to test memory. Are children being asked to recognize or recall information? If the latter, are they being asked open-ended free recall questions, or are they being cued to recall specific types of information?

The second set of factors relates to the focus of the study, or the level and type of detail that is asked about. This could be focal information about critical actions in an event (e.g., 'did the man hit the girl?'), or it could be peripheral information (e.g., 'what colour was the girl's

▶

sweater?'). It might not be details at all, but rather a gist memory of the event. Third, there are characteristics of the children to consider. Individual differences with respect to social and cognitive skills, age, personality, knowledge and motivation can affect the information they store and retrieve.

Lindberg, Keiffer and Thomas (2000) designed a study to examine many of these variables together. They showed 329 children aged 9 to 16 a film in which a mother appeared to slap her 5-year-old son after he failed to help her pick up some spilled groceries, choosing to continue playing a video game he had previously started instead. The participants saw the boy being knocked to the floor, crying. The mother then roughly pulled him to his feet and seemed to hit him a second time as they exited the room. There is obvious potential for negative effects on the participants, given the nature of the study, so they were very carefully debriefed, and were shown an out-take from the film that featured the actors laughing after the boy forgot his lines. It was also clear from the out-take that the sound of the slap given by the mother was a sound effect, as it was out of time with the pretend action.

Three groups of participants each heard a different introduction prior to viewing the film as a manipulation of how they encoded what they saw. One group was told that the mother was mean and had previously been arrested for child abuse, another was told that the boy was always bad and that his mother was usually very gentle with him, and a third group received no information about the mother or the boy. Storage was manipulated by asking a series of questions after the film, including some leading questions. Some participants in each of the first two encoding conditions were given leading questions in which the mother was characterized as mean, and some were given questions characterizing the boy as bad. Those who had not had the introduction were given neutral questions. With respect to retrieval, three types of questions were asked: recognition, cued-recall and free recall.

In general, the youngest group, 9-year-olds, performed more poorly on the tests of memory than 13- or 16-year-olds, and recognition questions elicited more incorrect responses than recall across the age groups. The youngest group made more confabulations (made-up answers) than the older age groups when asked, for example, about what items were in the mother's grocery bag, when it was not possible to tell what was in the bag from the film. One of the key issues in eyewitness memory is suggestibility, which was manipulated by asking leading questions. Some of the participants were asked a question about what the mother said as she went to the kitchen 'to wipe the blood from his bloody nose' and then all the participants were asked how many drops of blood fell from the boy's nose. Those who received the leading question reported three times as much blood as those who did not have the presence of blood suggested to them, and the youngest age group reported more blood than the older age group. In the film, there was no blood. This finding shows how easy it is for children, particularly pre-teens, to be misled by suggestive questions. There were also effects of the encoding manipulations; the participants in the 'bad boy' condition rated the boy as more deserving of being hit than those in the 'mean mother' condition. There was also an effect of age, with younger children giving higher ratings of this item. As with the 'blood' question, this illustrates the power of suggestion, but the difference lies in the memory stage. The rating of deserving to be hit reflects suggestions made at the encoding stage whereas the answers about the amount of blood reflect the effect on storage.

Lindberg *et al.* summarize these and many other findings from this study with an analogy:

> '... digging for memories may be something like digging for snow. If you dig too deep, you will stop getting snow and get dirt instead. Memories are even more complicated in that the nature of the snow shovelled will depend on the type of shovel and who is doing the digging.' (p. 587)

patients with frontal lobe damage both tasks and found worse performance for retrospective confidence judgement compared to healthy controls, but no differences in feeling of knowing. These studies suggest that metamemory is not a unitary construct, which may explain why children's performance is inconsistent across tasks.

Concluding comments

As with most areas of science, the development of memory is not a phenomenon that can be explained simply. We have seen that maturation of the nervous system, availability and use of strategies for encoding information, prior knowledge and metacognitive skills all contribute to increasing memory abilities throughout infancy, childhood and adolescence. Is it, then, possible to determine how all these factors interact? DeMarie and Ferron (2003) aimed to answer this question by using **structural equation modelling** to examine how well metamemory, strategies and capacity predicted children's recall. Using data from 179 children aged from 5 to 11 years, who completed a battery of memory tasks, DeMarie and Ferron found that around two-thirds of the variance in recall could be explained by these three constructs. Figure 3.7 illustrates the model; only strategies had a statistically significant direct effect on recall. The authors note that there may be indirect effects of metamemory and capacity on recall, however.

structural equation modelling Similar to path analysis, this is a statistical method for examining causal relationships between variables. Theoretical models of the relationships between variables can be tested in order to see how well they fit the data.

Figure 3.7

Model of three constructs predicting recall. The bold numbers are the path coefficients for 5- to 8-year-olds and the non-bold numbers are the path coefficients for 8- to 11-year-olds. Asterisks indicate statistically significant paths.

Source: Reprinted from Journal of Experimental Child Psychology, 84, DeMarie, D. & Ferron, J., Capacity, strategies, and metamemory: Tests of a three-factor model of memory development, 167–193, Copyright (2003), with permission from Elsevier.

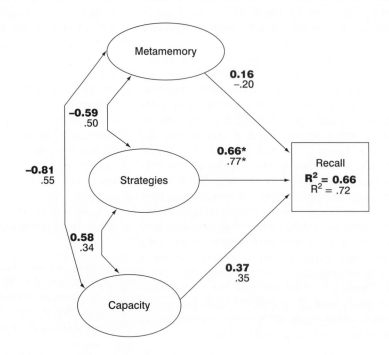

Subsequently, DeMarie *et al.* (2004) used path analysis to test two different theoretical accounts of the interaction of metamemory, strategies and capacity. The two models were the Würzburg Model (Schneider, Schlagmüller and Visé, 1998) and DeMarie *et al.*'s own Utilization Deficiency Model. According to the Würzburg Model, capacity and intelligence influence metamemory, which influences strategies; both metamemory and strategies affect recall. The Utilization Deficiency Model proposes direct influences of both capacity and metamemory on strategies, but the main way in which it differs from the Würzburg Model is that it also includes strategy effectiveness, which is moderated by metamemory and capacity. Recall is influenced by three variables: Strategy, the interaction between metamemory and strategies, and the interaction between capacity and strategies. The models were fitted to data from the same children studied by DeMarie and Ferron (2003). The path analysis showed that the Würzburg Model did not fit the data collected from the children, but that the Utilization Deficiency Model could have produced the data. This finding suggests that the effectiveness of strategy use is determined by both capacity and metamemory. If both capacity and metamemory are high, then a change in strategy will lead to increased recall whereas, if both are low, new strategies will not lead to large improvements. This could explain why some children, in some situations, exhibit utilization deficiency, and others do not.

Ornstein and Haden (2001) also note the importance of basic processes, strategies and knowledge. In addition, they point out that the research on eyewitness testimony has led to psychologists having an appreciation of how what is going on at the time of an event can affect children's memory for the event, as well as their subsequent experiences. The context of an event, and adults' explanations of experiences, contribute to how memories are encoded. Knowledge and experience can not only facilitate memory, as in Chi's (1978) work, but also lead to distortions, as in Lindberg *et al.*'s (2000) study. Ornstein and Haden argued (ten years ago) that in order for us to have a full understanding of what develops, developmental psychologists need to (a) carry out more longitudinal research in order to examine children's changing skills, and (b) integrate the information processing approach with a social constructivist perspective in order to consider children's social and communicative interactions with adults. To some extent, these aims have been addressed. Several of the studies mentioned in this chapter are longitudinal (e.g., Bauer *et al.*, 2000; Kron-Sperl et al., 2008; Schlagmüller and Schneider 2002), and researchers are also looking at the social and communicative factors affecting memory (e.g., Topal *et al.*, 2008).

Another major development in recent years has been the use of cognitive neuroscience techniques to address some of the questions concerning the development of memory. Adult studies have provided a map of brain regions associated with different aspects of memory, but developmental research is still in its infancy. Knowing which neural structures are active in different memory tasks, and knowing when they develop, goes some way to explaining why some memory abilities are used earlier than others, but this does not tell us the whole story. Howe, Courage and Rooksby (2009) point out that the network of brain structures necessary for declarative memory is mature by 12 months of age, a whole year before autobiographical memories emerge. In order to understand why this ability develops when it does, we need to understand the role of physical maturation and the way in which cognitive factors such as knowledge develop.

path analysis A statistical method for examining causal relationships between variables.

Summary

What is memory? Memory can be divided into short-term memory and long-term memory. Short-term memory contains information that is currently active or in consciousness. Items can be held in short-term memory for short durations of up to 20 seconds. Long-term memory is our permanent store of information, and is made up of semantic memory, episodic memory and procedural memory. Both semantic and episodic memory are also referred to as declarative memory or explicit memory. Procedural memory is also referred to as implicit memory.

Theories of memory development. Most theories of memory adopt an information processing approach. Atkinson and Shiffrin explained cognitive processing in terms of the organization and structure of memory. Input hits the sensory register, which has a large capacity but extremely short duration. A subset of the information that gets into sensory memory is processed further in short-term memory. The short-term store has very limited capacity and a duration of up to 20 seconds. Information can be kept active in the short-term store, and subsequently transferred to the long-term store by control processes such as rehearsal. Baddeley and Hitch proposed a more sophisticated account of short-term memory called the working memory model, which takes into account the differences between auditory and visual stimuli. This model consists of a central executive, the phonological loop, the visuospatial sketchpad and the episodic buffer.

Memory in infancy. Some aspects of memory are available early in infancy, and others do not develop until about 12 months of age. The tasks that young infants can do involve implicit procedural memory whereas the tasks that they cannot yet do involve explicit declarative memory and working memory. Newborns have at least minimal recognition memory and by 6 weeks demonstrate the ability to recall the actions needed to imitate facial expressions. By 9 months of age, infants start to demonstrate an ability to imitate actions performed on objects after a delay of 24 hours, and by 13 months they can imitate a sequence of actions after a 3 month delay. The lack of autobiographical memory from the first few years of life has been termed 'infantile amnesia'. One explanation for this lack of memory is that infants are not capable of encoding and storing memories, but Rovee-Collier's work using the mobile conjugate reinforcement procedure suggests that it may be due to limitations on the retrieval process.

Episodic memory. Children as young as 2 are able to talk about events that happened in the past but require a lot of prompting from adults. By 3 or 4 years of age, children can answer questions with fewer prompts, suggesting that episodic memory develops gradually through the preschool years. Some argue that memory for events in children younger than 4 or 5 is actually semantic memory involving scripts, rather than episodic memory.

How does memory develop? The development of memory may be the result of an increase in capacity of working memory, the development of more efficient strategies for getting information into memory, the development of metamemory, or an increase in knowledge. Young children are less effective than older children at using encoding strategies, such as rehearsal, organization and elaboration. These strategies can be learned by young children, but are not spontaneously utilized until later. Two explanations for this are that children have a *mediation deficiency* or a *production deficiency*. Sometimes, however, children use a strategy that does not lead to any immediate increases in recall. This has been termed *utilization deficiency*. With respect to the role of knowledge, Chi's work demonstrates that highly structured knowledge can lead to greater recall of information related to the knowledge domain. Another key aspect of effective use of memory is our metacognitive knowledge about the contents and processes of memory, or metamemory.

Eyewitness testimony. It has long been known that adults' eyewitness reports can be unreliable, and the same can be said of children. Young children tend to recall fewer details of an event than older children, but what they do recall tends to be accurate. However, when given suggestive cues, children of all ages often remember details that were not there, and children's accuracy of recall is more likely to decrease over time than adults. Preschoolers are more suggestible than older children and adults, but there is mixed evidence with respect to the susceptibility of children aged 4 to 11.

Discussion questions

1 Why do you recall little or nothing from the first few years of your life?

2 How does strategy use develop throughout childhood?

3 What is metamemory and why is it important?

4 Imagine you are helping a child study for a test. What advice would you give them in order to help them remember key facts or ideas? How would this advice change depending on the age of the child?

5 Given what we know about the suggestibility of young children, what should interviewers do, and avoid doing, when seeking eyewitness testimony?

Further Reading

Books and chapters

Courage, M. L. and Cowan, N. (Eds) (2009). *The development of memory in infancy and childhood*. Hove: Psychology Press.

Mary Courage and Nelson Cowan have gathered many key figures together in this edited volume to present a state-of-the-art overview of developmental research on memory.

Ornstein, P. A., Haden, C. A. and San Souci, P. P. (2008). The development of skilled remembering in children. In J. H. E. Byrne (Series Ed.) and H. L. Roediger, III (Vol. Ed.), *Learning and memory: A comprehensive reference: Volume 2. Cognitive psychology of memory* (pp. 715–744). Oxford: Elsevier.

In this chapter, Peter Ornstein, Catherine Haden and Priscilla San Souci discuss research on the roles of strategy and knowledge in the development of memory.

Schneider, W. and Bjorklund, D. F. (1998). Memory. In W. Damon, D. Kuhn and R. S. Siegler (Eds), *Handbook of child psychology, Volume 2: Cognition, perception and language* (pp. 467–521). New York: John Wiley and Sons.

Wolfgang Schneider and David Bjorklund provide a thorough overview of the topic.

Articles

Bauer, P. J. and Fivush, R. (2010). Autobiographical memory: Context and consequences [Special issue]. *Cognitive Development*, 25(4).

In this special issue of *Cognitive Development*, editors Patricia Bauer and Robyn Fivush bring together a series of papers examining the social-emotional context of remembering, and the implications of autobiographical memories for the development of identity and well-being.

Ceci, S. J. and Bruck, M. (1993). Suggestibility of the child witness: A historical review and synthesis. *Psychological Bulletin*, 113(3), 403–439.

Stephen Ceci and Maggie Bruck present a comprehensive survey of research on children's memory and suggestibility within the context of eyewitness testimony.

Rovee-Collier, C. (1999). The development of infant memory. *Current Directions in Psychological Science*, 8, 80–85.

In this paper, Carolyn Rovee-Collier discusses research on the development of infant memory, including her classic 'mobile' studies.

Gathercole, S. E. (1998). The development of memory. *Journal of Child Psychology and Psychiatry*, 39, 3–27.

Susan Gathercole presents a comprehensive review of research on the development of memory. The first half of the paper focuses on Gathercole and her colleagues' information processing approach to the development of working memory.

Chapter 4

Language

Learning Outcomes

At the end of this chapter you should be able to:

- Describe the components of language.

- Critically compare and evaluate the behaviourist, nativist and constructivist views of language acquisition.

- Outline the sequence of acquisition of grammar.

- Describe and evaluate research on statistical learning.

- Discuss the biological basis of language.

In 1958, Jean Berko set out to see if young children understand the rules of inflections – the bits we add to words to indicate tense or number (e.g., jump<u>ed</u>, cat<u>s</u>). A simple test of this is to provide children with some nouns and verbs and ask them to produce past tense endings, plurals, etc. However, one of the problems facing language researchers is that we don't know what children already know. If a child is able to produce all the different inflections for a given word, we cannot tell whether this is because they understand the rules of grammar or because they have rote-learned all the variations of the word. Berko got round this problem by creating a set of novel nouns, such as 'wug' and 'gutch', and verbs, such as 'rick' and 'gling'. As it is fair to assume that children would not have heard these words before, any ability to generate the appropriate inflections must indicate the ability to use grammar productively.

> Q. At what age would you expect children to be able to produce 'gutches' as the plural of 'gutch'? What about the past tense: When do you think children will be able to produce 'glinged' as the past tense of 'gling'?

Berko recruited 56 children aged 4 to 7. Those aged 4 to 5½ were in preschool and the children aged 5½ to 7 were in the first grade. She presented them with a series of pictures drawn on cards to illustrate the novel words. The nouns were illustrated with drawings of cartoon animals and the verbs were illustrated with pictures of men performing various tasks. One of the cards is shown in Figure 4.1. In this case, a novel noun, 'wug', is presented and the task is to generate the regular plural 'wugs'. In addition to the novel words, several real words (glass, melt, ring), were also included to see if children had the appropriate endings in their vocabularies. Most of them knew the regular endings 'glasses' and 'melted', but not the irregular 'rang'.

THIS IS A WUG

NOW THERE IS ANOTHER ONE.
THERE ARE TWO OF THEM.
THERE ARE TWO _____

Figure 4.1

Berko's Wug test.

Source: From Berko, J. (1958). The child's learning of English morphology. *Word*, 14, 150–177. Reprinted with permission.

The results are shown in Table 4.1. The older children performed significantly better than the younger children on fewer than half of the items. Although the pattern of correct answers is not consistent across all items, it is clear that, in general, children aged 4 to 7 are able to apply the rules of grammatical inflection to novel words.

Table 4.1

Results from Berko's study.

Source: From Berko (1958), reproduced with permission.

Item	Percentage of correct answers: Preschoolers	Percentage of correct answers: First-graders
Plural		
Glasses	75	99*
Wugs	76	97*
Luns	68	92*
Tors	73	90
Heafs	79	80
Eras	58	86*
Tasses	28	39
Gutches	28	38
Kazhes	25	36
Nizzes	14	33
Progressive		
Zibbing	72	97*
Past tense		
Binged	60	85*
Glinged	63	80
Ricked	73	73
Melted	72	74
Spowed	36	59
Motted	32	33
Bodded	14	31*
Rang	0	25*
Third singular		
Oodges	57	56
Nazzes	47	49
Possessive		
Wug's	68	81
Bik's	68	95*
Niz's	58	46
Wugs'	74	97*
Biks'	74	99*
Nizzes'	53	82*

*Denotes a significant difference between the two age groups

Q. Can you explain how it is that young children know the rules of grammar? Do you think they have innate knowledge that helps them to acquire language, or do you think they are able to learn from listening to the language that is in their environment?

As we shall see later, there are two broad categories of theories concerning the acquisition of language. Some argue that the impressive ability of young children to apply the rules of grammar to novel nouns and verbs implies some innate knowledge of the structure of language. Others claim that children are exposed to a lot of speech and are able to learn how to construct appropriate inflections for novel words.

A special ability

Consider the phrases 'he hasn't got an umbrella' and 'he have to go to hospital', both spoken by 3-year-old Becky (Theakston *et al.*, 2001). Two questions immediately arise. First, how is it that such a young child is capable of producing the adult-like first sentence? Second, why is it that she uses 'have' instead of 'has' in the second sentence? Children acquire language very quickly – mere months after they first start stringing words together they appear to have a firm grasp of a very complex structure. They also, however, make errors that adults do not make. Theories of language acquisition are an attempt to explain the speed with which language is acquired, whilst taking the idiosyncrasies of children's speech into account.

There is a distinction between human language and animal communication. Whilst other species communicate with body movements and vocalizations, such as the 'waggle dance' of bees (von Frisch, 1967, 1974) or the warning calls of vervet monkeys (Demers, 1988) these messages typically have fixed meanings which relate to concrete events or needs in the present. Most other species cannot combine bits of messages with bits of other messages to create new meanings, although Ouattara, Lemasson and Zuberbuhler (2009) have found that Campbell's monkeys can combine calls into different sequences. Human language is extremely flexible, allowing for an infinite number of combinations of words carrying meaning about abstract and hypothetical events which may be in the past or in the future. Both adults and children produce utterances they have never heard before. In doing so, we adhere to the rules of grammar. We cannot just stick words together in any order; children do not produce phrases such as:

want shops I go to the to

Whilst there have been attempts to get other species (notably chimps and gorillas) to use sign language (e.g., Gardner and Gardner, 1969; Patterson, 1978) or artificial symbol systems (Premack, 1976; Rumbaugh, 1977; Savage-Rumbaugh, 1986), these animals use very few combinations of words other than those they have been taught and any they do produce tend to be limited to the concrete. In addition, language is something that arises spontaneously in all typically developing human infants; there are few cases of animals attempting to use language without human teaching. The strongest case for human-like language in an animal without formal training comes from Kanzi, a bonobo studied by Savage-Rumbaugh and colleagues (Savage-Rumbaugh and Lewin, 1994; Savage-Rumbaugh *et al.*, 1986). By the age of 4, Kanzi knew 50 symbols and had combined them in around 800 different ways.

Humans become very good at comprehending and producing language in a relatively short period of time. English-speaking adults can produce 20 000–50 000 words, and many of these are learnt in early childhood (Clark, 1995). By the age of 6, children can produce around 6000 words and comprehend 14 000 words (Dollaghan, 1994). Some argue that this rapid development means that we must have innate knowledge of linguistic structures. Others argue that we have very powerful learning mechanisms.

The components of language

Phonology

Phonology is the study of phonemes, the basic units of sound used in a language. The international phonetic alphabet contains over 100 different phonemes, but only a subset of these are used in English. Table 4.2 lists 44 common English phonemes.

In order to produce consonants, we interrupt or obstruct the flow of air. Different consonants are produced when the airflow is obstructed in different places. For example, *b* is produced by obstructing air at the lips, whereas *g* is produced towards the back of the mouth, at the soft palate. A second distinction is between different manners of articulation. Like *b*, *m* is also produced by closing the lips, but the airflow is not entirely obstructed as some escapes through the nose. So although the two sounds have the same place of articulation, they have a different manner of articulation. The third way in which consonants can vary is in voicing, which is whether the vocal cords are vibrating at the time at which the air is released. *B* and *p* are both produced at the lips (labial) and are produced in the same manner (plosive), but differ in that *b* is voiced and *p* is not. Table 4.3 shows how these three dimensions – place of articulation, manner of articulation and voicing – result in the different consonant sounds.

Vowels do not involve fully obstructing the airflow; instead the airflow is affected by the shape of the tongue. By varying the position (high, middle or low) of

Table 4.2	Consonants		Vowels	
English phonemes.	p	pit	ɪ	pit
	b	bit	e	bet
	t	tip	æ	bat
	d	dip	ɒ	pot
	k	cat	ʌ	pun
	g	got	ʊ	book
	f	fit	ə	laughter
	v	have	iː	seen
	θ	thin	ɜː	turn
	ð	that	ɑː	star
	s	sit	ɔː	torn
	z	zoo	Uː	moon
	ʃ	shop	aɪ	fight
	ʒ	treasure	eɪ	wait
	h	hot	ɔɪ	toy
	tʃ	cherry	əʊ	foe
	dʒ	badger	aʊ	house
	m	mouse	ʊə	more
	n	nut	ɪə	fear
	ŋ	sing	eə	hair
	l	lit		
	r	ripe		
	w	wine		
	j	yes		

Table 4.3 Consonants.

Manner of articulation		Stop		Fricative		Affricative		Nasal	Lateral Approximant	Approximant
Voiced (+v) or voiceless (−v)		+v	−v	+v	−v	+v	−v	+v	+v	+v
Place of articulation	Bilabial	b	p					m		w
	Labiodental			v	f					
	Dental			ð	θ					
	Alveolar	d	t	z	s			n	l	
	Postalveolar			ʒ	ʃ	dʒ	tʃ		r	
	Velar	g	k					ŋ		
	Glottal				h					

different parts of the tongue (front, central or back), different vowels are formed (see Table 4.4). A second group of vowels, called diphthongs, are produced by combining two vowels together.

Table 4.4 Vowels.

	Front	Central	Back
High	iː		u
	ɪ		uː
Middle	e	ə	o
			ɔː
Low	æ	ʌ	aː

Grammar

Grammar can be divided into syntax and morphology. Syntax is concerned with how to fit words together into sentences. Children have to learn what grammatical categories words fit into. Table 4.5 contains a list of grammatical categories with examples of words which belong in them:

Table 4.5 Grammatical categories.

Nouns	dog, cat, bird, mummy, house, thing
Pronouns	I, we, you, she, that, these
Verbs	like, love, run, jump, kiss
Adjectives	big, hot, little, red
Adverbs	quietly, loudly, fast, slow
Prepositions	on, in, under, up
Conjunctions	and, because, but
Determiners	a, this, the, some, my, your
Infinitive	to (as in to run, to jump)
Quantifiers	half, all
Wh-words	what, who, when

Children also have to learn what grammatical relations exist between these categories. Some examples of grammatical relations are *subject*, *verb* and *object*.

John   kissed   Mary
Subject   Verb   Object

These relations are important as they contribute to the way in which sentences are constructed. For example, the rule *subject–verb agreement* means that the form of the verb (i.e., whether it is singular or plural, past or present tense) *agrees* with the subject of a sentence. In the phrase 'Gemma loves cats' the verb 'loves' takes a form relative to the subject ('Gemma'). If verbs agreed with objects, we would end up with 'Gemma love cats'.

In the example 'John kissed Mary', it would seem that the grammatical relations of subject and object are the same as the grammatical category of noun. However, the categories of relations are broader than the categories of words. All the following sentences have the same subject-verb-object order:

John   kissed   Mary
The boy   kissed   the girl
The tall dark boy gently kissed   the attractive pale girl

The subject and object can be either nouns or noun phrases and the verb can be a verb or a verb phrase. A simple noun phrase can consist of an optional determiner, optional adjectives and a noun. A simple verb phrase can consist of an optional adverb and a verb.

It is these grammatical relations we manipulate, rather than words, to create different types of sentences. The passive construction, for example, has the order object-verb-participle-subject. We have to move the whole grammatical relation (subject/object) not just the words (boy/girl) to create the same sentence in the passive.

The attractive pale girl   was kissed   by   the tall dark boy
Object   Verb   Participle   Subject

Questions are another example:

Did   the tall dark boy   gently kiss   the attractive pale girl?
Auxiliary Subject   Verb   Object

In addition to learning about the relations between grammatical categories, children have to learn about morphology. Morphology refers to the inflections (or 'little bits') of words, such as the '-ed' which is added to regular verbs to create the past tense (kiss-ed) and the '-s' which is added to nouns to make plurals (cat-s). These added bits of words are called morphemes, a term which refers to the smallest meaningful units of language. Thus, 'cats' is composed of two morphemes: 'cat' and 's'. Short *function* words such as 'on', 'the' and 'are' are also morphemes, as they cannot be subdivided into smaller units. This can make things confusing but when we talk about the acquisition of morphology we're usually talking about the addition of endings to words to make plurals, past tenses, etc.

Theories of language acquisition

A theory of language acquisition must account for the rapid acquisition of language, children's correct language use, children's mistakes and the sequence of acquisition, or why some aspects of language are always acquired before others. The basic problem of grammatical acquisition is for language-learning children to be able to successfully manipulate grammatical categories. This is not a trivial problem, as more than five decades of theorizing, experimentation and no small amount of argument will attest to. Theories of grammatical acquisition fall broadly into two categories: nativist theories and constructivist theories. The basic argument of nativists is that children are born with innate knowledge of grammar, whereas constructivists argue that language is learned via a process of extracting information available in the linguistic environment. These two camps represent a highly polarized community of language researchers; this duality is possibly due to the fact that many nativist theorists are linguists, whereas a lot of constructivists approach the problem of language acquisition from a psychological perspective. Whereas some deplore the polarization (e.g. Rispoli, 1999), Maratsos (1999b) is swift to point out that many of the differences between the two groups are non-negotiable.

Behaviourism

Skinner (1957) argued that language could be and was learnt, with no need for innate knowledge. Skinner suggested that language is acquired according to the general laws of learning, including operant conditioning, and is therefore no different to any other learnt behaviour. According to the behaviourist view, language develops as a result of children's imitation of adult speech and adults' reinforcement and gradual shaping of children's babbling and speech. However, if this were the case, we would expect children to produce only those utterances they have heard and the syntactic structures they use should be the same as those found in adult speech. Evidence from children's speech data demonstrates that this is not the case:

Me maden that
Me tippen that over
Me haden strawberries at lunchtime
Me just buyen it
Something maken a funny noise
(Fletcher, 1983; cited in Aitchison, 2008, p. 135)

Although these examples do not conform to a full adult grammar, they are not random combinations of words. They have a clear grammatical structure and they are clearly novel utterances (i.e., combinations of words that the children had not heard before). Also, Brown and Hanlon (1970) noted that parents do not correct their children's grammar. Even when they do, children do not seem to pay attention to the corrections, which suggests that children do not learn via behaviourist principles. Here is an example of Braine's attempt to correct his 2-year-old daughter:

Child: Want other one spoon, Daddy.
Father: You mean, you want *the other spoon*.
Child: Yes, I want the other one spoon, please, Daddy.
Father: Can you say 'the other spoon'?
Child: Other ... one ... spoon.
Father: Say 'other'.
Child: Other.
Father: Spoon.
Child: Spoon.
Father: 'Other spoon'.
Child: Other ... spoon. Now give me other one spoon?
(Braine, 1971, p. 161)

Here is another example from McNeill (1970, pp.106–107):

> Child: Nobody don't like me.
> Mother: No, say 'nobody likes me'.
> Child: Nobody don't like me.

(Eight repetitions of this dialogue)

> Mother: No, now listen carefully; say 'nobody likes me'.
> Child: Oh! Nobody don't likes me.

Nativism

In response to Skinner's (1957) claims that language is learned by imitation, Chomsky (1957, 1959) published the original nativist account of language acquisition. Chomsky argued that children learn languages that are governed by highly subtle and abstract principles, and they do so without explicit instruction or any other environmental clues to the nature of such principles. Hence language acquisition depends on an innate, species-specific module that is distinct from general intelligence. Various modifications and updates have been made to basic nativist theory, however there are three main arguments used to justify an approach which specifies innate linguistic knowledge.

First, the poverty of the stimulus argument states that the language heard by children does not contain all the information necessary to 'decode' it or interpret it correctly. Not all language addressed to children consists of well-formed utterances. Children hear utterances that contain incomplete and ungrammatical sentences and have a limited exposure to the full range of structures present in the language. Any given word may have a number of different interpretations, depending on context. The Chomskyan argument is that this information is not present in the stimulus itself, so therefore must be present in the child. In addition children are exposed to poor, incorrect grammar; how do children, in the face of complex spoken language, decide which utterances are grammatical and which are not unless they have innate principles to guide them?

Second, children come to use sentences that never occur in their language-learning environment but they form very few ungrammatical utterances. They make errors that suggest that they're not simply imitating or mimicking the language they hear but are actually working out what the rules of language are. Children make overgeneralization errors; they create words such as 'runned' or 'goed' which follow the rules of grammar for regular verbs, but are extremely unlikely to have been heard by the child. They seem to know somehow what the rules of English are – that '-ed' is added to the end of a verb to create the past tense and that '-s' is added to a noun to make it plural. They then use these rules in situations where adults will never have used them. The implication of this is that children are being guided by rules that govern the grammaticality of their production.

The third argument is the problem of no negative evidence; children do not generally receive feedback regarding the grammaticality of their speech (Bowerman, 1988). Without this feedback (or negative evidence) children cannot learn which utterances are ungrammatical. Even in cases where children do receive feedback, they do not seem to incorporate this information into their speech. This suggests that children are not being 'taught' language by their elders. These three arguments – poverty of the stimulus, overgeneralization errors and no negative evidence – have been used to argue that language learning is an impossible task, unless one posits innate linguistic knowledge. All nativist theories attempt to discover and define

poverty of the stimulus The argument that the linguistic input children receive is impoverished in that it (i) contains mistakes, and (ii) does not contain a full range of grammatical constructions.

overgeneralization errors Errors in which regular inflections are added to irregular words.

no negative evidence The lack of feedback children receive regarding the grammaticality of their speech.

exactly what the properties of this innate knowledge are and how children are able to access this information. The Chomskyan linguistic goal, therefore, is to define a grammar which is capable of generating all legal sentences in a language, but none of the illegal ones.

Chomksy's theory. Linguistic nativism has been dominated by the work of Chomsky. Chomsky contends that the capacity to comprehend and generate language is innate, and the principles by which it develops are not the same as those underlying other human behaviours. Chomsky's (1965) response to the problems noted above was to propose a mental language organ which came to be known as the Language Acquisition Device (LAD), a device through which Universal Grammar (UG), the universal rules of all human languages, could be accessed. Nativist researchers have tended not to be interested in the mechanism by which the LAD works, concentrating instead on working out what the rules of UG are and how children come to apply them to the specific language they are learning. The LAD is an innate structure containing knowledge about the structure of language. It also includes some abilities specialized to language learning so that children can work out the rules of syntax.

Of course, not all human languages share the same grammar and it is possible for any child to be raised in any linguistic community, and therefore have the potential to learn any language. A nativist solution to the problem of acquiring language has to account for the presence of errors in children's speech and the ability to acquire any one of a set of grammars. Chomsky's Principles and Parameters Theory (PPT) (1981), which has replaced the LAD, deals with both of these problems by giving the child's linguistic input a role in the acquisition process. The notion of a set of rules governing grammar is removed in favour of the idea that UG contains some universal principles – features that are present in all languages – such as the existence of a noun category, and some features that are subject to parametric variation depending on the language, such as whether the subject is obligatory. In French and English a subject is required. We cannot say 'Am a good kid'; we need to include the subject: 'I am a good kid'. In Spanish and Italian, on the other hand, subjects are obligatory. In Italian, both 'Io sono bravo tato' (I am good kid) and 'sono bravo tato' (am good kid) are allowed (Valian, 1991). These differences are called parametric variation. Acquiring language involves identifying the correct parameter from a range of innately specified possibilities. So if we are learning English we would have to learn to set the subject parameter to the *obligatory* option. As very little learning about grammar takes place, language must necessarily contain 'trigger' information which enables parameter setting (Meisel, 1995). Errors occur when these parameters are not yet set correctly.

Chomsky's theory is thus able to explain how it is that children are able to acquire language quickly and how language is learnt despite the problems of the poverty of the stimulus and no negative evidence. However, three major problems with this theory have been noted. First, empirical studies of child language data have failed to find any evidence that children are operating with adult-like, abstract grammatical knowledge (Tomasello, 2000). For example, Bowerman (1976), Braine (1976) and MacWhinney (1978) reported that children's early utterances are much more restricted in their terms of reference than would be expected if they were working with adult-like grammatical categories. If children have such categories, they should be able to use words productively in a variety of contexts. For example, once they learn the word 'hit' and understand it belongs to the verb category, they should be able to use the word 'hit' in all the positions in an utterance that they know verbs can be used in, such as 'John hit', 'hit ball', 'Sarah hit John', 'hit with bat'. However, child speech data shows that although children do use some words productively, they use other words in only one context. Thus it may be the case that a child uses 'hit' in all the ways mentioned above, in conjunction with subjects and objects, but only produces another verb, 'break', on its own, without subjects and objects. The structure of such utterances could be captured more accurately in terms of semantic or positional formulae (e.g., agent+action, hitter+hit).

Second, children make errors which do not fit in with Chomsky's theory. For example, they omit obligatory constituents such as determiners, subjects and auxiliaries. Third, children make grammatical errors not only when very young, but for many years afterwards, having had extensive exposure to their language. For example, English children continue to omit subjects in sentences for a very long time. According to the theory, they should learn very quickly that subjects are obligatory in English. This suggests that children either do not have access to UG or that access is in some way limited.

In response to these criticisms, nativist theorists have developed ideas which try to account for the differences between adult and child speech, while remaining true to the assumptions that a complex structure such as grammar cannot be learnt without access to innate linguistic principles. In order to achieve this, theorists have begun to argue that children are somehow prevented from making use of their full knowledge, although such knowledge is available to them. What it is that prevents children using their knowledge is, however, hotly debated. Modern nativist theory can be broadly divided into two camps: Those that suggest that children have access to adult-like grammatical knowledge but are prevented from utilizing this knowledge in their production (continuity theories), and those that suggest that some aspects of linguistic knowledge only become available to the child at a later point in time (competence theories).

Continuity theories. Continuity theorists such as Valian (1991) argue that children have access to the full blueprint for language, but that this knowledge is not reflected in their speech production, which is constrained. Valian (1991) and Bloom (1990) suggest performance limitations due to processing factors which affect both adults and children, but are more discernable in children as they are not expert at manipulating language. Adults are constrained by factors including those related to planning, organizing syntactic structures and choosing appropriate lexical items. Children have these constraints and, in addition, as young children have a smaller working memory than adults (see Chapter 3), they are more likely to produce shorter utterances with shorter constituents. Other proposed performance-related limits on production include length, the content of the message the child wants to convey, syntactic and discourse requirements and pragmatic factors. Processing factors also come into play: Valian (1986) suggests that there is a high processing load at the beginning of utterances. As children get older, these constraints are either reduced or cease to have such a large impact on speech production as the child's linguistic competence increases.

Although this can be considered a parsimonious explanation, due to the fact that no discontinuity between adult and child knowledge of grammar has to be accounted for, there are two major problems with this approach. First, it has been argued by Theakston *et al.* (2001) that the theory does not make clear predictions. Logically, it is hard to see how any data could contradict such an account. This is because a combination of different performance limits could, in theory, predict any pattern of acquisition. For example, auxiliary omission could be predicted if we argue that restrictions on utterance length lead children to omit items that carry the least semantic information. Conversely, subject omission could be explained by a performance limit that acts on the beginning of the sentence. Second, Pine, Lieven and Rowland (1998) argue that this approach attributes too much knowledge to the child and cannot explain the restricted grammar found in children's speech. For example, Valian argues that children as young as two know that if you want to say that you ate a cake you say 'I ate a cake' not 'me ate a cake'. Knowledge about which pronoun to use (I, me, my) is called case-marking. Valian argues that 2-year-olds correctly use the nominative case (I) in subject position. Pine *et al.* report that although children do correctly put subjects at the start of sentences, the children's use of the accusative pronoun (me) in the correct position is not significantly different from chance. In other words, children should treat 'me' and 'I' equally but children make many more errors with 'me' than with 'I'.

Competence theories. Competence theorists such as Radford (1990) and Hyams (1986) explain the discrepancy between adult and child speech by arguing that certain aspects of innate linguistic knowledge are not accessible by the child initially, coming 'on-line' as maturation progresses. One of the main driving forces behind the development of both competence and continuity theories is the phenomenon of subject omission, in which obligatory subjects are omitted to produce phrases such as 'want milk' rather than 'I want milk'. Hyams (1986) accounts for this finding in her 'pro drop hypothesis', in which she argues that the category of subject is mandatory, but that the 'subject' parameter is initially set to a null value (correct for some languages, such as Italian); English-speaking children have to reset this parameter value before they will achieve the correct grammar. This is accomplished by paying attention to features in the linguistic input which inform the child that subjects are obligatory. Valian (1991) argues that this explanation cannot be correct as her analysis of American children (who regularly omitted subjects) and Italian children shows a different pattern of subject use between the two populations. It is not the case, therefore, that young English-speaking children are mis-identifying English as Italian. An additional problem with this sort of parameter-setting account is that one would expect an abrupt transition between the production of subjectless utterances and grammatically correct utterances once the parameter is correctly set. Bloom (1990) notes that this does not occur – the transition is a gradual one. Furthermore, Valian (1990) points out that it is hard to explain how the 'triggering' process which re-sets parameters can consistently be relied upon given that the linguistic environment contains a lot of noise and examples of incorrect grammatical rules.

A quite different example of a competence theory is Radford's (1990) 'small clause hypothesis'. For Radford, the difference between child and adult speech is that children's sentences lack functional categories. Radford argues for three stages of acquisition. First, children's speech is acategorical. Children seem to have little or no knowledge of how to access grammatical properties and rules. Second, at about 20 months, children enter the categorical stage in which grammatical knowledge starts to mature, but they only have access to some categories such as noun, verb, adjective and preposition. Finally at about 24 months, the functional categories of determiner, inflection and complementizer mature. The absence of functional categories in the child's linguistic system before age 2 means that there are a range of structures the child cannot produce. Radford uses evidence from a large number of child speech corpora that structures such as the possessive 's', case-marked pronouns, modal auxiliaries, the infinitive 'to' and nominative case-marking do not appear in children's data until at least age 2.

Unfortunately, evidence from other studies seems to suggest that the data does not fit the predictions of the theory. In fact, it is now generally agreed that, contrary to the small clause hypothesis, items associated with the functional categories (e.g., 'a doggie') are present in the earliest multi-word speech and that children continue to make grammatical errors well after the functional categories are hypothesized to come on-line (Rowland, 2000).

What are the universal rules of grammar? A final problem with nativism is the lack of an adequate description of the universal rules of grammar. Other languages are often very different to our own. For example, English and Dutch are actually very similar grammatically when compared to the differences between English and Japanese. However, even between these two languages there are some large differences. For example, in English we use the preposition 'on' to mean 'on' anything, regardless of the means of support: A cup on the table, a coat on the hook, words on the page. In Dutch there are two words for 'on' – 'op' and 'aan' – 'op' for on the table or on the chair and 'aan' for on the wall or on the hook. For languages that are even more different the situation seems even less universal. We have already looked at the 'pro drop' or 'obligatory/optional subject' parameter. Hyams first suggested that there is a universal rule that states that the subject of a sentence is either obligatory or optional, all children had to learn to do was to learn whether their language had optional or obligatory subjects and set their subject parameter accordingly. However, recent research on the Asian languages suggests that this is far too simplistic. In Japanese, children can leave the subject out, but only in certain situations. The optionality is decided by discourse factors such as whether the information carried by the subject is new or old. It is hard to see how to create a universal grammatical rule that takes these subtleties into account.

Constructivism

Constructivist theorists argue that language can be learnt, although not in the simple behaviourist way suggested by Skinner. They agree that something must be innate; there must be something in us all that allows us all to learn language. However, they differ from nativists in two important respects. First, they do not believe that there is an innate language acquisition device; rather there is a predisposition to be good at picking up the types of things that are necessary to learn language. Second, they do not believe that the innate mechanism is all that important in learning language. Most of the work is done by children learning from their experiences with the environment. There are many different types of constructivist theory, some of which are variously known as *interactionist* or *emergentist* theories, however all will here be referred to as *constructivist*.

Social interactionist theory. The fundamental argument of constructivist accounts of language acquisition is that the input received by children is not impoverished – rather, it contains all the information necessary for language learning. Snow (1977) argues that child-directed speech is different to adult-directed speech in that it is simpler and 'cleaner', therefore easier to learn language from, though it is still complex and consistent with 'full' adult speech. Child-directed speech – also referred to as *motherese, babytalk* and *infant-directed speech* – is characterized by things that make it easier for children to decode the meaning of sentences. These include slow speech rate, making it easier for the child to segment words from the speech stream; exaggerated intonation, making stress patterns more obvious to the child; a high fundamental frequency (or pitch), which children are 'tuned' to; repetition; simple syntax, making the grammatical rules of language more obvious; and simple and concrete vocabulary. Although Brown and Hanlon (1970) found that parents do not explicitly correct children's grammar (the 'no negative evidence' problem), social interactionists have found that parents do provide children with

Child	Mother
Baby highchair	Baby is in the highchair
Mommy eggnog	Mommy had her eggnog
Eve lunch	Eve is having lunch
Mommy sandwich	Mommy'll have a sandwich
Sat wall	He sat on the wall
Throw Daddy	Throw it to Daddy
Pick glove	Pick the glove up

Table 4.6

Expansions of child speech produced by mothers.

Source: Brown and Bellugi (1964).

more subtle feedback. They expand or recast children's utterances into a grammatically correct equivalent and they prompt for more details and ask follow-up questions. These responses contain an implicit correction of children's grammar. Brown and Bellugi (1964) offered a few examples of such expansions (see Table 4.6). Some of the responses from adults are confirmations and others were said with a questioning intonation.

There are, however, some problems with the idea that children learn language via listening to a special type of speech. First, child-directed speech contains a lot of questions. Interrogatives (e.g., 'what are you doing?') have a more complex linguistic structure than declaratives (e.g., 'Susie likes the horse') which may make child-directed speech harder for children to understand and learn from. Second, child-directed speech as described above is not universal. In some languages (e.g., Quiche Mayan) child-directed speech is used, but is characterized by different patterns such as a low fundamental frequency rather than a high one (Bernstein Ratner and Pye, 1984). It has also been claimed that adults in some cultures do not use a simplified mode of speech to children at all (Heath, 1989; Ochs and Schieffelin, 1995).

Semantic and cognitive accounts. Although the issue of whether child-directed speech is necessary for language learning has been debated, the claim that the speech children hear is impoverished has been undermined. In order to assess whether or not there really is a 'poverty of the stimulus', adult speech to children has to be examined more closely. Regardless, an explanation of *how* children learn language is still necessary. One explanation is that children access grammar through a more salient route. Early constructivist accounts of acquisition, therefore, argued that children could learn the grammatical categories underlying sentences by associating them with their semantic or cognitive equivalents.

Semantic accounts (e.g., Bates and MacWhinney, 1982; Schlesinger, 1982) are based on the notion that syntax is learned by associating grammatical categories with their semantic equivalents; semantic roles (agent, action, patient, etc.) are mapped onto their syntactic counterparts (subject, verb, object, etc.). In a typical semantic constructivist theory, words are classified by semantic properties and the grammatical properties of these words are gradually analyzed. Words that cannot be classified in this straightforward manner are compared in terms of their grammatical properties as well as their semantic properties. The key idea is that words are analyzed both in form and function and narrow categories are formed on this basis. These eventually become adult-like syntactic categories. In Schlesinger's (1982, 1988) semantic assimilation theory, children initially construct narrow relational categories which are generalized by a process of semantic assimilation, which is a generalization on the basis of form and function across instances. These eventually become adult-like syntactic categories (Tomasello and Brooks, 1999). Bates and MacWhinney's (1982, 1987) 'competition model' likewise posits a direct mapping between form and function. Maratsos (1979, 1999a) proposes two arguments against semantic theories. First, he notes that it is not clear that children construct initial semantic categories. Second, he argues that grammar cannot be acquired in this way as not all languages have reliable semantic-syntactic correspondences. Ninio (2005), for example, provides evidence that there is little semantic similarity between a group of early-acquired verbs in Hebrew.

Another proposal (e.g., Bates *et al.*, 1979) is that language development follows on from the child's mastery of the relevant cognitive achievements. According to Piaget (1926), conceptual development provides the basis for linguistic development. Piaget thus accounted for the fact that language does not develop until the second year of life by arguing that children spent the first 18 months exploring the world, discovering the natures of things in the world and constructing the ability to use symbols to represent objects. It is not until 18 months that we have the conceptual structures necessary for language. We have seen (e.g., Chapters 2 and 6) that children's knowledge and abilities develop at a much younger age than Piaget thought. However, other theorists have used Piaget's ideas to develop theories of language development which predicate linguistic achievements on cognitive achievements. For example, according to Gopnik and Meltzoff (1986), disappearance words (e.g., 'gone') appear when children have mastered object permanence, and words denoting success or failure (e.g., 'did it') are acquired once they have solved problems such as using a stick to get an object. However, correlation does not equal cause – just because two things occur together doesn't mean that one causes the other. Without evidence of a causal relationship, the theory is not really supported.

Distributional accounts. A third type of constructivist theory is based on the idea that children use the statistical and distributional information about language, that is present in language, to learn from the input they receive (e.g., Lieven, Pine and Baldwin, 1997; Maratsos, 1988; Maratsos and Chalkley, 1980; Pine, Lieven and Rowland, 1998; Tomasello, 1992). The distributional approach includes a number of different accounts with one aspect in common. They are based on the idea that distributional or positional commonalties in the language guide children's learning of grammatical categories and rules. Theorists such as Braine (1987) argue that nativist and traditional semantic accounts attribute to children categories and rules that are more abstract than the data would indicate they possess. They suggest instead that children learn language by picking up distributional patterns (as well as the semantic regularities and similarities common to certain word classes) and use these to form syntactic categories. For example, the phrases 'a dog', 'a cat', 'a bird' and 'a car' all follow the pattern 'a + noun'. Grammatical rules and categories are implicit in the distributional characteristics of language. Children attend to the patterns present in language and are able to form syntactic categories on the basis of these patterns, using general cognitive tools. Other examples of such patterns are 'noun + s' for plurals and 'verb + ed' for the past tense. Braine (1987) suggests that we first learn individual words, then we build up connections between related words (e.g., grow, show, mow; growed, showed, mowed). In this way, we learn the grammatical patterning of our language. Distributional theories are often implemented as computer programs – cognitive (or computational) models, which will be discussed in Chapter 11.

Braine's model has been criticized as being too simplistic by the nativists, such as Pinker (1984), who argues that there are simply too many possible interconnections for the child to keep track of. Also, Sabbagh and Gelman (2000) note that although domain-general learning mechanisms are undoubtedly powerful (and necessary), they query whether these are sufficient. They ask how we are able to classify words in terms of abstract categories, unless we already have knowledge of these categories. Similarly, Pinker (1987) notes that distributional learning can explain the identification of items with respect to their syntactic categories on the basis of context, but identifies this as problematic as these contexts have to already exist. MacWhinney (1999) argues that this is something of a red herring – there is no need for abstract categories to exist prior to language learning. These can emerge from the information present in the linguistic environment, when coupled with powerful, yet constrained, learning mechanisms.

Constructivist models have also been criticized on logical grounds. Certain formal properties of human languages, such as the presence of long-distance dependencies, have been seen as ruling out such accounts. Consider the following sentences:

The cats chase mice
The girl who likes cats chases mice

It the first sentence, the verb 'chase' agrees with 'cats' (this is an example of 'subject-verb' agreement). In the second sentence, the subject is 'the girl who likes cats' and the verb 'chases' agrees with 'the girl'. This is an example of a long-distance dependency. There is some 'distance' between 'girl' and 'chases' whereas, in the first sentence, 'cats' directly precedes 'chase'. The argument against distributional accounts is that it would be impossible for either children or computer programs to use the long-distance information in the second sentence. However, Elman (1993) demonstrated that it is possible for a relatively simple distributional learning mechanism to learn such dependencies. This suggests that *a priori* arguments should be treated with a certain amount of scepticism since they are based on a particular way of conceptualizing language acquisition. In this case it is viewing language as a single logical problem to be solved, rather than as a complex developmental process.

Learning and innateness

We know that almost all humans possess language (either spoken or signed, with the exception of some individuals with severe mental handicaps), but animals have relatively limited language skills, so the capacity for language must involve heredity. However, a child growing up in Tokyo speaks Japanese whereas the same child brought up in Derby would speak English, so the environment must also be involved. Any theory of language acquisition has to take both factors into account. It can be argued that a theory which does not consider innate structure will result in a hypothetical child who does not have a complex, true language, and that a theory which does not consider the environment will result in a child capable of acquiring one specific language but not another. If we knew the degree to which language can be learned, it would give us some idea of how much innate structure or knowledge is necessary. One way of answering this question is to use a branch of computer science called learnability theory.

Gold (1967) used a formal theoretical proof to assert that no natural human languages are learnable as they contain a massive number of positive examples but no negative examples. This means that children hear only examples of sentences that are grammatical; they are not given examples of syntactic structure that are not permissible within a language. According to learnability theory, the task of language learning involves (i) a class of languages – all the possible human languages – of which one is the 'target' language; (ii) a linguistic environment; (iii) a strategy for creating and testing hypotheses about the target language; and (iv) some way of judging whether a hypothesis is correct. The basis of Gold's argument is that if a language-learning child has a set of possible solutions to the problem of identifying the grammar of the target language which includes at least one incorrect grammar, then the child will not be able to learn the target grammar, as an incorrect grammar can be used to generate incorrect utterances. Gold's work has satisfied many nativist theorists that language is not learnable, that learning language is not a problem that can be solved by attending to the language available in the environment alone. However, MacWhinney (2004) lays out a number of solutions to this problem, including evidence that complex languages *can* be learned from positive examples alone (e.g. Kanazawa, 1998; Shinohara, 1994; Jain et. al., 1999). He also notes that although children do produce errors, there are ways in which these can be recovered from without negative evidence. One explanation is that there is competition between incorrect forms (e.g., 'goed') and correct forms (e.g., 'went'). As the correct form will be of higher frequency than the incorrect form, its representation will grow in strength and it will override and eventually displace the competing incorrect form. Also, research using computational models has shown that it may indeed be possible to learn language on the basis of information contained in that language. We will look at such models in detail in Chapter 11.

The sequence of acquisition

Children vary in terms of the age at which particular milestones are reached. One child may start stringing words together before she is 18 months old, whereas another may not do so until a year later. However, the sequence of development – the order in which children use aspects of language – remains the same across children.

Phonology

Infants can discriminate speech sounds soon after birth and can even discriminate between different languages. Mehler *et al.* (1988) tested forty 4-day-old French infants on their ability to distinguish between two short (13 to 22 second) language samples. In one condition infants heard two French samples, in another they heard two Russian samples, in the third they heard a French sample followed by a Russian sample, and in the fourth condition they heard Russian followed by French. Mehler *et al.* used a variation of the high amplitude sucking technique to see if the infants could discriminate between the speech samples. The difference between the technique as it was used in this study and the technique as it was explained in Chapter 2 is that the speech samples were not played in response to the rate of sucking in Mehler *et al.*'s study. Instead, the researchers just measured the sucking rate for each speech sample. They found the infants could discriminate between the two languages and that they preferred French, as evidenced by a higher sucking rate.

By 9 months of age, they seem to know which sounds can appear next to one another in their native language. Jusczyk, Luce and Charles-Luce (1994) presented 6- and 9-month-old American infants with two lists of syllables. One list was composed of phonetic patterns that do not often appear in English words, such as 'youdge', 'shawch' and 'gushe'. The second list contained frequently occurring patterns such as 'riss', 'gen' and 'kazz'. Jusczyk *et al.* used the conditioned head rotation procedure to see whether the infants listened to one set of items more than the other, and found that the 6-month-olds showed no preferences whereas the 9-month-olds listened longer to the list containing frequent English phoneme patterns.

In addition to developing the ability to listen to language, young infants also start to produce sounds. In the first two months of life they make reflexive vocalizations, such as crying, which are basic reactions to physiological stimuli such as hunger. Over the following two months they start to make laughing and cooing sounds. Around 6 months of age, infants start to babble. This consists of sequences of consonant-vowel syllables, such as 'babada'.

First words

At around 12 months children produce their first adult-like words. Infants' first words tend to consist of syllables in which consonants are followed by vowels (e.g., 'dada'), rather than words ending in consonants. First words usually refer to objects that infants interact with (Nelson, 1973) rather than function words or abstract words. As well as referring to objects, children use single words to communicate their desires, such as recurrence ('more'), non-existence ('gone') or negation ('no'). Many early words are initially used in highly specific ways. Barrett (1986) described how a 12-month-old used the word 'dut' ('duck') when he knocked his duck off the edge of the bath, but did not use the word when the duck was not being knocked over. Similarly, infants have been observed to use the word 'bye' only in the context of playing with a toy telephone (Bates *et al.*, 1979).

In contrast to this highly specific use of words, children's early speech includes many examples of over-extension, whereby children use a word for a wider variety of referents than is appropriate. For example, the word 'moon' may be used to refer to a grapefruit half, a lemon slice or a hangnail (Bowerman, 1976), or 'clock' may be used to refer to a clock, a dial, a timer, a radio, a telephone or a medallion (Rescorla, 1980). These over-extensions are probably due to children's efforts to communicate beyond their vocabulary. For example, if a child over-extends the word 'dog' to another four-legged animal such as a horse, this does not mean the child thinks the word for horse is 'dog', but rather that they do not yet know the word 'horse' and use 'dog' as it is the closest word they do know, based on the similarities between the two animals.

By 18 months, infants can produce about 60 words (Fenson *et al.*, 1994). Over the following 6 months there is a 'vocabulary spurt' in which another 150–250 words are learnt (Barrett, 1995). By 30 months, children can produce 600 words and by 6 years they can produce 6000 words (Dollaghan, 1994).

Grammar

Towards the end of their second year, children start to put words together into two-word utterances. These are very simple utterances but they are constructed, not rote-learned. This is often referred to as the telegraphic speech stage. This is a reference to the pre-internet equivalent of emails. When sending telegrams people paid by the word, so they kept their messages as brief as possible (e.g., 'horse dead send money'). Children's speech is like a telegram in that the more subtle aspects are omitted. Children in the two-word stage leave out the grammatical morphemes. For example, they may say 'mummy shoe' rather than 'mummy's shoe' or 'two cat' instead of 'two cats'. This, however, is a generalization and there are individual variations. Some children are 'analytic' and stick to the telegraphic style, whereas others are 'gestalt' and seem to be trying to put the morphemes in even when they don't know what they are. Also there are languages in which it is impossible to speak without the grammatical inflection. In English we can use the bare stem of a verb such as 'talk' (e.g., 'I talk', 'you talk'). In Spanish there always has to be an inflection. The

telegraphic speech An early type of speech in which function words are omitted.

bare stem of 'talk' in Spanish is 'habl-', which cannot be used without an inflectional morpheme. We can say 'hablo', 'hablas', 'hablamos' and 'habla', but not just 'habl-'.

Some of the first two-word utterances tend to have very simple meanings, such as recurrence, non-existence and negation, similar to the meanings present in the single word stage. Other early two-word utterances express semantic relations between the two words (Brown, 1973). A list of these early two-word utterance types is listed in Table 4.7. Slobin (1970) noted that these initial meanings are largely the same across languages.

Over the next two years, children start to add function words, verb endings and plurals. Within any language, most children acquire these morphemes in about the same order (Brown, 1973; see Table 4.8). As children acquire these morphemes, they use this new knowledge of verb morphology to create new verbs from nouns. Some examples of these, collected by Clark (1995) are listed in Table 4.9. The sequence of producing single words, then combining them, may be similar for all children learning a language through immersion (rather than in language classes), regardless of age. Snedeker, Geren and Shafto (in press) found that international preschool-age adoptees being raised in the USA went through a one-word stage before combining words together in much the same way as infant adoptees. This suggests that the aspect of the sequence of language acquisition is not a result of maturation or cognitive development.

By the time they are 24 months old, children can produce sentences of up to four or five words; by 30 months they can produce sentences of up to eight words (Fenson *et al.*, 1994). Later developments include the production of complex sentence types such as questions, negatives, passives and compound sentences (sentences consisting of two simple sentences linked by 'and', 'but' or 'or'). As children get older their sentences increase in terms of number of words, but the words in their utterances also get more complex and carry more information as they use longer words and add grammatical morphemes to words. As a result, just counting how many words they use is not a good measure of language development. For instance 'I play drum' contains three morphemes and is, therefore a less grammatically sophisticated utterance than 'They're playing drums', which contains six morphemes (they+re play+ing drum+s). As a result, language researchers use Mean Length of Utterance (MLU) as an index of development. A child's MLU is derived by taking a sample of utterances, counting the morphemes present, and calculating the average number of morphemes. Brown (1973) used this technique to chart an increase in utterance length for three children, Eve, Adam and Sarah. Brown noted two interesting

Table 4.7			
Early two-word utterances.	Operations of reference	recurrence	more milk
		non-existence	allgone egg
		nomination	this truck
	Semantic relations	agent-action	mummy push
		action-object	eat dinner
		agent-object	mummy pigtail
		action-location	play garden
		entity-location	cookie plate
		possessor-possession	mummy scarf
		attribute-entity	green car
		demonstrative-entity	that butterfly

Morpheme	Example
present progresssive '-ing'	walking
prepositions	on, in
plural '-s'	cats
irregular past tense	broke
possessive	Mummy's
uncontractible copula (full form of 'to be' when it is the main verb)	he **is** hot, they **are** ready
articles	a, the
regular past tense	kissed
third person singular –s	wants
irregular third person singular	has, does
uncontractible auxiliary (full form of 'to be' when it is the auxiliary verb)	she **is** swimming, they **are** coming
contractible copula (shortened form of 'to be' when it is the main verb)	he**'s** hot, they**'re** ready
contractible auxiliary (shortened form of 'to be' when it is an auxiliary verb)	she**'s** swimming, they**'re** coming

Table 4.8

The order of morpheme acquisition.

findings. First, individual children's MLU growth is rapid, and second, there are large variations between individual children. Eve's MLU progressed from two items at around 20 months of age to four items at 28 months. Adam's and Sarah's MLU growth was later and slower. Adam and Sarah did not achieve MLUs of two items until around 27 months and 29 months, respectively, and were around 3½ years old before they had MLUs of four items.

Age	Context	Utterance
2;7	Hitting baby sister with toy broom	I broomed her
2;9	Playing with a toy lawnmower	I'm lawning
3;0	Pretending to be superman	I'm supermanning
3;1	Watching a cement truck revolving, not pouring	That truck is cementing
3;2	Realizing his father was teasing	Daddy, you joked me
3;3	Of a doll that disappeared	I guess she magicked
4;0		Maybe it rained or it fogged yesterday
4;11		We already decorationed our tree

Table 4.9

Novel verbs coined by 2- to 5-year-olds (Clark, 1995).

Is there a critical period?

The speed with which young children acquire a language seems particularly impressive when you compare it to your experience of trying to learn a second language as a teenager or as an adult. Johnson and Newport (1989) tested 46 native Korean or Chinese speakers on their English proficiency. The participants had moved to the USA between the ages of 3 and 39 and had lived there between 3 and 26 years by the

Figure 4.2

The relationship between age of arrival in the United States and total score correct on a test of English grammar.

Source: Reprinted from Cognitive Psychology, 21, Johnson, J. S., & Newport, E. L., Critical period effects in second language learning: The influence of maturational state on the acquisition of English as a second language, 60–99, Copyright (1989), with permission from Elsevier.

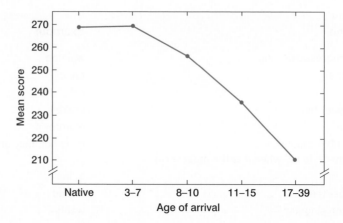

critical period hypothesis The idea that there is a window of time in the first few years of life in which exposure to language is necessary for normal linguistic development to occur.

time of testing. They were tested on a wide variety of structures of English grammar. Figure 4.2 shows scores on the grammar test plotted against age. There is a clear and strong advantage for participants who started learning English earlier in life.

For many other skills and knowledge domains, adults are much faster at learning than young children, but language, it seems, is easier to learn the younger one is. So is there something special about language?

Lenneberg (1967) claimed that there is a 'critical period' for language learning, a window of time during which two key things happen. First, the brain develops. At birth, the brain is not yet lateralized, it has a higher degree of plasticity, and can adapt to changes and recover from damage. Lenneberg argued that hemispheric specialization takes place between 2 and 5 years of age and (usually) the left hemisphere becomes specialized for language. The second factor is exposure to language. According to the critical period hypothesis, children have to be exposed to a rich source of language during this period of flexibility, before the brain has matured. This idea has been used to explain why second language acquisition is harder for older children and adults, and it has also been used to explain why there are a number of cases of children deprived of linguistic input early in life who were unable to acquire full linguistic competence later in life. The most famous of these is Victor, the 'wild boy of Aveyron'. Victor was a small child discovered in the woods in France in the year 1800. He was given language instruction, but never learned to speak more than two words.

The evidence for a critical period is not clear cut. With respect to brain maturation, we now know that some lateralization is present very soon after birth (Entus, 1977; Molfese, 1977), but research on older infants' event-related potentials shows that further lateralization occurs between 13 and 20 months (Mills, Coffrey-Corina and Neville, 1997). With respect to children who are not exposed to language early in life, this is usually accompanied by other forms of deprivation, such as social, physical and nutritional deprivation (Curtiss, 1977). As a result, it is hard to tell whether underdeveloped language skills are a consequence of lack of linguistic input or a combination of factors.

Statistical learning

As we have already seen, some theorists claim that the sequence of development described above is based on innate knowledge, whereas others argue that children learn how to put the elements of language together in a meaningful way. The most recent constructivist approach is to explain that language learning occurs as a result of analysing the statistical properties of the language. Initially, this argument was made on the basis of the observation that a lot of information about language is present in the way that language is organized. For example, Redington, Chater and Finch (1993) used cluster analysis techniques to examine a large corpus of adult speech data, and demonstrated that grammatical categories are implicit in the linguistic input children receive. The results of this cluster analysis, based on the distributional statistics of language, provide evidence that syntactic categories are clearly differentiated in adult speech. The argument for statistical learning was further supported by computational simulations of how such an analysis might take place (Cartwright and Brent, 1997; Rohde and Plaut, 1999), without the need for innate knowledge. This does, however, leave the problem of explaining whether or not children do use statistical information, and how they use it to learn language. Recently, a body of work has emerged in which psychologists have examined infants' and children's use of statistical information which has, in turn, provided some insight into the nature of language (Saffran, 2003).

Phonology

In order to understand speech we have to be able to perceive the different sounds that make up words. As we saw in Chapter 2, young infants can perceive different phonemes, and they become tuned to the sounds present in their native language by 12 months of age, losing the ability to distinguish between sounds that occur only in foreign languages. For example, Japanese-speaking people find it hard to discriminate between the English *r* and *l* phonemes (Miyawaki *et al.*, 1975). In Japanese, the sounds that English speakers hear as two distinct phonemes belong to just one category: *r* and *l* are, in Japanese, the *same* phoneme. Phonemes differ with respect to place of articulation, manner of articulation and voicing. The difference between *r* and *l* is the place of articulation; make both sounds and notice where your tongue is. In English, there is a bimodal distribution for *r* and *l*. We perceive sounds as belonging to either the *r* category or the *l* category depending on how the speaker makes the sound. In Japanese, there is a unimodal distribution: all *r* and *l* sounds are perceived as belonging to just one category. Other sounds differ in their voicing, or voice onset time – the period during which the vocal cords begin to vibrate relative to the release of air by the vocal apparatus. *D* and *t* differ in that the period between vibration of vocal chords and release of air is different. *D* has zero or negative voice onset time; the vocal cords vibrate either before or at the same time as the air is released (this is also true of *b* and *g*). *T* has positive voice onset time; the vocal cords vibrate after the air is released (it is the same for *p* and *k*).

Maye, Werker and Gerken (2002) proposed that the developmental pattern of phoneme perception occurs as a result of the statistical distribution of sounds in an infant's native language. In order to test this, they created two sets of stimuli to present to 6- and 8-month-old infants. One stimulus set had a bimodal distribution, and consisted mostly of sounds that fall at the two ends of the voiced/voiceless continuum; sounds that were clearly voiced *d* sounds or voiceless *t* sounds. The second stimulus set contained a unimodal distribution of sounds that occurred in the middle of this continuum. After the participants were familiarized with one of the stimulus sets, Maye *et al.* measured their ability to discriminate between *d* and *t* sounds using the preferential looking technique. They found that the participants in the bimodal group, but not the unimodal group, could discriminate the test stimuli. This finding could certainly explain why infants lose the ability to discriminate sounds not heard in their native language. However, not all the contrasts that are present in a

Figure 4.3

The two distributions of stimuli used by Maye, Weiss and Aslin (2008). The bimodal distribution is shown by the dashed line and the unimodal distribution is shown by the solid line. In the test phase of the experiment, the sounds with voice onset times of −50 ms and +7 ms were used.

Source: From Maye, J., & Weiss, D. (2003). Statistical cues facilitate infants' discrimination of difficult phonetic contrasts. Proceedings of the 27th Annual Boston University Conference on Language Development. Reprinted with permission from the authors.

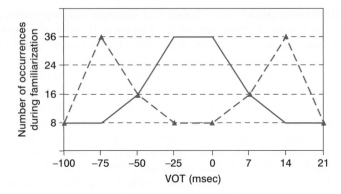

language are as easy to discriminate as the bimodal stimuli presented by Maye *et al.* For example, infants find it harder to discriminate *d* and a hard *th* sound (as in 'the', rather than as in 'thin') (Polka, Colantonio and Sundara, 2001).

Maye, Weiss and Aslin (2008) conducted a study that aimed to address these more difficult contrasts. They wanted to see whether a bimodal distribution would enhance infants' ability to discriminate between such pairs of phonemes. The researchers constructed a set of stimuli of a Hindi speaker saying *da* and *ga*, which are voiced, and *ta* and *ka*, which are voiceless. Each of the one hundred and fifty-three 8-month-old participants was placed in one of three conditions. In one condition, the infants were presented with a bimodal distribution of the sounds, and in the second condition, infants were given a unimodal distribution to listen to (see Figure 4.3). A third group of infants were given a sequence of tones that were irrelevant to the task at hand, in order to be able to determine baseline performance on the test items. In the test phase, participants in all three conditions were habituated to the sound with a voice onset time +7 ms. They were then played the −50 ms sound and the length of time they took to dishabituate was measured. The infants in the bimodal condition dishabituated whereas infants in the other conditions didn't, suggesting that the exposure to the bimodal distribution enhanced their infant's ability to discriminate the phonemes.

Words

With regard to lexical learning, Huttenlocher *et al.* (1991) demonstrate that there is a relationship between individual differences in vocabulary growth and the amount of parental speech input children receive. Aslin, Saffran and Newport (1999) argue that the transitional probabilities between sounds heard by children are logically sufficient for some aspects of word segmentation. But is it possible to demonstrate that the meanings of words can be learnt via analysis of the statistical properties of language? One of the potential problems with this idea is that parents say 300 to 400 words per hour to their children (Hart and Risley, 1995). If parents only directed a few words to children, and made it clear what the referent of the word was, then it would seem like an easy task for children to learn words. But with the quantity of words they do hear, the referents of the words are much more ambiguous. Yu and Smith (2007) argue that this huge amount of information may, in fact, lead to word learning. In a study on university students, Yu and Smith demonstrated that young adults can learn word-meaning mappings from an ambiguous context in which multiple words and pictures were presented.

Lany and Saffran (2010) showed that infants can learn word categories on the basis of statistical information. They familiarized 22-month-olds with words from an artificial language, then paired the words with pictures of animals and vehicles. In the test phase, the infants heard the words again and were presented with two pictures, one of which had previously been paired with the words The experimenters measured looking times, and found that the participants showed greater increases in looking at the target picture than a control group who had been trained on another artificial language that did not possess the same statistical cues. Thus, the participants were able to combine their phonological and distributional cues of the artificial language with their semantic knowledge to learn the meanings of novel words.

Syntax

Infants can use transitional probabilities between sounds to segment the speech stream into words, but can this be scaled up to the next level? Can language learners use the transitional probabilities between words to segment speech into phrases, the units of grammar? Thompson and Newport (2007) demonstrated that adults can achieve this by using the probability that two words will occur together to learn the syntax of an artificial language. Some aspects of syntax, however, depend on relations between words that are not adjacent to each other. One example of this is where the morpheme added to the end of a verb depends on the auxiliary before the verb (e.g., '**is** eat**ing**' as opposed to '**has** eat**en**'). Another example that we saw earlier is number agreement (e.g., 'the **girl** who **likes** cats **chases** mice' or 'the **girls** who **like** cats **chase** mice').

Gómez (2002) tested whether adults could learn this type of information by training 48 undergraduate students on three-item sentences from one of two artificial languages. The two languages were made up of the same nonsense words (e.g., 'pel wadim rud', 'pel wadim jic') but differed in the dependencies between the first and third elements. For example, in language one, 'pel' and 'rud' co-occurred in positions one and three, as did 'vot' and 'jic', whereas in language two, 'pel' and 'jic' co-occurred in positions one and three, as did 'vot' and 'tood'. If the participants had been able to learn these dependencies as a result of training on one of the languages, they should be able to discriminate between sentences from the two different languages. Gómez also wanted to know whether the amount of variety in the language would have an effect. The participants were split into four groups who were exposed to different numbers of items (2, 6, 12 or 24) in position two. The group with the smallest variety only heard phrases consisting of 'x wadim y' and 'x kicey y'. There were three x-y pairs (e.g., 'pel – rud', 'vot – jic', and 'dak – tood') so there were only six different phrases in total. For those in the group with the largest variety, there were 24 different nonsense words that occurred in position two, so the total number of phrases was 72. Each participant heard a total of 432 three-word sentences in the training set. This means that, depending on which group they were in, they heard each three-item phrase either 6, 12, 24 or 72 times.

In the test phase, participants were presented with six strings from each of the two languages and asked to indicate which were consistent with the training set they had been exposed to. Gómez found that the participants were able to discriminate the two languages, even though they contained the same 'words' and the 'words' appeared in the same positions in both languages (e.g., 'pel' was always in position one). There was also an interaction with variety of the training set, such that the participants who had been trained on a wider variety of items in position two made more accurate judgements on whether the test items were consistent with the language they had heard.

Having demonstrated that adults could succeed on this task, Gómez moved on to 18-month-old infants. The task she gave them was almost exactly the same task as the one given to adults. The main difference was that there were two, rather than three, $x - y$ pairs in each of the languages. In the test phase, the phrases were played from speakers to the left or right of the participants, and a head rotation procedure was used to measure how long they looked towards the sound source. Infants who were exposed to a training set with a wide variety of items in position two listened longer to test phrases from the language they had not been trained on than to phrases from the language they had been trained on. Infants who had been trained on samples with less variety did not seem to discriminate between the two languages. This finding not only demonstrates that infants can learn non-adjacent dependencies from the input they hear, but also that a richer language environment with lower transitional probabilities between adjacent items helps with this process.

Theakston (2004) examined the evidence for learning from the distributional properties of linguistic input in explaining the development of overgeneralization errors in verb argument structure. From around the age of 3, children produce utterances such as 'don't giggle me', in which an intransitive verb (a verb that doesn't have an object) has been used as a transitive verb (one in which an object is necessary). We have already seen that children do not learn from negative evidence, either because they are not corrected when they make mistakes, or because they ignore corrections, yet they manage to decrease the number of such errors they make over the coming years. Theakston presented 5- and 8-year-olds with four types of sentence. Some were fully grammatical (e.g., 'The cat drank the milk'), some were fully ungrammatical (e.g., 'Jump the cat the mouse'), some contained argument structure errors with high frequency verbs, and some contained argument structure errors with low frequency verbs. The latter two groups of sentences are shown in Table 4.10. The sentences were presented in a random order and, for each sentence, participants were asked to decide whether the sentence was grammatical or not. The children in both age groups judged the sentences with argument structure errors containing low frequency verbs to be significantly more grammatical than those containing high frequency verbs. The 5-year-olds were also more likely than the 8-year-olds to accept both types as correct. This finding suggests that the frequency with which particular verbs are found in the input children receive, plays an important part in determining their understanding of grammar. With greater exposure to verbs, children develop a greater understanding of the contexts in which they are acceptable.

Table 4.10	High frequency verbs	Low frequency verbs
Ungrammatical sentences with high and low frequency verbs used in Theakston's (2004) study.	She came me to school	She arrived her to the park
	I'm gonna disappear it	I'm gonna vanish it
	Somebody fell it off	Somebody tumbled it off
	Don't laugh me	Don't giggle me
	I poured you with water	I dribbled teddy with water
	Shall I shout you something?	Shall I whisper you something?

Box 4.1 The biological basis of language

Humans are the only species in full possession of language. An obvious explanation for this is that language evolved in humans and has not done so in other species (the alternative would be that other species have also evolved this ability but do not use it). What, then, has led to the evolution of language? Is there a survival benefit to having language that was selected for? Or did language evolve as a by-product of something else? Hauser, Chomsky and Fitch (2002) argued for the latter. They claim that the only species-specific aspect of language is syntactic recursion, and that this developed for reasons other than language. Humans developed the computational mechanisms needed for recursion in the service of number, navigation and social relations. Although other species use recursion in these non-communicative domains, only humans went on to apply this ability to language. Alternatively, language may have evolved because it is adaptive. It provides us with advantages over non-linguistic species such as the ability to communicate our knowledge and intentions to others (Jackendoff and Pinker, 2005; Pinker and Jackendoff, 1995).

Exactly when we evolved the ability to use language is another difficult question to answer. Fossil evidence suggests that Broca's area (see below) was present two million years ago, and the physical apparatus we use to speak has been in its present form for about 60 000 years. This suggests that the development of the physical structures necessary for language took a long time. With respect to genetics, there is a single gene that is associated with grammar called FOXP2. Damage to this gene leads to difficulties in acquiring language. It has been suggested that the modern structure of the FOXP2 gene came about some time in the last 100 000 years, so it is likely that we did not use language before this (Corballis, 2004; Enard *et al.*, 2002).

Language functions are predominantly located in the left hemisphere (this is the case for 96 per cent of right-handers and 70 per cent of left-handers) (Rasmussen and Milner, 1977). We know which areas of the brain are important for language as a result of studies of people with brain damage. Brain damage can lead to **aphasia**, which is impaired language production or comprehension skills. In the 1860s, Broca found that damage to the left frontal lobe led to an impairment in speech production, but that patients with this damage could still understand language. Wernicke, in 1874, found that damage to the temporal gyrus results in impaired language comprehension and the production of fluent but nonsensical speech. Figure 4.4 illustrates the locations of the areas discovered by Broca and Wernicke.

More recent evidence for the left-hemisphere specialization for language comes from work in

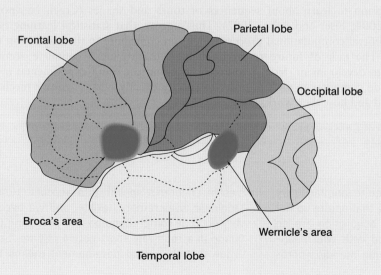

Frontal lobe

Parietal lobe

Occipital lobe

Broca's area

Wernicle's area

Temporal lobe

aphasia A disorder in which language comprehension and/or production are affected as a result of brain damage.

Figure 4.4

The locations of Broca's and Wernicke's areas.

cognitive neuroscience. EEG studies show that adults, children and even young infants show greater activity in the left hemisphere when listening to speech sounds as opposed to non-speech auditory stimuli (Molfese and Betz, 1988). Peña *et al.* (2003) used near infra-red spectroscopy to measure activation in response to infant-directed speech, reversed speech and silence. They found that 2- to 5-day old infants showed greater activation in the left temporal areas when listening to speech sounds than when listening to non-speech sounds.

Concluding comments

The last 15 years have seen a move away from accounts of the cognitive structures necessary for language and towards explanations of how language learning actually takes place. Cognitive models of language acquisition (e.g., Croker, 2007; Elman *et al.*, 1996) have demonstrated that language can theoretically be acquired without innate knowledge by proving that the language present in a child's environment contains enough information for simple mechanisms to learn language. Following on from these demonstrations of statistical learning by computer programs, psychologists have conducted studies examining the extent to which children and adults can use the statistical properties of language to learn the regularities, categories and structures of language (Gómez 2002; Lany and Saffran, 2010; Maye *et al.*, 2002, 2008; Theakston, 2004). This shift was largely due to a landmark paper by Saffran, Aslin and Newport (1996), in which they demonstrated that 8-month-old infants could use the statistical relationships between speech sounds to segment words from a speech stream. What was particularly exciting about this study was that the infants were only familiarized to two minutes of an artificial language, hearing just 180 three-syllable words in a continuous stream with no cues as to where the word boundaries were (e.g., 'bidakupadotigolabubidaku …').

However, just because we can use statistical learning to learn different aspects of language, it doesn't mean that is necessarily how we do it, particularly given the sheer amount of knowledge we learn (McMurray and Hollich, 2009). Our ability to learn from statistical information is not restricted to language; we can also use this information to learn about sequences of tones and shapes (Creel, Newport and Aslin, 2004; Fiser and Aslin, 2002). This suggests that statistical learning is a domain-general computational process which can contribute to the acquisition of language. The task of future research, then, is to provide a complete account of language development, from phonology to grammar, using experimental methods alongside computer models in order to specify exactly what cognitive mechanisms are used and how they work.

Summary

A special ability. Children acquire language very quickly, but they make errors that adults do not make. Theories of language acquisition are an attempt to explain the speed with which language is acquired, whilst taking the idiosyncrasies of children's speech into account. Human language is extremely flexible, and we become very good at comprehending and producing language in a relatively short period of time. Some argue that this rapid development means that we must have innate knowledge of linguistic structures. Others argue that we have very powerful learning mechanisms.

The components of language. Phonology is the study of phonemes, the basic units of sound used in a language. The international phonetic alphabet contains over 100 different phonemes, but only a subset of these are used in English. Grammar can be divided into syntax and morphology. Syntax is concerned with how to fit words together into sentences. Children have to learn what grammatical categories words fit into and what grammatical relations, such as *subject*, *verb* and *object* exist between these categories. Different types of sentences are created by manipulating these grammatical relations. Morphology refers to the inflections of words, such as the past tense '-ed' and the plural '-s'.

Theories of language acquisition. Skinner argued that language is acquired according to the general laws of learning, and develops as a result of children's imitation of adult speech and adults' reinforcement and gradual shaping of children's babbling and speech. However, children produce words and structures that are not found in adult speech, and do not change their verbal behaviour as a result of parental feedback. Chomsky argued against the behaviourist approach on the basis of the poverty of the stimulus argument, the presence of overgeneralization errors in child speech and the observation that children are not provided with negative evidence. He proposed a mental language organ, the Language Acquisition Device (LAD), through which Universal Grammar (UG) could be accessed. Modern variants of nativism include continuity theories and competence theories. An alternative to the nativist approach is constructivism (or interactionism). Constructivist theorists argue that language can be learnt. Some constructivist theories focus on social interaction and the nature of child-directed speech. Others are based on the idea that children access grammar through their knowledge of semantics, or that language is predicated on cognitive equivalents. A third type of constructivist theory is that children use the statistical and distributional information about language that is present

in language to learn from the input they receive. Children learn language by picking up distributional patterns and use these to form syntactic categories.

The sequence of acquisition. Infants can discriminate speech sounds soon after birth and can even discriminate between different languages. By 9 months of age, they seem to know which sounds can appear next to one another in their native language. In the first two months of life infants make reflexive vocalizations, such as crying, which are basic reactions to physiological stimuli e.g., hunger. Over the following two months they start to make laughing and cooing sounds. Around 6 months of age, infants start to babble. At around 12 months children produce their first adult-like words. Many early words are initially used in highly specific ways, but children's early speech also includes many examples of over-extension, whereby children use a word for a wider variety of referents than is appropriate. By 18 months, infants can produce about 60 words. Over the following 6 months there is a 'vocabulary spurt' in which another 150–250 words are learnt. By 30 months, children can produce 600 words and by 6 years they can produce 6000 words. Towards the end of their second year, children start to put words together into two-word utterances. This is often referred to as the telegraphic speech stage. Over the next two years, children start to add function words, verb endings and plurals. By the time they are 24 months old, children can produce sentences of up to four or five words, and by 30 months they can produce sentences of up to eight words. According to the critical period hypothesis, children have to be exposed to a rich source of language between 2 and 5 years of age, before the brain has matured. However, the evidence for a critical period is not clear cut as language deprivation is usually accompanied by other forms of deprivation.

Statistical learning. Recent research on language development has focused on infants' and children's use of statistical information. Young infants can perceive different phonemes, and they become tuned to the sounds present in their native language by 12 months of age. There is evidence that this developmental pattern of phoneme perception occurs as a result of the statistical distribution of sounds in an infant's native language. There is a relationship between individual differences in vocabulary growth and the amount of parental speech input children receive, and research shows that infants can learn word categories and syntactic on the basis of statistical information.

The biological basis of language. Human language is the product of evolution, and it is likely that the ability to communicate our knowledge and intentions to others led to selection for language. Broca's area was present two million years ago, and the physical apparatus we use to speak has been in its present form for about 60 000 years. There is a gene, FOXP2, that is associated with grammar, and damage to this gene leads to difficulties in acquiring language. Language functions are predominantly located in the left hemisphere. Damage to Broca's area or Wernicke's area can lead to aphasia, which is the impairment of language production or comprehension skills. Further evidence for the left-hemisphere specialization for language comes from work in cognitive neuroscience using EEG and NIRS.

Discussion questions

1 What are the arguments in support of the claim that we need innate grammatical knowledge in order to develop language?

2 Why do constructivists argue that we do not need innate knowledge?

3 How has research on statistical learning contributed to our understanding of language development?

4 Do you think there is a critical period for language acquisition? What is the evidence for your point of view?

5 Why do you think that humans developed language? What is the adaptive value of being able to communicate in a more flexible and generative way than other species?

Further Reading

Books and chapters

Barrett, M. (Ed). (1999). *The development of language*. Hove: Psychology Press.

In this edited volume, Martyn Barrett brings together a collection of specially-authored chapters on speech perception, phonology, lexical development, the acquisition of grammar, discourse skills, bilingualism, sign language and language in children with developmental disorders.

Harley, T. A. (2008). *The psychology of language: From data to theory*. Hove: Psychology Press.

Trevor Harley's textbook is an excellent resource on psycholinguistics. Only a fraction of the book focuses specifically on the *development* of language, but the rest is also very useful.

Maratsos, M. (1998). The acquisition of grammar. In W. Damon, D. Kuhn and R. S. Siegler (Eds), *Handbook of child psychology, Volume 2: Cognition, perception and language* (pp. 421–466). New York: John Wiley and Sons.

Woodward, A. L. and Markman, E. M. (1998). Early word learning. In W. Damon, D. Kuhn and R. S. Siegler (Eds.), *Handbook of child psychology, Volume 2: Cognition, perception and language* (pp. 371–420). New York: John Wiley and Sons.

These two chapters from the fifth edition of the *Handbook of child psychology* offer a comprehensive view of theoretical issues in word learning (Amanda Woodward and Ellen Markman) and the acquisition of grammar (Michael Maratsos).

Articles

Maye, J., Weiss, D. J. and Aslin, R. N. (2008). Statistical phonetic learning in infants: Facilitation and feature generalization. *Developmental Science, 11*, 122–134.

Maye, J., Werker, J. F. and Gerken, L. (2002). Infant sensitivity to distributional information can affect phonetic discrimination. *Cognition*, *82*(3), B101–B111.

In these two papers, Jessica Maye and her colleagues demonstrate how infants can learn speech sounds using the statistical properties of language.

Saffran, J. R. (2003). Statistical language learning: Mechanisms and constraints. *Current Directions in Psychological Science*, *12*(4), 110–114.

Jenny Saffran presents a brief overview of the evidence for statistical learning in language development.

Chapter 5

Theory of mind

Learning Outcomes

At the end of this chapter you should be able to:

- Define 'theory of mind'.

- Describe and evaluate competing theories of the development of theory of mind.

- Describe and evaluate research on the development of theory of mind.

- Discuss whether false belief tasks accurately test theory of mind skills.

- Discuss the evidence for early abilities and later development of theory of mind.

In 1983 Heinz Wimmer and Josef Perner carried out a series of experiments in which they presented 3- to 9-year-olds with the following scenario. They used paper cut-outs of a boy and a girl to represent the characters in the story (a boy called Maxi and his mother) and three coloured matchboxes glued to a piece of upright polystyrene to represent kitchen drawers:

> Mother returns from her shopping trip. She brought chocolate for a cake. Maxi may help her put away the things. He asks her: 'Where should I put the choco- late?' 'In the blue cupboard', says the mother. 'Wait, I'll lift you up there because you are too small'. Mother lifts him up. Maxi puts the chocolate into the blue cupboard.
> *[A toy chocolate is put into the blue matchbox.]*
> Maxi remembers exactly where he put the chocolate so he could come back and get some later. He loves chocolate. Then he leaves for the playground.
> *[The boy doll is removed]*
> Mother starts to prepare the cake and takes the chocolate out of the blue cup- board. She grates a bit into the dough and then she does *not* put it back into the *blue* but into the *green* cupboard.
> *[Toy chocolate is thereby transferred from the blue to the green matchbox.]*
> Now she realizes that she forgot to buy eggs. Then Maxi comes back from the playground, hungry, and he wants to get some chocolate.
> *[Boy doll reappears.]*
> He still remembers where he had put the chocolate.
> (Wimmer and Perner, 1983, p. 109)

Participants were asked a *belief* question: 'Where will Maxi look for the choco- late?' and had to point to one of three matchboxes (blue, green or red). The correct answer is, of course, that Maxi will look in the blue cupboard as he is unaware that the chocolate has been moved to the green cupboard (the **unexpected transfer**). The participants were then told another story with the same structure. The second story was about a girl who had hidden her favourite book. While she was out on a walk the caretaker put her book back on another shelf. Participants were asked to indicate in which of three locations the girl would look for her book upon her return. Table 5.1 shows the number of correct responses to these two stories in Wimmer and Perner's first experiment. Only 33 per cent of the 4- to 5-year-olds gave the correct answer to both stories, whereas 92 per cent of the 6- to 9-year-olds gave the correct answer both times.

unexpected transfer task Task in which an object is moved from one location to another without the knowledge of the story character who placed the object in its initial location. This task tests the ability of children to understand that the character has a false belief about the location of the object.

Table 5.1

Number of participants giving correct answers in experiment 1.

	Number of correct answers		
Age (years)	2	1	0
4–5	4	2	6
6 to 7	11	0	1
8 to 9	11	1	0

> Q. Why do you think the younger children were less successful on the task?

One explanation might be that the younger children simply forget key elements of the story, such as which drawer the chocolate was originally in or where Maxi was when his mother moved the chocolate. However, Wimmer and Perner controlled for this by also asking participants a *reality* question: 'Where is the chocolate really?', and a *memory* question, 'Do you remember where Maxi put the chocolate in the beginning?' Of the children who gave incorrect responses to the belief question, 80 per cent gave correct answers to the memory question. Of the children who gave correct responses to the belief question, 100 per cent gave correct answers to the reality question. This shows that neither the correct nor the incorrect answers to the belief question were due to incorrect recall of the story.

Wimmer and Perner followed this up with a second experiment in which they introduced two new conditions. In the *Stop-and-Think Displacement* condition the participants were told: 'Think carefully! What did Maxi do before he went off to the playground? Now he wants to eat the chocolate. Where will he look for the chocolate?' In the *Disappear* condition the story was altered such that Maxi's mother used up all the chocolate. In this version of the task the toy chocolate is removed completely.

> Q. Why do you think the experimenters introduced these two new conditions?

The *Stop-and-Think Displacement* condition was introduced to control for the possibility that children were giving 'impulsive' answers whereby they were pointing automatically to the true location of the chocolate without reflecting on what was being asked of them. The *Disappear* condition was introduced as the correct 'blue drawer' answer and the incorrect 'green drawer' answer are very similar and may be confused. Table 5.2 shows the results of experiment 2. None of the 3- to 4-year-olds chose the correct answers, whereas 50 per cent of the 4- to 5-year-old children and 83 per cent of the 5- to 6-year-olds answered both questions correctly. The 5- to 6-year-olds in the two new conditions performed perfectly and the 4- to 5-year-olds scored more highly in the *Disappear* condition than the *Standard Displacement* and *Stop-and-Think-Displacement* conditions.

Wimmer and Perner concluded that children aged 6 years and older have no problems with representing two different models of the world, one that reflects the true state of affairs (the chocolate is in the green box) and one that reflects Maxi's *false belief* that the chocolate is in the blue box. Three-year-olds, on the other hand, were unable to correctly represent Maxi's false belief, answering the belief question with the true location of the chocolate. The 4- to 6-year-olds showed some ability to represent both true and false beliefs, but their performance varied with modifications to the task.

			Number of correct answers		
Age (years)	Condition	*n*	2	1	0
3–4	Stop-and-Think Displacement	10	0	0	10
	Disappear	10	0	3	7
4 to 5	Standard Displacement	14	6	1	7
	Stop-and-Think Displacement	14	4	2	8
	Disappear	14	11	0	3
5 to 6	Standard Displacement	10	5	0	5
	Stop-and-Think Displacement	10	10	0	0
	Disappear	10	10	0	0

Table 5.2

Number of participants giving correct answers in experiment 2.

What is theory of mind?

Wimmer and Perner's experiments have been replicated and extended by a number of psychologists with the general finding that children aged 4 years and older pass false belief tasks and children under 3½ years fail them (Wellman, Cross and Watson, 2001). These findings have classically been interpreted as showing that young children cannot understand the minds of others and cannot understand that another person can hold a belief that is different from reality and different from the child's own belief. This is similar to Piaget's (1926; Piaget and Inhelder, 1956) idea of egocentrism, whereby children in the preoperational stage cannot adopt the perspective on another person. However, Piaget's egocentrism cannot explain performance on false belief tasks as, according to Piaget, children do not start to take the perspective of others until around 7 years of age, when they enter the concrete operational stage. The ability to understand that other people can have beliefs that differ from our own is often seen as a critical aspect of theory of mind. The term theory of mind refers to our everyday understanding of mental states. According to Mitchell and Lewis (1994), having a theory of mind means having the 'ability to make inferences about others' representational states and to predict behaviour accordingly' (p. 2). For example, when we see someone behaving in a certain way, such as putting their umbrella up or saying 'it is raining hard', we will make the inference that they have a belief about the current weather conditions (i.e., they believe that it is raining). We can use our understanding of their mental state to predict other behaviour, such as driving to the shops rather than walking. The term 'theory of mind' was coined by Premack and Woodruff (1978) and was actually used to refer to chimpanzees rather than humans. However, since the early 1980s, a vast body of research on theory of mind in humans (particularly in children and clinical populations) has been carried out. The main questions that this research has attempted to answer are *what* develops, *when* does it develop, and *how* does it develop? Several theoretical perspectives have been proposed in order to answer these questions. These accounts can be broadly split into domain-general theories and domain-specific theories.

epistemic state A mental state of knowledge or belief; from the Greek *episteme* (knowledge).

mental representation A mental object or structure with semantic content. This may be an image (e.g., a bar of chocolate) or a proposition (the chocolate is in the green drawer).

metarepresentation A representation of a representation. In order to understand another person's false belief, one has to hold a mental representation of the other person's representation. In the unexpected transfer task, Maxi has a representation (belief) that the chocolate is in the blue cupboard. Participants who pass the task have a representation (knowledge) of Maxi's representation of the location of the chocolate.

Theories of theory of mind

Representational mind theory

Wimmer and Perner's answer to these questions is that an ability to understand false beliefs emerges between the ages of 4 and 6 as a result of a new cognitive skill, the ability to represent two different **epistemic states**. Children under the age of 4 are unable to mentally represent both reality and a false view of reality at the same time. This inability to hold two conflicting mental representations has been explained by Perner (1991) as a lack of understanding of **mental representations**. Specifically, Perner argues that younger children have not acquired the concept of **metarepresentation**. A metarepresentation is representation of a representation. When one has a belief that the bar of chocolate is in the blue drawer, this belief is a representation. In order to pass the false belief task, one must have a mental representation of Maxi's mental representation that the chocolate is in the blue drawer. Metarepresentation involves the ability to distinguish between what is being represented and how it is being represented. The representational mind theory has been an influential theoretical view of the development of theory of mind. As with Piaget's theory of cognitive development, the **representational mind theory** is a stage theory of development. Stage theorists such as Perner suggest that theory of mind cannot be

representational mind theory The theory that domain-general representational abilities underlie theory of mind. Around the age of 4 children come to understand metarepresentation and are thus able to understand false beliefs.

acquired by children until there is a radical shift in their thought processes. Once this shift in understanding has taken place, children have a theory of mental states which they can use to explain and predict behaviour. The representational mind theory offers a universal, domain-general, discontinuous account of the development of theory of mind. This idea is supported by evidence that this shift in thought processes is universal, regardless of cross-cultural boundaries. Avis and Harris (1991), noting that all false belief tasks had been conducted on children in Western cultures, went to Cameroon to investigate theory of mind with a tribe of hunter-gatherer Baka pygmies who had had little contact with Western civilization. Avis and Harris adapted the unexpected transfer test to involve a mango, a cooking pot and a bowl. They found that, just as in Western children, there seemed to be a radical shift in thought processes, although a little later than that experienced by Western children. Generally, children under 5 could not give the correct answer; children over 5 could. They concluded that the acquisition of theory of mind as part of a stage of development was universal. Other researchers have had mixed results. Vinden (1999) presented children from non-Western cultures with a false belief task, with different results. She found that in Mofu children from Cameroon, and Tolai children from Papua New Guinea, false belief understanding did not emerge until around 7 years of age. Knight *et al.* (2004) found similar results when they tested Maya children from the Yucatán peninsula in South-eastern Mexico. In order to try to resolve the question of whether children from different cultures develop a theory of mind at different rates, or whether the mixed results were an artifact of small sample sizes and differing procedures, Callaghan *et al.* (2005) examined the performance of 3- to 5-year-olds from five countries on a false belief task. Two-hundred-and-sixty-seven children from Canada, Peru, Samoa, India and Thailand, with a mix of socioeconomic statuses, were given a task in which an experimenter hid a toy under one of three bowls, then left the room. A second experimenter asked the participants to hide the toy under a different bowl. The children were then asked where the first experimenter would look for the toy upon their return. Only fourteen of the ninety-seven 3-year-olds passed the task, just under half (39/85) of the 4-year-olds passed the task and most (72/85) of the 5-year-olds passed the task. Figure 5.1 shows the results for the children from Peru, India, Samoa and Canada (participants from Thailand are excluded from this graph as no 4-year-olds were tested). The authors argue that their results demonstrate that there is a universal fundamental shift in false-belief understanding between the ages of 3 and 5.

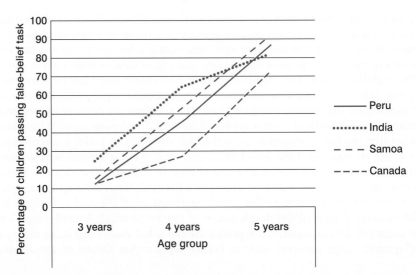

Figure 5.1

Number of children passing and failing the false-belief task for each culture and age group.

Source: Callaghan *et al.*, 2005.

The deceptive box task. There are two basic types of false belief task. The first is the unexpected transfer task, used in the studies mentioned above. The second is the deceptive box task (Hogrefe, Wimmer and Perner, 1986; Perner, Leekam and Wimmer, 1987), also often referred to as the 'Smarties experiment'. In this task, children are shown a container, such as a Smarties tube, and asked 'What is in here?' The children will answer 'Smarties'. The tube is then opened and it is revealed that there is actually a pencil in the box. The pencil is then put back in the box and the box is closed. Participants are then asked three questions: a control question ('Can you remember what's inside here?'), a prior belief question ('But what did you think was in here?') and a false belief question. For the false belief question, participants are told that a friend would see the closed box and be asked what was in it. Each participant is asked 'What will [name of friend] think is in here?' In Perner *et al.*'s study, 32 children aged between 3 and 4 took part. The data from three children were excluded as they failed to recall that there was actually a pencil in the box. Of the remaining 29 children, only 12 correctly answered both the prior belief and false belief questions. The authors interpret this as demonstrating that an understanding of false belief develops around 3 to 4 years of age. As with the unexpected transfer task, successful performance on the deceptive box task requires the child to represent not only the true state of affairs (that there is a pencil in the box) but also to represent another person's false belief (that there are Smarties in the box). Interestingly, Gopnik and Astington (1988) have shown that younger children not only fail to predict their friend's false belief but fail to remember their own false belief. After the participants (43 children aged 3 to 5) had been shown the pencil, they are asked 'When you first saw the box, before we opened it, what did you think was inside it? Did you think there were Smarties inside it or did you think there were pencils inside it?'. More than half of the 3-year-olds answered 'a pencil' although they originally said 'Smarties'. This can be interpreted as an inability to hold metarepresentations. In this case, they are apparently unable to hold both a representation of reality and a representation of their own initial false belief.

deceptive box task
Task in which the contents of a box differ from what would be expected to be in it. Children are asked what someone else will think is in the box in order to determine whether they can (a) understand that another person can hold a false belief and (b) understand their own initial false belief.

Appearance-reality. Perner *et al.* (1987) argue that in order to pass false belief tasks, it is necessary to understand that someone who wants to give a correct answer can actually give a wrong answer, and that this requires an understanding of conflicting truth values. In false belief tasks, the conflict is between the true belief of the participant and the false belief of the story character (in the unexpected transfer task) or the participant's friend (in the deceptive box task). Flavell, Flavell and Green (1983) carried out an experiment in which participants' own conflicting truth values were examined. Their appearance-reality task allows us to see whether children can distinguish between the way the world really is and the way the world seems. In order to see whether children confused representations of appearance with representations of reality, Flavell *et al.* showed participants aged 3 to 5 a series of deceptive objects such as a sponge that had been shaped and painted to look like a rock. At first the participants were only allowed to look at each object. They were then allowed to hold the objects and were asked a series of questions including 'What did you think this was when you first saw it?', 'When you look at this with your eyes right now, does it look like a rock or does it look like a piece of sponge?', and 'What is this really really? Is it really really a rock or really really a piece of sponge?'. The 4- to 5-year-olds were generally able to report that the object appeared to be one thing but was, in reality, another, whereas half the 3-year-olds confused appearance and reality. This is more evidence in support of the view that children under the age of 4 have difficulties with metarepresentation.

appearance-reality task
Task in which an item has an appearance which conflicts with what it really is (e.g., a sponge that looks like a rock or a candle that looks like an apple). The aim of the task is to see whether children can hold two different representations of the same object.

Theory theory

Theory theory shares some similarities with representational mind theory, but whereas Perner (1991) offers a domain-general account of conceptual change, Gopnik and Wellman (1994) and Wellman and Gelman (1992) posit domain-specific changes within a number of domains, including biology and physics as well as mind. Perner's representational mind theory is often cited as an example of **theory theory**, but Wellman (2002) draws distinctions between the two. More specifically, whereas Perner focuses on children's developing understanding of representations in general, including physical representations such as photographs as well as mental representations, Gopnik, Slaughter and Meltzoff (1994) and Gopnik and Wellman (1992, 1994) describe a series of conceptual changes in the development of theory of mind. They identify an understanding of perception and desire as precursors to a true theory of mind. Gopnik, Wellman and colleagues argue that children initially understand misrepresentation in the context of desire and perception and then extend it to belief. Each new 'theory' replaces the previous one. Before 30 months, children have a foundational non-representational understanding of perception, evidenced by their use of joint attention, social referencing and understanding of object permanence. From 30 months onwards, children develop an understanding of perception and desire. They can understand that if someone desires something, this will affect their actions. At around 3 years, children show a more complex understanding of desires and perspectives. They can understand that other people's desires may conflict with their own and they begin to understand perceptual misrepresentation (e.g., that a pink object covered with a green filter can look green (Flavell, Green and Flavell, 1986)). Finally at about 4 years, children realize that they can generalize the notion of misrepresentation (that what you see isn't necessarily what is real) from perspective contexts to belief contexts. They now realize that people's beliefs about the world, and not the true state of the world, determine their behaviour; they possess a theory of mind. Theory theory offers a constructivist account of conceptual change as this developmental progression is driven by an accumulation of information from experiencing social interactions, but does not specify the mechanisms that underlie these changes (Sodian, 2005).

Gopnik and Wellman (1992, 1994) describe 2-year-old children as having a theory based on desire psychology. They claim that, even at this young age, they have some understanding of psychological states. This knowledge is largely based around desires and perceptions. At this stage in development the child has a non-representational understanding. Desires are understood as drives towards objects; a person's desire for an object can cause them to behave in a certain way. If a person wants a toy, for example, they will go and get it. Wellman and Woolley (1990) found that 2-year-olds could predict behaviours based on desire, but were poor at predicting behaviours based on belief. Repacholi and Gopnik (1997) demonstrated that infants as young as 18 months old are able to engage in desire reasoning. They gave eighty-one 14-month-old and seventy-eight 18-month-old infants a task in which the infants had to predict what food the experimenter would desire once she had tasted two foods and expressed disgust at one of them and happiness at the other. In one condition the experimenter liked crackers and disliked broccoli, in line with the infants' preferences. In a second condition the experimenter's preference was reversed so as to be mismatched to the infants' preferences. Repacholi and Gopnik found that 14-month-olds chose the crackers in both conditions, whereas 18-month-olds chose the food the experimenter had indicated she enjoyed. Importantly, this finding held true even when the experimenter had opposing tastes to the infants, demonstrating that the older infants understood that the experimenter had a desire and would make choices based on this desire.

The theory of 3-year-olds is more sophisticated and is based on a belief-desire psychology. They predict actions on the basis of both beliefs and desires, where beliefs are based on perceptions (see Figure 5.2). For example, an emotion (dislike of dogs) coupled with a perception (the dog went under the table), mediated by a desire (to put the dog outside) and a belief (the dog is under the table) can lead to an action (reaching for the dog under the table) (Bartsch and Wellman, 1989). Around the age of 3, children start to use mental state terms such as think, know and believe (Wellman and Bartsch, 1994), however their understanding of belief is initially non-representational. According to Gopnik and Wellman (1994), the 3-year-old's conception of belief, as with the early conception of desire, involves a direct link between people and objects. Beliefs are expected to mirror the real world, which is why children at this stage still fail false belief tasks. As children progress through their third year, they start to understand desires and perceptions as representing a view of objects in the world, rather than as a mere mirroring of copy of reality. By the age of 4 or 5, children develop a representational understanding of beliefs, and can hold a representation of a belief of an object which contradicts reality. This understanding enables them to pass false belief tasks.

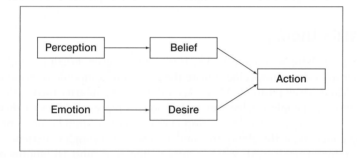

Figure 5.2

Belief-desire reasoning.

Simulation theory

An alternative account of the development of theory of mind, **simulation theory**, explains reasoning about minds in terms of first-hand experiences, rather than the concepts or representations posited by representational mind theory and theory theory. According to this view, we are able to understand other people's mental states in terms of the mental states we have experienced. When we try to understand what someone else believes in a particular situation, we simulate what it would be like to be in that situation and imagine what we would feel and believe. We then take this simulated experience and attribute it to the others. Our own mind is a model of other people's minds and we do not, therefore, need to develop a theory of how other people's minds work. Gordon (1986) introduced simulation theory as a general explanation of folk psychology, our everyday understanding of mental states, within the field of philosophy of mind. He does, however, make reference to developmental psychology, suggesting that what distinguishes a 4-year-old child who passes false belief tasks from a younger child who fails them, is the ability to simulate (or 'put himself in Maxi's shoes'), the capacity for which enables him to overcome the younger child's limited, egocentric view of the world.

simulation theory The theory that we can understand other people's beliefs by imagining ourselves to be in their situation.

Harris (1992) took Gordon's ideas and developed a version of simulation theory which is based specifically on developmental psychology. In this account, developmental differences are explained in terms of some simulations being harder than others, depending on how many adjustments have to be made to children's default settings, which are their own mental states. Harris argues that the process which leads to the apparent understanding of mind observed in 4-year-olds is an increase in imaginative flexibility. Whereas Wellman and colleagues assert a theory of belief-desire psychology, Harris proposes that 2- and 3-year-olds can imagine having different wants and desires from their own. With an increase in imaginative power, they come to acknowledge that two people may have different beliefs about a situation, and can imagine – or simulate – a belief that is different from their own. Harris cites children's pretend play abilities (discussed below) as evidence for simulation theory. When children pretend that a toy doll has a desire for a drink, for example, they are simulating thirstiness (which they have first-hand experience of) and attributing this to the doll. In doing so they need to temporarily alter their default setting (not desiring a drink) to match that of the doll (desiring a drink). False belief tasks are harder as they require two sets of default settings, reality and own mental state, to be altered. To pass false belief tasks, children have to imagine a counterfactual reality in which they do not know the true location of an object or the true contents of a box, and they have to imagine that they are in a different mental state with respect to that reality; they have to simulate a belief that is different to their own.

Modularity theory

modularity theory The theory that there is a cognitive module which is innately specified to process mental representations. Theory of mind develops as this module matures.

Leslie (1994a, 1994b; Scholl and Leslie, 1999, 2001; Leslie, Friedman and German, 2004) proposes a domain-specific, innate theory of mind module referred to as the Theory of Mind Mechanism (ToMM). According to **modularity theory**, this mental module interprets people's behaviour and produces representations of their beliefs and desires. Leslie argues that the development of theory of mind is not a product of developing concepts or the ability to simulate, learned through experience, but is a result of the maturing ToMM, which comes online at around 18 months of age. If this is true, it means that children have metarepresentational abilities long before they are 4 years old. Leslie argues that the reason younger children fail false belief tasks is not because they lack a theory of mind, but because they fail to inhibit their own belief when making judgements. He posits a selection processing mechanism, which has not yet fully matured in younger children, which enables us to inhibit competing contents of the ToMM. True beliefs are also present in the ToMM and these are preferred as a default to false beliefs. This is because beliefs often are true and, according to Scholl and Leslie (2001), this default attribution of beliefs as true should have been favoured in the evolutionary history of the ToMM. Early false belief task failure is, therefore, a result of performance limitations, not any kind of conceptual deficit. Leslie supports this assertion with evidence from the literature on autism (see Chapter 10), arguing that the reason why autistic children fail false belief tasks is because they do not have a ToMM. Surian and Leslie (1999) also argue that the many examples of children younger than 4 passing false belief tasks is evidence for an innate representational system. Some of these studies are discussed below.

Do false belief tasks underestimate children's abilities?

Most of the evidence for the changes in children's theory of mind ability comes from false belief tasks, which are generally experiments conducted in a lab. There have been many researchers who suggest that this reliance on such experiments distorts our view of children's ability (e.g., Birch and Bloom, 2004; Bloom and German, 2000). In part, this is because the false belief tasks themselves are flawed. In much the same way that researchers have criticized Piaget's experiments for underestimating children's ability, researchers have criticized false belief tasks for misleading children. There are a number of variations of false belief tasks that try to show that young children under 4 years can actually pass these tasks.

For example, Lewis and Osborne (1990) suggest that the question in the deceptive box task confuses children. They argue that asking children 'What will [name of friend] think is in the box?' may be interpreted as 'What will your friend think when she looks in the box'. If children really do interpret the question in this way, then any answers in which they say that their friend will think there is a pencil in the box cannot be taken as evidence of a lack of theory of mind. Similarly, Gopnik and Astington's (1988) finding that children appear to have difficulty in acknowledging their original false belief may be because they are misinterpreting the time reference. Although they are asked 'When you first saw the box, before we opened it, what did you think was inside it?', they may interpret the question as asking what is inside the box now, which would lead to an incorrect answer. To test this, Lewis and Osborne compared the standard wording of the question with two modified versions of the task. They split 131 children (29 aged 3 to 3½, 49 aged 3½ to 4 and 53 aged 4–4½) into three groups. The first group were given the standard (Perner *et al.*, 1987) questions: 'What did you think was in the box?' / 'What will [name of friend] think is in the box?' The second group were given the standard questions but were also asked when questions: 'What did you think was in the box when the top was still on it?' / 'What will [name of friend] think is in the box when the top is still on it?' The third group were given the standard questions and before questions: 'What did you think was in the box before I took the top off?' / 'What will [name of friend] think is in the box before I take the top off?' Children in all three age groups performed better in the before condition, demonstrating that by making precise time references they were able to help young children acknowledge the false belief of another person. The implication of this is that the linguistic features of task are important; subtle changes of wording can have an effect on the age at which children are able to pass the task. Similarly, Siegal and Beattie (1991) argue that the wording used in false beliefs tasks may be misinterpreted. They suggest that children may take the question 'Where will a person (with the false belief) look for the object?' to mean 'Where will the person have to look (or go to look) to find the object?' rather than 'Where will the person look first?' They took Wellman and Bartsch's (1988) explicit false belief task, which includes stories such as 'Jane wants to find her kitten. Jane's kitten is really in the playroom. Jane thinks the kitten is the kitchen', and modified the wording to ask 'Where will Jane look first for her kitten?' They found that 3-year-olds were often able to pass this version of the task. However, Perner (2000) claims that Lewis and Osborne's finding is not replicable, and that while some studies have replicated Siegal and Beattie's finding the results are variable. Surian and Leslie (1999), for example, found that while only 30 per cent of 3-year-olds passed the standard question, 83 per cent passed the 'look first' question, but Clements and Perner (1994) failed to find this effect, with only 36 per cent of children passing the 'look first' version, compared to a 32 per cent pass rate on the standard version.

Another demonstration that false belief task failure in 3-year-olds may be a result of comprehension difficulties was made by Lewis *et al.* (1994). They adapted the traditional unexpected transfer story such that participants were shown a picture book, rather than dolls acting out the story, with the aim of helping the children to understand the narrative. In a series of experiments, they found that narrating the book back to the experimenter or being taken through the story twice led to greater task success. This suggests that failure may be due to not having a clear understanding of the sequence of events in the story. Freeman, Lewis and Doherty (1991) argue that children are not able to articulate their false beliefs because they have implicit, rather than explicit, knowledge. Freeman *et al.* modified the unexpected transfer task such that instead of asking children to tell them where the character in the story would look for the item, they asked the children to act out what the character would do. They found that 59 of 75 older 3-year-olds and young 4-year-olds, correctly acted out the character's journey to the empty location, whereas only 23 of the same participants could verbalize the character's false belief. This suggests that younger children may have an understanding of theory of mind but not be able to verbalize it.

All the above arguments concern linguistic factors. Wimmer and Hartl (1991) devised a modified version of the deceptive box task in order to determine whether children's incorrect report of their initial false belief was due to a failure to understand the question, or a failure to understand belief. In order to discriminate between these two hypotheses, they introduced an extra stage to the task, in which there actually were Smarties in the box. After guessing the contents and being shown that their guess was correct, the children observed as the Smarties were taken out and replaced with a pencil. This manipulation, known as the state change task, ensures that children's initial observation of the contents of the box would contrast with the final contents of the box. Therefore, if children interpret the initial belief question as asking 'What was in the box?', their predicted answer is 'Smarties'; if they interpret the question as 'What is in the box now?', they should answer 'A pencil'. Over 80 per cent of their 3- and 4-year-old participants answered 'Smarties'. In contrast, only 40 per cent of participants gave this answer when they were presented with the standard version of the task. If children were making an error in interpreting the question, thinking that they were being asked 'What is in the box now?', we would not expect any difference between the two conditions. As a result, Wimmer and Hartl claim that the reason children fail these tasks is because they lack a concept of belief. Mitchell (1997), however, offers an alternative explanation. He argues that the reason younger children fail to acknowledge their false beliefs is because their attention is dominated by their current knowledge. Older children are able to shift their attention between their current knowledge and their prior belief. When younger children are shown a pencil inside the box, the pencil competes more successfully for the child's attention as a candidate for judging what they used to think, owing to its tangible existence. Mitchell suggests that this is why Wimmer and Hartl's state change procedure, in which the child's initial belief was instantiated in reality, produced a greater number of 'Smarties' responses. To test the idea that reality is more salient for young children, Mitchell and Lacohee (1991) modified the experiment to embody the child's original belief in a physical reality. They first asked their participants what was in the tube. The children answered 'Smarties'. The experimenters then asked the children to identify a picture of Smarties from a set of pictures presented, and to post this picture into a special post box where it remained out of sight until the end of the experiment. The tube was then opened to reveal the pencil. The tube was closed again and the children were asked what they had thought was in the tube when they posted the picture into the postbox. In the standard version of the task (without the pictures and the postbox), only 23 per cent of 3- and 4-year-olds correctly remembered their false belief. In the modified version, 63 per cent of 3- and 4-year-olds correctly remembered their previous false belief. On the basis of this finding, along with others (Robinson and Mitchell, 1995; Saltmarsh, Mitchell and Robinson, 1995), Mitchell argues that the difference between older and younger children is not that the younger children lack a concept of belief, but rather that younger children rely more heavily on reality when making judgements about belief.

A further problem was identified by Wimmer, Hogrefe and Perner (1988; see also Wimmer, Hogrefe and Sodian, 1988). They suggested that all the false belief tasks show is that young children do not understand the relationship between access to an informational source and the resulting knowledge. In other words, they do not know that 'seeing is believing', that what someone believes or knows depends on what they have seen or heard. Adults and older children know, for example, that if a person has seen inside a box, they know what the contents are. Wimmer *et al.* suggested that younger children do not make this link. They demonstrated this with an experiment in which they showed pairs of children a box and asked one child whether the other child knew what was in it. Three groups of children (16 each of 3-, 4- and 5-year-olds) were split into two groups. In one condition, one member of each pair was given visual access to the contents of the box. In the other condition, one member of each pair was told what was in the box by the experimenter. The children in each pair alternated between being the participant who was asked questions and the 'other child'. In half the trials, the participant knew what was in the box and the other child didn't. In the other half, the participant didn't know what was in the box and the other child did. Each participant answered four questions in total, two about their own knowledge: 'Do you know what is in the box or don't you know that?' (one with and one without informational access), and two about the knowledge of the other child: 'Does [name of other child] know what is in the box or does she [he] not know that?' (one with and one without informational access). All the 5-year-olds were able to correctly state whether they and the other child knew what was in the box or not, but the 3- and 4-year-olds found it easier to judge whether they knew what was in the box, rather than the other child. The most frequent error was stating that the other child did not know what was in the box when they had, in fact, either looked into it or been told about it. A follow-up experiment demonstrated that this error was not due to a failure to recognize that the other child had informational access; 3- and 4-year-olds were able to correctly answer the question: 'Did [name of other child] look into the box or didn't he [she] look into the box?' Wimmer *et al.* suggest that what distinguishes a 3-year-old from a 5-year-old is the understanding that information leads to knowledge and belief.

Evidence for earlier abilities

One of the limitations of false beliefs tasks noted above was the requirement that children are able to verbalize their understanding of other people's actions and beliefs. A number of studies have used direction and duration of gaze to measure young children's implicit understanding of belief (see Sodian, 2011, for a brief overview). Using an unexpected transfer task, Clements and Perner (1994) reported that 77 per cent of children aged 2 years 11 months to 3 years 7 months looked at the location the protagonist believed the object to be in, even though only 23 per cent gave this correct location as their answer. Children younger than 2 years 11 months did not look at the false belief location. Although it can be argued that these results indicate an implicit theory of mind at 3 years of age, it is also possible that children are looking at the location the protagonist has seen the contents of, in line with Wimmer *et al.*'s (1988) ideas about the link between seeing and knowing. Garnham and Ruffman (2001) devised an experiment to discriminate between these two explanations. They used a modified unexpected transfer task in which there were three possible locations for the object. Participants were told the following story:

> Sam is looking for his ball. He looks in the yellow box but there is no ball in the yellow box. Sam sees his ball on the ground. He picks up the ball and plays with it. When Sam has finished playing with the ball he puts it in the blue box. Sam is tired now so he goes inside and falls fast asleep. Along comes Katy. Katy is look-ing for something to play with. She looks in the blue box and takes out the ball. Katy plays with the ball. When Katy has finished playing with the ball she puts it in the pink box. Then Katy goes away again. When Katy has gone away, Sam wakes up. He says 'I will go outside and play with my ball again now'.
> (Garnham and Ruffman, 2001, p. 99)

> Q. Why do you think Garnham and Ruffman included three boxes instead of just two?

This was a clever modification designed to determine which of the two explana-tions for young children's looking behaviour (implicit understanding of belief or looking where the protagonist has looked) was correct. Because Sam has looked in both the yellow and blue boxes, we would expect children to look at both of these if they were looking at the locations Sam had looked at. If, on the other hand, they have an understanding of Sam's false belief, they should look at the blue box and not the yellow box. Of the thirty-two 2 to 4-year olds who took part, only six gave the correct verbal response, but twenty-three looked in anticipation at the correct location. When gaze duration was analyzed, it was found that children looked at the blue box for a significantly longer period of time than either the yellow or pink boxes. The authors conclude that young children's anticipatory looking is governed by their implicit knowledge of the protagonist's false belief.

Although Clements and Perner (1994) found that children under the age of 3 did not demonstrate anticipatory looking, more recent research by Onishi and Baillar-geon (2005) has found this behaviour in 15-month-olds. Onishi and Baillargeon gave fifty-six 15-month-old infants a non-verbal task using the **violation-of-expectation** method. The infants watched an actor hide a toy in either a yellow or a green box. The infants then watched one of four changes that led to the actor holding either a true belief or a false belief regarding the location of the toy (see Figure 5.3). In the true belief/green condition the actor hid the toy in the green box and watched while the yellow box moved towards the green box then away again. In the true belief/yellow condition the actor watched the toy move from the green box into the yellow box. In the false belief/green condition the toy moved from the green to the yellow box with-out the actor seeing it, and in the false belief/yellow condition the actor watched the toy move from the green box to the yellow box but didn't see it move back to the green box again. Following this the infants observed the actor reaching into either the green box or the yellow box. Seven infants were placed in each of the eight condi-tions (four changes of location × two search locations). If infants base their expecta-tions about where the actor will search for the toy on the basis of her belief rather

violation-of-expectation
A methodology used in infant cognition studies. If an infant looks for a longer duration at one event than others, it is interpreted as a surprise – a violation of expectation – which enables researchers to infer the infant's knowledge.

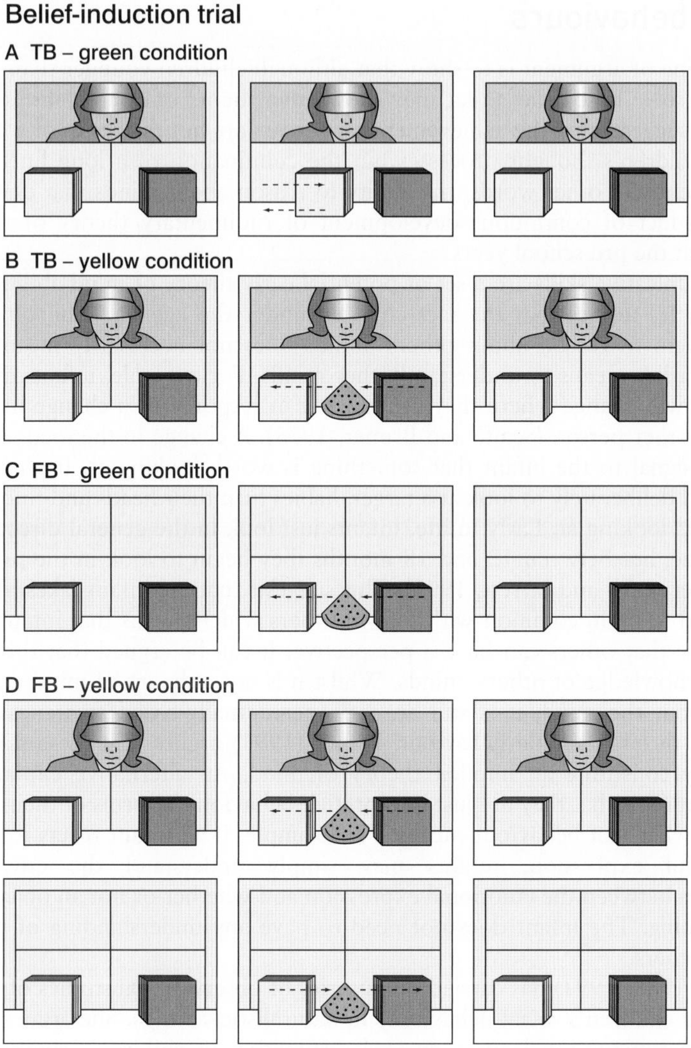

Belief-induction trial

A TB – green condition

B TB – yellow condition

C FB – green condition

D FB – yellow condition

Figure 5.3

Belief induction trial in Onishi and Baillargeon's study. The light grey box on the left of each panel is 'yellow' and the darker grey box on the right is 'green'.

Source: From Onishi, K. H., & Baillargeon, R. (2005). Do 15-month-old infants understand false beliefs? *Science*, 308, 255–258. Reprinted with permission from AAAS.

than their knowledge of the actual location, they should look longer at the instances where their expectations are violated. The results showed that for all four location change conditions, the infants looked longer when the actor reached for the toy in the location that the actor did not believe it to be in. However, Sodian and Thoermer (2008) carried out a series of looking-time experiments and found that 16-month-old infants' success on the task depended not on an understanding of what other people can see, but rather on situational cues such as whether the actor was absent or present while the toy was moved. They argue (based on studies conducted by Poulin-Dubois *et al.*, and Schnoeppner, 2007) that although 14-month-olds are able to understand what another person can or cannot see, it is not until 18 months that infants are able to use this information to predict actions, and even then the behavioural cues (such as head-turning and body orientation) need to be present. Perner and Ruffman (2005) suggest that Onishi and Baillargeon's findings might be explained by infants applying rules about behaviour, such as 'people look for objects where they last saw them', rather than as a result of infants representing actors' false beliefs.

Social behaviours

Another line of argument is to show that although children younger than 4 may not be able to solve false belief tasks, they show other theory of mind abilities very early on which suggests that the achievements at 4 years are not the result of a conceptual shift in children's thought processes but the culmination of a long line of related developments. In other words, the ability to reason about minds that develops at 4 is the product of continuous development of rudimentary theory of mind skills throughout the pre-school years.

Communicative skills are a set of potential early theory of mind abilities. Butterworth (1994) argues that the fact children under the age of 4 fail on tasks that require them to reason about others' minds does not necessarily mean that they have no earlier means to understand other minds. For example, infants as young as 6 months will change where they are looking in response to a change in the attention of another person (Scaife and Bruner, 1975). A change in the focus of an adult seems to signal to the infant that something is worth looking at. If an adult turns slowly and deliberately to look at a target, babies turn their heads and find the target the adult is looking at. Early in life, infants just look in the general direction of the adult's gaze, but between 12 and 18 months they begin to look in the precise location (Butterworth and Jarrett, 1991). This suggests that the infant takes his/her own visual field to be in common with that of others which means that infants know in some sense that others can have a perspective. It can be argued that this is a rudimentary knowledge of others' minds. Whilst it is not a theory of mind and not reasoning about the mind, it is still an early perceptually-based awareness of mind, expressed through simple behaviour. Perner (1991) argues that these skills do not necessarily constitute an implicit theory of mind. An alternative explanation for joint attention is that they are just interpreting behaviour in terms of their past experience of what that behaviour means. For example, if an infant reacts to her mother's fearful expression, infants may simply understand the environmental correlation between the emotional expression and whether or not an object or event is threatening. The infant does not need to have any understanding of the mental states of others.

Dunn (1988, 1991) has carried out a series of observational studies of 18- to 36-month-old children's social behaviours in naturalistic settings. She argues that laboratory experiments can lead to an underestimation of children's abilities whereas the home has emotional significance for them. Moreover, observation allows the study of child-initiated behaviours as opposed to just the responses to questions from psychologists that are generated in experiments. She argues that these studies provide evidence for the development of young children's understanding of the feelings, intentions and beliefs of others. Dunn studied 52 second-born children in their homes when the children were playing with their mothers and their siblings. She examined several domains of social behaviour, such as disputes, jokes, cooperation and conversations about others. With respect to disputes, she found a growth in sophistication between 2 and 3 years. Young 2-year-olds engaged in simple teasing behaviours, such as stealing their siblings' special toys. Children aged between 2 and 3 demonstrated more frequent and elaborate teasing. One example she gives is of a girl who pretended to be one of her sister's imaginary friends. Dunn argues that carrying out this pretence involves an understanding of what would upset the girl's sister and the ability to pretend to be someone else, both of which imply some comprehension of mental states. She also shows evidence that 3-year-olds can anticipate the actions of their mothers. Children this age frequently blamed their siblings in situations where the mother might be predicted to administer a punishment.

Their excuses for transgressions also show a growth in sophistication between the ages of 2 and 3. Whereas a 26-month-old child made a simple reference to intention, saying 'I didn't mean to', a 33-month-old child concocts a much more elaborate intention-based excuse for refusing to get down from the settee:

> Mother: Get off!
> Child (sits down): Look. I'm not—(stands up). Mummy. I'm not—I'm not standing on there. I'm trying to get a paint off (rubs TV).
> Mother: —
> Child: I going try and get a paint off. All I'm trying to do is— there.
> (Dunn, 1988, p. 33)

Deception

There is also evidence of other early abilities that seem to indicate early proto-theory of mind, such as deception. Deception involves theory of mind skills; in order to deceive someone we have to have some knowledge of what they are likely to be thinking in order to determine what is most likely to mislead them. Lewis, Stanger and Sullivan (1989) devised an experiment to test if 3-year-old children could lie. They told 33 children aged 33 to 37-months that the experimenter was going to show them a surprise toy. Each participant was seated with his back to a table while the experimenter set up a toy zoo. Participants were told that the experimenter was going to leave the room, but they were not allowed to peek; they could play with the toy when the experimenter returned. While the experimenter was out of the room, the children were observed and videotaped through a one-way mirror. Of course, many were unable to resist peeping under the cloth; 29 children looked at the toy. When the experimenter came back, the children were asked if they had peeked. Of the 29 children who had peeked, 18 attempted to conceal their behaviour. Seven of them told a straight lie and 11 refused to answer the question. The remaining 11 children admitted to peeking. Importantly, when Lewis *et al.* showed videos of the children's answers to a panel of 60 adults (aged 21 to 25), the adults were unable to detect which children were lying and which children were telling the truth. This shows that by 3 years of age children are able to deceive adults by integrating their verbal and facial behaviour.

Chandler, Fritz and Hala (1989) also demonstrated that young children could engage in deceitful behaviour in order to prevent someone from finding some hidden treasure. Their experimental setup consisted of a white washable surface, five opaque plastic containers, some 'treasure' (a bag of gold coins and jewels) and a puppet mounted on a wheel with feet on it. The feet were dipped in ink so that the doll left a trail of footprints as it was rolled over the white surface. First, there were a series of warm-up sessions in which it was demonstrated to the participants that the treasure could be removed from its initial location (one of the five containers) and hidden in one of the remaining four containers. It was also demonstrated that the puppet could be used to take the treasure to a hiding place. In doing so, the puppet would leave inky footprints behind, but these could be wiped clean using a sponge. Next, the participants were asked to help the puppet hide the treasure. One of the two experimenters left the room and the children were told to hide the treasure in one of the containers so that the absent experimenter would not be able to find it. After the experimenter had returned and searched for the treasure, making use of any footprints on the surface, the children were asked to explain the deceptive strategies they had employed. The 50 children aged 2½ to 5 who participated in the study employed a range of deceptive strategies: wiping away the footprints leading to the correct location, lying about which container the treasure was in, laying false trails to empty containers and combining false trails with the removal of the original footprints. The latter strategy is the most sophisticated and was adopted by 20 of the participants. What is most striking is that even some of the 2-year-olds were capable of carrying out these deceptions. These results suggest that even very young children can behave in a way that shows that they can predict the mental states of others, and modify their behaviour accordingly in order to deceive. Chandler *et al.*'s findings seem to refute the idea that children do not develop a theory of mind until the age of 4. However, this study has been criticized by Sodian, Taylor, Harris and Perner (1991), who replicated the experiment. Sodian *et al.* modified the task by introducing two more puppets: a robber and a king. Their participants, 20 children aged 3 and 16 children aged 4, were instructed to make it hard for the robber to find the treasure and (in separate trials) make it easy for the king to find the treasure. As in Chandler *et al.*'s study, children in both age groups were capable of wiping out footprints and laying false trails. However, many of the younger participants used these strategies indiscriminately, laying false trails or wiping out footprints on trials in which they were supposed to be helping the king, and leaving correct trails for the robber. Most of the 4-year-olds, in contrast, helped the king and deceived the robber. Sodian *et al.* argue that these results demonstrate that an understanding of false beliefs emerges around 4 years of age. Although younger children can engage in deceptive acts, they do not appear to understand the impact of the deception.

Pretence

Leslie (1987, 1994a) discusses children's early ability to pretend as an important development in understanding of mental states. Children start to engage in pretend play from about 18 months onwards (McCune-Nicolich, 1981). Leslie argues that, as with theory of mind, pretence relies on metarepresentational ability. If, for example, an infant pretends that a banana is a telephone, they have to hold two representations of the banana. The primary representation is of the banana as what it really is: a banana. In order to suspend its real identity and pretend that it is a telephone, the infant must take a copy of the primary representation and decouple it from its literal real-world reference. This second order copy is a representation of a representation: a metarepresentation (see Figure 5.4). Leslie takes this early ability to pretend, and to understand pretence in others, as evidence for the existence of an innate theory of mind mechanism. Perner (1991) argues that pretence and false belief differ in that in pretence it is not necessary to hold the representation as being true of the world. In the unexpected transfer task, children have to be able to know that Maxi *really* holds a false belief, whereas in pretence children only have to acknowledge that someone is pretending; there is not a conflict between belief and reality. Furthermore, Perner, Baker and Hutton (1994) showed that children do not understand pretence as a state of mind. They conducted an experiment in which 34 participants aged 3 years 2 months to 4 years 4 months were told three stories. Each story had three variants, think, pretend and reality; story variants were randomly assigned to participants so that each child heard one of the stories in its think form, one in its pretend form and one in its reality form. One of the stories was about a doll that was being dressed as a girl. In the think version, the protagonist, Jessica, thinks that the doll, who is really a boy, is a girl. In the pretend version, Jessica knows the doll is really a boy, but pretends that it is a girl. In the reality version, the doll is really a girl. Participants were then asked 'Did Jessica really think it was a girl, or did she just pretend?' Seven of the eight participants aged 4 were able to discriminate between thinking and pretence, but only six of the twenty-six 3-year-olds made

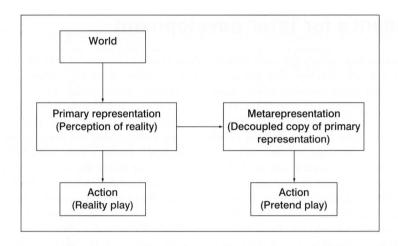

Figure 5.4

Metarepresentation in pretend play.

Source: Copyright © 1987 by the American Psychological Association. Adapted with permission. The official citation that should be used in referencing this material is Leslie, A.M. (1987). Pretense and representation: The origins of "theory of mind". *Psychological Review*, 94(4), 412–426. The use of APA information does not imply endorsement by APA.

this distinction. The rest either said that Jessica was pretending in the reality or think conditions or said she thought the doll really was a boy in the pretend condition. It can therefore be argued that children do not have a proper grasp of pretence until the age at which they are able to pass false belief tasks.

Meta-analysis of false belief tasks

In 2001, Wellman, Cross and Watson conducted a meta-analysis on 77 articles that reported results on false belief tasks. This encompassed 178 studies in which there were a total of 591 conditions. In a meta-analysis, it is the conditions, rather than the studies or the participants, which are the unit of analysis. The dependent variable was the proportion of children in a condition who made correct false belief judgements. Wellman *et al.* looked at a large number of variables, but these are the significant findings:

There were six main effects (factors which influenced task performance), five of which did not interact with age. First, they found a better performance if deception was the motive for the change (e.g., if the chocolate was moved in order to trick the protagonist). Second, children were more likely to pass if they carried out transformation themselves. In some studies, children passively watched the narrative, in others they helped to enact the story by, for example, moving the chocolate themselves. Third, performance was improved if the target object was not present when the false belief question was asked (e.g., if the chocolate had been moved from the drawer and eaten). The fourth facilitating factor was if the protagonist's belief is explicitly stated, for example if children were told 'Maxi believes the chocolate is in the green drawer – where will he look for it?' Fifth, there was an effect of country of origin. Children from the USA, the UK and Korea performed similarly, whereas children from Australia and Canada performed somewhat better and children from Austria and Japan performed somewhat worse. Finally, emphasis of time frame facilitated performance. In other words, if children were asked 'Where will he look *first*?' they had a greater chance of success. However, this factor interacted with age such that an effect was only found in children older than 4. This is possibly because including this information increases the length and complexity of the questions, which may affect younger children's performance. However, the basic development trend was still observed. Wellman *et al.* reported that children aged 4 and over performed above chance, whereas children aged 3 years 5 months and younger performed below chance.

meta-analysis An analysis of the findings from multiple studies. Whereas the unit of analysis in a single study is usually the individual children, the unit of analysis in a meta-analysis is the conditions within the studies.

Evidence for later development

In addition to evidence for early abilities, there is also evidence for aspects of theory of mind which develop after the age of 4. Knowledge about the minds of others doesn't just mean knowing when someone is holding a false belief. There are other developments that take place later. For example, Perner and Wimmer (1985) studied second order belief attribution. They were interested in determining whether children understand that people hold beliefs not just about reality but about other people's beliefs. Participants were told a story which was enacted with dolls. Mary and John saw the ice-cream van in the park. Mary went home for some money and meanwhile John saw the ice-cream van move to the church. On her way back to the park, Mary unexpectedly saw the ice-cream van at the church, so her belief about the van's location remains true. John sets out to look for Mary whom, he is told, has gone for an ice-cream. Participants were asked 'Where will John think that Mary has gone?' Obviously, the correct answer is the park as John holds a false belief about Mary's belief, but children don't tend to get the answer right until they are 7 years old. It could be argued that if there is a conceptual shift at age 4 we also need some way to explain the development of later stages.

There is also evidence that older children and adults can be manipulated to fail theory of mind tasks. Mitchell (1997) argues that the reason young children fail false belief tasks is that they pay too much attention to reality. If this is the case the young child is not qualitatively different from older children and adults. Instead young children, older children and adults differ only in the degree to which they rely on reality in making judgements. Therefore, it should be possible to induce false belief failure in older children and even adults. Steverson (1996; cited in Mitchell, 1997) carried out a variant of the deceptive box task, in which participants were asked to make a judgement about the false belief held by a puppet called Sweep. In this task, the standard Smarties tube task was presented to 5- and 6-year-old children. They were told that Sweep had said there were Smarties inside before the tube was opened to reveal a pencil inside. The experimenter then suggested to the children that Sweep's initial judgement was that the tube contained a pencil, a suggestion that the participants agreed with. It seems that hindering the children by asserting (incorrectly) a true belief on the part of the puppet meant they failed the task. Could it be, however, that children simply agreed with experimenter? No. There was also a control condition in which the same procedure was used with the sole difference that the experimenter claims that Sweep's initial belief was that there were jelly babies inside the tube. In this condition, children did not agree with the experimenter. This suggests that it remains tempting for children to judge all beliefs to be true even after they are 5 years old. This can be induced by manipulating the task to make it harder to judge the correct answer.

Birch and Bloom (2007) demonstrated that even adults can show a deficit on a false belief task when their own knowledge interferes with their reasoning about another person's false beliefs. One-hundred-and-fifty-five undergraduate students were presented with a variant of the unexpected transfer task with four containers (blue, red, purple and green) in which a character called Vicki puts her violin in the blue container then goes outside to play. While Vicki is outside, her sister, Denise, moves the violin. Participants were assigned to one of three conditions. In the *ignorance* condition they were told that the violin was moved to another container, in the *knowledge-plausible* condition they were told that the violin was moved to the red container and in the *knowledge-implausible* condition they were told that the violin was moved to the purple container. Participants in all conditions were then told that Denise rearranged the room such that the containers were swapped around (see Figure 5.5). Importantly, the red container was moved to the original location of the blue container, so we might expect Vicki to look in either the blue container or the red container on her return. The participants were then asked what the chances (expressed as a percentage) were that Vicki will look first in each of the containers. Participants in the *knowledge-plausible* condition assigned a higher probability (34 per cent) to the red container than participants in the *ignorance* condition (23 per cent), and a lower probability to the blue container (59 per cent vs 71 per cent).

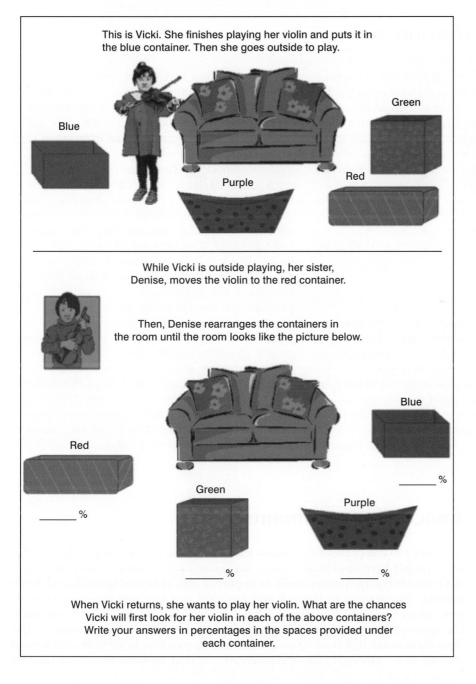

Figure 5.5

The knowledge-plausible condition in Birch and Bloom's study.

Source: Birch, S. A. J., & Bloom, P., *Psychological Science*, *18*(5), pp. 382–386, copyright © 2007 by SAGE publications. Reprinted by Permission of SAGE Publications.

This shows that participants' own knowledge of the true location of the violin affected their judgements of Vicki's false belief. However, participants in the *knowledge-implausible* condition gave similar answers to those in the *ignorance* condition (mean probability of 73 per cent for the blue container). Although these participants also had knowledge of the location of the violin, the purple container was not a plausible place for Vicki to look. Birch and Bloom argue that this shows that the bias adults have as a result of their knowledge is mediated by their perception of the plausibility of an explanation for Vicki to look in the true location.

Box 5.1 An adult false belief task

The following information is based on a study by Mitchell *et al.* (1996). There is a kitchen with a jug in it. Sometimes the jug has orange juice in it and sometimes it has milk in it. Kevin stood on a chair and looked into a jug on a shelf. He saw there was orange juice in the jug. Kevin then left the room. While Kevin was out of the room, Rebecca entered the room, poured out the orange juice and replaced it with milk. Kevin returned to the room with Rebecca, who announced to Kevin that there was milk in the jug.

What does Kevin think is in the jug? Choose an answer:

Orange juice
Milk

If you chose orange juice, it is likely that you think Kevin will believe the evidence of his own senses rather than information supplied by Rebecca. If you chose milk, it is likely that you think that Kevin will believe Rebecca's statement, rather than the evidence of his own senses. In reality, there is no way of judging whether Kevin will believe what he saw with his own eyes some time ago or whether he will believe what Rebecca

told him. All other things being equal, we could argue that he would believe what he saw rather than what he was told. However it is also possible that, all other things being equal, we could say he would believe the most recent information in preference to earlier information. When Mitchell *et al.* carried out this study, they found that adults were more likely to judge that Kevin would believe Rebecca if they themselves had been told that Rebecca's statement was true – as you were told. If they had been told that Rebecca's statement was false, they were less likely to judge that Kevin would believe Rebecca. Mitchell *et al.* argue that under these conditions when there's no right or wrong answer it may be possible for participants' own beliefs to distort their judgement of what Kevin would believe. So, in certain circumstances, we can observe a false belief task 'failure' in adults whereby they allow their privileged knowledge of reality to contaminate their judgement of someone's belief. Does this mean that adults have no theory of mind? Obviously not. Therefore, we shouldn't conclude that children who can be manipulated to fail false belief tasks have no theory of mind either.

Concluding comments

The ability to comprehend that minds are a fundamental aspect of people, and that other people have knowledge, beliefs, desires and perceptions, which may or may not resemble reality, is undoubtedly an important part of human psychological development. The quantity of research into this topic that has been generated over the past twenty-five years is enormous. However, there is still much debate concerning the nature of the changes that take place in the pre-school years. It is reasonably clear from the research that children do not consistently pass false belief tasks until around the age of 4. Although task manipulations can lead to some success in younger children, there are still 3-year-olds who do not pass these modified tasks, and the manipulations that hinder performance in older children and adults are probably placing a greater demand on memory and inhibitory processes, rather than revealing deficits in mentalizing competence. What is less clear, however, is the relationship between theory of mind and early social cognitive skills, such as joint attention, pretence, deception and the understanding of emotions, desires and perceptions.

A number of theories have been put forward to explain the developmental shift observed in experimental studies. All make the prediction that children will be able to pass false belief tasks around the age of 4, but for different reasons. Some very clever studies have been designed in order to test the theories along their lines of difference, but at present all are still contenders. Doherty (2009) points out that it is not necessarily the case that one theory has to emerge victorious; it may be that simulation enables us to understand emotion, whereas a succession of concepts, developed within a specialized neural module, may be required to understand belief.

Although the experimental path has been well trodden, it is possible that developments in cognitive neuroscience will allow the issues surrounding the development of theory of mind to be addressed. A number of neural structures have been shown to play a role in mentalizing. The medial prefrontal cortex (MPFC), right temporo-parietal junction (rTPJ) and posterior cingulate cortex (PC) are associated with understanding mental states in the self and in others in adults (Frith and Frith, 2003; Perner *et al.*, 2006; Sommer *et al.*, 2007). Recent studies have confirmed that these same cortical regions are recruited in child samples (Sabbagh *et al.*, 2009; Saxe *et al.*, 2009). However, it is not clear how these brain mechanisms develop in young children with respect to their mentalizing abilities. This is largely due to the fact that there are practical limitations to conducting neuroimaging studies with young children. Therefore, the knowledge we do have does not, at present, tell us which theory of the development of theory of mind is most likely to be correct, although it has been argued that the evidence does not support a domain-specific modular view (Apperly, Samson and Humphreys, 2005; Saxe *et al.*, 2009). On the other hand, the modular view is given support by research on children with autism, the vast majority of whom do not develop the ability to pass false belief tasks at the age of 4. We will look at this evidence in Chapter 10.

Summary

Theory of mind. Theory of mind is our everyday understanding of mental states. The ability to understand that other people can have beliefs that differ from our own is often seen as a critical aspect of theory of mind. One of the classic experimental tests of false belief is the unexpected transfer task, in which an object is moved from one location to another without the knowledge of the story character who placed the object in its initial location. The general finding is that children are not consistently able to understand that the character has a false belief about the location of the object until around 4 years of age.

Theories of theory of mind. Several theoretical perspectives have been proposed to account for the development of theory of mind. These accounts can be broadly split into domain-general theories and domain-specific theories. According to representational mind theory, younger children have not acquired the concept of metarepresentation; theory of mind cannot be acquired until there is a radical shift in thought processes. The representational mind theory offers a universal, domain-general, discontinuous account of the development of theory of mind. Support for this position comes from studies in which the deceptive box and appearance-reality tasks are used. Evidence from cross-cultural research shows that children all round the world demonstrate a shift in ability to pass fail belief tasks at around 4 to 5 years of age. Theory theory posits series of domain-specific conceptual changes in the development of theory of mind. Two-year-olds have a basic understanding of perception and desires, 3-year-olds have a more sophisticated belief-desire psychology and 4- to 5-year-olds develop a representational understanding of beliefs which enables them to pass false belief tasks. Simulation theory is the theory that, rather than experiencing changes in concepts and understanding, the ability to pass false belief tasks comes from increasing imaginative flexibility. Two and 3-year-olds can imagine having different wants and desires from their own, whereas 4-year-olds can simulate holding a belief that is different from their own. According to modularity theory, there is a domain specific, innate theory of mind module (ToMM). This mental module interprets people's behaviour and produces representations of their beliefs and desires. The ToMM matures at around 18 months old, but young children are not able to pass false belief tasks as they have an immature selection processor, a device which eventually allows them to inhibit their own beliefs.

Do false belief tasks underestimate children's abilities? Many researchers have argued that a reliance on traditional false belief tasks distorts our view of children's abilities. One argument is that the linguistic demands of these tasks are too high, and studies have shown that by altering the wording of the task, or allowing children a greater opportunity to comprehend the story, more 3-year-old children pass. However, other studies have failed to replicate these findings. It has also been proposed that the children fail false belief tasks because of a tendency to favour reality over belief or because they don't understand the relationship between seeing an event and holding a belief as a result.

Evidence for earlier abilities. Several studies have used direction and duration of gaze to measure young children's implicit understanding of belief, with the general finding that children look at the location which corresponds to the protagonist's false belief at an earlier age to that at which they can verbalize the false belief, possibly even in infancy. A number of other early social behaviours may also be related to theory of mind. Joint attention in infancy, and disputes, jokes and prosocial behaviour in early childhood, are arguably precursors of theory of mind. It has been suggested that the ability to deceive and pretend play require children to mentalize, but studies show that young children do not have a full understanding of what other people are thinking when they engage in deception or pretend play.

Meta-analysis of false belief tasks. As a result of the many criticisms of false belief tasks and claims for earlier development, Wellman, Cross and Watson (2001) carried out a meta-analysis of 77 published studies. They found six variables which affected the age at which children were able to pass false belief tasks: deception as the motive for change, participation in the transformation, absence of the target object, an explicit statement of the protagonist's belief, country and temporal marking. However, the basic developmental trend was still observed; children aged 4 and over performed above chance, whereas children aged 3 years 5 months and younger performed below chance.

Evidence for later development. Although children can pass basic false belief tasks around the age of 4, there is some evidence that theory of mind abilities continue to develop and are not completely reliable even in adulthood. Children do not pass second-order false belief tasks (John thinks that Mary thinks . . .) until the age of 7 or older. The performance of older children and adults can be affected by manipulating the task, demonstrating that even though they have a theory of mind, their judgements can be swayed by their true beliefs.

Discussion questions

1 Are false belief tasks a good way of testing for the presence of a theory of mind? If not, why not?

2 Is the development of theory of mind stage-like or continuous?

3 Which theory of the development of theory of mind do you think best accounts for the available data? Are there any data that this theory cannot explain?

4 If the development of theory of mind is universal (i.e., the same across cultures), does this mean that theory of mind is innate?

5 What might future cognitive neuroscientific studies reveal about the nature of theory of mind?

Further Reading

Books and chapters

Doherty, M. J. (2009). *Theory of mind*. Hove: Psychology Press.

Martin Doherty presents 25 years of theory of mind research in this book. As well as discussing false belief tasks and theories of theory of mind, he covers pretence, visual attention, executive functions and language.

Mitchell, P. (1997). *Introduction to theory of mind*. London: Arnold.

Peter Mitchell's book, although over a decade old, offers a clear and easy-to-read account of some of the key ideas in the field, in addition to discussing autism and offering an evolutionary perspective on the development of theory of mind.

Sodian, B. (2005). Theory of mind – the case for conceptual development. In W. Schneider, R. Schumann-Hengsteler and B. Sodian (Eds), *Young children's cognitive development* (pp. 95–130). Mahwah, NJ: Lawrence Erlbaum Associates.

Beate Sodian gives an up-to-date and succinct account of the research and theoretical issues in theory of mind.

Articles

Callaghan, T., Rochat, P., Lillard, A., Claux, M. L., Odden, H., Itakura, S., Tapanya, S. and Singh, S. (2005). Synchrony in the onset of mental-state reasoning – Evidence from five cultures. *Psychological Science*, 16(5), 378–384.

Callaghan *et al.* describe an impressive study, in which they gave a false belief task to 3- to 5-year-old children from Canada, India, Peru, Samoa and Thailand. They found similar results in all five cultures and discuss the implications of this finding.

Gopnik, A. and Astington, J. W. (1988). Children's understanding of representational change and its relation to the understanding of false belief and the appearance-reality distinction. *Child Development*, 59(1), 26–37.

In this classic study, Gopnik and Astington compare performance on the deceptive box task with several appearance-reality tasks.

Wellman, H. M., Cross, D. and Watson, J. (2001). Meta-analysis of theory-of-mind development: The truth about false belief. *Child Development*, 72(3), 655–684.

In one of the most important theory of mind articles, Wellman *et al.* demonstrate which factors have an effect on false belief task performance.

Scholl, B. J. and Leslie, A. M. (2001). Minds, modules and meta-analysis. *Child Development*, 72(3), 696–701.

Wellman, H. M. and Cross, D. (2001). Theory of mind and conceptual change. *Child Development*, 72(3), 702–707.

These two articles feature a debate between the modularity theory and theory theory camps, following on from Wellman *et al.*'s (2001) meta-analysis.

Chapter 6
Reasoning

Learning Outcomes

At the end of this chapter you should be able to:

- Define deductive and analogical reasoning.

- Describe and evaluate theories of deductive reasoning.

- Discuss research on the development of deductive reasoning.

- Describe and evaluate theories of analogical reasoning.

- Discuss research on the development of analogical reasoning in infancy.

One of most heavily used tasks in reasoning research is Wason's (1966) selection task. It has appeared in many forms and been used for a variety of purposes.

In this task, participants are told that there is a deck of cards, and on each card there is a letter on one side and a number on the other. Participants are then shown four cards, such as those in Figure 6.1 and told that two of the cards are presented with the letter side up and two with the number side up. They are then told the following rule:

If a card has a vowel on one side then it has an even number on the other side.

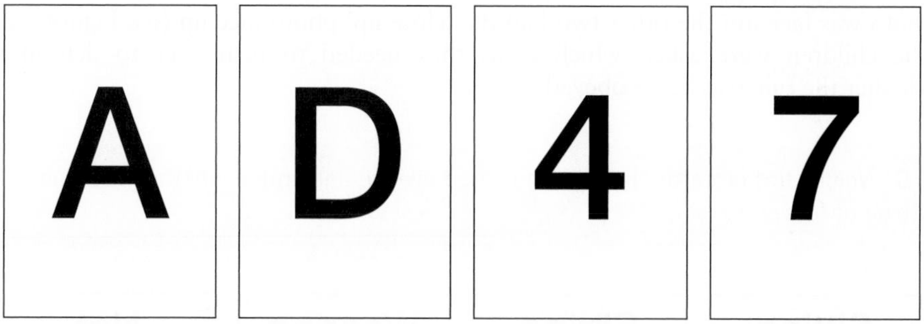

Figure 6.1

Wason's selection task.

Q. Before reading on, select which card or cards need to be turned over to determine whether the rule is true or false.

Note that the four cards are a vowel, a consonant, an even number and an odd number. To solve this task, participants must appreciate that the rule would be false if a vowel was paired with an odd number, and that it is logically necessary to choose cards which could reveal the falsifying combination. The correct answer, therefore, is to choose the vowel (*A*) and the odd number (*7*) as this is the only choice that can falsify the rule. If there is an odd number on the reverse of the vowel, or a vowel on the reverse of the odd number, then the rule is falsified. Wason and Johnson-Laird's (1972) review of studies using the selection task had rather surprising results. Fewer than 10 per cent of adult participants gave the correct answer, so don't feel too bad if you didn't pick the correct cards! The most common response patterns are for participants to select either *A* alone or *A* and *4*, even though both selection patterns are logically incorrect. Many adults find it hard to understand why picking the *7* is necessary and why it is not necessary to turn the *4* card over. Even when Wason convinced people to turn over the odd number, and showed them a vowel on the other side (thus showing that the rule was falsified), they still said that it was not necessary to select this card (Evans and Newstead, 1995). Regarding the *4*, think about what it would tell you if you were to turn it over. Regardless of whether there is a vowel or a consonant on the other side, the rule is not being falsified. The rule states that if there is a vowel on one side then there is an even number on the other side, it does not say that consonants cannot also have an even number on the other side.

Since it was created, the Wason selection task has been modified in many ways. One of these modified tasks was conducted on a sample of 160 French children by Vittorio Girotto, Michael Gilly, Agnes Blaye and Paul Light (1989). Half of the participants were aged 10 to 11, and the other half were 14- to 15-year-olds. Children were assigned to one of four different problem types (two of which will be discussed later in the chapter). One of these was the standard selection task, as presented above. In another, they were given the rule 'If one is sitting in the front of a car, then one must wear a seatbelt'. The participants were asked to imagine that they were policemen whose job it was to check whether road safety rules were being obeyed. They were then told that policemen used a concealed camera to take two photographs of each car. The first photo is taken at a distance and can be used to see whether a person is sitting in the front or the back. The second is taken close-up; this photo reveals whether the person is wearing a seatbelt or not. They were then presented with four cards, each of which had a 'distance' photo on one side and a 'close-up' photo on the other. Two cards were placed so that the 'distance' photo was face up; the other two had the 'close-up' photo face up (see Figure 6.2). The children were asked which cards they needed to turn over to determine whether the rule was being obeyed.

Q. Which card or cards need to be turned over to determine whether the rule is true or false?

Figure 6.2
Girotto *et al.*'s (1989) modified selection task.

Sitting in the front	Sitting in the back	Wearing a seat-belt	Not wearing a seat-belt

As with the standard version, the correct answer is to select the first and last cards. The 'sitting in the front' card needs to be selected, as a picture of someone not wearing a seatbelt on the back would falsify the rule. The 'not wearing a seat-belt' card needs to be examined as a photo of someone sitting in the front would falsify the rule. The second card does not need to be turned over as it doesn't matter if someone sitting in the back is wearing a seatbelt or not. The third card depicts someone wearing a seatbelt, so regardless of whether they are in the front or the back, they are not breaking the rule. Girotto *et al.* found that in the standard version of the task (letters and numbers), the children performed very poorly. None of the twenty 10- to 11-year-olds assigned to this condition selected the correct response, and only three of the twenty older children got it right. However, in the 'seat-belt' task, 80 per cent of the younger children and 85 per cent of the older children selected the correct cards.

Q. Why do you think the participants in Girotto *et al.*'s study were able to pass the modified version of the task so easily when children and adults perform so poorly on the standard version?

Some suggested answers to this question will be revealed later on in the chapter.

Types of reasoning

From the examples above, it is clear that something about Girotto *et al.*'s modified version of the selection task made it easier than the standard version. Hopefully you have thought of some ideas based on the differences between the tasks. One is more 'linguistic' than the other, it has more meaning for participants, it is more familiar. In looking at these two examples and trying to formulate a general rule as to why one task is easier, you are engaging in inductive reasoning. Induction involves drawing inferences from specific examples and trying to generalize them or apply them to other situations, such as in analogies. In contrast, participants on the selection task are engaging in deductive reasoning. Whereas induction involves making generalizations from specific examples, deduction involves the opposite. Given the general premise 'if one is sitting in the front of a car, then one must wear a seatbelt', participants have to reason about the more specific examples they are presented with in the selection task. The other main difference between deductive and inductive reasoning is that deduction leads to one logically valid conclusion, whereas inductive inferences are not logically valid. This is because, in situations in which we use inductive reasoning, we can never have conclusive proof of a conclusion, although it can be strongly supported by the evidence. This is not, however, to say that induction is not an incredibly useful way of reasoning. When you use inductive reasoning to try to generate a hypothesis as to why children found the 'seat-belt' version of the selection task easier, you are doing what scientists have been doing for centuries: making observations and attempting to account for those observations with a more general explanation. Scientific reasoning is covered in Chapter 7, so it will not be discussed here. Instead, we will focus on one type of inductive reasoning: analogy.

inductive reasoning
Reasoning in which inferences are drawn from specific examples and generalized, or applied to other situations, such as in analogies.

deductive reasoning
Reasoning in which a specific, logically valid, conclusion can be drawn from more general premises.

Theories of deductive reasoning

Piaget's theory of logical development

Logical reasoning is central to Piaget's theory of cognitive development. The developing child is seen as gradually and progressively re-structuring the logical structures of the mind, the endpoint of which is the attainment of full logical competence during adolescence (Inhelder and Piaget, 1958, 1964). Piaget's stage theory is primarily a theory of the development of logical capabilities. In the sensory-motor period a child's knowledge is action-based and dependent upon physical interaction with the world. An infant's initial knowledge is derived through reflexes such as sucking and grasping as well as perceptual processing. Subsequently, the child makes trial-and-error explorations of the world, which are a basic form of hypothesis-testing behaviour, such as dropping an object in different ways to see what happens. By acting upon the world, the child builds a logical framework for the development of reasoning. In the pre-operational stage, this action-based knowledge is organized into representation-based or symbolic knowledge. However, the child's use of this symbolic or internalized knowledge is limited. The child does not relate separate patterns of action to one another. For example, adults and older children understand that actions are reversible, whereas pre-operational children do not. This is demonstrated by Piaget's conservation and class inclusion tasks (Inhelder and Piaget, 1964; see Chapter 1) and Piaget's studies on transitivity, discussed later in this chapter. In the concrete operational stage, children develop the ability to mentally reverse actions and begin to understand the relationships between different patterns of action. Their representational systems start to be organized according to logical groupings or concrete operations, such as transitivity, class inclusion and conservation. An understanding of transitivity means that the child understands that transitive relations hold between entities that can be organized in an ordinal series. An understanding of class inclusion means the child knows that a set of items can simultaneously be part of a combined set and embedded set. Knowledge of conservation is the knowledge that quantity is conserved across changes in appearance.

Although children in the concrete operational stage can pass the tasks mentioned above, their operations are restricted to concrete objects and events. Their logical understanding only extends as far as reversing specific physical actions. The child is unable to represent logical relationships in abstract form or think about hypothetical ideas. Cognitive change beyond the stage of concrete operations depends on the ability to take the results of concrete operations and to generate hypotheses about their logical relationships. This was described by Piaget as 'operating upon operations' or 'second-order reasoning', and enables children to derive predictions from such hypotheses which can then be tested empirically. Inhelder and Piaget's (1958) pendulum task (see Chapter 7) illustrates these principles. With respect to deductive reasoning tasks, such as the selection task, Piaget's theory predicts that children will acquire the necessary logical competence during the formal operations stage. More specifically, Inhelder and Piaget claimed that children acquire an ensemble of rules of deductive inference, which are described later in this chapter. As a result of possessing these rules, adults should perform very well on these tasks, and children under the ages of 11 or 12 should find them very difficult. As we saw above, the story is more complicated than that.

Mental models

mental models Mental representations of the premises of a reasoning problem, which can be used to test whether conclusions are valid.

An alternative to Piaget's idea that we develop a mental logic with which we can reason deductively, is the idea that we construct **mental models**. According to Johnson-Laird (1983, 2004), in order to solve problems we construct mental representations of the possibilities described in the premises. Mental models may be likened to mental images, or they may be more abstract. When given the rule, 'if a card has a vowel on one side then it has an even number on the other side', we may visualize a playing card, or we might imagine two overlapping circles, representing vowels and even numbers. Having constructed a model, we then use it to propose tentative conclusions. In order to determine whether our conclusions are valid, we attempt to formulate further mental models based on the premises. If the conclusion doesn't hold true in these alternative models, we reject it and look for another conclusion that is true in all models. We encode the information that is explicitly stated in a problem into our mental models, so a mental model for the standard selection task may just contain one card which has a vowel on one side and an even number on the other (Johnson-Laird and Byrne, 1991) (the square brackets indicate that this should be true for *all* vowels):

[Vowel] = Even number

From this, we would conclude that it is necessary to look at any cards with vowels and maybe cards with even numbers as well, to check whether the rule is falsified. This, as described above, is what many adults do when presented with this task. But it is, of course, an incorrect solution. What is missing from the above model is the implicit information that consonants can be paired with either odd or even numbers, and an explicit representation of the vowel/odd number combination that is not allowed. We can, therefore, construct an alternative model of the premises that include all this information. The following model contains a card with a vowel on one side and an even number on the other, a card with an even number on one side that can have either a vowel or a consonant on the other side, and a card that has a vowel on one side and doesn't have an odd number on the other side ('¬' means negation):

[Vowel] = Even number

= Even number

[Vowel] = ¬Odd number

From this model, we can draw the conclusion that it is necessary to check the card with a vowel to confirm that there isn't an odd number on the other side, and the card with an odd number to confirm that there isn't a vowel on the other side. Johnson-Laird and Byrne can, therefore, explain the common adult error on the selection task. They predict that, if the task is structured so as to induce people to construct alternative models, people will have a higher degree of success. Some examples of variants of the selection task which facilitate success are discussed later in the chapter.

> Q. What is your mental model for Girotto *et al.*'s seatbelt problem?

Markovits (2000, 2004; Markovits and Barrouillet, 2002) argues that Johnson-Laird's theory, which is largely a theory of adult reasoning, relies on quite complicated cognitive processes, so he formulated a developmental theory of mental models to account for children's reasoning abilities. In this account, it is assumed that children have greater information-processing limitations than adults. As a result of a smaller working memory capacity, younger children are not able to construct and hold as many models as older children. Furthermore, younger children's memory retrieval is less efficient than older children's which may lead to reduced access to previously stored information. Markovits also suggests that younger children have greater difficulty in inhibiting irrelevant information and, because they have a smaller knowledge base, they will be unable to easily generate alternative models for a wide variety of problems. As a result, reasoning with premises that have familiar content should be easier than reasoning with abstract or unfamiliar premises. This account could, therefore, explain why children in Girotto *et al.*'s (1989) study found the seatbelt task much easier than the standard selection task.

Deductive reasoning

Syllogisms

A syllogism is the simplest form of deductive reasoning, dating back to Aristotle, who described it in his *Prior Analytics* (written around 350 BC) as a 'discourse in which, certain things being stated, something other than what is stated follows of necessity from their being so'. I mean by the last phrase that they produce the consequence, and by this, that no further term is required from without in order to make the consequence necessary' (*Prior Analytics*, I.2, 24b18–20). What he meant by this is that syllogisms consist of (usually) two premises from which just one logical conclusion can be drawn, without the need for any further information. Here is an example:

Premise 1: O'Grady is a cat
Premise 2: All cats like fish
Conclusion: O'Grady likes fish

This is the easiest form of syllogism to solve, and can be rewritten without the specific content as:

All A are B
All B are C
All A are C

Table 6.1	A–B		B–A		A–B		B–A
	B–C		C–B		C–B		B–C

Four figures of the syllogism.

There are four types of premise, referred to as moods, labelled A, I, E and O:

A: All A are B
I: Some A are B
E: No A are B
O: Some A are not B

There are also four different configurations of the two premises, know as figures (Johnson-Laird, 1983). These are shown in Table 6.1. In each figure, the conclusion should describe the logical relationship between A and C. Because the two premises and the conclusion can each be in any one of the four moods, and the syllogism as a whole can be in any one of the four figures, there are 256 possible syllogisms ($4 \times 4 \times 4 \times 4$). Of these, most are invalid in the sense that no conclusion follows logically from the premises. Although the example presented above is quite easy to solve, some of the other valid combinations are harder. For example, try to deduce the conclusion to the following syllogisms:

No Beekeepers are Artists
Some Chemists are Beekeepers

Some Artists are not Beekeepers
All Chemists are Beekeepers

In both cases, the valid conclusion is 'Some Artists are not Chemists'. Many adults find most syllogisms to be very difficult (Johnson-Laird and Bara, 1984), and various factors have been shown to have an effect on success at solving syllogisms and judging the validity of given conclusions. According to the atmosphere hypothesis (Woodworth and Sells, 1935), negative premises (no A are B; some A are not B) lead to people accepting negative conclusions, whereas positive premises (all A are B; some A are B) lead to the acceptance of positive conclusions. People also demonstrate belief bias, whereby they are more likely to accept the conclusion if it is true or consistent with their beliefs, even if it is logically invalid (de Neys and

Van Gelder, 2009; Evans, Barston and Pollard, 1983; Evans and Feeney, 2004). A further mediator is familiarity with the content of problems. Luria (1976), in a study with villagers from Uzbekistan, found they performed more poorly on syllogisms about snow, with which they had no experience. Scribner (1975, 1977) also found a role for experience and familiarity, which she termed the 'empirical bias'. This bias has also been found in children. Hawkins *et al.* (1984) gave 4- and 5-year-olds syllogisms with familiar, unfamiliar and fantasy content. They found that the participants did not do as well on the unfamiliar problems as the familiar and fantasy problems. These findings are problematic for a Piagetian account of deductive reasoning as, according to this view, adults should possess full logical competence, and young children should have difficulty with syllogistic reasoning, regardless of content.

Following on from Hawkins *et al.*'s study, Dias and Harris (1988) wanted to find out whether young children's ability to reason with familiar and fantasy content could be extended to problems with content that runs counter to their knowledge. They gave forty-eight 5- and 6-year-olds three types of syllogism: *known facts* problems that were consistent with participants' knowledge; *unknown facts* problems that were outside the participants' experience; and *contrary facts* problems which were inconsistent with their knowledge. The problems were phrased so that the participants just had to answer 'yes' or 'no' when asked whether the conclusion was correct. There were eight problems of each type, four of which had 'yes' as the correct answer, and four with 'no' as the correct answer. The experimenters also used probe questions to test whether their assumptions about children's knowledge and beliefs were correct. Examples of their syllogisms and probe questions are shown in Table 6.2. Participants were subdivided into a *verbal* group and a *play* group, with 24 children in each. Children in the *verbal* group were read the problems, whereas children in the *play* group acted out the syllogisms with toys. Eight of the children in each group (four 5-year-olds and four 6-year-olds) were given the *known facts* problems, eight were given the *unknown facts* problems, and eight were given the *contrary facts* problems. Dias and Harris found an interaction between group and type of fact; although children in both groups answered the *known facts* problems correctly, the children in the play group produced more correct replies for the *unknown* and *contrary facts* problems. In another experiment, they compared the performance of thirty-two 4-year-olds with that of thirty-two 6-year-olds on the contrary facts problems. In this experiment the children were again split into two groups, but this time there were no toys in the play condition. Instead, the experimenter presented the problems in a fantasy context, explaining that what the children were being told was happening on another planet. The results revealed two main effects: age and group. The 4-year-olds got fewer answers correct than the 6-year-olds, but participants of both ages performed better in the play condition. The younger children in the verbal group got an average of 18 per cent of the answers correct, whereas the younger children in the play group averaged 54 per cent correct answers. In a later study, Dias and Harris (1990) explored three different types of fantasy, or make-believe, contexts. They allocated their participants to groups in which one, two, all three, or none of the following manipulations were made: (1) children were told to use their imagination to mentally visualize the contrary facts; (2) the contrary facts were presented as occurring on another planet; (3) the experimenter adopted a dramatic tone of voice when describing the problems, to imply that the stories were unusual. The results showed that any of these three cues led to improved performance, suggesting that children as young as 4 can judge the logical validity of syllogisms with contrary-to-fact conclusion as long as the syllogisms are presented in a fantasy context.

The syllogisms given to children in the studies reported so far have all been of one figure (A–B, B–C ⇒ A–C) and one mood (all A are B). Johnson-Laird, Oakhill and Bull (1986) gave twenty 9- to 10-year-olds and twenty 11- to 12-year-olds twenty syllogisms, five of each of the four figures, to solve. The problems were designed such that the content would be familiar to the children, using footballers, musicians and runners in the premises, and so that no obvious plausible conclusion could be drawn. An example, with the B–A, B–C figure and I and A moods, is:

Some of the footballers are musicians
All of the footballers are runners

Table 6.2	Syllogisms used in Dias and Harris' study.

'Yes' answers	'No' answers
Known fact problem:	
All cats miaow Rex is a cat Does Rex miaow? (Probe question: What noise do cats make?)	All fishes live in water Tot is a fish Does Tot live in a tree? (Probe question: Where do fishes live?)
Unknown fact problem:	
All hyenas laugh Rex is a hyena Does Rex laugh? (Probe question: What noise do hyenas make?)	All molluscs live in shells Tot is a mollusc Does Tot live in a tree? (Probe question: Where do molluscs live?)
Contrary fact problem:	
All cats bark Rex is a cat Does Rex bark? (Probe question: What noise do cats make?)	All fishes live in trees Tot is a fish Does Tot live in water? (Probe question: Where do fishes live?)

Source: Dias and Harris (1988), reproduced with permission.

According to mental models theory, the difficulty of the syllogism is a function of the difficulty of constructing a mental model, which depends on the figure of the syllogism, and the number of mental models that it is necessary to construct in order to solve the problem. Box 6.1 contains a fairly simple explanation of how mental models are constructed for syllogisms. For each figure, Johnson-Laird *et al.* constructed some one-model and three-model syllogisms with valid conclusions, and a two-model syllogism with no valid conclusion. None of the participants were able to solve the three-model problems, but they demonstrated some competence on the two-model problems. The 9- to 10-year-olds got 38 per cent correct and the 10- to 11-year-olds got 35 per cent correct. They were much better at solving the one-model problems (see Figure 6.3) and, as predicted by the theory, there was an effect of figure. Bara, Bucciarelli and Johnson-Laird (1995) took this finding even further, demonstrating that, in a sample of twenty 7-year-olds, fourteen of the participants were able to draw correct conclusions to simple one-model problems 43 per cent of the time, and gave correct responses to problems with no valid conclusion 45 per cent of the time.

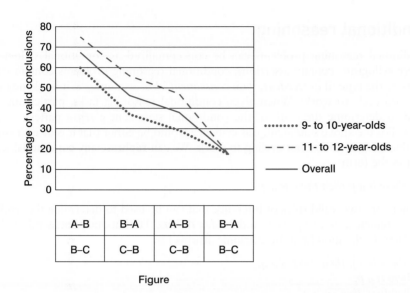

Figure 6.3

Percentage of valid conclusions to one-model problems as a function of figure.

Box 6.1 Mental models of syllogisms

When presented with a syllogism, people first construct a model, which can be conceived of as imagining a scenario in which the premises are true. They then use this model to see if they can arrive at a conclusion. Finally, they test the validity of the conclusion by trying to construct alternate models of the premises in which the conclusion is falsified. Johnson-Laird *et al.* (1986) give the following examples of how syllogisms are solved using mental models:

All Artists are Beekeepers
All Beekeepers are Chemists

A reasoner might construct an initial model, in which she imagines two artists who are beekeepers and also chemists, a third person, who is a chemist but may or may not be a beekeeper and a fourth – a chemist – who may or may not exist ('may or may not' is denoted by a 'o'):

Artist = Beekeeper = Chemist
Artist = Beekeeper = Chemist
  oBeekeeper = Chemist
      oChemist

In this case, there are no other models of the premises which can be constructed, so our rea-

soner is free to draw the conclusion suggested by this model, 'All artists are chemists'.

Other problems require two or more models to be constructed.

Some of the Artists are Beekeepers
Some of the Beekeepers are Chemists

A reasoner might construct an initial model, in which she imagines two artists who are beekeepers and also chemists, and an additional third person, who may or may not be an artist, a beekeeper, or a chemist:

Artist = Beekeeper = Chemist
Artist = Beekeeper = Chemist
oArtist oBeekeeper oChemist

This model suggests the conclusion, 'Some of the Artists are Chemists'. However, the creation of a second model refutes this conclusion and shows that there is, in fact, no valid answer to this syllogism (because some, or all, of the artists may, or may not, be chemists):

Artist = Beekeeper
Artist = Beekeeper oChemist
oArtist   Beekeeper = Chemist
           Beekeeper = Chemist

Conditional reasoning

Conditional reasoning problems can be conceptualized as conditional syllogisms. Where syllogisms contain assertions, conditional reasoning problems contain statements of the type 'if *antecedent*, then *consequent*.' For example, 'if it is a sunny day, then you cycle to work'. When given conditional reasoning tasks, participants are asked to determine the truth of the conditional statement given a pattern of evidence. For the above statement, this evidence would be either that it is or isn't sunny and that you are or are not cycling to work. We can rephrase any conditional statement in the form:

If there is a p then there is a q

There are two valid rules of inference that can be used to determine the truth of such statements, *modus ponens* and *modus tollens*. The modus ponens rule (which translates as 'the mood that by affirming affirms') is:

If there is a p then there is a q,
There is a p,
Therefore, there is a q.

A simple rule of inference such as *modus ponens* allows one to deduce the logically valid conclusion **q** from the conditional statement 'if there is a **p** then there is a **q**' together with the premise 'there is a **p**'. For example, when we take the conditional statement 'if it is a sunny day, then you cycle to work', together with the premise 'it is sunny', we can come to the conclusion 'you cycle to work'. Another simple rule, *modus tollens,* allows one to deduce the logically valid conclusion 'not **p**' when given the conditional statement plus the information that 'there is not a **q**'. The *modus tollens* rule (which translates as 'the mood that by denying denies') is:

If there is a p then there is a q,
There is not a q,
Therefore, there is not a p.

To continue with the cycling example, we can use this rule to deduce that if you are not cycling to work, then it is not sunny. These two rules of inference constitute the fundamental aspect of formal operational competence that Piaget viewed as characterizing adult thinking. There are also two other principles people use, both of which are logical fallacies. First, the *denial of the antecedent*:

If there is a p then there is a q,
There is not a p,
Therefore, there is not a q.

The cycling example demonstrates that this leads to an error, namely the conclusion that, as it is not sunny, you are not cycling to work. This may appear to make sense, but the conditional rule – 'if it is a sunny day, then you cycle to work' – says nothing about not cycling to work on days that aren't sunny. The second fallacy is the *affirmation of the consequent*:

If there is a p then there is a q,
There is a q,
Therefore, there is a p.

The error here is that this way of thinking allows one to draw the invalid conclusion that it is sunny, given the premise that you are cycling to work. Again, this is not covered by the conditional rule.

The Wason selection task. We can think of the four cards in the Wason selection task as mapping onto the **p** and **q** of the rules of inference. 'If there is a vowel on one side of the card, then there is an even number on the other side of the card' can be rephrased as 'if there is a **p**, then there is a **q**'. So, the *A* card corresponds to **p** and the *4* card corresponds to **q**. We can call the *D* card **not-p** (written as ¬**p**) and the *7* card **not-q** (written as ¬**q**). *Modus ponens* should lead to people selecting the **p** card as one that is necessary to turn over to discover the truth of the rule. Generally, people do select the **p** card (*A* in this case). However, if people are able to use the *modus tollens* rule of inference, then they should have no problem selecting the ¬**q** card (*7* in this case), since the choice of the ¬**q** card follows easily from the application of this rule: There is not a **q** (even number), therefore there should not be a **p** (a vowel on the other side). According to the Piagetian view, children acquire an ensemble of rules of deductive inference which allow them to reason independently of any specific contents or contexts during adolescence. If this is the case, then we would expect adults to perform very well on tests of logical reasoning. However, as we saw at the beginning of the chapter, very few adults correctly select both the **p** and ¬**q** cards. There are two ways of interpreting this logical failure in adults. Either reasoning with this task reflects a sophisticated stage of formal operational thought that adults haven't yet achieved, or adults haven't yet reached the stage of formal operations advanced under Piaget's theory. Neither of these seems plausible and matters are further complicated by evidence that under suitable circumstances adults are able to solve the selection task.

There have been many variants of the selection task. Some of these retained the 'abstract' nature of the original task, using letters and numbers, but changed the wording of the rules in order to clarify the implication of the conditional statement (Hoch and Tschirgi, 1985; Kroger, Cheng and Holyoak, 1993; Platt and Griggs, 1993). Most of the subsequent research, however, involves *thematic* versions of the task (Cheng and Holyoak, 1985; D'Andrade, 1982; Griggs and Cox, 1982; Johnson-Laird, Legrenzi and Legrenzi, 1972; Wason and Shapiro, 1971). Johnson-Laird *et al.* asked their participants to imagine they were postal worker sorting letters who had to check whether the following rule was being obeyed: 'If a letter is sealed then it has a 50 lire stamp on it'. They were told that some of the envelopes were sealed and some were not sealed and that if a letter was lying face up, they could not see whether it was sealed or not (see Figure 6.4). Participants were then asked to indicate the card or cards that need to be turned over to determine whether the rule was being obeyed. When Johnson-Laird *et al.* carried out this experiment with British participants, they found that this thematic version of the selection task facilitated performance: 39/48 participants (81 per cent) gave the correct answer. Interestingly, the participants were familiar with the now defunct postal rule which required higher value postage stamps on sealed letters.

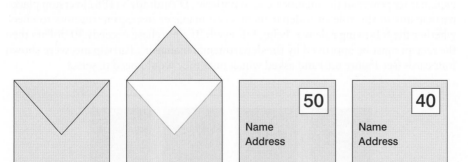

Figure 6.4

The postal rule problem.

Griggs and Cox (1982) attempted a replication of this study with 24 undergraduate students at the University of Florida. They presented the students with two slightly different versions of Johnson-Laird *et al.*'s task alongside two abstract versions of the task. The rules for the four tasks were:

If a letter is sealed, it has a 15 cent stamp on it.
A letter is sealed only if it has a 3 peso stamp on it.
If a letter has an A on one side, then it has a 3 on the other side.
A letter has a D on one side only if it has a 5 on the other side.

They failed to get the facilitation; participants were only correct on five of the 48 thematic problems given to them (two per participant). Golding (1981) also attempted to replicate Johnson-Laird *et al.*'s study and found that only older British participants, who were familiar with the postal rule, showed facilitation. Manktelow and Evans (1979) suggested that on the postal rule problem people are not reasoning at all but are just retrieving the solution from memory. The ¬q instance – a sealed, understamped letter – would be available from experience. This explains why younger British participants and participants in the US failed the task – the relationship between sealing a letter and the amount of postage paid is not part of their experience. This theory was referred to as the memory cue hypothesis and was tested in a further study by Griggs and Cox (1982). Griggs and Cox asked participants to imagine they were police officers whose job it was to ensure that people conform to certain rules. They were presented with cards displaying information about four people sitting at a table. One side of each card had the person's age and the other side of the card showed what the person was drinking (see Figure 6.5). The rule they were given was: 'If a person is drinking beer, then that person must be over 19 years of age'. Participants were then told to select the card or cards that they definitely needed to turn over to determine whether or not the people were violating the rule.

Figure 6.5

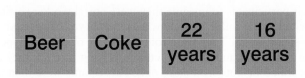

The drinking age problem.

This rule is, of course, a real rule in Florida, so the participants were familiar with it. The results showed a massive facilitation – 29/40 participants got it right – which suggested that the memory-cue hypothesis was right. However, other thematic tasks failed to find the same facilitation and so caused doubt about the explanatory power of the memory-cue hypothesis. D'Andrade's (1982) version placed participants in the role of a department store manager inspecting receipts to check whether the following rule was being followed: 'If a purchase exceeds 30 dollars then the receipt must be approved by the departmental manager'. Participants were shown four cards (see Figure 6.6) and asked which ones they would need to select.

Figure 6.6

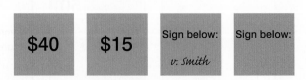

The Sears store-manager problem.

As with the previous examples, this task produced a big facilitation. However, it cannot be claimed that this is the result of participants' familiarity with the rule! So memory cueing cannot account for this facilitation.

Pragmatic reasoning schemas. What is it about these thematic versions of the rule that facilitates conditional reasoning on the Wason selection task? One explanation is that these tasks make it easier for participants to construct more accurate mental models. Another explanation, proposed by Cheng and Holyoak (1985, 1989) is that we reason using abstract knowledge structures called pragmatic reasoning schemas which develop through ordinary life experience. For example, all of the rules that facilitate reasoning performance in the tasks above can be viewed as being permission rules. According to Cheng and Holyoak, people have a permission schema which they use in permission contexts. Permission is a specific instance of a pragmatic reasoning schema, others include obligations and causations. Whenever people are confronted by a permission context the schema is elicited by both the content of the problem and the associated context. The elicited permission schema encapsulates knowledge which is derived from the long and extensive everyday experience that people have with permission contexts. The permission schema is based around four conditional statements – also known as production rules – which enable people to reason effectively in any permission situation:

Rule 1: If the Action is to be taken, then the Precondition must be satisfied.
Rule 2: If the Action is not to be taken, then the Precondition need not be satisfied.
Rule 3: If the Precondition is satisfied, then the Action may be taken.
Rule 4: If the Precondition is not satisfied, then the Action must not be taken.

Consider these rules in terms of the drinking age problem. In this specific context, the rules become:

Rule 1: If a person if drinking beer, then they must be over 19 years of age.
Rule 2: If a person is drinking Coke, they need not be over 19 years of age.
Rule 3: If a person is over 19 years of age, then they may drink beer.
Rule 4: If a person is under 19 years of age, then they must not drink beer.

Notice that rules 1 and 4 contain the **deontic** terms must and must not, whereas the other rules do not. The inclusion of these terms frames the problem as one involving permission, and leads people to realize that they need to search for potential violations of the rule. This leads to the need to check the cards relevant to rule 1 and rule 4. In selecting the 'Beer' card, you are checking whether rule 1 is being obeyed. This has the same effect as *modus ponens*. In selecting the '16 years' card, you are checking whether rule 4 is being obeyed, which has the same effect as *modus tollens*. Rules 2 and 3 can be said to block the logical fallacies of denying the antecedent and affirming the consequent as they show that the cases of ¬p and q are irrelevant to the rule. According to Girotto (1991), the mixed results of adult selection task studies can be explained in terms of pragmatic reasoning schemas; adults' performance in tasks which are interpreted as being about permission and obligation is superior to tasks in which this interpretation is not available.

deontic Concerning rules or obligations, such as permission.

Although the studies reported above are not developmental in nature, these findings are important for theories of cognitive development. The fact that adults find the abstract version of the task much harder than the thematic versions poses a serious problem for Piaget's theory. According to Piaget, adults have reached the formal operations stage, which means they should possess logical thought. If this were the case, they should have no problems with the abstract version of the task. Evidence from studies on adults suggests that people reason using semi-abstract clusters of domain-specific rules, such as those relating to permission. Whilst these rules produce responses that coincide with logical choices, such choices do not actually reflect any process of logical reasoning of the type envisaged by Piaget. The other prediction made by Piagetian theory is that, prior to the formal operations stage, children will perform very poorly. However, it appears that under suitable circumstances even quite young children seem to be able to solve deductive reasoning tasks. Moreover, the same content and context factors which seem to help adults with their reasoning also seem to help children.

Children's performance on the selection task. Several key studies by Girotto and colleagues have employed a *reduced array* version of the selection task (Girotto, Blaye and Fariolli, 1989; Girotto, Light and Colbourn, 1988; Light *et al.*, 1989). In this version participants only have the **q** and the **¬q** cases to choose from. This allows a reduction in cognitive load whilst still allowing the main difficulty with selection tasks to be investigated. Adults rarely have difficulty in selecting the **p** card; it is the choice of the **q** and **¬q** cards which is problematic. Even with this reduced-array task, the difficulty for participants is in correctly selecting the **¬q** card. Girotto *et al.* (1989) gave children a reduced array task in which they were presented with a computer screen displaying some schematic bees. Some of the bees were 'buzzers' and some were 'non-buzzers'; when touched on the screen with a light pen the buzzers emitted a buzz whilst the silent bees did not. The screen also showed where the bees live – a hive with a central area which was inside and a peripheral area which was outside (see Figure 6.7).

It was explained that the Queen Bee had made a rule: 'If a bee buzzes then it must stay outside.' The rationale for this was that the Queen Bee had made the rule so that she could rest and not be disturbed by the buzzing. The children were asked to imagine that they were officers of the Queen Bee. They had to check that her rule was being followed. They were asked which of the bees they would need to check

Figure 6.7

The reduced array 'bees' task.

Source: Reproduced with permission of Lawrence Erlbaum Associates, from Girotto, V., & Light, P. (1992). The pragmatic bases of children's reasoning. In P. Light & G. Butterworth (Eds.), *Context and cognition: Ways of learning and knowing* (pp. 135–156); permission conveyed through Copyright Clearance Center, Inc.

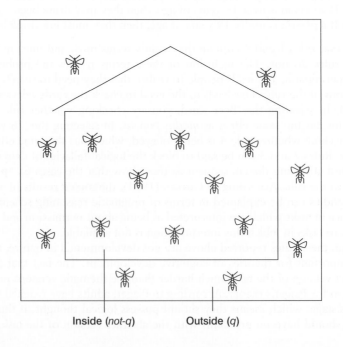

Inside (*not-q*)   Outside (*q*)

to see if the rule was being obeyed. They were asked to use the light pen to test any of the bees and then to determine whether the rule was being obeyed. We can map the rule onto the **p** and **q** terms we have been using such that:

    p = buzzing bees
    ¬**p** = silent bees
    q = bees outside the hive
    ¬**q** = bees inside the hive

The only options available to the participants were **q** and ¬**q**; they could choose to test bees outside the hive, bees inside the hive, or both. In order to pass this task, participants needed to understand that they needed to test all of the ¬**q** bees – those inside the hive. Seventy per cent of 7-year-olds succeeded on the task. When the rule 'If a bee buzzes then it is outside' was presented without a supporting context then this condition produced a mere five per cent success rate from the 7-year-olds. The high success rates on the permission form of the rule presents a major problem for the Piagetian account of reasoning development and the memory-cue hypothesis. This high success rate, coupled with the poor success rate on the non-permission version of the task, offers support for the Cheng and Holyoak's permission schemas explanation. Further support for the role of permission schemas comes from Harris and Núñez (1996), who developed a version of the selection task that was suitable for use with even younger children. In one experiment, they gave sixteen 3-year-olds and sixteen 4-year-olds a series of six permission stories. For three of the stories a rationale for the permission rule was given, for the other three it was left out. For each story, a set of four pictures were laid down. These four pictures corresponded to all the different combinations of **p** and **q** (**p** and **q**, **p** and ¬**q**, ¬**p** and **q**, ¬**p** and ¬**q**). For example, one rule was 'if Sally wants to play outside she must wear her coat). The four pictures depicted Sally outdoors with her coat on, Sally outdoors with no coat, Sally indoors with her coat on and Sally outdoors with no coat. The experimenter described all four pictures to the children and then asked them to identify the picture in which Sally is being naughty and not obeying her mother. The younger children picked the correct card 65 per cent of the time when a rationale was given and 60 per cent of the time when no rationale was given. The mean scores for the older children were 94 per cent for stories with a rationale and 96 per cent for stories without a rationale. Even though the 3-year-olds didn't pick the correct picture as often as the 4-year-olds, their performance is still surprising given the results of previous conditional reasoning studies. Harris and Núñez's task is much less demanding than the full selection task, as it only requires one selection that depicts both **p** and ¬**q** rather than making two independent selections of **p** and ¬**q**. However, this finding clearly demonstrates that very young children understand violations of permission rules and do not need a rationale. Also, some of the rules used in the study were unfamiliar to the participants, such as 'if Sally wants to do some painting, she must wear an apron' and 'if Sally wants to ride on her bicycle, she must wear her helmet'. Because children were still able to identify violations of permission for these rules, Harris and Núñez conclude that familiarity with a rule is not necessary.

The tasks discussed above are based on the selection task, but are clearly easier. Girotto *et al.* (1989) conducted some full array selection task studies with permission rules with 10- to 11-year-olds and 14- to 15-year-olds, as discussed at the beginning of the chapter. In addition to the abstract selection task and the thematic 'seat-belt' task, there were two other conditions in which participants were presented with a novel permission rule. In one condition they were just given the rule, in the other they were also given a rationale for the rule. The children were asked to imagine they were policemen in an imaginary country whose job it was to check that the following rule was being obeyed: 'If one drives over 100 km/h, then one must have a fluorescent car'. The four cards showed a speedometer indicating 140 km/h, a speedometer indicating 60 km/h, a fluorescent car and a white car. The participants in the rationale condition were told that the rule had been introduced to increase road safety. At high speeds, cars need to be visible from a distance, so the fluorescent bodywork is a safety measure. Remember that 80 per cent of the younger participants and 85 per cent of the older participants selected the correct cards in the familiar rule (seat-belt) condition. For the novel permission rule with rationale condition, the results were exactly the same. However in the condition with the novel permission rule but no rationale, only 65 per cent of the 10- to 11-year-olds and 45 per cent of the 14- to 15-year-olds chose correctly. Although it seems as though the older children performed more poorly than the younger children, there was no main effect of age. These results confirm the findings of the reduced-array task, illustrating the fact that direct experience with a specific permission rule is not a necessary condition for searching for potential violators of a rule. It even appears that simply having the word 'must' in the rule is sufficient to support the elicitation of a pragmatic reasoning schema.

Further studies on children's performance on the full selection task have been carried out by Overton and colleagues (Overton *et al.*, 1987; Ward and Overton, 1990), who found much poorer performance than Girotto *et al.* In one experiment Overton *et al.* gave sixty 10-, 12- and 14-year-olds eight variations on the selection task. In addition to the standard version and Johnson-Laird *et al.*'s (1972) postage rule version, they devised three novel problems related to school discipline, in which the rules were familiar to the participants:

Halls problem: If a student is in the school halls then the student is not running.
Absent problem: If a student is absent, then the student brings a note from his or her parent.
Radio problem: If a student is in school, then the student is not playing a radio.

They also presented these latter three problems in a reversed form, such that the antecedent and consequent were swapped:

Halls-reverse problem: If a student is not running, then the student is in the school halls.
Absent-reverse problem: If a student brings a note from his or her parent, then the student is absent.
Radio-reverse problem: If a student is not playing a radio, then the student is in school.

Across all eight problems, the success rates for the three ages groups (10-, 12- and 14-year-olds) were 24 per cent, 29 per cent and 39 per cent, respectively. For just the three familiar rules (the halls, absent and radio problems), the children's performance was higher: 40 per cent for the 10-year-olds, 47 per cent for the 12-year-olds and 59 per cent for the 14-year-olds. The participants found the reverse problems much harder, frequently selecting the ¬p and q answers, rather than the p and ¬q answers. As a result, Overton *et al.* conclude that although there is a role for familiarity, the semantic content of the task is a variable that moderates an underlying logical competence, which develops throughout adolescence. This conclusion is supported by Ward and Overton's (1990) study on one-hundred-and-eighty 11-, 14- and 17-year olds, in which they found a steady developmental progression on versions of the selection task in which the two parts of the rule were associated or highly relevant (e.g., 'drinking beer' and 'over 21'). In tasks in which the consequent was less relevant to the antecedent (e.g., 'drinking beer' and 'goes to church'), fewer participants chose the correct answer. However, there was no significant difference between high and low relevance problems for the two younger age groups, whereas the 17-year-olds showed a facilitation effect of high-relevance problems. However, as Girotto and Light (1992) observe, many of the problems presented in these studies were presented as descriptive covariation (e.g., 'If a student is not playing a radio, then the student is in school') and did not contain the deontic term 'must'. Therefore, these problems are less likely to be interpreted in terms of permission contexts. When Girotto's and Overton's results are compared, there appears to be facilitation for problems containing familiar rules, a clear structure (i.e., not reversed), permission rules, and a rationale for the permission rule, all of which suggest that children's reasoning is highly susceptible to subtle task differences.

Transitive reasoning

Just as conditional reasoning problems can be thought of as conditional syllogisms, transitive reasoning problems can be conceived of as linear syllogisms. Transitive relations hold between any entities that can be organized in an ordinal series. Take a series of five entities, A, B, C, D and E. Let's say these are five people – Anna, Brian, Charlotte, Derek and Elizabeth – and that they are organized by height such that A > B > C > D > E; Anna is the tallest and Elizabeth is the shortest. There are four transitive relations between neighbouring members of the series: A > B, B > C, C > D and D > E. From these relations, we can make inferences about non-adjacent pairs. If we know that A > B and B > C, we can conclude that A > C. Piaget (1921), conducted experiments with problems such as this and found that children in the pre-operational stage demonstrated poor performance. According to Piaget (1960), children cannot reason with transitive relations until they know how to use the rules of logic. More specifically, it is not until the concrete operations stage that children understand reversibility. Once children can mentally manipulate relationships between two items, they can understand that A > B is the same as B < A. Once they can understand that B can be both shorter than one thing and longer than another, they combine A > B with B > C to conclude that A > C.

Remembering all the transitive relations between five people places a large demand on memory, so Bryant and Trabasso (1971) designed a transitive reasoning task that reduced the demands on memory. They used a series of five coloured rods placed in a box so that only the top inch stuck out: a 3 ft white rod, 4 ft red rod, 5 ft blue rod, 6 ft yellow rod and 7 ft green rod. In an initial training phase, they asked 4-, 5- and 6-year-old children to guess which rod of a given pair was longer, then removed the rods from the box so the children could see which was actually longer. In the testing phase, children were again asked which rod in a given pair was longer, but did not receive the visual feedback. The most important result is how well the participants did on the red–yellow comparison. As the white and green rods were the longest and shortest, respectively, it is possible to answer questions involving these from memory. In order to judge the correct relationship between the second and fourth items in the series, children had to make transitive comparisons about the relationship between red–blue and blue–yellow. Participants in all age groups performed well: 78 per cent of 4-year-olds, 88 per cent of 5-year-olds and 92 per cent of 6-year-olds gave the correct answer. As a result of this and other studies (Trabasso, 1977; Trabasso, Riley and Wilson, 1975), Trabasso concluded that training children so they remember all the transitive relations is sufficient to pass the task, which means that memory, rather than the development of general logical rules, is the most important factor. However, Halford and Galloway (1977) and, more recently, Bouwmeester, Vermunt and Sijtsma (2007) have demonstrated that the ability to remember the pairs is not sufficient to draw a transitive inference. Halford and Andrews (2004) point out that because the pairs Bryant and Trabasso presented were in order in the training phase (A > B, B > C, C > D, D > E), this helped participants to construct an ordered set, which means that rather than remembering individual pairs of relations, all children had to do was remember where each rod was in the sequence. In experiments in which the presentation order was randomized (Halford and Kelly, 1984; Kallio, 1982), 4-year-olds performed more poorly.

Pears and Bryant (1990) removed memory and learning from the equation altogether by making the problem entirely visible. Rather than using rods, they showed children pairs of coloured bricks which were placed on top of one another: Red on top of blue, blue on top of green, green on top of yellow, yellow on top of white and white on top of purple. Their participants, twenty-four 4-year-old children, were asked to build 4-, 5- or 6-block towers, using the pairs they had been shown as guides for which blocks could go on top of each other. Prior to building the tower the children were asked inferential questions, such as whether the yellow or blue brick would be higher in the tower. Pears and Bryant found that 4-year-olds were above chance in their performance. The number of children who gave the correct answer on critical questions involving reasoning about pairs of blocks that were each neither at the top nor the bottom of the tower varied between 14 and 21 on different trials. From this they concluded that children of this age had the ability to make transitive inferences about spatial position.

Analogical reasoning

The following is a problem originally posed by Duncker (1945), who was studying insight problem solving:

> You are a doctor faced with a patient who has a malignant tumour in his stomach. It is impossible to operate on the patient, but unless the tumour is destroyed the patient will die. There is a kind of ray that may be used to destroy the tumour. If the rays reach the tumour all at once and with sufficiently high intensity, the tumour will be destroyed, but surrounding tissue may be damaged as well. At lower intensities the rays are harmless to healthy tissue, but they will not affect the tumour either. What type of procedure might be used to destroy the tumour with the rays, and at the same time avoid destroying the healthy tissue?
> (Gick and Holyoak, 1980, pp. 307–308)

> Q. Can you think of a solution to this problem?

If not, here is another story:

> A general wishes to capture a fortress located in the centre of a country. There are many roads radiating outward from the fortress. All have been mined so that while small groups of men can pass over the roads safely, a large force will detonate the mines. A full-scale direct attack is therefore impossible. The general's solution is to divide his army into small groups, send each group to the head of a different road, and have the groups converge simultaneously on the fortress.
> (Gick and Holyoak, 1980, p. 309)

Q. Go back to the first story. What type of procedure might be used to destroy the tumour with the rays, and at the same time avoid destroying the healthy tissue? Here's a hint: Use the information about the general and the fortress to help solve the tumour problem.

Gick and Holyoak (1980) gave this problem to college students. They found that only 10 per cent managed to solve the tumour problem immediately. However, when told the fortress story as well, 40 per cent of participants solved the tumour problem. When they expressly told participants that the fortress story was a hint to help solve the problem, 80 per cent managed to get it right. This is an example of solving a problem by analogy. **Analogical reasoning** involves finding correspondences between new and old problems in order to transfer knowledge from the old problem to the new one. Some of the correspondences between the two problems presented above are fortress – tumour, roads – rays, general – doctor, capture fortress – destroy tumour and so on. The solution to the tumour problem is, therefore, to use several weak rays that can pass through the healthy tissue without damaging it, but can converge on the tumour and so destroy it. The ability to draw analogies is an important reasoning skill. This ability enables us to transfer understanding across problems between or within domains.

analogical reasoning A type of reasoning that involves finding correspondences between new and old problems in order to transfer knowledge from the old problem to the new one.

Theories of analogical reasoning

Structural theory

As with deductive reasoning (and just about every aspect of developmental psychology), one of the earliest theories of inductive reasoning was formulated by Piaget (Inhelder and Piaget, 1958; Piaget, Montangero and Billeter, 1977). According to Piaget's theory, it is not until the formal operations stage (11 to 12 years and over) that children are able to make the sorts of inductive inferences necessary for full scientific and analogical reasoning. This is because younger children do not possess the cognitive structures necessary to make a comparison between two problems on the basis of abstract similarities. Piaget *et al.* (1977) presented children with problems such as 'A bicycle is to handlebars as a ship is to ... ?', Problems such as these are known as relational similarity problems. To solve relational similarity problems, it is necessary to identify a conceptual relationship between two items (e.g., handlebars are what steers a bicycle). When presented with a third item (ship) we can search for an item which has the same relationship to the third item as the second to the first. In this case, helm, as it is what is used to steer the ship. This type of problem follows the pattern A is to B as C is to D, or A:B :: C:D. Before presenting children with these problems, Piaget *et al.* asked them to sort a series of pictures (e.g., dog, ship, feather, bicycle, bird, handlebars, hair, helm) into pairs. The children were then asked to combine these pairs into groups of four, which involves creating analogies between the pairs. Finally, the children would be presented with an alternative fourth item and asked if it was as good as the current fourth item. For example, it would be asked whether a picture of a bicycle pump was as good as the picture of handlebars in the ship:helm :: bicycle:handlebars analogy. Some children in the preoperational stage had difficulty constructing the initial pairs. One child put ship and bird together on the basis that they can both be found near water. Other preoperational children were able to sort the pictures into pairs, but had trouble combining these pairs into appropriate groups of four. An example of this is the child who correctly linked bicycle to handlebars and car to petrol, but then placed them together in a foursome on the basis that both cars and bicycles go on the road. Although it is true that bicycles and cars have a functional similarity, there is no relational similarity between the bicycle:handlebars and car:petrol pairs. From the way in which they constructed pairs and foursomes, Piaget concluded that pre-operational children use associations to try to solve these problems. Children in the concrete operations stage were able to construct the groups of four but would often accept the alternative fourth item suggested by the experimenter, leading Piaget to conclude that they did not have a full understanding of analogy. Piaget explained that this was because they are restricted to lower-order relations between items, whereas thinking about higher-order relations is necessary to pass the task. Lower-order relations are those that hold between a particular pair (e.g., bicycle and handlebars are related because handlebars are part of a bicycle). Higher-order relations are those that hold across both pairs in a group of four (e.g., steering is the higher-order relation in both the bicycle:handlebar and ship:helm pairs). Only the children in the formal operations stage consistently grouped appropriate pairs together, were able to justify their choices and rejected the suggestions for an alternative fourth item. This evidence was taken by Piaget as support for his theory of stages in which structural changes in cognition lead to qualitatively different logical reasoning abilities as children develop. According to Goswami (1992), this conclusion depends on three assumptions. First, it assumes that there is a clear difference between lower-order and higher-order relations. Second, it assumes that children have the knowledge of the relations that they need in order to solve the problems. Third, it assumes that children know that they need to look for relational similarities, rather than just searching for any relationships. Goswami argues that all these assumptions are problematic.

Knowledge-based theory

An alternative to Piaget's structural theory proposed by Goswami and colleagues (Brown, 1989; Goswami and Brown, 1990a, 1990b; Goswami, 1989, 1992, 2001) is that the basic ability to reason analogically is present from early childhood, but increases with age as a function of conceptual knowledge. According to this account, children will not demonstrate global shifts in their ability to reason, but will show a gradual improvement over time as they acquire more knowledge. Children may well be able to recognize relational similarities from infancy, although this ability will often be masked by lack of relational knowledge. A greater level of knowledge enables the perceptions of parallels and commonalities. Therefore, it is possible that young children's failure to reason adeptly by analogy on Piaget's tasks is the result of a lack of knowledge of the situations involved in the problems he gave them. Piaget's tasks, such as the bicycle–ship example, involve unfamiliar relations. If it is the case that knowledge plays a key role, then providing children with more familiar relations between items should facilitate their reasoning. This idea is supported by the work of Goswami and Brown (1990b), who used relations which are more familiar to younger children. Goswami and Brown gave 4-, 5- and 9-year-olds analogy tasks presented as a series of pictures (see Figure 6.8). The experimenter places the A, B and C items on a board. The child is asked to name each item to ensure they know what they are. The child then has to select the item which completes the set.

Whereas Piaget's bicycle–ship problem requires knowledge of the working of ships and also features a problem with no perceptual similarity and only a limited functional similarity, Goswami and Brown's problem involves items, properties and

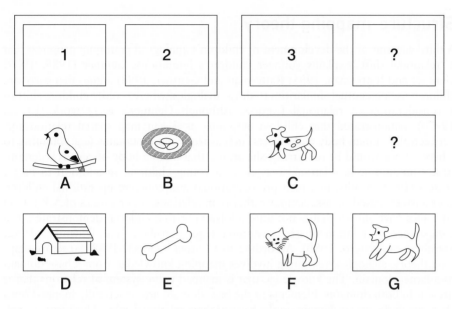

Figure 6.8

Analogical reasoning task.

Source: Reprinted from Cognition, 30, Goswami, U. & Brown, A. L., Higher-order structure and relational reasoning – contrasting analogical and thematic relations, 207–226, Copyright (1990), with permission from Elsevier.

relations with which children are familiar. In this example, the bird–dog analogy, the relational similarity is 'lives in' and the correct answer is the kennel. The other choices were also designed so as to reveal the way in which children approached the problem. If Piaget was correct in his assertion that young children use associations, we would expect the bone to be chosen. The second dog is a 'mere appearance match' and the cat is a category match. The results showed that all children performed above chance. The correct answer was chosen 59 per cent of the time by 4-year-olds, 66 per cent of the time by 5-year-olds and 94 per cent of the time by 9-year-olds. Prior to presenting the four possible answers, the experimenters asked children to make a prediction as to the identity of the fourth item, which would be evidence of sophisticated analogical reasoning. Even younger children showed quite advanced abilities on this part of the task. One 4-year-old participant, Lucas, predicted that the correct solution was puppy, arguing that 'Bird lays eggs in her nest – dog – dogs lay babies, and the babies are – umm – and the name of the babies is puppy!' Although this was not the 'correct' answer to the task – and Lucas chose kennel when presented with the four choices – he has solved the analogy using the relation 'offspring'. In addition to this demonstration that 4-year-olds can solve analogy problems based on conceptual relations such as 'lives in', Goswami and Brown (1990a) have shown that children as young as 3 can reason about physical causal relations. They gave 4-, 5- and 6-year-olds analogy problems with causal relations such as cutting, wetting and melting, e.g., 'Playdoh is to cut playdoh as apple is to … ?'. All of the 6-year-olds, 90 per cent of the 4-year-olds and 52 per cent of the 3-year-olds tested were able to solve problems such as this, choosing answers which represented the causal relationship rather than answers based on association (a banana), appearance (a round ball), or a different transformation (bruised apple). Therefore, as long as they have knowledge of the relations involved, even 3-year-olds can reason by analogy. Goswami *et al.* (1998) extended this task to see if children aged 3 to 6 could solve the same sorts of problems if *two* causal relations (e.g., cutting and wetting) were used to describe the relationship between one item and another. Although 3-year-olds had difficulties with this more complex task, 4-year-olds were fairly successful, demonstrating that young children can perform analogical reasoning tasks in which there is more than one relational change.

Structure-mapping theory

A third account of the development of children's analogical reasoning proposes that a 'relational shift' explains younger children's limitations. Gentner (1988, 1989; Gentner and Ratterman, 1991; Ratterman and Gentner, 1998) argues that early on, children use perceptual similarities to draw analogies, whereas older children shift to a consideration of relational features. Although Gentner's early work (1977a, 1977b) demonstrated that children as young as 4 can map spatial relationships between the human body and objects such as trees and mountains (e.g., pointing to where a knee would be on a tree), she argues that a large body of research demonstrates limitations in relational reasoning in young children. In addition to Piaget *et al.*'s (1977) results, in which pre-operational and concrete operational children gave answers based on associations rather than relations, other studies of A:B :: C:D analogies have shown that is not until adolescence that children demonstrate a full competence in relational-based reasoning (e.g., Sternberg and Downing, 1982; Sternberg and Nigro, 1980). According to Gentner's (1983, 1988) structure-mapping theory, analogical reasoning involves mapping knowledge from a base domain to a target domain. The knowledge that is mapped is the system of relations that is present in both domains. Elements in the base domain are structurally mapped onto elements in the target domain on the basis of their relational roles. This view of analogy explains how people are able to identify correspondences between two problems (such as Gick and Holyoak's tumour and fortress stories) without any need for perceptual similarities. Gentner and Ratterman (1991) argue that children's use of similarity and analogy progresses from matching objects based on superficial commonalities (e.g., shape, colour) to matches based on higher-order relations. This progression may proceed at different speeds in different domains as, similar to Goswami, Gentner proposes that development is driven by knowledge acquisition rather than maturational of cognitive structures. However, Goswami and Brown's (1990a) study poses a problem for Gentner's theory. Goswami and Brown found that, in cases where children did not choose the causal relation item from the list of possible answers in their analogy task, they did not select the appearance-match item more often than the other alternatives. According to Gentner's theory, this should be the most attractive choice for children who have yet to make the relational shift. Ratterman and Gentner (1998) suggest that Goswami and Brown's appearance-match choices (e.g., yellow balloon for lemon) were no more similar than the alternatives (e.g., slice of lemon, squeezed lemons) and that they therefore failed to offer their participants a real choice between answers based on causal relations and mere appearance. Ratterman and Gentner carried out a replication of Goswami and Brown's study, but replaced the original answers relating to appearance with items rated by undergraduate students as being more similar than the original choices. They found that although 5-year-olds mostly chose the correct relational item, 4-year-olds either chose the correct item or the appearance-match item, which they interpret as support for the shift from perceptual-based to relation-based reasoning.

Analogical reasoning in infancy

As the research on perception demonstrates (see Chapter 2), studying the abilities of very young children requires different methodologies to those used on older children. We would not expect infants to be able to carry out Goswami and Brown's tasks. In order to investigate analogical reasoning skills in younger children, physical activity-based tasks are necessary. Chen, Sanchez and Campbell (1997) presented

10- and 13-month-olds with a puzzle they had to solve by transferring the solution from a similar problem they had already seen. The problem was to obtain an attractive toy which was out of reach. The toy was hidden behind a barrier and had a piece of string attached to it which was itself out of reach but rested on a cloth that was within grasping distance (see Figure 6.9). Once they had been presented with the solution (remove the barrier, pull the cloth, pull the string), the infants were presented with similar problems which included similar materials. However, the boxes, pieces of cloth and bits of strings were dissimilar to the ones used in the source problem. In addition, there were two pieces of cloth, each with a length of string resting on them; only one of the cloth/string pairs led to the toy. Twenty-nine per cent of the infants solved the first of the target problems they were presented with. Sixty-seven per cent solved the third of the target problems. This demonstrates that even infants can solve problems based on the similarity of two situations. It is arguable whether this is 'true' problem-solving in the Piagetian sense, as the task is purely perceptual. However, we can be certain that 3- or 4-year-olds, at least, are capable of 'true' analogical reasoning. What of children in between these ages? Singer-Freeman (2005; Singer-Freeman and Bauer, 2008) investigated whether 2-year-olds were capable of solving the sort of formal analogical reasoning tasks used by Goswami and Brown. She gave children aged 24 and 30 months a series of formal relational reasoning tasks over two sessions. The relations used in both types of task were stretching, fixing, opening, rolling, breaking and attaching. Whereas older participants given formal relational reasoning tasks are usually presented with one A:B pair before solving the C:? problem, Singer-Freeman gave these younger children two A:B examples in order to increase their familiarity with the relation between the two. She also gave them three C:? trials, rather just one. For example, in the stretching task, participants were first shown loose yarn and stretched yarn, then loose nylon and stretched nylon. In the three test trials, they were shown a loose rubber band, a loose ribbon and a loose gold band, and had to choose from three alternatives. One of these was the target item – a stretched rubber band/ribbon/gold ribbon, the other two were distracter items, such as stretched yarn or a loose rubber band. If children answered incorrectly, they were allowed to choose again from the remaining two items. For both age groups, their initial answers were not different from chance. However, the total success rate (when their second answers were taken into

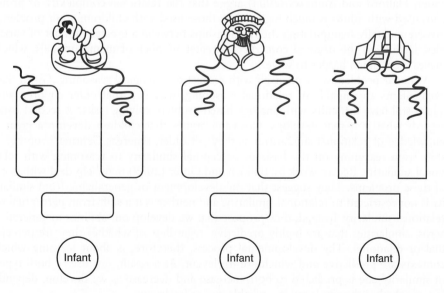

Figure 6.9

'Reaching for a toy' analogical reasoning problem.

Source: Copyright © 1997 by the American Psychological Association. Adapted with permission. The official citation that should be used in referencing this material is Chen, Z., Sanchez, R. P., & Campbell, T. (1997). From beyond to within their grasp: The rudiments of analogical problem solving in 10- and 13-month-olds. *Developmental Psychology*, 33(5), 790–801. The use of APA information does not imply endorsement by APA.

account) was significantly above chance (we would expect 67 per cent by chance for two choices from three), with 24-month-olds selecting the correct answers 78 per cent of the time and 30-month-olds responding correctly 81 per cent of the time. Singer-Freeman and Bauer conducted a similar study, but used more complex objects and relations, such as a horse changing colour or a comb getting smaller. They found that 2-year-olds were able to solve these problems as long as they were given explicit information about the object and the nature of the transformation. The results from these two studies lead the authors to conclude that 2-year-olds are capable of analogical reasoning as long as they are given supporting circumstances.

Concluding comments

It is clear from the research presented in this chapter that, unless they have studied logic and are capable of thinking about problems in terms of logical propositions, adults' deductive reasoning is highly susceptible to content effects, and both deductive and inductive reasoning can be facilitated by the way in which a task is presented. It is also clear that similar effects are found in children's reasoning, with some studies showing very early ability. What, then, is the role of the formal logical reasoning abilities described by Piaget? Is it the case that only a few adults reach full logical competence? Or does the research on children suggest that this competence develops very early, or is, perhaps, innate? If the latter is true, then it must also be true that our logical powers are very fragile, as we can easily be manipulated to fail reasoning tasks. Part of the problem, according to Markovits and Barrouillet (2004), is that although there has been a vast amount of research on both adults and children, these two literatures do not interact, and that studies on adults may be measuring different things to child studies, which have to be simplified in order for children to understand the task. One possible explanation for the contradictory patterns of performance seen in adults and children is that different tasks place greater or lesser information processing demands on participants. Handley *et al.* (2004) have shown a correlation between children's working memory and their performance on logical reasoning tasks. This suggests that simple problems, which make fewer demands on memory, may be making the tasks used in child reasoning studies easier. Halford and Andrews (2004) argue that the relational complexity of problems used with adults is much higher than those used with children; adult problems involve mentally manipulating the relationships between a greater number of variables, leading to the need to construct a greater number of mental models, which makes them much harder to solve.

A similar problem presents itself with respect to analogical reasoning. Given that even infants are capable of relational reasoning, why is it that older children and adults still have difficulty with analogy-based problem solving tasks? A second issue regards what it is that develops. Goswami argues that children develop a greater knowledge of relational similarities as they get older, whereas Gentner proposes a shift from reasoning on the basis of perceptual similarity to reasoning with relational similarity. Recent work by Bulloch and Opfer (2009) may help deal with both of these problems. They suggest that the development of generalizing from similarity is not restricted to relational similarity, and neither is it a shift from perceptual to relational similarity. Instead, they propose that we develop our abilities to generalize across similarities that are highly predictive, regardless of whether they are perceptual or relational. The developmental process, therefore, is about learning which contexts are predictive and which are irrelevant. As a result, our use of both types of similarity cue is predicted to both increase and decrease as we develop, depending on whether the similarity is a reliable cue or irrelevant.

Summary

Types of reasoning. There are two broad types of reasoning: inductive reasoning and deductive reasoning. Induction involves drawing inferences from specific examples and trying to generalize them or apply them to other situations, such as in analogies. Deduction involves reaching a specific conclusion from more general premises. Deduction leads to one logically valid conclusion, whereas inductive inferences are not logically valid. One form of induction is analogical reasoning, in which we look for correspondences between new and old problems in order to transfer knowledge from the old problem to the new one.

Theories of deductive reasoning. Piaget's stage theory is primarily a theory of the development of logical capabilities. The developing child is seen as gradually and progressively re-structuring the logical structures of the mind, the endpoint of which is the attainment of full logical competence during adolescence. In the sensory-motor period, infants' knowledge and rudimentary hypothesis-testing behaviour is based around actions. In the pre-operational stage, this action-based knowledge is organized into representation-based or symbolic knowledge. In the concrete operational stage, children develop the ability to mentally reverse actions and begin to understand the relationships between different patterns of action. Their representational systems start to be organized according to logical groupings or concrete operations, such as transitivity, class inclusion and conservation, but their operations are restricted to concrete objects and events. In the formal operations stage, children develop a full logical competence, as a result of the ability to mentally operate upon their mental representations. Piaget's theory predicts that adults should perform very well on deductive reasoning tasks, and children under the age of 11 or 12 should find them very difficult. An alternative to Piaget is Johnson-Laird's mental models theory. According to mental models theory, we construct mental representations of the possibilities described in the premises of a reasoning problem. Having constructed a model, we then use it to propose tentative conclusions. In order to determine whether our conclusions are valid, we attempt to formulate further mental models based on the premises. If the conclusion doesn't hold true in these alternative models, we reject it and look for another conclusion that is true in all models. Markovits proposed a developmental version of mental models theory in order to account for age-based differences. In this account, working memory capacity, efficiency of retrieval, inhibition and knowledge, all affect children's ability to construct, and reason with, mental models.

Deductive reasoning. Syllogisms are the simplest form of deductive reasoning, consisting of two premises from which just one logical conclusion can be drawn, without the need for any further information. Syllogisms can be in any one of four different figures, and each of the premises and the conclusions can be in one of four different moods. As a result, adults and children find some syllogisms much harder than others. In studies on adults, it has been shown that the beliefs and knowledge of the reasoner have an effect on task success. These same factors can affect children's reasoning, but young children have greater success with counterfactual syllogisms if they are induced to think of the premises as being true in a fantasy context. Conditional reasoning problems can be conceptualized as conditional syllogisms, constructed of statements of the type 'if p, then q'. There are two valid rules of inference that can be used to determine the truth of such statements, *modus ponens* and *modus tollens*, and two other principles people use, both of which are logical fallacies: the *denial of the antecedent* and the *affirmation of the consequent*. The Wason selection task is an example of a conditional reasoning problem. On the standard, abstract, version of the task, adults and children alike do very poorly, however thematic versions facilitate performance. One explanation for this effect of thematic versions is Cheng and Holyoak's pragmatic reasoning schemas, whereby contexts involving permission or obligation elicit a reasoning schema which encapsulates knowledge derived from everyday experience with such contexts. Studies on younger children, which have employed a simpler version of the selection task with only two of the four card choices made available, have found that children as young as 7 can solve the task if they are given a permission context. On an even simpler version, in which each card represents a combination of p and q terms, children as young as 3 have demonstrated that they can identify when a rule is being violated. Transitive reasoning problems can be conceived of as linear syllogisms, in which the reasoner has to make inferences about the relationships between items in an ordinal series. Piaget's early work demonstrated that children in the pre-operational stage found these problems very difficult. However, later studies have shown that children as young as 4 can solve transitive inference problems in which items are ordered along the dimensions of length or height.

Theories of analogical reasoning. According to Piaget's theory, it is not until the formal operations stage that children are able to make the sorts of inductive inferences necessary for full scientific and analogical reasoning. This is because younger children do not possess the cognitive structures necessary to make a comparison between two problems on the basis of abstract similarities. Piaget presented children with relational similarity problems, in which it is necessary to identify a conceptual relationship between two pairs of items. Many pre-operational stage children fail this task, and Piaget explained that those who do show some success solve the problems on the basis of associations, rather than relational similarities. An alternative theory proposed by Goswami and Brown is that the basic ability to reason analogically is present from early childhood, but increases with age as a function of conceptual knowledge. According to this account, children will not demonstrate global shifts in their ability to reason, but will show a gradual improvement over time as they acquire more knowledge. Goswami and Brown demonstrated that 4-year-olds can solve analogy problems in which the items and causal relations are familiar to them. A third account of the development of children's analogical reasoning proposes that a 'relational shift' explains younger children's limitations. Gentner argues that early on, children use perceptual similarities to draw analogies, whereas older children shift to a consideration of relational features. This view of analogy explains how adolescents and adults are able to identify correspondences between two problems without any need for perceptual similarities.

Analogical reasoning in infancy. Studying the abilities of very young children requires different methodologies to those used on older children. In order to investigate analogical reasoning skills in younger children, physical activity-based tasks are necessary. Research with this type of task has demonstrated than 1-year-old infants can solve problems based on the similarity of two situations. Other studies have used more complex tasks, based on the type of formal analogy problems used with older children. Two-year-olds are able to solve these problems as long as they are given supporting circumstances, such as being provided with explicit information about the objects used in the tasks and the nature of the relationships between them.

Discussion questions

1 What factors seem to affect the performance of children of different ages on deductive reasoning tasks?

2 To what extent does research on deductive reasoning present a challenge to Piaget's theory of cognitive development?

3 What are the strengths and weaknesses of Piaget's theory with respect to analogical reasoning?

4 What are the differences between the skills used by infants in simple analogical reasoning tasks, and those used by adolescents and adults in conditional reasoning tasks?

5 Why do you think it is important to understand the reasoning abilities of children of different ages?

Further Reading

Books and chapters

Goswami, U. (1992). *Analogical reasoning in children*. Hove: Lawrence Erlbaum Associates.

Usha Goswami proposes her relational difficulty account of analogical reasoning in this book, which includes a discussion of her studies with Ann Brown.

Girotto, V. and Light, P. (1992). The pragmatic bases of children's reasoning. In P. Light and G. Butterworth (Eds), *Context and cognition: Ways of learning and knowing* (pp. 135–156). Hemel Hempstead: Harvester Wheatsheaf.

Vittorio Girotto and Paul Light discuss a number of selection task studies and the pragmatic reasoning schemas explanation.

Articles

Bara, B. G., Bucciarelli, M. and Johnson-Laird, P. N. (1995). Development of syllogistic reasoning. *American Journal of Psychology*, 108(2), 157–193.

Bruno Bara, Monica Bucciarelli and Philip Johnson-Laird present a mental models account of the development of syllogistic reasoning.

Chen, Z., Sanchez, R. P. and Campbell, T. (1997). From beyond to within their grasp: The rudiments of analogical problem solving in 10- and 13-month-olds. *Developmental Psychology*, 33(5), 790–801.

Zhe Chen, Rebecca Polley Sanchez and Tammy Campbell present their classic study on analogy in infants.

Harris, P. L. and Núñez, M. (1996). Understanding of permission rules by preschool children. *Child Development*, 67(4), 1572–1591.

In this paper, Paul Harris and Maria Núñez investigate conditional reasoning in 3- and 4-year-olds.

Markovits, H. and Barrouillet, P. (2004). Development and reasoning [Special issue]. *Thinking and Reasoning*, 10(2).

In this special issue of *Thinking and Reasoning*, editors Henry Markovits and Pierre Barrouillet bring together a series of papers examining the development of reasoning.

Overton, W. F., Ward, S. L., Black, J., Noveck, I. A. and Obrien, D. P. (1987). Form and content in the development of deductive reasoning. *Developmental Psychology*, 23(1), 22–30.

Willis Overton and his colleagues present a series of three studies looking at the development of conditional reasoning.

Pears, R. and Bryant, P. (1990). Transitive inferences by young children about spatial position. *British Journal of Psychology*, 81, 497–510.

This is Rosalind Pears and Peter Bryant's 'blocks' task, used to demonstrate early competence on transitive reasoning.

© Rubberball/iStock

Chapter 7
Scientific thinking

Learning Outcomes

At the end of this chapter you should be able to:

- Describe the difference between scientific knowledge and scientific reasoning.

- Describe and compare theories of scientific conceptual change.

- Discuss research on children's knowledge of scientific concepts.

- Compare and evaluate theories of the development of scientific reasoning.

- Discuss research on children's scientific reasoning skills.

Deanna Kuhn, Eric Amsel and Michael O'Loughlin (1988) report a series of six studies they (and other colleagues) carried out in which they examined the development of scientific thinking. In one experiment, twenty children aged 10 to 12, twenty adolescents aged 14 to 16 and twenty-five adults, five of whom were working towards a PhD in philosophy, participated in an evidence evaluation task. They were given information about the following fictional study:

> Some scientists have been studying whether the kinds of foods children eat make any difference in whether or not they get lots of colds. The scientists decided to do their study at a boarding school, where children live. The children eat all their meals in the school dining room and they all eat the same food. They sit in the dining room at tables of six children each. The scientists wanted to see if what the children eat makes a difference in whether or not they get lots of colds. So for six months they asked the dining room workers to serve certain foods at certain tables. During that time, the school nurse kept careful records of children's colds. I'm going to ask you some questions about the foods the scientists studied and what they discovered.
> (Kuhn *et al.*, 1988, p. 38)

Participants were then told that the nurse had discovered that the children who sat at some tables had had lots of colds, whereas children who sat at other tables had not had any. They were shown a series of eight pictures of children with or without colds alongside the foods they had eaten (four example pictures are shown in Figure 7.1). For each of the eight pictures they were asked 'Does the kind of

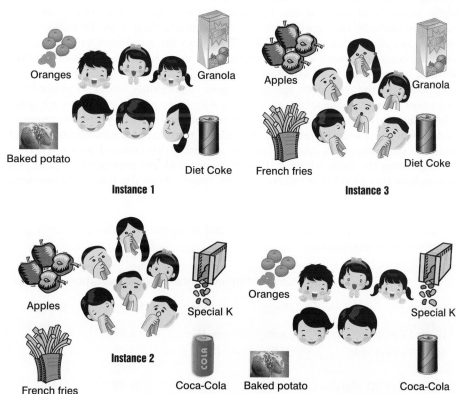

Figure 7.1

Covariation of food and colds from Kuhn *et al.*'s study.

Source: Kuhn, D., Amsel, E., & O'Loughlin, M., *The development of scientific thinking skills*, Copyright Elsevier (1988).

[fruit/cereal/potato/drink] the children have make any difference in whether they get lots of colds or very few colds?'

> Q. Have a look at Figure 7.1. Does the kind of fruit children have make any difference in whether they get colds or not? What about the kind of cereal, potato or drink?
>
>   If you answered 'yes' or 'no' for any of the variables, how do you know that it does/doesn't make a difference? If you answered 'maybe', why can't you tell whether it makes a difference?

Participants were each presented with different types of foods on the basis of an earlier session in which they were asked to rate the extent to which they thought each food would have an effect. Two of the foods that were rated as most likely to have an effect and two of the foods that were rated as least likely to have an effect were selected. One each of the foods rated most likely/least likely to have an effect were presented as covarying with colds (fruit and potato in the example given in Figure 7.1), and the remaining two were presented as non-covarying or independent (e.g., cereal and cola). Participants' responses to whether they thought each food had an effect on colds were coded as either evidence-based or theory-based. Evidence-based responses were those in which the participants made reference to the pattern of data made available to them. Theory-based responses were those in which participants referred to why a particular food stuff might cause colds (e.g., 'Orange juice makes you healthier because it has lots of vitamins'). As there were eight instances of each of the two covariation variables, the total number of responses made by each participant was 16. Similarly, there were 16 responses for the two noncovariation variables. Table 7.1 shows the mean number and range of evidence-based responses made by participants in each group. Statistical analyses showed a significant main effect of age for both types of variable; post-hoc tests revealed that the youngest age group gave significantly fewer evidence-based responses than the adolescents and adults, who were not different to each other. The results show that only around 30 per cent of the 10- to 12-year-olds' responses and half of the 14- to 16-year-olds' and adults' responses were based on evidence. Many of the participants paid attention to a variable that covaried on a single occasion, ignoring the cases where it did not covary with the presence of a cold. The researchers also found that children's prior beliefs about the foodstuffs interfered

| **Table 7.1** | Frequencies of spontaneous evidence-based responses to covariation and noncovariation evidence. |

Group	Covariation evidence Mean	Range	Noncovariation evidence Mean	Range
10- to 12-year-olds	4.85	0–12	4.95	0–13
14- to 16-year-olds	7.95	0–14	8.10	0–13
Adults	8.05	2–13	9.60	5–13
Philosophy PhD students	10.20	1–16	12.00	11–14

Source: Adapted from Kuhn, Amsel and O'Loughlin (1988). ©Elsevier (1988).

with their reasoning with the evidence. Kuhn *et al.* concluded that the younger participants showed a very limited ability to evaluate how evidence bears on a theory.

Two perspectives on scientific thinking

Traditionally, young children have been characterized as intuitive scientists who develop hypotheses in order to arrive at conclusions (Inhelder and Piaget, 1958). Children's naïve beliefs about the world, based on everyday experiences, are often scientifically invalid. Kuhn *et al.*'s study demonstrates that, although adults and older children were able to reason (to an extent) about the evidence they were presented with, younger children made fewer references to the evidence and relied more heavily on their beliefs about which variables were more likely to lead to a particular outcome. A large body of evidence suggests that even teenagers continue in their naïve (and incorrect) conceptions of physical, biological and psychological phenomena. As children get older and encounter new evidence, their theories are modified in a process often referred to as conceptual change. It has been claimed that their incorrect understanding is either a result of a lack of a consistent conceptual system (Kuhn, 1989) or possession of well-organized but incorrect conceptual systems (Carey, 1985). Some of the research into children's scientific thinking has focused on the concepts and knowledge children possess at different points in development (e.g., Carey, 1985; Wellman and Gelman, 1992, 1998), whereas others have studied the strategies children use in order to apply their knowledge to solve problems (e.g., Kuhn and colleagues; Inhelder and Piaget, 1958). According to Duschl, Schweingruber and Shouse (2006), science consists of two elements, 'a body of *knowledge* that represents current *understanding* of natural systems and the *process* whereby that body of knowledge has been established and is being continually extended, refined and revised' (p. 26, italics added). It is therefore necessary to make a distinction between two aspects of scientific thought: *scientific knowledge* and *scientific reasoning*. In order to advance their scientific knowledge, children need to be able to develop scientific reasoning skills. Whilst some researchers have focused on what children know, others have investigated the possible mechanisms by which conceptual change and theory revision occur (Kuhn, 2002).

Research on children's scientific thinking has focused on three domains: Physics, biology and psychology. We will look at some examples of research into children's knowledge of, and reasoning about, physics and biology. We will not look at children's understanding of psychology as this is really about the development of theory of mind (see Chapter 5). The development of reasoning skills is also relevant to scientific thought, so bear in mind the issues and results covered in Chapter 6 as well.

Theories of scientific conceptual change

The development of scientific thought requires conceptual change, for example thinking of heat and temperature as distinct concepts. How does this conceptual change take place? The general consensus is that children create models or theories to explain and account for everyday physical events. As new evidence arises, these theories are revised. As we saw in Chapter 1, Piaget's (1967/1971) view was that when children are confronted with a result that challenges an existing way of thinking – when children are faced with a conflict – they realize that they need to rethink how they solve problems. This conflict brings about disequilibrium which sets off the process of equilibration which produces cognitive change. Change is, therefore, driven by solving problems. According to Carey (1986; 1991), there are two differing views of developmental change: weak restructuring and strong restructuring. Weak restructuring involves incremental change. A child starts with some basic assumptions and adds or modifies information which leads to changes in concepts. The child's theories have not been radically altered, but simply enriched. This is somewhat similar to Piaget's idea of assimilation. For example, a 10-year-old sees more relations among processes such as growing, eating, dying and having babies than a 4-year-old and has a richer theory of biology. This gradual enrichment can be seen as similar to the process by which a beginner in a particular domain (e.g., physics) gains expertise: the novice-expert shift (Chi, Glaser and Rees, 1982). This view is supported by Gutheil, Vera and Keil (1998) who argue that 4-year-olds possess a limited biological theory which can develop into a more mature understanding. Strong restructuring involves a more radical conceptual shift in which children change their basic assumptions and construct a new theory which is completely incompatible with their old theory and replaces it, as with Piaget's notion of accommodation.

Radical restructuring

Carey (1985) proposed a theoretical framework which appeals to domain-specific conceptual change rather than domain-general development. According to Carey young children have knowledge of facts about biology, but it is not until the age of 7 that these facts are assimilated into a coherent theory or conceptual structure. According to Carey, a preschooler's theory of biology is based on their understanding of wants and desires; it is essentially a psychological theory. Younger children's explanations for biological phenomena centre on motivation and social convention, not on biological processes. For example, eating is seen by younger children as *psychologically* necessary to fulfil a desire for food, rather than *biologically* necessary to fuel the body. This early conception of biology-as-psychology is later transformed into a true biological theory. Up until around the age of 6, children learn facts, such as animals are alive, babies come from inside mothers, one can get sick from playing with a sick friend and medicine can make people better. It is not until children connect these facts together into a conceptually coherent framework that they can be said to have a theory of biology. By the age of 10, children give the same sorts of responses as adults to questions about living things, animals, people and bodily processes. Carey claims that this is a process of strong restructuring as a new domain – intuitive biology – emerges from a previous domain – naïve psychology. One example of conceptual change is the construction of a 'living things' category from two separate categories of animals and plants. Young children deny that plants and animals share any biological properties, arguing that plants aren't alive, can't die and don't eat. After the age of 6, this knowledge undergoes conceptual change and restructuring. The concepts of plants and animals become joined to create a new concept of 'living things'. Alongside this, children's conceptions of something that is 'not alive' become more precise; they differentiate biological death from inanimate objects and non-real entities (such as cartoon characters, which are not alive).

With respect to physics, Carey and Spelke (1994) describe a transition from a basic knowledge of the principles that guide the behaviour of physical objects to a concept of matter that is not like an adult's until around the age of 12. Infants understand that objects are coherent, do not change identity as they move in space and time, and act upon each other via physical contact. Young children, therefore, make a distinction between solid objects and non-solid substances such as liquid, as liquids do not maintain cohesion. However, it is not until the school years that children begin to have an understanding of the distinction between material and immaterial entities. Carey (1991) asked 4- to 12-year-old children to sort a list of items into two piles – material and immaterial. Over 90 per cent of the children in all age groups correctly placed items such as car, tree and Styrofoam in the material pile, and less than 20 per cent in each age group identified wish and dream as material, but there were differences for water and cola. Although 6- to 12-year-olds said that cola was material, only 30 per cent of 4-year-olds gave this response, and only 25 per cent of 6-year-olds said that water was material. According to Carey, results such as these show that concepts of matter develop throughout early and middle childhood. Furthermore, she argues that this conceptual change is not simply a matter of enriching existing concepts, but evidence for radical restructuring.

Theory theory

Some developmental psychologists think that Carey underestimates what children understand, and that we have separate domain-specific theories from the beginning. Wellman and Gelman (1992, 1998) and Gopnik and Wellman (1994) present Theory theory, the idea that preschool children possess coherent knowledge and distinct frameworks in the domains of physics, biology and psychology. In Chapter 5, we saw how Theory theory accounts for the conceptual changes that occur as preschool children develop their understanding of psychology. Wellman, Gelman and Gopnik argue that a similar process of change occurs with respect to biological and physics concepts. Children form domain-specific naïve theories, which undergo a process of revision when their theories do not account for their experiences. This can lead to stage-like, qualitative shifts in concepts. The 'theories' possessed by young children are not fully-fledged scientific theories in the sense of Piaget's theory of cognitive development, rather they are 'framework' theories consisting of basic concepts and causal processes for a particular set of phenomena. A framework theory defines which entities (e.g., physical objects, animate organisms or people) and which processes (e.g., physical force, biological motion, or intentional actions) can be explained by that theory. As these entities and processes differ between domains, the Theory theory predicts domain-specific development. Children's basic understanding of the physical world develops in infancy, for example, whereas their understanding of psychology (i.e., the development of theory of mind) occurs in early childhood.

Although it may seem that the Theory theory account of conceptual change is fundamentally very similar to Carey's view, there are a couple of key differences. First, according to Gopnik (1996b, 2003) children are born with basic innate theories, which are revised as a result of experience. Carey and Spelke (1996), in contrast, argue that although infants are born with core knowledge, this knowledge is not organized into theories. Second, as a result of these innate theories, Theory theory predicts that young children will make distinctions between domains in the preschool years, whereas Carey and Spelke describe later developing theories of biology and physics.

Scientific knowledge

Scientific understanding is not just about the accumulation of facts, but also about ways of thinking about those facts. Primary school children know facts about the world, for example that it is round, but their thinking does not reflect this factual knowledge. Rather, when they reason about the world, their answers suggest that their reasoning is largely based on the idea that the world is flat. Various psychologists have explored children's conceptions of the earth (Mali and Howe, 1979; Nussbaum, 1979, 1985; Nussbaum and Novak, 1976; Sneider and Pulos, 1983). The general finding from these studies was that children aged from 8 to 13 years said that the earth is round, but gave answers to follow-up questions indicating that they were working with naïve conceptions of what the idea of a 'round earth' actually means. Nussbaum and Novak described five different conceptions of the earth held by young children: (1) a flat earth, extending infinitely, with a parallel sky above the ground; (2) a ball-shape, but with a sky above it and ground below; (3) a sphere, but objects fall off the bottom; (4) a sphere from which objects do not fall, but with the origin of gravitational pull at the bottom; (5) a scientifically accurate conception of the earth as a sphere with gravity pulling towards the centre. Following the above studies, Vosniadou and Brewer (1992) investigated the mental models of the earth held by 6- to 11-year-olds, and developed a classification scheme that built upon the notions described by Nussbaum and Novak. Vosniadou and Brewer's six categories are illustrated in Figure 7.2, with examples of children's drawings shown in Figure 7.3. What this body of research demonstrates is that although children may have access to scientific facts, they may not fully comprehend these facts, and their reasoning about a scientific domain is not necessarily based on such facts. Scientific thinking, therefore, is not just about facts; it also involves thinking about problems appropriately.

Figure 7.2

Mental models of the earth.

Source: Reprinted from Cognitive Psychology, 24, Vosniadou, S., & Brewer, W.F., Mental models of the earth: A study of conceptual change in childhood, 535–585, Copyright 1991, with permission from Elsevier.

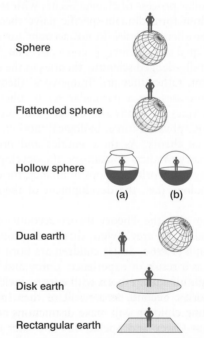

Sphere

Flattended sphere

Hollow sphere

(a) (b)

Dual earth

Disk earth

Rectangular earth

Children's understanding of scientific facts is mediated by the logical aspects of a concept, the situations that give meaning to a concept and the way a problem is represented (Nunes and Bryant, 2004). But everyday experiences often conflict with learned scientific concepts. Children's everyday experience with a ground that is perceptibly flat is at odds with the concept of a spherical earth. One of the difficulties children face when learning science is that they often have to make distinctions that are not made in everyday life. For example, temperature and heat are not the same concept. Two differently sized ice cubes are the same temperature, but the larger one will be better at cooling a drink. This can lead people to think that

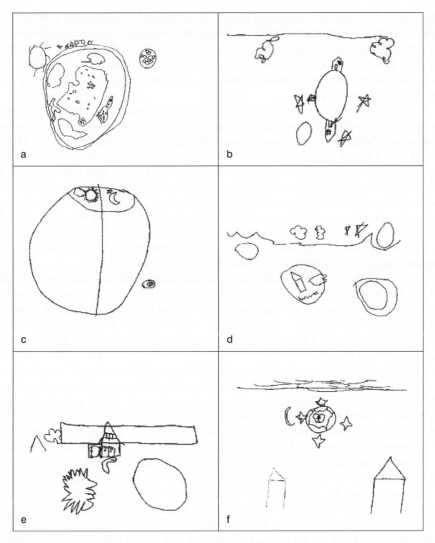

Figure 7.3

Children's drawings of the Earth, the Moon, the stars and the sky: (a) spherical earth, (b) flattened sphere, (c) hollow sphere, (d) disc earth, (e) rectangular earth, (f) dual earth.

Source: Reprinted from Cognitive Psychology, 24, Vosniadou, S., & Brewer, W.F., Mental models of the earth: A study of conceptual change in childhood, 535–585, Copyright 1991, with permission from Elsevier.

the large one is actually colder, when the distinction really involves the ability of the larger ice cube to cool the drink more effectively. Another difficulty is that science can require reasoning about non-perceptible aspects of the physical world, such as the particulate nature of matter. This is hard to think about when we understand objects to be solid and undivided. However, these are problems which affect thinking about fairly advanced concepts. Before children can engage in reasoning about such phenomena, they need to have a basic understanding of how the world works.

Understanding physics

Infants and young children are surprisingly knowledgeable about basic scientific facts. Infants of just 4 to 5 months use contiguity (occurrence close in time and space) to infer that events are related. For example, Leslie (1982) used a habituation technique to show that infants expect an object to move when a second object collides with it and that they do not expect an object to move unless a force is applied to it. Infants looked longer at an object when it started moving on its own, or when an object did not move after a collision. By 4 to 6 months infants seem to understand the principles of gravity. Spelke (1990) found that infants expected a falling object to fall even if they could no longer see it. Work by Baillargeon (1987b) suggests that infants have a good understanding of the physical world (see Chapter 2). By 3 to 4 years, children understand causation. Bullock and Gelman (1979) showed children three events (A, B, C) in order, and asked what made B happen. The children were more likely to choose A than C, indicating that they understand that causes occur before effects.

Given this, we might expect that it would not take long for children to develop a more sophisticated understanding of scientific facts. However, the evidence shows that older children are surprisingly *un*knowledgeable. Winer and Cottrell (1996) found that 11-year-olds thought that when we see an object, energy or rays come out of our eyes. Kaiser, Proffitt and McCloskey (1985) found that children aged 11 and older thought that if you dropped an object from a moving vehicle it would fall down in a straight line. Levin, Siegler and Druyan (1990) asked college students questions about cars travelling around an oval track and found that they thought that all the doors on such a car would move at the same speed. This is not the case as the outer doors covers more distance than the inner doors. The students were assuming that all parts of an object must move at the same speed.

The first person to study children's understanding of physics was Piaget (1946/1970). He studied whether and how children understand the relationship between time and speed as a result of a question posed to him by Albert Einstein at a conference in 1928: 'Which concept develops first, time or speed?' Piaget's answer (almost 20 years later) was that the acquisition of these concepts is a lengthy developmental process and that it seemed to be the case that they either developed at the same time or that the concept of speed developed first. A typical Piagetian task involved presenting children with two trains on parallel tracks and varying the speed at which the trains travelled and the distance they had to cover. 4- to 11-year-old children were asked which train travelled longer, which train travelled at the greatest speed and which train covered the greatest distance. Piaget's general finding was that correct answers for speed and distance were given at an earlier age than those for time.

A number of studies in the 1980s looked at children's and adults' understanding of the trajectories of moving objects. Kaiser, McCloskey and Proffitt (1986) asked participants to predict the trajectory of a ball leaving a C-shaped tube (see Figure 7.4). Most participants predicted a curvilinear arc (the dotted line), rather than the correct answer of a straight line. Interestingly, preschool children correctly predicted a straight line trajectory. McCloskey, Washburn and Felch (1983) asked participants to predict the trajectory of an object dropped from a moving aeroplane. Both adults and children predicted a 'straight down' trajectory, and some participants even

Figure 7.4

C-shaped-tube.

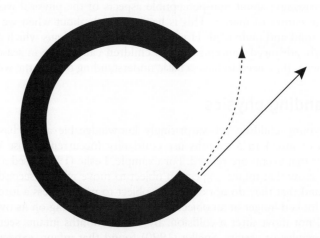

predicted that the object would move 'backwards' with respect to the aeroplane. In a similar study, McCloskey, Caramazza and Green (1980) gave students a scenario of running across a room and dropping a ball into a box. There were two groups of participants, physics students and students of other disciplines. The participants were shown pictures of someone letting go of the ball in three locations – before reaching the box, above the box or after the box – and asked to judge which was correct. The responses of the physics students were more accurate: 73 per cent chose the correct picture whereas only 13 per cent of non-physics students chose the correct picture. The physics students took the fact that the ball was already in motion into account; they considered this initial force plus gravity. The non-physics students only took gravity into account and, as a result, 80 per cent of them said that the ball should be dropped from directly above the box.

Another area which has been studied is the understanding of force and weight. Pauen (1996) used a force table (see Figure 7.5) to give a problem in which two force vectors had to be solved. Participants were asked to predict the trajectory of the central object, once it had been released. They were asked to place the opening in the place they thought the object would move to. The problem was placed in the context of a king (the central object) who had become tired of skating on a frozen lake (the platform) and wanted to be pulled into his bed on the shore (the opening). 6- to 10-year-olds were presented with several different combinations of angles and weights. Most of the younger children predicted that the king would move in the direction of the stronger force only and 45 per cent of the 10-year-olds failed to properly consider both forces.

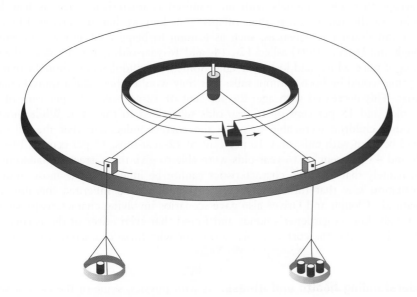

Figure 7.5

Force table.

Source: Reprinted from Journal of Experimental Child Psychology, 67, Pauen, S., & Wilkening, F., Children's analogical reasoning about natural phenomena, 90–113, Copyright (1997), with permission from Elsevier.

Understanding biology

Around 3 years of age, children can start to distinguish between animate and inanimate objects (Gelman, Spelke and Meck, 1983); this marks the beginnings of thinking about biology and biological processes. By the time they start school, children know that bodies contain brains, bones, blood and a heart, although they do not yet understand the functions of the organs in the body. Johnson and Wellman (1982) asked 5- to 11-year-olds and adults questions about the brain. All participants were able to say where the brain is and all agreed that the brain is needed for mental acts such as thinking and remembering, but the youngest children denied the brain was involved in walking. According to them, you just need feet. This superficial understanding of biology is also apparent from studies looking at children's conceptions of processes of change. Although 3- and 4-year-olds understand that people, animals and plants grow, whereas artifacts do not (Carey, 1985; Rosengren *et al.*, 1991), children under 7 also accept impossible physical transformations. For example, Keil (1986) told children aged 5, 7 and 9 a story about a raccoon that was shaved, dyed black, given a white stripe and dipped in a sack of odour such that it looked and smelled like a skunk. Almost two-thirds of the youngest children thought that the operation changed the raccoon into a skunk, whereas only a third of the 7-year-olds, and less than a quarter of the 9-year-olds, made this mistake. A similar progression can be seen with children's conceptions of death. Whereas children under 5 do not appreciate that everyone dies or that death is final, around the age of 9 children understand that death is universal and inevitable (Slaughter, Jaakkola and Carey, 1999).

It is clear that many biological concepts take some time to develop, although Inagaki and Hatano (2002) have argued that Carey has overestimated the time it takes to view biology as a separate domain. As with physics, however, some concepts seem to be more simple than others and some of the more advanced concepts in biology may never be fully grasped by some, even in adulthood. One example of a common and persistent misconception which can survive into adulthood is the idea that genetics is based on the inheritance of acquired characteristics. Springer and Keil (1989) found that 4- to 7-year-old children were more likely than adults to accept that adult animals with an acquired characteristic, such as hair loss, would pass this feature on to their offspring, as long as that property had biological or functional consequences, such as leading to being cold and sick in winter. Clough and Driver (1991) asked 12-, 14- and 16-year-olds questions about the offspring of mice which had lost their tails. Some of the adolescents thought that the offspring would be born without tails, that they would inherit the acquired characteristic. This decreased with age: 26 per cent of 12-year-olds, 17 per cent of 14-year-olds and 15 per cent of 16-year-olds subscribed to this idea. While most of the other children were able to make the correct judgement that the offspring would be born with tails, only 10 per cent of 12-year-olds, 17 per cent of 14-year-olds and 43 per cent of 16-year-olds were able to give the correct explanation for this, namely that acquired characteristics cannot be inherited. The most common explanation was that these characteristics could not be inherited 'because it is unnatural'. Clough and Driver also gave scenarios involving characteristics such as the rough skin on gardener's hands and found that even fewer of the participants were able to offer the correct explanations for why these characteristics could not be inherited.

Understanding health and illness. As with physics, some of the earliest work on children's understanding of biology was conducted by Piaget. He presented 167 children aged 6 to 12 with stories such as this:

> Once there were two children who were stealing apples in an orchard. Suddenly a policeman comes along and the two children run away. One of them is caught. The other one, going home by a roundabout way, crosses a river on a rotten bridge and falls into the water. Now what do you think? If he had not stolen the apples and had crossed the river on that rotten bridge all the same, would he also have fallen into the water?
> (Piaget, 1932, pp. 250–251)

The answers that children – particularly the younger ones – gave suggested that they believe that bad behaviour will lead to punishment. Illness and misfortune are explained in terms of **immanent justice**. Piaget found that 86 per cent of 6-year-olds, 73 per cent of 7- to 8-year-olds, 54 per cent of 9-year-olds and 34 per cent of 11- to 12-year-olds gave answers based on immanent justice.

Piaget aside, the investigation of children's understanding of health and illness is a relatively recent field of enquiry (Siegal and Peterson, 1999). Early work suggested a developmental trend from naïve to sophisticated concepts. Millstein, Adler and Irwin (1981) examined conceptions of illness in 11- to 15-year-olds and found that, compared to previously established child norms, adolescents gave more sophisticated definitions. Millstein and Irwin (1987), in a study on 11- to 18-year-olds, found that older adolescents were less likely to conceptualize health as an absence of illness. Similarly, Schmidt and Frohling (2000) found that older children and adults gave richer definitions of illness than younger children. In addition they found a developmental progression in concepts of specific diseases. Kister and Patterson (1980) presented stories similar to the ones used by Piaget to children aged 4 to 9 years old. The 4- and 5-year-olds were more likely than the older children to say illnesses result from disobedient behaviour. Bibace and Walsh (1980) also claimed that younger children view illness as having social or moral causes, rather than biological causes. They found that most 4-year-olds conceptualized all illnesses as things people catch as a product of contagion, even 'illnesses' with obvious physical causes such as cut and scrapes. Seven-year-olds explained illness in terms of contamination, either through physical contact with an object or a person that is 'bad' or by engaging in bad behaviour. Eleven-year-olds specify the mechanisms by which illnesses are caught, knowing that physical contact may be necessary as germs have to be swallowed or inhaled. Children in this age group talked about viral transmission of colds. As a result of findings such as this, Bibace and Walsh proposed a neo-Piagetian stage account. They mapped stages of children's knowledge onto Piaget's stages of logical development. On this view, children in the pre-operational stage (2 to 7 years old) account for illness by superstition or magical causes (e.g., the sun, trees, or God or sources of illness). Concrete-operational children (7 to 11 years old) give contamination and immanent justice-based explanations. Children in the formal operational stage (11 years onwards) have a much more sophisticated understanding, differentiating between internal and external causal agents. Although a cold may be transmitted externally, the illness is in the body and develops through the malfunctioning of specific organ or process. One problem with this is that Piaget theorizes logical structures which do not contain knowledge; it is not clear that domain-specific knowledge should necessarily follow domain-general logical abilities (Hergenrather and Rabinowitz, 1991). Also, adults may not have a scientific understanding of illness. Bibace and Walsh (1979) give an example of a 30-year-old woman who claimed that a pain in her side resulted from contact with her sister who was under a curse. Others have offered methodological criticisms, arguing that beliefs of sick children are not adequately compared to those of healthy children (Burbach and Peterson, 1986) and that questions are biased towards specific illnesses without addressing everyday aspects of health (Eiser, 1989).

Criticism of the neo-Piagetian stage approach of Bibace and Walsh (1980; also adopted by Perrin and Gerrity, 1981) has led to developmental models in which the role of experience is acknowledged. Charman and Chandiramani (1995) compared children's understanding of physical illness and psychological illness and found that 5-, 7- and 9-year-olds all had a basic knowledge of chicken pox and depression. They also found developmental change, stating that older children's more

immanent justice The belief that negative experiences are punishments for breaking rules.

sophisticated understanding reflected greater experience of both types of illness. Other recent research has explored what children know about different illnesses and has utilized more open questioning techniques to try and elicit detailed explanations. Myant and Williams (2005) interviewed children aged 4 to 12 to explore their concepts of health and illness in general and three different types of illness (contagious, non-contagious and injury) in particular. They used a series of short vignettes followed by a series of questions, based on Leventhal, Nerenz and Steele's (1984) illness representations, to probe children's explanations for the causes, prevention and time course of each illness. They found that knowledge of illness increases in sophistication with age and that levels of understanding differed for different illnesses, with participants demonstrating a greater understanding of injury than of illness. McQuaid *et al.* (2002) investigated knowledge and causal concepts of asthma in children with asthma and their parents. They found age-related changes in both factual asthma knowledge and causal reasoning about the illness. Both parents and children had more sophisticated concepts of asthma than headaches, which the authors interpret as evidence for a role of education and experience.

Within Wellman and Gelman's (1992) theory, children's understanding of health and illness is part of a larger framework theory of biology concerned with living things and biologically specific causal processes. As a result, children's reasoning about illness should focus on inheritance and contagion as casual factors. (Siegal, 1988) investigated children's knowledge of contagion and found that even preschoolers were aware that injury is caused by a physical process and not by contagion, demonstrating a further understanding of domain-specific causes of illness. Au and Romo (1999), on the other hand, argue that children do not have a domain-specific biological understanding of illness as, in interviews with 5- to 10-year-olds, they found very few biological explanations of the causes of illness.

Domain-specific or domain-general knowledge?

Another area of investigation is whether children use scientific concepts in the same way, independent of task domain. Carey and Spelke (1994) argue that scientific thought is domain-specific, that entities and explanations go together. When a task involves people children give psychological explanations, when a task involves inanimate objects they give physical explanations and when plants or animals are involved they give biological explanations. This idea is supported by Smith (1978) who showed 4- and 5-year-old children videos of an actor engaging in voluntary activities (e.g., chewing something or doing arm exercises), reflex reactions (e.g., yawning or saying 'Ow!' when poked) and object-like movement (e.g., being pushed across a room like a box). Four-year-olds judged that all three types of movement were intentional; they gave psychological explanations for human behaviour. Five-year-olds were, however, able to distinguish reflex and object-like movements from intentional movements.

Schult and Wellman (1997), on the other hand, argue that children's reasoning is flexible and interchangeable across domains. They gave 3- and 4-year-olds stories involving humans and asked the children to explain the protagonists' behaviours. There were four types of story, which featured intended behaviours, mistakes, behaviours which resulted from biological factors and behaviours which resulted from physical factors. An example of an 'intended story' is one in which it is breakfast time and Jimmy wants milk on his cereal; Jimmy pours milk on his cereal. An example of a mistake story is one in which it is breakfast time and Jimmy wants milk on his cereal, but Jimmy pours orange juice on his cereal. One of the 'biological' stories told of how Robin climbs a tree and hangs from a branch; she wants to hang on forever and never let go. Robin drops to the ground. A 'physical' story featured Bobby, who climbs on top of a stool. He wants to step off and float up into the air. Bobby steps off the stool and lands on the floor. Children gave three types of explanation for these stories: psychological, biological and physical. The results are shown in Figure 7.6. For the 'intended' story, all of the explanations were psychological and for the 'mistake' story, 87.5 per cent of the 3-year-olds and 93 per cent of the 4-year-olds gave a psychological explanation. However, contrary to the domain-specific hypothesis, they found that children explained the 'physical' story in terms of physical principles such as gravity: 75 per cent of the 3-year-olds and 80 per cent of the 4-year-olds gave physical answers. The 'biological' stories elicited a biological answer from 60 per cent of the 4-year-olds whereas most of the 3-year-olds gave a psychological explanation or gave no explanation. Wellman *et al.* concluded that young children can explain human behaviour in terms of all three domains and that the domains were, therefore, interchangeable.

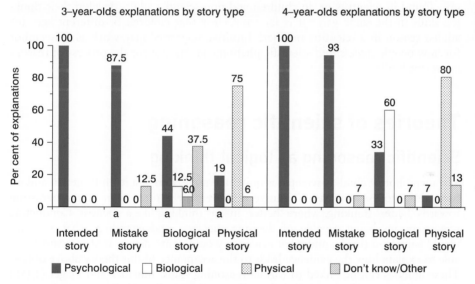

Figure 7.6

Schult and Wellman's results.

Source: Reprinted from Cognition, 62, Schult, C. A. & Wellman, H. M., Explaining human movements and actions: Children's understanding of the limits of psychological explanation, 291–324, Copyright (1997), with permission from Elsevier.

However, there is some evidence that the domains are separate. Children with autism, as we shall see in Chapter 10, have extreme difficulties with false belief tasks, suggesting they have an impaired intuitive psychology. However, they have an intact, or even advanced, intuitive physics. The status of these children's biological theories is less clear. Gopnik, Capps and Meltzoff (2000) argue that children with autism have a limited intuitive biology, but Binnie and Williams (2002) argue that it is intact. Binnie and Williams gave children with autism and verbal-mental-age-matched preschool children a story in which Craig plays with a friend who has a cold and sneezes on him. The participants were asked whether, after his friend has gone, Craig does not have a cold, he maybe has a cold, or he definitely has a cold. Around 30 per cent of children in both groups got it right. But, regardless of the status of biology in autism, it is clear that physics and psychology are very different, which casts some doubt on whether all three systems can be interchangeable in the way that Wellman suggests. Even if they are interchangeable, it is perhaps a process of learning that enables children to integrate three domains which develop independently.

Scientific reasoning

As we saw in Chapter 6, many adults cannot reason in a formal way and perhaps this is because, in many situations, we do not actually need to be able to do so. However, one area in which we do need to manipulate abstract concepts in a logical way is reasoning about scientific phenomena. Although young children may have scientific knowledge, it is not clear that they have a way of thinking scientifically; of reasoning with this knowledge. Scientific thinking involves reasoning about theories and asking whether the evidence supports or refutes a theory. Theories are necessary as they provide a framework for organizing and interpreting evidence and deciding what evidence is necessary to find conclusive answers. Theory revision can certainly be seen as an essential component of cognitive development. Our understanding and abilities (our 'theories') develop as we encounter a broader range of examples (or 'evidence') within different domains. Likewise, scientific thought can be characterized as relating evidence and theories. What, then, is the process that leads to a fully scientific way of thinking? Is this something which is only found in scientists or do children and non-scientist adults develop their thinking skills in the same way? It is far from clear that children of different ages (or adults) reason in a scientific manner. 'Intuitive scientists' may work as a metaphor for how people *understand* scientific phenomena, but not for the process of reasoning scientifically.

Theories of scientific reasoning

Scientific reasoning as logical thinking

The metaphor of child-as-scientist is quite pervasive, deriving from Piagetian and information-processing ideas. Cognitive development is often seen as a progression towards 'better' thinking, where 'better' means thinking like a scientist. Conducting science means being capable of devising theories, understanding what evidence would support a theory, and what evidence would contradict it. It also means being able to explain how the evidence leads to the acceptance of this theory above others. These abilities can be linked to formal reasoning skills. Inhelder and Piaget (1958) thought that formal reasoning skills and an understanding of the scientific method do not develop until the formal operations stage. They argued that children need to develop appropriate cognitive structures before they can master scientific concepts. Once these have developed, children should be able to discover scientific concepts on their own. In support of the relationship between formal reasoning and scientific thinking, Piburn (1990) found a correlation between success in science courses and performance on a test of propositional (if–then) reasoning. Interestingly, an item analysis indicated that the correlation relied on the test items that Inhelder and Piaget expected to develop in the formal operations stage, whereas aspects of reasoning which develop at the concrete operations stage were not related to success in science. Of course, the finding of a correlation does not necessarily mean there is a causal relationship. Inhelder and Piaget also predicted that when the appropriate cognitive structures have developed, children should be able to generalize across contexts. This is based on the idea that during the formal operations stage, children learn to think in a formal way; they can learn about any scientific domain without the development of new operations of reasoning. However, much of the research over the last 20 years has shown that scientific thought can be affected by the content of the propositions, in much the same way that research on conditional reasoning has demonstrated that children can reason within certain contexts (e.g., permission contexts; see Chapter 6).

Box 7.1 Inhelder and Piaget's pendulum problem

Inhelder and Piaget (1958) present a series of tasks they used to examine the development of logical reasoning. One of the most famous of these is the pendulum problem, in which they asked children to determine which of four factors – the length of the string, the weight of the object, the height from which the object is set in motion, or the force of the initial push – determines the frequency of the oscillation (how fast the pendulum moves) (see Figure 7.7). To solve this problem it is necessary to isolate one variable at a time and manipulate the value of the variable (e.g., vary the weight) whilst holding the other variables constant. This is known as

the **control of variables strategy** (CVS). Inhelder and Piaget found that children in the concrete operational stage would often manipulate more than one variable at a time (e.g., compare a long string and heavy weight with a shorter string and a lighter weight). Although these children demonstrate some understanding of carrying out different experiments, the experiments are confounded and, as a result, the children are not able to solve the problem. According to Inhelder and Piaget, it is not until the formal operations stage that children are able to test their hypotheses and arrive at logical conclusions

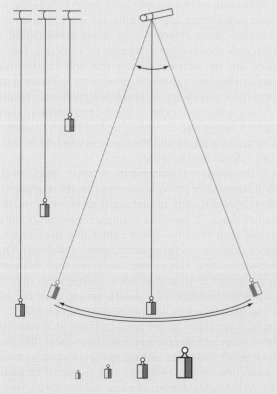

control of variables strategy A domain-general strategy in which unconfounded experiments are designed such that valid causal inferences can be made. For example, designing a series of experiments in which only one variable is manipulated at a time enables one to determine which variables have an effect on the outcome.

Figure 7.7

The pendulum problem.

Source: Inhelder, B., & Piaget, J. *The Growth of Logical Thinking from Childhood to Adolescence*. Copyright 1958 Basic Books, Inc. Reprinted by permission of Basic Books, a member of the Perseus Books Group.

The development of metacognition

Kuhn (1989) argues that both children and lay adults do not think like scientists. Kuhn and her colleagues have carried out a body of research which looks at how people relate theory and evidence, such as the example given at the beginning of the chapter. In one of their other studies, Kuhn *et al.* (1988) studied 8- to 10-year-olds, 11- to 13-year-olds, 14- to 15-year-olds and adults. The participants were given problems such as 'Why do some types of tennis balls result in a better serve?' and were asked to hypothesize about what factors may influence the quality of the serve. They were given the options of balls which were large or small, dark or light, rough or smooth, balls that were ridged, or balls with no ridges. They were then presented with theories, such as 'Mr S believes size is important' and 'Ms C thinks colour is important', and evidence. The evidence consisted of two baskets, one containing balls which had resulted in 'good serves' and one which had resulted in 'bad serves'. The youngest participants did not see evidence as separate from theory, they did not know what kind of evidence would support a theory and did not know what kind of evidence would contradict a theory. As a result of this, and other studies, Kuhn argues that children have little understanding of how hypotheses are supported or contradicted by evidence until they are 11 or 12 years old.

Kuhn (1989) suggests there are three main problems with children and lay adults which result in a failure to think scientifically. They are *theory bound*, they are *data bound* and they *need theories*. Children are theory bound in that they ignore discrepant evidence or attend to it selectively. They may also adjust the evidence to fit in with their theories. This is because they do not differentiate between theory and evidence. This seems to be true particularly when people have prior beliefs (or, at least, theories that they favour) and when there are multiple causes. Children are *data bound* in that they focus on their most recent results when constructing a theory. They can formulate a theory to account for a pattern of evidence, but if there is older evidence which does not fit the new theory, this will be ignored. Finally, they seem to *need theories* as they are apparently unable to consider data without a theory. If enough contradictory evidence is presented, they will finally acknowledge it, but only after a theory which can explain it has been devised. They need a plausible causal link between a factor and its results before they can accept the data. Ideally, evidence should be acknowledged and then a theory should be constructed which takes the pattern of evidence into account.

According to Kuhn (1989), it is the ability to differentiate between and coordinate theories and evidence which distinguishes individuals who can think scientifically from those who can't. Children have difficulty in revising their theories and do not distinguish between theory and evidence. If asked to evaluate the evidence for a theory, children will often just restate their theories. Kuhn argues that the effective coordination of theory and evidence depends on three metacognitive abilities: The ability to encode and represent evidence and theory separately, so that relations between them can be recognized; the ability to treat theories as independent objects of thought; and the ability to be open to the falsity of a theory, setting aside the acceptance of a theory so evidence can be assessed to determine the truth or falsity of the theory. Kuhn says metacognition is necessary as we need to know that theories are theories. We need to be aware of them and be able to think about them. We also need metacognitive abilities to think about strategies and when they should be used. Metacognition allows a general awareness of our thoughts and a control of high-order reasoning. Although Piaget never described them as such, the 'operating upon operations' or 'second-order operations' with which he characterized formal operational thinking are essentially metacognitive skills. Kuhn suggests that problems involving relating evidence to theory arise because the acquisition of metacognitive skills is a gradual process. As a result, early strategies for coordinating theory and evidence are replaced with better ones, but there is not a stage-like change from using an older strategy to a newer one. Multiple strategies are concurrently available so the process of change is very much like Siegler's (1996) 'overlapping waves' model (as discussed in Chapter 11). This account suggests that scientific reasoning skills are domain-general. Evidence to support this comes from Kuhn *et al.*, (1995) who found that improvement in the strategies used to solve problems in one domain can lead to a similar improvement in another domain.

The role of causal mechanisms

Koslowski (1996) argues that psychology often focuses on the covariation aspect of scientific thinking at the expense of other principles (such as theories and mechanisms) and that if these principles are taken into account, people's scientific reasoning abilities emerge as much superior. There are lots of examples of covariation and correlation in the world, but we only take seriously those in which there is a causal mechanism. This consideration allows us to decide which correlations are causal and which are not. Considering causal mechanisms requires a knowledge base (e.g., theories describing the mechanism). Thus, in order to test scientific reasoning, we need to see whether participants use their knowledge in a methodological way. Koslowski argues that many of the responses judged to be scientifically flawed by Kuhn and colleagues are, in fact, reasonable because theories and mechanisms provide a plausible way for mediation between cause and effect. When participants give theory-based answers, they are explaining why they give weight to some patterns of covariation and not to others. Kuhn and Koslowski agree that children and adolescents rely on their beliefs when making judgements about covariation evidence, but Koslowski states that as professional scientists rely on their accumulated knowledge, this is legitimate scientific behaviour. She suggests that where there are flaws in children's reasoning, it is a result of information-processing limitations (e.g., in capacity or strategies) rather than an inability to coordinate theory and evidence. Thus, this view of scientific reasoning conceptualizes the inclusion of a consideration of plausible mechanisms as a useful way of excluding artifactual causes and deciding whether a theory requires outright rejection or modification in the face of disconfirming evidence (Koslowski and Masnick, 2002).

Koslowski (1996) reports a series of studies she carried out with various colleagues, with the aim of demonstrating that participants make judicious and appropriate use of theoretical considerations, such as plausible causal mechanisms. One of the studies (Koslowski *et al.*,1989) looked at the effects of four types of evidence – *covariation, causal mechanism, sample size* and *sample method* – on judgements of the likelihood that a target factor caused an effect. They presented three groups of participants, with mean ages of 11, 14 and 20, with story problems in which a character was trying to determine whether a target factor caused an effect. One of the story problems was about a man who wanted to find out whether using a special type of petrol with an additive to cover up odour was responsible for getting worse mileage than regular petrol. Four variables were manipulated in the stories. First, the *sample method*: In the *direct intervention* condition the man tries two cars of the same model; in the *natural occurrence* condition he tries one model that uses normal petrol and one that uses the special petrol. Second, the *sample size*: in one condition he tests a *small* sample of two cars, in another he tests a *large* sample of eight cars. Third, the presence of *covariation*: In the *covariation present* condition, the special petrol gets worse mileage whereas in the *covariation absent* condition there is no difference. Finally, *causal mechanism*: In the *causal mechanism present* condition, the special additive has impurities that interfere with efficient combustion, in the *causal mechanism ruled out* condition there is no evidence for how the special petrol could make a difference, and in the *control* condition no information is available. For each story, participants were asked to rate the likelihood that the target factor was causally related to the effect on a nine-point scale.

As well as finding main effects of *causal mechanism* and *covariation* on the ratings given, Koslowski *et al.* found several two- and three-way interactions. The three-way interaction between *covariation*, *age* and *mechanism* is illustrated in Figure 7.8. Taken as a whole, the results suggest that adolescents and adults consider both mechanism and covariation when evaluating evidence, with the younger participants' consideration of mechanism overruled by the presence of covariation. The authors conclude that, over time, we learn that other factors, such as sample size and mechanism, limit the extent to which covariation evidence indicates a causal effect.

Figure 7.8

Results from Koslowski *et al.*

Source: Reprinted from Koslowski, B., Okagaki, L., Lorenz, C., & Umbach, D. (1989). When covariation is not enough: The role of causal mechanism, sampling method, and sample size in causal reasoning. *Child Development*, 60(6), 1316–1327, with permission from Wiley.

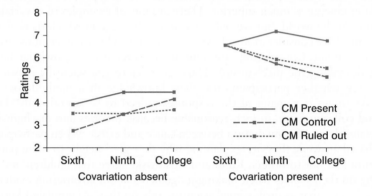

Scientific discovery as problem solving

Klahr and Dunbar (1988; Dunbar and Klahr, 1989; Klahr, 1996) view scientific discovery as a type of problem solving, in which scientific reasoning is conceptualized as a search through two problem spaces. They extended a classic model of problem solving from the field of cognitive science (Simon and Lea, 1974) to explain how adults and children carry out scientific reasoning. There are three major components to their Scientific Discovery as Dual Search (SDDS) model: Searching the hypothesis space, testing hypotheses and evaluating evidence (see Figure 7.9). The two problem spaces to be searched are the space of possible hypotheses and the space of possible experiments. The experiment-space search can be carried out in the hypothesis generation phase and/or the hypothesis testing phase. In generating a hypothesis, we start with some knowledge about a domain and aim to produce a hypothesis that can explain that knowledge. The hypothesis may be generated by considering what we already know; our initial hypothesis may be based on our knowledge, beliefs and biases. Alternatively, or if our prior-knowledge-based hypothesis is falsified, we may conduct experiments to generate further information which can then inform our hypothesis. Once a hypothesis has been generated, we test the hypothesis by designing an experiment, which involves searching through the experiment space in order to produce an experiment which will give us some evidence against which we can measure the hypothesis. In the final phase the evidence we have generated is evaluated to see if the hypothesis should be accepted or rejected. Alternatively, the evidence may be inconclusive, in which case we move back to the hypothesis testing

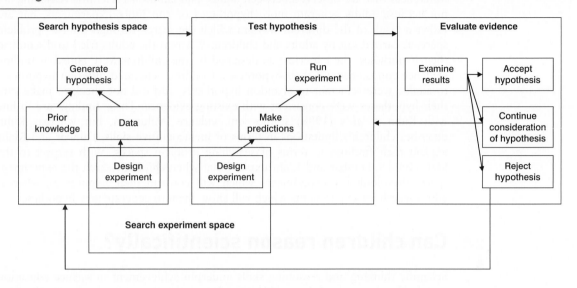

Figure 7.9 Simplified version of SDDS framework.

phase and search for another experiment which may give us some more conclusive evidence.

Dunbar and Klahr (1989) carried out three studies on adults' and children's scientific discovery using 'BigTrak', a robot vehicle that is programmed by entering a series of commands (move forwards, move backwards, rotate left, rotate right, pause, fire-cannon) on a keypad mounted on the top. There is also a key marked 'RPT'; when RPT is pressed, followed by a numerical value n, the last n instruction steps are repeated. Participants in these studies, twenty undergraduate students and twenty-two children aged 8 to 11, were not told what RPT does. Instead, they were asked to find out what the RPT key does by writing programs and observing the results. After a period of experimentation, they were asked to generate hypotheses regarding the function of the RPT key and run experiments to test their hypotheses. Many participants started with the hypothesis that the RPT key causes the entire instruction set to repeat n times. Other popular hypotheses were that it causes the last step to repeat n times or that it repeats the subsequent steps n times. The results from these studies are shown in Table 7.2. Both adults and children took an average of 20 minutes to decide that they had worked out the answer. They also generated similar numbers of hypotheses and experiments. However, the adults were much

Table 7.2 Performance on Dunbar and Klahr's (1989) BigTrak task.

	Adults	Children
Solvers	19/20	2/22
Mean time	20 mins	20 mins
Number of hypotheses	4.6	3.3
Number of programs	18	13

Source: Klahr (1996). Reproduced with permission of Lawrence Erlbaum Associates, permission conveyed through Copyright Clearance Center, Inc.

more successful at discovering the correct answer. Dunbar and Klahr argue that the differences that are observed between adults' and children's scientific reasoning are not because adults generate more hypotheses or run more experiments, but are rather a result of the different ways in which the search through the two problem spaces is carried out by adults and children. Whereas the adults tried to disconfirm their hypotheses, the experiments designed by the children were aimed at finding evidence consistent with their hypotheses. Children generated different hypotheses to adults, were reluctant to abandon hypotheses, and did not check to make sure their hypotheses were consistent with existing evidence. These findings are in line with Kuhn *et al.*'s (1988) studies on evidence evaluation, but whereas Kuhn describes children's limitations in terms of metacognitive skills, Dunbar and Klahr explain their findings in terms of searching problem spaces. With respect to the SDDS model, Dunbar and Klahr explain that when children search the experiment space, they look for experiments which will confirm their hypotheses, whereas adults search for experiments which will allow them to generate new hypotheses.

Can children reason scientifically?

Scientific thinking and reasoning skills underpin achievement in science education and the development of these skills is fundamental to becoming a scientifically literate adult. Research into children's scientific thinking and reasoning is multifaceted and includes the investigation of the formation and revision of theories and the principles of scientific inquiry. The scientific reasoning process consists of four key abilities: hypothesis generation, experimental design, hypothesis testing and evidence evaluation (Klahr and Dunbar, 1988). The evidence presented so far suggests that children are not able to reason scientifically until 11 or 12 years of age and that this reasoning skill depends on the development of metacognitive abilities. However, the sorts of experiments carried out by Kuhn and colleagues may underestimate children's abilities. There is a large body of evidence which suggests that children can carry out some level of scientific thinking at a much younger age. We have looked at the development of theory of mind (Chapter 5) and it seems that scientific theories can be like false beliefs; children who fail false belief tasks cannot hold both a true and false belief in mind at the same time and do not know that a theory could be a false belief. However, 4-year-olds can pass false belief tasks and can be argued to be reasoning about beliefs as theories in the domain of psychology.

Hypothesis testing

Hypothesis testing involves searching through a space of experiments in order to select a test that will discriminate among competing hypotheses. In order to achieve this, predictions about experimental results must be made (Klahr, Fay and Dunbar, 1993). Prior knowledge can often guide the selection of predictions and the strategy for selecting a hypothesis. This is evidenced by the finding that participants in scientific reasoning studies often select or design experiments that will generate data that will potentially confirm, rather than disconfirm, their hypotheses (Klayman and Ha, 1987). An important first step in the scientific reasoning chain is to select a test of a hypothesis which will generate valid data, regardless of whether the data confirm or disconfirm the hypothesis. The Control of Variables Strategy (CVS) is a domain-general processing strategy that enables us to make a distinction between confounded and unconfounded experiments and gives us the ability to draw valid inferences from experiments (Chen and Klahr, 1999).

Findings from research on children's ability to design or select unconfounded experiments tend to reveal a pattern of poor performance prior to adolescence (e.g., Kuhn *et al.*, 1988, 1995; Schauble, 1996). In these studies, children were unable to design experiments which would allow valid inferences to be made and had difficulty evaluating evidence with respect to hypotheses. Klahr *et al.* (1993) agree that children have limited domain-general reasoning skills compared to adults, but argue that when hypotheses are plausible and there are few alternatives to choose from, children are able to succeed in scientific reasoning tasks. A number of studies demonstrate that domain-specific knowledge is also a relevant factor (e.g., Carey, 1985; Chi and Koeske, 1983; Penner and Klahr, 1996) and recent approaches to scientific reasoning take into account both domain-general strategies and domain-specific concepts, suggesting that the two bootstrap one another (Lehrer and Schauble, 2006; Schauble, 1996; Zimmerman, 2007).

Sodian, Zaitchik and Carey (1991) asked children aged between 6 and 9 to choose between two tests of a theory, one which was conclusive and one which was inconclusive. The children were told the following story:

> Jim and Steven are brothers. They know there is a mouse in their house, but they never see it because it only comes out at night. They know there is just one mouse. Jim thinks it's probably a big daddy mouse, but Steven thinks it's probably a little baby mouse.
>
> The boys decide they want to feed the mouse. Here are two boxes. One has a large opening and one has a small opening. The boxes aren't traps; they're just plain old boxes, like mouse houses. If the mouse can fit through the opening, he can go inside the house, eat the food, and then leave again. The boys want to leave food for the mouse in one of the boxes. Remember, they don't know whether the mouse is a big daddy mouse or a small baby mouse.
>
> Which box should they use if they want to make sure the mouse will be able to get the food, whether it's a big mouse or a little mouse? Why?
>
> The next day they decide to find out whether it's a big mouse or a little mouse. Now they don't care anymore about feeding the mouse. What they want to know now is if it's a big mouse or a small mouse. Remember, if they put food into a box and in the morning the food is no longer there, then they know that the mouse came inside the box during the night and ate it.
>
> Which box should they put the food into if they want to find out if the mouse is a big mouse or a baby mouse? Why?
>
> (Sodian, Zaitchik and Carey, 1991, p. 757)

Note that the participants were asked two questions. The first question (the *feed* question) was included to see whether children could distinguish between testing a hypothesis and producing an effect. In the feed question, participants were being asked to ensure that the mouse gets the food, whereas the aim of the *find out* question was to see if they could differentiate between a conclusive and inconclusive test of the theory. The majority of the children correctly answered that the box with the small opening was required, demonstrating that even 6-year-olds can identify whether a hypothesis is supported by a piece of evidence.

Tschirgi (1980) examined hypothesis testing in familiar contexts, providing participants with scenarios such as baking a cake and making a paper airplane. In these scenarios the outcome could either be positive or negative (e.g., a great cake or a terrible cake). Tschirgi tested the prediction that outcome is important in hypothesis testing performance. If one variable is hypothesized to be the cause of a bad outcome, people will change that variable alone. However, if the outcome is positive, there is a desire to reproduce the effect by holding the variables that are hypothesized to cause the good outcome constant. Tschirgi found children were more likely to use a VOTAT (vary-one-thing-at-a-time) strategy when presented with a bad outcome and a HOTAT (hold-one-thing-at-a-time) strategy when presented with a good outcome. Younger children (6- to 7-year-olds) were also more likely to 'change all' in a bad outcome situation in attempt to make a change for the better. Similarly, Zimmerman and Glaser (2001) provided 11- to 12 year-olds with hypotheses about whether certain liquids were good or bad for plant health. When a negative outcome was presented, participants tended to propose experiments using a VOTAT/CVS strategy, whereas a positive outcome led to attempts to preserve the outcome by manipulating other variables (e.g., type of plant).

Croker and Buchanan (in press) examined how hypothesis testing strategies are affected by prior belief. We examined the responses given by 144 children aged 3 to 11 in a contextualized scientific reasoning task in which children have strong prior beliefs. Oral health was selected for two key reasons: (a) it is a domain in which behaviours have a direct causal link with outcomes (e.g., regular consumption of sugar results in tooth decay); and (b) from an early age, children have beliefs regarding this link and the behaviours which mediate it. Specifically, we predicted that whether the evidence is consistent or inconsistent with prior beliefs will have an effect on task performance and, in line with Tschirgi's findings, that a good or bad outcome will affect task performance. In order to test these predictions, an experimental task was devised in which pictures of oral health behaviours (brushing teeth, visiting the dentist and drinking either cola or milk) were presented alongside pictures of healthy (good outcome) or unhealthy (bad outcome) teeth. The task involved choosing the set of behaviours that should be carried out in order to test the hypothesis. There were four hypothesis-testing tasks in all: Two in which the evidence presented was consistent with participants' beliefs (*belief-consistent* condition) and two in which the evidence presented was inconsistent with their beliefs (*belief-inconsistent* condition). For both sets of tasks, one featured a *good outcome* (healthy teeth) and the other featured a *bad outcome* (unhealthy teeth). Half the participants were presented with stories in which the evidence presented was consistent with their own beliefs (belief-consistent) and the other half were presented with stories in which the evidence was inconsistent with their beliefs (belief-inconsistent). Each participant completed two tasks, one with a good outcome and one with a bad outcome. Interestingly, there were no main effects of age. The results showed that in the *good outcome* condition, participants were more likely to answer correctly (i.e., select the VOTAT strategy) when the information presented in the task was consistent with their beliefs, whereas in the *bad outcome* condition they were more likely to pass the task when the information was inconsistent with their beliefs. These effects of context suggest that domain-general reasoning processes, such as the control of variables present in the VOTAT strategy, can be mediated by domain-specific knowledge regarding the plausibility of a hypothesis.

Evidence evaluation

Kuhn *et al.*'s (1988) evidence evaluation studies ('food and colds' and 'tennis balls') were described earlier in the chapter. Their conclusion that pre-adolescent children cannot differentiate between theory and evidence as separate entities has been criticized (Leach, 1999; Samarapungavan, 1992) on the grounds that they do not distinguish between *ability* and *performance*. Samarapungavan argues that because

Kuhn *et al.* gave the same tasks to children, adults and scientists, higher task demands were placed on the children. Carey *et al.* (1989) describe the theories presented in Kuhn *et al.*'s tasks as *correlational* hypotheses, as opposed to theories which are presented as *causal*, which would normally be accompanied with explanations of the mechanisms involved in science education. In an electric circuits task involving coordination of theory and evidence, given to pairs of 9- to 16-year-olds, Leach (1999) found that, although many 9-year-olds did not explicitly refer to evidence, some of the children in this age group still seemed to be able to consider theory and evidence separately. Leach suggests that the difference in performance between younger and older children may be a result of science education. By the age of 16, adolescents have been taught how to relate observations and explanations, whereas 9-year-olds draw more on their knowledge of the domain. There are important practical implications of this debate. If primary children lack the ability to coordinate theory and evidence, then there seems to be little point in including it in the curriculum. If, on the other hand, the *ability* is present in younger children, then science education can be modified to address their poor *performance*.

Samarapungavan (1992) conducted an evidence evaluation study, in which she demonstrated that when children are given a causal hypothesis, they are capable of evaluating evidence with respect to theories. She presented 150 children aged 6 to 12 years old with a series of pictures showing the phases of the moon. The children were also given two theories as to why these phases may occur. One theory was that clouds cover different portions of the moon at different times; the other was that the moon has a dark side and a light side. The children were then given some evidence with which to evaluate the two theories. They were told that an astronaut who had landed on the moon reported that the moon was dry and had no water and that he landed on white rock but later walked on black gravel. Most of the participants correctly selected the second theory as being supported by the evidence.

Ruffman *et al.* (1993) found even earlier ability when they gave 4- and 5-year-olds a task, which was based on false belief tasks, in which the children had to work out how a pattern of evidence relates to a hypothesis. The task involved ascertaining whether red or green food leads to tooth loss. The participants were shown pictures of ten boys eating food. Five of the boys ate green food and had healthy teeth; five ate red food and had missing teeth. All the participants correctly answered that red food leads to tooth loss. The evidence was then rearranged (or 'faked'), with bits of green paper (representing green food) placed in front of the pictures of boys with missing teeth and bits of red paper placed in front of the pictures of boys with healthy teeth. A doll was then introduced and the children were asked 'which food will Sally say makes teeth fall out?' The majority of the 5-year-olds gave the correct answer and even 4-year-olds seemed to understand the principles of causal reasoning. It is possible that young children found this task relatively easy as there is no conflict between the evidence presented and the participants' own causal beliefs; both causal factors (red food and green food) are equally plausible.

What happens when there is a conflict between beliefs and evidence? Successful scientific reasoning often involves suspending prior beliefs when the evidence encountered contradicts these beliefs (Greenhoot *et al.*, 2004), and we have seen that belief can have an effect on hypothesis-testing behaviours. Kuhn *et al.* (1988) and Amsel and Brock (1996) found that children's answers were biased by their prior beliefs. In addition, Kuhn *et al.* found that even when the covariation data was correctly interpreted, participants justified their answers in terms of new beliefs about the causal mechanisms which would lead a variable to have an effect. Koerber *et al.* (2005) also demonstrated an effect of prior belief on evidence evaluation. Their results showed that 5-year-olds were able to perform better on tasks that were belief-neutral, such as whether red or yellow fire causes dragons to catch colds, than on tasks where they had a prior belief, such as whether seeing a ghost or a princess makes you scared.

Integrated experimentation skills

Whereas the aims of the studies discussed above were to examine either hypothesis testing or evidence evaluation, many researchers have conducted microgenetic studies in order to assess children's abilities with respect to the whole process of scientific investigation. In these studies, participants are usually presented with multiple variables which may have an effect on an outcome. Their task is to generate hypotheses, design experiments to test the hypotheses, record the outcomes of their experiments and evaluate the evidence with respect to the hypotheses. Some studies have used hands-on physical systems, such as the canal boat problem in which various sizes and shapes of boat, with variable mass, can be placed in a water tank with a movable floor. The aim of the task is to determine which factors affect the speed of the boat (Kuhn *et al.*, 1995; Schauble, 1996; Schauble, Klopfer and Raghavan, 1991). Other studies have used computer simulations, which enables a wider range of tasks to be used. Examples include a virtual version of the BigTrak robot, in which a spaceship can be programmed to move about the screen (Klahr, Fay and Dunbar, 1993), and earthquake and avalanche prediction software, which allow the user to see whether factors such as soil type and water quality, or windspeed and slope angle, affect the likelihood of the occurrence of earthquakes and avalanches, respectively (Dean and Kuhn, 2007; Kuhn and Dean, 2005; Kuhn *et al.*, 2008; Kuhn, Pease and Wirkala, 2009).

Schauble (1990) also used a virtual environment to explore children's integrated experimentation skills. Twenty-two children aged 9 to 11 were presented with a computer microworld in which they had to determine the effects of five factors on the speed of racing cars: Engine size, wheel size, presence of muffler, presence of tailfins and colour. As Schauble was interested in whether children's strategies and beliefs would change over time, a microgenetic research design was employed. The participants were given eight sessions, spread over eight weeks, in which to conduct experiments. Initially, the children tended to believe that a large engine, large wheels and the presence of a muffler increased speed. In reality, the microworld was set up so that a large engine and medium-size wheels increased speed, presence or absence of a muffler and the colour of the car were irrelevant, and the absence of tailfins only increased speed when the engine was large. If the children were behaving like scientists, they should take one factor to manipulate and hold the rest of the variables constant and record the results of each experiment (i.e., what the value of each variable was and what the outcome was in terms of the speed of the car). This did not happen. The children often varied several factors at the same time and none of them wrote down which set of features led to which speed. Some recorded features without outcomes, or outcomes without features, but most wrote down nothing at all, relying on their memory of the experiments they had carried out over the eight-week period. Only 22 per cent of the experiments they carried out could be classed as valid tests. When they did conduct valid experiments they often drew conclusions consistent with their beliefs and not necessarily consistent with the evidence generated. Only 38 per cent of the judgements made were valid on the basis of the experimental findings. The children didn't know what they needed to know to come to a valid conclusion. They used a positive test strategy, testing variables they believed would influence speed (e.g., engine size) as opposed to variables they believed would not have an effect (e.g., colour). Most of the children managed to discover simple effects, but only two of the twenty-two participants discovered the interaction effect between tailfin and engine size. Other microgenetic studies have revealed similar limitations in 8- to 12-year-old children's abilities to generate unconfounded experiments, attempt to disconfirm hypotheses, keep accurate and systematic records and evaluate evidence (Klahr *et al.*, 1993; Kuhn *et al.*, 1995; Schauble, 1996; Zimmerman, Raghavan and Sartoris, 2003).

Concluding comments

Scientific thinking is a complex domain as it involves both knowledge and reasoning skills. The nature of what it is that develops is therefore confounded. Some researchers have attempted to avoid this problem by either interviewing children to find out what they know or by devising reasoning tasks that involve little prior knowledge. However, it is not clear that this provides a true picture of children's scientific thinking. The evidence presented in this chapter shows that there is more to children's understanding of biology and physics than simply acquiring facts and that children's knowledge and beliefs have a role to play in how they reason. Although it may or may not be the case that the knowledge domains of psychology, biology and physics are separate, it may be necessary to have some understanding of psychology in order to be able to reason scientifically. Sodian *et al.* (1991) argue that two basic skills are needed for scientific reasoning. First, children need to understand that inferences can be drawn from evidence. The theory of mind literature (see Chapter 5) demonstrates that it is not until the age of 4 that children understand that knowledge and beliefs are based on perceptual experience. Second, they need to understand that inference is itself a mechanism with which further knowledge can be acquired. Four-year-olds base their knowledge on perceptual experiences and do not realize that there may be other evidence with which to draw inferences. Sodian and Wimmer (1987) carried out an experiment in which one doll moves an object from one bag to another and tells a second doll what they have done. Four to 6-year-olds tended to say that the second doll didn't know what was in the second bag, whereas children aged 6 and over understood that the second doll could infer the contents of the bag from what the first doll had told them. This may explain why, at around the age of 6, children are able to pass some of the simple hypothesis testing and evaluation tasks, such as those carried out by Sodian *et al.* and Ruffman *et al.* (1993).

How are these findings of early scientific thinking skills reconciled with the research on integrated experimentation skills, which shows major limitations in 8- to 12-year-olds' reasoning? Kuhn (2000; Kuhn and Pearsall, 2000) argues that successful performance on the tasks investigated by Ruffman *et al.* and Sodian *et al.* depends on skills other than the differentiation and coordination of theory and evidence. She claims that a competency in recognizing that determinate evidence is superior to indeterminate evidence enables children to pass the 'mouse size' task and that passing the 'green/red food' task results from the ability to recognize correspondences between theory and evidence. In fact, the ability to identify correspondences between theory and evidence may well develop a lot earlier than the age of 5. Kuhn points out that infants who have a rattle attached to their leg can infer that moving their leg causes the rattle to move. The abilities studied by Ruffman *et al.* and Sodian *et al.* do support the development of scientific thought, but are not central to it.

On the basis of recent research into scientific reasoning, Sodian and Bullock (2008) pose three questions and draw two conclusions. Their first question is whether metaconceptual (or metacognitive) understanding matters; does the ability to examine our own reasoning enable us to overcome biases and develop our conceptual knowledge? Second, they ask how domain knowledge and domain-general reasoning strategies interact, suggesting that more experiments looking at reasoning in knowledge-rich contexts are needed. Third, they ask whether education matters; is it possible to induce long-term improvements in scientific thinking by teaching children appropriate strategies? Their first conclusion is that scientific reasoning involves the metastrategic process of being able to think explicitly about hypotheses and evidence; their second conclusion is that the abilities to reason scientifically and understand scientific knowledge are difficult, and that neither is fully mastered until adolescence at the very earliest. Perhaps this is why many adults privilege their own beliefs and biases over scientific knowledge and logical reasoning.

Summary

Scientific thinking. Children have been characterized as intuitive scientists, yet their conceptions are often scientifically invalid and studies on scientific reasoning show that, rather than making judgements based on evidence, they rely heavily on their prior knowledge and beliefs. There are two broad types of research on scientific thinking: Research into the concepts and knowledge children possess at different points in development, and the strategies children use in order to apply their knowledge to solve problems. These can be defined, respectively, as the study of *scientific knowledge* and *scientific reasoning*.

Theories of scientific conceptual change. According to the radical restructuring account, young children have knowledge of facts about biology and principles of physics, but it is not until the age of around 7 that these facts are assimilated into a coherent theory or conceptual structure. Prior to this, the child's theory of biology is based on their understanding of psychology. Although younger children possess factual knowledge, it is not until children connect these facts together into a conceptually coherent framework that they can be said to have a theory of biology or physics. By the age of 10 to 12 years old, these theories have developed into an adult-like understanding. Theory theory posits innate framework theories of psychology, biology and physics. These initial naïve theories undergo a process of revision when their theories do not account for their experiences which can lead to stage-like, qualitative shifts in concepts. As these entities and processes differ between domains, the Theory theory predicts domain-specific development, where advances in understanding in one domain are independent from advances in another.

Scientific knowledge. Infants and young children show a surprising knowledge of basic principles of physics, yet older children are surprisingly unknowledgeable. Piaget conducted early research on children's understanding of physics, but most of what we know is the result of work from the 1980s onwards. Studies examining how children and adults predict trajectories show that even adults have an incorrect understanding of how forces affect motion. Children start to discriminate between animate and inanimate objects around the age of 3, but their conceptions of biology are limited until middle childhood. Prior to this, they do not understand the functions of the organs in the body, do not understand that death is universal and inevitable and accept impossible transformations of identity based on superficial appearances. Some misconceptions, such as the idea that acquired characteristics can be inherited, continue into adolescence. Children's conceptions of health and illness also show a long period of development, from naïve beliefs that illness is a punishment for bad behaviour in the preschool years, to a scientific understanding of illness transmission in adolescence. Recent research suggests that experience has a role in developing concepts of illness; as children come into contact with specific illnesses, they develop a more sophisticated understanding of them.

Scientific reasoning. As well as developing concepts and theories, scientific thinking involves reasoning about theories and asking whether the evidence supports or refutes a theory. Many studies have shown severe limitations in children's ability to reason scientifically.

Theories of scientific reasoning. There are various theoretical perspectives on scientific reasoning. The logical thinking account views scientific reasoning as part of the domain-general development of logical thinking skills which do not develop fully until (at least) the formal operations stage. According to the metacognitive account, children are not capable of scientific reasoning until 11 or 12 years of age, but this is not because of the development of formal logical thinking. Children younger than this are seen as generally incapable of coordinating theory and evidence, particularly when evidence contradicts their prior beliefs. The effective coordination of theory and evidence depends on metacognitive skills such as the ability to treat theories and strategies as independent objects of thought. The causal mechanism account, however, suggests that allowing prior knowledge of plausible causal mechanisms to mediate the interpretation of evidence is scientifically legitimate. When children give answers based on their theories, rather than the evidence, they are explaining why they give weight to some patterns of covariation and not to others. A fourth view of scientific reasoning conceptualizes it as a type of problem solving, which involves a search through two problem spaces. There are three major components to the Scientific Discovery as Dual Search (SDDS)

model: Searching the hypothesis space, testing hypotheses and evaluating evidence. The two problem spaces to be searched are the space of possible hypotheses and the space of possible experiments.

Can children reason scientifically? The scientific reasoning process consists of four key abilities: hypothesis generation, experimental design, hypothesis testing and evidence evaluation. Successful hypothesis testing involves using the Control of Variables Strategy (CVS) to select a test that will discriminate among competing hypotheses. Although some research has revealed a pattern of poor performance prior to adolescence, other studies have demonstrated that children as young as 6 are capable of choosing a valid test of a hypothesis. This ability is mediated by prior beliefs and whether participants are trying to replicate a good outcome or remove a bad outcome. Similarly, some studies on evidence evaluation skills have found poor performance in children, whereas others have shown that children aged 6 or younger are able to pass simple tasks. Also – as with hypothesis testing – prior beliefs seem to play a role in how easy children find the tasks. Many researchers have conducted microgenetic studies in order to assess children's abilities with respect to the whole process of scientific investigation, including the generation of hypotheses, experimental design, record keeping and evidence evaluation. In general, these studies have revealed limitations in 8- to 12-year-old children's abilities to generate unconfounded experiments, attempt to disconfirm hypotheses, keep accurate and systematic records and evaluate evidence.

Discussion questions

1 Does the development of children's scientific knowledge result from the development of domain-general knowledge and processes, or changes in domain-specific concepts?

2 What are the implications of research on children's knowledge of biology, health and illness for how health professionals communicate with children?

3 Do you think that children's existing knowledge, and/or beliefs, help or interfere with scientific reasoning? What evidence is there in support of your answer?

4 Is scientific reasoning a skill that can be applied equally across domains? Do you think that learning to reason scientifically about physics problems will transfer to reasoning about psychological experiments?

5 What impact could the psychological study of scientific reasoning have on how school curricula are designed?

Further Reading

Books and chapters

Siegal, M. and Peterson, C. C. (Eds). (1999). *Children's understanding of biology and health*. Cambridge: Cambridge University Press.

Michael Siegal and Candida Peterson bring together a collection of essays on children's understanding of biology and health.

Wellman, H. M. and Gelman, S. A. (1998). Knowledge acquisition in foundational domains. In D. Kuhn and R. S. Siegler (Eds), *Handbook of child psychology, Vol. 2: Cognition, perception, and language* (pp. 523–573). New York: Wiley.

Henry Wellman and Susan Gelman offer an overview of theory theory and discuss evidence from the domains of physics, psychology and biology.

Articles

Gopnik, A. (1996). The scientist as child. *Philosophy of Science*, 63(4), 485–514.

Carey, S. and Spelke, E. (1996). Science and core knowledge. *Philosophy of Science*, 63(4), 515–533.

In these two papers, Alison Gopnik argues for the theory theory account of scientific knowledge, and Susan Carey and Elizabeth Spelke discuss where they disagree and agree with Gopnik.

Kuhn, D. (1989). Children and adults as intuitive scientists. *Psychological Review*, 96(4), 674–689.

Deanna Kuhn summarizes some of the work presented in her 1988 book and presents her theory of the development of scientific reasoning.

Sodian, B. and Bullock, M. (2008) Scientific reasoning – where are we now? [Special issue]. *Cognitive Development*, 23(4).

In this special issue of Cognitive Development, editors Beate Sodian and Merry Bullock present a collection of six papers offering a 'state of the art' view of the current issues, themes and research in scientific reasoning.

Sodian, B., Zaitchik, D. and Carey, S. (1991). Young children's differentiation of hypothetical beliefs from evidence. *Child Development*, 62(4), 753–766.

This is Beate Sodian and colleagues' classic 'mouse house' hypothesis testing paper.

Zimmerman, C. (2007). The development of scientific thinking skills in elementary and middle school. *Developmental Review*, 27(2), 172–223.

Corinne Zimmerman gives a comprehensive overview of themes and research in scientific reasoning.

© Bonnie Jacobs/iStock

Chapter 8
Numeracy and literacy

Learning Outcomes

At the end of this chapter you should be able to:

- Describe and evaluate theories of numeracy.
- Describe the basic skills that are necessary for numeracy.
- Discuss research on the development of numeracy.
- Describe the basic skills that are necessary for literacy.
- Describe and evaluate theories of the development of reading.
- Discuss research on the development of literacy.

In 1985, Terezinha Nunes Carraher, David Carraher and Analúcia Schliemann published a study in which they looked at the mathematical abilities of Brazilian children who came from poor families and sold food on the street. Selling food requires adding, subtracting and multiplying. Children who do this need to be able to tell customers how much their purchases cost and calculate the correct change. As such, they clearly have mathematical abilities, but it is likely that these are derived from practical experience, rather than formal education. Carraher *et al.* wanted to compare real-life mathematical problem-solving to formal mathematics problems in children who had learned their mathematics skills in an applied context.

They studied five children aged from 9 to 15 years, who had a range of schooling. One participant had one year of school, two had three years, one had four years and one had eight. Each participant took part in an informal test and a formal test. In the informal test, the researchers played the role of customers and asked the children to sell them items. Here is one example from participant 'M', a 12-year-old coconut vendor.

Customer: How much is one coconut?
M: 35.
Customer: I'd like ten. How much is that?
M: (Pause) Three will be 105; with three more that will be 210. (Pause) I need four more. That is … (pause) 315 … I think it is 350.
(Carraher *et al.*, 1985, p. 23)

> Q. How did M solve the problem of 10 × 35? How is it different from the way in which you might expect a 12-year-old to solve the problem?

After the informal test, the participants were given a formal test, in which they were asked to solve problems that were numerically identical to some of the ones they had solved in the informal test. Each participant was presented with a mix of mathematical operations or word problems in the formal test. For example, in the informal test, one participant was asked how much 12 lemons costing 5 cruzeiros each would cost. In the formal test, the problem was posed as a mathematical operation: 12 × 5. An example of a word problem is: 'A fisherman caught 50 fish. The second one caught five times the amount of fish the first fisherman had caught. How many fish did the lucky fisherman catch?'

> Q. How well do you think the children did on the word problems? How well do you think they did on the mathematical operations?

The results are shown in Table 8.1. Each child's score was calculated by dividing the overall percentage by 10. This gives a maximum score of 10 for each of the three problem types. As you can see, the participants got almost all of the questions on the informal test correct. However, they only got 74 per cent of the word problems correct, and did poorly on mathematical operations test, scoring an overall 37 per cent. These results demonstrate that the participants knew how to perform arithmetic, but could not transfer the skill across situations.

Table 8.1						

Results from
Carraher *et al.*'s
study.

Source: Carraher, Carraher
and Schliemann (1985).
Reprinted with permission.

			Formal test			
			Mathematical operations		Word problems	
	Informal test					
Subject	Score	Number of items	Score	Number of items	Score	Number of items
M	10	18	2.5	8	10	11
P	8.9	19	3.7	8	6.9	16
Pi	10	12	5.0	6	10	11
MD	10	7	1.0	10	3.3	12
S	10	7	8.3	6	7.3	11
Overall per cent correct	98		37		74	

> Q. What do you think the implications of this study are with respect to teaching mathematics?

It is clear from these results that we cannot assume that children automatically transfer their knowledge of mathematics from an informal context, such as selling goods, to the more formal context of the classroom. Therefore, one goal of educators should be to teach children how the knowledge they already have applies to the classroom and, conversely, how skills taught in school are relevant in a wide variety of settings.

Numeracy

dyscalculia A learning
disability characterized
by impairments in
mathematical ability that
cannot be explained by a
general intellectual
impairment.

An estimated 6.5 per cent of children have **dyscalculia** (also known as mathematics disability; see Chapter 10) (Gross-Tsur, Manor and Shalev, 1996). They have difficulties with basic skills such as counting and arithmetic operations (Geary, Hamson and Hoard, 2000). This leads to problems with more complex arithmetic and algebra. Why do some children have these problems? There are a variety of sociocultural factors, such as limited exposure to numbers before entering school. Many children who have difficulties with mathematics come from impoverished families with little formal education; these children are behind their peers in their counting skills and knowledge of arithmetic facts. However, in order to understand how numeracy develops, we need to examine the basic skills and cognitive processes underlying this ability. For example, working memory plays a role. In order to solve a problem, we need to hold the details of the problem in memory whilst computing the answer so that the problem and the answer can be associated. Siegler and Shipley (1995) used a computational model to demonstrate that the speed and accuracy of retrieval of an answer depends on this strong association (see Chapter 11). Children with dyscalculia cannot hold as much information in memory as other children (Geary, Bow-Thomas and Yao, 1992; Passolunghi and Siegel, 2001) and they demonstrate impairments in other aspects of working memory (besides capacity), such as visual-spatial and executive processes (McLean and Hitch, 1999).

It is not just those labelled as having dyscalculia that have difficulties with numeracy. The Concepts in Secondary Mathematics and Science (CSMS) study at Chelsea College, London (Hart, 1981) examined ten thousand 11-year-old children's ability in 10 mathematical subjects. One of the conclusions from the study was that mathematics is a very difficult subject for most children. It was also noted that the introduction of mathematics teaching techniques which attempted to give children a greater conceptual understanding of the foundations of mathematics had not succeeded. More recently, the focus in the UK has been on mathematical skills, not conceptual understanding. In this chapter we will look at the skills and concepts required for numeracy, but first we will consider a few theoretical approaches to the development of numeracy.

Theories

Piaget's constructivism. For Piaget, a child's understanding of number is based on the discovery of number invariance, which is reflected in **conservation** of number tasks. This refers to the fact that the number of items in a set is the same unless some items are added or taken away (see the discussion of Piaget's conservation tasks in Chapter 1). Children aged 4 to 5 realize that adding items increases quantity and subtracting items decreases quantity, but they still make conservation errors, believing that spreading items out over a greater area increases quantity. This error led Piaget to argue that children in the pre-operational stage base their judgements on appearance, and thus do not have a conceptual understanding of number. At around 6 to 7 years, when they enter the concrete operations stage, children realize that despite the spatial arrangement of items, the number of items remains the same (Piaget, 1952a). Children can now do simple addition and subtraction problems, but they cannot solve problems in which a proportional relationship between two variables has to be established. Inhelder and Piaget (1958) report an experiment in which children were told that eels have to be fed amounts of food that vary with their size. The children were given several pairs of values for two variables: the length of the eel and the amount of food it needed. The children were then asked to say how much food an eel of a given length needs. Seven-year-olds correctly suggested greater amounts of food for longer eels, but they did not use proportional reasoning to determine quantities of food that were related to the size of the eels. Children aged 11 to 13, on the other hand, considered both variables – size and amount of food – together, and attempted to work out the relationship between the two variables, such as 2 grams of food for every 1 cm of length. Understanding proportion involves recognizing that the relationship between the two variables remains invariant, even though the values of both variables change. The achievement of proportional reasoning marks the transition to Piaget's formal operations stage (Nunes and Bryant, 2004).

Information processing. The availability of computers for use in psychology experiments led researchers to use computers to present mathematical problems. The advantage of this is that, in addition to recording whether responses are correct, **reaction times** can be measured (Ashcraft, 1995). By looking at reaction times, it is possible to infer whether children are solving arithmetic problems by counting or whether they are retrieving the answers from memory. Retrieval will lead to short reaction times, whereas counting will lead to larger reaction times for larger addends. For example, children will take longer to arrive at the answer for $9 + 8$ than for $2 + 3$ if they are counting. By studying children's arithmetic problem-solving and measuring reaction times, Siegler (1987) arrived at the conclusion that children use a mix of strategies, depending on experience and the type of problem. Children who have greater experience with a range of problems are more likely to retrieve answers from memory, whereas children who have not had much experience will use counting strategies. However, regardless of whether they usually retrieve answers, children will use counting when presented with a novel problem. According to

reaction time A measure of the time elapsed between the presentation of a stimulus and the response; longer reaction times indicate that more mental operations are being used.

Siegler, this holds for a variety of arithmetic tasks. For example, Siegler (1988) gave twenty-six 8- and 9-year-olds a hundred single-digit multiplication problems. The children were videotaped and two raters made judgements as to which strategy each child used for each problem. The results are shown in Table 8.2.

Table 8.2

Results of Siegler's multiplication study.

Source: Siegler (1988). © 1988 by the American Psychological Association, adapted with permission.

Strategy	Per cent use of strategy	Mean reaction time (seconds)	Per cent correct
Retrieval	68	5.5	78
Writing the problem	5	14	39
Repeated addition	22	23.3	59
Counting sets of objects	4	30.1	55

Note that when children use retrieval they arrive at an answer much faster than when using other strategies, and that answers retrieved from memory are more accurate than answers resulting from other strategies. Siegler and Crowley (1991) demonstrated that any one child's problem-solving ability cannot be characterized as a result of any one strategy. Siegler (1995, 1996) refers to his model of children's strategy use as the overlapping waves model because a visual representation of strategy use over time looks like the graph shown in Figure 8.1. According to this model, children may have multiple strategies, or ways of thinking about a problem, available to them at any one point in time. Some strategies are dominant early on, but decrease in frequency over time (e.g., strategy 1, which might be using pencil and paper to solve the problem), some become more prevalent over time (e.g., strategy 5, which might be retrieval from memory) and others start to exhibit a rise-and-fall pattern (e.g., strategy 4, which might be repeated addition). We will return to the overlapping waves model in Chapter 11.

Figure 8.1

Siegler's overlapping waves model.

Source: Reprinted from Cognitive Psychology, 28, Siegler, R. S., How does change occur: A microgenetic study of number conservation, 225–273, Copyright (1995), with permission from Elsevier.

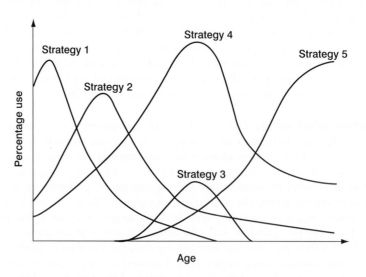

Nativism. Whereas Piaget discusses the development of concepts and Siegler ascribes development to variable strategy use, nativist theorists such as Gelman and Gallistel (1978) and Wynn (1992a, 1992b, 1995a, 1998) posit innate principles that guide early knowledge of number. According to Gelman and Gallistel, there are five principles that underlie children's counting ability. The 1–1 principle refers to the knowledge that each item in a set is referred to by one, and only one, number. The stable-order principle is that the order of numbers is stable and repeatable. The cardinal principal states that the number of the final item in a set also represents the quantity of the entire set. The abstraction principle allows children to apply the preceding three principles to any set of physical or non-physical items. Finally, the order-irrelevant principle is the knowledge that is does not matter what order items are counted in.

Wynn (1992a) demonstrated that 5-month-olds can perform addition and subtraction on small numbers. She placed 32 infants into two groups who were presented with an addition problem and a subtraction problem, respectively. Infants in the addition group were presented with a display case into which a single object was placed (see Figure 8.2). A screen was placed in front of the object and a second

| Figure 8.2 | The sequence of events shown in Wynn's study. |

Sequence of events 1 + 1 = 1 or 2

1. Object placed in case   2. Screen comes up   3. Second object added   4. Hand leaves empty

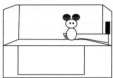 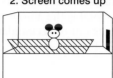 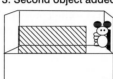 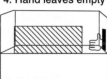

Then either : possible outcome   or : impossible outcome

5. Screen drops...   revealing 2 objects   5. Screen drops...   revealing 1 object

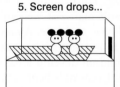 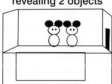  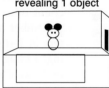

Sequence of events 2 – 1 = 1 or 2

1. Object placed in case   2. Screen comes up   3. Empty hand enters   4. One object removed

 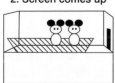 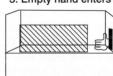 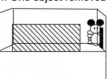

Then either : possible outcome   or : impossible outcome

5. Screen drops...   revealing 1 object   5. Screen drops...   revealing 2 objects

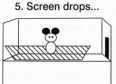 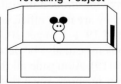  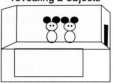

object was added. The screen was then lowered and the infants were shown either one or two objects remaining. In the subtraction condition, the procedure was the same except that each trial started with two objects, one of which was removed from behind the screen. In both groups, each of the infants was given 6 trials: 3 with one object and 3 with two objects. If the infants had no counting ability, they should have looked at the two displays equally. If, however, they were able to add, they would expect there to be two objects at the end of the addition scenario. An ability to subtract would lead them to expect just one object at the end of the subtraction scenario. Wynn found that both groups of infants looked longer at the unexpected outcomes than the expected outcomes, leading her to argue that humans have innate arithmetical abilities.

Wynn's explanation for these innate abilities is a mental mechanism called the *accumulator*, originally proposed by Meck and Church (1983) as a way of explaining the numerical abilities found in rats. According to Wynn (1992b, 1995a, 1995b), the accumulator mechanism produces pulses at a constant rate that pass into the accumulator by the closing of a switch. For each item counted, the switch closes for a fixed interval, which means that the accumulator fills up in equal amounts for each item counted. The final level of the accumulator represents the number of items counted. Addition and subtraction are accomplished by using more than one accumulator. For addition, one accumulator pours its contents into a second accumulator that already has some content. The total is the amount in the final accumulator. Subtraction involves pouring the contents out of accumulator A into accumulator C until the content of A are the same as B. The quantity in C represents A–B.

Basic skills

An important skill we need to master in order to do maths is 1–1 correspondence. This means understanding that one number refers to one thing. For example, if we count out equal numbers of counters to two people, it doesn't matter if we can't remember how many were counted out, both people will still have the same. A mastery of 1–1 correspondence lays down some of the necessary foundations for counting, adding and subtracting (Gelman and Gallistel, 1978). Children develop a basic understanding of number before they start school, with most 4-year-olds being able to count up to 10 (Dowker, 2008). Once children can count, they can start to learn about simple addition of single-digit numbers. This is more complex than it may appear at first as there are a number of different strategies children can employ in solving addition problems. As children gain experience, their strategy use changes and the speed and accuracy with which they solve problems increases.

When children are 4 or 5 years old, they count on their fingers or with blocks. Given the problem 2 + 5, they will count 2 fingers, then count 5 more fingers, then count them all up to arrive at 7. The next strategy is *counting on*, in which children start with 2 and count from there (3, 4, 5, 6, 7). However, in using this strategy, children often start with the first figure in the sum, regardless of whether it is larger or smaller than the second. They soon learn to start with the biggest number, regardless of whether it is first or last, and then just count on from there. After this, children begin to be able to do this in their heads, without fingers. Having mastered these simple techniques, children use *decomposition*, a mixture of addition and subtraction strategies which are used when they are most efficient. For example, in solving the problem 19 + 3, children may add 19 + 1 to get 20, add 3 to 20 to get 23, then take away the 1, arriving at 22. Problems can also be decomposed into tens and units (e.g., 15 + 4: 5 + 4 = 9, 10 + 9 = 19). Alongside all these strategies children are able to retrieve answers directly from memory, once they have memorized the answers. There is a general trend towards more complex strategies as children get older, which leads to the question of whether there are age-related stages. According to Siegler's overlapping waves theory (1987; Siegler and Jenkins, 1989; Siegler and Shrager, 1984), strategy changes do not occur as a function of age. Rather, use of different strategies is driven by success. Children will use the most efficient strategy that they can use in any given situation. Younger children use complex strategies less often (or not at all) as these are hard for them to understand and use and are therefore not efficient. For older children, the more complex strategies are more automatic and therefore more effective. When a complex strategy is not efficient, perhaps due to a high cognitive load, children will regress to easier strategies.

Another skill we need to be numerate is understanding cardinal numbers. The ordinal use of a number name is when the number refers to one of the set. If we have a set of 5 fingers, each number (1, 2, 3, 4, 5) is an ordinal number; it represents one finger. Cardinal use of a number name refers to the use of that number to identify the set. The number 5 can be used to refer to the 5th finger (ordinal use) or the set of 5 fingers (cardinal use). Similarly, a 10 pence coin represents a set of ten 1-penny coins. This understanding of cardinal number, achieved by most children before the age of 5 (Dowker, 2008), is an important landmark in number concepts. Having achieved this, children start to understand the relationships between numbers and understand that numbers are organized around a base (base 10 in our case). The next step is to understand that a cardinal number can be assembled or disassembled into various combinations (e.g., $7 = 1 + 6, 2 + 5, 3 + 4$). Around 60 per cent of 6-year-olds understand that the same cardinal number can be formed in different ways and still be the same number (Nunes and Bryant, 1996).

As is the case with science (see Chapter 7), mathematics isn't just about facts (e.g., what numbers there are) and procedures (e.g., how you add two numbers together), but also about understanding. Children need to think about facts and procedures so they can reveal the underlying principles. In order to understand children's learning, knowing what they know (their factual knowledge) is not enough, it is necessary to analyze their productions – to look at how they count, how they write numbers and how they solve problems.

cardinal number A number that refers to the quantity of items in a set.

ordinal number A number that refers to the position of one item in a set.

Research on children's arithmetic

As we have seen with other areas of development, Piaget's ideas have not been left uncriticized. More recent research shows that both children and adults show different levels of success on problems which involve the same intellectual structures but differ in other respects, such as content, social situation or mathematical representation (e.g., written or oral). As with conditional reasoning (see Chapter 6), if Piaget's ideas concerning logical thinking were correct, we would not expect these factors to affect task performance. At the beginning of the chapter, we saw that the content of a problem (whether it was expressed in terms of numbers or food items) has an effect on children's success. Lave (1988) illustrated the effect of social situation by giving proportion problems to adults in California in different situations. The participants performed more successfully in a supermarket than when given a formal written test.

Nunes (1993) demonstrated that the mathematical representation used could have an effect. In her study, Brazilian children in grades 4 to 6 were able to solve problems which involved negative numbers orally, but made more errors if asked to write the information down. The children were given problems about a farmer's profits and losses. They were told about the farmer's financial situation at the start of the season, and whether he made a profit or loss during the season. Their task was to calculate his financial situation at the end of the season. The participants were placed in either a written or oral condition. Those in the oral condition made a significantly higher percentage of correct responses. Some of the children in the written condition made mistakes when trying to solve the problems with pencil and paper, but were able to solve the problem when they talked about it. For example, one of the participants was presented with a problem in which a farmer started with a debt of 10 cruzados. He planted two crops and gained 10 cruzados on one and 20 on the other. The participant wrote the following down:

$$
\begin{array}{r}
10 \\
+10 \\
\underline{20} \\
40
\end{array}
$$

Note that he omitted a minus sign on line one and a plus sign on line three. Having arrived at the answer of '40' the participants said that this was incorrect and that he couldn't do it on paper. He could, however, solve it orally: 'He had a profit of 10, paid the 10 he owed. Then he still has a profit from the beans, he has 20' (Nunes, 1993, p. 69). In this case, the content and the social situation are the same across conditions, but the written representation has characteristics which confuse people.

Piagetian intellectual structures may influence performance, but it is clear that there are other factors involved. Two factors which have been identified are children's conceptual understanding of aspects of the system of mathematics and the context in which mathematical problems are presented.

Concepts. The concept of inversion is the understanding that adding and subtracting the same number leaves the original quantity unchanged. Children aged as young as 3 understand inversion in sets of objects (Sherman and Bisanz, 2007), but they do not understand inversion when it is applied to numerical problems (Villette, 2002). They have difficulties with problems such as $3 + 7 - 7 = ?$. Children aged 6 to 9 demonstrate better performance on '$a + b - b$' problems (Canobi and Bethune, 2008; Robinson and Dubé, 2009), but even 9-year-olds take longer on problems where b is a large number, suggesting they are actually adding and subtracting the number, rather than applying the principle of inversion (Bisanz and Lefevre, 1990). It is not until about 11 years that children ignore the value of b and solve all such problems equally quickly.

Another important concept is mathematical equality. This refers to the understanding that the equals sign means that values on either side of it represent the same quantity. Most 7- and 8-year-olds think that the equals sign is a signal to execute an arithmetic operation. They do not have difficulties with problems such as $3 + 4 + 5 = ?$, but when faced with a problem of the form $3 + 4 + 5 = ? + 5$, they either add all the numbers to the left of the equals sign or add all the numbers including the 5 on the right (Rittle-Johnson and Alibali, 1999). This pattern of performance is a result of learning that the equals sign is a marker placed to the right of the numbers to be operated upon and to the left of the answer, and that it signifies that the child should calculate the total of the numbers to the left (McNeil and Alibali, 2004; McNeil and Alibali, 2005a; Seo and Ginsberg, 2003). McNeil (2007; 2008; McNeil *et al.*, 2006) argues that this misconception is not helped by exposure to typical arithmetic problems which follow the format $x + y = ?$ because this type of problem does not make the interchangeable nature of the two sides of the equation clear. As a result of this limited experience with the equality, children form knowledge structures that only lead to success on typical problems (McNeil and Alibali, 2005b).

After the basic arithmetic facts are learned children begin to use algorithms for solving more complex, multi-digit problems. However, many children fail to see the relationship between the procedures for solving problems and the concepts that underlie them. Memorizing problem-solving algorithms without a deeper conceptual understanding can lead to misconceptions. Box 8.1 shows an example of this.

Many children perform poorly on problems which involve fractions. For example, when presented with 1/3 + 1/4, children are likely to give 2/7 as the answer. Again, this is the result of a lack of deep conceptual understanding; children are not considering the magnitude of the numbers and are unaware that this solution does not seem to be sensible. But it is not just young children who lack conceptual understanding where fractions are concerned. As part of a national assessment test in the US, Carpenter *et al.* (1981) gave the following task to American 13- and 17-year-olds: 'Estimate the answer to 12/13 and 7/8'. Only 24 per cent of the 13-year-olds and 37 per cent of 17-year-olds correctly estimated 2. Most of the remaining participants guessed 19 or 21. Again, Korean children don't have such a problem. One-third is spoken as 'sam bun ui il' in Korean, which translates as 'of 3 parts, 1'; the relation between fractions is more explicit (Miura *et al.*, 1999).

In order to perform well on tasks such as the one presented above, children need to have an understanding of fractions, but they also need to be able to estimate. Estimation is involved in a huge variety of everyday tasks, such as thinking about time (how long will it take to get to school?), distance (how far is to the shops?), weight (how heavy is this book?) and money (how much will all the food in my shopping trolley cost?) (Siegler and Booth, 2004). Siegler and his colleagues (Booth and Siegler, 2006, 2008; Siegler and Booth, 2004, 2005; Siegler and Opfer, 2003) have carried out a number of studies examining the development of estimation using a number line task. In this task, participants are presented with a line (either on a piece of paper or a computer screen) with 0 marked at one end and 100 marked at the other end, and they are asked to estimate where on the line numbers between 0 and 100 fall. This seems like an easy task; if given the number 48, you would mark a point half way along the line; if given the number 12, you would mark a point a little above a tenth of the way along the line. However, when this task was given to children, there were some surprising results.

Box 8.1 Subtraction errors

Brown and Burton (1978) analysed data from 1300 Nicaraguan students aged from 10 to 13 who had each attempted to solve 30 addition and subtraction problems. Here is a sample of the solutions to subtraction problems by one student (Brown and Burton, 1978, p. 178):

103	257	1039	6523	7001
−64	−161	−44	−1280	−94
139	96	1995	5243	7007

Q. Some of these problems have been solved correctly, others have not. What errors has the child made?

This student has answered two of the problems correctly, but has given incorrect answers to the first, third and fifth problems. Looking at the incorrect problems in isolation may lead one to think that the student just doesn't know how to subtract, or cannot solve subtraction problems that involve carrying tens. However, problems two and four also involve borrowing tens. These errors can be explained as a result of one 'bug' in the student's behaviour. The three incorrect problems all involve borrowing from a column in which the top number is 0. The student has borrowed 10, and decremented the 0 to 9, but has not then gone on to borrow 10 from the column to

▶

the left of the 0. For example, in the first problem the student has carried 10 from the middle column to the right column and solved 13–4. The 0 at the top of the middle column was replaced with a 9, leading to 9–6. But the 1 in the left column was not decremented to 0. Once we understand this error children make, we can reconceptualize this student as someone who can perform the procedures for subtraction problems correctly, with the exception of the one 'bug'.

Fuson and Kwon (1992) found that patterns of performance such as this are not common in Korean children. In a study of 72 children aged 7 to 9, they found very few errors on 2- and 3-digit addition and subtraction problems. Fuson and Kwon suggest this high level of performance is at due to a better conceptual understanding of the base 10 system, which is supported by the Korean language. For example, the Korean terms for numbers from 11 to 19 are 'ten and x ones'.

Booth and Siegler (2006) tested four groups of children, 5- to 6-, 6- to 7-, 7- to 8-, and 8-to 9-year-olds, and found that the 5- to 6-year-olds' estimates were less accurate than those of the older children. Figure 8.3 shows the actual magnitude of the numbers plotted against children's estimations of where the numbers are on the line. The older children's estimates were the most accurate and also fit a linear function. That is, they represent all numbers in the set as being equidistant; the distance between 6 and 8 is the same as the distance between 79 and 81. The data from the youngest group, on the other hand, provides a better fit to a logarithmic curve. This means that they estimate the differences between smaller numbers as being larger than the distance between larger numbers. For example, they represent 20 and 40 as being further apart than 60 and 80. Why should young children represent numbers in this way? Siegler and Booth (2004) suggest that when children are first learning about numbers, it is useful to use a logarithmic representation as this provides a greater discrimination between numbers at the lower end of the scale, which are more frequently encountered, than a linear representation. There are other, very practical reasons why we may have developed a bias towards logarithmic representations of number. The difference between 2 and 3 food items is more important to a hungry organism, than the difference between 87 and 88 food items (Opfer and Siegler, 2007). The estimations made by the group of 6- to 7-year-olds fit both logarithmic and linear functions, suggesting that these children were using a mix of logarithmic and linear representations. This may be because, at this age, the children were gaining greater experience with numbers from 20 to 100.

When the scale is increased from 0–100 to 0–1000 or 0–100 000, the same developmental trend emerges, but at a later point. Between 7 and 9 years of age, children shift from a logarithmic to a linear representation of values from 0 to 1000 (Booth and Siegler, 2006; Opfer and Siegler, 2007). The shift for larger values of up to 100 000 occurs between 8 and 11 years (Thompson and Opfer, 2010). As with smaller numbers, the utility of logarithmic representations for these large numbers can be explained in practical terms. For example, the difference between £1 and £100 is much more important than the difference between £100 001 and £100 100 (Opfer and Siegler, 2007). In turn, this knowledge of the development of numerical representations can be put to practical use. Booth and Siegler (2008) found that the linearity of children's estimations correlated with their mathematics achievement, and Thompson and Siegler (2010) found a correlation between accuracy of number line and recall for numbers. Booth and Siegler (2008) also found that training on a number line increased the linearity of children's representations and led to improved performance on arithmetic problems. Ramani and Siegler (2008; Siegler, 2009; Siegler and Ramani, 2008, 2009) used this information to develop an intervention for low-income preschoolers, who develop linear representations later than

Figure 8.3

Results from Booth and Siegler's study showing the progression from a logarithmic to a linear pattern of estimation.

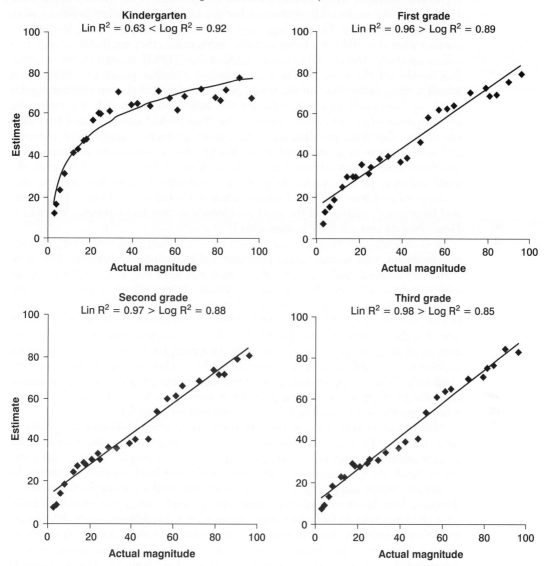

higher-income children. Ramani and Siegler gave their participants a race traversing a linear board marked with the numbers 1 to 10. The idea behind this intervention is that such a board game is like a number line, and that playing the game should lead to a more linear representation of the numbers 1 to 10. Ramani and Siegler found that playing with the board game led to an improvement in preschoolers' number-line estimation, magnitude comparison, numeral identification, counting and ability to learn the answers to novel arithmetic problems. Moreover, these gains were still in place two months later.

Context. As we saw at the beginning of the chapter, unfamiliar contexts prevent children from using the procedures they are able to use successfully in other contexts. The Brazilian street vendors studied by Carraher *et al.* (1985) could solve arithmetic problems in a selling context, but did not do so well when problems were presented numerically. The findings suggest that the participants were not able to connect what they did for a living with the mathematics they studied in school. In a follow-up study, Nunes, Schliemann and Carraher (1993) wanted to see whether they would get the same effects if they studied a similar group of children in a school setting, rather than on the street. Nunes *et al.* tested sixteen children aged 8 to 13 on three problem types. Although this may seem like a wide age range, the children were all in third grade; some of the children had started school later than the others. The three problem types were word problems, computation exercises and selling items in a simulated store setting. The computation exercises were straightforward numerical problems such as 'What is 200 minus 35?', while the word and store problems gave the problems a concrete context. For example, one of the word problems was 'I had *x* soccer cards in my collection. I lost *y*. How many do I have now?', and one of the store problems was 'You had *x* pencils. You sold *y*. How many do you still have in your store?'

In each setting, participants were given three addition problems, three subtraction problems, two multiplication problems and two division problems. The questions were all presented orally, but the participants were free to solve them with or without pencil and paper. For the store problems, the participants chose to solve the problems orally (i.e., without pencil and paper) over 80 per cent of the time, regardless of whether the problems involved addition, subtraction, multiplication or division. For the word problems, about half of the addition problems, and over 60 per cent of all other types, were solved orally. However, for most of the computation problems, the children used a written procedure. This finding demonstrates the children's choice of procedure was largely dependent on the context. A second interesting finding was the participants were more likely to get the answers correct when using the oral procedure rather than the written procedure.

Nunes *et al.*'s explanation of this difference is that when children solve problems using pencil and paper they work from smaller to larger values; the algorithm for written calculations involves starting with units, then moving on to tens, then moving to hundreds. This means that any error at the unit level has the potential to be magnified. When using oral procedures, children tend to work in the opposite direction, from larger to smaller quantities. For example, when presented with 200 − 35, a child may take 30 from 200, then take another 5. In addition, when children use the written procedure they are manipulating symbols, whereas oral problem solving involves mentally manipulating quantities. The oral procedure preserves the relative values being dealt with; 'two hundred and twenty-two' includes clear information about the values of the three different '2's. The written procedure represents value as position; we only know that the three '2's in '222' are different because of the relative position. A concrete context, therefore, invokes mental operations on actual values, rather than abstract algorithmic procedures, which means we are less likely to make the sort of mistakes shown in Box 8.1.

Bjorklund and Rosenblum (2002) also demonstrated the power of context to affect how children approach mathematical problems. In a study on 6- and 7-year-olds, they found that children used more sophisticated strategies to solve arithmetic problems when the problems were placed in an academic context (e.g., 'How much is 2 + 2?') than when the problems were presented in a game context (e.g., 'How many spaces are you going to move' in a game of 'snakes and ladders' after rolling two dice). In the academic context, children used retrieval or count-up strategies. In the game context, they used the count-all strategy – the most basic of the addition strategies and much less efficient than count-up or retrieval. It seems that the context of a problem influences strategy choice.

McNeil and Alibali (2005a) asked children and young adults to define the equals sign in three different contexts: by itself, a typical addition context (e.g., 4 + 8 + 5 + 4 = ?), and an equivalence context in which there were addends on both sides (e.g. 4 + 8 + 5 = 4 + ?).

Participants' definitions were coded as expressing either an operational view (e.g., 'the total,' 'add up all the numbers'), a relational view (e.g., 'two amounts are the same'), or an 'unspecified equal' view (e.g., 'equal,' or 'equals'). The adults (undergraduate and graduate students) gave a relational definition most of the time, and the youngest children (aged 10 to 12) gave operational definitions most of the time. However, older children (aged 13 to 14) gave an interesting pattern of responses. The equals sign by itself, and the typical addition context led to answers indicating an operational definition, but the equivalence context led to relational definitions in almost all cases. This shows us that not only is the *concept* of mathematical equality important for numeracy, but that the *context* can influence any conceptual knowledge children may have.

Why do children have difficulties with mathematics?

We know what skills and concepts children need in order to be numerate, so why do children find school mathematics so hard? Nunes and Bryant (1996) argue that in order to do mathematics we must have an understanding of written numerical values and mathematical symbols and an understanding of logical relations. Both of these are hard to grasp. Children's difficulties in understanding written numerical values and mathematical symbols are tied up with problems in understanding language. Children in the CSMS study (Hart, 1981) often misunderstood common expressions such as *shared between*, *bigger* and *straight*. A problem such as '10 sweets are shared between two boys so that one has 4 more than the other; how many does each get?' can be misunderstood. One child said 'that's wrong, if you share they each have 5 so one can't have more'. *Straight* for many children means perpendicular; a slanting line can't be straight. Thus, the mathematical meaning of a word can be slightly different from its everyday meaning. Wood (1998) gives an example of this in a secondary school child:

> Interviewer: Do you know what volume means?
> Child: Yes.
> Interviewer: Could you explain to me what it means?
> Child: Yes, it's what is on the knob of the TV set.

There are more basic problems with language and number. The English number system is arbitrary, especially the 'teens' (eleven, twelve, thirteen, etc.). Children often learn these numbers verbally before learning how to write them. The problem is the decimal relation between the teens and the single-digit numbers 1–9 is not transparent. In China, the decimal relation is more obvious: 11 is 'ten one', 12 is 'ten two' (Miller *et al.*, 1995). Similarly, numbers like 52 are 'five ten two' which highlights the fact that the 5 refers to 5 sets of 10. The implication is that it is easier for children exposed to more regular or obvious base relations to master the mapping between oral numbers and written systems. Fuson (1992) noted that Japanese children start solving problems with two or more digit numbers (e.g., 11 + 3) earlier than American children. Chinese pre-schoolers find constructing amounts such as

11 from 10 and a 1 easier than English-speaking children. The language of numbers may present a significant handicap for children exposed to an irregular oral number system. This may impact on written mathematics as written numbers defined as 'three ten' instead of thirteen will be easier to manipulate. Siegler and Mu (2008) tested Chinese and American 5- and 6-year-olds on the number line estimation task and found that the Chinese children's estimates were comparable to those of American children one to two years older. Siegler and Mu suggest this may be due to cultural differences in the amount of time spent engaged in mathematical activities even before school (Zhou *et al.*, 2006).

Nunes and Bryant's (1996) second point relates to the difficulties children have in understanding logical relations. Children get better at problem solving and logical thinking as they get older. Perhaps this means that in order to master mathematical concepts children need to have the prerequisite conceptual understanding. Schools may be trying to teach children things that they are incapable of grasping. According to Piaget, children in the concrete operations stage of development cannot do abstract and logical hypothetical reasoning. They can only grasp procedural knowledge (e.g., knowing how to solve equations) but not conceptual knowledge (e.g., the deeper relations underlying the equation). However, as we have seen, Piaget's theory is insensitive to the importance of content and meaning in children's mathematical capabilities. Logical relations may be important, but need to be integrated within a framework that acknowledges the part played by content and culture in children's learning. Nunes and Bryant dispense with the concept of stages but maintain the idea that development involves conceptual change. They also note that acquiring skill and expertise in executing procedures without developing a sense of the nature of the logical relations involved in different kinds of problems will lead the child to using surface structure strategies that do not give them deep understanding. In essence, they are arguing that conceptual knowledge is needed, but that this is not necessarily inaccessible to children younger than 11.

If school maths is *not* too hard, why isn't it being taught successfully? Fuson (1992) argues that this is due to what she calls the poverty of the mathematics curriculum. Fuson identified a wide range of different problem types in whole-number addition and subtraction but an analysis of the textbooks used in the USA showed that only a few of the different types of problems were used as examples. Children were, therefore, learning procedures from a restricted set of problems. This means they were not being given a chance to encounter all the tasks that could develop their conceptual understanding. Children can be led into making mistakes when they attempt to generalize the procedures they've learnt, to problems beyond the restricted range they have encountered. Fuson also argues that too little time is spent on the use of concrete materials such as blocks, fingers and number lines. This means children are not helped to bridge the gap between the early conceptual understanding they develop in the pre-school years and mathematical symbol systems. Too little time spent on these activities, and too much emphasis on mental arithmetic, means that children develop surface strategies to deal with problems rather than developing a true conceptual understanding of the nature of the relation between the numbers in a problem. On the other hand, the introduction of the National Numeracy Strategy into British schools in 1998, which has a strong focus on oral and mental practices, appears to have led to some improvements in both mental and written arithmetic (Ineson, 2007).

Greer (1992) argues that children who are only taught rules and procedures arrive at a false conceptualization of what maths actually is. Some children (and adults) believe that multiplication makes numbers bigger and division makes numbers smaller. This is not true: When fractions are multiplied, numbers get smaller (e.g., 1/2 × 1/2 = 1/4), but children are led to believe this by the limited range of situations in which they experience mathematics in the classroom. Greer argues that a greater use of real world examples would allow children to learn the underlying concepts behind maths, not just a series of rules and procedures. In schools, there has been a tendency to dismiss 'non-academic' maths. This means children do not have the right conceptualization of what maths is. They fail to see its relevance to the real world. Nunes (1992) found that expert darts players did not conceptualize their subtraction of scores as real maths even though they were using successful, generative and consistent mathematical calculations. Similarly, the young Brazilian street vendors studied by Carraher *et al.* (1985; see also Nunes, Schliemann and Carraher, 1993) carried out mathematical procedures in calculating the cost of various items. Whilst they could perform these calculations in their heads, they could not solve identical problems on paper. They failed to see the link between 'street' maths and 'school' maths. Nunes and Bryant (1996) argue that educators are mistaken in making the distinction between street and school maths as they are both useful in that they are different contexts in which children can exploit their conceptual knowledge of mathematical relations. Although Greer and Fuson argue for increased practical ability, they do not want these to come in the form of word puzzles or word problems but think that numerical concepts should be used instead. Consider problems such as 'if we mix 4 cups of orange concentrate with 2 cups of water and 2 cups of lemon concentrate with 1 cup of water, will one taste stronger or will they taste the same?'. They argue that in the real world we would just mix the substances together and taste them; we wouldn't solve the problem using mathematics. These types of problems are potentially misleading for children. It is more effective to use real world examples that demand computation in the real word, such as problems to do with price or speed.

Literacy

Around 33 per cent of 10-year-olds, 25 per cent of 14-year-olds and 23 per cent of 18-year-olds in the USA score below the basic reading level for their age (Donahue *et al.*, 1999; National Center for Education Statistics, 2009; Perie, Grigg and Donahue, 2005), where 'basic' is defined as 'partial mastery of prerequisite knowledge and skills that are fundamental for proficient work at each grade' (National Center for Education Statistics, 2009, p. 5). At the turn of the century, an estimated 25 per cent of adults in the USA had the reading level of an 8- or 9-year old (Adams, Treiman and Pressley, 1998). In the UK, 16 per cent of adults (5.2 million people) have entry-level literacy skills, meaning they would not get a passing grade on a GCSE exam (Grinyer, 2006). Those who have achieved functional levels of literacy are able to read text at a much faster rate than they can hear speech. This is because the grammatical structures in text are more compressed and more varied than those of speech, the level of redundancy is low and there are no pauses, hesitations or false starts. A reader can read at their own pace, re-reading some information or skipping some paragraphs. Generally, there is a greater efficiency and autonomy in reading than in hearing speech. Those who have not made the shift to functional literacy are unable to engage in simple and useful tasks such as reading tabloid newspapers and recipes. Why is this? There are a vast number of issues including debates on how we teach children to begin to read, how we teach text comprehension, how we teach children awareness of text structure and how we teach literary appreciation and literary evaluation. However, in order to effectively teach the skills needed for literacy, we need to know what these skills are.

Skills we need to be literate

In order to achieve a functional level of literacy, there are a few basic skills we must master. First, we need to be able to recognize letters. This does not just mean recognizing that an 'a' is different to a 'b', but also recognizing that the same letter may take several differing forms. All of these letters look different but are, of course, the same: A a A a *A a A*

Second, we need to understand grapheme-phoneme correspondence rules. We need to recognize which sounds correspond to which letter symbols. In Italian there is a nearly perfect one-to-one grapheme-phoneme relationship; words are pronounced in accordance with their spelling. It is harder in English as the relationship is more variable and often depends on the letters surrounding the words. For example the *i* in 'bit' sounds different to the *i* in 'bite'. We also need to be aware of how to segment words into their constituent phonemes (e.g., 'cat' = *k, æ, t*). Early preschool interaction with nursery rhymes can often help with this process.

Third, we need to be able to recognize words. We must understand that letter strings represent conventional words. When we can recognize whole words, we no longer have to spell each word out as a series of component sounds. Fourth, we need to recognize the meanings of words and their relations to real-world referents; we need to know that the word 'chair' means an object designed to be sat on and we need to know that there are specific objects this word applies to. Finally, we need comprehension and interpretation skills. We need to be able to comprehend and interpret texts, which relies on automatic word recognition, having a large vocabulary, working memory capacity and knowledge of the world.

Theories of reading development

There are many theories of reading. Because of the way in which reading develops, many of these theories are stage theories. Most are not strict stage theories in the Piagetian sense in which mastery of one stage is a prerequisite for transition to the next, but refer to phases or stages of development in which there is a typical pattern of progression (Ehri, 2005). In addition, some are not so much explanatory theories, but descriptive models of the sequence in which children acquire reading skills. Because reading is unlike many of the other topics in this book in that it is not something that develops without the supporting context of education, it is difficult to discriminate between the development of the cognitive skills used in reading, and the sequence in which reading skills are learnt as a result of formal schooling.

Chall (1979, 1983) identified five stages of reading covering the lifespan from prereading skills that are mastered before school, to highly skilled adult reading. In the first stage (stage 0), young children learn to identify the letters of the alphabet and may have learnt to recognize a few words, particularly those that they are frequently exposed to through signs and adverts. Stage 1 covers the first year of school, in which children are formally taught to read. During this period, children learn the skill of **phonological recoding**, which is the translation of letters into sounds and, by extension, words. Stage 2 covers the next two years of school, in which children's reading becomes more fluent. However, reading is still effortful. Because a lot of mental resources go into identifying words, children in this stage are not able to use reading to acquire new knowledge. In stage 3, from about 10 to 14 years, children make the transition from learning to read, to reading to learn, and can obtain new information through reading. Stage 4 covers the final school years. At this point, children come to be proficient readers, integrating information from a variety of written sources, making inferences, and appreciating multiple viewpoints.

phonological recoding
The translation of a written representation into sounds and words.

Whereas Chall's model largely describes a typical pattern of progression, Frith (1985) developed a theory which describes the skills children use at different points in this progression. Frith's theory is based on the earlier theory of Marsh *et al.* (1981) who proposed four stages of reading development. In the first stage, children use rote learning to associate written words with their spoken forms, and guess unfamiliar words from context. In stage 2, the guesses are based on some letters as well as context. In stage 3, words are decoded sequentially, letter by letter. In the fourth stage, context is taken into account when determining how letters are pronounced, and children guess unfamiliar words using analogy as a strategy. Frith adapted this theory into a three-stage account of reading development. The first stage, called the *logographic* stage, equates to the rote-learning stage of Marsh *et al.* In this stage, children recognize familiar words without analyzing individual letters. The second stage is the *alphabetic* stage, corresponding to Marsh *et al.*'s sequential decoding, during which children analyze words in terms of their letters and use their knowledge of grapheme-phoneme correspondence to work out how to pronounce words. The third stage is the *orthographic* stage, which is related to Marsh *et al.*'s strategy of analogy. In this stage children use their knowledge of patterns of letters, usually morphemes, to determine pronunciation.

Ehri's (1992, 1999, 2002, 2005) four-stage theory is based on the connections between written words and their mental representations. The first stage (or phase) is the pre-alphabetic phase and, as with the other theories, this stage is characterized by rote-learned connections between a written word and its meaning. In the second stage, the partial alphabetic phase, children start make connections between letters and sounds, particularly the first and final letters in a word. In the full alphabetic phase, children have learnt a complete set of connections between letters and the corresponding phonemes. In the consolidated alphabetic phase, adult-like reading emerges, in which children can make direct use of morphemes and syllables without having to explicitly decode each individual letter.

Although there are variations in the number of stages or phases in the development, the theories outlined above agree that reading starts with visual cues as to the identity of words. This is followed by the acquisition of decoding skills, which is then built upon by using more sophisticated contextual cues. Other theories, such as those proposed by Gough and Hillinger (1980), Mason (1980), Seymour and Duncan (2001) and Stuart and Coltheart (1988) describe a similar progression.

In contrast to stage theories, Goswami and Bryant (1990) and Siegler (1986, 1996) propose that several different strategies are available to children, and that it is the relevant frequency of the use of each strategy, rather than their availability, that varies as a function of age and experience. You were introduced to Siegler's overlapping waves model earlier in the chapter. Siegler argues that children's strategy use in reading is similar to their strategy use in mathematics in that children make variable use of multiple strategies at any one point in time. If the word is one they know well, children will use retrieval, but if it is less familiar, they will sound it out or use a combination of visual retrieval and phonological recoding. There is also evidence for variable strategy use in spelling. In a study on children tested once when they were 6 years old, and again when they were 7, Rittle-Johnson and Siegler (1999) found that the children used six different spelling strategies: retrieval, sounding out, a combination of retrieval and sounding out, drawing analogies to the spelling of other words, using rules (such as adding an 'e' at the end of a word to make a long vowel sound, as in 'mile') and visual checking, which is where children write an approximation of the word and change letters until it looks correct.

Phonological awareness

An important precursor to the development of reading is phonological awareness – the awareness of the sound structure of language. If children fail to make the phonological connection they are destined to find learning to read and write very difficult (Bryant *et al.*, 1990). Several studies have found that adults with literacy problems perform poorly on tasks on phonological awareness (e.g., Morais *et al.*, 1979; Morais *et al.*, 1986). Phonological awareness manifests itself in a number of abilities such as the ability to monitor and correct speech errors, the ability to play with sounds, the ability to compare words for rhyme or alliteration, the ability to split words into phonemes (e.g., 'cat' = k, æ, t) and the ability to manipulate phonemes (e.g., changing 'cat' to 'mat'). This involves an awareness of how language can be manipulated.

There are many different tasks that have been used to test phonological processing and awareness. Some are based on retrieval, such as verbal short-term memory, and rapid automatized naming tasks. In the latter task, participants are presented with a matrix of objects, colours, letters or digits and have to name them as quickly as possible, which requires retrieving the phonological forms from memory. Other tasks include sound-to-word and word-to-word matching, phoneme counting and segmentation, and rhyme recognition. According to Yopp (1988) many of these tasks actually involve two abilities: holding sounds in working memory and manipulating sounds. Muter *et al.* (1997) suggested that tests of phonological awareness measure rhyming skills and segmentation skills. We can characterize both of these distinctions between two types of skill as a distinction between implicit phonological processing, which involves verbal short-term memory, and explicit phonological awareness. Implicit phonological awareness refers to abilities such as detecting words that start with the same letter, or words that rhyme, whereas explicit phonological awareness refers to the ability to segment words into phonemes, map letters to sounds and manipulate sounds to produce words.

Implicit phonological processing develops in the preschool years before explicit phonological awareness, and both have been shown to predict later reading ability (Bowey, 2005; Goswami, 1993; Goswami and Bryant, 1990; Gottardo, Stanovich and Siegel, 1996; Liberman and Shankweiler, 1977). Bradley and Bryant (1983) followed 400 children between the ages of 4 and 8. They found that performance on tasks measuring the large phonological units of rhyme and alliteration at age 4 predicted reading and spelling performance at age 8. As a result of this, Goswami and Bryant (1990) theorized that the developmental progression starts with an awareness of syllables and proceeds to the phoneme level. The gap between syllable and phonemes is bridged by *onset* (the consonant, or cluster of consonants, that precede the vowel in a syllable) and *rime* (the vowel and any consonants that follow it). They suggest that awareness of onsets, which are often single phonemes, leads to phonemic awareness.

However, more recent studies have found that although awareness of large units such as rhyme leads to phonemic awareness, rhyme itself does not predict reading ability; the key skill is the ability to segment words into smaller phonological units: phonemes (Hulme *et al.*, 2002; Muter *et al.*, 1997; Nation and Hulme, 1997). Hulme *et al.* gave 72 children aged 5 and 6-years-old three tasks which were each used to measure awareness of initial phoneme, final phoneme, onset and rime. In the detection task, participants were asked to choose one of three spoken nonwords which was similar to another spoken nonword with respect to first phoneme, final phoneme, onset or rime, depending on which was currently being assessed. For example, when they were being tested on onset, participants would be presented with a target such as 'blipe', and would have to choose whether 'bleug', 'sook' or 'thad' was similar. In the oddity task, participants were presented with three spoken nonwords and asked to pick the odd one. For example, of 'blipe', 'skeep' and 'zook', the final nonword is the odd one out with respect to final phoneme. In the deletion task, participants were asked to repeat a series of nonwords with a sound (initial, final, etc.) missing from each. Initial and final phoneme awareness were the best predictors of reading ability, whereas onset and rime did not account for any further variance beyond that shared with phoneme awareness. However, several commentators criticized this study on the grounds that the participants had already started to learn to read (Bowey, 2002; Bryant, 2002; Goswami, 2002).

In order to overcome this concern and determine the relative roles of phonemes and onset-rime in predicting later reading ability, Muter *et al.* (2004) followed 90 children for two years from the time they started school. At time 1 (mean age 4 years 9 months), the children were given a series of tasks, including measures of rhyme detection, production and oddity, phoneme completion and deletion, letter knowledge and receptive vocabulary. One year later, the participants completed all these tasks again, except for the measure of vocabulary. They were also given three additional tasks measuring syntactic awareness, the ability to generate morphemes such as plurals and grammatical inflections and reading ability. At time 3, when the children's mean age was 6 years and 9 months, they were given several reading tests. Muter *et al.* conducted a path analysis in order to ascertain which measures at times 1 and 2 predicted reading at time 3. The path model illustrated in Figure 8.4

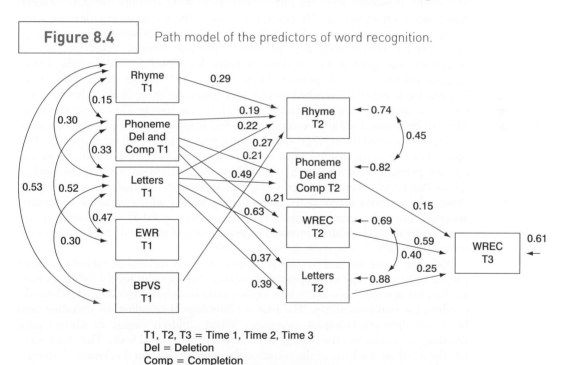

Figure 8.4 Path model of the predictors of word recognition.

T1, T2, T3 = Time 1, Time 2, Time 3
Del = Deletion
Comp = Completion
EWR = Early Word Recognition Test
BPVS = British Picture Vocabulary scale II
WREC = Word Recognition

shows that letter knowledge and phonemic awareness are the most important predictors of word recognition, whereas rhyme and vocabulary are relatively unimportant. However, reading does not just involve recognizing words, it also requires comprehension. When Muter *et al.* constructed a path model for reading comprehension at time 3, they found that phonological skills were less important, and that vocabulary knowledge and grammatical skills were the most important predictors. These results suggest that different aspects of reading are predicted by different linguistic skills.

Influences on literacy

Home life is the first important influence in literacy. Children who learn to read, at least a few words, before they get to school tend to be better at reading in school than children who have not started reading (Durkin, 1966). The prevailing view in the 1960s was that reading should be left to school. It is now known that the home environment has a big impact on how well children learn to read. However, it is not necessarily the case that a high level of literacy in the home immediately leads to better reading in school. Phillips and McNaughton (1990) showed that parents who spend a lot of time in literary activities with preschoolers and who have lots of books in their home don't necessarily have preschoolers who can learn to read. It seems more likely that there is an indirect link. Parents who encourage literary activities at the preschool level are more likely to provide support for their children when they do start to read. However, *failure* of home life to support literary activities can have an effect on reading ability. In some cases, this may be due to the lack of financial resources needed to provide books and materials (Orr, 1995). Lack of privacy and space makes working at home hard (Wilson and Dupuis, 1992). Parental interest is also important. Snow *et al.* (1991) found that children from low-income homes who also had literacy problems were more likely to have parents who were unaware of the difficulties their child was having They were also more likely to be satisfied with lower grades and less likely to engage in communication with the school and the teacher. Another important influence on reading skill is attitude. Exposure to the printed word and experience of being read to at home are significant pre-school predictors of vocabulary and success in learning to read at school (Stanovich, West and Harrison, 1995; Wells, 1981). Children can learn a lot about reading from listening to and watching skilled adults engaging in reading activities. However, passive exposure to the printed word is not enough. Active experiences that get children involved in letter manipulation and word reading contribute to literacy development (Levy *et al.* 2006).

Although home life and parents are important early influences, school obviously plays a huge role in the development of literacy. The big educational debate in literacy has, for decades, been about how skills should be taught. In order to read words, children use two procedures. The first is phonological recoding, or decoding, and builds on their phonological awareness. When children engage in phonological recoding, they translate the printed word into a phonological form. They then identify the word on the basis of the sound of the word. The second is visually based retrieval, in which the visual form is used to identify the word by retrieving it from long-term memory without phonological recoding. Early on, during Frith's (1985) logographic stage, visually based retrieval is used to identify familiar signs, logos and adverts on the basis of the overall word shape, without any phonological knowledge. Once children start school, they can use a variety of cues, such as the shape of individual letters and the surrounding context, as well as the overall appearance of the word. However, these cues do not guarantee accurate word iden-tification. For example, 'stop' and 'shop' look very similar and may not be differen-tiated by context (e.g., 'she stood under the stop/shop sign'). The accuracy of visually based retrieval can be influenced by phonological recoding. By sounding out the first two letters in the ambiguous word, the child can then retrieve the cor-rect word. Both phonological recoding and visually based retrieval have been used as the basis of educational approaches to reading. Phonics instruction is based on phonological recoding, whereas the whole word approach is based on visually based retrieval.

For a long time educators thought we should teach children by phonics, in which children are taught to read by starting with the simplest elements and matching let-ters to phonemes. However, many 5-year-olds have difficulty analyzing a word into its component sound units or phonemes. Unless they can conceive of 'cat' as a sequence of separable sounds, children cannot take the next step of matching the sounds to letters. Children who do succeed in learning phonics find that the com-plex spelling system of English doesn't always work as it ideally should; words such as 'one' and 'two' do not have a match between letters and sounds. For words such as these, it is simpler to identify them by using context cues or learning to recognize the visual form of the words.

This led to a move towards the opposite extreme. The whole word approach replaced phonics instruction with memorization of whole word shapes. Children taught by this method alone are heavily dependent on the teacher and on repetitive graded tests in which a restricted set of commonplace words is drilled and regi-mented to ensure repeated exposure. This means that children can only read the words they have been taught, and make many errors (Seymour and Elder, 1986). For decades, competition between phonics and the whole word approach was intense. Today, in both Britain and the USA, the focus has returned to phonological skills, and children are taught using phonics-based methods in order to help them learn the basics. The evidence supports this move (Adams, 1990). A meta-analysis conducted by Ehri *et al.* (2001) showed that phonics training produced a positive effect on learning to read. There is not just one approach to phonics, though. Until 2006, analytic phonics was a common type of instruction in the UK. This method involves the gradual introduction of letter sounds alongside words that use those let-ters. This approach can be contrasted with synthetic phonics, in which all the letters and letter sounds are introduced first. A longitudinal study by Johnston and Watson (2005) demonstrated that children who were taught using the synthetic method developed reading and spelling skills more quickly than children taught using the analytic method or a combination of analytic and synthetic phonics. As a result of the Rose Review (Rose, 2006), the UK government recommended that schools in England use synthetic phonics.

However, all of this does not mean that phonics alone provides the best outcome. The best approach probably involves a combination of the two approaches. Chil-dren do need to develop an awareness of phonemes, and their relations to letters, in order to learn to read. It is also the case that skilled readers use visually based re-trieval, so it is important that children learn to do this as well. However, reading is not just about word recognition, it is also about comprehension. It is the meaning of the text that provides the impetus for reading it. Children should, therefore, be introduced to real books in order to help them see the purpose of reading as well as concentrating on the mechanics of learning to read. When an appreciation of read-ing books is added to the basic skills of reading, we potentially have children who are not only good at reading, but enjoy it.

Concluding comments

Neither numeracy nor literacy are monolithic; both are comprised of many skills, some of which have been discussed in this chapter. Even when we break numeracy and literacy down into their components at the next level, such as arithmetic and reading, it is clear that these aspects are, in turn, comprised of many skills. There is no single arithmetic ability skill, but rather there are several different arithmetic abilities (Dowker, 2005). Many researchers have proposed different models, in which different components are taken into account. Baroody (2003; Baroody and Ginsberg, 1986) proposes a model in which conceptual, procedural and factual knowledge all interact to produce the development of mathematical abilities. Geary and Widaman (1987, 1992) account for individual differences in arithmetic in terms of information-processing factors such as retrieval of facts from long-term memory and the efficiency with which information can be manipulated in working memory.

If it is the case that mathematical ability depends on a number of lower-level abilities, then children's performance on different mathematical tasks should differ depending on which components are used in each task. Jordan *et al.* (2006) found that children's developmental trajectories differed for story problems and nonverbal calculations. In a longitudinal study of 5- to 7-year-olds, Jordan, Mulhern and Wylie (2009) gave their participants seven tasks at six month intervals. For tasks that involved procedural knowledge, or arithmetic skills, performance at the first measurement time was correlated with performance 18 months later. In contrast, there was not a significant correlation over time for performance on tasks based on conceptual knowledge. However, the intercorrelations between different conceptual tasks, and between conceptual and procedural tasks, which were weak at time 1, became stronger at time 4. This suggests that the relationship between procedural and conceptual knowledge increases over time, supporting Baroody's (2003) model. Jordan *et al.* (2009) also note that their participants showed greater increases over time for tasks on which children may have developed alternative strategies, which supports Siegler's ideas regarding the role of strategies in the development of arithmetic ability. Overall, studies such as these provide evidence for the componential nature of mathematical ability, an implication of which is that different children may have different profiles of strengths and weaknesses, which can be hidden when mathematical ability is viewed as a unitary construct.

As we saw earlier, Siegler's (1996) adaptive strategy choice model can also be applied to reading. According to Siegler, when children can use visually based retrieval to identify a word, they will do so. If this strategy does not work for a particular word, they can use phonological recoding – a more effortful strategy – to read the word. Over time, as children's knowledge of words grows, phonological recoding will be used less frequently and direct access will be used most of the time. As with mathematical ability, the phonological skills necessary for reading are not one unitary ability and theorists have argued for the relative importance of different levels of phonological awareness, such as onset-rime or individual phonemes (Bryant, 1998; Muter *et al.* 1997). The path analysis carried out by Muter *et al.* (2004), discussed earlier, suggested that phoneme and letter level knowledge are more important than rhyme and word level knowledge for word recognition, but that vocabulary is needed for comprehension.

However, it is also possible that literacy has an effect on phonological awareness such that early reading leads to greater phonological skills (Adrian, Alegria and Morais, 1995; Castles and Coltheart, 2004). This hypothesis is difficult to test as, by the time children are old enough to be tested for their phonological skills, they have usually started learning to read. In order to get round this problem, Alcock, Ngorosho, Deus and Jukes (2010) studied Tanzanian children, many of whom start their education late. Alcock *et al.* recruited 108 children aged 7 to 10 years. Some of the participants had no education, some were in the first grade and some were in the second grade. They completed several tests measuring phonological awareness, reading ability and other cognitive abilities. The results showed that children who had not yet started learning to read performed more poorly on tests on phonological awareness than children who could read. Performance on phonological awareness tasks, regardless of unit size (e.g., phoneme, syllable, word) was related to letter-reading ability. Alcock *et al.* conclude that phonological awareness starts to develop before experience with reading, but that its ongoing development requires the acquisition of literacy.

One final point to note is that whereas we humans have been using many of our cognitive abilities – such as our perceptual skills, our memories, our verbal language skills and our theory of mind abilities – for thousands of years, numeracy and literacy are relative newcomers to human culture. Although we have been counting and writing in a very basic way for a long time, it takes formal education to provide us with the advanced skills discussed in this chapter, and mass education is a recent phenomenon that is still not universal. As such, numeracy and literacy, along with the knowledge and skills discussed in Chapter 7, are qualitatively different cognitive abilities from those discussed in Chapters 2 to 5. Whereas we might reasonably expect perception and memory to develop along similar lines in children throughout the world, the development of reading and sophisticated mathematical knowledge and skills will clearly vary as a function of culture and education.

Summary

Numeracy. This is an important issue as many children have difficulties with basic skills such as counting and arithmetic operations, which leads to problems with more complex mathematics. There are many important skills needed for mathematics, including 1–1 correspondence, counting strategies and an understanding of cardinal numbers. However, mathematics isn't just about facts and procedures, but also about understanding. According to Piaget, children's understanding of number is based on the discovery of number invariance. Piaget argued that children in the pre-operational stage do not have a conceptual understanding of number. Information-processing theorists often use reaction time data in order to infer which strategies children use at different ages and on different problems. Siegler arrived at the conclusion that children use a mix of strategies, depending on experience and the type of problem. Children who have greater experience with a range of problems are more likely to retrieve answers from memory, whereas children who have not had much experience will use counting strategies. Nativist theorists posit innate principles that guide early knowledge of number. This idea is supported by the work of Wynn, who demonstrated that 5-month-olds can perform addition and subtraction on small numbers.

Research on mathematics reveals that both children and adults show different levels of success on problems which involve the same intellectual structures but differ in other respects, such as content, social situation or mathematical representation, contrary to Piaget's ideas. Two important factors that influence children's mathematical abilities are their conceptual understanding of aspects of the system of mathematics and the context in which mathematical problems are presented. Children aged as young as 3 understand the concept of inversion in sets of objects, but do not understand inversion when it is applied to numerical problems until late primary school, and most 7- and 8-year-olds do not have a good understanding of mathematical equality. With respect to fractions, even teenagers have problems. One of the differences between younger and older children is the way in which they conceptualize and estimate magnitudes. In a series of studies using number lines, Siegler and his colleagues demonstrated that children progress from a logarithmic to a linear representation of number. Unfamiliar contexts prevent children from using the procedures they are able to use successfully in other contexts. Nunes and her colleagues have conducted several studies illustrating a failure to transfer arithmetic skills between contexts. For example, Brazilian street vendors could solve arithmetic problems in a selling context, but did not do so well when problems were presented numerically. The findings suggest that the participants were not able to connect what they did for a living with the mathematics they studied in school.

In order to do mathematics we must have an understanding of written numerical values and mathematical symbols and an understanding of logical relations. Both of these are hard to grasp. Children's difficulties in understanding written numerical values and mathematical symbols are tied up with problems in understanding language. The mathematical meaning of a word can be slightly different from its everyday meaning, and some aspects of the English number system are arbitrary. Children get better at problem solving and logical thinking as they get older, suggesting that in order to master mathematical concepts children need to have the prerequisite conceptual understanding. Although logical relations may be important, they need to be integrated within a framework that acknowledges the part played by content and culture in children's learning.

Literacy. As with mathematics, many children and adults have problems with reading and spelling, which can have a major impact on daily life. If people do not have functional literacy they are unable to engage in simple and useful tasks such as reading newspapers and recipes. There are a vast number of issues including debates on how we teach children to begin to read, how we teach text comprehension, how we teach children awareness of text structure and how we teach literary appreciation and literary evaluation. In order to achieve a functional level of literacy, there are a few basic skills we must master, including letter recognition, grapheme-phoneme correspondence rules and word recognition.

Many theories of reading are stage theories. Chall identified five stages of reading covering the lifespan, from prereading skills that are mastered before school to highly skilled adult reading. Frith developed a theory which describes the skills children use at different points in this progression. In Frith's first stage, the logographic stage, children rote-learn associations between written and spoken words. The second stage is the alphabetic stage, in which children analyze words in terms of their letters and use their knowledge of grapheme-phoneme correspondence to work out how to pronounce words. The third stage is the orthographic stage, in which children use their knowledge of patterns of letters, usually morphemes, to determine pronunciation. Ehri's four-stage theory is based on the connections between written words and their mental representations. In contrast to stage theories, Siegler proposes that several different strategies are available to children, and that it is the relevant frequency of the use of each strategy, rather than their availability, that varies as a function of age and experience.

An important precursor to the development of reading is phonological awareness – the conscious awareness of the sound structure of language. If children fail to make the phonological connection they are destined to find learning to read and write very difficult. There is a distinction between implicit phonological processing, which involves verbal short-term memory, and explicit phonological awareness. Implicit phonological awareness refers to abilities such as detecting words that start with the same letter, or words that rhyme, whereas explicit phonological awareness refers to the ability to segment words into phonemes, map letters to sounds and manipulate sounds to produce words. Implicit phonological processing develops in the preschool years before explicit phonological awareness, and both have been shown to predict later reading ability. However there is some debate as to whether large units such as rhyme, or the smaller units of phonemes, are most important. It is likely that different aspects of reading are predicted by different linguistic skills.

Both home life and school life, including how reading is taught, are important influences on literacy. Children who learn to read, at least a few words, before they get to school tend to be better at reading in school than children who have not started reading, and parents who encourage literary activities at the preschool level are more likely to provide support for their children when they do start to read. Active experiences that get children involved in letter manipulation and word reading contribute to literacy development. The big debate in education has, for decades, been about whether to teach literacy skill using phonics, based on phonological recoding, or the whole word approach, based on visually based retrieval. Although it is generally agreed that phonics-based instruction leads to the best outcomes, reading also needs to be contextualized. If children do not enjoy reading, they are less likely to develop higher levels of literacy.

Discussion questions

1 What cognitive factors affect the development of numeracy?

2 What do psychological theories and research tell us about how we learn the skills and concepts necessary to be numerate?

3 What skills do children need to master to be literate? What influences the development of literacy?

4 Do you think that reading development progresses in stages, or that variable strategy use is a better explanation?

5 How can psychological theory and research be used to inform curriculum development? Can this knowledge be used to address the difficulties with literacy or numeracy that many children have?

Further reading

Books and chapters

Donlan, C. (Ed.) (1998). *The development of mathematical skills*. Hove: Psychology Press.

Chris Donlan's edited volume brings together several of the researchers and theorists discussed in this chapter. It includes contributions from Karen Wynn on infant's numerical competence, and Bethany Rittle-Johnson and Robert Siegler, among others, on conceptual and procedural knowledge.

Ehri, L. (2005). Development of sight word reading: Phases and findings. In M. J. Snowling and C. Hulme (Eds). *The science of reading: A handbook*. Oxford: Blackwell.

In this chapter, Linnea Ehri presents some of the different theories of reading development.

Nunes, T. and Bryant, P. (Eds) (1997). *Learning and teaching mathematics: An international perspective*. Hove: Psychology Press.

In this edited volume, Terezinha Nunes and Peter Bryant have included chapters on pre-school mathematical understanding, proportional reasoning, cultural influences and classroom practice.

Nunes, T. and Bryant, P. (2009). *Children's reading and spelling: Beyond the first steps*. Chichester: Wiley-Blackwell.

Nunes and Bryant offer an account of the development of literacy through the school years.

Articles

Hulme, C., Hatcher, P. J., Nation, K., Brown, A., Adams, J. and Stuart, G. (2002). Phoneme awareness is a better predictor of early reading skill than onset-rime awareness. *Journal of Experimental Child Psychology, 82*, 2–28.

Bowey, J. A. (2002). Reflections on onset–rime and phoneme sensitivity as predictors of beginning word reading. *Journal of Experimental Child Psychology, 82*, 29–40.

Bryant, P. E. (2002). It doesn't matter whether onset and rime predicts reading better than phoneme awareness or vice versa. *Journal of Experimental Child Psychology, 82,* 41–46.

Goswami, U. (2002). In the beginning was the rhyme? A reflection on Hulme, Hatcher, Nation, Brown, Adams and Stuart. *Journal of Experimental Child Psychology, 82,* 47–57.

Hulme, C. (2002). Phonemes, Rimes and the Mechanisms of Early Reading Development. *Journal of Experimental Child Psychology, 82,* 58–64.

This collection of papers deals with the issue of whether phoneme awareness or onset-rime awareness is more important for developing reading skills. Charles Hulme and colleagues present a study demonstrating that phonemic awareness is more important than onset-rime awareness, and Judith Bowey, Peter Bryant and Usha Goswami provide critical commentaries. In the final paper, Hulme responds to the issues raised by Bowey, Bryant and Goswami.

McNeil, N. M. (2007). U-shaped development in math: 7-year olds outperform 9-year olds on mathematical equivalence problems. *Developmental Psychology, 43,* 687–695.

Nicole McNeil presents a study in which she examines the development of primary school children's performance on equivalence problems.

Siegler, R. S., Thompson, C. A. and Opfer, J. E. (2009). The logarithmic-to-linear shift: One learning sequence, many tasks, many time scales. *Mind, Brain and Education, 3,* 143–150.

Robert Siegler, Clarissa Thompson and John Opfer review the work of Siegler and his colleagues on number line estimation and numerical representations.

Chapter 9

Intelligence

© Chris Schmidt/iStock

Learning Outcomes

At the end of this chapter you should be able to:

- Describe and evaluate theories of intelligence.

- Discuss different ways of testing intelligence and the problems associated with them.

- Discuss the issue of whether intelligence is stable over time and be able to describe and evaluate the relevant research

- Describe and evaluate studies that explore the roles of genetic inheritance and the environment.

Between 1972 and 1977, Craig Ramey admitted 57 infants from low-income families, ranging in age from 6 weeks to 6 months, to a special day care programme in North Carolina. These infants were provided with a special curriculum, featuring game-like learning activities, focused on perceptual-motor, cognitive, language and social development (Sparling and Lewis, 1979, 1984). From the age of 3, the children also received mathematics, reading and science instruction. They received full-time year-round day care along with nutritional meals, healthcare and social services, until the age of 5. A further 54 infants were recruited for a control group. The latter group received nutritional supplements, healthcare and social benefits but did not get the day care.

The rationale behind this programme, the Carolina Abecedarian project (Campbell and Ramey, 1994, 1995, 2007; Ramey and Campbell, 1984; Ramey and Ramey, 1998, 2000), was that Ramey had previously found that intelligence test scores of children from poor families tended to drop well below average after infancy. Although it had been suggested that intelligence was fixed and could not, therefore, be altered (Jensen, 1973), Ramey and his team worked with the idea that this deficit was the result of a deprived environment, rather than due to innate differences. Ramey and his colleagues designed the Abecedarian study in order to see what effect full-time child care, with an emphasis on enhancing development, would have. The name of the project – Abecedarian – refers to someone who is learning basics, such as the first letters of the alphabet: An *A-B-C-darian*.

Throughout the programme several different measures of intelligence were used. The Bayley Scales of Infant Development (Bayley, 1969) were administered every three months from 3 to 18 months of age. The Stanford-Binet Intelligence Scale (Terman and Merrill, 1972) was administered at 2, 3 and 4 years, the McCarthy General Cognitive Index (McCarthy, 1972) was used at 2½, 3½ and 4½ years, and the Wechsler Preschool and Primary Scale of Intelligence (Wechsler, 1967) was given at 5 years.

When the children in the intervention group entered the programme, they had a mean age of 4.4 months. Figure 9.1 shows the IQ scores for the two groups of children up to 5½ years. After 3 months, both groups were averaging around 95 on the Bayley Scales, but at almost all subsequent measurement points, the intervention

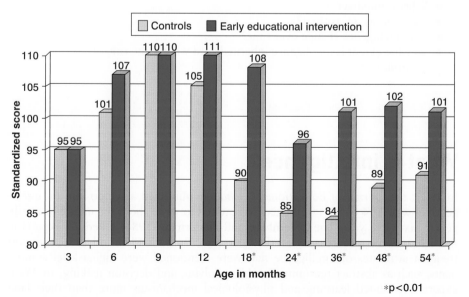

Figure 9.1

IQ scores for the treatment and control groups in the Carolina Abecedarian Project.

Source: Ramey, S. L. & Ramey, C. T. (1999) Early experience and early intervention for children "at risk" for developmental delay and mental retardation. *Mental Retardation and Developmental Disabilities Research Reviews*, 5, 1–10. Copyright 1999 John Wiley & Sons. This material is reproduced with permission of John Wiley & Sons, Inc.

group scored higher. By 3 years of age, the intervention group showed normal IQ scores on the Stanford-Binet test, averaging 101, whereas the control group were 17 points lower. When the children were 12 years old, the participants' IQs were measured using the Wechsler Adult Intelligence Scale–Revised (Wechsler, 1981). The average IQ scores were 94 for the intervention group and 88 for the control group (Campbell and Ramey, 1994). Over 15 years after the programme had finished, when the participants were 21 years old, their IQ was measured again. The intervention group had an average IQ of 90, whereas the control group had an average IQ of 85 (Campbell *et al.*, 2001; Campbell *et al.*, 2002). Even though the early difference had been reduced, the effect of the intervention programmes was still there.

In addition to the higher IQ scores, the group who had received the treatment showed other positive outcomes. At 12 years of age, the intervention group had higher scores on measures of academic achievement, including reading, writing, written language and knowledge. At age 21, 35.9 per cent of the participants from the intervention group had entered higher education, compared to just 13.7 per cent of the control group. The intervention group were more likely to hold skilled jobs than the control group, less likely to become teenage parents and less likely to be regular smokers. Also, it was not just the participants who benefited from the Abecedarian programme. Having their children in full-time day care enabled the mothers to gain greater educational and occupational success (Campbell *et al.*, 2002).

The fascinating findings from the Abecedarian project show an obvious effect of the environment on intelligence, leading to improved cognitive and social development. These findings also raise a number of interesting questions. The different intelligence tests administered at different ages measure different things, as we shall see later in the chapter. Does this mean that there is an underlying entity called 'intelligence' that is captured by these different tests? Or is it the case that intelligence is made of several different, yet correlated, abilities? The findings demonstrate that day care can have a positive impact on intelligence. Does this mean that intelligence is not something that is fixed from birth, that it is not the case that children are born with a particular IQ? Or does it mean that we are born with a particular level of intelligence that can be changed through experience?

Throughout the rest of the chapter, we will consider questions such as:

- What is intelligence?
- How can we measure it?
- Can intelligence change over time?
- To what extent is intelligence inherited, and what is the role of the environment?

Q. How do you define intelligence?

What is intelligence?

In 1921, the *Journal of Educational Psychology* published a symposium on intelligence in which 14 experts of the day were asked to write about the nature of intelligence. Sixty-five years later, Sternberg and Detterman (1986) asked 24 experts in the field to write a short essay on the same topic. In both 1921 and 1986, the most frequent attributes of intelligence that were mentioned were higher-level components, such as abstract reasoning, problem solving and decision making. In 1921, experts mentioned learning and physiological mechanisms more than their later counterparts, whereas the 1986 contributors placed a greater emphasis on metacognition, executive processes and cultural values (Sternberg and Berg, 1986). Sternberg's (1997a) own definition of intelligence is that it 'comprises the mental abilities necessary for adaptation to, as well as shaping and selection of, any environmental context' (p. 1030). This reflects Piaget's (1950, 1952b) view, in which he considered adaptation to be the defining characteristic of intelligence. Thus, finding a definition of intelligence is not hard, but the chances are that the first definition will not be the same as the next one you find! There is little consensus on how to define intelligence and the definitions that do exist tend to be rather vague and, as we have seen, change over time. If we do not know exactly what intelligence is, it is hard to construct tests that measure it. If, over time, definitions change, tests have to change as well.

In the late nineteenth century, Francis Galton noted that abilities such as musical talent and the capacity for sophisticated thinking seemed to run in families. He proposed that our general capacity for learning and reasoning differs between individuals and is inherited from our parents (Galton, 1883). Early psychometric research concerned itself with the ability to differentiate this capacity – intelligence – between individuals, rather than attempting to discover the processes underlying intelligence. It was originally thought that intelligence was a unitary concept and ways of measuring it were devised. The classic IQ test is based on the test developed by Binet and Simon (1905) for the French Ministry of Education, who were interested in differentiating between children so they could provide an adequate education for those who were mentally retarded. Interestingly, it was whilst working as an assistant on this programme that Piaget became interested in children. Binet devised tests to create the concept of mental age. A child who scored lower than other children of the same age would have a lower mental age than chronological age, and a child scoring above average would have a mental age higher than their chronological age. This led William Stern to propose an **Intelligence Quotient (IQ)**, calculated by dividing mental age by chronological age and multiplying by 100. Thus, a 10-year-old with a mental age of 11 would have an IQ of 110 (11/10 × 100). Now referred to as the Stanford-Binet test (Terman, 1916), the score achieved by a child is compared to a population, with the average around 100. Over the years, IQ tests have changed but the original idea was that intelligence was something (as opposed to lots of different things) that could be measured. In the late nineteenth and early twentieth centuries, intelligence was thought to be the ability to solve problems and carry out abstract reasoning, whereas some of the more recent views of intelligence include other factors, such as social intelligence and practical skills.

The concept of a mental age implies that intelligence rises consistently as we get older, which is not the case, so the scoring of IQ tests moved from the calculation of a ratio IQ (mental age ÷ chronological age) to a deviation IQ, in which the mean of a population is 100, with a standard deviation of 15. Modern IQ tests are designed to produce a normal distribution, which means that 67 per cent of the scores are within one standard deviation of the mean and 96 per cent are within two standard deviations. Most IQ tests are designed to produce a normal distribution with a standard deviation of 15. Figure 9.2 shows a typical distribution of modern IQ tests.

However, people do not always perform at a similar level across different cognitive tasks. Some theorists, such as Thurstone, challenged the idea that a single score could represent human intellectual performance. Intelligence tests include a variety of tasks such as defining words or concepts, extracting meaning from different passages of text, answering general knowledge questions, reproducing geometric designs with blocks and solving arithmetic puzzles. Some people are better at verbal puzzles or visuospatial tasks and others may be better at learning languages. Perhaps these different tasks were measuring different mental abilities, which suggests that

intelligence quotient (IQ) A score on a standardized test designed to measure intelligence.

Figure 9.2

A normal distribution of IQ scores.

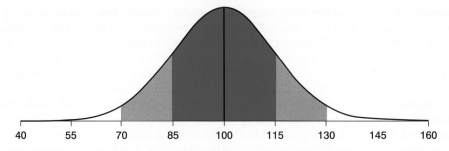

factor analysis A statistical method that is used to determine whether the variability in several observed variables can be described in terms of fewer underlying variables, or factors.

our abilities are not determined by a single factor. But there is still some correlation between abilities, and this needs to be explained. This led to the suggestion that general intelligence has more than one dimension and that these dimensions could be discovered by using factor analysis. This statistical procedure enables psychologists to see whether different test items are measuring the same underlying ability (i.e., general intelligence) or whether there are more basic abilities, such as verbal ability and visuo-spatial ability. Factor analysis works by examining the variability of scores on observed variables across a sample of the population. If several items on a test are highly correlated, then it is likely that they reflect the same underlying factor. Uncorrelated items are likely to be measures of different factors.

Spearman (1904, 1927) was the first to use factor analysis. He found that children's scores across tests were moderately correlated and inferred the existence of a general mental factor: *g*. Spearman proposed that in addition to the general factor (*g*), there were other factors (*s*), which were specific to a particular task, and explained differential task performance. Thurstone (1938) disagreed with Spearman about the existence of a single general intelligence factor. Thurstone's factor analysis uncovered seven factors, each of which related to some (but not all) tasks. Thurstone's seven 'primary mental abilities' are: Word fluency, which involves the speed with which we recognize words, and generating words – words that all start with a particular letter, for example; verbal meaning, which involves defining words; reasoning (e.g., inductive reasoning); spatial visualization, such as the mental manipulation of geometric forms or symbols; numbering, or the ability to solve arithmetic problems; rote memory, which includes our ability to recall lists of words, sentences or pictures; and perceptual speed – how quickly we can process visual information (e.g., recognizing symbols).

Theories of intelligence

It is now generally agreed that intelligence does not consist of one simple component, but there is still disagreement as to the structure of intelligence – whether there is an overarching general ability with a number of subcomponents or whether there are a number of relatively separate intelligences. The former view has led to the creation of hierarchical models (e.g., Cattell, Carroll) and the latter to models of multiple intelligences (e.g., Gardner, Sternberg).

Hierarchical models

Proponents of hierarchical models view intelligence as consisting of a general ability factor at the top of the hierarchy and a number of specialized ability factors. Cattell (1963, 1971) argued for two basic components under general intelligence: Fluid intelligence and crystallized intelligence. Fluid intelligence is our general capacity for reasoning, independent of cultural factors and experience. Fluid intelligence consists of our biologically-based abilities and includes the acquisition of new knowledge and grasping new relations. Crystallized intelligence is the result of cultural experience and acquired knowledge and skills. These include things like vocabulary, reading comprehension and general information about the world. These two intelligences can be used to explain the development of intellectual skills over the lifespan. Crystallized intelligence increases through childhood and adulthood and is maintained at a high level into old age. Fluid intelligence, on the other hand, does not take so much time to develop fully, but may start declining before the age of 40.

Another example of a hierarchical model is that of Carroll (1993, 1997). This is the most elaborate hierarchical model, the three-stratum theory of intelligence, based on an analysis of over 400 sets of cognitive ability test scores. Table 9.1 illustrates the three strata. The first layer (on the left) is general intellectual ability, the second layer (in the middle) is our broad intellectual abilities. We have strengths and weaknesses according to these abilities. Items further down the list have a decreasing correlation with *g*; fluid intelligence and crystallized intelligence are strongly associated with *g*. The third layer (on the right) consists of specific factors which make up the second stratum factors. This model can account for why it may be that we have a high level of general ability, but are not very creative, or why we may have below-average general ability, yet excel at memory tasks. Performance on third-stratum tasks results from our second-stratum abilities, which may be different to our general abilities.

General intellect (g)		
	Fluid intelligence	Quantitative reasoning, analogical reasoning
	Crystallized intelligence	Language comprehension, vocabulary
	General memory and learning	Memory span, associative memory
	Visual perception	Visual and spatial discrimination
	Auditory perception	Phonemic and musical discrimination
	Retrieval ability	Creativity, naming facility
	Cognitive speed	Perceptual speed, rate of test-taking
	Processing speed	Reaction time, speed of decision-making

Table 9.1

Carroll's hierarchical model.

Gardner's theory of multiple intelligences

Gardner (1993a, 1993b) argues for the existence of eight independent intelligences or *frames of mind*. Each of these frames of mind is a biologically specified module that may differ in strength from person to person. Each module has its own computational mechanisms and is based on distinct neural architecture. Gardner has linked each of these modules to vocational end-states. For example, someone with a strong spatial intelligence may be an engineer. Table 9.2 shows the eight intelligences, along with examples of abilities related to each area and examples of vocations.

In support of this model, there is evidence from neuroscience showing that brain damage can disrupt certain intelligences. For example, damage to Broca's area or Wernicke's area (see Chapter 4) can cause aphasia, or language impairment. Another example is brain damage leading to impaired interpersonal intelligence (Damasio, 1999). Also, it seems to be the case that most children excel in one or two of these eight areas and may be mediocre or poor in others. Savant skills, similar to those seen in autism (see Chapter 10), are apparent in many individuals who are mentally retarded; they may have exceptional abilities in art, music or calculation. But, as Gardner himself notes, these modules and intelligences 'exist not as physically

Table 9.2	Gardner's eight frames of mind.	

Frame of mind	Abilities	Examples of vocation
Linguistic	Sensitivity to sounds and meanings of words and structure of language	Poet, novelist, journalist
Logical-mathematical	Understand abstract symbol systems; think logically and systematically	Mathematician, scientist
Spatial	Perceive visual-spatial relationships accurately; recreate aspects of visual experience in absence of perceptual stimuli	Engineer, sculptor, cartographer
Bodily-kinesthetic	Use body to express oneself, handle objects skilfully	Dancer, athlete
Musical	Sensitivity to pitch and melody; understanding of emotional aspects of music	Musician, composer
Interpersonal	Detect others' moods, temperaments, motives and intentions; react appropriately	Therapist, PR specialist, spokesperson
Intrapersonal	Sensitivity to own inner states; recognition of own strengths and weaknesses; adapt behaviour accordingly	Success in any walk of life
Naturalist	Sensitivity to factors influencing and influenced by organisms in the natural environment	Biologist, naturalist

Source: Gardner (1993a); Torff and Gardner (1999).

verifiable entities, but only as potentially useful scientific constructs' (Gardner, 1993a, p. 70). Although Gardner's multiple intelligences seem intuitively appealing, the evidence does not point towards these intelligences as statistically independent (Sternberg, 1988). Most of the abilities are correlated, suggesting that there are more general underlying factors.

Sternberg's triarchic theory

One criticism of many of the models of intelligence is that they focus on the child's knowledge, rather than the processes by which knowledge is acquired, retained and used to solve problems. Sternberg's (1985, 1986, 1997b) triarchic theory addresses this. Sternberg argued that IQ tests were only measuring one type of intelligence and that in fact we can and should distinguish three types. He developed the Sternberg Triarchic Abilities Test (Sternberg et al., 2001) to measure these three intelligences. Analytical intelligence (also referred to as componential intelligence) is concerned with analytic thinking and abstract reasoning. This is the intelligence we use when planning, organizing and remembering, and refers to the relationship between intelligence and the internal world. Creative intelligence (also called experiential intelligence) is our ability to have insightful and creative thinking, and to see connections between ideas. It describes the relationship between intelligence and experience. Practical, or contextual, intelligence refers to our 'street smarts' and 'practical know-how' – our common sense. This is intelligence used in relation to the external world, and includes our social skills, for example knowing when to tell someone something and when to keep your mouth shut!

According to Sternberg (2003), children who have strengths in different aspects of intelligence will display different patterns of strengths and weaknesses in school.

Children who have high analytical intelligence will tend to do well in school, as school tests tend to measure analytic skills. Children who are high in creative intelligence or practical intelligence may not do well on traditional tests. In terms of skills needed to succeed in life, Sternberg argues that practical and creative intelligence may be required just as much as the type of skills (analytical intelligence) measured in a traditional IQ test. This is interesting as the research we will look at in this chapter involves various issues to do with intelligence, but only considers analytic intelligence. We don't know anything about the origins of, or variations in, creative and practical intelligence, yet these may be just as important as analytical intelligence in daily life (Sternberg and Grigorenko, 2006).

According to Sternberg's theory, intelligence draws upon three basic information-processing components that operate on our internal representations of objects, events or symbols. The first of these components are the metacomponents. These are the brains of the operation, in charge of planning and decision making, combining new information with old, allocating capacity to other components, keeping track of what has been done, deciding how to respond to feedback and constructing appropriate strategies from among the performance components. The second components are the performance components that actually solve the problem, and the third are the knowledge-acquisition components. The latter acquire the knowledge needed to solve the problem if it is not already possessed.

Consider the following problem:

> If you have black socks and brown socks in your drawer, mixed in the ratio of 4 to 5, how many socks will you have to take out to make sure of having a pair the same colour?
> (Sternberg and Davidson, 1983)

Why can some people do this and not others? Why, in particular, might children find it difficult? According to Sternberg, children and adults differ in the effectiveness of the components. The metacomponents allocate capacity more effectively in adults than in children. Also, children need to acquire more knowledge, which means that more capacity must be allocated to knowledge acquisition components, so there is less left for problem solving. The metacomponents in children are also more likely to choose the wrong strategy or fail to shift to an alternative strategy if the chosen one is not successful. Children's knowledge acquisition components are less effective than those of adults in three ways. First, children are poorer at selective encoding, or differentiating relevant information from irrelevant information. In the case of the 'socks' tasks, the ratio of black to brown socks is irrelevant. Second, children are poorer at selective combination, or integrating new information in a meaningful way. Finally, children are poorer at selective comparison, or relating new information to previously acquired information. Children and adults also differ in the degree of automaticity they possess. In adults, increased automaticity of the components frees capacity for other tasks. To take reading as an example, children have to expend a lot of their capacity on recognizing letters, which means less is available for recognizing words and other higher order skills. This leads to less smooth reading than adults whose letter recognition is automated and effortless. Children and adults also differ in the amount of contextual information available to them. Adults are more aware of their environment and their cultural and social context. They are more able to choose their environment to play to their strengths. Children do not have the knowledge of the world or themselves to do this.

(The solution to the socks problem is that you only have to take three socks out to be sure of having a pair. Even if the first two socks you draw are mismatched, the third is bound to make a pair with one of the first two.)

Anderson's minimal cognitive architecture

Anderson's (1992) model is quite different from the other theories we have looked at, although it shares some features with them. Anderson proposed a basic processing mechanism which underlies intelligence. Differences between individuals are a result of the speed and efficiency with which we process information, which are part of our inherited neurophysiology. Anderson argues that people who can process information more quickly and more efficiently can process more information and, therefore, learn faster and reason more effectively. This explains why there is a weak correlation across different measures of cognitive ability, but does not explain differences across tasks within individuals. According to Anderson, these differences occur because the basic processing mechanism is not involved in all mental activity. There are other, more specialized, processors for dealing with higher-level cognitive skills such as verbal reasoning and spatial processing. There are individual variations in the speed and efficiency of each of these processors, as with the basic processor, but the specialized processors also draw on the basic processor and so are not independent modules. A strength or weakness in any given area of cognition reflects the combined strengths or weaknesses of both the basic processing mechanism and the relevant specialized processor. This, argues Anderson, explains the pattern of varied abilities both between and within individuals. In addition to the basic processor and specialized processors, there is an additional route to knowledge, which does not involve these processors. This route is through dedicated information-processing modules, which deal with areas such as language acquisition, theory of mind and face recognition. Anderson's theory argues for two dimensions of *g*, one based on speed of processing and related to IQ scores, the other based on the development of cognitive modules and related to developmental changes.

Anderson (1999, 2005) notes that his theory accounts for three main observations of the development of intelligence. First, as we get older, our cognitive abilities, such as memory, perception and language, increase. Second, there is evidence for stability of intelligence over time with respect to individual differences. Third, our cognitive abilities tend to correlate, such that a person who scores highly on tests of, for example, verbal skills, is likely to score highly on tests of spatial reasoning.

Testing intelligence

Some of the models of intelligence have associated tests (e.g., the Sternberg Triarchic Abilities Test), but the most widely used tests are the Stanford-Binet Intelligence Scale and the Wechsler Scales. The Stanford-Binet Scale, described earlier, has undergone many revisions. The current version (Thorndike, Hagen and Sattler, 1986) is based on a three-stratum hierarchical model. The model has *g* at the top level, and crystallized abilities, fluid-analytic abilities and short-term memory at the second level. The third level consists of three factors: Verbal reasoning and quantitative reasoning (aspects of crystallized abilities), and abstract/visual reasoning (fluid-analytic abilities). There are 15 subtests of the test, measuring the three third-level factors and the second level memory factor.

The Wechsler intelligence scales come in three forms: The Wechsler Intelligence Scales for Children (WISC; Wechsler, 2003), the Wechsler Preschool and Primary

Scale of Intelligence (WPPSI; Wechsler, 2002) and the Wechsler Adult Intelligence Scales (WAIS; Wechsler, 2008). The WISC is similar to other IQ tests, but items are grouped according to 12 subscales which allow an insight as to the areas of mental performance that an individual is best or worst at. Wechsler felt that earlier tests were too loaded with items requiring verbal skills, so his scales contain verbal and non-verbal subscales, providing three scores: A verbal score, a non-verbal score and an overall score. There are six verbal subscales: Information ('How many dimes makes a dollar?'), comprehension ('Why are cheques signed?'), arithmetic ('How much would three pieces of candy cost if each piece cost 15 cents?'), similarities ('In what way are a finger and a toe alike?'), vocabulary ('What does save mean?') and digit span (participants are asked to repeat a series of numbers in order). There are also performance subscales. Picture completion involves showing children pictures such as a car with no wheels and asking 'What part of this picture is missing?' Picture arrangement involves arranging a series of pictures in the right order so they tell a story. The block design test is where children are given nine cubes, each of which has two red sides, two white sides and two sides with a red triangle and white triangle (so that half of the side is red and half white). The children are then shown a picture of a square and they have to put the blocks together to match the picture (see Chapter 10, in which the block design task is discussed with reference to autism). Object assembly involves putting an object together from several parts (e.g., a shaped jigsaw puzzle). Coding involves giving children a piece of paper with 100 small geometric shapes: 25 each of squares, circles, triangles and diamonds in a random order. The children have to write a different symbol (e.g. a cross or a dash) under different shapes. Finally, the maze task involves drawing a line through a printed maze.

Problems

There are a number of problems with both concepts of intelligence and intelligence testing. First, there is not a lot of evidence to demonstrate that any one method of testing is superior to the others, despite the amount of research into intelligence. Second, there is a debate over whether intelligence stems from one general ability, whether there are many separate kinds of relatively independent intelligence, or whether there is a hierarchical organization of specific skills stemming from one or two factors. Third, within the multiple intelligence/hierarchy camp, there is no agreement as to how many intelligences there are. Both practical intelligence (Sternberg) and musical intelligence (Gardner) have been proposed. Why not also have intelligences in the areas of chess, law, writing or poetry? People excel in a huge variety of ways. Why should an outstanding musician be characterized by a specific musical intelligence, but not an outstanding chess player? We need to either find categories of intelligence under which all skills can be included or to expand our number of intelligences to a huge number to include all the different skills. Guilford's (1988) model includes 180 different factors of intelligence, by multiplying five content areas by six types of mental operations by six kinds of product that can result from applying operations to content. However, any test that measures individuals on a large number of different factors would be hard to administer and the results would be hard to interpret.

Another problem for testing is the effect of the environment. There is evidence that changing children's environments can help improve their IQ. Is it fair, then to categorize people according to the environment in which they've been brought up? This issue will be discussed in more detail later on.

Cultural bias

A further problem for testing is cultural bias. In Western cultures we emphasize the importance of abstract thinking and problem solving. In other cultures, such as African and Eastern cultures, intelligence is not necessarily viewed as the same set of skills (Cole, 2006; Cole and Cigagas, 2010; Serpell, 2000). In Kenya, more emphasis is placed on responsible participation in family and social life as an integral part of intelligence (Harkness and Super, 1992; Grigorenko *et al.*, 2001). In Uganda and Zimbabwe, an intelligent person is one who knows what to do in order to benefit the community (Irvine, 1970, 1988; Mpofu, 2004; Wober, 1974). Zambian children are viewed as intelligent if they respect their elders and obey them, as well as having good mental skills (Serpell, 1977, 1993). Similarly, the Taiwanese conception of intelligence includes both cognitive and social factors (Yang and Sternberg, 1997a, 1997b). For the Poluwat islanders of Micronesia, the skill of navigating to neighbouring islands, hundreds of miles away, is an important and complex aspect of intelligence (Gladwin, 1970). IQ tests do not test these skills but rather ones that are considered important in Western cultures. Therefore people from cultures that do not emphasize the skills that we think are important may fail our IQ tests for this reason. Even within Western cultures, people from different ethnic groups place different emphases on whether cognitive or social aspects of intelligence are most important (Heath, 1983; Okagaki and Sternberg, 1993).

For these, among other reasons (e.g., people from other countries may not speak English) many modern tests are what are called *culture-fair* tests, which are intended to be free of cultural bias. There are two broad types of such tests. In the first type, questions that should be familiar to all people, despite socioeconomic and ethnic backgrounds, are asked. For example 'How are a dog and cat different?' In the second type, all verbal questions are removed. Examples of these are Raven's Progressive Matrices and Cattell's (1971) culture-fair test. Even so, people with higher levels of education tend to get higher scores. Perhaps there is no such thing as a culture free test. If tests have time limits, they are biased against cultures which are not concerned with time. If tests have drawings or photos (which is necessary if verbal components are removed), they are biased against cultures where people have less experience with them or interpret drawings differently. Perhaps there is no such thing as an objective definition of intelligence.

Does intelligence change over time?

One of the major questions is whether intelligence remains stable or changes over the years. Although there is evidence that intelligence scores at different stages of life correlate, there is also evidence that levels of intelligence can change over time. The question of stability relates to the nature–nurture debate; to what extent is our intelligence innate and to what extent is it shaped by the environment?

If intelligence is a unitary construct (e.g., Spearman's *g*), we would expect it to be highly heritable. The heritability of intelligence refers to the proportion of variation in intelligence in the population that can be attributed to genetic variation. Thus, if intelligence is a unitary construct, we would be born with a greater or lesser degree of intelligence. This may mean that intelligence is stable (Jensen, 1969, 1988), or it may be that there is room for environmental influences. If this is the case, our genetic endowment would place constraints on the range of intellect any individual may develop as a result of experience. If, on the other hand, there are many factors that make up intelligence, it may be that the environment has a larger role in the development of intelligence. The range of experiences we encounter, and the range of contexts we encounter them in, could therefore contribute to our intelligence, meaning that intelligence is changeable over time and situations (Ceci, 1996).

Infant intelligence

In order to assess the stability of intelligence, it is useful to know what the intelligence levels of infants are, so that these can be compared to later measures. It is possible to measure infant intelligence, but infant intelligence scales have, obviously, no measures of verbal intelligence. They contain more items measuring perceptual motor development and social interaction. Gesell (1925) devised a test to differentiate potentially normal babies from abnormal ones. This test looks at four categories of behaviour: Motor skills, language skills, adaptive skills and personal-social skills. Another scale which is widely used is the Bayley Scales of Infant Development (BSID; Bayley, 1933, 1969, 1993). The Bayley Scales have two components: A motor scale and a mental scale. The scales are aimed at assessing infants from 1 to 42 months old. Table 9.3 shows some of the items used for infants of different ages. Administering this test results in two scores, a psychomotor developmental index (PDI) and mental developmental index (MDI), both of which are normalized with a mean score of 100. This allows comparisons with infants of the same age.

Anderson (1939) looked at intelligence at 3 months, as measured by Bayley Scales, and intelligence at 5 years and found no correlation. The BSID seems to be measuring quite different things to IQ tests, so it is not surprising that scores derived from this measure do not correlate with later IQ scores (Birney *et al.*, 2005). This

Age	Mental scale	Motor scale
2 months	Turns head to sound Plays with rattle Reacts to disappearance of face	Holds head erect and steady for 15 seconds Turns from side to back Sits with support
6 months	Lifts cup by handle Looks for fallen spoon Looks at pictures in book	Sits alone for 30 seconds Turns from back to stomach Grasps foot with hands
12 months	Builds tower of two cubes Turns pages of book	Walks with help Throws ball Grasps pencil in middle
17 to 19 months	Imitates crayon stroke Identifies objects in photograph	Stands alone on right foot Walks up stairs with help
23 to 25 months	Matches pictures Uses pronouns Imitates a two-word sentence	Laces three beads Jumps distance of four inches Walks on tiptoe for four steps
38 to 42 months	Names four colours Uses past tense Identifies gender	Copies circle Hops twice on one foot Walks down stairs, alternating feet

Table 9.3

Items from the Bayley Scales of Infant Development.

Source: Bayley (1993).

means that although the BSID can be useful for making judgements about the developmental status of infants, and has been useful in picking up some cognitive delays (Langley, 1989), it has little to tell us about the stability of intelligence over time.

Evidence for stability

Some early measures, however, do seem to correlate with later intelligence measures. Speed of habituation and visual recognition memory correlate with IQ scores, suggesting that there is continuity between infancy and childhood (Domsch, Lohaus and Thomas, 2009; Gaultney and Gingras, 2005; Kavšek, 2004; Slater, 1995). These two measures reflect basic information-processing capacity. Taking speed of habituation first, an infant who habituates to a stimulus quickly may be fast at processing information and therefore capable of learning quickly. Bornstein and Sigman (1986) carried out a meta-analysis of studies which looked at habituation or novelty preference and later intelligence. Their results suggested that there was continuity: They found a correlation of 0.44 between early measures and follow-up studies at 2 to 3 years old and a correlation of 0.56 between early measures and follow-up studies at 6 years and over. Sigman and her colleagues (Sigman et al., 1986; Sigman et al., 1991; Sigman, Cohen, and Beckwith, 1997) followed 93 children for a period of 18 years, taking measures of fixation times and habituation with simple checkerboard patterns at birth and 4 months of age. When the children were 8, they were given the WISC-R; Sigman et al. (1986) found that the neonate fixation measure predicted IQ at 8 years. Infants who spent longer looking at the stimuli at birth and 4 months did not perform as well on later assessments of intellectual ability. Also, more efficient processing as an infant was related to good performance on an analogical reasoning task at age 12 (Sigman et al., 1991). When the participants were tested again 6 years later, Sigman et al. (1997) found that longer looking times in infancy were negatively associated with IQ (measured using the WAIS-R) at age 18.

The second early measure which suggests continuity is visual recognition memory. Recognition involves encoding a stimulus, recognizing it, and recognizing that other stimuli are novel – all basic information-processing abilities. Fagan (1984) measured preference for a novel face over a familiar face at 7 months and correlated this with performance on the Peabody Picture Vocabulary Test at 3 years and 5 years. He found a correlation of 0.42 between the infant measure and the later measures. Rose and Feldman (1995) looked at the scores of 90 infants of tests of visual recognition memory and visual attention and correlated these with performance on the WISC-R at 11 years. They found a correlation of 0.41 between early visual recognition memory and later intelligence. A meta-analysis of studies looking at both habituation and visual recognition memory as predictors of intelligence was carried out by McCall and Carriger (1993). They found correlations of around 0.45 for both measures with later intelligence. McCall and Carriger suggested that the reason for the equivalent predictive power of these two measures was that they both involve the ability to inhibit responses to familiar stimuli.

Later childhood measures also show correlations over time, suggesting that there is some stability in intelligence. Honzik, MacFarlane and Allen (1948) tested 250 children repeatedly between the ages of 4 and 18. The lowest correlation they found was a correlation of 0.42 between IQ scores at ages 4 and 18, and the highest was a correlation of 0.88 between scores at 8 and 10. Correlations between two adjacent years tend to fall in the range of 0.65 to 0.80 (Bartels et al., 2002; Honzik, 1986).

Evidence against stability of intelligence over time

There is also a lot of evidence against the stability of intelligence over time. The correlations mentioned above were averaged scores across many children. When looked at as individuals, there is some variability. Around 15 per cent of children will show a substantial change in IQ score over time (Sattler, 2008). McCall, Applebaum, and Hogarty (1973) looked at IQ score variations for 140 individual children and found that IQ scores fluctuated widely from test to test for a single child. They found an average IQ shift of 28.5 points between 2½ and 17 years of age, and one in seven of the children's scores fluctuated by as much as 40 points. This could mean a difference between a score of 90 (below average) and 130 (highly intelligent). In a longitudinal study of children in New Zealand, Caspi *et al.* (1996) found that 10 per cent of the children displayed a change in IQ score of 15 points over a two-year period. A few of the children (15 of 1037) shifted by 50 points or more over a six-year period. If intelligence were totally stable and unaffected by environmental influences, we would expect the actual scores of children to change very little over the years.

There is further evidence for an effect of environment. IQ scores are highly predictive of success in school and likelihood of going into tertiary education (Brody 1992, 1997). Low IQ scores are associated with negative outcomes, such as illiteracy and delinquency (Birney *et al.*, 2005; Stattin and Klackenberg-Larsson, 1993). Lots of programmes have attempted to intervene in manipulating the environment for children who are at risk of impoverished intelligence. Such schemes may work to improve the environment of both parents and children and thus provide more intellectual stimulation.

The Abecedarian project, discussed at the start of the chapter, is an example of an intervention that demonstrated an environmental effect, suggesting that intelligence is not stable throughout the school years. Another intervention project, the Head Start programme, started in the 1960s and has provided services such as medical care and nutrition to more than 20 million American children (Zigler and Finn-Stevenson, 1999). This programme was designed to help disadvantaged children, mostly pre-schoolers. The programme has led to immediate academic gains and rising IQ scores in the participating children, but these gains have not been permanent or consistent, so it is harder to draw any firm conclusions (McKey *et al.*, 1985; McLoyd, 1998). As we shall see, intelligence can be highly heritable, but it may also be susceptible to change through environmental changes such as educational interventions. The common agreement is that although some aspect of intelligence is undisputably inherited it doesn't mean that that aspect is rigidly fixed in the child and unchangeable from that point on.

How much of intelligence is inherited?

Research into the interaction between genetics and the environment follows several lines. In trying to assess the relative contributions of heredity and the environment, there are three useful populations: People who are genetically related and share the same environment, people who are genetically related and do not share the same environment and people who are genetically unrelated and share the same environment. In particular, twins and adopted siblings have been very important as, between them, they provide all three groups. There are two types of twins, identical or monozygotic twins, and fraternal or dizygotic twins. Monozygotic twins are the

monozygotic twins Also known as 'identical twins', the result of one fertilized egg splitting in two, creating two embryos with identical genes.

dizygotic twins Also known as 'fraternal twins', the result of two eggs that are fertilized by two different sperm cells.

result of one fertilized egg (zygote) splitting in two, creating two embryos with identical genes. Dizygotic twins, on the other hand, occur when two eggs are fertilized by two different sperm cells. As with any other pair of siblings, dizygotic twins share, on average, 50 per cent of their genes. If two monozygotic twins were to be separated at birth and raised in two different environments, they would have an identical genetic makeup but no (or very little) shared environment. If many pairs of such twins were studied and found to have highly correlated intelligence, we could infer that intelligence has a strong genetic basis. If, on the other hand, we took pairs of genetically unrelated children and raised them together, and found that intelligence scores were highly correlated, this would suggest a strong environmental role. Similarly, any differences between monozygotic twins would be due to non-genetic factors, and any differences in the unrelated children raised together can be ascribed to hereditary factors.

heritability The amount of variance of a trait, such as intelligence, that can be ascribed to genetic factors.

The amount of variance in a trait (in this case, IQ scores) in a population that can be attributed to genetics is known as the **heritability** of intelligence. A heritability coefficient can be calculated by taking the difference between correlations of monozygotic twins and dizygotic twins (for twin pairs who were raised together) and doubling it. Thus, a correlation of 1.0 between monozygotic twins and a correlation of 0.5 between dizygotic twins would lead to a heritability index of 1 (1–0.5 × 2), meaning that all differences in intelligence can be explained in terms of genetics. If genetics played no part in determining intelligence, we would not expect to see any differences between monozygotic and dizygotic twins, and the heritability coefficient would be 0. For monozygotic twins raised apart, where there is no shared environment, the correlation of intelligence scores gives a direct estimate of heritability.

Bouchard and McGue (1981) constructed a survey of the literature on studies in which correlations of intelligence between family members were reported. Some of the pooled results of the 111 studies they included are shown in Figure 9.3. If intelligence was entirely a matter of genetics, we would expect to see correlations of 1 for both groups of identical twins, and 0.5 for fraternal twins, siblings, and parent–child pairs, regardless of whether they were raised together or apart. We would also expect correlations of 0 between adopted children and adoptive parent–child pairs.

| **Figure 9.3** | IQ correlations. |

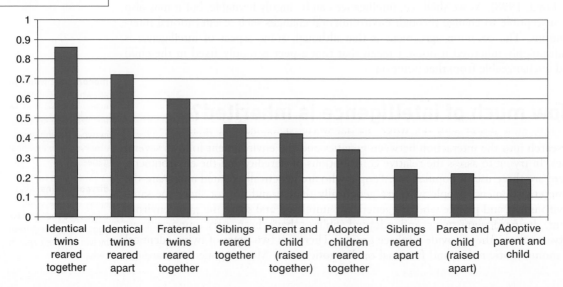

The fact that the correlations between identical twins, siblings and parent–child pairs are smaller than those predicted by a purely genetic view shows that there is a role for the environment. The higher-than-predicted values for fraternal twins and adoptive pairs also illustrates the role of the environment. However, for identical twins, environmental factors appear to lead to reduced similarity, whereas, in fraternal twins and adoptive pairs, environmental factors appear to lead to greater similarity. We can term these two distinctive roles for the environment non-shared environment and shared environment. The fact that identical twins do not have identical experiences means they end up less than perfectly correlated; their differences are therefore due to non-shared environmental experiences. Fraternal twins are more similar than genetics alone can account for; their shared environmental experiences can explain this. Although genetic similarities and differences do not account for everything, it is clear that they still have a dominant role. As Bouchard and McGue point out, a higher genetic similarity between two family members leads to a higher correlation between their IQ scores.

We can calculate the heritability of intelligence from these data by doubling the difference between correlations for identical twins raised together (0.86) and fraternal twins raised together (0.6). From this we get a heritability coefficient of 0.52 (.86–.60 × 2), meaning that 52 per cent of the variability of intelligence can be explained by genetic factors. On the other hand, using the data from the identical twins raised apart, we get a much higher estimate of 0.72.

Over the last three decades, psychologists at the University of Minnesota have set up several projects based around the study of twins, including the Minnesota Twin Family Study, the Minnesota Twin Study of Adult Development and the Minnesota Study of Twins Reared Apart (MISTRA). As part of the latter project over 100 pairs of twins from the UK, the USA and several other countries, who were separated early in life, were recruited between 1979 and 2000. Bouchard et al. (1990) gave a set of intelligence tests, including the WAIS, to 48 pairs of monozygotic twins reared apart. They found correlations of 0.69 to 0.78, suggesting that around 70 per cent of variation in IQ scores can be explained by genetics. Another study, in which 48 pairs of Swedish monozygotic twins who had been raised apart were given intelligence tests, led to a similar correlation of 0.78 (Pederson et al., 1992). These two studies, along with three studies on monozygotic twins raised apart (Juel-Nielsen 1965; Newman, Freeman and Holzinger, 1937; Shields, 1962), yield an average heritability index for intelligence of 0.75 (McGue and Bouchard, 1998). More recently, Johnson et al. (2007) gave intelligence tests to 74 pairs of monozygotic twins and 52 pairs of dizygotic twins from the MISTRA project, and found a heritability of 0.77 for general intelligence.

Further evidence for the heritability of intelligence can be derived by looking at the similarities and differences between adopted children and their adoptive and biological parents. In the Texas Adoption Project (Horn, 1983), 300 adoptive families, and the biological mothers of the adopted children, were given IQ tests. The children were tested with the WISC or the WAIS, depending on their age. Horn found that the IQ scores of the adopted children were more highly correlated with their biological mothers (0.28) than with their adoptive mothers (0.15) or fathers (0.12). This, of course, suggests that genetic factors play a larger role than environmental factors. Ten years later, when the children were, on average, 17 years old, they were tested again. Loehlin, Horn and Willerman (1997) used these data to compute a rough heritability for intelligence of 0.78.

Loehlin et al. note that the genetic effect on intelligence increased with age, from an earlier estimate of 0.37 (Loehlin, Horn and Willerman, 1989). There are many other sources of evidence for the development of heritability, which may explain why studies of adult twins tend to report heritability estimates of around 75 per cent, whereas other studies (e.g. Loehlin, 1989; Plomin, DeFries and McClearn, 1990; Scarr, 1978) report lower estimates of around 50 per cent. It is possible that correlations between parents and children tend to be small when the children are very young because, as we have seen, it is difficult to make accurate measurements of young children's IQs. However, a common finding is that the correlations between adopted children and their biological parents increase over time, and that the correlation with adoptive parents decreases over time. This leads to heritability increasing from around 0.45 in childhood to 0.75 by late adolescence (McCartney, Harris and Bernieri, 1990; McGue, Bouchard, Iacono, and Lykken, 1993; Neisser *et al.*, 1996). Polderman *et al.* (2006) collected data from 237 pairs of twins when they were 5 years old. In this study, both monozygotic and dizygotic twins were recruited, and each pair was raised together. Seven years later, the researchers obtained a second dataset from 172 of the original twin pairs. The researchers found that the heritability of intelligence rose from 30 per cent at age 5, to 80 per cent at age 12. Although different values have been obtained from different studies, there is a clear trend: Genetic factors become stronger influences on intelligence as we develop.

Although the evidence in favour of a high level of heritability seems quite conclusive, there are a couple of issues to bear in mind. First, the majority of studies looking at the heritability of intelligence use traditional IQ tests, such as the WAIS, WISC and Stanford-Binet tests. As we saw earlier, there are many theorists, such as Gardner and Sternberg, who do not think these tests adequately measure intelligence as they conceptualize intelligence as a broad construct, not just the analytical or logical abilities measured by IQ tests. Second, there is often an assumption that genetic and environmental influences are distinct from one another. In reality, genes do not exist in isolation; they are always in an environment, and that environment shapes their activity. As a result, statistical models of intelligence in which genetic variance and environmental variance are included, but interactions between genes and environments are omitted, may not accurately identify the relative contributions of all three factors.

Plomin, DeFries and Loehlin (1977) refer to the ways in which heredity and environment interact as the genetic-environment correlation. The basic idea is that our genes influence the environments to which we are exposed. There are three types of genetic-environment correlation: Passive, evocative and active. The developmental role of genetic-environment correlations was expanded on by Scarr and McCartney (1983). Passive correlation refers to an interaction over which the child has no control. In this case, parents provide environments for their children that are influenced by the parents' own heredity. For example, parents who are athletic are likely to emphasize outdoor activities, such as swimming lessons or gymnastics lessons. Their children are likely to become good athletes for both genetic and environmental reasons; they have inherited some athleticism from their parents and have also experienced an environment with an emphasis on sport. The second type of interaction is the evocative correlation, whereby children evoke responses from others that are influenced by their heredity. These responses in turn reinforce the children's style of responding. An active, friendly baby is more likely to evoke social stimulation and attention than a passive, quiet baby. The stimulation received will reinforce the baby's friendliness. The third interaction, active correlation, becomes more common as children get older, and is also referred to as niche-picking. Children seek out environments, or pick niches, that are consistent with their genetically-derived tendencies. A child with good coordination who is physically muscular is likely to choose to participate in sports clubs at school; a child who has inherited a talent for music is likely to join a school orchestra or play in a band; an intellectually curious child may spend a lot of time in the library. What all of this means is that if we want to understand nature and nurture, we have to be open to subtlety and complexity, as development is a series of complex interactions between nature and nurture.

Concluding comments

We have seen that intelligence is, arguably, an entity that can be decomposed into a range of more basic abilities. How the structure of intelligence is viewed depends, at least in part, on whether a bottom-up or top-down perspective is taken (Pretz and Sternberg, 2005). The bottom-up approach involves the attempt to identify basic processes that underlie intelligence, such as information processing speed. The top-down approach, on the other hand, measures higher-level cognitive abilities, such as problem solving and reasoning, and ascribes differences in intelligence to knowledge and metacognitive abilities, such as cognitive control and flexibility in strategy use. We saw earlier that many studies on infant intelligence have shown that measures such as habituation speed and visual recognition memory are predictors of later intelligence. We also know that information processing speed increases with age (Kail, 1991a), and that reaction time is correlated with general intelligence (Fry and Hale, 1996, 2000; Jensen, 1993). It may also be the case that greater processing speed allows working memory to be used more effectively, leading to higher scores on intelligence tests (Kail, 2000). Although processing speed and memory are clearly linked to intelligence, they do not tell the whole story. In order to perform well on tasks measuring intelligence, we not only need to be able to process information quickly and make effective used of memory, we also need to direct our attention to salient aspects of the task, inhibit automatic responses and switch between strategies (Pretz and Sternberg, 2005).

All of the above are domain-general aspects of intelligence; they can be employed across tasks and contexts. However, the type of task, the knowledge an individual has about the task domain, and the context in which the task is carried out can also have an effect. For example, Ceci and Bronfenbrenner (1985) found an effect of context for children's behaviour on two prospective memory tasks: taking cupcakes out of the oven and disconnecting charging cables from a motorcycle battery. Children performed the tasks more efficiently, and were better able to engage in concurrent tasks, in their own homes than in a university laboratory. In a similar vein, we saw in Chapter 3 that when given tasks concerning the specific knowledge domains of chess and football, children's performance depended on their domain-specific knowledge rather than their intelligence (Chi, 1978; Schneider, Korkel and Weinert, 1989). This means that in addition to domain-general processes, intelligent behaviour is also affected by domain-specific knowledge and experience.

Summary

What is intelligence? Over the years, experts have given many different definitions of intelligence, although many include abstract reasoning, problem solving and decision making. Psychological research into intelligence started in the late nineteenth century, and it was initially assumed that intelligence was a unitary construct. The concept of the intelligence quotient (IQ) was devised in the early twentieth century as a way of comparing the mental ages of children to their chronological ages. IQ tests, such as the Stanford-Binet test, are now normalized such that the mean score of any population is 100, with a standard deviation of 15, such that 67 per cent of the scores are within one standard deviation of the mean and 96 per cent are within two standard deviations. Some theorists challenged the idea that a single score could represent human intellectual performance, and instead proposed hierarchical models or multiple intelligences. Factor analysis can be used to see whether different items on intelligent tests measure the same underlying ability (i.e., general intelligence) or whether there are more basic abilities, such as verbal ability and visuospatial ability.

Theories of intelligence. Proponents of hierarchical models view intelligence as consisting of a general ability factor at the top of the hierarchy and a number of specialized ability factors. Cattell's model included fluid intelligence and crystallized intelligence. Fluid intelligence is our general capacity for reasoning, independent of cultural factors and experience, whereas crystallized intelligence is the result of cultural experience and acquired knowledge and skills. Carroll's model is more elaborate, with three strata. General intellectual ability is at the top level, broad intellectual abilities are at the second level and the third level consists of specific factors which make up the second stratum factors. This model can account for strengths and weaknesses in different domains. Whereas the different levels are linked in hierarchical models, Gardner's theory of multiple intelligences includes eight independent intelligences or frames of mind. Each of these intelligences may differ in strength from person to person. Although Gardner's multiple intelligences seem intuitively appealing, the evidence does not point towards these intelligences as statistically independent. Sternberg distinguishes three types of intelligence in triarchic theory: Analytical intelligence, creative intelligence and practical intelligence. Sternberg argues that practical and creative intelligence may be required just as much as the type of skills (analytical intelligence) measured in a traditional IQ test. Anderson's minimal cognitive architecture theory is based around a processing mechanism which underlies intelligence. According to

Anderson, differences between individuals are a result of the speed and efficiency with which we process information. People who can process information more quickly and more efficiently can process more information and, therefore, learn faster and reason more effectively. Differences in performance across tasks are explained by other, more specialized, processors. Anderson proposes two dimensions of general intelligence, one based on speed of processing and related to IQ scores, the other based on the development of cognitive modules and related to developmental changes.

Testing intelligence. The most widely used tests are the Stanford-Binet Intelligence Scale and the Wechsler Scales. The current version of the Stanford-Binet test is based on a three-stratum hierarchical model, with g at the top level; crystallized abilities, fluid-analytic abilities and short-term memory at the second level; and verbal reasoning, quantitative reasoning and abstract/visual reasoning at the third level. The Wechsler intelligence scales come in three forms: The Wechsler Intelligence Scales for Children (WISC), the Wechsler Preschool and Primary Scale of Intelligence (WPPSI), and the Wechsler Adult Intelligence Scales (WAIS). The WISC has 12 subscales, containing both verbal and non-verbal subscales. There are a number of problems with both concepts of intelligence and intelligence testing. First, there is not a lot of evidence to demonstrate that any one method of testing is superior to the others. Second, there is the debate over whether intelligence stems from one general ability, whether there are many separate kinds of relatively independent intelligence, or whether there is a hierarchical organization of specific skills stemming from one or two factors. Third, there is no agreement as to how many intelligences there are. Fourth, there is the problem of cultural bias. Whereas abstract thinking and problem solving are emphasized in Western cultures, other cultures view intelligence as comprising different sets of skills.

Does intelligence change over time? Although there is a lot of evidence that intelligence scores at different stages of life correlate, there is also evidence that levels of intelligence can change over time. The question of stability relates to the nature–nurture debate; to what extent is our intelligence innate and to what extent is it shaped by the environment? Infant intelligence scales, such as the Bayley Scales of Infant Development, do not correlate with later IQ scores. However, speed of habituation and visual recognition memory in infants *do* correlate with IQ scores, suggesting that there is continuity between infancy and childhood. These two measures reflect basic information-processing capacity; an infant who habituates to a stimulus quickly may be fast at processing information and therefore capable of learning quickly, and recognition also involves the ability to inhibit a response to a familiar stimulus. There is also a lot of evidence against the stability of intelligence over time. Around 15 per cent of children show a substantial change in IQ score over time. If intelligence were totally stable and unaffected by environmental influences, we would expect the actual scores of children to change very little over the years. The Abecedarian project is an intervention that demonstrated an environmental effect, suggesting that intelligence is not stable throughout the school years.

How much of intelligence is inherited? In order to determine the role of heredity in intelligence, researchers have employed a number of methods, including twin studies and adoption studies. There are two types of twins, identical or monozygotic twins, and fraternal or dizygotic twins. Monozygotic twins have identical genes, whereas dizygotic twins share 50 per cent of their genes. When monozygotic twins have been raised apart, any similarities are assumed to be hereditary, and any differences assumed to be environmental. The amount of variance in IQ scores is known as the heritability of intelligence. A heritability coefficient of 1 means that all variance can be explained by genetic factors, whereas a coefficient of 0 means that genetics does not explain any of the variance. Results from twin, adoption and other family studies show that a higher genetic similarity between two family members leads to a higher correlation between their IQ scores. The consensus is that the heritability of intelligence is about 0.75, although some have reported lower estimates of 0.50. This may be because the genetic effect on intelligence increases with age. The correlations between adopted children and their biological parents increase over time, and the correlation with adoptive parents decreases over time.

Discussion questions

1 Is it important to have a universal definition of intelligence? Are there any advantages to not having such a definition?

2 What tasks have you done today that you would class as requiring intelligence? What intelligent behaviours were necessary?

3 Do you consider yourself to be equally intelligent across all domains of knowledge and situations? If not, how do you account for the differences?

4 If intelligence is largely heritable and stable across time, what are the implications for education?

5 If intelligence is largely a result of environment and experience, what are the implications for education?

Further Reading

Books and chapters

Anderson, M. (Ed.) (1999). *The development of intelligence.* Hove: Psychology Press.

In this edited volume, Mike Anderson collects a set of chapters on theories of intelligence, intelligence testing and behavioural genetics.

Loehlin, J. C., Horn, J. M. and Willerman, L. (1997). Heredity, environment and IQ in the Texas Adoption Project. In R. J. Sternberg and E. L. Grigorenko (Eds), *Intelligence, heredity, and environment* (pp. 105–25). Cambridge: Cambridge University Press.

John Loehlin, Joseph Horn and Lee Willerman describe the findings from the Texas Adoption Project.

Sternberg, R. J. (1985). *Beyond IQ: A triarchic theory of human intelligence*. New York: Cambridge University Press.

In his classic book, Robert Sternberg lays out his triarchic theory of intelligence, and describes how the three components of intelligence can be tested.

Articles

Bouchard, T. J., Jr, Lykken, D. T., McGue, M., Segal, N. L. and Tellegen, A. (1990). Sources of human psychological differences: The Minnesota study of twins reared apart. *Science*, 250(4978), 223–228.

Thomas Bouchard and his co-authors describe the findings from the Minnesota study of twins reared apart.

Campbell, F. A., Pungello, E. P., Miller-Johnson, S., Burchinal, M. and Ramey, C. T. (2001). The development of cognitive and academic abilities: Growth curves from an early childhood educational experiment. *Developmental Psychology*, 37, 231–242.

Frances Campbell and colleagues present an analysis of the long-term effects of the Abecedarian programme.

Neisser, U., Boodoo, G., Bouchard, T. J., Boykin, A. W., Brody, N., Ceci, S. J., Halpern, D. F., Loehlin, J. C., Perloff, R., Sternberg, R. J. and Urbina, S. (1996). Intelligence: Knowns and unknowns. *American Psychologist*, 51(2), 77–101.

Ulrich Neisser, along with the other members of an APA task force on intelligence, present a readable summary of the psychological literature on intelligence, testing, and genetic and environmental effects.

Sigman, M., Cohen, S. E. and Beckwith, L. (1997). Why does infant attention predict adolescent intelligence? *Infant Behavior and Development*, 20(2), 133–140.

Marian Sigman, Sarale Cohen and Leila Beckwith present a study in which they demonstrate that infant attention predicts intelligence in 18-year-olds.

Sternberg, R. J. and Grigorenko, E. L. (2000). Theme-park psychology: A case study regarding human intelligence and its implications for education. *Educational Psychology Review*, 12(2), 247–268.

In this paper Robert Sternberg and Elena Grigorenko discuss the limitations of conventional intelligence testing in the light of studies on non-Western populations.

Chapter 10

Developmental disorders

Learning Outcomes

By the end of this chapter you should be able to:

- Describe the characteristics of different developmental disorders.
- Describe the criteria for diagnosis of these disorders.
- Combine and evaluate cognitive theories of autism, ADHD, dyslexia and dyscalculia.
- Describe and evaluate research on developmental disorders.

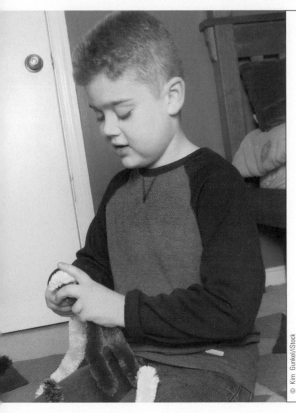

© Kim Gunkel/iStock

Chapter 10

Developmental disorders

Learning Outcomes

At the end of this chapter you should be able to:

- Describe the characteristics of different developmental disorders.

- Describe the criteria for diagnosis of these disorders.

- Compare and evaluate cognitive theories of autism, ADHD, dyslexia and dyscalculia.

- Describe and evaluate research on developmental disorders.

This chapter is organized a little differently from the previous chapters. Rather than discussing a single topic in cognitive development, I will present descriptions of four developmental disorders, along with relevant theories and research. Many academic disciplines contribute to the study of developmental disorders, including psychiatry, medicine and biology, but I will focus on cognitive explanations for these disorders, rather than discussing behavioural or genetic explanations. Most of the aspects of cognitive development covered so far in this book have a role to play in attempting to describe and explain developmental disorders. Memory and executive functioning are implicated in ADHD, for example. Knowledge of memory, language and literacy can help us to understand dyslexia, while an understanding of memory and numeracy are important for investigating dyscalculia. First, however, we will examine a disorder on which studies of perception, memory, language, theory of mind and intelligence are all brought to bear – autism.

Simon Baron-Cohen, Alan Leslie and Uta Frith (1985) gave three groups of children a task that is very similar to Wimmer and Perners's (1983) 'Maxi and the chocolate' task that we looked at in Chapter 5. In Baron-Cohen *et al.*'s 'Sally-Anne' task, participants are presented with a story about two dolls, Sally and Anne, illustrated in Figure 10.1. Sally has a basket and Anne has a box. Sally places a marble in her basket, then leaves. In her absence, Anne retrieves the marble from the basket and puts it in her box. Sally then returns. Participants are asked 'Where will Sally look for her marble?' If they point to the basket, which was the location of the marble at the time that Sally left, they pass the task. If they point to the box, which is the current location, they fail the task. As with the Maxi task, this is a test of false-belief reasoning. In order to pass the task, children must show that they appreciate Sally has a false belief about the location of the marble.

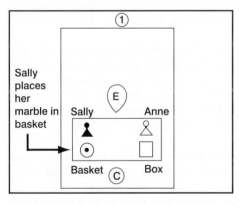
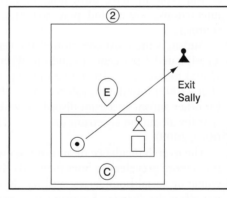
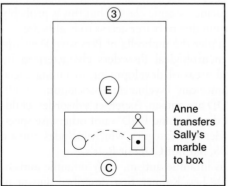
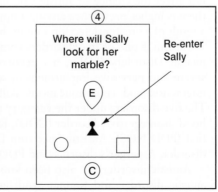

Figure 10.1

The Sally-Anne task.

Source: Reprinted from Cognition, 21, Baron-Cohen, S., Leslie, A.M., & Frith, U., Does the autistic child have a "theory of mind"?, 37–46, Copyright (1985), with permission from Elsevier.

The three groups of participants were twenty children with autism aged 6 to 16, with a mean verbal mental age of 5 years, and a mean non-verbal mental age of 9 years; twenty-seven typically-developing children aged 3 to 5; and fourteen children with Down's syndrome aged 6 to 17, with IQ levels just below those of the children with autism. Twenty-three of the twenty-seven typically-developing children, and twelve of the fourteen children with Down's syndrome passed the task, but only four of the twenty children with autism passed.

> Q. What does this finding tell us about theory of mind in children with autism?

If we assume that this traditional false belief task is a fair way of measuring whether participants have a theory of mind or not, then the findings of Baron-Cohen *et al.*'s study lead to the implication that children with autism do not possess a theory of mind. However, as we saw in Chapter 5, there is some debate over whether false belief tasks allow us to see the full picture. We will look at the implications of this study, and other studies on theory of mind and autism, later in the chapter.

Autism

autism A developmental disorder characterized by a triad of impairments in socialization, communication and imaginative or symbolic play.

Autism is a complex developmental disorder. It is one of the most severe childhood neuropsychiatric conditions and typically appears during the first three years of life. Autism is characterized by a triad of impairments in socialization, communication and imaginative or symbolic play (Wing and Gould, 1979). Children and adults with autism typically have difficulties in verbal and non-verbal communication, social interactions, leisure and play activities, and engage in repeated behaviours and routines.

Autism is the most common of the Pervasive Developmental Disorders, affecting an estimated 1 per cent of children. With respect to the UK population, Green *et al.* (2005) found a prevalence rate of 0.9 per cent for autism spectrum disorders. Baird *et al.* (2006) found a prevalence rate of 0.39 per cent for autism, and 0.77 per cent for other autism spectrum disorders, which gives a total prevalence rate of 1.16 per cent for all autism spectrum disorders. The US rate is estimated to be 0.91 per cent (Rice, 2009).

The overall incidence of autism is consistent around the globe, but is around four times more prevalent in boys than girls (Green *et al.*, 2005). Autism knows no racial, ethnic or social boundaries, and family income, lifestyle and educational levels do not affect the chance of autism's occurrence. Having said that, it often appears that there is higher prevalence amongst upper socioeconomic classes, but this is probably a result of a greater detection rate in this group due to better access to healthcare.

Autism is one of five disorders coming under the umbrella of Pervasive Developmental Disorders (PDD), a category of neurological disorders characterized by severe and pervasive impairment in several areas of development, including social interaction and communications skills (American Psychiatric Association, 2000). The five disorders under the category of PDD are autism, Asperger's disorder, childhood disintegrative disorder (CDD), Rett's disorder and PDD – not otherwise specified (PDD-NOS). Autistic Spectrum Disorder is a category which includes autistic disorder, Asperger's disorder and PDD-NOS, but not CDD or Rett's.

Autistic disorder has also been known as infantile autism, early infantile autism, autistic disorder and Kanner syndrome. Dr Leo Kanner first described autism in

1943, after he had observed a group of 11 patients (9 boys and 2 girls) who exhibited a lack of interest in other people, but were highly interested in objects and exhibited repetitive verbal and physical behaviour. Over the following decades there was a lack of consensus on aspects of the syndrome definition. It was many years before researchers and clinicians were sure that autism was not an early stage of schizophrenia.

Hans Asperger, a Viennese physician, published a paper in 1944 in which he described a group of patients who had deficits in social interaction and autistic behaviour patterns. Asperger was, at the time, unaware of Leo Kanner's work on autism. Asperger's disorder is a condition marked by a severe and sustained impairment in social interaction when not accompanied by the other autism-like symptoms. In Asperger's, there is no language delay and no problems with the development of self-help skills. The classical Kanner-type autism is also often accompanied by mental retardation whereas this is not seen in Asperger's. As the two syndromes are very similar, there is often some confusion as to the difference between them and debate over whether they constitute two different disorders. In 1994, Asperger's was recognized as a unique disorder, although many experts agree that they are related forms of the same underlying disorder. Children diagnosed as having Asperger's usually have symptoms too mild to be classed as autism. Asperger's disorder tends to be diagnosed later than autism, in later childhood or adolescence and sometimes even in adulthood. Although this is largely due to the apparent 'mildness' of the condition in the early years, the effects can become a lot more obvious with age. This can be extremely difficult for the individual with Asperger's as there are greater demands on our social and communicative skills as adults.

Pervasive Developmental Disorder – Not Otherwise Specified (PDD-NOS) is a somewhat loosely defined category in which some (but not all) features of autism can appear. Children are diagnosed as having PDD-NOS when there is impairment of social or communicative skills and/or stereotyped behaviour patterns, but when the criteria for autism (or any other PDD) are not met.

Characteristics of autism

As autism is a spectrum disorder, the symptoms and characteristics can present themselves in a wide variety of combinations, from mild to severe. This means that two individuals could be diagnosed as autistic, yet have very different skills and behaviours. Some, for example, may exhibit only slight delays in language and experience greater difficulties with social interactions. Here are some of the traits which *may* be exhibited by an autistic person (Autism Society of America, 2008):

spectrum disorder One of a range of linked disorders that can form a continuum from mild to severe.

- insistence on sameness; resistance to change
- difficulty in expressing needs; uses gestures or pointing instead of words
- repeating words or phrases in place of normal, responsive language
- laughing, crying, showing distress for reasons not apparent to others
- prefers to be alone; aloof manner
- tantrums
- difficulty in mixing with others
- may not want to cuddle or be cuddled
- little or no eye contact
- unresponsive to normal teaching methods
- sustained odd play
- spins objects

- inappropriate attachments to objects
- apparent over-sensitivity or under-sensitivity to pain
- no real fears of danger
- noticeable physical over-activity or extreme under-activity
- uneven gross/fine motor skills
- not responsive to verbal cues; acts as if deaf although hearing tests in normal range.

Some of these characteristics have come to be stereotypes of autistic behaviour. Although it may be true for some individuals, many people with autism do not refuse eye contact. Similarly, many are affectionate and many develop communication skills. Generally, the clinical picture is similar to that of schizophrenia, but autism is evident in early childhood, whereas schizophrenia typically appears in adolescence or early adulthood.

Many people with autism have delayed language development and some never develop spoken language. There is often an idiosyncratic and peculiar use of sounds and words. Wing (1976) found a strange use of the suffix '-ing' in a 9-year-old girl. She said 'daddy piping' when referring to her father smoking a pipe and 'boy bubbling' when referring to a boy who was blowing bubbles. Echolalia, in which the child echoes the utterances of another individual, is frequently observed. Children with autism often reverse pronouns, using 'I' where 'you' is meant and vice-versa. For example, a child may say 'do you want a drink' instead of 'I want a drink'. This could be taken to be a denial of personal identity, but a more prosaic explanation is that it is related to echoing (Bartak and Rutter, 1974).

Children with autism often have both a physical and an emotional distance from others. They fail to develop social attachments and do not participate in cooperative group play. They also have difficulties in reacting to or recognizing other people's feelings. Many children with autism do gradually improve their social relationships at around the age of 5, but these relationships are still difficult.

In terms of intellectual ability, children with autism tend to score poorly on tests of verbal ability, although they may perform at an above-average level on memory or spatial tasks and they may be talented in music or drawing. Despite these islands of intelligence, they have traditionally been perceived as possessing poor cognitive and intellectual abilities. In a review of studies conducted between 1966 and 2001, Fombonne (2003) reported that only 30 per cent of children with autism achieve IQ scores above 70. The remaining 70 per cent ranged from mild intellectual impairment to profound mental retardation. This perception has, however, been changing in recent years. Baird *et al.* (2000) found that 60 per cent of their sample was estimated to have IQ scores above 70. As we saw in Chapter 9, the tool we use to measure intelligence can have an effect on IQ scores. Dawson *et al.* (2007) gave 38 children with autism the Wechsler Intelligence Scales for Children – Third Edition (WISC-III; Wechsler, 1991) and Raven's Progressive Matrices (Raven, Raven and Court, 2000). Dawson *et al.* found that although the children's WISC-III scores were in the 26th percentile, their scores on Raven's Matrices were in the 56th percentile. The latter score indicates an average, rather than poor, overall level of intelligence. Although this seems like an astonishing difference, Bölte, Dziobek and Poustka (2009) replicated this study and found a much smaller difference of nine percentile points between scores on the WISC-III and Raven's Matrices. In a recent study on 8848 pairs of twins without autism, autistic traits and IQ were found to be only moderately negatively correlated (Hoekstra, Happé, Baron-Cohen, and Ronald, 2010). The authors conclude that most of the genetic influences on autistic traits are independent of the genetic influences on intelligence.

Diagnosing autism

There are no medical tests for diagnosing autism. Diagnoses are based on observation of communication skills, behaviours and general developmental levels. In order to make an accurate diagnosis, the input of parents is necessary as a clinician cannot make a full judgement on the basis of short observations. To confuse the issue, some children may appear to have one or more of a number of other disorders, such as mental retardation, deafness or a behavioural disorder. Unfortunately, these disorders can co-occur with autism, making diagnosis even harder. It is, however, important to accurately diagnose autism and to distinguish it from other conditions so that an appropriate educational programme can be started. Early diagnosis is generally perceived to be valuable as individuals who are diagnosed late may have poorer outcomes due to missing out on intervention programmes. The behaviours listed in the DSM-IV definition of autism (see Box 10.1) are usually apparent between 2 and 6 years of age. Whilst diagnosis is difficult, Filipek *et al.* (1999) list these five behaviours that signal further evaluation is warranted:

Box 10.1 Diagnostic criteria for autistic disorder
From the DSM-IV-TR (APA, 2000)

A. A total of six (or more) items from (1), (2) and (3), with at least two from (1), and one each from (2) and (3):

(1) Qualitative impairment in social interaction, as manifested by at least two of the following:

(a) Marked impairment in the use of multiple nonverbal behaviours such as eye-to-eye gaze, facial expression, body postures and gestures to regulate social interaction.

(b) Failure to develop peer relationships appropriate to developmental level.

(c) A lack of spontaneous seeking to share enjoyment, interest or achievements with other people (e.g., by a lack of showing, bringing or pointing out object of interest).

(d) Lack of social or emotional reciprocity.

(2) Qualitative impairments in communication as manifested by at least one of the following:

(a) Delay in, or total lack of, the development of spoken language (not accompanied by an attempt to compensate through alternative modes of communication such as gesture or mime).

(b) In individuals with adequate speech, marked impairment in the ability to initiate or sustain a conversation with others.

(c) Stereotyped and repetitive use of language or idiosyncratic language.

(d) Lack of varied, spontaneous make-believe play or social imitative play appropriate to developmental level.

(3) Restricted repetitive and stereotyped patterns of behaviour, interests and activities, as manifested by at least one of the following:

(a) Encompassing preoccupation with one or more stereotyped and restricted patterns of interest that is abnormal either in intensity or focus.

(b) Apparently inflexible adherence to specific, nonfunctional routines or rituals.

(c) Stereotyped and repetitive motor mannerisms (e.g., hand or finger flapping or twisting, or complex whole-body movements).

(d) Persistent preoccupation with parts of objects.

B. Delays or abnormal functioning in at least one of the following areas, with onset prior to age 3 years: (1) social interaction,

▶

(2) language as used in social communication, or (3) symbolic or imaginative play.

C.   The disturbance is not better accounted for by Rett's Disorder or Childhood Disintegrative Disorder.

Source: Reproduced with permission of the American Psychiatric Association, from American Psychiatric Association. (2000). *Diagnostic and statistical manual of mental disorders* (4th edn, text revision); permission conveyed through Copyright Clearance Center, Inc.

No babbling by 12 months
No gesturing (pointing, waving bye-bye, etc.) by 12 months
No single words by 16 months
No two-word spontaneous *(not just echolalic)* phrases by 24 months
ANY loss of ANY language or social skills at ANY age.

If a child demonstrates any of these behaviours, it does not necessarily mean they have autism, but it does suggest that a more detailed analysis of their behaviours should be carried out by a team of specialists.

Cognitive theories of autism

We now look at three theories that have been prominent in psychological research into autism (Rajendran and Mitchell, 2007). These theories are attempts to explain autism at the cognitive level, as opposed to the behavioural level or the genetic level.

Theory of mind deficit. One of the key theories of autism at the cognitive level is that children with autism fail to develop a theory of mind as the result of an inability to engage in metarepresentational activity. This is partly based on finding that children with autism don't seem to show pretend or symbolic play which, according to Leslie (1987) is an early indication of metarepresentational ability. In a study by Baron-Cohen (1987), typically-developing 4-year-olds and children with autism who were matched for mental age were given toys such as stuffed animals, a toy kitchen stove and playpeople. The typically-developing 4-year-olds engaged in pretend play whereas the children with autism engaged in functional or sensorimotor play. If the theory of mind deficit theory is correct, we would of course expect to find poor performance on false belief tasks and other measures of theory of mind. As we saw at the beginning of this chapter, Baron-Cohen *et al.* (1985) found this poor performance. The implication of this study is that the ability to infer mental states may be an aspect of social intelligence that is relatively independent of general intelligence, otherwise the children with Down's syndrome would also have had difficulty on the task.

executive functions
Cognitive processes used to control thought and actions, including planning and initiating behaviours, shifting between activities and inhibiting responses.

Executive dysfunction. Executive functions are the supervisory processes controlling thought and actions. They are involved in planning and initiating behaviours, shifting between activities and inhibiting responses. When participating in a false belief task, children must suppress their true belief whilst simultaneously holding in mind the requirement to answer a question about what protagonist will do. These are processes controlled by the executive functions so it may be that failing a false belief task is due to difficulties with executive processes, not because of a lack of mentalizing ability. Hughes and Russell (1993) suggested that this was, in fact, the case; children with autism could not inhibit the perceptual salience of the true location of the object. They also argue that this could account for other, apparently related, phenomena such as poor performance on deception tasks. In order to test this idea, a lot of studies have been carried out in which participants with autism are given tasks that are associated with executive function, such as the Tower of Hanoi, Tower of London and the Wisconsin Card Sorting Task (Hughes, Russell and Robbins, 1994; Ozonoff, Pennington and Rogers, 1991).

Weak central coherence. Most people have a need and a desire for understanding events in terms of a high-level meaning. Central coherence refers to the way in which we process information in context for high-level meaning, and often fail to recall surface features. Bartlett (1932) showed that people remember the general outline of a story, but do not recall the specific details. A preference for low-level, or local, processing is often in people with autism. Frith (2003; Happé and Frith, 2006) argues that the normal tendency towards global processing is absent in autism and that people with autism demonstrate local processing. As a result, they perceive and remember features, but have difficulties with overall meaning. She refers to this as weak central coherence. The weak central coherence theory offers the ability to explain patterns of both excellent and poor performance on various tasks. Weak central coherence predicts relatively good performance where attention to local information is advantageous, and poor performance on tasks requiring the recognition of global meaning or the integration of stimuli in context. This means that this account of autism is best characterized in terms of a cognitive *style* rather than a cognitive *deficit*. This idea has received empirical support from many studies. Detail-focused processing has been demonstrated at several levels, including the perceptual, the visuospatial and the verbal-semantic levels (Happé, 1999).

weak central coherence A tendency to process information for fine details, rather than broad gist.

Research on autism

False belief and 'mentalizing' tasks. If the theory of mind deficit theory is correct, we would expect to find that children with autism perform poorly on a number of tasks that involve mentalizing, an addition to the standard unexpected transfer task conducted by Baron-Cohen *et al.* (1985). Results from a number of different studies support this theory (Baron-Cohen and Swettenham, 1997). Baron-Cohen (1989) demonstrated that children with autism perform at chance on tasks involving a mental-physical distinction, demonstrating no clear understanding of how physical objects differ from thoughts about objects. They have a poor understanding of functions of the mind. They can understand functions of the brain (it makes you move, do things, etc.), but they don't mention functions of the mind such as thinking, dreaming and wishing. They also do poorly on fail appearance-reality tasks, finding it hard to distinguish between what an object looks like and what it really is.

Several studies have found that children with autism have difficulty understanding that seeing leads to knowing; they often do not know that the act of observing something means that the observer has knowledge of what they have observed (Baron-Cohen and Goodheart, 1994; Leslie and Frith, 1988; Lind and Bowler, 2010; Perner *et al.*, 1989). Further evidence for this failure to understand the role of visual access in knowledge formation comes from a study by Baron-Cohen (1992). He carried out a study using a penny hiding game in which participants were asked to hide a penny in one hand. The majority either didn't close the hand that the penny wasn't in, opened the hand with the penny before the other person could make a guess, or 'hid' the penny in full view. As we saw in Chapter 5, it has been argued that the ability to deceive is related to theory of mind. Baron-Cohen's (1992) study, along with other studies (Russell *et al.*, 1991; Sodian and Frith, 1992) suggests that children with autism have difficulty with deception. Recent research has shown that higher-functioning children with autism *do* tell lies, both in order to hide misbehaviour and to be polite, but that they have greater difficulty than typically-developing children in maintaining these lies (Li *et al.*, 2011).

Children with autism perform at chance on recognizing mental state words such as think, know or imagine (Baron-Cohen *et al.*, 1994). Typically developing 4-year-olds can pick out words that refer to the mind from a list, which they easily distinguished from non-mental state words such as jump, eat or move. Also, children with autism do not produce a range of mental state words in spontaneous speech when asked to describe picture stories involving action and deception (Tager-Flusberg, 1992). Baron-Cohen (1991) found that they have difficulty understanding complex causes of emotion. They can understand that situations and desires can cause emotion, but not more complex causes such as belief. For example, they can understand Jane will feel sad if she falls over and cuts her knee, or that John will feel happy if he gets what he wants, but they don't understand that John will feel happy if he *thinks* he's getting what he wants – even if he isn't.

Other theory-of-mind related difficulties include a failure to understand intentionally non-literal statements (Happé, 1994). Children with autism tend not to appreciate metaphor ('she's got a sharp tongue'), sarcasm ('how clean your room looks today!') and irony. They also have difficulty with pragmatics (Baron-Cohen, 1988), failing to recognize violations of pragmatic rules, such as an irrelevant answer to a question.

Executive function tasks. If impaired executive function plays a causal role in autistic behaviours, then certain predictions can be made. In particular, we should see poor performance on tasks specifically designed to reflect planning, inhibition, working memory or set shifting. In general, this prediction has been borne out. Pennington and Ozonoff (1996) reviewed 14 such studies and found that people with autism performed significantly worse than controls in 25 of 32 tasks reported. Also, difficulties in planning actions can account for the perseverative and rigid behaviours commonly found in autism. More recently, Dichter *et al.* (2010) found that children with autism were slower and less accurate on Zelazo, Frye and Rapus' (1996) Dimensional-Change Card Sort task.

Although there is a wide range of studies demonstrating poor performance on tasks involving executive functioning in children with autism, there are other studies which call the executive dysfunction theory into question. For example, children with autism are not always impaired on tasks that have the same structure as the false belief task, but no mentalizing aspect. Leekam and Perner (1991) used Zaitchik's (1990) false photograph test to try and distinguish between the theory of mind and executive dysfunction theories. In this task, participants are presented with a doll in a red dress and watch a photo of the doll being taken with a Polaroid camera. Whilst the photo is developing, the doll is put in a green dress. Participants are asked 'What colour dress will the doll be wearing in the photo?' Leekham and Perner claim that this task makes very similar executive function demands to the false belief task, but does not require mindreading. Children with autism were not impaired on this task, suggesting that the reason why they fail false belief tasks is not that the children have executive difficulties.

Russell, Saltmarsh and Hill (1999) argue that it is not necessarily the case that this task makes executive demands of same severity as false belief tasks. To test this, they compared the standard false photograph test with a modified version. In the standard task, they took a photo of a Barbie doll in front of a screen then swapped the Barbie for an Action Man. Children were asked 'When I took the photo, where was

Dimensional-Change Card Sort A simplified version of the Wisconsin Card Sort Task in which cards can be sorted by colour or shape. The task involves switching from sorting according to one dimension (colour) to the other dimension (shape).

Barbie?' and 'What will we be able to see in the photo when it's ready?' Twenty-two of the 25 participants with autism passed this task, as did 22 of the 25 participants with moderate learning difficulties used as a control group. In the modified version of the task, they took a photo of a screen with no toy in front of it. Barbie or Action Man was then placed in front of screen and the children were asked 'When I took the photo, where was Barbie?' (control question) and 'What will we be able to see in the photo when it's ready?' (test question). Eighteen of the 25 moderate learning difficulties group passed the test, but only 10 of the 25 children with autism passed; the same level of performance found on a false belief task given as part of the study. Sabbagh, Moses and Shiverick (2006) conducted a pair of studies in which they gave typically developing 3- to 5-year-olds a series of false belief, false photograph and executive function tasks. They found that whilst false belief task performance was related to performance on executive function tasks, false belief and false photograph tasks were not related. This suggests that, at the very least, we cannot dismiss the idea that false belief failure in autism is due to executive dysfunction.

Perceptual tasks. According to weak central coherence theory, children with autism should do well on certain perceptual tasks, such as the Children's Embedded Figures Test (Witkin *et al.*,1971), in which a shape has to be found 'hidden' in a larger picture, as this requires detail-focused processing. Shah and Frith (1983) found that children with autism were faster and more accurate at identifying the embedded figures than typically-developing children matched for mental age. A later study by Jolliffe and Baron-Cohen (1997) revealed the same difference between adults with and without autism.

Happé (1996) found that children with autism do not succumb to visual illusions to the same extent as typically-developing children. She presented individuals with autism aged 8 to 16, with an IQ range of 40 to 92, with standard textbook visual illusions, such as the Ebbinghaus illusion (see Figure 10.2), and they were asked to make simple judgements about them. If people with autism have a tendency towards fragmented perception, they should succumb less to the typical mis-perceptions. This proved to be the case – children with autism were better able to make accurate judgements of the illusions than typically developing children or developmentally delayed controls. They resisted, for example, the illusion that the two central circles in the Ebbinghaus illusion are not the same size. However, subsequent studies by Ropar and Mitchell (1999, 2001) failed to find this reduced susceptibility to illusions. Other examples of detailed perceptual processing are superior processing of musical pitch in the autistic population (Heaton, 2003; Heaton, Hermelin and Pring, 1998; Järvinen-Pasley and Heaton, 2007), reduced susceptibility to visually-induced motion (Gepner *et al.*, 1995), and a reduced McGurk effect (i.e., less influence from visual to auditory speech perception) (deGelder, Vroomen and Van der Heide, 1991).

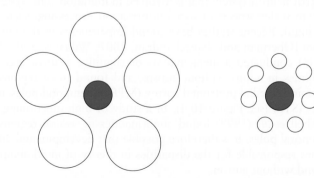

Figure 10.2

The Ebbinghaus illusion.

In terms of visuospatial coherence, Shah and Frith (1993) showed that the reason people with autism perform well on the standard Wechsler Block Design task is due specifically to segmentation abilities. In this task (see Figure 10.3), participants are presented with a pattern and asked to construct that pattern using blocks. For normally-developing and intellectually-impaired groups, a sizable advantage was gained from the pre-segmentation of designs, but this advantage was not observed in individuals with autism, suggesting that the latter were already processing the design in terms of its constituent blocks.

Figure 10.3

The block design task. The top row contains blocks that can be combined patterns, the bottom row shows an unsegmented and pre-segmented target pattern.

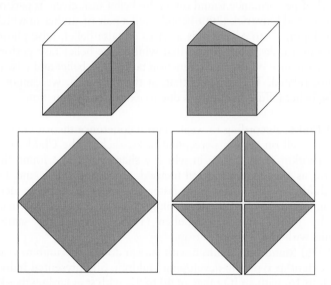

The poor performance on tasks requiring the recognition of global meaning or integration of stimuli in context, predicted by weak central coherence, is supported by research looking at verbal-semantic coherence. We would expect people with autism to perform poorly on homograph tests where context is necessary for disambiguating between two meanings and pronunciations of two words spelt the same. For example, 'lead' could be a metal (pronounced 'led') or a verb (pronounced 'leed'). In several studies (Frith and Snowling, 1983; Snowling and Frith, 1986; Happé, 1997), individuals with autism failed to use preceding sentence context to determine the pronunciation of homographs. For example, the word 'tear' is disambiguated by context: 'In her eye there was a big tear' versus 'In her dress there was a big tear'.

Evidence from cognitive neuroscience. As we saw in Chapter 2, there is evidence for a mirror neuron system that is involved in imitation. This system may also play a key role in wider aspects of social information processing, such as empathy and theory of mind. Recent studies have found impairments in the mirror neuron system in autism (Oberman and Ramachandran, 2007; Williams *et al.*, 2006). Frith and Frith (2003) conducted a meta-analysis of cognitive neuroscience studies on mentalizing abilities in adults without autism, and found three regions associated with theory of mind: medial prefrontal cortex (MPFC), temporal poles and superior temporal sulcus (STS) (see Figure 10.4). In a study of high-functioning individuals with autism, Abell *et al.* (1999) found abnormalities in several regions, including MPFC and temporal poles. It is therefore possible that developmental differences in these regions are responsible for the disparities in theory of mind abilities between children with and without autism.

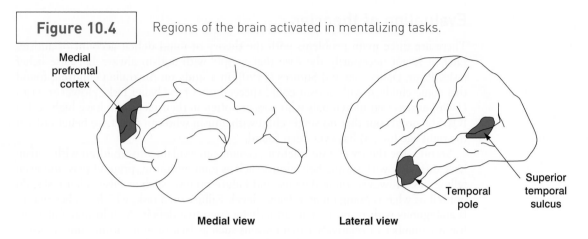

Figure 10.4 Regions of the brain activated in mentalizing tasks.

Medial
prefrontal
cortex

Superior
temporal
sulcus

Temporal
pole

Medial view **Lateral view**

Source: Adapted from Frith, U., & Frith, C.D., Development and neurophysiology of mentalising, Philosophical Transactions of the Royal Society of London – Series B: Biological Sciences, 358, 459–473, 2003, the Royal Society, with permission from the Royal Society and the authors.

Given that there is mixed evidence as to whether failure on false belief tasks is a result of a specific theory of mind deficit or a wider impairment in executive function, it is important to discover whether these regions are specifically involved in mentalizing or whether they are also activated in non-mentalizing tasks. Saxe and her colleagues (Saxe and Kanwisher, 2003; Saxe and Powell, 2006; Saxe and Wexler, 2005) report evidence that the temporo-parietal junction (TPJ) (see Figure 10.5) is more important than the MPFC for false belief tasks. This finding is reinforced by evidence from brain damage patients that shows theory of mind deficits in patients with left TPJ lesions, whereas patients with medial frontal damage are more widely impaired in terms of cognitive and executive abilities as well as theory of mind (Apperley *et al.*, 2004; Samson *et al.*, 2004). Perner and Leekam (2008) reviewed imaging studies of theory of mind, and classified them into studies using tasks that involve contrasting perspectives, such as false belief tasks, and studies that used non-contrasting perspective tasks (e.g., tasks involving pretence or photos). They found that tasks with contrasting perspectives are associated with TPJ activity, whereas tasks without contrasting perspectives are associated with the STS. Therefore, differences between people with and without autism may arise from differences in the temporo-parietal junction, rather than the superior temporal sulcus.

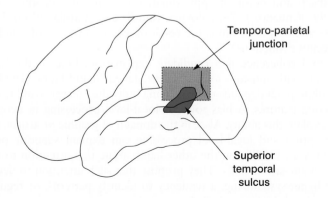

Temporo-parietal
junction

Superior
temporal
sulcus

Figure 10.5

Temporo-parietal junction and superior temporal sulcus.

Evaluation of theories

There are three main problems with the theory of mind deficit account of autism. First, it is not necessarily the case that people with autism always fail false belief tasks. Prior, Dahlstrom and Squires (1990), in a study on Australian children, found that some children with autism could succeed on a false belief task. However, Frith (1996) argues that individuals who pass are often in their teens and have high verbal IQs. She points out that no single child with autism who can pass false belief tasks at the right age (i.e., 4) has ever been found.

Second, the theory of mind deficit account can explain why children with autism have difficulty with simple behaviours such as joint attention, pretend play and even telling lies. However, these deficits, and failure on tests such as false belief tasks, do not tell us what is going on at a deeper level. Failure on a task, which is a behaviour, is ambiguous with respect to an underlying cognitive deficit. A child may fail a test for any number of relatively banal reasons such as lack of motivation, limited attention or failure to comprehend the task, not because they lack a theory of mind.

Third, although this account addresses the triad of impairments in social, communicative and imaginative skills, it does not address the characteristic rigidity and perseveration of autism. These latter factors are, however, accounted for by executive dysfunction theory. But there are problems with this theory as well. Impaired executive functioning is not specific to autism. Executive difficulties are also present in schizophrenia, obsessive-compulsive disorder, Tourette syndrome, ADHD, Parkinson's disease and frontal lobe damage. So, by itself, executive dysfunction cannot explain autism, but it may co-occur with a theory of mind deficit. Ozonoff, Pennington and Rogers (1991) argue that executive dysfunction offers a better explanation for autism, but that there must also be a mentalizing deficit in order to account for many other autistic behaviours.

The theory of mind account, the executive dysfunction account, and any other theory which attempts to explain autism in terms of deficits, fails to explain why people with autism show not only preserved, but also superior, skills in certain areas. Examples of such skills are children who are lightning calculators, twin brothers who can remember what the weather was like, every day of their adult lives, and the man who inspired Dustin Hoffman's character in *Rain Man*, who has memorized thousands of books and can simultaneously read one page with his left eye and another with his right (Treffert, 2006, 2009). More common skills are exemplified by the child who can construct jigsaw puzzles very quickly, even when the picture is face-down, and the adult who recalls the exact date and time of your last meeting twenty years ago (Frith, 2003). Savant skills in areas such as music, art, calculation and memory are ten times more common in people with autism than in others with mental handicap and occur in approximately one in ten individuals with autism (Happé, 1999; Rimland, 1978; Saloviita, Ruusila and Ruusila, 2000). How can we explain these abilities, if autism is the result of a lack of theory of mind or difficulties with executive functions?

Weak central coherence is a candidate explanation. One of the 'savant' skills found in people with autism is musical talent. Takeuchi and Hulse (1993) argue that learning absolute pitch depends on perceiving individual features and not perceiving relations among features. A bias towards local-level processing in people with autism would explain this ability. Also, in the domain of graphic or artistic ability, fragmented perception and local-level processing can explain superior performance. Baron-Cohen *et al.* (2009), on the other hand, argue that attention to detail is not enough to explain savant skills. They propose that such attention to detail is a consequence of hyper-systemizing, a tendency to identify patterns, or regularities, and seek out the rules that govern the behaviour of a system.

We have considered three accounts which attempt to explain aspects of autism at the cognitive level. The theory of mind deficit theory focuses on social and communicative impairments, the executive dysfunction theory additionally considers stereotyped behaviour and the weak central coherence theory explains special talents and peaks in performance. Few theorists argue that any one of these three can explain the behavioural profile of autism. Ozonoff *et al.* (1991) argue that executive dysfunction needs to be coupled with a theory of mind deficit; Frith (2003) also supports the theory of mind deficit alongside her own weak central coherence theory; and Tager-Flusberg (2007) states that no single hypothesis can account for all the characteristics of autism. Is it perhaps the case that these theories address three primary deficits affecting different brain systems? Happé, Ronald and Plomin (2006) present data that show only modest correlations between the three core areas of autism, suggesting that there are different genetic causes for the behavioural, social and communicative impairments that are symptomatic of autism.

Attention deficit hyperactivity disorder (ADHD)

Attention deficit hyperactivity disorder (ADHD) is a neurobiological condition affecting attention, impulses and concentration. The inability to concentrate, to control attention and to inhibit impulsive behaviour, which is frequently accompanied by physical overactivity, can lead to many negative outcomes, including academic underachievement and antisocial behaviour. ADHD affects an estimated 3 to 7 per cent of children (Barkley, 1998; Wolraich *et al.*, 1996). As with autism, ADHD is more common in boys than in girls (Green and Chee, 1997). For up to half of the children who have this disorder, the symptoms continue into adulthood. (Murphy and Barkley, 1996).

attention deficit hyperactivity disorder (ADHD) A disorder characterized by hyperactive-impulsive and/or inattentive behaviour.

Although ADHD-like symptoms have been noted for over 100 years, it was not until 1980 that the term ADD (attention deficit disorder) was used. Prior to this point, ADHD had been variously named hyperkinetic impulse disorder, hyperactive child syndrome and hyperkinetic reaction of childhood. The 'H' was added to 'ADD' in the DSM-III-R (American Psychiatric Association, 1987), as a result of a move towards emphasizing the hyperactive-impulsive element of the disorder (Barkley, 2003).

There are now three subtypes of ADHD: Predominantly hyperactive-impulsive, predominantly inattentive, and combined hyperactive-impulsive and inattentive. As a result, some children display more symptoms of hyperactivity and impulsivity, some display more symptoms of inattentivity, but the majority of those diagnosed with ADHD display both hyperactive-impulsive and inattentive symptoms.

Characteristics of ADHD

According to the National Institute for Mental Health (2008), some of the characteristics of ADHD associated with inattentiveness are that children may be easily distracted, and have difficulty focusing on one thing at a time. They may become bored quickly and frequently switch between tasks. They may appear not be listening to people who are speaking to them, daydream, and have difficulty in following instructions. Characteristics associated with hyperactivity include fidgeting, nonstop talking and running around. Impulsivity is characterized by impatience, inappropriate comments, unrestrained emotional responses and difficulty with waiting.

In addition to the core symptoms of inattention and hyperactivity-impulsivity, children with ADHD may show a number of other cognitive and emotional deficiencies (Barkley, 2003). These include lowered scores on intelligence tests, poor academic achievement, decreased working memory, speech impairments, underdeveloped moral reasoning, delayed motor coordination and poor emotion regulation.

Diagnosing ADHD

As is the case with autism, there is no single medical test that can be used to diagnose ADHD. Instead, a pediatrician or mental health specialist will examine a child's behaviour, and try to rule out other possible causes of the symptoms. According to the DSM-IV-TR (APA, 2000), a diagnosis of ADHD can only be made if the child has displayed symptoms before the age of 7, has been experiencing the symptoms for at least six months and has been experiencing the symptoms to a developmentally deviant extent. Diagnosis is difficult as the behavioural symptoms of ADHD may be the result of another disorder, such as autism, in which case a diagnosis of ADHD should not be made. However, it is possible for a child to have *both* ADHD and one or more other disorders, including autism, dyslexia or obsessive-compulsive disorder. The diagnostic criteria from the DSM-IV-TR are shown in Box 10.2.

Box 10.2 Diagnostic criteria for ADHD
From the DSM-IV-TR (APA, 2000)

I. Either A or B.
A. Six or more of the following signs of inattention have been present for at least six months to a point that is disruptive and inappropriate for developmental level:
Inattentive:
- Often does not give close attention to details or makes careless mistakes in schoolwork, work or other activities.
- Often has trouble keeping attention on tasks or play activities.
- Often does not seem to listen when spoken to directly.
- Often does not follow instructions and fails to finish schoolwork, chores or duties in the workplace (not due to oppositional behaviour or failure to understand instructions).
- Often has trouble organizing activities.
- Often avoids, dislikes, or doesn't want to do things that take a lot of mental effort for a long period of time (such as schoolwork or homework).
- Often loses things needed for tasks and activities (such as toys, school assignments, pencils, books, or tools).
- Is often easily distracted.
- Often forgetful in daily activities.
B. Six or more of the following signs of hyperactivity-impulsivity have been present for at least six months to an extent that is disruptive and inappropriate for developmental level:
Hyperactivity:
- Often fidgets with hands or feet or squirms in seat.
- Often gets up from seat when remaining in seat is expected.
- Often runs about or climbs when and where it is not appropriate (adolescents or adults may feel very restless).
- Often has trouble playing or enjoying leisure activities quietly.
- Is often 'on the go' or often acts as if 'driven by a motor'.
- Often talks excessively.
Impulsiveness:
- Often blurts out answers before questions have been finished.
- Often has trouble waiting one's turn.
- Often interrupts or intrudes on others (example: butts into conversations or games).
II. Some signs that cause impairment were present before age 7 years.
III. Some impairment from the signs is present in two or more settings (such as at school/work and at home).
IV. There must be clear evidence of significant impairment in social, school, or work functioning.

V. The signs do not happen only during the course of a pervasive developmental disorder, schizophrenia or other psychotic disorder. The signs are not better accounted for by another mental disorder (such as mood disorder, anxiety disorder, dissociative identity disorder or a personality disorder).

Executive function deficit theory

Candidate causes for ADHD include genes (Faraone *et al.*, 2005; Khan and Faraone, 2006) and environmental factors, such as alcohol use and cigarette smoking during pregnancy (Linnet *et al.*, 2003; Mick *et al.*, 2002). At the cognitive level, a theory must explain both the inattentive and hyperactive-impulsive aspects of ADHD. The dominant cognitive-level explanation for ADHD is similar to one of the theories of autism discussed above: a deficit in executive functioning (Barkley, 1997; Pennington and Ozonoff, 1996).

Barkley (1997) argues that the central cognitive cause of ADHD symptoms is poor inhibition. He outlines four executive functions that depend on inhibition, and shows how they affect behaviour (see Figure 10.6). Importantly, he does not claim

Figure 10.6 Barkley's theory of the role of inhibition in ADHD.

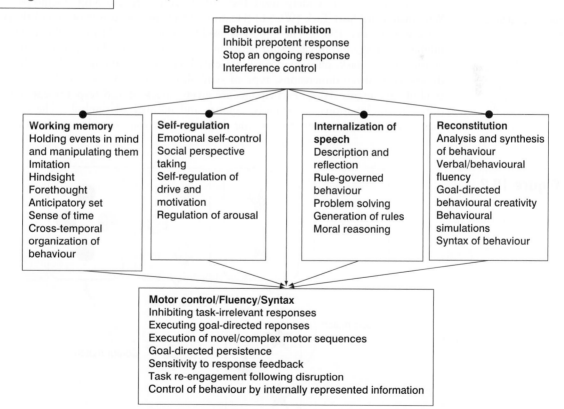

that behavioural inhibition directly causes executive functions, but rather that it allows them to work. Inhibition does, however, have direct causal effect on the motor system. The motor system is referred to as 'motor control/fluency/syntax' as it reflects the generation of complex, goal-directed sequences of responses. Just as syntax in language refers to the ordering of lexical items, the syntax of behaviour refers to the ordering of actions.

Barkley's model predicts that, as a result of a deficiency in behavioural inhibition, the four executive abilities are diminished in ADHD. In consequence, there are effects on self-control and goal-directed behaviour. In typically-developing children, behaviour is goal-directed and results from information that is represented internally, such as plans and rules. In children with ADHD, behaviour is controlled less by internal representations and more by the immediate context.

Research on ADHD

There is a substantial amount of neurophysiological evidence showing differences in the structure and function of the prefrontal cortex between people with and without ADHD, along with differences in the connections between the prefrontal cortex and the striatum (Castellanos *et al.*, 1994; Heilman, Voeller and Nadeau, 1991; Seig *et al.*, 1995). As executive functions are associated with the prefrontal cortex, these findings lend themselves to an executive function deficit explanation of ADHD. However, data from behavioural studies suggests that the picture may be more complex.

There are several widely used tests of executive functioning, including the Wisconsin Card Sort Task (WCST) (Heaton, 1981) and the Tower of Hanoi (Borys, Spitz and Dorans, 1982). The WCST is used to measure set-shifting – the ability to inhibit responses and flexibly shift between 'cognitive sets', or different stimulus categories. In this task, participants are presented with four stimulus cards. Each card differs along three dimensions: type of symbol, colour of symbols and number of symbols (see Figure 10.7). Participants are given a deck of 128 response cards with different combinations of symbols, colours and number of symbols. The experimenter directs participants to sort the deck onto the four stimulus cards, without

Wisconsin Card Sort Task A task in which cards can be sorted by colour, shape or number. The task involves switching from sorting according to one dimension (colour) to another dimension (shape).

Figure 10.7

The Wisconsin Card Sort Task.

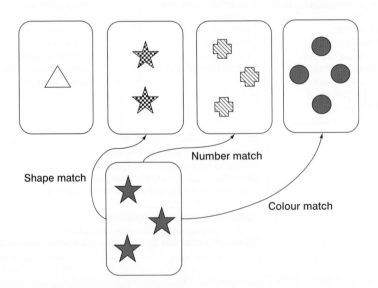

asking for a particular dimension (symbol, number or colour) to be used for the sorting. Participants are told that the rule for sorting will change during the task. Once participants start placing the response cards in piles, the experimenter says 'right' or 'wrong' for each card placed. The experimenter can thus control which dimension is used for the sorting rule. If for example, participants initially sort cards by colour (placing all cards with red symbols, regardless of symbol shape or numerosity, by the single red triangle), the experimenter can choose to change to a different sorting rule by saying 'wrong'. At this point, participants have to work out whether to sort by number or symbol shape. Each time the rule is changed, the experimenter can see how long participants take to learn the new rule and what mistakes are made. If a participant is unable to shift from the first sorting rule to a different rule, this may indicate frontal lobe damage.

The Tower of Hanoi is a test of planning ability. The aim of the task is to move three rings, one at a time, from the leftmost peg to the rightmost peg such that the rings are in the same order with the smallest at the top (see Figure 10.8). The catch is that a larger ring may not be placed on a smaller one. This task involves planning and monitoring as, if one makes the wrong first move, the pile of rings will end up on the middle peg rather than the peg on the right. If a participant has impaired executive functions, he may exhibit poorer performance on the task.

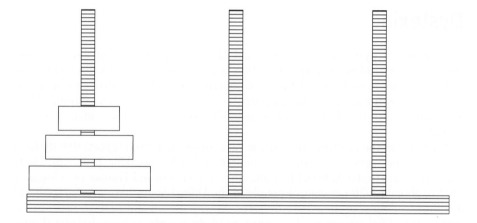

Figure 10.8

The Tower of Hanoi.

The Stop-Signal Task (Schachar and Logan, 1990) has been widely used in research on ADHD as it tests the ability of participants to inhibit proponent responses. In a typical version of this task, participants are presented with repeated trials in which they have to make a response according to which one of two visual stimuli is presented on a screen. For example, they are asked to press the 'x' or 'o' key on the keyboard depending on whether an 'x' or 'o' is displayed. On some trials, the visual stimulus is followed immediately by a beep. Participants are instructed that they should not make a key press on trials where there is a beep. Because the visual stimulus has already been presented before the beep, the task requires participants to inhibit a behaviour that they have already started planning or executing. If Barkley is correct in his theory that the root of ADHD is a lack of inhibition, then we would expect children with ADHD to perform poorly on this task. Some studies (e.g., Rubia *et al.*, 2001) have found impaired performance for children with

ADHD, whereas others (e.g., Kuntsi, Oosterlaan and Stevenson, 2001) have not. The latter did, however, find differences in reaction times; children with ADHD take longer to respond and have more variable reaction times. This evidence could be taken as support for Barkley's theory, but it could also be viewed as the result of a more general difference in information processing speed (Sergeant, Oosterlaan and van der Meere, 1999).

Pennington and Ozonoff (1996) conducted a meta-analysis in which they included 18 studies on ADHD. Of these 18 studies, 15 reported a difference between people with and without ADHD on measures of executive function. Participants with ADHD performed more poorly on two-thirds of the tasks used across the studies, including the Tower of Hanoi, the Stroop test and measures of motor inhibition. A decade later, Wilcutt *et al.* (2005) carried out another meta-analysis on 83 studies of ADHD. They found that ADHD is associated with impairments on most executive function tasks, but the largest effects were on measures of response inhibition, vigilance, spatial working memory and planning. However, because many of the effect sizes were moderate, and because different individuals with ADHD do not show the same patterns of executive function deficits, Willcutt *et al.* conclude that executive functions cannot be a cause of all cases of ADHD.

Dyslexia

dyslexia A learning disability characterized by poor reading and spelling that cannot be explained by a general intellectual impairment.

Developmental dyslexia is a reading and language-based learning disability, also referred to as reading disability. Children with dyslexia may have problems with word recognition, spelling and reading comprehension. There is strong evidence for a genetic basis for the disorder (Grigorenko, 2005; Pennington and Olson, 2005), but there is also a role for environmental factors in how these genetic factors unfold.

Estimates of the incidence of dyslexia vary. Snowling (2008) reports that dyslexia affects 4–8 per cent of school-aged children in English-speaking countries. However, according to the National Institute for Child Health and Human Development (2010), about 15–20 per cent of people in the United States have a language-based disability, and most of these have dyslexia. As with autism and ADHD, males are at greater risk. They are up to three times as likely as girls to have dyslexia (Rutter *et al.*, 2004). Dyslexia persists into adulthood. Although adults may have developed their reading abilities, Rutter, Kim-Cohen and Maughan (2006) report that 80 per cent of children with dyslexia, from a study in the 1970s, still had low spelling scores when they were in their mid-40s.

Characteristics of dyslexia

Dyslexia is characterized by difficulties in phonological awareness, verbal memory and verbal processing speed. Children with dyslexia may also have difficulties with language, motor coordination, mental calculation, concentration and personal organization (Rose, 2009). However, without the reading-specific components, these problems do not themselves signify dyslexia. Depending on the age of the individual, different aspects of reading disability are present. Table 10.1 shows common characteristics that appear at different ages.

Developmental phase	Signs of dyslexia
Preschool	Delayed or problematic speech Poor expressive language Poor rhyming skills Little interest/difficulty learning letters
Early school years	Poor letter-sound knowledge Poor phoneme awareness Poor word attack skills Idiosyncratic spelling Problems copying
Middle school years	Slow reading Poor decoding skills when faced with new words Phonetic or non-phonetic spelling
Adolescence and adulthood	Poor reading fluency Slow speed of writing Poor organization and expression in work

Table 10.1

Developmental phases of dyslexia.

Source: Snowling (2008).

Diagnosing dyslexia

In order to be diagnosed as dyslexic, a child must meet the criteria outlined in Box 10.3. Note that reading achievement must be below what would normally be expected, given age and intelligence. This is referred to as discrepancy definition – rather than defining dyslexia in terms of an absolute score on a reading, it is defined with respect to what might be expected from an individual, given what else is known about them. This means that if poor reading can be explained by low intelligence, then dyslexia can be ruled out. It also means that children with dyslexia have, by definition, normal intelligence levels.

Theories

The predominant cognitive theory of dyslexia is the phonological deficit theory (Siegel, 1992; Snowling, 2000; Stanovich, 1988; Stanovich and Siegel, 1994; Swan and Goswami, 1997). According to this view, the disorder is caused by a phonological processing impairment, which leads to difficulty mapping words to speech sounds. More specifically, people with dyslexia have an impaired ability to represent segments of words at the phonological level, which means that word recognition is impeded, with the result that reading is difficult. If the theory is correct, we would expect to see impairments in any phonologically-based tasks in people with dyslexia. We would also expect poor performance on measures of verbal working memory as, according to the working memory model (Baddeley and Hitch, 1974), verbal information is processed in the phonological loop (see Chapter 3 for a more detailed description of the working memory model).

There are some competing theories of dyslexia. Livingstone *et al.* (1991) proposed the magnocellular theory, in which dysfunction of magnocells in the lateral

> **Box 10.3** Diagnostic criteria for reading disorder
> From the DSM-IV-TR (APA, 2000)
>
> A. Reading achievement, as measured by individually administered standardized tests of reading accuracy or comprehension, is substantially below that expected given the person's chronological age, measured intelligence and age-appropriate education.
> B. The disturbance in Criterion A significantly interferes with academic achievement or activities of daily living that require reading skills.
>
> C. If a sensory deficit is present, the reading difficulties are in excess of those usually associated with it.
>
> Source: Reproduced with permission of the American Psychiatric Association, from American Psychiatric Association. (2000). *Diagnostic and statistical manual of mental disorders* (4th edn, text revision); permission conveyed through Copyright Clearance Center, Inc.

geniculate nucleus gives rise to a visual impairment that causes dyslexia. Tallal (1980) suggested that dyslexia may be caused by an auditory impairment, and Nicolson and Fawcett (1990) argued for cerebellar dysfunction as the cause. According to the latter theory, cerebellar dysfunction has an impact on motor control and automaticity, which results in speech articulation problems. This in turn leads to deficient phonological representations and difficulties in learning the correspondences between graphemes (letters) and phonemes (sounds). The main difference between the phonological deficit theory and the other theories is that the latter all posit sensorimotor impairments as the cause of phonological impairments downstream.

Research on dyslexia

Studies of people with dyslexia have shown impairments in a range of tasks that require phonological awareness – an understanding of the phonological structure of words (Goswami and Bryant, 1990; Metsala, Stanovich and Brown, 1998). Phonological awareness tasks require explicit, rather than implicit, processing of speech sounds. In a longitudinal study of 400 children without dyslexia, followed between the ages of 4 and 8, Bradley and Bryant (1983) showed that phonological awareness in preschool predicts later reading ability independently of intelligence. In an earlier study, Bradley and Bryant (1978) had found that a group of 12-year-olds with dyslexia performed worse than reading-age-matched children on a task that involved picking the odd one out from a group of words in which all but one are phonologically similar, such as 'cat', 'fat', 'hat' and 'net'. Taken together, these studies suggest that a failure to develop good phonological skills leads to reading disability.

Rack, Snowling and Olson (1992) found that people with dyslexia do poorly on tests of nonword reading. Nonwords are wordlike sequences of letters that are not real words, such as 'tafflest' and 'perplisteronk'. In order to read nonwords, knowledge of correspondences between graphemes and phonemes is needed. If someone is unable to read nonwords, it may be the case that they have a phonological deficit. A meta-analysis of 16 studies of nonword reading by van Ijzendoorn and Bus (1994) confirmed that children with dyslexia are impaired in nonword reading. In addition to nonword reading tasks, researchers have used the nonword repetition task to investigate phonological abilities in children with dyslexia. In this task, participants are asked to repeat a spoken nonword. Snowling (1981; Snowling *et al.*, 1986) found that children with dyslexia were not as good as reading-age-matched children at repeating nonwords. The nonword repetition test is a measure of verbal working memory (see Chapter 3). According to Gathercole and colleagues (Gathercole and Baddeley, 1989, 1993; Gathercole *et al.*, 1994), when a child hears a word or nonword, it is placed in the phonological loop before it can be repeated. Thus the working memory model offers an explanation of the verbal memory and vocabulary learning difficulties found in dyslexia; the phonological deficit means that items cannot be processed in the phonological loop which means it is hard to learn and remember new words.

In order to compare the phonological deficit theory to the sensorimotor accounts of dyslexia, White *et al.* (2006) compared the performance of 23 children with dyslexia to that of 22 children without dyslexia on a battery of tasks that assessed their literacy, and their phonological, visual, auditory and motor skills. All participants were aged 8 to 12 and had non-verbal IQs of at least 85. Unsurprisingly, there were differences between the two groups with respect to reading and spelling, as measured using the Wide Range Achievement Test (Wilkinson, 1993). The two groups differed on six of seven phonology tasks, including a nonword reading task and a rhyme task similar to the one used by Bradley and Bryant (1978). There were no differences on the visual and auditory tasks, but there were differences on two of four motor tasks. When the participants were examined individually, it was found that 14 of the 23 children with dyslexia, and 13 of the 22 children *without* dyslexia had at least one sensorimotor impairment. White *et al.* compared the children with dyslexia and sensorimotor impairments to those with dyslexia only, and found no differences in literacy performance. As a result of these findings, they argue that sensorimotor impairments cannot explain the symptoms of dyslexia as well as a primary phonological deficit can.

Dyscalculia

Developmental dyscalculia, also called mathematics disability, is a learning disability in which there is a specific difficulty with numbers and mathematics, including learning number facts and performing calculations (Geary, 1993). As with dyslexia, dyscalculia is independent of general intelligence; it is possible to be highly intelligent on non-mathematical measures yet have severe impairments on tasks involving numbers and arithmetic. As a result, children with dyscalculia can find their difficulties frustrating, and are at risk of low self-esteem, stigmatization and disruptive behaviour in class (Butterworth, 2005).

In a study of 3029 children aged 11, Gross-Tsur, Manor and Shaley (1996) found that 6.5 per cent of their sample had dyscalculia. Twenty-six percent of the children with dyscalculia had symptoms of ADHD, and 17 per cent had dyslexia. A lower estimate of 3.6 per cent is reported by Lewis, Hitch and Walker (1994). This means the incidence of dyscalculia is similar to that of dyslexia. Unlike the other disorders discussed in this chapter, dyscalculia appears to affect males and females equally (Gross-Tsur *et al.*, 1996; Lewis *et al.*,1994; von Aster, 1994).

Characteristics of dyscalculia

A child with dyscalculia may have difficulty with understanding number concepts, learning multiplication tables, and distinguishing between the different arithmetic operators ($+$, $-$, $\times$, $\div$). In addition to difficulties with number facts and procedures, children with dyscalculia may have low digit spans, reduced processing speed for numbers and problems with counting and representing single-digit numbers (Butterworth, 2003). This means that it will take children and adults with dyscalculia longer than their peers to solve single-digit addition and subtraction problems, and they will rely more heavily on counting on their fingers. They may not be able to solve double-digit subtraction or multiplication problems at all. Some children with dyscalculia exhibit difficulties with transcoding numbers between spoken verbal, written verbal and Arabic numeral format (Sullivan, Macaruso and Sokol, 1996; Sokol, Macaruso and Gollan, 1994; Temple, 1991). Dyscalculia is frequently accompanied by other disorders, including ADHD and dyslexia, which can make it hard to tell whether particular impairments are caused by dyscalculia or not. For example, Sokol *et al.* (1994) present data from a number of students with both dyslexia and dyscalculia. One of their participants, Doug, performed very well on single- and multi-digit arithmetic problems, but performed poorly on tasks involving estimating the answer. Conversely, another participant, Tom, performed very poorly on the arithmetic problems, but outperformed Doug on the estimation tasks. Because language and reading are intimately tied to mathematics, it may be the case that some individuals who perform poorly on tests of mathematical ability, do so for reasons other than dyscalculia.

Diagnosing dyscalculia

The DSM-IV diagnostic criteria for mathematics disability are shown in Box 10.4. However, 'mathematical ability, as measured by … standardized tests' is a fairly loose definition, in that the standardized tests usually administered in schools measure many things, including verbal and spatial abilities. As a consequence, a low score may not indicate the specific deficits associated with dyscalculia, but may result from any number of factors, such as poor school attendance or ineffective teaching (Butterworth, 2005). As it is difficult to define exactly what dyscalculia is, it follows that it is difficult to diagnose.

Different researchers have used different operational definitions of dyscalculia. Shalev, Manor and Gross-Tsur (1997), use a criterion of mathematics achievement level two years below chronological age. Butterworth (2003) uses scores in the eleventh percentile on two tests. Landerl, Bevan and Butterworth (2004) use a criterion of three standard deviations below the mean on tests of mental arithmetic.

Box 10.4 Diagnostic criteria for mathematics disorder
From the DSM-IV-TR (APA, 2000)

A. Mathematical ability, as measured by individually administered standardized tests, is substantially below that expected given the person's chronological age, measured intelligence and age appropriate education.

B. The disturbance in Criterion A significantly interferes with academic achievement or activities of daily living that require mathematical ability.

C. If a sensory deficit is present, the difficulties in mathematical ability are in excess of those usually associated with it.

Source: Reproduced with permission of the American Psychiatric Association, from American Psychiatric Association. (2000). *Diagnostic and statistical manual of mental disorders* (4th edn, text revision); permission conveyed through Copyright Clearance Center, Inc.

Theories

Butterworth (1999, 2005) argues for a specific deficit with respect to numerosity, or a basic understanding of cardinality (see Chapter 8). He claims that abnormal development of a specific number module in the parietal lobes leads to the impairments associated with dyscalculia. Failure to understand basic number concepts, such as numerosity, prevents children with dyscalculia learning the meanings of numerical expressions, and leads to difficulties in learning number facts and operations. As a result, these children display poor memory for number facts and the incorrect use of calculation procedures. This theory does not predict impairments in non-numerical domains, so we should not find impairments on language tasks, unless the dyscalculia is accompanied by an additional disorder, such as dyslexia.

An alternative account, based on memory, has been proposed by Geary (1993). According to Geary there are two deficits in dyscalculia – an impairment of use of arithmetic procedures, and difficulty with representing and retrieving number facts from semantic memory. He claims that these are caused by a deficit in semantic memory, and impaired working memory. If this view is correct, we would expect to find poor performance on tasks involving working memory, specifically the phonological loop, which is used for the rehearsal and storage of verbal information such as number facts.

Research on dyscalculia

If, as Butterworth claims, a specific impairment in numerosity is the cause of dyscalculia, we should expect to find impairments in tasks that involve cardinal sets or the use of subitizing. Subitizing refers to the ability to make a fast and accurate judgement as to how many items are in a set, when the set contains up to four items (Kaufman et al., 1949). For example, when you look at the patterns on the cards used for the Wisconsin Card Sort Test (Figure 10.8), you 'automatically' know that there are four circles or three crosses without having to count them. Subitizing can be assessed using tasks in which arrays of dots are presented, and participants are asked to report the number of dots.

Koontz and Berch (1996) used a dot matching task, in which participants were asked to make judgements as to whether two numerical stimuli were the same or not. Each item in the pair could be the numeral 2, the numeral 3, a set of two dots or a set of three dots. They found that children with dyscalculia were slower on trials involving three dots than trials involving two dots, leading them to suggest that the children were counting rather than subitizing. Geary, Hamson and Hoard (2000) gave 6- to 7-year-old children with and without dyscalculia a battery of tasks including one in which the participants were asked to compare the magnitude of pairs of numbers (e.g., 1 9, 3 2, 5 7, 9 8). Geary et al. found differences between the children with dyscalculia and the control group on this task.

Landerl, Bevan and Butterworth (2004) studied 8- and 9-year-olds with dyscalculia alongside a comparison group matched on reading ability and knowledge of arithmetic facts. They found that the children with dyscalculia performed more poorly on tests of single-digit subtraction and multiplication, and were slower on tests of dot counting and of number magnitude comparison. However, they performed at a normal or above average level on tasks involving phonological working memory, non-verbal intelligence and language abilities, suggesting that dyscalculia involves a number-specific impairment. This does not, therefore, support Geary's memory-based account.

There are also other studies showing normal performance on memory tasks in children with dyscalculia. McLean and Hitch (1999) used a nonword repetition task, which – as we saw earlier – makes use of the phonological loop. They found no differences between children with and without dyscalculia, suggesting that children with dyscalculia do not have a general working memory impairment. Temple and Sherwood (2002) used several working-memory measures, including digit span and word span, and found no group differences.

Converging evidence from developmental, comparative and neuroscientific approaches suggests that basic number processing is a fundamental process and therefore not mediated by language-based processes such as verbal short-term memory or semantic long-term memory. Wynn (1992a, 1995a; McCrink and Wynn, 2004) has found basic numerical abilities in preverbal infants, and there is evidence for a sense of number in animals (Gallistel, 1990). Several neuroimaging studies have shown that arithmetic processes are dependent on specialized systems in the parietal lobes and the anterior intraparietal sulcus (IPS) (Castelli, Glaser and Butterworth, 2006; Dehaene, Molko and Cohen, 2004; Dehaene et al., 2003; Zago et al., 2001). Taken together, these findings support Butterworth's theory of a specific number-processing deficit.

Concluding comments

In this chapter we have looked at four developmental disorders. This is by no means an exhaustive list. We have not, for example, considered specific language impairment or Williams syndrome, both of which are of great interest to cognitive developmental psychologists. I have chosen to focus on just four disorders for reasons of space, and I have tried to pick a range of disorders that are related to material covered elsewhere in this book.

The study of developmental disorders is important for at least three reasons. First, understanding the nature of these disorders can help us understand why people with such disorders behave in the way that they do, and why they find some tasks – which may seem trivial to us – difficult. Understanding disorders in this way will ideally lead to a lessened stigmatization of those with the disorders.

Second, if we can discover the causes of behavioural or cognitive difficulties, we can develop interventions to assist with the social and intellectual development of children with psychological disorders. For example, if dyslexia is a result of a phonological deficit, tailored educational interventions can be designed for children with dyslexia. Hatcher, Hulme and Ellis (1994) found that poor readers, including children with dyslexia, demonstrated an improvement when given a reading programme that emphasized phonological skills, phonological awareness and made explicit links between phonology and reading. Other groups that just received reading instruction or phonological skills training alone did not show the same improvements. Similarly, if dyscalculia is the result of an impairment in basic number sense, interventions can focus on developing relevant conceptual knowledge. Wilson et al. (2006) developed an intervention for children with dyscalculia in which the participants used a computer program that focused on developing their number sense. Although Wilson et al. did not find improvements in all arithmetic skills, they did find increased performance on measures of subitizing speed and magnitude comparison speed.

The third reason for studying developmental disorders is that we can gain additional insights into the normal development of cognition. For example, the research on theory of mind in autism can inform the study of the development of theory of mind in typically-developing children. Similarly, studies of children with autism and ADHD have caused researchers to distinguish between the effects of executive functions and other cognitive processes. Theories of reading have to account for patterns of performance in dyslexia as well as in those without reading disorders. Compared to dyslexia, there has been relatively little research into dyscalculia. We also know less about the processes involved in mathematical skills than we know about reading. By studying both the typical and atypical development of mathematical skills together, psychologists will be able to build a more complete picture of what exactly it is we do when we work with numbers.

Summary

Autism. Autism is a disorder that is characterized by a triad of impairments in socialization, communication and imaginative or symbolic play. Children and adults with autism typically have difficulties in verbal and non-verbal communication, social interactions, leisure and play activities, and engage in repeated behaviours and routines. Autism affects an estimated 1 per cent of children. There are no medical tests for diagnosing autism; diagnoses are based on observation of communication skills, behaviours and general developmental levels. There are three main cognitive theories of autism: theory of mind deficit theory, executive dysfunction theory and weak central coherence theory. According to the theory of mind deficit theory, children with autism are unable to engage in metarepresentational activity, such as thinking about false beliefs. The executive dysfunction theory posits difficulties with executive functions (such as planning, shifting and inhibition), are the cause of the behavioural profile of children with autism. According to weak central coherence theory, the normal tendency towards global processing is absent in autism; people with autism demonstrate local processing. As a result, they perceive and remember features, but have difficulties with overall meaning. Evidence for the theory of mind deficit theory comes from research using mentalizing tasks, on which children with autism tend to perform poorly. Evidence in support of the executive dysfunction theory is provided by research using tasks involving planning, inhibition, working memory or set shifting. However, children with autism are not always impaired on executive function tasks. The weak central coherence theory is supported by studies on perceptual processing, visuospatial coherence and verbal-semantic coherence. Few theorists argue that any one of these three theories alone can explain the behavioural profile of autism, and there may be different genetic causes for the behavioural, social and communicative impairments that are symptomatic of autism.

Attention deficit hyperactivity disorder (ADHD). ADHD is a neurobiological condition affecting attention, impulses and concentration, in an estimated 3–7 per cent of children. There are three subtypes of ADHD: Predominantly hyperactive-impulsive, predominantly inattentive and combined hyperactive-impulsive and inattentive. As a result, some children display more symptoms of hyperactivity and impulsivity, some display more symptoms of inattentivity, but the majority of those diagnosed with ADHD display both hyperactive-impulsive and inattentive symptoms. As with autism, diagnosis is difficult. The dominant cognitive theory of ADHD is that there is a deficit in executive functioning, caused by poor inhibition. There is evidence showing differences in the structure and function of the prefrontal cortex between people with and without ADHD which supports the executive dysfunction hypothesis. However, data from behavioural studies does not unequivocally support the theory. Meta-analyses of studies in which planning, set-shifting and inhibition tasks were used have found impairments on most, but not all, executive function tasks.

Dyslexia. Developmental dyslexia is a reading and language-based learning disability, also referred to as reading disability. Estimates of the incidence of dyslexia vary, ranging from 4–8 per cent upwards. Dyslexia is characterized by difficulties in phonological awareness, verbal memory and verbal processing speed. Diagnosis is defined by a discrepancy between the level reading achievement children have, and the level expected, given their age and intelligence. The dominant cognitive theory of dyslexia is the phonological deficit theory. According to this view, the disorder is caused by a phonological processing impairment, which leads to difficulty mapping words to speech sounds. Competing theories include the magnocellular theory, in which dysfunction of magnocells in the lateral geniculate nucleus gives rise to a visual impairment that causes dyslexia, auditory impairment theory and cerebellar dysfunction. Studies of people with dyslexia have shown impairments in a range of tasks that require phonological awareness, and on nonword reading and repetition tasks.

Dyscalculia. Developmental dyscalculia, also called mathematics disability, is a learning disability in which there is a specific difficulty with numbers and mathematics, including learning number facts and performing calculations. Children with dyscalculia may have low digit spans, reduced processing speed for numbers and problems with counting and representing numbers. As with dyslexia, dyscalculia is independent of general intelligence. Between 3 and 7 per cent of children are thought to have dyscalculia. Dyscalculia is frequently accompanied by other disorders, including ADHD and dyslexia, which can make it hard to tell whether particular impairments are caused by dyscalculia or not. One theory of dyscalculia is that there is a specific deficit with respect to numerosity. According to this theory, failure to understand numerosity prevents children with dyscalculia learning the meanings of numerical expressions, and leads to difficulties in learning number facts and operations. An alternative account is based on memory deficits, specifically with respect to semantic long-term memory and the phonological loop in working memory. There is evidence that children with dyscalculia perform poorly on tests of magnitude judgement, supporting the numerosity theory. There are also many studies which have found normal performance on memory tasks, suggesting that dyscalculia is not the result of memory deficits. Converging evidence from developmental, comparative and neuroscientific approaches also supports the theory of a specific number-processing deficit.

Discussion questions

1 How has the study of theory of mind contributed to our understanding of autism?

2 Which cognitive theory do you think best accounts for the findings from research on autism? What are the strengths and weaknesses of each theory?

3 What does research on executive functioning tell us about (a) autism, and (b) ADHD?

4 Does research on literacy help us to understand dyslexia?

5 How does our knowledge of the development of numeracy help us to understand dyscalculia?

Further Reading

Books and chapters

Barkley, R. A. (2003). Attention deficit hyperactivity disorder. In Mash, E. J. and Barkley, R. A. (Eds), *Child Psychopathology* (2nd ed.). New York: Guilford Press.

In this chapter, Russell Barkley gives an overview of the history, characteristics and diagnosis of ADHD, and describes his theory of behavioural inhibition.

Butterworth, B. (2005). Developmental dyscalculia. In J. I. D. Campbell (Ed.), *Handbook of mathematical cognition* (pp. 455–467). Hove: Psychology Press.

In this chapter, Brian Butterworth provides a description of dyscalculia, and discusses research with respect to different theories of the disorder.

Frith, U. (2003). *Autism: Explaining the enigma*. Oxford: Blackwell.

Uta Frith's book is an excellent read for both scientists and laypeople. She offers an accessible account of characteristics of autism and some of the theories that attempt to explain it.

Hulme, C. and Snowling, M. J. (2009) *Developmental disorders of language learning and cognition*. Chichester: Wiley-Blackwell.

Charles Hulme and Margaret Snowling's book includes chapters on autism, ADHD, dyslexia and dyscalculia, alongside other developmental disorders, making it a very worth while read.

Articles

Baron-Cohen, S., Leslie, A.M. and Frith, U. (1985). Does the autistic child have a 'theory of mind'? *Cognition*, 21, 37–46.

This is the classic paper, discussed at the beginning of the chapter, in which Simon Baron-Cohen, Alan Leslie and Uta Frith first investigated theory of mind in children with autism.

Geary, D. C. (2004). Mathematics and learning disabilities. *Journal of Learning Disabilities*, 37, 4–15.

David Geary reviews patterns of performance in dyscalculia and presents his framework theory for the study of the disorder.

Rajendran, G., and Mitchell, P. (2007). Cognitive theories of autism. *Developmental Review*, 27(2), 224–260.

Gnanathusharan Rajendran and Peter Mitchell discuss the three main theories of autism, along with the evidence for and against them.

White, S., Milne, E., Rosen, S., Hansen, P., Swettenham, J., Frith, U. and Ramus, F. (2006). The role of sensorimotor impairments in dyslexia: a multiple case study of dyslexic children. *Developmental Science*, 9(3), 237–269.

Sarah White and colleagues present a study in which they investigated the roles of sensorimotor and phonological impairments in dyslexia. This target article is followed by commentaries from other dyslexia researchers.

Willcutt, E. G., Doyle, A. E., Nigg, J. T., Faraone, S. V. and Pennington, B. F. (2005). Validity of the executive function theory of Attention-Deficit/Hyperactivity Disorder: A meta-analytic review. *Biological Psychiatry*, 57, 1336–1346.

Erik Wilcutt and colleagues review the evidence for an executive function deficit in ADHD.

Neurocognitive Approaches to Developmental Disorders: A Festschrift for Uta Frith (2008). *The Quarterly Journal of Experimental Psychology*, 61(1).

This special issue of *The Quarterly Journal of Experimental Psychology* celebrates the retirement of Uta Frith, who spent over 40 years studying autism and dyslexia. It contains many papers on autism and a few on dyslexia.

© Corbis RF/Alamy

Chapter 11

Computational models of development

Learning Outcomes

At the end of this chapter you should be able to:

- Understand what a computational model is.

- Explain how computational modelling can help psychologists understand cognitive development.

- Discuss and evaluate models of children's development.

Computational modelling is a technique used by many people, including engineers and computer scientists, as well as cognitive psychologists. A computational model is a simulation of a real world phenomenon implemented as a computer program. When used in psychology, such models are usually simulations of cognitive processes and are referred to as cognitive models. Increasingly, developmental psychologists are starting to use cognitive models as a way of exploring their theories. A theory of cognitive development is, as we saw in Chapter 1, an explanation of children's behaviour. As well as explaining behaviour, a theory has to be able to make testable predictions. A cognitive model of behaviour on a task allows us to test theories and the predictions made by them. In order to see what a cognitive model is and why modelling is a useful tool for developmental psychologists, we will look at an example of how such a model can be used to test the predictions of a theory.

The Tower of Nottingham

Figure 11.1 shows the 'Tower of Nottingham' task, devised by Wood and Middleton (1975). The 'Tower of Nottingham' is a wooden pyramid which consists of 21 blocks. There are five layers of four blocks and a final top block. The task involves giving participants the 21 blocks and asking them to assemble the pyramid. The four blocks that make up each layer are labelled A through D in the diagram. In order to complete each layer, it is necessary to join A and B together and C and D together before joining the AB and CD halves. A and B (and C and D) are joined by slotting a peg into a hole. It is necessary to make these two halves first as A and B together make a half with a hole in which to slot the peg created by joining C and D.

This task involves coordinating mental representations as, in order to complete each layer, participants have to understand that the peg in C must go into the hole in D in order to bring the two half pegs together to create a whole peg, and that A and B must be joined to bring the two half holes together. According to Piaget's (1952b) theory, children younger than 7 years of age should find this task harder than older children because pre-operational stage children do not have the ability to coordinate their internal mental representations (see Chapter 1).

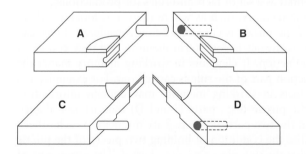 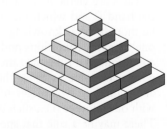

Figure 11.1

The Tower of Nottingham.

Source: Reproduced with permission of Lawrence Erlbaum Associates, from Jones, G., & Ritter, F. E. (1998). Simulating Development by Modifying Architectures. *Proceedings of the Twentieth Annual Conference of the Cognitive Science Society* (pp. 543–548); permission conveyed through Copyright Clearance Center, Inc.

In Chapter 3, we saw that working memory span increases with age. Therefore Pascual-Leone's (1987) information-processing theory would also predict that older children's performance would be superior to that of younger children, as a result of being able to hold more elements, such as representations of tower pieces, in working memory at once. Case (1985) and Halford (1993) also theorize developmental changes in working memory capacity, so they would also predict age-related differences in performance. But, as we saw in Chapter 3, there are other factors hypothesized to affect the amount of information we can manipulate in memory, including speed and strategy use. This means that Kail's (1991b) theory that increasing processing speed is a major factor in cognitive development would predict that older children would be better at the task. Siegler and Shipley's (1995) theory of developmental changes in strategy use makes the same prediction, but for a different reason.

Wood and his colleagues (Murphy and Wood, 1981, 1982; Wood, Bruner and Ross, 1976; Wood and Middleton, 1975) carried out several studies in which the Tower of Nottingham task was given to children aged 3 to 8. They demonstrated that older children show better performance on this task than younger children, in terms of speed of completion of the tower, and the number of correct and incorrect constructions made.

So how do we know which theory is correct? Unfortunately, even with cognitive neuroscience techniques, we cannot look inside children's heads and see what type of knowledge, or how much knowledge, they have, or what the contents of working memory are. We can only guess at their knowledge, memory and strategies from their behaviour on a task. This makes it hard to test predictions as we do not know whether the older children are better at this task because they are able to coordinate mental representations, whether they have greater processing speed or mental capacity, or whether their strategy use is more efficient.

A model of the task

One way to compare theories is to construct a computational model of the cognitive processes involved in completing the Tower of Nottingham task. Jones, Ritter and Wood (2000) built a computer model into which they programmed all the information necessary to perform the task, including knowledge of the task, instructions on directing eye gaze to different components of the Tower, and instructions for moving a hand to a particular piece. This particular model is a **production system**, which means its knowledge is represented as a set of facts and rules (or productions).

production system A type of cognitive model in which knowledge is stored as a list of 'if . . . then' (or condition-action) rules.

Facts are elements in working memory, such as where the eye is looking, where the hand is and which piece of the puzzle is currently being considered. Rules can be thought of as knowledge or strategies in long-term memory and they consist of one or more conditions and an action. If elements in working memory match the conditions of a rule, then the action part of the rule is carried out. For example, at a particular point in time, the facts in working memory may contain information about holding two pieces of the puzzle (e.g., parts C and D) that are not aligned with one another (i.e., such that the two parts of the peg are not next to each other). There may be a rule that specifies the condition of holding two pieces of the puzzle and also specifies a condition that the two parts are not aligned. The action part of the rule may state that the hand must then rotate the second piece 180 degrees, so that they are aligned.

By carrying out a sequence of rules, the model is able to start with the goal of building the Tower. First, it will select the largest pieces to form the bottom layer. It will select parts A and B, make sure they are correctly oriented, and put them together. It can then select parts C and D, align them and fit them together. It can then take the two assembled parts, A–B and C–D, and build the entire bottom layer. It can then carry out the same process to build the next layer, and so on.

Jones *et al.* started by building a model of adult performance on the task. This model had 317 rules, including the knowledge and strategies that adults can be expected to have, such as knowing that blocks of the same size go together, and that pegs go in holes. Each rule has a 'strength' value which is altered on the basis of success or failure. If using a particular rule helped to construct the Tower, the strength of that rule increases. If a rule turned out not to help with the task, the strength is decreased. When the 'facts' in working memory can be matched to the conditions of more than one rule, then the rule with the highest strength will be picked. Manipulating the strength of the rules has the effect of increasing or decreasing the likelihood that a particular strategy will be used.

In addition to knowledge, there are other factors affecting task performance that were programmed into the model, including the amount of time needed to make a saccade to a new piece (50 ms), to fixate on a piece (200 ms) and to carry out a motor action e.g., fitting two pieces together (550 ms). Also – as we saw in Chapter 3 – working memory has a limited duration; items soon decay and disappear from working memory if they are not kept active. This was also built into the model. Any element that gets put in working memory has a base level of activation. This activation decreases every time a rule is used, until it falls below a particular value (called the *retrieval threshold*), at which point the element can no longer be used in selecting rules.

This model, which contains a working memory, a knowledge base and values for how long it takes to carry out each aspect of the task, was compared to adult performance on the Tower of Nottingham. Five adults were given the task and their performance was measured in two ways: the amount of time it took to complete the Tower, and the number of constructions they made. Figure 11.2 shows the performance of the five adults and ten attempts at the task by the model. It is clear that the model's performance is a close match to that of the adults.

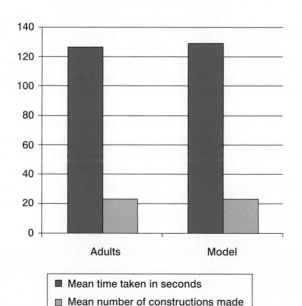

Figure 11.2

Comparison of adult and model data.

Adapting the model to test developmental theories

Whereas adults take about two minutes to complete the task, and make around 23 constructions, children take longer and make more mistakes. Reichgelt *et al.* (1993) gave five 7-year-olds the task and found that they took, on average, almost three minutes to build the Tower and made around 28 constructions. As we saw earlier, this difference between 7-year-olds and adults can be explained in several different ways, including differences in working memory capacity and choice of strategies.

Jones *et al.* made modifications to the model in order to test some of the competing theories of development. They tested two different theories of capacity limitations, and one theory of strategy choice. The first capacity-based theory is Pascual-Leone's (1987) M-Power theory, in which development is accounted for by increasing working memory. Jones *et al.* instantiated M-Power theory in the model by raising the retrieval threshold for elements in working memory. As items in working memory have to be above this threshold in order to be matched against rules, raising the threshold effectively reduces the number of active elements in working memory.

The second capacity-based theory is the proposal by Case (1985) and Halford (1993) that the number of elements that can be simultaneously processed in working memory increases with age. This means that a rule with a large number of conditions (some of the rules in the adult model had 12 conditions) would not be accessible to younger children. To model this theory, Jones *et al.* split some of the larger rules into two smaller ones and deleted any rules with more than nine conditions that could not be split into two.

The third variant of the model was an instantiation of Siegler and Shipley's (1995) strategy choice theory. According to this account, children's use of strategies changes with experience. As children get older, they are better able to identify the most appropriate strategy to use in a given situation. In the model, strategies are implemented as individual rules or sequences of rules. In order to reduce the model's knowledge of which strategies are best (which is reflected in the strength of each rule), Jones *et al.* introduced random noise to the strength values, thus making it more likely that the model would choose a sub-optimal strategy.

Figure 11.3 shows how well each model performed with respect to time taken to complete the task and number of constructions. Jones *et al.* also measured how long it took, and how many constructions were made, to complete each layer. All three models led to an increase in total time taken and total number of constructions compared to the adult model, but the best fit to the child data, when behaviour on individual layers was also taken into account, was provided by model 3: the strategy choice model.

This example of a cognitive model shows us that a theory (or set of independent theories) can be implemented within a computer program, the behaviour of which can be compared to human data. If the output of the model provides a good match to human data, then support for the theory is provided. In this case, the best match to the human data was provided by the version of the model in which the strategy-choice theory was implemented. This provides support for the idea that cognitive development is at least partially due to changes in strategy use.

Q. What are the limitations of this study? What else would be needed for a more thorough test of strategy change as the mechanism by which cognitive development occurs?

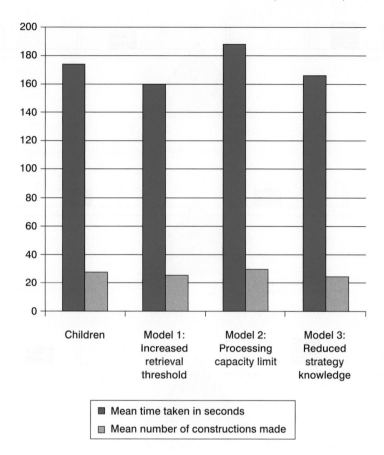

Figure 11.3

Comparison of child
and model data.

Jones *et al.* (2000) compared the performance of the model to five adults, and to the five 7-year-olds from Reichgelt *et al.*'s (1993) study. One potential limitation of Jones *et al.*'s study is that the sample sizes are fairly small. It may be the case that a larger group of 7-year-olds would produce data that are more similar to a version of the model other than the one in which the strategy choice theory was implemented. Even if these 7-years-old are highly representative of the population of all 7-year-olds, this study only tells us that strategy choice theory can explain their behaviour on the Tower of Nottingham task. In order to see if the theory can explain children's behaviour on a wider range of tasks, those tasks would also have to be modelled. Also, to test the claim that strategy choice accounts for developmental changes, the behaviour of children of different ages would need to be examined, and models of children of these different ages would have to be constructed.

The balance beam task

The second example we will consider is the balance beam task (Inhelder and Piaget, 1958). Figure 11.4 shows three examples of a balance beam. This is a beam which rests on a central fulcrum and has several pegs on each side onto which weights can be placed. The task involves placing weights on pegs to either side of the fulcrum

Figure 11.4

Three examples of
balance beam
problems.

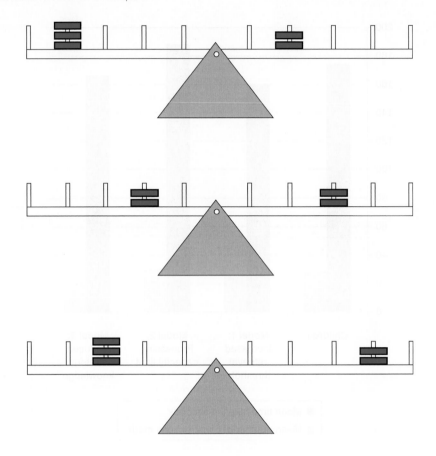

and asking participants whether they think one side or the other will go down, or
whether it will balance.

> Q. I am sure that you are able to predict which side will go down in the exam-
> ples in Figure 11.4, but *how* do you know? On what basis did you make your
> judgements? Did you use the same knowledge or principles for all three bal-
> ance beams?

Siegler's theory

Siegler (1976, 1981) theorized that children use a series of rules of increasing complexity to solve balance beam problems. The first (and simplest) rule is that the side
with the most weight will go down. Rule two is that when the weights on the two
sides are equal, the side with weights furthest away from the fulcrum will go down.
Rule three states that both weight and distance should be taken into account, but
that if there is greater distance on one side and greater weight on the other, a guess
should be made. Rule four states that, for each side, the weight and the distance
should be multiplied. The side with the greatest product of weight and distance will
go down. All four rules predict that the beam will balance if weight and distance are
the same on both sides. Figure 11.5 shows the four rules as 'decision trees'.

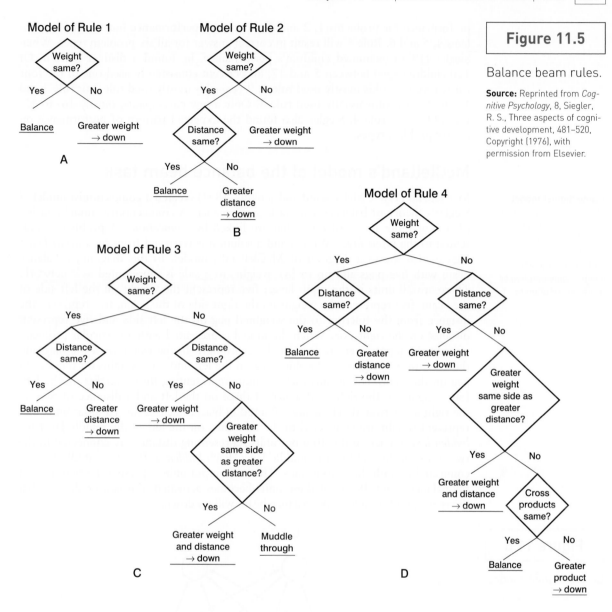

Figure 11.5

Balance beam rules.

Source: Reprinted from *Cognitive Psychology*, 8, Siegler, R. S., Three aspects of cognitive development, 481–520, Copyright (1976), with permission from Elsevier.

In order to determine which rules children were using, Siegler devised six problem types; performance on these different problems differentiates between the four rules.

1 Balance problems: Same configuration of weights on both sides.
2 Weight problems: Same distance, different weights.
3 Distance problems: Same weights, different distances.
4 Conflict-weight problems: One side has more weight, the other has more distance; the side with the greater weight goes down.
5 Conflict-distance problems: One side has more weight, the other has more distance; the side with the greater distance goes down.
6 Conflict-balance problems: One side has more weight, the other has more distance; the two sides balance.

Children using Rule 1 will only be able to solve problems 1, 2 and 4. Children using Rule 2 will get 1, 2, 3 and 4 correct. Use of Rule 3 will result in correct performance for problems 1, 2 and 3 and chance performance (guessing) for problems 4, 5 and 6. Rule 4 will result in correct answer for all six problem types. When Siegler (1976) examined children's performance, he found a distinct pattern. Of 120 children aged between 5 and 17, 80 per cent consistently used one of the four rules. Five-year-olds mostly used rule 1, 9-year-olds mostly used rule 2 or rule 3 and 13- to 17-year-olds usually used rule 3. Only a few participants, mostly 16- to 17-year-olds, used rule 4. Siegler also found the expected pattern of performance on the six problem types.

McClelland's model of the balance beam task

connectionist model
Also known as a neural network. A cognitive model in which knowledge is stored as a pattern of connection weights between two or more layers of units.

McClelland (1989; McClelland and Jenkins, 1991) created a **connectionist model** of Siegler's theory of balance beam task performance. A connectionist model consists of two or more layers of *units* that are linked by *connections*. A problem is presented to the *input layer* of units and a solution is retrieved from the *output layer*. Figure 11.6 shows a diagram of McClelland's model. In this diagram, a balance beam with five pegs and up to five weights to a side is represented as a network. There are 20 units in the input layer: five represent the weight on the left side of the beam, five represent the weight on the right side of the beam, five represent the distance from the fulcrum to the weighted peg on the left side and five represent distance on the right side. When the model is presented with a particular problem, units in the input layer are 'activated' accordingly. In the example in the diagram, there are three weights on the third peg on the left and four weights on the second peg on the right. This means that the units representing three weights on the left, four weights on the right, a distance of three on the left and a distance of two on the right are activated. These are coloured in black. Each of the 10 input units that represent weight are connected to the two units on the left of the middle layer (or *hidden layer*). Each of the 10 input units representing distance are connected to the two units on the right of the middle layer. Each *hidden unit* in the middle layer is connected to both the output units. The two output units represent the two sides of the balance beam. If one of these units becomes activated, this is a prediction that the corresponding side of the balance beam will go down.

Figure 11.6

Connectionist model of the balance beam.

Source: Reproduced with permission of Lawrence Erlbaum Associates, from McClelland, J. L., & Jenkins, E. (1991). Nature, nurture, and connections: Implications of connectionist models for cognitive development. In K. Van Lehn (Ed.), *Architectures for Intelligence* (pp. 41–73); permission conveyed through Copyright Clearance Center, Inc.

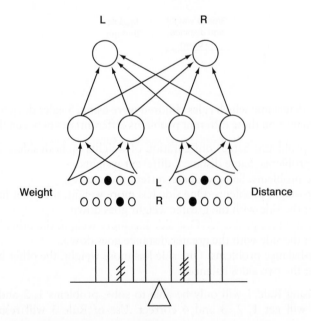

How the model works. When an input unit (such as one of the weight units) is activated it sends a signal to all the units that it is connected to. In this case, this is two of the hidden units in the middle layer of the network. If any of these hidden units become activated, they send a signal to both units in the output layer. A very important feature of connectionist networks is that each connection between two units has a value (or 'weight'), usually between −1 and +1. For each input unit that a middle layer unit is connected to, the signal from the input unit is multiplied by the weight of a connection, and these values are added up. If this value is above a certain threshold, then the middle layer unit will become activated, and will pass a signal to the output units. Therefore, if the signal from the 'left weight three' input unit is connected to a middle layer unit by a connection of value +1, the middle layer unit will receive a strong positive signal which means it will be activated. In reality, any middle unit or output unit will be receiving a number of signals from all the units in the preceding layer, and it may be that some of these connections have negative weights. So while there is an *excitatory* effect from an activated unit with a positive connection weight, there may also be an *inhibitory* effect from a unit with a negative connection weight.

Don't worry if this all sounds complicated; the point is that quite complex behaviour can be produced by these sorts of systems as the connection weights change over time. By changing weights of connections, the system is capable of learning. The model is initially given a random set of values for the connections, ranging from −0.5 to +0.5. The model is trained by presenting a series of balance beam problems and telling it the correct answer. If the model has made an incorrect prediction, it will alter the weights of the connections in order that it might give the right answer. If trained on enough examples, the model will have a set of connection weights that will result in the right answer to any problem presented to it.

Performance on the task. The model was trained on 100 problems from the full range of 625 (5 left weights × 5 right weights × 5 left distances × 5 right distances), with a bias to problems based on weight. This is based on an assumption that children know more about weight than they do about distance. The training given can be thought of as 'experience'. If given a different set of problems to learn, its eventual behaviour would be different. After training, the model was given 24 problems, four of each of the six problem types devised by Siegler. The model was then trained on 100 more examples, then tested on the 24 problems again; this was done 100 times.

When a child is initially shown the balance beam task, they may just have a wild guess as to the answer. They then start to realize that weights are important. Then they realize that they have to take distance into account as well. The model learns in a similar way to children: It is given problems, shown which side goes down, and has to learn about the task.

On the test problems, the model was assessed on the basis of whether the answers conformed to rule 1, rule 2, rule 3 or rule 4. The performance of the model changed over time as a result of its experience. Initially, performance was poor. The model only gave 'balance' answers rather than predicting left or right. This can be interpreted as behaviour in which neither weight nor distance cues are used, which is similar to the random guessing displayed by children under the age of 5. After this, the model showed 'rule 1' behaviour, then 'rule 2' behaviour, then a mixture of 'rule 3' and 'rule 4' behaviour. In other words, it showed the same developmental pattern as children. This finding, therefore, shows support for Siegler's theory that children's performance on the tasks improves as a result of increasingly complex rules.

Simple addition

In addition to being responsible for theories tested in the above two examples, Siegler (1987; Siegler and Robinson, 1982; Siegler and Shrager, 1984) has also carried out research in the area of children's simple addition. As we saw in Chapter 8, when children attempt to add two numbers together, they have a number of strategies available to them, including the *count-all*, *count-up*, *decomposition* and *retrieval* strategies. As children get older, their use of strategy changes. Children initially use the *count-all* strategy, which involves counting on their fingers or with blocks. If given the problem 2 + 4, they will count 2 fingers, then count 4 more fingers, then count them all up to arrive at 6. The next strategy is *count-up* (also referred to as *counting on* or the *min* strategy), in which children start with the first number and count up from there (e.g., 2, then 3, 4, 5, 6). Older children and adults tend to use *retrieval* on simple addition problems; this means retrieving the answer from memory. A fourth strategy, *decomposition*, also increases with age. *Decomposition* is where a problem is broken down into two or more simple problems. For example, when asked to solve 5 + 6, a child may know that 5 + 5 = 10, and note that 5 + 6 is the same as 5 + 5, with another one added.

Children will use the most efficient strategy that they can use in any given situation. Younger children use complex strategies less often (or not at all), whereas for older children the more complex strategies are more efficient. Younger children make less errors when using the count-all and count-up strategies than when attempting to retrieve answers from memory. As they gain more experience with addition problems and the problems become more familiar, they become better at using the retrieval strategy. Table 11.1 shows the frequency with which children of different ages use different strategies (Siegler, 1987). Five-year-olds use *count-all*, but 6- and 7-year-olds do not. Use of *min* and *retrieval* increases as children get older.

It is important to recognize that children use several different strategies at the same time, not just one. Development, therefore, is not about moving from stage to stage where each stage involves a more sophisticated strategy than the last. Children do move towards more frequent use of more sophisticated strategies, but they make use of all the strategies available to them. Also, children use different strategies on the same problem at different times. For example, on one day a child may use *count-all* to solve 2 + 3, but use *count-up* on the same problem the following day (or vice versa); children do not always use the most efficient strategy. Siegler theorized that this is true for children's thinking in a number of different domains. He named this the overlapping waves model, illustrated in Figure 11.7 (note that this is not a computational 'model', but a 'model' in the theoretical sense). The idea is that at any one

---

Table 11.1

Percentage use of each addition strategy.

Source: Siegler (1987). © The American Psychological Association (1987), adapted with permission. (The use of APA information does not imply endorsement by APA.)

Age (years)	Strategy				
	Retrieval	Min	Decomposition	Count-all	Guess or no response
5	16	30	2	22	30
6	44	38	9	1	8
7	45	40	11	0	5
Overall	35	36	7	8	14

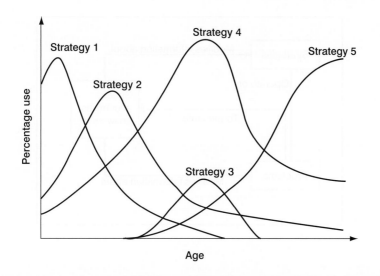

Figure 11.7

Siegler's overlapping
waves model.

Source: Reprinted from *Cognitive Psychology*, 28, Siegler, R. S., How does change occur: A microgenetic study of number conservation, 225–273, Copyright (1995), with permission from Elsevier.

time, children have several different ways of thinking about problems, as we saw in Chapter 8. There is competition between the strategies and those that are more efficient come to be used more frequently. Early on, children are able to use *retrieval* for 1 + 1, but not for harder problems such as 4 + 3. A simpler strategy, such as *count-all*, will be slower but is more likely to result in the correct answer. After some experience with 4 + 3, children will gradually come to always use the retrieval strategy.

Siegler's adaptive strategy choice model

According to Siegler, development involves understanding which strategies are best. An idea that is central to his theory is that children are adaptive – they adapt their strategy use according to the current problem. As well as addition, he has studied children's strategy use in areas such as multiplication and spelling (Lemaire and Siegler, 1995; Rittle-Johnson and Siegler, 1999; Siegler, 1988; Siegler and Lemaire, 1997). Siegler and Shipley (1995) tested this theory with a cognitive model of the theory. This model is called the Adaptive Strategy Choice Model (ASCM), which is a model of children's development of single-digit addition from 4 to 12 years. ASCM is structurally quite different from the McClelland's connectionist model described previously. ASCM consists of a database containing information about the different strategies and problems, and uses mathematical equations to decide which strategy will be used on each problem. The organization of the model is shown in Figure 11.8.

For each strategy, the database holds information about past speed and accuracy on problems. These data are used to make projections about how likely each strategy is to solve a particular problem. If the strategy chosen is retrieval, the performance of the model depends on a probability of the correct answer being retrieved. This probability is higher for simpler problems (e.g. 2 + 1) than it is for harder problems (e.g. 5 + 3). If this probability is low, a backup strategy (e.g., count-all or count-up) is used. Initially, the model was given just two strategies – count-all and retrieval – on the basis that these are the strategies commonly used by 4-year-olds. The model was then trained on the 81 possible single-digit addition problems (all the combinations with values of 1–9 for both addends). After each problem had been presented 60 times, the count-up strategy was added. Figure 11.9 shows the model's use of the different strategies over time. After the initial training period (i.e., after each problem had been seen 60 times), the model used count-all on

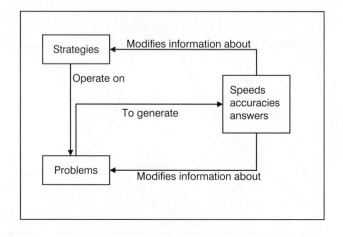

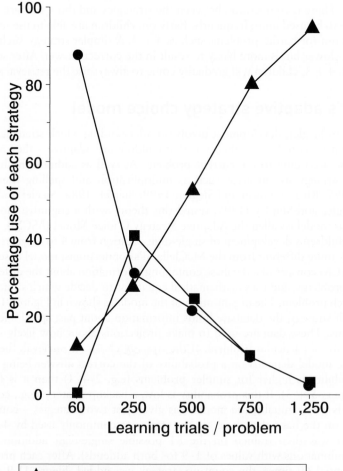

almost all the problems. After 250 presentations of each problem, the use of count-all decreased dramatically and the model started to use the count-up and retrieval strategies. After this, the use of retrieval increased and the use of the other two strategies decreased. In accordance with Siegler's 'overlapping waves' idea, the model used different strategies to a different degree at different points in time. The model exhibited the same pattern of strategy use observed in children.

There are four key components of Siegler's theory – variability, adaptiveness, change and generalization – which are demonstrated in the behaviour of the model (and children). *Variability* is illustrated by the probability of a strategy being selected. For $2 + 1$, there is a higher probability of retrieval than for $5 + 3$. The model displays *adaptiveness* in that better strategies are sought for complex problems. Both children and the model adapt their strategy choice to the problem being solved. *Change* is demonstrated by the probability of strategy use, which changes over time as a function of previous speed and accuracy. As the model gains experience and sees a problem such as $5 + 3$ more often, the chance of using retrieval increases. The model uses generalization in that problems with similar features will be solved by using similar strategies. For example, problems with large numbers such as $9 + 3$ are best solved using the count-up strategy. The model learns to solve most of the large number problems with the count-up strategy.

In summary, Siegler's Adaptive Strategy Choice Model is an implementation of his theory of how children's use of strategies changes over time. The theory predicts that simple strategies will be used at first, that multiple strategies are available to children (and used by them) at the same time, and that use of retrieval will increase over time until all simple additions problems are solved using this strategy. The model's performance conforms to these predictions and so the theory is supported.

Language acquisition 1: The past tense

One of the classic computational models in the domain of language acquisition is Rumelhart and McClelland's (1986) past tense acquisition model. This is a connectionist model (similar to the balance beam model discussed above) so there are no explicit rules in the system, just patterns of weights between units. This approach is in opposition to the view that language has rules stored in an explicit form. For example, the idea that we have a mental rule that says 'add *ed* to a verb to make a past tense construction' or 'add *s* to make a plural'. Rumelhart and McClelland's model was an attempt to account for the three stages of past-tense acquisition found in English-speaking children. As we saw in Chapter 4, young children make overgeneralization errors in which the regular past tense ending is applied to irregular verbs as well as regular verbs.

There are three stages in children's development of the past tense (Kuczaj, 1977). In the first stage, children are able to use the regular past tense correctly. They also produce irregular verbs, for which the past tenses are generally given correctly. In the next stage, a greater number of verbs are used, most of which are regular. At this point, children appear to have some knowledge of the relevant linguistic rules as they are able to create past tenses for verbs. Regular tense endings are applied to irregular verbs in an overgeneralization of the '-ed' rule (e.g., 'wented', 'goed', 'eated'). Lastly, both irregular and regular verb endings are correctly produced and novel verbs are given regular endings, as Berko (1958) demonstrated (e.g., 'ricked', 'glinged'). This developmental pattern is a U-shaped curve, in which children make few errors in stages 1 and 3, but make many errors in stage 2 (see Figure 11.10).

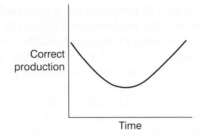

One interpretation of this pattern is the dual route model (Pinker, 1994, 1999). According to this view children first learn individual words, then learn the rule for forming the past tense. At this point they use the rule incorrectly on irregular verbs as well as on regular forms. Later, they learn a list of exceptions to the rule. From this point, children produce past tense forms through two routes: either using the rule to generate regular past tense forms, or using the list of irregular forms. This view has been challenged by the work of Rumelhart and McClelland (1986).

Rumelhart and McClelland's model

Rumelhart and McClelland's (1986) model is a type of connectionist network known as a single layer pattern associator. 'Single layer' refers to the fact that, unlike McClelland's balance beam network it does not have a hidden layer, it just has input and output units. There is, therefore, just a single layer of connections between the input and output layer. It is called a pattern associator because its job is to associate the root, or uninflected, forms of verbs with their past tense forms. The basic idea is that a verb, such as 'come' is inputted and, after extensive training, the model produces 'came' as the output.

One of the difficulties in creating such a model is determining how to encode the information given as input. An obvious thing to do in this case would be to have 44 or so input units, and the same number of output units, representing each of the phonemes in English. In order to input 'came', one would activate the k, $e\partial$ and m units (see Chapter 4 for a list of phonemes). However, this does not encode any information about the *order* in which the phonemes occur. Does the activation of k, $e\partial$ and m mean 'came', 'cmae', 'akem', 'aimk', 'make' or 'mkae'?

In order to include information about the order of the phonemes, Rumelhart and McClelland proposed using a system of Wickelphones, named after a system devised by Wickelgren (1969), in which words are represented as a sequence of context-sensitive phonemes. Each phoneme is represented as a triple, containing the preceding, current, and succeeding sounds. For example, 'came' can be represented as three wickelphones: # $k\ e\partial$, $k\ e\partial\ m$, $e\partial\ m$ # (the # represents a word boundary). However, this scheme would require a lot of input units. Even if just 35 phonemes were used, there would need to be 35^3 units in each layer – which works out at 42 875! With 42 875 input units and 42 875 output units, there would be 2×10^9 connections (that's 2 000 000 000). Something more compact was needed.

Rumelhart and McClelland decided to use features of the phonemes as input, rather than the actual Wickelphones. If you refer back to Tables 4.3 and 4.4, you will see that phonemes can be described in various ways. For example, k is a voiceless, velar, stop consonant. Rumelhart and McClelland simplified the ways in which phonemes can be described into the four-dimensional scheme illustrated in Table 11.2. The first dimension splits sounds into interrupted consonants,

Table 11.2	Categorization of phonemes.

Place of articulation		Front		Middle		Back	
Voiced (+v) or voiceless (−v) (consonants) Long (l) or short (s) (vowels)		+v / l	−v / s	+v / l	−v / s	+v / l	−v / s
Interrupted consonant	Stop	b	p	d	t	g	k
	Nasal	m		n		ŋ	
Continuous consonant	Fricative	v / ð	f / θ	z	s	ʒ / dʒ	ʃ / tʃ
	Liquid	w/l		r		j	h
Vowel	High	iː	ɪ	əʊ		uː	ʌ
	Low	æ	e	aɪ	æ / aː	aʊ	ɔː / ɒ

continuous consonants and vowels. Dimension two further subdivides these into stop and nasal consonants, fricatives and sonorant consonants, and high and low vowels. Place of articulation – front, middle or back – is the third dimension, and the fourth dimension further divides sounds into voiced or voiceless consonants, and long or short vowels. Under this scheme, k is referred to as a voiceless, back, stop, interrupted consonant, and $e\partial$ is a long, low, front vowel.

The upshot of this scheme is that each phoneme can be represented as a pattern of these features, termed Wickelfeatures, across a number of input units. In order to include a different input unit for each feature of each phoneme in each position of the word, including the word boundary marker for the first and third phonemes, there would still need to be 1210 input and output units. By reducing some of the redundancy in this scheme (each feature of each phoneme would activate 16 input units) Rumelhart and McClelland managed to reduce the network to 460 input and output units. The result of all this is that each present tense verb can be inputted as a unique pattern of activated units in the input layer, and its past tense form can be represented as a unique pattern in the output layer.

The pattern associator has an encoding network attached to the front, and a decoding network attached to the back. These were added so that the model could convert a phonological representation of the input to Wickelfeatures for processing, and convert the output back into phonological form. The structure of the model is shown in Figure 11.11. The actual model is much larger than shown in the Figure as it has 460 input units and 460 output units, rather than just the four shown.

Training and results. The model was trained on lists of verbs given to the model in two stages. The first group contained ten high-frequency verbs, of which eight were irregular (come, get, give, make, take, go, have, feel) and two were regular (live and look). Each of these ten verbs was presented to the network ten times. This first group represents the verbs that children are likely to hear most often. Once the pattern associator was trained on these, the second group was added. This group contained 410 medium-frequency verbs, of which 76 were irregular. The network was trained on both the high- and medium-frequency verbs a further 190 times. At first there were many errors during this second phase, corresponding to the second stage of acquisition in which overgeneralization occurs, but by the end the model was able to produce the correct past tense forms.

Figure 11.11

Structure of the
past-tense network.

Source: McClelland, James L.,
David E. Rumelhart, and PDP
Research Group., *Parallel Distributed Processing, Volume 2:
Explorations in the Microstructure of Cognition: Psychological
and Biological Models*, figure 1,
p. 222 © 1986 Massachusetts
Institute of Technology, by permission of The MIT Press.

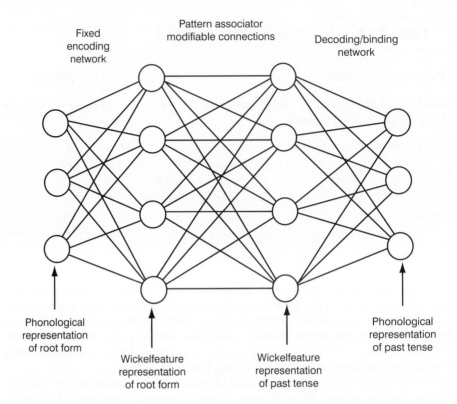

During the training phase the model was presented with the correct past-tense
form as well as the present-tense input. If the output produced by the model did not
match the correct past-tense form, the weights of the connections between the input
and output units were adjusted. If an output unit was inactive and should have been
active, all the weights for the connections from active input units were increased. If
an output unit was active and should not have been, the weights were decreased. In
this way, the model learns from being 'taught' the correct answers.

After these two training phases the model was tested on 86 low-frequency verbs,
of which 14 were irregular. Performance was poorer on the irregular verbs, as is to
be expected, but the endings given for regular verbs were mostly correct. This, also,
is in accord with the behaviour of children presented with novel verbs, in that irregular verbs are often regularized but not all regular verbs are given regular endings.
For six of the 72 regular verbs, the model did not generate a clear past-tense form,
but it produced the correct form for 48 of them. The remaining 18 resulted in either
an incorrect output, or two or more different answers, of which one may be correct.
These, along with the outputs for the irregular verbs, are shown in Table 11.3.

In summary, the model produced the U-shaped curve found in children. After
training, it was able to produce most of the correct regular past-tense endings, and
some correct irregular past-tense endings. The main implication of these results is
that although the link between regular verb stems and past tense forms can be
described using rules, past-tense creation can be achieved by a mechanism which does
not use explicit rules. Rather than a rule, knowledge of how to form the past tense is
distributed across the network. In addition, the links between irregular verb stems
and past tense forms are encoded in the same set of weights as the regular forms,
whereas the dual-route account requires two components: a rule for producing regular past tense forms and a list of irregular verbs that are exceptions to the rule.

Regular verb input	Regular verb past tense output	Irregular verb input	Irregular verb past tense output
Guard	Guard	Bid	Bid
	Guarded		
Kid	Kid	Thrust	Thrusted
	Kidded		
Mate	Mated	Bend	Bended
	Maded		
Squat	Squated	Lend	Lended
	Squat		
	Squawked		
Carp	Carped	Creep	Creeped
	Carpted		
Drip	Dripted	Weep	Weeped
	Dripped		Wept
Map	Mapted	Catch	Catched
	Mapped		
Shape	Shaped	Breed	Breeded
	Shipped		
Sip	Sipped	Grind	Grind
	Sepped		
Slip	Slept	Wind	Wind
Smoke	Smokted	Cling	Clinged
	Smoke		Clung
Snap	Snapted	Dig	Digged
Step	Stepted	Stick	Sticked
Type	Typted	Tear	Teared
Brown	Browned		
	Brawned		
Hug	Hug		
Mail	Mailed		
	Mumbled		
Tour	Toureder		
	Toured		

Table 11.3

Some of the past-tense forms produced by the model.

Source: McClelland, Rumelhart and PDP Research Group (1986). © Massachusetts Institute of Technology (1986) reproduced with permission.

Criticisms. A critique of Rumelhart and McClelland's work is given by Pinker and Prince (1988). One of their arguments is that the U-shaped curve produced by the model is the result of the way in which the input was presented, rather than the result of a learning process similar to that of children. However, the U-shaped curve displayed by children is, in this case, also input-driven. Children are first exposed to high-frequency verbs, then medium-frequency and so forth. Although children receive continuous input, rather than discrete chunks, the U-shaped curve is still a reflection of the language they hear. Another of Pinker and Prince's arguments concerns the errors made by the model. They point out that some of the errors were unlike those encountered in children. For example, the model generated 'membled' as a past tense form of 'mail'. This is probably due to the fact that the model does not 'conceive' of verbs in terms of stems + suffixes. This also means that although the model is capable of encoding specific verbs' endings, it cannot encode the general formula for creating a past-tense ending. It is, however, possible to argue that the general rule is encoded implicitly in the regularity extractions performed on a whole corpus of verbs. Pinker and Prince also note that the Wickelfeature structure is inappropriate for this situation. For example, homophones are not represented in a distinct way. 'Ring' (as in 'to ring a bell'), 'ring' (as in 'to ring the answer on a test'), and wring (as in 'to wring someone's neck') would all be treated identically by the model, yet the past tense forms are 'rang', 'ringed' and 'wrung' respectively.

An attempt to address some of these issues was made by Plunkett and Marchman (1991). They created a connectionist network with an input layer, an output layer and a hidden layer, with 20 units in each layer. One of the main differences between this model and the earlier one by Rumelhart and McClelland is that Plunkett and Marchman did not use Wickelfeatures. The units in the input and output layers still represent features of the phonemes, but in a much simpler way. Each of three phonemes can be represented by a pattern of activation across six units. One unit corresponds to whether the phoneme is a consonant or a vowel, the second is for the voiced/voiceless distinction. There are two units each for place and manner of articulation. Eighteen of the input units are thus used to encode the three phonemes. The final two units are unused in the input layer, and represent different suffixes. A second key difference is that Plunkett and Marchman focused on the way in which they presented input to the model, claiming that verb morphology development and 'U'-shaped learning can still be modelled when a continuous (rather than discontinuous) training set is employed.

Plunkett and Marchman trained their network on 700 verbs, but carried out a series of simulations in which they varied the frequency with which different words occurred. When 74 per cent of the input set consisted of irregular verbs, the model did not learn the regular past tense. When they changed the frequencies such that 74 per cent of the input consisted of regular verbs, irregular past tense forms were not learnt. When the regular/irregular ratio was 50/50 (which is similar to what children hear), the model performed well.

The debate between Pinker and McClelland, and their colleagues, has demonstrated incredible longevity, turning to the wider issue of whether connectionist systems in general are capable of providing an explanation of the acquisition of past-tense morphology. Pinker and Ullman (2002) argued that connectionist models that have succeeded in modelling this phenomenon (e.g., Hare, Elman and Daugherty, 1995) have done so because they specify mechanisms dedicated to dealing with the past tense, which could easily be characterized as innate rules. Pinker and Ullman advocate, instead, the dual-route system. According to this 'words and rules' theory, irregular past tense endings are individually learned and retrieved from a lexical subdivision of declarative memory whilst regular endings are generated using a rule stored in a grammatical subdivision of procedural memory. Overregularization errors are avoided by a process of blocking, whereby the default regular ending is blocked when there is an alternative irregular ending available. McClelland and Patterson (2002) discuss three predictions implied by the words and rules model. First, that there will be a sudden acquisition of the regular-ending rule; second, that this rule will be applied in a uniform manner – its effects will not be affected by phonology, semantics or other factors; third, that the two mechanisms in the model will be genetically and neurologically separable. McClelland and Patterson present evidence that these three predictions are not upheld: Child language data does not show a sudden acquisition of regularization (Brown, 1973), regularization is not uniform (Ramscar,

2002), and there is no evidence of genetic and neurological separability (Bird *et al.*, 2003). They also argue that three predictions of a connectionist account are upheld. The regular past tense inflection is acquired gradually, there is a graded sensitivity to phonological and semantic content, and there is a single, integrated mechanism for both regular and irregular forms. Westermann (1997, 1998) presents just such a connectionist model, which models past tense acquisition with single mechanism. This is achieved by utilizing two representational forms, applied to all words, which allows the double dissociation between regular and irregular endings to emerge.

Language acquisition 2: MOSAIC – Model Of Syntax Acquisition In Children

We will now consider a cognitive model which has been used to test several theories in the domain of language acquisition (see Chapter 4 for a description of some of the key theoretical positions). Nativists explain children's language acquisition by positing innate knowledge, whereas constructivists argue that children learn a lot about language from the linguistic input they receive. The model we will look at is a model of how children learn from their input. The basic idea is that if a computer model is given the sort of input that a child will get from his or her mother, we can see to what extent children's speech can be explained by learning about language from the input.

MOSAIC (Model Of Syntax Acquisition In Children) is a constructivist cognitive model that embodies a distributional theory of language acquisition (see Chapter 4). This model has been used by a group of researchers to examine a number of different phenomena in child language such as optional infinitive errors (Croker, 2007; Croker, Pine and Gobet, 2000, Freudenthal *et al.*, 2007, Freudenthal, Pine and Gobet, 2001, 2002a, 2006, 2009); case-marking errors (Croker, Pine and Gobet, 2001); negation errors (Croker, Pine and Gobet, 2003); subject omission errors (Freudenthal, Pine and Gobet, 2002b, 2007); vocabulary acquisition (Jones, Gobet and Pine, 2000a, 2007, 2008); and verb islands (Jones, 2007; Jones, Gobet and Pine, 2000b).

How the model learns

The theory behind MOSAIC is that a lot of children's language can be explained just from the input a child receives. An important feature of MOSAIC is its ability to deal with semi-naturalistic data. Cognitive models of aspects of language acquisition are often criticized for producing output that looks very little like natural language, derived from input that has been transformed into an abstraction of language. The input given to MOSAIC is *semi-* or *pseudo-naturalistic* data, taken from maternal speech. This input consists of transcribed speech presented as text (e.g., 'he liked it'). Whilst not *fully* naturalistic (i.e., an unsegmented audio stream), this input representation is more 'naturalistic' than the representations used by other models. The output produced by MOSAIC also appears in this form. This means that the predictions made by the model can be feasibly compared to child speech data, transcribed similarly.

MOSAIC consists of a hierarchical network that grows as input is presented to the model. This is not a network in the connectionist sense of the term (i.e., it is not like the balance beam or past tense models described above). The network is a structure that contains a list of words and phrases. MOSAIC is given maternal speech, taken from recorded mother–child interactions as its input, and uses this to gradually build up the network of knowledge about language. Initially, the model has no knowledge – it is, in a sense, a 'blank slate'. When an input utterance contains words

Figure 11.12

Network formed after the utterance 'he sings loudly' is presented three times to the model.

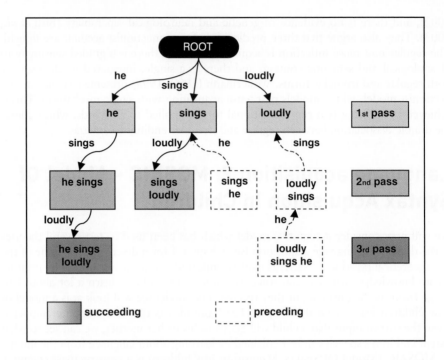

that are not yet known to the model, each word is stored as a piece of information (a 'node' in the network). These new nodes are created at the first layer of the network. This first layer may be seen as the layer where the 'primitives' of the network (i.e., the individual words that have been seen by the model) are learned and stored. When a word that is already known is inputted, the model starts to learn about the context of the word. It stores information about which words preceded and succeeded the current word. Thus, over time, the model learns the distributional statistics of both words that follow and words that precede a given word. Figure 11.12 depicts a fragment of a network created in this manner.

Another feature of MOSAIC is probabilistic learning. There is a parameter which determines how likely it is that any given word in the input is learnt. If this parameter is set to 0.1, a word must be seen, on average, 10 times before it is added to the network. This form of learning gives a positive bias to words and phrases that occur many times in the input corpus. If a particular mother's speech is used as the input sample, and the sample contains frequent use of a verb such as 'walk', the model will learn a lot about the word 'walk', including what words are used before and after it. If another verb (e.g. 'talk') is not used much, the model will not learn so much about it. As a result, the model will learn more about aspects of language that occur more frequently in maternal speech. The output is therefore a reflection of the frequency with which words occur, rather than a reflection of which items are present in the input.

Creating links between words. What has been described so far is essentially rote learning. In addition to this rote learning of utterances, MOSAIC is able to generate novel utterances that were not present in the input sample using *generative links*, an important feature of the model. Generative links are 'horizontal' links between nodes that have contextual similarities. If two words occur frequently in similar contexts (e.g., if they are succeeded by the same items), then a generative link can be made between these items. In Figure 11.13, an example is given in which the model

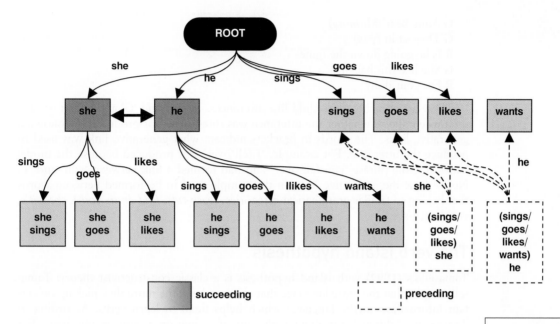

Figure 11.13

Generative link formation: 'he' and 'she' are linked by virtue of possessing child nodes in common.

is trained on a data set in which the items 'he' and 'she' are followed by the verbs 'sings', 'jumps' and 'likes'. On the basis of the similarity of the contexts in which 'he' and 'she' have been seen, a generative link is created. So words that are used in similar contexts become interchangeable. If, for example, 'need' and 'want' are used in similar contexts – if they are preceded and succeeded by similar items (e.g., the model may have learned phrases such as 'do you need it?' and 'do you want it?') – a generative link can be created between them. This means that if the model has learnt the phrase 'Tigger needs sweeties', it will also be capable of producing 'Tigger wants sweeties'. This is a novel utterance – it does not appear in the mother' speech. According to the theory behind MOSAIC, children produce novel utterances by analyzing the distributional properties of the input they receive and learning about similarities between words.

Producing output. Once a network has been created, it can be used to produce utterances in two ways – by recognition and by generation. Utterances produced by recognition are essentially rote-learned phrases and portions of phrases that occur in the input. Production by generation utilizes the generative links to create utterances not seen in the input. From the example network in Figure 11.13, 'she sings', 'she goes' and 'she likes' would be produced by recognition. 'She wants' would be produced by generation. Here are some examples of the output produced by the model when trained on a full corpus of maternal utterances:

G Tidy your feet *(wash)*
G I fell over *(you)*
R That's Mummy and Daddy
G Draw you some more in a bit *(find)*
R Mummy do it
G It's gonna read a book *(she's)*
G Does you say *(did)*
R Coming to the party too

G Anne Bear *(Mummy)*
G They sit in *(you)*
R Is he going down the mine
G She like this baby *(I)*
R For your dolly

These are arguably quite child-like utterances. The 'R' and 'G' at the start of each utterance indicate whether the utterance was rote-learned or produced by following generative links. The words in brackets indicate what generative link was used to produce the utterance. For example, 'I fell over' was produced because the model had learnt the phrase 'you fell over' and had formed a link between 'you' and 'I'. Notice how the generative links in this sample tend to be formed between words that belong to similar grammatical categories: *wash-tidy, find-draw, you-I, she's-it's, you-they, I-she*.

The verb island hypothesis

Tomasello's (1992) verb island hypothesis is a classic constructivist theory. Tomasello argues that the more language that children hear, the more they pick up on certain information in the language which helps them to learn verbs. According to Tomasello, children learn about verbs one at a time on a verb-specific basis. For example, when a child hears 'I hit the ball', they learn that 'hit' can be preceded by a hitter ('I') and succeeded by a hittee ('the ball'). The words 'I' and 'ball' will not be used with other verbs (such as 'kick') unless the child learns that these words can be used together by hearing a phrase such as 'I kick the ball'. The more sentences which include the verb 'hit' that a child hears, the more they will know about the verb in terms of the sorts of words that can precede and succeed it. Similarly, once the child has heard a lot of 'kick' sentences, they will then know a lot about that verb. A 'verb island' is a knowledge structure based around a verb that is not connected to other verb-based knowledge structures.

Here are some examples from child data taken from the Manchester corpus (Theakston *et al.*, 2000) of the CHILDES database (MacWhinney and Snow, 1990).

Tom walked to town
You walk there
He's walking the dog
She walks him
Cindy walked Mr Snowman
I want to walk pooh bear
She talked to him
Can I talk

As you can see, the child has learnt a lot about the verb 'walk'. He/she has learnt that lots of different subjects can precede 'walk', and that lots of things of different objects can succeed 'walk'. He/she has less knowledge about 'talk'. He/she does not, for example, say 'I want to talk to Mr Snowman'. According to the theory, this is because he/she has heard of phrases containing 'walk', and fewer phrases containing 'talk'. In Tomasello's terms, the child has a *verb island* for 'walk' but not for 'talk'. This argument goes against nativist theories as nativists would predict that children will learn the same aspects of all verbs at the same time as a result of their innate knowledge of language. According to Tomasello, children build up grammatical structures in which verbs are the items that take *arguments*. The arguments of verbs are subjects (preceding items) and objects (succeeding items). Tomasello predicts that while pronouns (I, you, she, they, we), proper nouns (Mummy, Daddy), and common nouns (Baby, Dolly) will be the arguments of verb structures, verbs will not be arguments of other structures. Therefore, when examining children's speech, we would expect to find that some verbs are followed by many other items, but that non-verb items (such as pronouns) do not follow this pattern.

MOSAIC and the verb island hypothesis. What can this model tell us about the verb island hypothesis? According to Tomasello, children learn in a verb-specific way and should therefore show evidence of having verb islands. Tomasello also predicts that children will not have islands for other word categories. Jones *et al.* (2000a) analyzed child speech and found 10 verb islands. A verb was counted as having an 'island' if it was used with at least 10 different nouns. When the output from MOSAIC was analyzed in the same way, 10 verb islands were also found. What is particularly interesting, however, is that when the child data was analyzed, other island types were also found. The child had a lot of pronoun islands and also a few islands for proper nouns and common nouns. None of these are predicted by Tomasello. Figure 11.14 shows the number of each type of island demonstrated in the speech of the child and the output from the model. Notice that MOSAIC predicts the existence of all four island types. While the verb island hypothesis is correct with respect to verbs, it doesn't take into account other word categories, so is only partially correct. MOSAIC accounts for phenomena which are consistent with the verb-island hypothesis (the verb islands) and also accounts for phenomena which are inconsistent with the verb-island hypothesis (e.g. pronoun islands). This suggests that there are several aspects of child language which can be explained from the input a child receives.

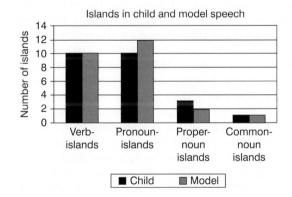

Figure 11.14

Verb islands produced by MOSAIC and a child.

The optional infinitive hypothesis

The optional infinitive hypothesis (Wexler, 1994, 1996) is an attempt to provide a unified nativist account of young children's knowledge of verb inflection across a variety of different languages. According to this view, by the time children begin to produce multi-word utterances they have basic knowledge of grammar. However, there is an initial stage – the optional infinitive stage – during which they lack the knowledge that tense is obligatory in certain utterance types. For example, 'she *goes* for a walk' is grammatical but 'she *go* for a walk' is not. Children in this stage are, however, assumed to know everything else about tense and agreement. Tense refers to verb morphology used to situate the verb in time (e.g., *-s* as in 'she goes' or *-ed* as in 'they walked'). Agreement refers to the form of the verb with respect to the subject (e.g., 'I run', 'he runs', 'they run').

The optional infinitive hypothesis can be used to explain why children sometimes fail to use appropriately tensed forms (e.g., 'that go in there' instead of 'that goes in there' or 'that going in there' instead of 'that's going in there'). Such errors are interpreted not as the dropping of inflections or auxiliaries, but as the use of untensed forms in contexts where tensed forms are obligatory. Wexler makes very clear predictions about what a child in the optional infinitive stage of development should and should not say. Children are predicted to produce forms such as 'she hide' alongside forms in which the -*s* is present ('she hides') as tense is optional.

MOSAIC and the optional infinitive hypothesis. An alternative explanation for the phenomena described by Wexler is that the formation of syntactic relationships in children's speech can be accounted for in the input the child receives from external sources, in particular parental input. The pattern of verb forms used by a child is a result of the distribution of these forms in the input. For example, a child may produce the utterance 'she going' which is accounted for in the optional infinitive hypothesis as the use of an untensed form in a position where tense is required, rather than the omission of an auxiliary. Obviously, a child should not hear her mother saying 'she going'; however, she will hear utterances such as 'where is she going?' and 'is she going to the shops?'

Croker (2007) compared the output of MOSAIC to the data from three children, taken from the Manchester corpus (Theakston *et al.*, 2000) of the CHILDES database (MacWhinney and Snow, 1990). Table 11.4 shows the rate at which the three children (Anne, Aran, Becky) and MOSAIC made optional infinitive errors, such as 'he go/going/gone', 'she go/going/gone' or 'I going/gone'. The rates of error of this type are fairly similar with respect to masculine utterances. The rate for feminine utterances is more variable across children, but the main difference between the children lies in the error rate for 'I' errors. Anne makes 38 errors in 633 utterances and Becky makes 87 errors in 1007 utterances, whereas Aran only makes 7 in 1583 utterances. Although it *could* be argued that these rates appear negligible, Becky's error rate is 19 times that of Aran. The data in Table 11.4 illustrate three things. First, children make optional infinitive errors in conjunction with both first- ('I') and third-person-singular ('he', 'she') subjects. Second, the error rates are much higher for third-person-singular subjects – this is largely due to the fact that for most verbs in English the correct form of a present-tense verb for the first (and second) person is identical to the uninflected form (e.g., 'I go'). Third, although the rate at which such errors are made is not consistent across children, the number of errors produced by MOSAIC is comparable to the error rates of the children.

As well as English, MOSAIC has been used to model Dutch, German and Spanish-speaking children's use of optional infinitives (Freudenthal *et al.*, 2006, 2007, 2009). These results suggest that the constructivist theory embodied by MOSAIC can go some way towards explaining the acquisition of language. Children's speech errors can be explained without assuming any domain-specific knowledge of linguistic structure. Therefore such errors cannot, by themselves, be taken as evidence for innate grammatical knowledge on the part of the child.

Table 11.4		Anne	Aran	Becky	MOSAIC
	He	17.09	12.68	17.89	20.4
	She	24.39	33.33	9.26	13.6
	I	6.00	0.44	8.64	1.6

Percentage of optional infinitive errors produced by MOSAIC and three children.

Concluding comments

One of the main points illustrated in the above examples is that cognitive models can be used to test theories and predictions. In order to do this, we need to know what predictions are made by a theory, and what processes, mechanisms, knowledge and abilities are hypothesized to account for developmental change. However, some theories are not well specified. They do not give enough information about exactly which processes are involved in development and how these processes work. For example, Piaget explains development in terms of accommodation and assimilation, but it is not clear how to go about applying these concepts to a developmental task. This means that it is hard to make very precise predictions about exactly how children will perform on a task and how and why performance will change over time.

Cognitive models can be used to help 'tighten up' theories. A cognitive model is a simulation of children's performance; it is a computer program which carries out a task in the same way as a child is theorized to do. When creating a model, we have to specify everything about the task, such as the initial knowledge of children, their mental capacity, their perceptual capabilities and so on. A model is, therefore, a theory of task performance and is very similar to a written theory. The only difference is that instead of a verbal description of the theory, it is 'embodied' within a computer programme. A written theory can be turned into a cognitive model and this model can be used to test the predictions of the theory.

The examples presented above are just a small fraction of the many instances in which cognitive models have been employed to test theories of cognitive development. Mareschal and Shultz (1999) developed a connectionist model of seriation in transitive reasoning. They demonstrated that the stages of development proposed by Piaget are not necessarily a result of qualitative shifts in knowledge, but can be achieved by a system in which very gradual changes to connection weights occur, alongside modifications to the architecture of the network. These modifications consisted of the automatic addition of new hidden units to the network when no further learning could take place. Shultz (1998) was similarly able to demonstrate that the abrupt changes in performance on conservation tasks (Piaget, 1954) can be accounted for by the addition of hidden units. Mareschal, Plunkett and Harris (1999) created a model of object perception in infancy. They used this model to explain why young infants show surprise when their expectations about physical objects are violated (e.g., Baillargeon, 1987a, 1987b; see Chapter 2), yet they do not manually search for hidden objects until months later (e.g., Piaget 1954; see Chapter 3).

Cognitive models have also been used to help us understand developmental disorders. Thomas and Karmiloff-Smith (2003) modified Plunkett and Marchman's (1991) model of past-tense acquisition to test different hypotheses of past-tense formation in children with Williams syndrome. Harm and Seidenberg (1999) modified a model of normal reading development to simulate dyslexia, Joanisse and Seidenberg (2003) have modelled specific language impairment, and Cohen (2007) presents a model of autism.

The most recent development is the emerging field of neuroconstructivism (Mareschal *et al.*, 2007). This approach is an attempt to combine constructivism, cognitive neuroscience and computational modelling, so that cognitive development can be studied from multiple perspectives at once. Neuroconstructivism is concerned with different levels of explanation that are not independent of one another, from neural activity, through cognitive processes, to behaviour. The idea behind this view is that it will encourage theories and models that attempt to explain cognitive development at multiple levels.

Summary

A cognitive model is a simulation of cognitive processes that is used to explore theories of performance on a task. The Tower of Nottingham is a task that has been used by Jones, Ritter and Wood to compare different theories of cognitive development. Jones *et al.*'s model is a production system, which means its knowledge is represented as a set of facts and rules. Having built a model of adult performance on the task, they made several modifications to it in order to construct different models of children's performance. Two of the modifications involved limiting the working memory capacity of the model, and the third involved manipulating the likelihood that different strategies would be used. All three models led to a more child-like performance on the task, but the strategy choice model provided the best fit to the child data.

The balance beam task. Initially used by Inhelder and Piaget, this task has been studied extensively by Siegler, who theorized that children use a series of rules of increasing complexity to solve balance beam problems. McClelland created a connectionist model of Siegler's theory of balance beam task performance. The model was trained by presenting a series of balance beam problems and telling it the correct answer. If the model made an incorrect prediction, the connection weights were altered. After training, the model was given balance problems to solve. The model was assessed on the basis of which of Siegler's rules the answers conformed to. The performance of the model changed over time as a result of its experience, showing the same developmental pattern as children. This finding shows support for Siegler's theory.

Simple addition. When children attempt to add two numbers together, they have a number of strategies available to them, including the *count-all*, *count-up*, *decomposition* and *retrieval* strategies. As children get older, their use of strategy changes. Younger children use complex strategies less often, whereas for older children the more complex strategies are more efficient. Siegler's theory is that although children move towards more frequent use of more sophisticated strategies, they make use of all the strategies available to them and will thus use different strategies at the same time. At any one time, children have several different ways of thinking about problems. There is competition between the strategies and those that are more efficient come to be used more frequently. Siegler and Shipley tested this theory with a cognitive model of the theory, the Adaptive Strategy Choice Model, which consists of a database containing information about the different strategies and problems, and uses mathematical equations to decide which strategy will be used on each problem. The model was trained on single-digit addition problems. Initially, the model used count-all on almost all the problems. Later, the use of count-all decreased dramatically and the model started to use the count-up and retrieval strategies. After this, the use of retrieval increased and the use of the other two strategies decreased. In accordance with Siegler's 'overlapping waves' idea, the model used different strategies to a different degree at different points in time. The model exhibited the same pattern of strategy use observed in children.

Language acquisition 1: The past tense. Rumelhart and McClelland's connectionist model of past-tense acquisition was an attempt to account for the three stages of past-tense acquisition found in English-speaking children. In the first stage, children produce correct past tense forms of regular and irregular verbs. In the next stage, children apply regular tense endings to irregular verbs in an overgeneralization of the '-ed' rule. Lastly, both irregular and regular verb endings are correctly produced. Rumelhart and McClelland used a system of Wickelfeatures to encode information in the input and output units of their model. The model was trained on lists of verbs given to the model in two stages. The first group contained 10 high-frequency verbs and the second group contained 410 medium-frequency verbs. After training, the model was tested on 86 low-frequency verbs. Performance was poorer on the irregular verbs, but the endings given for regular verbs were mostly correct, in accord with the behaviour of children presented with novel verbs. Pinker and Prince offered a number of criticisms of the model, including the argument that the U-shaped curve produced by the model is the result of the way in which the input was presented. They also pointed out that some of the errors made by the model were unlike those encountered in children. In response to these criticisms, Plunkett and Marchman created a connectionist network in which the input was not staged and Wickelfeatures were not used. The performance of this model depended on this ratio of regular to irregular verbs in the input. When the ratio was 50/50 (which is similar to what children hear), the model performed well.

Language acquisition 2: MOSAIC – Model Of Syntax Acquisition In Children. MOSAIC is a constructivist cognitive model that embodies a distributional theory of language acquisition. It consists of a hierarchical network that grows as input is presented to the model. In addition to simple rote learning, the model forms links between words which can be used to generate novel utterances. MOSAIC has been used to test several theories, including Tomasello's verb island hypothesis. According to Tomasello, children learn about verbs one at a time on a verb-specific basis, creating 'verb islands'. Although children are predicted to have verb islands, they are not predicted to have islands for other word categories. Jones, Gobet and Pine analyzed child speech and found 10 verb islands. When the output from MOSAIC was analyzed in the same way, 10 verb islands were also found. Other island types were also found in child speech and were produced by the model. MOSAIC has also been used to test Wexler's optional infinitive hypothesis. This is a nativist account of children's knowledge of verb inflection, according to which children use untensed verb forms in phrases that require tensed forms as they lack one piece of linguistic knowledge. Croker compared the output of MOSAIC to the data from three children, and found similar rates of errors. The constructivist theory embodied by MOSAIC thus provides an alternative explanation of children's speech errors.

Discussion questions

1 What are the similarities and differences between computational models of cognition and theories of cognition?

2 Do the models discussed in this chapter have any 'innate' knowledge?

3 What built-in mechanisms do these models have in order to learn or perform a task?

4 Choose a cognitive task or behaviour you are interested in. What knowledge or learning mechanisms would you need to build in to a computational model in order to produce the behaviour?

5 What does it tell us if a model is able to simulate behaviour in several domains?

Further Reading

Books and chapters

Bates, E. A. and Elman, J. L. (2002). Connectionism and the study of change. In Mark Johnson (Ed.), *Brain development and cognition: A reader* (2nd Ed.). Oxford: Blackwell.

Elizabeth Bates and Jeffrey Elman present a historical overview of the role of computer metaphors and simulations in developmental psychology.

Klahr, D. and MacWhinney, B. (1998). Information Processing. In D. Kuhn and R. S. Siegler (Eds), W. Damon (Series Ed.). *Handbook of child psychology (5th ed.): Vol. 2: Cognition, perception, and language* (pp. 631–678). New York: Wiley.

In this readable chapter, David Klahr and Brian MacWhinney explain the differences between production systems and connectionist models, with reference to several examples of each.

McClelland, J. L. and Jenkins, E. (1991). Nature, nurture and connections: Implications of connectionist models for cognitive development. In K. Van Lehn (Ed.), *Architectures for intelligence* (pp. 41–73). Hillsdale, NJ: Erlbaum.

James McClelland and Eric Jenkins present the connectionist model of the balance beam task described above.

Thomas, M. S. C. and Karmiloff-Smith, A. (2002). Modelling typical and atypical cognitive development. In U. Goswami (Ed.), *Handbook of Childhood Development* (pp. 575–599). Oxford: Blackwell.

In addition to discussing some classic models of typical development, Michael Thomas and Annette Karmiloff-Smith survey models of atypical development, including dyslexia and Williams syndrome.

Articles

Freudenthal, D., Pine, J. M. and Gobet, F. (2009). Simulating the referential properties of Dutch, German and English Root Infinitives in MOSAIC. *Language Learning and Development*, 5, 1–29.

Daniel Freudenthal, Julian Pine and Fernand Gobet give a detailed description of how MOSAIC works and show how the model can explain optional infinitive phenomena in three languages.

Jones, G., Ritter, F. E. and Wood, D. J. (2000). Using a cognitive architecture to examine what develops. *Psychological Science*, 11(2), 93–100.

The way in which the Tower of Nottingham model was used to compare different theories of cognitive development is described by Gary Jones, Frank Ritter and David Wood.

McClelland, J. L., Patterson, K., Pinker, S. and Ullman, M. (2002). The Past Tense Debate: Papers and replies by S. Pinker and M. Ullman and by J. McClelland and K. Patterson. *Trends in Cognitive Sciences*, 6, 456–474.

In this series of papers and responses, James McClelland, Karalyn Patterson, Steven Pinker and Michael Ullman discuss the arguments for and against the ability of connectionist models to account for past tense acquisition.

Chapter 12

What have we learned?

© Science Photo Library/Alamy

Chapter 12

What have we learned?

Learning Outcomes

At the end of this chapter you should be able to:

- Discuss the roles of nature and nurture in development.
- Describe the interaction of domain-general and domain-specific knowledge and processes.
- Discuss the roles of knowledge and metacognition in development.
- Describe the contribution made to the filed by cognitive neuroscience.

We have covered quite a lot of ground in this book. In this final chapter I will attempt to summarize some of the themes that have emerged. I will refer back to the issues and themes that were introduced at the beginning of the book: nature and nurture, stages of development and domain-general versus domain-specific development. In addition to these, three other major themes have emerged. The first of these is the importance of knowledge in cognitive development. What we know about a specific domain (declarative knowledge), and what we know about *how* to approach a problem (procedural knowledge or strategies) influence how we perform on cognitive tasks. The second is the importance of metacognition: our ability to think about our knowledge, and the strategies we know, and to think about what we *don't* know. The third theme is the importance of cognitive neuroscience for informing our understanding of the neural basis for cognition.

Nature and nurture

We have seen a variety of evidence in support of the ideas that infants possess core knowledge. Baillargeon, Spelke and Wasserman (1985) demonstrated that 5-month-olds have some knowledge of how objects behave. Since then, Baillargeon and her colleagues have carried out many studies in which impossible events are presented to infants, using the violation of expectations method. The general finding is that infants are surprised when physically impossible events appear to occur. Further evidence that infants possess basic knowledge about physics is supplied by Leslie (1982) and Spelke (1990). According to Spelke (2000) and Baillargeon (2008), this is best explained in terms of an innate system of core knowledge. Wynn (1992a) demonstrated that 5-month-olds can perform addition and subtraction on small numbers, suggesting that we are also born with knowledge of numbers. Gopnik (1996b, 2003) argues that children are born with basic innate theories of biology, physics and psychology, which are revised as a result of experience. Carey and Spelke (1996), on the other hand, argue that although infants are born with core knowledge, this knowledge is not organized into theories until later in childhood.

We have a preference for faces over other stimuli from around 2 to 3 months of age. Morton and Johnson (1991) proposed two mechanisms to explain this. One contains innate knowledge of the visual structure of faces, and the second is used to guide the acquisition of further knowledge about faces. Around 1 month of age, infants can distinguish between the face of their mother and other faces (Bartrip, Morton and de Schonen, 2001). By the time infants are 6 or 7 months old, they have learned to discriminate between different facial expressions (Barrera and Maurer, 1981; Schwartz, Izard and Ansul, 1985; Nelson and Dolgin, 1985). Many studies have shown that infants just days or weeks old can imitate facial expressions (Field *et al.*, 1982; Meltzoff and Moore, 1977, 1983)

There is also some evidence for the existence of innate modules. Leslie (1994b; Scholl and Leslie, 1999) proposes a domain specific, innate theory of mind module referred to as the Theory Of Mind Mechanism (ToMM). Leslie argues that the development of theory of mind is not a product of the acquisition of a new concept, learned through experience, but is a result of the maturing ToMM, which comes online at around 18 months of age. Leslie argues that the reason younger children fail false belief tasks is because they have performance limitations relating to inhibition. The evidence for this theory comes in the form of cases where young children pass modified theory of mind tasks (Surian and Leslie, 1999), and the lack of theory of mind in children with autism (Baron-Cohen, Leslie and Frith, 1985).

The role of nature in development is also illustrated by studies on the contribution of heredity to intelligence. The results from a range of studies on twins and adopted children have led to the general conclusion that around 75 per cent of the individual differences in IQ scores can be explained by genetics. (Bouchard *et al.*, 1990; Horn, 1983; Johnson *et al.*, 2007; Pederson *et al.*, 1992). However, when we look at both children and adults, there is a clear trend: Genetic factors become stronger influences on intelligence as we develop (Polderman *et al.*, 2006). We also need to take account of the extent to which our genetic inheritance influences the environments to which we are exposed (Scarr and McCartney, 1983), which means that the roles of nature and nurture are not discrete, but rather interact in a complex way.

Although there is a lot of evidence in favour of innate (or at least very early developing) systems of knowledge, it is also clear that environment, experience and culture play important roles. With respect to speech perception, Werker and Lalonde (1988) showed that 6- to 8-month-old infants brought up in an English-speaking environment could distinguish phonemes that are used in Hindi but are not present in English, but that this ability declined in 11- to 13-month-olds. Werker and Desjardins (1995) report a series of studies in which various languages and phoneme pairs were used. Their results point to the loss of the ability to perceive non-native contrasts some time between 6 and 12 months of age. This ability to attend to statistical regularities in the environment has given us a way of explaining how language can be learnt, without the need for innate knowledge. Recent research has shown that it is possible that phonology, vocabulary and grammar can be learned using the statistical information present in the environment. (Gómez, 2002; Lany and Saffran, 2010; Maye, Weiss and Aslin, 2008; Theakston, 2004). These findings are supported by cognitive models of language acquisition (Croker, 2007; Elman *et al.*, 1996)

There is also an effect of culture on numeracy. Fuson (1992) noted that Japanese children start solving problems with two or more digit numbers earlier than American children. Siegler and Mu (2008) tested Chinese and American 5- and 6-year-olds on the number line estimation task and found that the Chinese children's estimates were comparable to those of American children 1 to 2 years older. They suggest this may be due to cultural differences in the amount of time spent engaged in mathematical activities even before school (Zhou *et al.*, 2006). It is also well-known that the home environment has a big impact on how well children learn to read

We also know that there are cultural differences in how we conceptualize intelligence. In Western cultures we emphasize the importance of abstract thinking and problem solving. In other cultures, such as African and Eastern cultures, intelligence is not necessarily viewed as the same set of skills (Cole, 2006; Cole and Cigagas, 2010; Serpell, 2000). Intelligence is also, at least partially, responsive to environmental manipulations. Ramey and his colleagues designed the Carolina Abecedarian study in order to see what effect full-time child care, with an emphasis on enhancing development, would have on intelligence. The fascinating findings from the Abecedarian project (Ramey, Campbell and Ramey, 1999) show an obvious effect of the environment on intelligence, leading to improved cognitive and social development. In fact, our experiences affect much of our cognition. For example, several researchers have found that children's understanding of health and illness develops with age, which is not surprising, but also that experience with specific illnesses is reflected in increased knowledge of those illnesses (Charman and Chandiramani, 1995; Myant and Williams, 2005).

Are there stages of development?

Although this has been a topic of much discussion for decades, we have seen very little evidence for the sort of qualitative shifts in cognition proposed by Piaget. It seems that development is mostly continuous and results from the development of knowledge, strategies and speed of information processing. For example, Mareschal and Schultz (1999) developed a connectionist model of seriation in transitive reasoning. They demonstrated that the stages of development proposed by Piaget are not necessarily a result of qualitative shifts in knowledge, but can be achieved by a system in which very gradual changes occur. One domain, however, in which there are still debates about stage-like transitions in knowledge is theory of mind. The general finding that children over the age of 4 can pass theory of mind tasks (Callaghan *et al.*, 2005; Wellman, Cross and Watson, 2001) has been taken by some (e.g., Perner, 1991) as evidence that this is the age at which the ability to represent mental states emerges, and that this marks a stage of development.

Domain specificity versus domain generality

As well as marking a stage of development, the emergence of theory of mind is, for Perner (1991), the development of a domain-general ability to hold metarepresentations. For Wellman and colleagues (Gopnik and Wellman, 1994; Wellman and Gelman, 1992), it is evidence for domain-specific development. The finding that children with autism do not pass theory of mind tasks, and that this does not seem to be due to impaired general intellectual abilities, is also supportive of the ideas of theory of mind as a domain-specific development. Wellman also proposes that children develop domain-specific naïve theories of physics and biology. However, when children are explaining human behaviour, Wellman, Hickling and Schult (1997) found they could refer to psychological, physical and biological explanations, suggesting they realize that all three domains apply to humans. In studies of scientific reasoning, Kuhn *et al.* (1995) found that improvement in the strategies used to solve problems in one domain can lead to a similar improvement in another domain. Klahr, Fay and Dunbar (1993) agree that children have limited domain-general reasoning skills compared to adults, but argue that when hypotheses are plausible and there are few alternatives to choose from, children are able to succeed in scientific reasoning tasks. A number of studies demonstrate that domain-specific knowledge is also a relevant factor (e.g., Carey, 1985; Chi and Koeske, 1983; Penner and Klahr, 1996). Recent approaches to scientific reasoning take into account both domain-general strategies and domain-specific concepts, suggesting that the two bootstrap one another (Lehrer and Schauble, 2006; Schauble, 1996; Zimmerman, 2007). Croker and Buchanan (in press) found that the domain-general control of variables strategy can be mediated by domain-specific knowledge regarding the plausibility of a hypothesis. Although they may, to some extent, develop as separate systems of knowledge, cognitive abilities do depend on one another. For example, we have seen that memory depends on the development of language. In Simcock and Hayne's (2002) study on the ability of 2- to 3-year-old children to recall an event six and twelve months later, they found that none of the children used words to describe the event that were not in their vocabulary at the time of the event. The children could recall more about the event than they could verbalize, but it seems that these memories could not be translated into the language they had acquired since the event. Thus, the reason we may not be able to remember events early in our lives is that we did not have the language skills and knowledge to encode these events.

Knowledge

In Chapter 3, we saw several instances of research demonstrating that performance on memory tasks can vary as a function of declarative knowledge. Chi (1978) found that children with a good knowledge of chess outperformed non-expert adults on a memory test. Similarly, knowledge of football leads to better performance on memory tasks involving these topics, independently of cognitive ability (Schneider, Korkel and Weinert, 1989). It can be argued that much of our general knowledge is represented as scripts, and that scripts can also have an effect on recall. Hudson (1988) told children stories about common events and then presented the participants with sentences that either had or had not been in the story. The children reported that they recognized sentences that were not in the story if the sentences conformed to the relevant script. Hudson and Nelson (1986) asked 3- and 5-year-olds questions about two events. Some of the questions were phrased in a general way so as to elicit a script, whereas others were more specific. Both the 3- and 5-year-olds found it easier to answer in more general terms, which implies that they were making use of scripts rather than episodic memories.

Knowledge is also implicated in the development of analogical and scientific reasoning. Goswami (1992) argues that the basic ability to reason analogically is present from early childhood, but increases with age as a function of conceptual knowledge. Children show a gradual improvement over time as they acquire more knowledge, because a greater level of knowledge enables the perceptions of parallels and commonalities. Koslowski (1996) argues that scientific reasoning abilities depend on our ability to consider plausible causal mechanisms, which require a knowledge base. She argues that because professional scientists rely on their accumulated knowledge, this is legitimate scientific behaviour.

A further way in which knowledge influences task performance is in terms of familiar content and contexts. Girotto *et al.* (1989) found that 10- and 11-year-olds performed poorly on the standard version of the Wason selection task, in which letters and numbers are used, but when given the problem with familiar content, most of the participants were able to give the correct answer. Hawkins *et al.* (1984) gave 4- and 5-year-olds syllogisms with familiar, unfamiliar and fantasy content. They found that the participants did not do as well on the unfamiliar problems as the familiar and fantasy problems. Other studies have also revealed an effect of the content of the problem (Dias and Harris, 1988, 1990). When Carraher, Carraher and Schliemann (1985) studied the mathematical abilities of Brazilian street vendors, they found that context played an important role. Although the children could perform arithmetic in the context of selling food, they could not easily transfer this skill to an academic context. Bjorklund and Rosenblum (2002) also demonstrated the power of context to affect how children approach mathematical problems. They found that children used more sophisticated strategies to solve arithmetic problems when the problems were placed in an academic context than when the problems were presented in a game context.

We have also seen that procedural knowledge, or strategy, affects children's cognitive abilities. According to Gathercole (1998), preschool and younger school-age children do not use subvocal rehearsal to keep items active in the phonological loop component of working memory. Without rehearsal, information decays after two seconds. Younger children recall fewer numbers because they are limited by the short duration of the loop, whereas older children can increase the length of time that auditory information remains in working memory. Children's use of the rehearsal strategy develops throughout childhood (Flavell, Beach and Chinsky, 1966; Naus, Ornstein and Aivano, 1977; Ornstein, Naus and Liberty, 1975), as does use of the organization strategy (Schlagmüller and Schneider, 2002; Schneider, 1986; Sodian, Schneider and Perlmutter, 1986). With respect to both literacy and numeracy, there is evidence that the ability to use different strategies is a key factor in performance. Siegler (1987) arrived at the conclusion that children use a mix of strategies in mathematics, depending on experience and the type of problem. Rittle-Johnson and Siegler (1999) found that the children use a variety of different strategies when spelling words, depending on their knowledge of individual words and the rules of spelling. Jones, Ritter and Wood's (2000) model of children's performance on the Tower of Nottingham task supported Siegler and Shipley's (1995) theory that development is a result of strategy change. Similarly, McClelland's (1989) model of the balance beam task and Siegler and Shipley's (1995) model of children's addition also provide support for Siegler's (1976) theory that children's performance on the tasks improves as a result of increasingly complex rules.

Metacognition

Much of what is described above with respect to children's declarative knowledge and use of strategies also depends on metacognition, what children know about their own knowledge and what they know about the availability and effectiveness of different strategies. Children's understanding of memory as a fallible process develops over middle childhood (Jaswal and Dodson, 2009; Kreutzer, Leonard and Flavell, 1975). Young children view all strategies on memory tasks as equally effective, whereas 8- to 10-year-olds start to discriminate between strategies, and 12-year-olds know which strategies work best (Justice, 1986; Schneider, 1986). The development of metacognitive abilities may also drive scientific reasoning. Kuhn (1989) argues that children do not think like scientists; she argues that children have little understanding of how hypotheses are supported or contradicted by evidence until they are 11 or 12 years old. It is the ability to differentiate between and coordinate theories and evidence which distinguishes individuals who can think scientifically from those who can't. Kuhn suggests that this is a metacognitive ability which develops gradually. The importance of metacognition is also supported by the changing way in which intelligence was viewed in the twentieth century. When Sternberg and Detterman (1986) asked 24 experts in the field to write a short essay on intelligence, the contributors placed a greater emphasis on metacognition than seen in older conceptions of intelligence.

Cognitive neuroscience

We have seen a number of cases in which the techniques of cognitive neuroscience have furthered our understanding of cognitive development. De Haan, Pascalis and Johnson (2002) examined event-related potentials (ERPs) of 6-month-olds to see if there is a specific electrical response to faces in the infant cortex. Although they found a negative potential that seems to correspond with the adult response to faces, it was delayed and had a smaller amplitude. De Haan *et al.* also found a later positive potential, which they argue may be involved in processes which are integrated into the negative potential by adulthood. This suggests that, at 6 months old, infants have not yet developed adult-like specialized face processing. This means that, even if there are specialized neural circuits for face processing, they need time to develop. In a study on responses to facial expressions in 4-month-olds, Rigato, Farroni and Johnson (2010) found that infant and adult processing of emotions is similar, although not identical, supporting the conclusion that neural processes develop throughout infancy. One ability that infants do possess very early is imitation. This can be explained in terms of mirror neurons, which have been found in monkeys. Mirror neurons fire both when monkeys observe an action being performed, and when they perform it themselves. There is evidence that a more complex system, involving several brain regions, with properties similar to monkey mirror neurons is present in humans (Iacoboni *et al.*, 1999; Rizzolatti and Craighero, 2004). In this system, cortical activity is similar when observing an action carried out and when imitating the action. This may, therefore, provide a neural basis for early imitative ability.

Cognitive neuroscience can also help us understand the development of categorical speech perception discussed earlier, as well as language in general. Rivera-Gaxiola, Silva-Pereyra and Kuhl (2005) examined infant ERPs responses to English and Spanish phonemes. They found that the neural responses at 7 months of age showed a discrimination of both native and non-native contrasts, but that the neural responses of 11-month-olds only showed a discrimination of native contrasts. It seems that we become 'tuned' to hear sounds that are present in our environment, which assists with the task of learning language. EEG studies show that adults, children and even young infants show greater activity in the left hemisphere when listening to speech sounds as opposed to non-speech auditory stimuli (Molfese and Betz, 1988). Peña *et al.* (2003) used near infra-red spectroscopy to measure activation in response to infant-directed speech, reversed speech and silence. They found that 2- to 5-day-old infants showed greater activation in the left temporal areas when listening to speech sounds than when listening to non-speech sounds.

A number of neural structures have been shown to play a role in theory of mind, including the medial prefrontal cortex (MPFC), right temporo-parietal junction (rTPJ), and posterior cingulate cortex (PC) (Sabbagh *et al.*, 2009; Saxe *et al.*, 2009). At present, we do not know how these brains mechanisms develop in young children, so we cannot tell which theory of the development of theory of mind is most likely to be correct. However, there is the potential for a greater understanding of this much-debated cognitive ability to be derived from brain imaging studies. For example, recent studies have found impairments in the mirror neuron system in autism (Oberman and Ramachandran, 2007; Williams *et al.*, 2006). In a study of high-functioning individuals with autism, Abell *et al.* (1999) found abnormalities in several regions, including MPFC and temporal poles. It is therefore possible that developmental differences in these regions are responsible for the disparities in theory of mind abilities between children with and without autism. Autism is not the only disorder that neuroscience can help us to understand. Several neuroimaging studies have shown that arithmetic processes are dependent on specialized systems in the parietal lobes and the anterior intraparietal sulcus (IPS) (Castelli, Glaser and Butterworth, 2006; Dehaene, Molko and Cohen, 2004; Dehaene *et al.*, 2003; Zago *et al.*, 2001). Taken together, these findings support the theory that dyscalculia is the result of a specific number-processing deficit (Butterworth, 1999).

In the future, it is highly likely that cognitive neuroscience will become more deeply integrated into cognitive development, along with cognitive models. The neuroconstructivist approach (Mareschal *et al.*, 2007) is an attempt to combine constructivism, cognitive neuroscience and computational modelling, so that cognitive development can be studied from multiple perspectives at the same time. Neuroconstructivism is concerned with different levels of explanation that are not independent of one another, from neural activity, through cognitive processes, to behaviour. The idea behind this view is that it will encourage theories and models that attempt to explain cognitive development at multiple levels. According to this view, the infant mind is not a blank slate or a collection of core knowledge modules. Rather, we are born with a flexible ability to learn, coupled with a set of minimal biases, which are distinct from nativist ideas of core knowledge, that place constraints on how we process incoming information. These biases are a result of differences between networks in the brain, such as types and density of neurons, which lead to some networks being more adept at processing particular types of stimuli than other networks. Over time, these networks become more specialized, which leads to increasing domain-specificity (Karmiloff-Smith, 2009). It is possible that, some time in the future, we may once again have a grand theory of cognitive development, in which the simplistic dichotomies of nature and nurture, and domain-generality and domain-specificity, are reinterpreted as more complex interactions between organism and environment.

Glossary

Accommodation One of two aspects of Piaget's concept of adaptation. Accommodation is the process by which cognitive structures are modified or created as a result of new experiences which do not fit into current structures.

Adaptation The process, described by Piaget, by which children meet environmental demands through the modification of cognitive structures by assimilation or accommodation.

Affordances Features of the environment that provide opportunities for a particular action.

Analogical reasoning A type of reasoning that involves finding correspondences between new and old problems in order to transfer knowledge from the old problem to the new one.

Aphasia A disorder in which language comprehension and/or production are affected as a result of brain damage.

Appearance-reality task Task in which an item has an appearance which conflicts with what it really is (e.g., a sponge that looks like a rock or a candle that looks like an apple). The aim of the task is to see whether children can hold two different representations of the same object.

Assimilation One of two aspects of Piaget's concept of adaptation. Assimilation is the process by which new experiences are incorporated into existing conceptual structures.

Attention deficit hyperactivity disorder (ADHD) A disorder characterized by hyperactive-impulsive and/or inattentive behaviour.

Autism A developmental disorder characterized by a triad of impairments in socialization, communication and imaginative or symbolic play.

Autobiographical memory Memory for episodes from one's personal life.

Cardinal number A number that refers to the quantity of items in a set.

Cognitive/computational model A simulation of cognitive processes instantiated in a computer program.

Cohort design A research design in which two or more groups of children who were born in different years are compared at the same age.

Conditioned head rotation A procedure in which responses in the form of orientation towards stimuli are reinforced.

Connectionist models Also known as neural networks. A cognitive model in which knowledge is stored as a pattern of connection weights between two or more layers of units.

Conservation The ability to understand that a quantity remains the same after a physical transformation.

Constructivist A theoretical position in which it is argued that meaning, in the form of mental representations, is constructed through interactions with the environment.

Control of variables strategy A domain-general strategy in which unconfounded experiments are designed such that valid causal inferences can be made. For example, designing a series of experiments in which only one variable is manipulated at a time enables one to determine which variables have an effect on the outcome.

Critical period hypothesis The idea that there is a window of time in the first few years of life in which exposure to language is necessary for normal linguistic development to occur.

Cross-sectional design A research design in which two or more groups of children of different ages are compared.

Deceptive box task Task in which the contents of a box differ from what would be expected to be in it. Children are asked what someone else will think is in the box in order to determine whether they can (a) understand that another person can hold a false belief and (b) understand their own initial false belief.

Declarative memory Conscious memory for facts (semantic memory) and events (episodic memory).

Deductive reasoning Reasoning in which a specific, logically valid, conclusion can be drawn from more general premises.

Deontic Concerning rules or obligations, such as permission.

Dimensional-Change Card Sort A simplified version of the Wisconsin Card Sort Task in which cards can be sorted by colour or shape. The task involves switching from sorting according to one dimension (e.g., colour) to the other dimension (e.g. shape).

Direct perception Picking up information from the environment without the mediation of mental representations.

Dizygotic twins Also known as 'fraternal twins', the result of two eggs that are fertilized by two different sperm cells.

Domain-general Referring to abilities or processes that operate across multiple domains of development.

Domain-specific Referring to abilities or processes that operate over just one domain of development.

Dyscalculia A learning disability characterized by impairments in mathematical ability that cannot be explained by a general intellectual impairment.

Dyslexia A learning disability characterized by poor reading and spelling that cannot be explained by a general intellectual impairment.

Episodic memory Memory for events.

Epistemic state A mental state of knowledge or belief; from the Greek *episteme* (knowledge).

Equilibration The process by which assimilation and accommodation are balanced to create stability.

Executive functions Cognitive processes used to control thought and actions, including planning and initiating behaviours, shifting between activities and inhibiting responses.

Explicit memory See declarative memory.

Factor analysis A statistical method that is used to determine whether the variability in several observed variables can be described in terms of fewer underlying variables, or factors.

Genetic epistemology The study of the origins of knowledge.

Habituation A decrease in response to a stimulus after repeated exposure to it.

Heritability The amount of variance of a trait, such as intelligence, that can be ascribed to genetic factors.

High amplitude sucking A rate of sucking above the baseline rate.

Immanent justice The belief that negative experiences are punishments for breaking rules.

Implicit memory See procedural memory.

Inductive reasoning Reasoning in which inferences are drawn from specific examples and generalized, or applied to other situations, such as in analogies.

Intelligence quotient (IQ) A score on a standardized test designed to measure intelligence.

Longitudinal design A research design in which the same group of children are tested repeatedly over a period of time.

Long-term memory Permanent or semi-permanent store of episodic, semantic and procedural memories.

Mental models Mental representations of the premises of a reasoning problem, which can be used to test whether conclusions are valid.

Mental representation A mental object or structure with semantic content. This may be an image (e.g., a bar of chocolate) or a proposition (the chocolate is in the green drawer).

Meta-analysis An analysis of the findings from multiple studies. Whereas the unit of analysis in a single study is usually the individual children, the unit of analysis in a meta-analysis is the conditions within the studies.

Metacognitive/metacognition Cognition about cognition. The ability to treat one's own thought processes as objects of thought.

Metamemory Knowledge of the contents and processes of memory.

Metarepresentation A representation of a representation. In order to understand another person's false belief, one has to hold a mental representation of the other person's representation. In the unexpected transfer task, Maxi has a representation (belief) that the chocolate is in the blue cupboard. Participants who pass the task have a representation (knowledge) of Maxi's representation of the location of the chocolate.

Microgenetic studies Studies which look at change over a brief period of time (often days or weeks).

Modularity theory The theory that there is a cognitive module which is innately specified to process mental representations. Theory of mind develops as this module matures.

Monozygotic twins Also known as 'identical twins', the result of one fertilized egg splitting in two, creating two embryos with identical genes.

No negative evidence The lack of feedback children receive regarding the grammaticality of their speech.

Object permanence The concept that objects exist independently of being directly perceived.

Ordinal number A number that refers to the position of one item in a set.

Overgeneralization errors Errors in which regular inflections are added to irregular words.

Path analysis A statistical method for examining causal relationships between variables.

Phonological recoding The translation of a written representation into sounds and words.

Poverty of the stimulus The argument that the linguistic input children receive is impoverished in that it (i) contains mistakes, and (ii) does not contain a full range of grammatical constructions.

Preferential looking A technique in which the relative amounts of time spent looking at two stimuli are compared in order to determine which stimulus is preferred.

Procedural memory Non-conscious memory of how to do things; skills and procedures.

Production system A type of cognitive model in which knowledge is stored as a list of 'if ... then' (or condition-action) rules.

Proprioception Awareness of the position of one's body, derived from receptors in muscles, joints, tendons and the inner ear.

Reaction time A measure of the time elapsed between the presentation of a stimulus and the response; longer reaction times indicate that more mental operations are being used.

Representational mind theory The theory that domain-general representational abilities underlie theory of mind. Around the age of 4 children come to understand metarepresentation and are thus able to understand false beliefs.

Scripts Mental structure containing a typical sequence of events.

Semantic memory Memory for facts and general knowledge.

Short-term memory Limited capacity, limited duration store of information.

Simulation theory The theory that we can understand other people's beliefs by imagining ourselves to be in their situation.

Spectrum disorder One of a range of linked disorders that can form a continuum from mild to severe.

Structural equation modelling Similar to path analysis, this is a statistical method for examining causal relationships between variables. Theoretical models of the relationships between variables can be tested in order to see how well they fit the data.

Telegraphic speech An early type of speech in which function words are omitted.

Theory of mind An understanding that people have minds and, via the attribution of mental states such as thinking, knowing and believing, that others may have mental states that differ to our own.

Theory theory The theory that our understanding of mind develops as a series of successively more sophisticated theories which are used to explain and predict behaviour.

Unexpected transfer task Task in which an object is moved from one location to another without the knowledge of the story character who placed the object in its initial location. This task tests the ability of children to understand that the character has a false belief about the location of the object.

Weak central coherence A tendency to process information for fine details, rather than broad gist.

Wisconsin Card Sort Task A task in which cards can be sorted by colour, shape or number. The task involves switching from sorting according to one dimension (e.g., colour) to another dimension (e.g. shape).

Violation-of-expectation A methodology used in infant cognition studies. If an infant looks for a longer duration at one event than others, it is interpreted as a surprise – a violation of expectation – which enables researchers to infer the infant's knowledge.

Working memory Temporary storage area in which information is processed, monitored and manipulated.

Zone of proximal development A conceptual space that describes the range of ability between what a child can do with and without support.

References

Abell, F., Krams, M., Ashburner, J., Passingham, R., Friston, K. J., Frackowiak, R., Happé, F., Frith, C. D. and Frith, U. (1999). The neuroanatomy of autism: A voxel based whole brain analysis of structural MRI scans in high functioning individuals. *NeuroReport*, 10, 1647–1651.

Adams, M. (1990). *Beginning to read: Thinking and learning about print*. Cambridge, MA: MIT Press.

Adams, M. J., Treiman, R. and Pressley, M. (1998). Reading, writing, and literacy. In I. Sigel and A. Renninger (Eds), *Handbook of child psychology, Volume 4: Child psychology in practice* (pp. 275–355). New York: Wiley.

Adams, R. J. and Courage, M. L. (1995). Development of chromatic discrimination in early infancy. *Behavioural Brain Research*, 67, 99–101.

Addis, D. R., Pan, L., Vu, M. A., Laiser, N. and Schacter, D. L. (2009). Constructive episodic simulation of the future and the past: Distinct subsystems of a core brain network mediate imagining and remembering. *Neuropsychologia*, 47, 2222–2238.

Addis, D. R., Wong, A. T. and Schacter, D. L. (2007). Remembering the past and imagining the future: common and distinct neural substrates during event construction and elaboration. *Neuropsychologia*, 45, 1363–1377.

Adrian, J. A., Alegria, J. and Morais, J. (1995). Metaphonological abilities of Spanish illiterate adults. *International Journal of Psychology*, 30(3), 329–353.

Aguiar, A. and Baillargeon, R. (1998). 8.5-month-old infants' reasoning about containment events. *Child Development*, 69, 636–653.

Aguiar, A. and Baillargeon, R. (1999). 2.5-month-old infants' reasoning about when objects should and should not be occluded. *Cognitive Psychology*, 39, 116–157.

Aguiar, A. and Baillargeon, R. (2003). Perseverative responding in a violation-of-expectation task in 6.5-month-old infants. *Cognition*, 88(3), 277–316.

Aitchison, J. (2008). *The articulate mammal: An introduction to psycholinguistics*. Abingdon: Routledge.

Alcock, K. L., Ngorosho, D., Deus, C. and Jukes, M. C. H. (2010). We don't have language at our house: Disentangling the relationship between phonological awareness, schooling and literacy. *British Journal of Educational Psychology*, 80, 55–76.

American Psychiatric Association. (1987). *Diagnostic and statistical manual of mental disorders* (3rd ed., revised). Washington, DC: American Psychiatric Association.

American Psychiatric Association. (2000). *Diagnostic and statistical manual of mental disorders* (4th ed., text revision). Washington, DC: American Psychiatric Association.

Amsel, E. and Brock, S. (1996). The development of evidence evaluation skills. *Cognitive Development*, 11(4), 523–550.

Anderson, J. E. (1939). The limitations of infant and preschool tests in the measurement of intelligence. *Journal of Psychology*, 8, 351–379.

Anderson, M. (1992). *Intelligence and development: A cognitive theory*. Oxford: Blackwell.

Anderson, M. (1999). Project development – the shape of things to come. In M. Anderson (Ed.), *The development of intelligence* (pp. 3–15). Hove: Psychology Press.

Anderson, M. (2005). Marrying intelligence and cognition: A developmental view. In R. J. Sternberg and J. E. Pretz (Eds), *Cognition and intelligence: Identifying the mechanisms of the mind* (pp. 268–287). New York: Cambridge University Press.

Apperly, I. A., Samson, D. and Humphreys, G. W. (2005). Domain-specificity and theory of mind: evaluating neuropsychological evidence. *Trends in Cognitive Sciences*, 9(12), 572–577.

Apperly, I. A., Samson, D., Chiavarino, C. and Humphreys, G. W. (2004). Frontal and temporo-parietal lobe contribution to theory of mind: Neuropsychological evidence from a false belief task with reduced language and executive demands. *Journal of Cognitive Neuroscience*, 16(10), 1773–1784.

Aristotle. (2007). *Prior analytics* (A. J. Jenkinson, Trans.). Adelaide, Australia: eBooks@Adelaide.

Retrieved from http://ebooks.adelaide.edu.au/a/ aristotle/a8pra/index.html (Original work published approx. 350 BCE).

Arterberry, M. E. (2008). Infants' sensitivity to the depth cue of height-in-the-picture plane. *Infancy, 13,* 544–555.

Arterberry, M. E., Yonas, A. and Bensen, A. (1989). Self-produced locomotion and the development of responsiveness to linear perspective and texture gradients. *Developmental Psychology, 25,* 976–982.

Ashcraft, M. H. (1995). Cognitive psychology and simple arithmetic: A review and summary of new directions. *Mathematical Cognition, 1,* 3–34.

Aslin, R. N. (1981). Development of smooth pursuit in human infants. In D. F. Fisher, R. A. Monty and J. W. Senders (Eds), *Eye movements: Cognition and visual perception* (pp. 31–51). Hillsdale, NJ: Lawrence Erlbaum Associates.

Aslin, R. N., Saffran, J. R. and Newport., E. L. (1999). Statistical learning in linguistic and nonlinguistic domains. In B. MacWhinney (Ed.) *The emergence of language* (pp. 359–380). Mahwah, NJ: Lawrence Erlbaum Associates.

Atkinson, R. C. and Shiffrin, R. M. (1968). Human memory: A proposed system and its control processes. In K. W. Spence and J. T. Spence (Eds), *The psychology of learning and motivation: Advances in research and theory (Vol. 2).* (pp. 742–775). New York: Academic Press.

Au, T. K. and Romo, L. (1999). Mechanical causality in children's 'Folkbiology'. In D. Medin and S. Atran (Eds), *Folkbiology* (pp. 355–401). Cambridge, MA: MIT Press.

Autism Society of America. (2008). *Autism FAQ.* Retrieved from: http://www.autism-society.org/site/ PageServer?pagename=about_FAQ.

Avis, J. and Harris, P. L. (1991). Belief-desire reasoning among Baka children: Evidence for a universal conception of mind. *Child Development, 62*(3), 460–467.

Baddeley, A. D. (1986). *Working memory.* Oxford: Oxford University Press.

Baddeley, A. D. (2000). The episodic buffer: a new component of working memory? *Trends in Cognitive Sciences, 4*(11), 417–423.

Baddeley, A. D. and Hitch, G. J. (1974). Working memory. In G. H. Bower (Ed.), *The psychology of learning and motivation: Advances in research and theory* (Vol. 8, pp. 47–90). New York: Academic Press.

Bahrick, L. E. (2000). Increasing specificity in the development of intermodal perception. In D. Muir and. A Slater. (Eds), *Infant development: The essential readings* (pp. 117–136). Oxford: Blackwell.

Bahrick, L. E., Hernandez-Reif, M. and Flom, R. (2005). The development of infant learning about specific face-voice relations. *Developmental Psychology, 41,* 541–552.

Bahrick, L. E., Walker, A. S. and Neisser, U. (1981). Selective looking by infants. *Cognitive Psychology, 13,* 377–390.

Baillargeon, R. (1987a). Object permanence in 3.5 and 4.5-month-old infants. *Developmental Psychology, 23,* 655–664.

Baillargeon, R. (1987b). Young infants reasoning about the physical and spatial properties of a hidden object. *Cognitive Development, 2*(3), 179–200.

Baillargeon, R. (1994). How do infants learn about the physical world? *Current Directions in Psychological Science, 3,* 133–140.

Baillargeon, R. (2008). Innate ideas revisited: For a principle of persistence in infants' physical reasoning. *Perspectives on Psychological Science, 3,* 2–13.

Baillargeon, R., Li, J., Ng, W. and Yuan, S. (2009). A new account of infants' physical reasoning. In A. Woodward and A. Needham (Eds), *Learning and the infant mind* (pp. 66–116). New York: Oxford University Press.

Baillargeon, R., Needham, A. and DeVos, J. (1992). The development of young infants' intuitions about support. *Early Development and Parenting, 1,* 69–78.

Baillargeon, R., Spelke, E. S. and Wasserman, S. (1985). Object permanence in 5-month-old infants. *Cognition, 20,* 191–208.

Baird, G., Cox, A., Charman, T., Baron-Cohen, S., Wheelwright, S., Swettenham, J., Drew, A. and Nightingale, N. (2000). A screening instrument for autism at 18 months of age: A six year follow-up study. *Journal of the American Academy of Child and Adolescent Psychiatry, 39,* 694–702.

Baird, G., Simonoff, E., Pickles, A., Chandler, S., Loucas, T., Meldrum, D., *et al.* (2006). Prevalence of disorders of the autism spectrum in a population cohort of children in South Thames: the Special Needs and Autism Project (SNAP). *The Lancet, 368*(9531), 210–215.

Ball, W. and Tronick, E. (1971). Infant responses to impending collision: Optical and real. *Science, 171*(3973), 818–820.

Bara, B. G., Bucciarelli, M. and Johnson-Laird, P. N. (1995). Development of syllogistic reasoning. *American Journal of Psychology, 108*(2), 157–193.

Barkley, R. A. (1997). Behavioral inhibition, sustained attention, and executive functions: constructing a unifying theory of ADHD. *Psychological Bulletin, 121*(1), 65–94.

Barkley, R. A. (1998). *ADHD: a handbook for diagnosis and treatment.* New York: Guilford Press.

Barkley, R. A. (2003). Attention deficit hyperactivity disorder. In E. J. Mash and R. A. Barkley (Eds), *Child psychopathology* (2nd ed.). New York: Guilford Press.

Baron-Cohen, S. (1987). Autism and symbolic play. *British Journal of Developmental Psychology, 5,* 139–48.

Baron-Cohen, S. (1988). Social and pragmatic deficits in autism: cognitive or affective? *Journal of Autism and Developmental Disorders, 18,* 379–402.

Baron-Cohen, S. (1989). Are autistic children behaviourists? An examination of their mental-physical and appearance-reality distinctions. *Journal of Autism and Developmental Disorders, 19,* 579–600.

Baron-Cohen, S. (1991). Do people with autism understand what causes emotion? *Child Development, 62,* 385–395.

Baron-Cohen, S. (1992). Out of sight or out of mind: another look at deception in autism. *Journal of Child Psychology and Psychiatry, 33,* 1141–1155.

Baron-Cohen, S. and Goodhart, F (1994). The 'seeing-leads-to-knowing' deficit in autism: the Pratt and Bryant probe. *British Journal of Developmental Psychology, 12,* 397–401.

Baron-Cohen, S. and Swettenham, J. (1997). The theory of mind hypothesis of autism: relationship to executive function and central coherence. In D. Cohen and F. Volkmar (Eds), *Handbook of autism and developmental disorders.* (pp. 880–893). New York: Wiley.

Baron-Cohen, S., Ashwin, E., Ashwin, C., Tavassoli, T. and Chakrabarti, B. (2009). Talent in autism: hyper-systemizing, hyper-attention to detail and sensory hypersensitivity. *Philosophical Transactions of the Royal Society B 364,* 1377–1383.

Baron-Cohen, S., Leslie, A. M. and Frith, U. (1985). Does the autistic child have a 'theory of mind'? *Cognition, 21,* 37–46.

Baron-Cohen, S., Ring, H., Moriarty, J., Shmitz, P., Costa, D. and Ell, P. (1994). Recognition of mental state terms: a clinical study of autism, and a functional neuroimaging study of normal adults. *British Journal of Psychiatry, 165,* 640–649.

Baroody, A. J. (2003). The development of adaptive expertise and flexibility: The integration of conceptual and procedural knowledge. In A. J. Baroody and A. Dowker (Eds), *The development of arithmetic concepts and skills: Constructing adaptive expertise* (pp. 1–33). Mahwah, NJ: Lawrence Erlbaum Associates.

Baroody, A. J. and Ginsburg, H. P. (1986). The relationship between initial meaningful and mechanical knowledge of arithmetic. In J. Hiebert (Ed.), *Conceptual and procedural knowledge: The case of mathematics* (pp. 75–112). Hillsdale, NJ: Lawrence Erlbaum Associates.

Barr, R., Rovee-Collier, C. and Campanella, J. (2005). Retrieval facilitates retrieval: Protracting deferred imitation by 6-month-olds. *Infancy, 7,* 263–283.

Barrera, M. E. and Maurer, D. (1981). The perception of facial expressions by the three-month-old. *Child Development, 52*(1), 203–206.

Barrett, M. (1986). Early semantic representations and early word usage. In S. A. Kuczaj and M. Barrett (Eds), *The development of word meaning* (pp. 39–67). New York: Springer Verlag.

Barrett, M. (1995). Early lexical development. In P. Fletcher and B. MacWhinney (Eds), *The handbook of child language* (pp. 362–392). Oxford: Blackwell.

Barrett, M. (Ed). (1999). *The development of language.* Hove: Psychology Press.

Bartak, L. and Rutter, M. (1974). The use of personal pronouns by autistic children. *Journal of Autism and Childhood Schizophrenia, 4,* 217–222.

Bartels, M., Rietveld, M. J. H., Van Baal, G. C. M. and Boomsma, D. I. (2002). Genetic and environmental influence on the development of intelligence. *Behavior Genetics, 32,* 237–249.

Bartlett, F. C. (1932). *Remembering: A study in experimental and social psychology.* Cambridge: Cambridge University Press.

Bartrip, J., Morton, J. and De Schonen, S. (2001). Responses to mother's face in 3-week to 5-month old infants. *British Journal of Developmental Psychology, 19*(2), 219–232.

Bartsch, K. and Wellman, H. (1989). Young children's attribution of action to beliefs and desires. *Child Development, 60*(4), 946–964.

Bates, E. and MacWhinney, B. (1982). Functionalist approaches to grammar. In E. Wanner and L. Gleitman (Eds), *Language acquisition: the state of the art* (pp. 173–218). New York: Cambridge University Press.

Bates, E. and MacWhinney, B. (1987). Competition, variation, and language learning. In B. MacWhinney (Ed.), *Mechanisms of language acquisition* (pp. 157–195). Hillsdale, NJ: Lawrence Erlbaum Associates.

Bates, E., Benigni, L., Bretherton, I., Camaioni, L. and Volterra, V. (1979). *The emergence of symbols: Cognition and communication in infancy.* New York: Academic Press.

Bates, E. A. and Elman, J. L. (2002). Connectionism and the study of change. In M. Johnson (Ed.), *Brain development and cognition: A reader* (2nd ed.) (pp. 421–440). Oxford: Blackwell.

Bauer, P. J. (2007). *Remembering the times of our lives: Memory in infancy and beyond.* Mahwah, NJ: Laurence Erlbaum Associates.

Bauer, P. J. and Fivush, R. (2010). Autobiographical memory: Context and consequences [Special issue]. *Cognitive Development, 25*(4).

Bauer, P. J., Wenner, J. A., Dropik, P. L., Wewerka, S. S. and Howe, M. L. (2000). Parameters of remembering and forgetting in the transition from infancy to early childhood. *Monographs of the*

Society for Research in Child Development, 65(4), i–213.

Bauer, P. J., Wiebe, S. A., Carver, L. J., Lukowski, A. F., Haight, J. C., Waters, J. M. and Nelson, C. A. (2006). Electrophysiological indices of encoding and behavioral indices of recall: Examining relations and developmental change late in the first year of life. *Developmental Neuropsychology*, 29, 293–380.

Bayley, N. (1933). Mental growth during the first three years. *Genetic Psychology Monographs*, 14, 1–92.

Bayley, N. (1969). *Bayley scales of infant development*. New York: Psychological Corporation.

Bayley, N. (1993). *Bayley scales of infant development (BSID-II)* (2nd ed.). San Antonio, TX: The Psychological Corporation.

Bentin, S., Allison, T., Puce, A., Perez, E. and McCarthy, G. (1996). Electrophysiological studies of face perception in humans. *Journal of Cognitive Neuroscience*, 8, 551–565.

Berko, J. (1958). The child's learning of English morphology. *Word*, 14, 150–177.

Bernstein Ratner, N. and Pye, C. (1984). Higher pitch in babytalk is not universal: acoustic evidence from Quiche Mayan. *Journal of Child Language*, 11(3), 515–522.

Bertenthal, B. I., Campos, J. J. and Haith, M. M. (1980). Development of visual organization: The perception of subjective contours. *Child Development*, 51(4), 1072–1080.

Beuhring, T. and Kee, D. W. (1987). Developmental relationships among metamemory, elaborative strategy use, and associative memory. *Journal of Experimental Child Psychology*, 44(3), 377–400.

Bibace, R. and Walsh, M. E. (1979). Developmental stages of children's conceptions of illness. In G. Stone, F. Cohen and N. Adler (Eds), *Health psychology: A handbook* (pp. 285–301). San Francisco, CA: Jossey-Bass.

Bibace, R. and Walsh, M. E. (1980). Development of children's concepts of illness. *Pediatrics*, 66(6), 912–917.

Binet, A. and Simon, T. (1905). Méthodes nouvelles pour le diagnostic du niveau intellectual des anormaux. *L'Année psychologique*, 11, 191–336.

Binnie, L. M. and Williams, J. M. (2002). Intuitive psychological, physical and biological knowledge in typically developing preschoolers, children with autism and children with Down's syndrome. *British Journal of Developmental Psychology*, 20(3), 343–359.

Birch, H. G. and Lefford, A. (1963). Intersensory development in children. *Monographs of the Society for Research in Child Development*, 28(5), 1–48.

Birch, S. A. J. and Bloom, P. (2004). Understanding children's and adults' limitations in mental state reasoning. *Trends in Cognitive Sciences*, 8(6), 255–260.

Birch, S. A. J. and Bloom, P. (2007). The curse of knowledge in reasoning about false beliefs. *Psychological Science*, 18(5), 382–386.

Bird, H., Lambon Ralph, M. A., Seidenberg, M. S., McClelland, J. L. and Patterson, K. (2003). Deficits in phonology and past tense morphology: What is the connection? *Journal of Memory and Language*, 48, 502–526.

Birney, D. P., Citron-Pousty, J. H., Lutz, D. J. and Sternberg, R. J. (2005). The development of cognitive and intellectual abilities. In M. H. Bornstein and M. E. Lamb (Eds), *Developmental science: An advanced textbook* (5th ed.) (pp. 327–358). Mahwah, NJ: Lawrence Erlbaum Associates.

Bisanz, J. and LeFevre, J. (1990). Strategic and nonstrategic processing in the development of mathematical cognition. In D. F. Bjorklund (Ed.), *Children's strategies: Contemporary views of cognitive development* (pp. 213–244). Hillsdale, NJ: Lawrence Erlbaum Associates.

Bjorklund, D. F. and Rosenblum, K. E. (2002). Context effects in children's selection and use of simple arithmetic strategies. *Journal of Cognition and Development*, 3(2), 225–242.

Bjorklund, D. F., Bjorklund, B. R., Brown, R. D. and Cassel, W. S. (1998). Children's susceptibility to repeated questions: How misinformation changes children's answers and their minds. *Applied Developmental Science*, 2, 99–111.

Bjorklund, D. F., Muir-Broaddus, J. E. and Schneider, W. (1990). The role of knowledge in the development of children's strategies. In D. F. Bjorklund (Ed.), *Children's strategies: Contemporary views of cognitive development* (pp. 93–128). Hillsdale, NJ: Lawrence Erlbaum Associates.

Bloom, P. (1990). Subjectless sentences in child language. *Linguistic Inquiry*, 21(4), 491–504.

Bloom, P. and German, T. P. (2000). Two reasons to abandon the false belief task as a test of theory of mind. *Cognition*, 77(1), B25–B31.

Bölte, S., Dziobek, I. and Poustka, F. (2009). Brief report: The level and nature of autistic intelligence revisited. *Journal of Autism and Developmental Disorders*, 39, 678–682.

Booth, J. L. and Siegler, R. S. (2006). Developmental and individual differences in pure numerical estimation. *Developmental Psychology*, 41, 189–201.

Booth, J. L. and Siegler, R. S. (2008). Numerical magnitude representations influence arithmetic learning. *Child Development*, 79, 1016–1031.

Bornstein, M. H. and Sigman, M. D. (1986). Continuity in mental development from infancy. *Child Development*, 57, 251–274.

Borys, S. V., Spitz, H. H., and Dorans, B. A. (1982). Tower of Hanoi performance of retarded young adults and nonretarded children as a function of solution length and goal state. *Journal of Experimental Child Psychology, 33*, 87–110.

Bouchard, T. J. and McGue, M. (1981). Familial studies of intelligence: A review. *Science, 212*(4498), 1055–1059.

Bouchard, T. J., Jr., Lykken, D. T., McGue, M., Segal, N. L. and Tellegen, A. (1990). Sources of human psychological differences: The Minnesota study of twins reared apart. *Science, 250*(4978), 223–228.

Bouwmeester, S., Vermunt, J. K. and Sijtsma, K. (2007). Development and individual differences in transitive reasoning: A fuzzy trace theory approach. *Developmental Review, 27*(1), 41–74.

Bower, T. G. R., Broughton, J. M. and Moore, M. K. (1970). Infant response to approaching objects: An indication of response to distal variables. *Perception and Psychophysics, 9*, 193–196.

Bowerman, M. (1976). Semantic factors in the acquisition of rules for word use and sentence construction. In D. M. Morehead and A. E. Morehead (Eds), *Normal and deficient child language* (pp. 99–179). Baltimore, MD: University Park Press.

Bowerman, M. (1988). The 'no negative evidence' problem: How do children avoid constructing an overly general grammar? In J. A. Hawkins (Ed.), *Explaining language universals* (pp. 73–101). Oxford: Blackwell.

Bowey, J. A. (2002). Reflections on onset–rime and phoneme sensitivity as predictors of beginning word reading. *Journal of Experimental Child Psychology, 82*, 29–40.

Bowey, J. A. (2005). Predicting individual differences in learning to read. In M. J. Snowling and C. Hulme (Ed.), *The science of reading: A handbook* (pp. 155–172) Oxford, UK: Blackwell.

Bradley, L. and Bryant, P. (1978). Difficulties in auditory organization as a possible cause of reading backwardness. *Nature, 271*, 746–747.

Bradley, L. and Bryant, P. E. (1983). Categorizing sounds and learning to read – a causal connection. *Nature, 301*, 419–421.

Braine, M. D. S. (1971). The acquisition of language in infant and child. In C. Reed (Ed.), *The learning of language* (pp. 7–95). New York: Appleton-Century-Crofts.

Braine, M. D. S. (1976). Children's first word combinations. *Monographs of the Society for Research in Child Development, 41*(1, Serial No. 164).

Braine, M. D. S. (1987). What is learned in acquiring word classes – a step towards an acquisition theory. In. B. MacWhinney (Ed.), *Mechanisms of language acquisition* (pp. 65–113). Hillsdale, NJ: Lawrence Erlbaum Associates.

Bremner, J. G. and Knowles, L. S. (1984). Piagetian stage IV errors with an object that is directly accessible both visually and manually. *Perception, 13*, 307–314.

Brennan, W. M., Ames, E. W. and Moore, R. W. (1966). Age differences in infants' attention to patterns of different complexities. *Science, 151*(3708), 354–356.

Brody, N. (1992). *Intelligence* (2nd ed.). San Diego, CA: Academic Press.

Brody, N. (1997). Intelligence, schooling and society. *American Psychologist, 52*, 1046–1050.

Brown, A. L. (1978). Knowing when, where and how to remember: A problem of metacognition. In R. Glaser (Ed.), *Advances in instructional psychology: Vol. 1* (pp. 77–165). Hillsdale, NJ: Lawrence Erlbaum Associates.

Brown, A. L. (1989). Analogical learning and transfer. What develops? In S. Vosniadou and A. Ortony (Eds), *Similarity and analogical reasoning* (pp. 369–412). New York: Cambridge University Press.

Brown, A. L., Bransford, J., Ferrara, R. and Campione, J. (1983). Learning, remembering, and understanding. In P. H. Musen (Ed.), *Handbook of child psychology: Vol. III* (pp. 77–166). New York: Wiley.

Brown, J. S. and Burton, R. R. (1978). Diagnostic models for procedural bugs in basic mathematical skills. *Cognitive Science, 2*(2), 155–192.

Brown, R. (1973). *A first language*. Cambridge, MA: Harvard University Press.

Brown, R. and Bellugi, U. (1964). Three processes in the child's acquisition of syntax. *Harvard Educational Review, 34*, 133–51.

Brown, R. and Hanlon, C. (1970). Derivational complexity and order of acquisition in child speech. In J. R. Hayes (Ed.), *Cognition and the development of language* (pp. 11–53). New York: Wiley.

Bruck, M. and Melnyk, L. (2004). Individual differences in children's suggestibility: A review and synthesis. *Applied Cognitive Psychology, 18*(8), 947–996.

Bruck, M., Ceci, S. J., Francoeur, E. and Barr, R. (1995). 'I hardly cried when I got my shot!' Influencing children's reports about a visit to their pediatrician. *Child Development, 66*, 193–208.

Bruner, J. (1966). *Toward a theory of instruction*. Cambridge, MA: Harvard University Press.

Bruner, J. and Haste, H. (Eds). (1987). *Making sense: The child's construction of the world*. New York: Methuen.

Bryant, P. and Trabasso, T. (1971). Transitive inferences and memory in young children. *Nature, 232*, 456–458.

Bryant, P., MacLean, M., Bradley, L. and Crossland, J. (1990). Rhyme and alliteration, phoneme detection and learning to read. *Developmental Psychology, 26*, 429–438.

Bryant, P. E. (1998). Sensitivity to onset and rhyme does predict young children's reading: A comment on Muter, Hulme, Snowling, and Taylor (1997). *Journal of Experimental Child Psychology, 71*(1), 29–37.

Bryant, P. E. (2002). It doesn't matter whether onset and rime predicts reading better than phoneme awareness or vice versa. *Journal of Experimental Child Psychology*, 82, 41–46.

Bulloch, M. J. and Opfer, J. E. (2009). What makes relational reasoning smart? Revisiting the perceptual-to-relational shift in the development of generalization. *Developmental Science*, 12(1), 114–122.

Bullock, M. and Gelman, R. (1979). Preschool children's assumptions about cause and effect: Temporal ordering. *Child Development*, 50(1), 89–96.

Burbach, D. J. and Peterson, L. (1986). Children's concepts of physical illness: A review and critique of the cognitive-developmental literature. *Health Psychology*, 5(3), 307–325.

Bushnell, I. W., Sai, F. and Mullin, J. T. (1989). Neonatal recognition of the mother's face. *British Journal of Developmental Psychology*, 7(1), 3–15.

Butterworth, B. (1999). *The mathematical brain*. London: Macmillan.

Butterworth, B. (2003). *Dyscalculia screener*. London: nferNelson.

Butterworth, B. (2005). Developmental dyscalculia. In J. I. D. Campbell (Ed.), *Handbook of mathematical cognition* (pp. 455–467). Hove: Psychology Press.

Butterworth, G. (1977). Object disappearance and error in Piaget's Stage IV task. *Journal of Experimental Child Psychology*, 23, 391–401.

Butterworth, G. (1994). Theory of mind and the facts of embodiment. In C. Lewis and P. Mitchell (Eds), *Children's early understanding of mind* (pp. 115–132). Hove: Lawrence Erlbaum Associates.

Butterworth, G. and Jarrett, N. (1991). What minds have in common is space: spatial mechanisms serving joint visual-attention in infancy. *British Journal of Developmental Psychology*, 9, 55–72.

Byers-Heinlein, K., Burns, T. C. and Werker, J. (2010). The roots of bilingualism in newborns. *Psychological Science*, 21, 343–348.

Callaghan, T., Rochat, P., Lillard, A., Claux, M. L., Odden, H., Itakura, S., Tapanya, S. and Singh, S. (2005). Synchrony in the onset of mental-state reasoning: Evidence from five cultures. *Psychological Science*, 16(5), 378–384.

Campbell, F. A. and Ramey, C. T. (1994). Effects of early intervention on intellectual and academic achievement: A follow-up study of children from low-income families. *Child Development*, 65, 684–698.

Campbell, F. A. and Ramey, C. T. (1995). Cognitive and school outcomes for high risk African-American students at middle adolescence: Positive effects of early intervention. *American Educational Research Journal*, 32, 743–772.

Campbell, F. A. and Ramey, C. T. (2007). *Critical issues in cost effectiveness in children's first decade*. Presented at the National Invitational Conference of the Early Childhood Research Collaborative.

Campbell, F. A., Pungello, E. P., Miller-Johnson, S., Burchinal, M. and Ramey, C. T. (2001). The development of cognitive and academic abilities: Growth curves from an early childhood educational experiment. *Developmental Psychology*, 37, 231–242.

Campbell, F. A., Ramey, C. T., Pungello, E. P., Sparling, J. J. and Miller-Johnson, S. (2002). Early childhood education: Young adult outcomes from the Abecedarian Project. *Applied Developmental Science*, 6, 42–57.

Campos, J. J. and Langer, A. (1971). The visual cliff: Discriminative cardiac orienting responses with retinal size held constant. *Psychophysiology*, 8, 264–265.

Campos, J. J., Hiatt, S., Ramsay, D., Henderson, C. and Svedja, M. (1978). The emergence of fear on the visual cliff. In M. Lewis and L. A. Rosenblum (Eds), *The development of affect* (pp. 149–182). New York: Plenum.

Campos, J. J., Langer, A. and Krowitz, A. (1970). Cardiac responses on the visual cliff in prelocomotor human infants. *Science*, 170(3954), 196–197.

Canobi, K. H. and Bethune, N. E. (2008). Number words in young children's conceptual and procedural knowledge of addition, subtraction and inversion. *Cognition*, 108, 675–686.

Carey, S. (1985). *Conceptual change in childhood*. Cambridge, MA: Bradford Books/MIT Press.

Carey, S. (1986). Cognitive science and science education. *American Psychologist*, 41(10), 1123–1130.

Carey, S. (1991). Knowledge acquisition: enrichment or conceptual change? In S. Carey and R. Gelman (Eds), *The epigenesis of mind: Essays in biology and cognition* (pp. 257–291). Hillsdale, NJ: Lawrence Erlbaum Associates.

Carey, S. and Spelke, E. (1996). Science and core knowledge. *Philosophy of Science*, 63(4), 515–533.

Carey, S. and Spelke, E. S. (1994). Domain specific knowledge and conceptual change. In L. Hirschfeld and S. Gelman (Eds), *Mapping the mind: Domain specificity in cognition and culture* (pp. 169–200). Cambridge: Cambridge University Press.

Carey, S., Evans, R., Honda, M., Jay, E. and Unger, C. (1989). 'An experiment is when you try it and see if it works': A study of grade 7 students' understanding of the construction of scientific knowledge. *International Journal of Science Education*, 11, 514–529.

Carpenter, G. (1974). Mother's face and the newborn. *New Scientist*, 61, 742–744.

Carpenter, T. P., Corbitt, M. K., Kepner, H. S., Lindquist, M. M. and Reys, R. E. (1981). *Results from the second mathematics assessment of the National Assessment of Educational Progress*. Washington, DC: National Council of Teachers of Mathematics.

Carraher, T. N., Carraher, D. W. and Schliemann, A. D. (1985). Mathematics in the streets and in schools. *British Journal of Developmental Psychology, 3,* 21–29.

Carroll, J. B. (1993). *Human cognitive abilities: A survey of factor-analytical studies.* New York: Cambridge University Press.

Carroll, J. B. (1997). The three-stratum theory of cognitive abilities. In D. P. Flanagan, J. L. Genshaft and P. L. Harrison (Eds), *Contemporary intellectual assessment: Theories, tests and issues* (pp. 122–130). New York: The Guilford Press.

Cartwright, T. A. and Brent, M. R. (1997). Syntactic categorization in early language acquisition: formalizing the role of distributional analysis. *Cognition, 63,* 121–170.

Case, R. (1985). *Intellectual development: Birth to adulthood.* Orlando, FL: Academic.

Case, R. (1992). The role of the frontal lobes in the regulation of cognitive development. *Brain and Cognition, 30,* 51–73.

Case, R., Kurland, M. and Goldberg, J. (1982). Operational efficiency and the growth of short-term memory span. *Journal of Experimental Child Psychology, 33,* 386–404.

Caspi, A., Harkness, A., Moffitt, T. E. and Silva, P. A. (1996). Continuity and change in human development: Lessons learnt from the study of intellectual performance. In P. A. Silva and W. A. Stanton (Eds), *From child to adult: The Dunedin study* (pp. 59–74). Oxford: Oxford University Press.

Cassel, W. S. and Bjorklund, D. F. (1995). Developmental patterns of eyewitness memory and suggestibility: An ecologically based short-term longitudinal study. *Law and Human Behavior, 19,* 507–532.

Castellanos, E. X., Giedd, J. N., Eckburg, P., Marsh, W. L., Vaituzis, C., Kaysen, D., Hamburger, S. D. and Rapoport, J. L. (1994). Quantitative morphology of the caudate nucleus in attention deficit hyperactivity disorder. *American Journal of Psychiatry, 151,* 1791–1796.

Castelli, F., Glaser, D. E. and Butterworth, B. (2006). Discrete and analogue quantity processing in the parietal lobe: A functional MRI study. *Proceedings of the National Academy of Science, 103,* 4693–4698.

Castles, A. and Coltheart, M. (2004). Is there a causal link from phonological awareness to success in learning to read? *Cognition, 91*(1), 77–111.

Cattell, R. B. (1963). Theory of fluid and crystallized intelligence: A critical experiment. *Journal of Educational Psychology, 54,* 1–22.

Cattell, R. B. (1971). *Abilities: Their structure, growth, and action.* Boston, MA: Houghton Mifflin.

Ceci, S. J. (1996). *On intelligence: A bio-ecological treatise on intellectual development* (2nd ed.). Cambridge, MA: Harvard University Press.

Ceci, S. J. and Bronfenbrenner, U. (1985). 'Don't forget to take the cupcakes out of the oven': Prospective memory, strategic time-monitoring, and context. *Child Development, 56*(1), 152–164.

Ceci, S. J. and Bruck, M. (1993). Suggestibility of the child witness: A historical review and synthesis. *Psychological Bulletin, 113*(3), 403–439.

Cernoch, J. M. and Porter, R. H. (1985). Recognition of maternal axillary odors by infants. *Child Development, 56*(6), 1593–1598.

Chall, J. S. (1979). The great debate: Ten years later, with a modest proposal for reading stages. In L. Resnick and P. A. Weaver (Eds), *Theory and practice of early reading* (pp. 29–56). Hillsdale, NJ: Lawrence Erlbaum Associates.

Chall, J. S. (1983). *Stages of reading development.* New York: Harcourt Brace and Co.

Chandler, M., Fritz, A. S. and Hala, S. (1989). Small-scale deceit: deception as a marker of 2-year-old, 3-year-old, and 4-year-olds early theories of mind. *Child Development, 60*(6), 1263–1277.

Charman, T. and Chandiramani, S. (1995). Children's understanding of physical illnesses and psychological states. *Psychology and Health, 10*(2), 145–153.

Chase, W. G. and Simon, H. A. (1973). Perception in chess. *Cognitive Psychology, 4*(1), 55–81.

Chen, Z. and Klahr, D. (1999). All other things being equal: Acquisition and transfer of the control of variables strategy. *Child Development, 70*(5), 1098–1120.

Chen, Z., Sanchez, R. P. and Campbell, T. (1997). From beyond to within their grasp: The rudiments of analogical problem solving in 10- and 13-month-olds. *Developmental Psychology, 33*(5), 790–801.

Cheng, P. and Holyoak, K. (1985). Pragmatic reasoning schemas. *Cognitive Psychology, 17,* 391–416.

Cheng, P. W. and Holyoak, K. J. (1989). On the natural selection of reasoning theories. *Cognition, 33,* 285–313.

Chi, M., Glaser, R. and Rees, E. (1982). Expertise in problem solving. In R. Sternberg (Ed.), *Advances in the psychology of human intelligence* (Vol. 1, pp. 7–75). Hillsdale, NJ: Lawrence Erlbaum Associates.

Chi, M. T. H. (1978). Knowledge structures and memory development. In R. Siegler (Ed.), *Children's thinking: What develops?* (pp. 73–96). Hillsdale, NJ: Lawrence Erlbaum Associates.

Chi, M. T. H. and Koeske, R. (1983). Network representation of a child's dinosaur knowledge. *Developmental Psychology, 19,* 29–39.

Chomsky, N. (1957). *Syntactic structures.* The Hague: Mouton.

Chomsky, N. (1959). A review of B. F. Skinner's 'Verbal Behavior'. *Language, 35,* 26–58.

Chomsky, N. (1965). *Aspects of the theory of syntax.* Cambridge, MA: MIT Press.

Chomsky, N. (1981). *Lectures on government and binding*. Dordrecht: Foris.

Chua, E. F., Schachter, D. L. and Sperling, R. A. (2009). Neural correlates of metamemory: A comparison of feeling-of-knowing and retrospective confidence judgments. *Journal of Cognitive Neuroscience, 21*, 1751–1765.

Clark, E. V. (1995). Later lexical development and word formation. In P. Fletcher and B. MacWhinney (Eds), *The handbook of child language* (pp. 393–412). Oxford: Blackwell.

Clements, W. A. and Perner, J. (1994). Implicit understanding of belief. *Cognitive Development, 9*(4), 377–395.

Clough, E. E. and Driver, R. (1991). A study of consistency in the use of students' conceptual frameworks across different task contexts. In P. Light, S. Sheldon and M. Woodhead (Eds), *Learning to think* (pp. 261–291). London: Open University.

Cohen, I. L. (2007). A neural network model of autism: implications for theory and treatment. In D. Mareschal, S. Sirois, and G. Westermann (Eds), *Neuroconstructivism, Vol. II: Perspectives and prospects* (pp. 231–264). Oxford: Oxford University Press.

Cole, M. (2006). Culture and cognitive development in phylogenetic, historical and ontogenetic perspective. In D. Kuhn and R. Siegler (Eds), *Handbook of child psychology, Vol. 2: Cognition, perception, and language* (6th ed.) (pp. 636–686). New York: Wiley.

Cole, M. and Cigagas, X. E. (2010). Culture and cognition. In M. H. Bornstein (Ed.), *Handbook of cultural developmental science* (pp. 127–142). New York: Psychology Press.

Corballis, M. C. (2004). The origins of modernity: Was autonomous speech the critical factor? *Psychological Review, 111*, 543–552.

Courage, M. L. and Cowan, N. (Eds) (2009). *The development of memory in infancy and childhood*. Hove: Psychology Press.

Creel, S. C., Newport, E. L. and Aslin, R. N. (2004). Distant melodies: Statistical learning of non-adjacent dependencies in tone sequences. *Journal of Experimental Psychology: Learning, Memory, and Cognition, 30*, 1119–1130.

Croker, S. (2007). Symbols without rules: A computational model of language acquisition using distributional analysis. In B. Wallace (Ed.), *The mind, the body and the world: Psychology after cognitivism?* (pp.185–207). Exeter: Imprint Academic.

Croker, S. and Buchanan, H. (in press). Scientific reasoning in a real world context: The effect of prior belief and outcome on children's hypothesis testing strategies. *British Journal of Developmental Psychology*.

Croker, S., Pine, J. M. and Gobet, F. (2000). Modelling optional infinitive phenomena. In N. Taatgen and J. Aasman (Eds), *Proceedings of the 3rd International Conference on Cognitive Modeling* (pp. 78–85). Veenendaal, Holland: Universal Press.

Croker, S., Pine, J. M. and Gobet, F. (2001). Modelling children's case-marking errors. In E. M. Altmann, A. Cleeremans, C. D. Schunn and W. D. Gray (Eds), *Proceedings of the 2001 Fourth International Conference on Cognitive Modeling* (pp. 55–60). Mahwah, NJ: Lawrence Erlbaum Associates.

Croker, S., Pine, J. M. and Gobet, F. (2003). Modelling children's negation errors using probabilistic learning in MOSAIC. In F. Detje, D. Dörner and H. Schaub (Eds), *Proceedings of the Fifth International Conference on Cognitive Modeling* (pp. 69–74). Bamberg: Universitäts-Verlag.

Crook, C. K. (1978). Taste perception in the newborn infant. *Infant Behavior and Development, 1*, 52–69.

Cultice, J. C., Somerville, S. C. and Wellman, H. M. (1983). Preschoolers' memory monitoring: feeling-of-knowing judgments. *Child Development, 54*(6), 1480–1486.

Curtiss, S. (1977). *Genie: A psycholinguistic study of a modern-day 'wild child'*. London: Academic Press.

D'Andrade, R. (1982). *Reason versus logic*. Paper presented at the Symposium on the Ecology of Cognition: Biological, Cultural, and Historical Perspectives, Greensboro, North Carolina.

Damasio, A. (1999). *The feeling of what happens: Body and emotion in the making of consciousness*. New York: Harcourt Brace and Co.

Dawson, M., Soulières, I., Gernsbacher, M. A. and Mottron, L. (2007). The level and nature of autistic intelligence. *Psychological Science, 18*, 657–662.

de Gelder, B., Vroomen, J. and Van der Heide, L. (1991). Face recognition and lip-reading in autism. *European Journal of Cognitive Psychology, 3*(1), 69–86.

de Haan, M., Pascalis, O. and Johnson, M. H. (2002). Specialization of neural mechanisms underlying face recognition in human infants. *Journal of Cognitive Neuroscience, 14*(2), 199–209.

De Neys, W. and Van Gelder, E. (2009). Logic and belief across the life span: The rise and fall of belief inhibition during syllogistic reasoning. *Developmental Science, 12*(1), 123–130.

Dean, D. and Kuhn, D. (2007). Direct instruction vs discovery: The long view. *Science Education, 91*(3), 384–397.

DeCasper, A. and Spence, M. J. (1986). Prenatal maternal speech influences newborns' perception of speech sounds. *Infant Behavior and Development, 9*, 133–150.

DeCasper, A. J. and Fifer, W. P. (1980). Of human bonding: Newborns prefer their mothers' voices. *Science, 208*(4448), 1174–6.

Dehaene, S., Molko, N. and Cohen, L. (2004). Arithmetic and the brain. *Current Opinion in Neurobiology, 14*, 218–224.

Dehaene, S., Piazza, M., Pinel, P. and Cohen, L. (2003). Three parietal circuits for number processing. *Cognitive Neuropsychology, 20*, 487–506.

DeMarie, D. and Ferron, J. (2003). Capacity, strategies, and metamemory: Tests of a three-factor model of memory development. *Journal of Experimental Child Psychology, 84*, 167–193.

DeMarie, D., Miller, P. H., Ferron, J. and Cunningham, W. R. (2004). Path analysis tests of theoretical models of children's memory performance. *Journal of Cognition and Development, 5*(4), 461–492.

Demers, R. A. (1988). Linguistics and animal communication. In F. J. Newmeyer (Ed.), *Linguistics: The Cambridge survey III. Language: Psychological and biological aspects.* (pp. 314–35). Cambridge: Cambridge University Press.

Dempster, F. N. (1981). Memory span: Sources of individual and developmental differences. *Psychological Bulletin, 89*, 63–100.

Desor, J. A., Maller, O. and Turner, R. E. (1973). Taste in acceptance of sugars by human infants. *Journal of Comparative and Physiological Psychology, 84*, 496–501.

Diamond, A. (1985). The development of the ability to use recall to guide action, as indicated by infants' performance on A-not-B. *Child Development, 56*, 868–883.

Dias, M. G. and Harris, P. L. (1988). The effect of make-believe play on deductive reasoning. *British Journal of Developmental Psychology, 6*, 207–221.

Dias, M. G. and Harris, P. L. (1990). The influence of the imagination on reasoning by young children. *British Journal of Developmental Psychology, 8*, 305–318.

Dichter, G. S., Radonovich, K. J., Turner-Brown, L. M., Lam, K. S. L., Holtzclaw, T. N. and Bodfish, J. W. (2010). Performance of children with autism spectrum disorders on the dimension-change card sort task. *Journal of Autism and Developmental Disorders, 40*(4), 448–456.

Doherty, M. J. (2009). *Theory of mind.* Hove: Psychology Press.

Dollaghan, C. A. (1994). Children's phonological neighbourhoods: Half empty or half full? *Journal of Child Language, 21*, 257–71.

Domsch, H., Lohaus, A. and Thomas, H. (2009). Prediction of childhood cognitive abilities from a set of early indicators of information processing capabilities. *Infant Behavior and Development, 32*, 91–102.

Donahue, P. L., Voelkl, K. E., Campbell, J. R. and Mazzeo, J. (1999). *NAEP 1998 reading report card for the nation and states.* Washington, DC: National Center for Educational Statistics.

Donlan, C. (Ed.) (1998). *The development of mathematical skills.* Hove: Psychology Press.

Dowker, A. (2005). *Individual differences in arithmetic.* Hove: Psychology Press.

Dowker, A. (2008). Individual differences in numerical abilities in preschoolers. *Developmental Science, 11*, 650–654.

Dufresne, A. and Kobasigawa, A. (1989). Children's spontaneous allocation of study time: Differential and sufficient aspects. *Journal of Experimental Child Psychology, 47*, 274–296.

Dunbar, K. and Klahr, D. (1989). Developmental differences in scientific discovery processes. In D. Klahr and K. Kotovsky (Eds), *Complex information processing: The impact of Herbert A. Simon* (pp. 109–143). Hillsdale, NJ: Lawrence Erlbaum Associates.

Duncker, K. (1945). On problem solving. *Psychological Monographs, 58* (Whole No. 270).

Dunn, J. (1988). *The beginnings of social understanding.* Oxford: Blackwell.

Dunn, J. (1991). Young children's understanding of other people: Evidence from observations within the family. In D. Frye and C. Moore (Eds), *Children's theories of mind* (pp. 97–114). Hillsdale, NJ: Lawrence Erlbaum Associates.

Durkin, D. (1966). *Children who read early.* New York: Teachers College Press.

Duschl, R. A., Schweingruber, H. A. and Shouse, A. W. (2006). *Taking science to school.* Washington, DC: National Academies Press.

Ehri, L. (1999). Phases of development in learning to read words. In J. Oakhill and R. Beard (Eds), *Reading development and the teaching of reading: A psychological perspective* (pp. 79–108). Oxford: Blackwell Publishers.

Ehri, L. (2002). Reading processes, acquisition, and instructional implications. In G. Reid and J. Wearmouth (Eds), *Dyslexia and literacy: Theory and practice* (pp. 167–185). West Sussex, UK: Wiley.

Ehri, L. (2005). Development of sight word reading: Phases and findings. In M. J. Snowling and C. Hulme (Eds), *The science of reading: A handbook.* Oxford: Blackwell.

Ehri, L., Nunes, R. S., Stahl, S. and Willows, D. (2001). Systematic phonics instruction helps students learn to read: Evidence from the National Reading Panel's meta-analysis. *Review of Educational Research, 71*, 393–447.

Ehri, L. C. (1992). Reconceptualizing the development of sight word reading and its relationship to recoding. In P. Gough, L. C. Ehri and R. Treiman (Eds), *Reading Acquisition* (pp. 107–143). Hillsdale, NJ: Lawrence Erlbaum Associates.

Eimas, P. D., Siqueland, E. R., Jusczyk, P. and Vigorito, J. (1971). Speech perception in infants. *Science, 171*(3968), 303–306.

Eiser, C. (1989). Children's concepts of illness: Towards an alternative to the 'Stage' approach. *Psychology and Health, 3*(2), 93–101.

Elman, J. L. (1993). Learning and development in neural networks: The importance of starting small. *Cognition*, 48, 71–99.

Elman, J. L., Bates, E., Johnson, M., Karmiloff-Smith, A., Parisi, D. and Plunkett, K. (1996). *Rethinking innateness: A connectionist perspective on development*. Cambridge, MA: MIT Press.

Enard, W., Przeworski, M., Fisher, S. E., Lai, C. S. L., Wiebe, V., Kitano, T., Monaco, A. P. and Paabo, S. (2002). Molecular evolution of FOXP2, a gene involved in speech and language. *Nature*, 418, 869–872.

Engen, T., Lipsitt, L. P. and Kaye, H. (1963). Olfactory responses and adaptation in the human neonate. *Journal of Comparative and Physiological Psychology*, 56(1), 73–77.

Entus, A. K. (1977). Hemispheric asymmetry in processing of dichotically presented speech and nonspeech stimuli by infants. In S. J. Segalowtiz and F. A. Gruber (Eds), *Language development and neurological theory* (pp. 63–73). New York: Academic Press.

Evans, J. S. B. T. and Feeney, A. (2004). The role of prior belief in reasoning. In J. P. Leighton and R. J. Sternberg (Eds), *The nature of reasoning* (pp. 78–102). Cambridge: Cambridge University Press.

Evans, J. S. B. T. and Newstead, S. E. (1995). Creating a psychology of reasoning: The contribution of Peter Wason. In S. E. Newstead and J. S. B. T. Evans (Eds), *Perspectives on thinking and reasoning* (pp. 1–16). Hove: Lawrence Erlbaum Associates.

Evans, J. S. T., Barston, J. L. and Pollard, P. (1983). On the conflict between logic and belief in syllogistic reasoning. *Memory and Cognition*, 11(3), 295–306.

Everett, D. (2005). Cultural constraints on grammar and cognition in Pirahã: Another look at the design features of human language. *Current Anthropology*, 46, 621–634.

Fagan, J. F. (1984). The relationship of novelty preferences during infancy to later intelligence and later recognition memory. *Intelligence*, 8, 339–346.

Fantz, R. L. (1958). Pattern vision in young infants. *Psychological Record*, 8, 43–47.

Fantz, R. L. (1961). The origin of form perception. *Scientific American*, 204(5), 66–72.

Fantz, R. L. and Miranda, S. B. (1975). Newborn infant attention to form of contour. *Child Development*, 46(1), 224–228.

Fantz, R. L., Ordy, J. M. and Udelf, M. S. (1962). Maturation of pattern vision in infants during the first six months. *Journal of Comparative and Physiological Psychology*, 55, 907–917.

Faraone, S. V., Perlis, R. H., Doyle, A. E., Smoller, J. W., Goralnick, J. J., Holmgren, M. A. and Sklar, P. (2005). Molecular genetics of attention-deficit/hyperactivity disorder. *Biological Psychiatry*, 57, 1313–1323.

Farroni, T., Menon, E. and Rigato, S. and Johnson, M. H. (2007). The perception of facial expressions in newborns. *European Journal of Developmental Psychology*, 4(1), 2–13.

Fenson, L., Dale, P., Reznick, J., Bates, E., Thal, D. and Pethick, J. (1994). Variability in early communication development. *Monographs of the Society for Research in Child Development*, 59(5, Serial No. 242).

Field, T. M., Cohen, D., Garcia, R. and Greenberg, R. (1984). Mother-stranger face discrimination by the newborn. *Infant Behavior and Development*, 7(1), 19–25.

Field, T. M., Woodson, R., Cohen, D., Greenberg, R., Garcia, R. and Collins, K. (1983). Discrimination and imitation of facial expressions by term and preterm neonates. *Infant Behavior and Development*, 6(4), 485–489.

Field, T. M., Woodson, R., Greenberg, R. and Cohen, D. (1982). Discrimination and imitation of facial expression by neonates. *Science*, 218(4568), 179–181.

Filipek, P. A., Accardo, P. J., Baranek, G. T., Cook, E. H., Dawson, G., Gordon, B. et al. (1999). The screening and diagnosis of autistic spectrum disorders. *Journal of Autism and Developmental Disorders*, 29(6), 439–484.

Fischer, K. W. (1980). A theory of cognitive development: The control and construction of hierarchies of skills. *Psychological Review*, 87, 477–531.

Fiser, J. and Aslin, R. N. (2002). Statistical learning of higher-order temporal structure from visual shape-sequences. *Journal of Experimental Psychology: Learning, Memory, and Cognition*, 28(3), 458–467.

Fivush, R. and Hamond, N. R. (1990). Autobiographical memory across the preschool years: Toward reconceptualizing childhood amnesia. In R. Fivush and J. A. Hudson (Eds), *Knowing and remembering in young children* (pp. 223–248). New York: Cambridge University Press.

Fivush, R. and Nelson, K. (2004). Culture and language in the emergence of autobiographical memory. *Psychological Science*, 15(9), 573–577.

Flavell, J. H. (1970). Developmental studies of mediated memory. In H. W. Reese and L. P. Lipsitt (Eds), *Advances in child development and behavior: Vol. 5* (pp. 181–211). New York: Academic Press.

Flavell, J. H. and Wellman, H. M. (1977). Metamemory. In R. V. Kail and J. W. Hagin (Eds), *Perspectives on the development of memory and cognition* (pp. 3–33). Hillsdale, NJ: Lawrence Erlbaum Associates.

Flavell, J. H., Beach, D. R. and Chinsky, J. M. (1966). Spontaneous verbal rehearsal in a memory task as a function of age. *Child Development*, 37(2), 283–299.

Flavell, J. H., Flavell, E. R. and Green, F. L. (1983). Development of the appearance-reality distinction. *Cognitive Psychology*, 15, 95–120.

Flavell, J. H., Green, F. L. and Flavell, E. R. (1986). Development of knowledge about the appearance-reality distinction. *Monographs of the Society for Research in Child Development, 51*(1, Serial No. 212).

Flin, R., Boon, J., Bull, R. and Knox, A. (1992). The effects of a five month delay on children's and adults' eyewitness memory. *British Journal of Psychology, 83*, 323–336.

Fodor, J. A. (1983). *The modularity of mind: An essay on faculty psychology.* Cambridge, MA: MIT Press.

Fodor, J. A. (1992). A theory of the child's theory of mind. *Cognition, 41*, 283–296.

Fombonne, E. (2003). Epidemiological surveys of autism and other pervasive developmental disorders: An update. *Journal of Autism and Developmental Disorders, 33*(4), 365–382.

Fox, R., Aslin, R. N., Shea, S. L. and Dumais, S. T. (1980). Stereopsis in human infants. *Science, 207*(4428), 323–324.

Frankel, M. T. and Rollins, H. A. (1985). Associative and categorical hypotheses of organization in the free recall of adults and children. *Journal of Experimental Child Psychology, 40*(2), 304–318.

Freeman, N. H., Lewis, C. and Doherty, M. J. (1991). Preschoolers grasp of a desire for knowledge in false-belief prediction: Practical intelligence and verbal report. *British Journal of Developmental Psychology, 9*, 139–157.

Freud, S. (2000). *Three essays on the theory of sexuality.* New York: Basic Books. (Original work published in 1905).

Freudenthal, D., Pine, J. M. and Gobet, F. (2001). Modeling the optional infinitive stage in MOSAIC: A generalisation to Dutch. In E. M. Altmann, A. Cleeremans, C. D. Schunn and W. D. Gray (Eds), *Proceedings of the 4th international conference on cognitive modeling* (pp. 79–84). Mahwah, NJ: Lawrence Erlbaum Associates.

Freudenthal, D., Pine, J. M. and Gobet, F. (2002a). Modelling the development of Dutch optional infinitives in MOSAIC. In W. D. Gray and C. D. Schunn (Eds), *Proceedings of the 24th annual meeting of the Cognitive Science Society* (pp. 328–333). Mahwah, NJ: Lawrence Erlbaum Associates.

Freudenthal, D., Pine, J. M. and Gobet, F. (2002b). Subject omission in children's language: the case for performance limitations in learning. In W. D. Gray and C. D. Schunn (Eds), *Proceedings of the 24th annual meeting of the Cognitive Science Society* (pp. 334–339). Mahwah, NJ: Lawrence Erlbaum Associates.

Freudenthal, D., Pine, J. M. and Gobet, F. (2006). Modelling the development of children's use of optional infinitives in English and Dutch using MOSAIC. *Cognitive Science, 30*, 277–310.

Freudenthal, D., Pine, J. M. and Gobet, F. (2007). Understanding the developmental dynamics of subject omission: the role of processing limitations in learning. *Journal of Child Language, 34*, 83–110.

Freudenthal, D., Pine, J. M. and Gobet, F. (2009). Simulating the referential properties of Dutch, German and English root infinitives in MOSAIC. *Language Learning and Development, 5*, 1–29.

Freudenthal, D., Pine, J. M., Aguado-Orea, J. and Gobet, F. (2007). Modelling the developmental patterning of finiteness marking in English, Dutch, German and Spanish using MOSAIC. *Cognitive Science, 31*, 311–341.

Frith, U. (1985). Beneath the surface of developmental dyslexia. In K. Patterson, J. Marshall and M. Coltheart (Eds), *Surface dyslexia, neuropsychological and cognitive studies of phonological reading* (pp. 301–330). London: Lawrence Erlbaum Associates.

Frith, U. (1996). Cognitive explanations of autism. *Acta Pædiatrica Supplement, 416*, 63–68.

Frith, U. (2003). *Autism: Explaining the enigma.* Oxford: Blackwell.

Frith, U. and Frith, C. D. (2003). Development and neurophysiology of mentalising. *Philosophical Transactions of the Royal Society of London – Series B: Biological Sciences, 358*, 459–473.

Frith, U. and Snowling, M. (1983). Reading for meaning and reading for sound in autistic and dyslexic children. *British Journal of Developmental Psychology, 1*, 329–342.

Fry, A. F. and Hale, S. (1996). Processing speed, working memory, and fluid intelligence: Evidence for a developmental cascade. *Psychological Science, 7*(4), 237–241.

Fry, A. F. and Hale, S. (2000). Relationships among processing speed, working memory, and fluid intelligence in children. *Biological Psychology, 54*(1–3), 1–34.

Furth, H. G. and Milgram, N. A. (1973). Labeling and grouping effects in the recall of pictures by children. *Child Development, 44*(3), 511–518.

Fuson, K. C. (1992). Research on learning and teaching addition and subtraction of whole numbers. In G. Leinhardt, R. T. Putnam and R. A. Hattrup (Eds), *The analysis of arithmetic for mathematics teaching* (pp. 53–187). Hillsdale, NJ: Lawrence Erlbaum Associates.

Fuson, K. C. and Kwon, Y. (1992). Korean children's understanding of multidigit addition and subtraction. *Child Development, 63*(2), 491–506.

Gallistel, C. R. (1990) *The organization of learning.* Cambridge, MA: MIT Press.

Galton, F. (1883). *Inquiry into human faculty and its development.* London: MacMillan.

Gardner, H. (1993a). *Frames of mind: The theory of multiple intelligences* (2nd ed.). London: Fontana.

Gardner, H. (1993b). *Multiple intelligences: The theory in practice*. New York: Basic Books.

Gardner, R. A. and Gardner, B. T. (1969). Teaching sign language to a chimpanzee. *Science*, *165*(894), 664–672.

Garnham, W. A. and Ruffman, T. (2001). Doesn't see, doesn't know: is anticipatory looking really related to understanding of belief? *Developmental Science*, *4*(1), 94–100.

Gathercole, S. E. (1998). The development of memory. *Journal of Child Psychology and Psychiatry*, *39*, 3–27.

Gathercole, S. E. (1999). Cognitive approaches to the development of short-term memory. *Trends in Cognitive Sciences*, *3*, 410–418.

Gathercole, S. E. and Baddeley, A. D. (1989). Evaluation of the role of phonological STM in the development of vocabulary in children: A longitudinal study. *Journal of Memory and Language*, *28*, 200–213.

Gathercole, S. E. and Baddeley, A. D. (1993). *Working memory and language*. Hove: Lawrence Erlbaum Associates.

Gathercole, S. E., Willis, C., Baddeley, A. D. and Emslie, H. (1994). The Children's Test of Nonword Repetition: A test of phonological working memory. *Memory*, *2*, 103–127.

Gaultney, J. F. and Gingras, J. L. (2005). Fetal rate of behavioral inhibition and preference for novelty during infancy. *Early Human Development*, *81*(4), 379–386.

Geary, D., Hamson, C. and Hoard, M. (2000). Numerical and arithmetical cognition: A longitudinal study of process and concept deficits in children with learning disability. *Journal of Experimental Child Psychology*, *77*, 236–263.

Geary, D. C. (1993). Mathematical disabilities: Cognition, neuropsychological and genetic components. *Psychological Bulletin*, *114*, 345–362.

Geary, D. C. (2004). Mathematics and learning disabilities. *Journal of Learning Disabilities*, *37*, 4–15.

Geary, D. C. and Widaman, K. F. (1987). Individual differences in cognitive arithmetic. *Journal of Experimental Psychology: General*, *116*, 154–171.

Geary, D. C. and Widaman, K. F. (1992). Numerical cognition: On the convergence of componential and psychometric models. *Intelligence*, *16*, 47–80.

Geary, D. C., Bow-Thomas, C. C. and Yao, Y. (1992). Counting knowledge and skill in cognitive addition: A comparison of normal and mathematically disabled children. *Journal of Experimental Child Psychology*, *54*, 372–391.

Gelman, R. and Gallistel, C. R. (1978). *The child's understanding of number*. Cambridge, MA: Harvard University Press.

Gelman, R., Spelke, E. S. and Meck, E. (1983). What preschoolers know about animate and inanimate objects. In D. Rogers and J. Sloboda (Eds), *The development of symbolic thought* (pp. 297–328). London: Plenum.

Gentner, D. (1977a). Children's performance on a spatial analogies task. *Child Development*, *48*(3), 1034–1039.

Gentner, D. (1977b). If a tree had a knee, where would it be? Children's performance on simple spatial metaphors. *Papers and Reports on Child Language Development*, *13*, 157–164.

Gentner, D. (1983). Structure-mapping: A theoretical framework for analogy. *Cognitive Science*, *7*, 155–170.

Gentner, D. (1988). Analogical inference and analogical access. In A. Prieditis (Ed.), *Analogica* (pp. 63–88). Los Altos, CA: Morgan Kaufmann.

Gentner, D. (1989). The mechanisms of analogical learning. In S. Vosniadou and A. Ortony (Eds), *Similarity and analogical reasoning* (pp. 199–241). London: Cambridge University Press.

Gentner, D. and Rattermann, M. J. (1991). Language and the career of similarity. In S. A. Gelman and J. P. Byrnes (Eds), *Perspectives on thought and language: Interrelations in development* (pp. 225–277). London: Cambridge University Press.

Gepner, B., Mestre, D., Masson, G. and De Schonen, S. (1995). Postural effects of motion vision in young autistic children. *Neuroreport*, *6*, 1211–1214.

Gesell, A. (1925). *The mental growth of the preschool child*. New York: Macmillan.

Gibson, E. J. (1969). *Principles of perceptual learning and development*. New York: Appleton.

Gibson, E. J. and Pick, A. D. (2000). *An ecological approach to perceptual learning and development*. Oxford: Oxford University Press.

Gibson, E. J. and Walk, R. D. (1960). The 'visual cliff'. *Scientific American*, *202*, 64–71.

Gibson, E. J., Owsley, C. J., Walker, A. and Megaw-Nyce, J. (1979). Development of the perception of invariants: Substance and shape. *Perception*, *8*(6), 609–619.

Gibson, J. J. (1950). *The perception of the visual world*. Boston, MA: Houghton Mifflin.

Gibson, J. J. (1966). *The senses considered as perceptual systems*. Boston, MA: Houghton Mifflin.

Gick, M. L. and Holyoak, K. J. (1980). Analogical problem-solving. *Cognitive Psychology*, *12*(3), 306–355.

Girotto, V. (1991). Reasoning on deontic rules: The pragmatic schemas approach. *Intellectica*, *1*(11), 15–52.

Girotto, V. and Light, P. (1992). The pragmatic bases of children's reasoning. In P. Light and G. Butterworth (Eds), *Context and cognition: Ways of learning and knowing* (pp. 135–156). Hemel Hempstead: Harvester Wheatsheaf.

Girotto, V., Blaye, A. and Farioli, F. (1989). A reason to reason: Pragmatic basis of children's search for counterexamples. *European Bulletin of Cognitive Psychology, 9*, 297–321.

Girotto, V., Gilly, M., Blaye, A. and Light, P. (1989). Children's performance in the selection task: Plausibility and familiarity. *British Journal of Psychology, 80*, 79–95.

Girotto, V., Light, P. and Colbourn, C. (1988). Pragmatic schemas and conditional reasoning in children. *Quarterly Journal of Experimental Psychology Section a-Human Experimental Psychology, 40*(3), 469–482.

Gladwin, T. (1970). *East is a big bird.* Cambridge, MA: Harvard University Press.

Gobbo, C. and Chi, M. (1986). How knowledge is structured and used by expert and novice children. *Cognitive Development, 1*(3), 221–237.

Gold, E. M. (1967). Language identification in the limit. *Information and Control, 10*, 447–474.

Golding, E. (1981). *The effect of past experience on problem solving.* Paper presented at the Annual Conference of the British Psychological Society, Surrey.

Gómez, R. L. (2002). Variability and detection of invariant structure. *Psychological Science, 13*(5), 431–436.

Gopnik, A. (1996a). The post-Piaget era. *Psychological Science, 7*(4), 221–225.

Gopnik, A. (1996b). The scientist as child. *Philosophy of Science, 63*(4), 485–514.

Gopnik, A. (2003). The theory theory as an alternative to the innateness hypothesis. In L. Antony and N. Hornstein (Eds), *Chomsky and his critics* (pp. 238–254). Oxford: Blackwell.

Gopnik, A. and Astington, J. W. (1988). Children's understanding of representational change and its relation to the understanding of false belief and the appearance-reality distinction. *Child Development, 59*(1), 26–37.

Gopnik, A. and Meltzoff, A. N. (1986). Relations between semantic and cognitive development in the one-word stage: The specificity hypothesis. *Child Development, 57*, 1040–1053.

Gopnik, A. and Wellman, H. M. (1992). Why the child's theory of mind really is a theory. *Mind and Language, 7*(1–2), 145–171.

Gopnik, A. and Wellman, H. M. (1994). The theory theory. In L. Hirschfeld and S. Gelman (Eds), *Mapping the mind: Domain specificity in cognition and culture* (pp. 257–293). New York: Cambridge University Press.

Gopnik, A., Capps, L. and Meltzoff, A. N. (2000). Early theories of mind: What the theory theory can tell us about autism. In S. Baron- Cohen, H. Tager-Flusberg and D. Cohen (Eds), *Understanding other minds: perspectives from autism and cognitive neuroscience* (2nd ed., pp. 50–72) Oxford: Oxford University Press.

Gopnik, A., Slaughter, V. and Meltzoff, A. (1994). Changing your views: How understanding visual perception can lead to a new theory of the mind. In C. Lewis and P. Mitchell (Eds), *Children's early understanding of mind* (pp. 157–181). Hove: Lawrence Erlbaum Associates.

Gordon, I. and Slater, A. (1998). Nativism and empiricism: The history of two ideas. In A. Slater (Ed.), *Perceptual development in infancy* (pp. 73–103). Hove: Psychology Press.

Gordon, R. M. (1986). Folk psychology as simulation. *Mind and Language, 1*(2), 158–171.

Gorman, J. J., Cogan, D. G. and Gellis, S. S. (1957). An apparatus for grading the visual acuity of infants on the basis of opticokinetic nystagmus. *Pediatrics, 19*, 1088–1092.

Gorman, J. J., Cogan, D. G. and Gellis, S. S. (1959). A device for testing visual acuity in infants. *Sight-Saving Review, 29*, 80–84.

Goswami, U. (1989). Relational complexity and the development of analogical reasoning. *Cognitive Development, 4*, 251–268.

Goswami, U. (1992). *Analogical reasoning in children.* Hove: Lawrence Erlbaum Associates.

Goswami, U. (1993). Toward interactive analogy model of reading development: Decoding vowel graphemes in beginning reading. *Journal of Experimental Child Psychology, 56*, 443–475.

Goswami, U. (2001). Analogical reasoning in children. In D. Gentner, K. J. Holyoak and B. N. Kokinov (Eds), *The analogical mind: Perspectives from cognitive science* (pp. 437–470). Cambridge, MA: MIT Press.

Goswami, U. (2002). In the beginning was the rhyme? A reflection on Hulme, Hatcher, Nation, Brown, Adams and Stuart. *Journal of Experimental Child Psychology, 82*, 47–57.

Goswami, U. and Brown, A. L. (1990a). Melting chocolate and melting snowmen: Analogical reasoning and causal relations. *Cognition, 35*(1), 69–95.

Goswami, U. and Brown, A. L. (1990b). Higher-order structure and relational reasoning: Contrasting analogical and thematic relations. *Cognition, 36*(3), 207–226.

Goswami, U. and Bryant, P. E. (1990). *Phonological skills and learning to read.* Hove: Psychology Press.

Goswami, U., Leevers, H., Pressley, S. and Wheelwright, S. (1998). Causal reasoning about pairs of relations and analogical reasoning in young children. *British Journal of Developmental Psychology, 16*, 553–568.

Gottardo, A., Stanovich, K. E. and Siegel, L. S. (1996). The relationships between phonological sensitivity, syntactic processing, and verbal working memory in the reading performance of third-grade children. *Journal of Experimental Child Psychology, 63*, 563–582.

Goubet, N., Rattaz, C., Pierrat, V., Allémann, E., Bullinger, A. and Lequien, P. (2002). Olfactory familiarization and discrimination in preterm and full-term newborns. *Infancy*, *3*(1), 53–75.

Gough, P. B. and Hillinger, M. L. (1980). Learning to read: An unnatural act. *Bulletin of the Orton Society*, *30*, 179–196.

Gratch, G. (1975). Recent studies based on Piaget's views of object concept development. In L. B. Cohen and P. Salapatek (Eds), *Infant perception: From sensation to cognition.* (Vol. 2, pp. 51–99). New York: Academic Press.

Green, C. and Chee, K. (1997). *Understanding ADHD – A parent's guide to Attention Deficit Hyperactivity Disorder in children.* London: Vermillion Publishing.

Green, H., McGinnity, Á., Meltzer, H., Ford, T. and Goodman, R. (2005). *Mental health of children and young people in Great Britain, 2004.* Basingstoke: Palgrave Macmillan.

Greenhoot, A. F., Semb, G., Colombo, J. and Schreiber, T. (2004). Prior beliefs and methodological concepts in scientific reasoning. *Applied Cognitive Psychology*, *18*(2), 203–221.

Greer, B. (1992). Multiplication and division as models of situations. In D. Grouws (Ed.), *Handbook of research on mathematics teaching and learning* (pp. 276–295). New York: Macmillan.

Griggs, R. A. and Cox, J. R. (1982). The elusive thematic-materials effect in Wason selection task. *British Journal of Psychology*, *73*, 407–420.

Grigorenko, E. L. (2005). A conservative meta-analysis of linkage and linkage-association studies of developmental dyslexia. *Scientific Studies of Reading*, *9*, 285–316.

Grigorenko, E. L., Geissler, P. W., Prince, R., Okatcha, F., Nokes, C., Kenny, D. A., Bundy, D. A. and Sternberg, R. J. (2001). The organization of Luo conceptions of intelligence: A study of implicit theories in a Kenyan village. *International Journal of Behavioral Development*, *25*(4), 367–378.

Grinyer, J. (2006). *Literacy, numeracy and the labour market: Further analysis of the Skills for Life survey.* Nottingham: DfES Publications.

Gross-Tsur, V., Manor, O. and Shalev, R. S. (1996). Developmental dyscalculia: prevalence and demographic features. *Developmental Medicine and Child Neurology*, *38*(1), 25–33.

Guilford, J. P. (1988). Some changes in the structure-of-intellect model. *Educational and Psychological Measurement*, *48*, 1–4.

Gutheil, G., Vera, A. and Keil, F. C. (1998). Do houseflies think? Patterns of induction and biological beliefs in development. *Cognition*, *66*, 33–49.

Halford, G. and Andrews, G. (2004). The development of deductive reasoning: How important is complexity? *Thinking and Reasoning*, *10*(2), 123–145.

Halford, G. and Galloway, W. (1977). Children who fail to make transitive inferences can remember comparisons. *Australian Journal of Psychology*, *29*(1), 1–5.

Halford, G. S. (1993). *Children's understanding: The development of mental models.* Hillsdale, NJ: Lawrence Erlbaum Associates.

Halford, G. S. (2000). Information-processing models of cognitive development. In U. Goswami (Ed.), *Blackwell handbook of childhood cognitive development.* Oxford: Blackwell.

Halford, G. S. and Kelly, M. E. (1984). On the basis of early transitivity judgments. *Journal of Experimental Child Psychology*, *38*(1), 42–63.

Hamond, N. R. and Fivush, R. (1991). Memories of Mickey Mouse: Young children recount their trip to Disneyworld. *Cognitive Development*, *6*(4), 433–448.

Handley, S. J., Capon, A., Beveridge, M., Dennis, I. and Evans, J. S. T. (2004). Working memory, inhibitory control and the development of children's reasoning. *Thinking and Reasoning*, *10*(2), 175–195.

Happé, F. (1994). An advanced test of theory of mind: Understanding of story characters' thoughts and feelings by able autistic, mentally handicapped, and normal children and adults. *Journal of Autism and Development Disorders*, *24*, 129–154.

Happé, F. (1999). Autism: Cognitive deficit or cognitive style? *Trends in Cognitive Sciences*, *3*, 216–222.

Happé, F. and Frith, U. (2006). The weak coherence account: Detail-focused cognitive style in autism spectrum disorders. *Journal of Autism and Developmental Disorders*, *36*(1), 5–25.

Happé, F. G. E. (1996). Studying weak central coherence at low levels: Children with autism do not succumb to visual illusions. A research note. *Journal of Child Psychology and Psychiatry and Allied Disciplines*, *37*(7), 873–877.

Happé, F. G. E. (1997). Central coherence and theory of mind in autism: Reading homographs in context. *British Journal of Developmental Psychology*, *15*, 1–12.

Happé, F., Ronald, A. and Plomin, R. (2006). Time to give up on a single explanation for autism. *Nature Neuroscience*, *9*(10), 1218–1220.

Hare, M., Elman, J. L. and Daugherty, K. G. (1995). Default generalization in connectionist networks. *Language and Cognitive Processes*, *10*, 601–630.

Harkness, S. and Super, C. M. (1992). Parental ethnotheories in action. In I. Sigel (Ed.), *Parental belief systems: The psychological consequences for children and families* (2nd ed.) (pp. 373–391). Hillsdale, NJ: Lawrence Erlbaum Associates.

Harley, T. A. (2008). *The psychology of language: From data to theory.* Hove: Psychology Press.

Harm, M. W. and Seidenberg, M. S. (1999). Phonology, reading acquisition and dyslexia: Insights from connectionist models. *Psychological Review, 106,* 491–528.

Harris, P. L. (1973). Perseverative errors in search by young infants. *Child Development, 44,* 28–33.

Harris, P. L. (1974). Perseverative search at a visibly empty place by young infants. *Journal of Experimental Child Psychology, 18,* 535–542.

Harris, P. L. (1992). From simulation to folk psychology: The case for development. *Mind and Language,* 7(1–2), 120–144.

Harris, P. L. and Núñez, M. (1996). Understanding of permission rules by preschool children. *Child Development,* 67(4), 1572–1591.

Hart, B. and Risley, T. R. (1995). *Meaningful differences in the everyday experience of young American children.* Baltimore, MD: Paul H. Brooks.

Hart, K. (1981). *Children's understanding of mathematics: 11–16.* London: John Murray.

Hassabis, D., Kumaran, D., Vann, S. D. and Maguire, E. A. (2007). Patients with hippocampal amnesia cannot imagine new experiences. *Proceedings of the National Academy of Sciences,* 104(5), 1726–1731.

Hasselhorn, M. (1992). Task dependency and the role of category typicality and metamemory in the development of an organizational strategy. *Child Development,* 63(1), 202–214.

Hatcher, P. J., Hulme C. and Ellis, A. W. (1994). Ameliorating early reading failure by integrating the teaching of reading and phonological skills: The phonological linkage hypothesis. *Child Development,* 65, 41–57.

Hauser, M. D., Chomsky, N. and Fitch, W. T. (2002). The faculty of language: what is it, who has it, and how did it evolve? *Science,* 298(5598), 1569–1579.

Hawkins, J., Pea, R. D., Glick, J. and Scribner, S. (1984). Merds that laugh don't like mushrooms: Evidence for deductive reasoning by preschoolers. *Developmental Psychology,* 20(4), 584–594.

Hayne, H., Rovee-Collier, C. and Borza, M. A. (1991). Infant memory for place information. *Memory and Cognition,* 19, 378–386.

Heath, S. B. (1983). *Ways with words: Language, life and work in communities and classrooms.* New York: Cambridge University Press.

Heath, S. B. (1989). Oral and literate traditions among Black Americans living in poverty. *American Psychologist,* 44(2), 367–373.

Heaton, P. (2003). Pitch memory, labeling and disembedding in autism. *Journal of Child Psychology and Psychiatry,* 44(4), 543–551.

Heaton, P., Hermelin, B. and Pring, L. (1998). Autism and pitch processing: a precursor for savant musical ability? *Music Perception,* 15(3), 291–305.

Heaton, R. K. (1981). *Wisconsin Card Sorting Test Manual.* Odessa, FL: Psychological Assessment Resources.

Heilman, K. M., Voeller, K. K. S. and Nadeau, S. E. (1991). A possible pathophysiological substrate of attention deficit hyperactivity disorder. *Journal of Child Neurology,* 6, 74–79.

Hepper, P. G. (1988). Foetal 'soap' addiction. *Lancet, 1,* 1347–8.

Hergenrather, J. R. and Rabinowitz, M. (1991). Age-related differences in the organization of children's knowledge of illness. *Developmental Psychology,* 27(6), 952–959.

Hernandez-Reif, M., Field, T., Diego, M. and Largie, S. (2003). Haptic habituation to temperature is slower in newborns of depressed mothers. *Infancy,* 4(1), 47–63.

Hespos, S. J. and Baillargeon, R. (2006). Décalage in infants' knowledge about occlusion and containment events: Converging evidence from action tasks. *Cognition,* 99, B31–B41.

Hoch, S. J. and Tschirgi, J. E. (1985). Logical knowledge and cue redundancy in deductive reasoning. *Memory and Cognition,* 13(5), 453–462.

Hoekstra, R. A., Happé, F., Baron-Cohen, S. and Ronald, A. (2010). Limited genetic covariance between autistic traits and intelligence: findings from a longitudinal twin study. *American Journal of Medical Genetics Part B: Neuropsychiatric Genetics,* 153B(5), 994–1007.

Hogrefe, G. J., Wimmer, H. and Perner, J. (1986). Ignorance versus false belief: A developmental lag in attribution of epistemic states. *Child Development,* 57(3), 567–582.

Honzik, M. P. (1986). The role of the family in the development of mental abilities: A 50-year study. In N. Datan, A. L. Greene and H. W. Reese (Eds), *Life-span developmental psychology: Intergenerational relations* (pp. 185–210). Hillsdale, NJ: Lawrence Erlbaum Associates.

Honzik, M. P., McFarlane, J. W, and Allen, L. (1948). The stability of mental test performance between two and eighteen years. *Journal of Experimental Education,* 17, 309–334.

Horn, J. M. (1983). The Texas Adoption Project: Adopted children and their intellectual resemblance to biological and adoptive parents. *Child Development,* 54, 268–275.

Howe, M. L., Courage, M. L. and Rooksby, M. (2009). The genesis and development of autobiographical memory. In M. L. Courage and N. Cowan (Eds), *The development of memory in infancy and childhood* (pp. 177–196). Hove: Psychology Press.

Hudson, J. A. (1988). Children's memory for atypical actions in script-based stories: Evidence for a disruption effect. *Journal of Experimental Child Psychology,* 46(2), 159–173.

Hudson, J. and Fivush, R. (1983). Categorical and schematic organization and the development of retrieval strategies. *Journal of Experimental Child Psychology, 36*(1), 32–42.

Hudson, J. and Nelson, K. (1983). Effects of script structure on children's story recall. *Developmental Psychology, 19*(4), 625–635.

Hudson, J. and Nelson, K. (1986). Repeated encounters of a similar kind: Effects of familiarity on children's autobiographic memory. *Cognitive Development, 1*(3), 253–271.

Hughes, C. and Russell, J. (1993). Autistic children's difficulty with mental disengagement from an object – its implications for theories of autism. *Developmental Psychology, 29*(3), 498–510.

Hughes, C., Russell, J. and Robbins, T. W. (1994). Evidence for executive dysfunction in autism. *Neuropsychologia, 32*(4), 477–492.

Hulme, C. and Snowling, M. J. (2009). *Developmental disorders of language learning and cognition.* Chichester: Wiley-Blackwell.

Hulme, C., Hatcher, P. J., Nation, K., Brown, A., Adams, J. and Stuart, G. (2002). Phoneme awareness is a better predictor of early reading skill than onset-rime awareness. *Journal of Experimental Child Psychology, 82*, 2–28.

Hulme, C., Thomson, N., Muir, C. and Lawrence, A. (1984). Speech rate and the development of short-term memory span. *Journal of Experimental Child Psychology, 38*, 241–253.

Huttenlocher, J., Haight, W., Bryk, A., Setzer, M. and Lyons, T. (1991). Early vocabulary growth: Relation to language input and gender. *Developmental Psychology, 27*(2), 236–248.

Hyams, N. M. (1986). *Language acquisition and the theory of parameters.* Dordrecht: Reidel.

Iacoboni, M., Woods, R. P., Brass, M., Bekkering, H., Mazziotta, J. C. and Rizzolatti, G. (1999). Cortical mechanisms of human imitation. *Science, 286*(5449), 2526–2528.

Inagaki, K. and Hatano, G. (2002). *Young children's thinking about the biological world.* New York: Psychology Press.

Ineson, G. (2007). Year 6 children: Has the new British mathematics curriculum helped their mental computation? *Early Child Development and Care, 177*, 541–555.

Inhelder, B. and Piaget, J. (1958). *The growth of logical thinking from childhood to adolescence.* New York: Basic Books.

Inhelder, B. and Piaget, J. (1964). *The early growth of logic in the child.* New York: Harper.

Irvine, S. H. (1970). Affect and construct: A cross-cultural check on theories of intelligence. *Journal of Social Psychology, 80*, 23–30.

Irvine, S. H. (1988). Constructing the intellect of the Shona: A taxonomic approach. In J. W. Berry, S. H. Irvine and E. B. Hunt (Eds), *Indigenous cognition functioning in a cultural context* (pp. 156–176). Dordrecht: Martinus Nijhoff Publishers.

Jackendoff, R. and Pinker, S. (2005). The nature of the language faculty and its implications for evolution of language (Reply to Fitch, Hauser and Chomsky). *Cognition, 97*, 211–225.

Jain, S., Osherson, D., Royer, J. and Sharma, A. (1999). *Systems that learn.* Cambridge, MA: MIT Press.

James, W. (1890). *The principles of psychology.* New York: Henry Holt.

Järvinen-Pasley, A. and Heaton, P. (2007). Evidence for reduced domain-specificity in auditory processing in autism. *Developmental Science, 10*(6), 786–793.

Jaswal, V. K. and Dodson, C. S. (2009). Metamemory development: Understanding the role of similarity in false memories. *Child Development, 80*, 629–635.

Jensen, A. R. (1969). How much can we boost I. Q. and scholastic achievement? *Harvard Educational Review, 33*, 1–123.

Jensen, A. R. (1973). *Educatability and group differences.* New York: Harper and Row.

Jensen, A. R. (1993). Why is reaction time correlated with psychometric *g*? *Current Directions in Psychological Science, 2*(2), 53–56.

Jensen, A. R. (1998). *The g factor: The science of mental ability.* Westport, CT: Praeger.

Joanisse, M. F. and Seidenberg, M. S. (2003). Phonology and syntax in specific language impairments: Evidence from a connectionist model. *Brain and Language, 86*, 40–56.

Johnson, C. N. and Wellman, H. M. (1980). Developing understanding of mental verbs: Remember, know and guess. *Child Development, 51*, 1095–1102.

Johnson, C. N. and Wellman, H. M. (1982). Children's developing conceptions of the mind and brain. *Child Development, 53*(1), 222–234.

Johnson, J. S. and Newport, E. L. (1989). Critical period effects in second language learning: The influence of maturational state on the acquisition of English as a second language. *Cognitive Psychology, 21*(1), 60–99.

Johnson, M. H., Dziurawiec, S., Bartrip, J. and Morton, J. (1992). The effects of movement of internal features on infants' preferences for face-like stimuli. *Infant Behavior and Development, 15*(1), 129–136.

Johnson, M. H., Dziurawiec, S., Ellis, H. and Morton, J. (1991). Newborns' preferential tracking of face-like stimuli and its subsequent decline. *Cognition, 40*(1–2), 1–19.

Johnson, W., Bouchard, T. J., Jr., McGue, M., Segal, N. L., Tellegen, A., Keyes, M., *et al.* (2007). Genetic and environmental influences on the Verbal-Perceptual-Image Rotation (VPR) model of the structure of mental abilities in the Minnesota study of twins reared apart. *Intelligence, 35*, 542–562.

Johnson-Laird, P. N. (1983). *Mental models: Towards a cognitive science of language, inference, and consciousness*. Cambridge, MA: Harvard University Press.

Johnson-Laird, P. N. (2004). Mental models and reasoning. In J. P. Leighton and R. J. Sternberg (Eds), *The nature of reasoning* (pp. 169–204). Cambridge: Cambridge University Press.

Johnson-Laird, P. N. and Bara, B. G. (1984). Syllogistic inference. *Cognition, 16,* 1–61.

Johnson-Laird, P. N. and Byrne, R. M. J. (1991). *Deduction*. Hillsdale, NJ: Lawrence Erlbaum Associates.

Johnson-Laird, P. N., Legrenzi, P. and Legrenzi, S. (1972). Reasoning and a sense of reality. *British Journal of Psychology, 63,* 336–400.

Johnson-Laird, P. N., Oakhill, J. and Bull, D. (1986). Children's syllogistic reasoning. *Quarterly Journal of Experimental Psychology Section A, 38,* 35–58.

Johnston, R. S, and Watson, J. (2005). *The effects of synthetic phonics teaching on reading and spelling attainment: A seven year longitudinal study*. Scottish Executive Education Department. Available at http://www.scotland.gov.uk/Publications/2005/02/20688/52449. Accessed 26 May, 2010.

Jolliffe, T. and Baron-Cohen, S. (1997). Are people with autism or Asperger's Syndrome faster than normal on the embedded figures task? *Journal of Child Psychology and Psychiatry, 38,* 527–534.

Jones, G. (2007). Distributional accounts of language: Explaining key phenomena in child language acquisition using a distributional account of the input the child receives. In B. Wallace (Ed.), *The mind, the body and the world: Psychology after cognitivism?* Exeter: Imprint Academic.

Jones, G. and Ritter, F. E. (1998). Simulating development by modifying architectures. *Proceedings of the Twentieth Annual Conference of the Cognitive Science Society* (pp. 543–548). Mahwah, NJ: LEA.

Jones, G., Gobet, F. and Pine, J. M. (2000a). A process model of children's early verb use. In L. R. Gleitman and A. K. Joshi (Eds), *Proceedings of the 22nd Annual Meeting of the Cognitive Science Society* (pp. 723–728). Mahwah, NJ: LEA.

Jones, G., Gobet, F. and Pine, J. M. (2000b). Learning novel sound patterns. In N. Taatgen and J. Aasman (Eds), *Proceedings of the 3rd International Conference on Cognitive Modeling* (pp. 169–176). Veenendaal, Holland: Universal Press.

Jones, G., Gobet, F. and Pine, J. M. (2007). Linking working memory and long-term memory: A computational model of the learning of new words. *Developmental Science, 10,* 853–873.

Jones, G., Gobet, F. and Pine, J. M. (2008). Computer simulations of developmental change: The contributions of working memory capacity and long-term knowledge. *Cognitive Science, 32,* 1148–1176.

Jones, G., Ritter, F. E. and Wood, D. J. (2000). Using a cognitive architecture to examine what develops. *Psychological Science, 11*(2), 93–100.

Jordan, J.-A., Mulhern, G. and Wylie, J. (2009). Individual differences in trajectories of arithmetical development in typically achieving 5- to 7-year-olds. *Journal of Experimental Child Psychology, 103*(4), 455–468.

Jordan, N., Kaplan, D., Olah, L. and Locuniak, M. (2006). Number sense growth in kindergarten: A longitudinal investigation of children at risk for mathematics difficulties. *Child Development, 77,* 153–175.

Juel-Nielsen, N. (1965). *Individual and environment: A psychiatric-psychological investigation of MZ twins reared apart*. Copenhagen: Munksgaard.

Jusczyk, P. W. (1985). On characterizing the development of speech perception. In J. Mehler and R. Fox (Eds), *Neonate cognition* (pp. 199–229). Hillsdale, NJ: Lawrence Erlbaum Associates.

Jusczyk, P. W., Luce, P. A. and Charles-Luce, J. (1994). Infants' sensitivity to phonotactic patterns in the native language. *Journal of Memory and Language, 33*(5), 630–645.

Justice, E. M. (1986). Developmental changes in judgments of relative strategy effectiveness. *British Journal of Developmental Psychology, 4,* 75–81.

Kail, R. (1991a). Developmental change in speed of processing during childhood and adolescence. *Psychological Bulletin, 109,* 490–501.

Kail, R. (1991b). Development of processing speed in childhood and adolescence. In H. W. Reese (Ed.), *Advances in child development and behavior* (Vol. 23, pp. 151–185). London: Academic Press.

Kail, R. (2000). Speed of information processing: Developmental changes and links to intelligence. *Journal of School Psychology, 38,* 51–61.

Kaiser, M. K., McCloskey, M. and Proffitt, D. R. (1986). Development of intuitive theories of motion: Curvilinear motion in the absence of external forces. *Developmental Psychology, 22,* 67–71.

Kaiser, M. K., Proffitt, D. R. and McCloskey, M. (1985). The development of beliefs about falling objects. *Perception and Psychophysics, 38,* 533–539.

Kaitz, M., Meschulach-Sarfaty, O., Auerbach, J. and Eidelman, A. (1988). A reexamination of newborns' ability to imitate facial expressions. *Developmental Psychology, 24*(1), 3–7.

Kallio, K. D. (1982). Developmental change on a 5-term transitive inference. *Journal of Experimental Child Psychology, 33*(1), 142–164.

Kanazawa, M. (1998). *Learnable classes of categorial grammars*. Stanford, CA: CSLI Publications.

Kanwisher, N., McDermott, J. and Chun, M. M. (1997). The fusiform face area: A module in human extrastriate cortex specialized for face perception. *Journal of Neuroscience, 17,* 4302–4311.

Karmiloff-Smith, A. (1992). *Beyond modularity: A developmental perspective on cognitive science.* Cambridge, MA: MIT Press.

Karmiloff-Smith, A. (2009). Preaching to the converted? From constructivism to neuroconstructivism. *Child Development Perspectives, 3,* 99–102.

Kaufman, E. L., Lord, M. W., Reese, T. W. and Volkmann, J. (1949). The discrimination of visual number. *American Journal of Psychology, 62,* 498–525.

Kavšek, M. (2004). Predicting later IQ from infant visual habituation and dishabituation: A meta-analysis. *Journal of Applied Developmental Psychology, 25,* 369–393.

Keil, F. C. (1986). The acquisition of natural kind and artifact terms. In W. Demopoulos and A. Marras (Eds), *Language learning and concept acquisition* (pp. 133–153). Norwood, NJ: Ablex.

Kellman, P. J. and Arterberry, M. E. (2006). Perceptual development. In W. Damon, D. Kuhn and R. Siegler (Eds), *The handbook of child psychology: Cognition, perception, and language* (6th ed.) (pp. 109–160). New York: Wiley.

Khan, S. A. and Faraone, S. V. (2006). The genetics of attention-deficit/hyperactivity disorder: A literature review of 2005. *Current Psychiatry Reports, 8,* 393–397.

Kinzler, K. D. and Spelke, E. S. (2007). Core systems in human cognition. *Progress in Brain Research, 164,* 257–264.

Kister, M. C. and Patterson, C. J. (1980). Children's conceptions of the causes of illness: Understanding of contagion and use of immanent justice. *Child Development, 51*(3), 839–846.

Klahr, D. (1996). Scientific discovery processes in children, adults, and machines. In D. Steier and T. Mitchell (Eds), *Mind matters: Contributions to cognitive and computer science in honor of Allen Newell* (pp. 325–355). Hillsdale, NJ: Lawrence Erlbaum Associates.

Klahr, D. and Dunbar, K. (1988). Dual-space search during scientific reasoning. *Cognitive Science, 12*(1), 1–48.

Klahr, D. and MacWhinney, B. (1998). Information Processing. In D. Kuhn and R. S. Siegler (Eds), W. Damon (Series Ed.), *Handbook of child psychology (5th ed.): Vol. 2: Cognition, perception, and language* (pp. 631–678). New York: Wiley.

Klahr, D. and Wallace, J. G. (1976). *Cognitive development: An information processing view.* Hillsdale, NJ: Lawrence Erlbaum Associates.

Klahr, D., Fay, A. L. and Dunbar, K. (1993). Heuristics for scientific experimentation: A developmental study. *Cognitive Psychology, 25*(1), 111–146.

Klayman, J. and Ha, Y. W. (1987). Confirmation, disconfirmation, and information in hypothesis-testing. *Psychological Review, 94*(2), 211–228.

Klingberg, T., Forssberg, H. and Westerberg, H. (2002). Increased brain activity in frontal and parietal cortex underlies the development of visuospatial working memory capacity during childhood. *Journal of Cognitive Neuroscience, 14*(1), 1–10.

Knight, N., Sousa, P., Barrett, J. and Atran, S. (2004). Children's attribution of belief to humans and God: Cross-cultural evidence. *Cognitive Science, 28,* 117–126.

Koerber, S., Sodian, B., Thoermer, C. and Nett, U. (2005). Scientific reasoning in young children: Preschoolers' ability to evaluate covariation evidence. *Swiss Journal of Psychology, 64*(3), 141–152.

Kohler, E., Keysers, C., Umiltà, M. A., Fogassi, L., Gallese, V. and Rizzolatti, G. (2002). Hearing sounds, understanding actions: Action representation in mirror neurons. *Science, 297*(5582), 846–848.

Koontz, K. L. and Berch, D. B. (1996). Identifying simple numerical stimuli: Processing inefficiencies exhibited by arithmetic learning disabled children. *Mathematical Cognition, 2*(1), 1–24.

Koslowski, B. (1996). *Theory and evidence: The development of scientific reasoning.* Cambridge, MA: MIT Press.

Koslowski, B. and Masnick, A. (2002). The development of causal reasoning. In U. Goswami (Ed.), *Blackwell handbook of childhood cognitive development* (pp. 257–281). Oxford: Blackwell Publishing.

Koslowski, B., Okagaki, L., Lorenz, C. and Umbach, D. (1989). When covariation is not enough: The role of causal mechanism, sampling method, and sample-size in causal reasoning. *Child Development, 60*(6), 1316–1327.

Kreutzer, M., Leonard, C. and Flavell, J. H. (1975). An interview study of children's knowledge about memory. *Monographs of the Society for Research in Child Development, 40*(1, Serial No. 159).

Kroger, J. K., Cheng, P. W. and Holyoak, K. J. (1993). Evoking the permission schema – the impact of explicit negation and a violation-checking context. *Quarterly Journal of Experimental Psychology Section A – Human Experimental Psychology, 46*(4), 615–635.

Kron-Sperl, V., Schneider, W. and Hasselhorn, M. (2008). The development and effectiveness of memory strategies in kindergarten and elementary school: Findings from the Würzburg and Göttingen longitudinal studies. *Cognitive Development, 23,* 79–104.

Kuchuk, A., Vibbert, M. and Bornstein, M. H. (1986). The perception of smiling and its experiential correlates in three-month-old infants. *Child Development, 57*(4), 1054–1061.

Kuczaj, S. A. (1977). The acquisition of regular and irregular past tense forms. *Journal of Verbal Learning and Verbal Behavior, 16*(5), 589–600.

Kuhl, P. K. and Miller, J. D. (1978). Speech perception by the chinchilla: Identification function for synthetic VOT stimuli. *Journal of the Acoustical Society of America*, 63(3), 905–917.

Kuhl, P. K. and Padden, D. M. (1982). Enhanced discriminability at the phonetic boundaries for the voicing feature in macaques. *Perception and Psychophysics*, 32(6), 542–550.

Kuhn, D. (1989). Children and adults as intuitive scientists. *Psychological Review*, 96(4), 674–689.

Kuhn, D. (1999). Metacognitive development. In L. Balter and C. S. Tamis-LeMonda (Eds), *Child psychology: A handbook of contemporary issues* (pp. 259–286). Philadelphia, PA: Psychology Press.

Kuhn, D. (2000). Theory of mind, metacognition, and reasoning: A life-span perspective. In K. J. Riggs and P. Mitchell (Eds), *Children's reasoning and the mind*. Hove: Psychology Press.

Kuhn, D. (2002). What is scientific thinking and how does it develop? In U. Goswami (Ed.), *The Blackwell handbook of childhood cognitive development* (pp. 371–393). Oxford: Blackwell.

Kuhn, D. and Dean, D. (2005). Is developing scientific thinking all about learning to control variables? *Psychological Science*, 16(11), 866–870.

Kuhn, D. and Pearsall, S. (2000). Developmental origins of scientific thought. *Journal of Cognition and Development*, 1, 113–129.

Kuhn, D., Amsel, E. and O'Loughlin, M. (1988). *The development of scientific thinking skills*. San Diego, CA: Academic Press.

Kuhn, D., García-Mila, M., Zohar, A. and Andersen, C. (1995). Strategies of knowledge acquisition. *Monographs of the Society for Research in Child Development*, 60(4, Serial No. 245).

Kuhn, D., Iordanou, K., Pease, M. and Wirkala, C. (2008). Beyond control of variables: What needs to develop to achieve skilled scientific thinking? *Cognitive Development*, 23(4), 435–451.

Kuhn, D., Pease, M. and Wirkala, C. (2009). Coordinating the effects of multiple variables: A skill fundamental to scientific thinking. *Journal of Experimental Child Psychology*, 103(3), 268–284.

Kuntsi, J., Oosterlaan, J. and Stevenson, J. (2001). Psychological mechanisms in hyperactivity: I. response inhibition deficit, working memory impairment, delay aversion, or something? *Journal of Child Psychology and Psychiatry*, 42(2), 199–210.

Kunzinger, E. L. and Witryol, S. L. (1984). The effects of differential incentives on second-grade rehearsal and free recall. *The Journal of Genetic Psychology*, 144, 19–30.

Landerl, K., Bevan, A. and Butterworth. B. (2004). Developmental dyscalculia and basic numerical capacities: A study of 8–9-year-old students. *Cognition*, 93, 99–125.

Langley, M. B. (1989). Assessing infant cognitive development. In D. B. Bailey and M. Wolery (Eds), *Assessing infants and preschoolers with handicaps* (pp. 249–274). Columbus, OH: Merrill Publishing Company.

Lany, J. and Saffran, J. R. (2010). From statistics to meaning. *Psychological Science*, 21(2), 284–291.

Lave, J. (1988). *Cognition in practice: Mind, mathematics, and culture in everyday life*. Cambridge: Cambridge University Press.

Leach, J. (1999). Students' understanding of the co-ordination of theory and evidence in science. *International Journal of Science Education*, 21(8), 789–806.

Leekam, S. and Perner, J. (1991). Does the autistic child have a metarepresentational deficit? *Cognition*, 40, 203–218.

Lehrer, R. and Schauble, L. (2006). Scientific thinking and science literacy. In W. Damon, R. Lerner, K. A. Renninger and I. E. Sigel (Eds), *Handbook of child psychology: Vol. 4. Child psychology in practice* (6th ed.) (pp. 153–196). Hoboken, NJ: Wiley.

Lemaire, P. and Siegler, R. S. (1995). Four aspects of strategic change: Contributions to children's learning of multiplication. *Journal of Experimental Psychology: General*, 124, 83–97.

Lenneberg, E. H. (1967). *Biological foundations of language*. New York: Wiley.

Leslie, A. (1988). Some implications of pretense for children's theories of mind. In J. W. Astington, P. L. Harris and D. R. Olson (Eds), *Developing theories of mind* (pp. 19–46). Cambridge, MA: Cambridge University Press.

Leslie, A. M. (1982). The perception of causality in infants. *Perception*, 11(2), 173–186.

Leslie, A. M. (1987). Pretense and representation: The origins of 'theory of mind'. *Psychological Review*, 94, 412–426.

Leslie, A. M. (1994a). Pretending and believing: Issues in the theory of ToMM. *Cognition*, 50(1–3), 211–238.

Leslie, A. M. (1994b). ToMM, ToBy, and Agency: Core architecture and domain specificity. In L. Hirschfeld and S. Gelman (Eds), *Mapping the mind: Domain specificity in cognition and culture* (pp. 119–148). New York: Cambridge University Press.

Leslie, A. M. and Frith, U. (1988). Autistic children's understanding of seeing, knowing and believing. *British Journal of Developmental Psychology*, 6, 315–324.

Leslie, A. M., Friedman, O. and German, T. P. (2004). Core mechanisms in 'theory of mind'. *Trends in Cognitive Sciences*, 8(12), 528–533.

Leventhal, H., Nerenz, D. R. and Steele, D. J. (1984). Illness representation and coping with health threats. In A. Baum, S. E. Taylor and J. E. Singer (Eds), *Handbook of psychology and health* (pp. 219–252). Hillsdale, NJ: Lawrence Erlbaum Associates.

Levin, I., Siegler, R. S. and Druyan, S. (1990). Misconceptions about motion: Development and training effects. *Child Development*, *61*(5), 1544–1557.

Levy, B. A., Gong, Z., Hessels, S., Evans, M. A. and Jared, D. (2006). Understanding print: Early reading developments and the contributions of home literacy experiences. *Journal of Experimental Child Psychology*, *93*, 63–93.

Lewis, C. and Osborne, A. (1990). Three-year-olds' problems with false belief: Conceptual deficit or linguistic artifact? *Child Development*, *61*(5), 1514–1519.

Lewis, C., Freeman, N. H., Hagestadt, C. and Douglas, H. (1994). Narrative access and production in preschoolers false belief reasoning. *Cognitive Development*, *9*(4), 397–424.

Lewis, C., Hitch, G. I. and Walker, P. (1994). The prevalence of specific arithmetic difficulties and specific reading difficulties in 9 to 10 year old boys and girls. *Journal of Child Psychology and Psychiatry*, *35*, 283–292.

Lewis, M., Stanger, C. and Sullivan, M. W. (1989). Deception in 3-year-olds. *Developmental Psychology*, *25*(3), 439–443.

Lewkowicz, D. J. and Ghazanfar, A. A. (2006). The decline of cross-species intersensory perception in human infants. *Proceedings of the National Academy of Sciences, USA*, *103*, 6771–6774.

Lewkowicz, D. J. and Ghazanfar, A. A. (2009). The emergence of multisensory systems through perceptual narrowing. *Trends in Cognitive Sciences*, *13*(11), 470–478.

Li, A., Kelley, E., Evans, A. and Lee, K. (2011). Exploring the ability to deceive in children with autism spectrum disorders. *Journal of Autism and Developmental Disorders*, *41*(2), 185–195.

Liberman, I. and Shankweiler, D. (1977). Speech, the alphabet and teaching to read. In L. B. Resnick and P. A. Weaver (Eds), *Theory and practice of early reading* (pp. 105–129). Hillsdale, NJ: Lawrence Erlbaum Associates.

Lieven, E. V. M., Pine, J. M. and Baldwin, G. (1997). Lexically-based learning and early grammatical development. *Journal of Child Language*, *24*, 187–219.

Light, P., Blaye, A., Gilly, M. and Girotto, V. (1989). Pragmatic schemas and logical reasoning in 6-year-old to 8-year-old children. *Cognitive Development*, *4*(1), 49–64.

Lind, S. E. and Bowler, D. M. (2010). Impaired performance on see-know tasks amongst children with autism: Evidence of specific difficulties with theory of mind or domain-general task factors? *Journal of Autism and Developmental Disorders*, *40*(4), 479–484.

Lindberg, M. (1991). An interactive approach to assessing the suggestibility and testimony of eyewitnesses. In J. Doris (Ed.), *The suggestibility of children's recollections: Implications for eyewitness testimony* (pp. 47–55). Washington, DC: American Psychological Association.

Lindberg, M. A., Keiffer, J. and Thomas, S. W. (2000). Eyewitness testimony for physical abuse as a function of personal experience, development, and focus of study. *Journal of Applied Developmental Psychology*, *21*(5), 555–591.

Linnet, K. M., Dalsgaard, S., Obel, C., Wisborg, K., Henriksen, T. B., Rodriguez, A., Kotimaa, A., Moilanen, I., Thomsen, P. H., Olsen, J. and Jarvelin, M. R. (2003). Maternal lifestyle factors in pregnancy risk of attention-deficit/hyperactivity disorder and associated behaviors: Review of the current evidence. *American Journal of Psychiatry*, *160*(6), 1028–1040.

Livingstone, M. S., Rosen, G. D., Drislane, F. W. and Galaburda, A. M. (1991). Physiological and anatomical evidence for a magnocellular defect in developmental dyslexia. *Proceedings of the National Academy of Sciences of the United States of America*, *88*(18), 7943–7947.

Loehlin, J. C. (1989). Partitioning environmental and genetic contributions to behavioral development. *American Psychologist*, *44*, 1285–1292.

Loehlin, J. C., Horn, J. M. and Willerman, L. (1989). Modeling IQ change: Evidence from the Texas adoption project. *Child Development*, *60*, 993–1004.

Loehlin, J. C., Horn, J. M. and Willerman, L. (1997). Heredity, environment and IQ in the Texas adoption project. In R. J. Sternberg and E. L. Grigorenko (Eds), *Intelligence, heredity, and environment* (pp. 105–25). Cambridge: Cambridge University Press.

Loftus, E. F. (1975). Leading questions and the eyewitness report. *Cognitive Psychology*, *7*, 560–572.

Loftus, E. F. and Palmer, J. C. (1974). Reconstruction of automobile destruction: An example of the interaction between language and memory. *Journal of Verbal Learning and Verbal Behavior*, *13*, 585–589.

Luria, A. R. (1976). *Cognitive development: Its cultural and social foundations*. Cambridge, MA: Harvard University Press.

MacWhinney, B. (1978). The acquisition of morphophonology. *Monographs of the Society for Research in Child Development*, *43*, 1–123.

MacWhinney, B. (1999). *The emergence of language*. Mahwah, NJ: Lawrence Erlbaum Associates.

MacWhinney, B. (2004). A multiple process solution to the logical problem of language acquisition. *Journal of Child Language*, *31*, 883–914.

MacWhinney, B. and Snow, C. (1990). The child language data exchange system: An update. *Journal of Child Language*, *17*, 457–472.

Makin, J. W. and Porter, R. H. (1989). Attractiveness of lactating females' breast odors to neonates. *Child Development*, *60*(4), 803–810.

Mali, G. B. and Howe, A. (1979). Development of earth and gravity concepts among Nepali children. *Science Education, 63*, 685–691.

Manktelow, K. I. and Evans, J. S. B. T. (1979). Facilitation of reasoning by realism: Effect or non-effect. *British Journal of Psychology, 70*, 477–488.

Maratsos, M. (1979). How to get from words to sentences. In D. Aaronson and R. W. Rieber (Eds), *Psycholinguistic research* (pp. 285–353). Hillsdale, NJ: Lawrence Erlbaum Associates.

Maratsos, M. (1988). The acquisition of formal word classes. In Y. Levy, I. M. Schlesinger and M. Braine (Eds), *Categories and processes in language acquisition* (pp. 31–44). Hillsdale, NJ: Lawrence Erlbaum Associates.

Maratsos, M. (1998). The acquisition of grammar. In W. Damon, D. Kuhn and R. S. Siegler (Eds), *Handbook of child psychology, Volume 2: Cognition, perception and language* (pp. 371–420). New York: Wiley.

Maratsos, M. (1999a). Some aspects of innateness and complexity in grammatical acquisition. In M. Barrett (Ed.), *The development of language* (pp. 191–228). Hove: Psychology Press.

Maratsos, M. (1999b). A sunny view of polarization. *Journal of Child Language, 26*, 239–242.

Maratsos, M. A. and Chalkley, M. P. (1980). The internal language of children's syntax: The ontogenesis and representation of syntactic categories. In K. Nelson (Ed.), *Children's language. Vol. 2* (pp. 127–214). New York: Gardner Press.

Marcus, G., Pinker, S., Ullman, M., Hollander, M., Rosen, T. J. and Xu, F. (1992). Overregularization in language acquisition. *Monographs of the Society for Research in Child Development, 57*(4, Serial No. 228).

Mareschal, D. and Shultz, T. R. (1999). Children's seriation: A connectionist approach. *Connection Science, 11*, 153–188.

Mareschal, D., Johnson, M. H., Sirois, S., Spratling, M., Thomas, M. and Westermann, G. (2007). *Neuroconstructivism, Vol. I: How the brain constructs cognition*. Oxford: Oxford University Press.

Mareschal, D., Plunkett, K. and Harris, P. (1999). A computational and neuropsychological account of object-oriented behaviours in infancy. *Developmental Science, 2*(3), 306–317.

Markovits, H. (2000). A mental model analysis of young children's conditional reasoning with meaningful premises. *Thinking and Reasoning, 6*(4), 335–347.

Markovits, H. (2004). The development of deductive reasoning. In J. P. Leighton and R. J. Sternberg (Eds), *The nature of reasoning* (pp. 313–338). Cambridge: Cambridge University Press.

Markovits, H. and Barrouillet, P. (2002). The development of conditional reasoning: A mental model account. *Developmental Review, 22*(1), 5–36.

Markovits, H. and Barrouillet, P. (2004). Introduction: Why is understanding the development of reasoning important? *Thinking and Reasoning, 10*(2), 113–121.

Marsh, G., Friedman, M., Welch, V. and Desberg, P. (1981). A cognitive-developmental theory of reading acquisition. In G. E. MacKinnon and T. G. Waller (Eds), *Reading research: Advances in theory and practice. Vol. 3* (pp. 199–221). New York: Academic Press.

Mason, J. (1980). When do children begin to read: An exploration of four year old children's letter and word reading competencies. *Reading Research Quarterly, 15*, 203–227.

Maurer, D. and Salapatek, P. (1976). Developmental changes in the scanning of faces by young infants. *Child Development, 47*(2), 523–527.

Maye, J. and Weiss, D. J. (2003). Statistical cues facilitate infants' discrimination of difficult phonetic contrasts. In B. Beachley, A. Brown and F. Conlin (Eds), *Proceedings of the 27th Annual Boston University Conference on Language Development* (pp. 508–518). Somerville, MA: Cascadilla Press.

Maye, J., Weiss, D. J. and Aslin, R. N. (2008). Statistical phonetic learning in infants: Facilitation and feature generalization. *Developmental Science, 11*, 122–134.

Maye, J., Werker, J. F. and Gerken, L. (2002). Infant sensitivity to distributional information can affect phonetic discrimination. *Cognition, 82*(3), B101–B111.

Mayer, D. L. and Dobson, V. (1982). Visual acuity development in infants and young children, as assessed by operant preferential looking. *Vision Research, 22*, 1141–1151.

McCall, R. B. and Carriger, M. S. (1993). A meta-analysis of infant habituation and recognition memory performance as predictors of later IQ. *Child Development, 64*, 57–79.

McCall, R. B., Appelbaum, M. I. and Hogarty, P. S. (1973). Developmental changes in mental performance. *Monographs of the Society for Research in Child Development, 38* (3, Serial No. 150).

McCarthy, D. (1972). *McCarthy scales of children's abilities*. New York: The Psychological Corporation.

McCartney, K., Harris, M. J. and Bernieri, F. (1990). Growing up and growing apart: A developmental meta-analysis of twin studies. *Psychological Bulletin, 107*, 226–237.

McClelland, J. L. (1989). Parallel distributed processing: Implications for cognition and development. In R. G. M. Morris (Ed.), *Parallel distributed processing: Implications for psychology and neurobiology* (pp. 8–45). Oxford: Oxford University Press.

McClelland, J. L. and Jenkins, E. (1991). Nature, nurture, and connections: Implications of connectionist models for cognitive development. In K. Van Lehn (Ed.), *Architectures for intelligence* (pp. 41–73). Hillsdale, NJ: Lawrence Erlbaum Associates.

McClelland, J. L. and Patterson, K. (2002). Rules or connections in past-tense inflections: What does the evidence rule out? *Trends in Cognitive Sciences*, 6, 465–472.

McClelland, J. L., Rumelhart, D. E. and the PDP Research Group. (1986). *Parallel distributed processing, Volume 2: Explorations in the microstructure of cognition: Psychological and biological models*. Cambridge, MA: MIT Press.

McCloskey, M., Caramazza, A. and Green, B. (1980). Curvilinear motion in the absence of external forces: Naive beliefs about the motion of objects. *Science*, 210(4474), 1139–1141.

McCloskey, M., Washburn, A. and Felch, L. (1983). Intuitive physics: The straight-down belief and its origin. *Journal of Experimental Psychology-Learning Memory and Cognition*, 9(4), 636–649.

McCrink, K. and Wynn, K. (2004). Large-number addition and subtraction in infants. *Psychological Science*, 15, 776–781.

McCune-Nicolich, L. (1981). Toward symbolic functioning: Structure of early pretend games and potential parallels with language. *Child Development*, 52(3), 785–797.

McGarrigle, J. and Donaldson, M. (1974). Conservation accidents. *Cognition*, 3, 341–350.

McGue, M. and Bouchard, T. J., Jr. (1998). Genetic and environmental influences on human behavioral differences. *Annual Review of Neuroscience*, 21, 1–24.

McGue, M., Bouchard, T. J., Jr., Iacono, W. G. and Lykken, D. T. (1993). Behavioral genetics of cognitive ability: A life-span perspective. In R. Plomin and G. E. McClearn (Eds), *Nature, nurture and psychology* (pp. 59–76). Washington, DC: American Psychological Association.

McKey, R. H., Condelli, L., Ganson, H., Barrett, B. J., McConkey, C. and Plantz, M. C. (1985). *The impact of Head Start on children, families, and communities. Final report of the Head Start evaluation, synthesis, and utilization project*. Washington, DC: US Department of Health and Human Services.

McLean, J. F. and Hitch, G. J. (1999). Working memory impairments in children with specific arithmetical difficulties. *Journal of Experimental Child Psychology*, 74, 240–260.

McLoyd, V. C. (1998). Children in poverty: Development, public policy, and practice. In W. Damon (Series Ed.), I. Sigel and K. A. Renninger (Eds), *Handbook of child psychology: Vol 4. Child psychology in practice* (5th ed.) (pp. 135–208). New York: Wiley.

McMurray, B. and Hollich, G. (2009). Core computational principles of language acquisition: Can statistical learning do the job? Introduction to special section. *Developmental Science*, 12, 365–368.

McNeil, N. M. (2007). U-shaped development in math: 7-year olds outperform 9-year olds on mathematical equivalence problems. *Developmental Psychology*, 43, 687–695.

McNeil, N. M. (2008). Limitations to teaching children 2 + 2 = 4: Typical arithmetic problems can hinder learning of mathematical equivalence. *Child Development*, 79, 1524–1537.

McNeil, N. M. and Alibali, M. W. (2004). You'll see what you mean: Students encode equations based on their knowledge of arithmetic. *Cognitive Science*, 28, 451–466.

McNeil, N. M. and Alibali, M. W. (2005a). Knowledge change as a function of mathematics experience: All contexts are not created equal. *Journal of Cognition and Development*, 6, 385–206.

McNeil, N. M. and Alibali, M. W. (2005b). Why won't you change your mind? Knowledge of operational patterns hinders learning and performance on equations. *Child Development*, 76, 883–899.

McNeil, N. M., Grandau, L., Knuth, E. J., Alibali, M. W., Stephens, A. S., Hattikudur, S. and Krill, D. E. (2006). Middle-school students' understanding of the equal sign: The books they read can't help. *Cognition and Instruction*, 24, 367–385.

McNeill, D. (1970). *The acquisition of language*. New York: Harper and Row.

McQuaid, E. L., Howard, K., Kopel, S. J., Rosenblum, K. and Bibace, R. (2002). Developmental concepts of asthma: Reasoning about illness and strategies for prevention. *Applied Developmental Psychology*, 23, 179–194.

Meck, W. H. and Church, R. M. (1983). A mode control model of counting and timing processes. *Journal of Experimental Psychology: Animal Behavior Processes*, 9, 320–324.

Mehler, J., Jusczyk, P., Lambertz, G., Halsted, N., Bertoncini, J. and Amiel-Tison, C. (1988). A precursor of language acquisition in young infants. *Cognition*, 29(2), 143–178.

Meisel, J. M. (1995). Parameters in acquisition. In P. Fletcher and B. MacWhinney (Eds), *The handbook of child language* (pp. 10–35). Oxford: Blackwell.

Meltzoff, A. N. (1988). Infant imitation and memory: Nine-month-olds in immediate and deferred tests. *Child Development*, 59(1), 217–225.

Meltzoff, A. N. and Borton, R. W. (1979). Intermodal matching by human neonates. *Nature*, 282, 403–404.

Meltzoff, A. N. and Moore, M. K. (1977). Imitation of facial and manual gestures by human neonates. *Science*, 198(4312), 75–78.

Meltzoff, A. N. and Moore, M. K. (1983). Newborn infants imitate adult facial gestures. *Child Development*, 54, 702–709.

Meltzoff, A. N. and Moore, M. K. (1994). Imitation, memory, and the representation of persons. *Infant Behavior and Development*, 17, 83–99.

Meltzoff, A. N. and Moore, M. K. (1997). Explaining facial imitation: A theoretical model. *Early Development and Parenting*, 6, 179–192.

Meltzoff, A. N. and Moore, M. K. (1999). Resolving the debate about early imitation. In A. Slater and D. Muir (Eds), *The Blackwell reader in developmental psychology* (pp. 151–155). Oxford: Blackwell.

Metsala, J. L., Stanovich, K. E. and Brown, G. D. A. (1998). Regularity effects and the phonological deficit model of reading disabilities: A meta-analytic review. *Journal of Educational Psychology*, 90, 279–293.

Mick, E., Biederman, J., Faraone, S. V., Sayer, J. and Kleinman, S. (2002). Case-control study of attention-deficit hyperactivity disorder and maternal smoking, alcohol use, and drug use during pregnancy. *Journal of the American Academy of Child and Adolescent Psychiatry*, 41(4), 378–385.

Miller, K. F., Smith, C. M., Zhu, J. and Zhang, H. (1995). Preschool origins of cross-national differences in mathematical competence: The role of number-naming systems. *Psychological Science*, 6, 56–60.

Miller, P. H. (1994). Individual differences in children's strategic behaviors: Utilization deficiencies. *Learning and Individual Differences*, 6(3), 285–307.

Miller, P. H. (2002). *Theories of developmental psychology*. New York: Worth.

Miller, P. H. and Seier, W. L. (1994). Strategy utilization deficiencies in children: When, where, and why. In H. W. Reese (Ed.), *Advances in child development and behavior* (Vol. 25) (pp. 7–32). New York: Academic Press.

Mills, D. L., Coffey-Corina, S. A. and Neville, H. J. (1997). Language comprehension and cerebral specialization from 13 to 20 months. *Developmental Neuropsychology*, 13(3), 397–445.

Millstein, S. G. and Irwin, C. E. (1987). Concepts of health and illness: Different constructs or variations on a theme? *Health Psychology*, 6(6), 515–524.

Millstein, S. G., Adler, N. E. and Irwin, C. E. (1981). Conceptions of illness in young adolescents. *Pediatrics*, 68, 834–839.

Milner, B., Corkin, S. and Teuber, H. L. (1968). Further analysis of the hippocampal amnesic syndrome: 14-year follow-up study of H. M. *Neuropsychologia*, 6(3), 215–234.

Mitchell, P. (1997). *Introduction to theory of mind*. London: Arnold.

Mitchell, P. and Lacohee, H. (1991). Children's early understanding of false belief. *Cognition*, 39(2), 107–127.

Mitchell, P. and Lewis, C. (1994). Critical issues in children's early understanding of mind. In C. Lewis and P. Mitchell (Eds), *Children's early understanding of mind* (pp. 1–16). Hove: Lawrence Erlbaum Associates.

Mitchell, P., Robinson, E. J., Isaacs, J. E. and Nye, R. M. (1996). Contamination in reasoning about false belief: An instance of realist bias in adults but not children. *Cognition*, 59(1), 1–21.

Miura, I. T., Okamoto, Y., Vlahovic-Stetic, V., Kim, C. C. and Han, J. H. (1999). Language supports for children's understanding of numerical fractions: Cross-national comparisons. *Journal of Experimental Child Psychology*, 74, 356–365.

Miyawaki, K., Strange, W., Verbrugge, R., Liberman, A. M., Jenkins, J. J. and Fujimura, O. (1975). An effect of linguistic experience: The discrimination of [r] and [l] by native speakers of Japanese and English. *Perception and Psychophysics*, 18, 331–40.

Molfese, D. L. (1977). Infant cerebral asymmetry. In S. J. Segalowitz and F. A. Gruber (Eds), *Language development and neurological theory* (pp. 21–35). New York: Academic Press.

Molfese, D. L. and Betz, J. (1988). Electrophysiological indices of the early development of lateralization for language and cognition, and their implications for predicting later development. In D. L. Molfese and S. J. Segalowitz (Eds), *Brain lateralization in children: Developmental implications* (pp. 171–190). New York: Guildford.

Morais, J., Bertelson, P., Cary, L. and Alegria, J. (1986). Literacy training and speech segmentation. *Cognition*, 24, 45–64.

Morais, J., Cary, L., Alegria, J. and Bertelson, P. (1979). Does awareness of speech as a sequence of phones arise spontaneously? *Cognition*, 7, 323–331.

Morrongiello, B. A., Fenwick, K. D. and Chance, G. (1998). Crossmodal learning in newborn infants: Inferences about properties of auditory-visual events. *Infant Behavior and Development*, 21(4), 543–553.

Morton, J. and Johnson, M. H. (1991). CONSPEC and CONLERN: A two-process theory of infant face recognition. *Psychological Review*, 98(2), 164–181.

Mpofu, E. (2004). Being intelligent with Zimbabweans: A historical and contemporary view. In R. J. Sternberg (Ed.), *International handbook on the psychology of human intelligence* (pp. 364–390). New York: Cambridge University Press.

Muir, D. W., Humphrey, D. E. and Humphrey, G. K. (1994). Pattern and space perception in young infants. *Spatial Vision*, 8(1), 141–165.

Mukamel, R., Ekstrom, A. D., Kaplan, J., Iacoboni, M. and Fried, I. (2010). Single-neuron responses in humans during execution and observation of actions. *Current Biology*, 20, 750–756.

Munakata, Y. (1997). Perseverative reaching in infancy: The roles of hidden toys and motor history in the AB task. *Infant Behavior and Development*, 20(3), 405–416.

Murphy, C. M. and Wood, D. J. (1981). Learning from pictures: The use of pictorial information by young children. *Journal of Experimental Child Psychology*, 32(2), 279–297.

Murphy, C. M. and Wood, D. J. (1982). Learning through media: A comparison of 4–8 year old children's responses to filmed and pictorial instruction. *International Journal of Behavioural Development*, 5, 195–216.

Murphy, K. R. and Barkley, R. A. (1996). The prevalence of DSM-IV symptoms in adult licensed drivers. Implications for clinical diagnosis. *Comprehensive Psychiatry*, 37, 393–401.

Muter, V., Hulme, C., Snowling, M. and Taylor, S. (1997). Segmentation, not rhyming, predicts early progress in learning to read. *Journal of Experimental Child Psychology*, 65, 370–396.

Muter, V., Hulme, C., Snowling, M. J. and Stevenson, J. (2004). Phonemes, rimes, vocabulary, and grammatical skills as foundations of early reading development: Evidence from a longitudinal study. *Developmental Psychology*, 40, 665–681.

Myant, K. A. and Williams, J. M. (2005). Children's concepts of health and illness: Understanding of contagious illnesses, non-contagious illnesses and injuries. *Journal of Health Psychology*, 10(6), 805–819.

Náñez, J. (1988). Perception of impending collision in 3- to 6-week-old human infants. *Infant Behavior and Development*, 11(4), 447–463.

Nation, K. and Hulme, C. (1997). Phonemic segmentation, not onset-rime segmentation, predicts early reading and spelling skills. *Reading Research Quarterly*, 32, 154–167.

National Center for Education Statistics. (2009). *The nation's report card: Reading 2009*. Washington, DC: National Center for Educational Statistics.

National Institute for Child Health and Human Development. (2010). *Learning disabilities*. Retrieved from: http://www.nichd.nih.gov/health/topics/learning_disabilities.cfm. Accessed 23 April, 2010.

National Institute for Mental Health. (2008). *Attention Deficit Hyperactivity Disorder (ADHD)*. Bethesda, MD: US Department of Health and Human Services.

Naus, M. J., Ornstein, P. A. and Aivano, S. (1977). Developmental changes in memory: The effects of processing time and rehearsal instructions. *Journal of Experimental Child Psychology*, 23, 237–251.

Nawrot, E., Mayo, S. L. and Nawrot, M. (2009). The development of depth perception from motion parallax in infancy. *Attention, Perception, and Psychophysics*, 71, 194–199.

Neil, P. A., Chee-Ruiter, C., Scheier, C., Lewkowicz, D. J. and Shimojo, S. (2006). Development of multisensory spatial integration and perception in humans. *Developmental Science*, 9, 454–464.

Neisser, U., Boodoo, G., Bouchard, T. J., Boykin, A. W., Brody, N., Ceci, S. J., Halpern, D. F., Loehlin, J. C.,

Perloff, R., Sternberg, R. J. and Urbina, S. (1996). Intelligence: Knowns and unknowns. *American Psychologist*, 51(2), 77–101.

Nelson, C. A. (1995). The ontogeny of human memory: A cognitive neuroscience perspective. *Developmental Psychology*, 31, 723–738.

Nelson, C. A. and Dolgin, K. G. (1985). The generalized discrimination of facial expressions by seven-month-old infants. *Child Development*, 56(1), 58–61.

Nelson, C. A. and Horowitz, F. D. (1987). Visual motion perception in infancy: A review and synthesis. In P. Salapatek and L. Cohen (Eds), *Handbook of infant perception* (Vol. 2, pp. 123–153). New York: Academic Press.

Nelson, K. (1973). Structure and strategy in learning to talk. *Monographs of the Society for Research in Child Development*, 38(1–2, Serial No. 149).

Nelson, K. (1984). The transition from infant to child memory. In M. Moscovitch (Ed.), *Infant memory* (pp. 103–130). New York: Plenum.

Nelson, K. and Fivush, R. (2004). The emergence of autobiographical memory: A social cultural developmental theory. *Psychological Review*, 111, 486–511.

Nelson, K. and Ross, G. (1980). The generalities and specific of long-term memory in infants and young children. In M. Perlmutter (Ed.), *New directions for child development: Children's memory* (pp. 87–101). San Francisco, CA: Jossey-Bass.

Nelson, T. O. and Dunlosky, J. (1991). The delayed-JOL effect: When delaying your judgements of learning can improve the accuracy of your metacognitive monitoring. *Psychological Science*, 2, 267–270.

Nelson, T. O. and Narens, L. (1990). Metamemory: A theoretical framework and new findings. In G. H. Bower (Ed.), *The psychology of learning and motivation: advances in research and theory, Vol. 26* (pp. 125–169). New York: Academic Press.

Nelson, T. O. and Narens, L. (1994). Why investigate metacognition? In J. Metcalfe and A. P. Shimamura (Eds), *Metacognition* (pp. 1–26). Cambridge, MA: MIT Press.

Newman, H. H., Freeman, F. N. and Holzinger, K. J. (1937). *Twins: A study of heredity and environment*. Chicago, IL: University of Chicago Press.

Nicolson, R. I. and Fawcett, A. J. (1990). Automaticity: A new framework for dyslexia research? *Cognition*, 35, 159–182.

Ninio, A. (2005). Testing the role of semantic similarity in syntactic development. *Journal of Child Language*, 32, 35–61.

Nunes, T. (1992). Ethnomathematics and everyday cognition. In D. A. Grouws (Ed.), *Handbook of research on mathematics teaching and learning* (pp. 557–574). New York: Macmillan.

Nunes, T. (1993). Learning mathematics: Perspectives from everyday life. In R. B. Davis and C. A. Maher

(Eds), *Schools, mathematics, and the world of reality* (pp. 61–78). Needham Heights, MA: Allyn and Bacon.

Nunes, T. and Bryant, P. (1996). *Children doing mathematics.* Oxford: Blackwell.

Nunes, T. and Bryant, P. (2004). Mathematical and scientific thinking. In J. Oates and A. Grayson (Eds), *Cognitive and language development in children* (pp. 259–302). Milton Keynes: Open University.

Nunes, T. and Bryant, P. (2009). *Children's reading and spelling: Beyond the first steps.* Chichester: Wiley-Blackwell.

Nunes, T. and Bryant, P. (Eds) (1997). *Learning and teaching mathematics: An international perspective.* Hove: Psychology Press.

Nunes, T., Schliemann, A. D. and Carraher, D. W. (1993). *Street mathematics and school mathematics.* New York: Cambridge University Press.

Nussbaum, J. (1979). Children's conceptions of the earth as a cosmic body: A cross age study. *Science Education, 63,* 83–93.

Nussbaum, J. (1985). Earth as a cosmic body. In R. Driver, E. Guesne and A. Tiberghien (Eds), *Children's ideas in science* (pp. 170–201). Philadelphia, PA: Open University Press.

Nussbaum, J. and Novak, J. D. (1976). An assessment of children's concepts of the earth utilizing structured interviews. *Science Education, 60*(4), 535–550.

O'Sullivan, J. T. (1993). Preschoolers' beliefs about effort, incentives, and recall. *Journal of Experimental Child Psychology, 55*(3), 396–414.

Oberman, L. and Ramachandran, V. (2007). The simulating social mind: The role of the mirror neuron system and simulation in the social and communicative deficits of autism spectrum disorders. *Psychological Bulletin, 133,* 310–327.

Ochs, E. and Schieffelin, B. (1995). The impact of language socialization on grammatical development. In P. Fletcher and B. MacWhinney (Eds), *Handbook of child language* (pp. 73–94). Oxford: Blackwell.

Okagaki, L. and Sternberg, R. J. (1993). Parental beliefs and children's school performance. *Child Development, 64,* 36–56.

Okamura, H., Kanazawa, S. and Yamaguchi, M. K. (2007). Development of chromatic induction in infancy. *Infant and Child Development, 16*(6), 629–648.

Onishi, K. H. and Baillargeon, R. (2005). Do 15-month-old infants understand false beliefs? *Science, 308,* 255–258.

Opfer, J. E. and Siegler, R. S. (2007). Representational change and children's numerical estimation. *Cognitive Psychology, 55,* 169–195.

Ornstein, P. A. and Haden, C. A. (2001). Memory development or the development of memory? *Current Directions in Psychological Science, 10*(6), 202–205.

Ornstein, P. A., Haden, C. A. and San Souci, P. P. (2008). The development of skilled remembering in children. In J. H. E. Byrne (Series Ed.) and H. L. Roediger, III (Vol. Ed.), *Learning and memory: A comprehensive reference: Volume 2. Cognitive psychology of memory* (pp. 715–744). Oxford: Elsevier.

Ornstein, P. A., Naus, M. J. and Liberty, C. (1975). Rehearsal and organizational processes in children's memory. *Child Development, 46*(4), 818–830.

Orr, E. (1995). *Australia's literacy challenge. The importance of education in breaking the poverty cycle for Australia's disadvantaged families.* Camperdown, Sydney: Smith Family.

Ouattara, K., Lemasson, A. and Zuberbuhler, K. (2009). Campbell's monkeys concatenate vocalizations into context-specific call sequences. *Proceedings of the National Academy of Sciences, 106*(51), 22026–22031.

Overton, W. F., Ward, S. L., Black, J., Noveck, I. A. and Obrien, D. P. (1987). Form and content in the development of deductive reasoning. *Developmental Psychology, 23*(1), 22–30.

Ozonoff, S., Pennington, B. F. and Rogers, S. J. (1991). Executive deficits in high-functioning individuals with autism: Relationships to theory of mind. *Journal of Child Psychology and Psychiatry, 32,* 1081–1105.

Pannu, J. K., Kaszniak, A. W. and Rapcsak, S. Z. (2005). Metamemory for faces following frontal lobe damage. *Journal of the International Neuropsychological Society, 11,* 668–676.

Paris, S. G. and Lindauer, B. K. (1982). The development of cognitive skills during childhood. In B. Wolman (Ed.), *Handbook of developmental psychology* (pp. 333–349). Englewood Cliffs, NJ: Prentice-Hall.

Paris, S. G. and Oka, E. R. (1986). Children's reading strategies, metacognition, and motivation. *Developmental Review, 6*(1), 25–56.

Pascalis, O., de Haan, M. and Nelson, C. A. (2002). Is face processing species-specific during the first year of life? *Science, 296*(5571), 1321–1323.

Pascalis, O., de Schonen, S., Morton, J., Deruelle, C. and Fabre-Grenet, M. (1995). Mother's face recognition by neonates: A replication and an extension. *Infant Behavior and Development, 18*(1), 79–85.

Pascual-Leone, J. (1987). Organismic processes for neo-Piagetian theories: A dialectical causal account of cognitive development. In A. Demetriou (Ed.), *The neo-Piagetian theories of cognitive development: Towards an integration* (pp. 531–569). Amsterdam: North-Holland.

Passolunghi, M. and Siegel, L. S. (2001). Short-term memory, working memory, and inhibitory control in children with difficulties in arithmetic problem solving. *Journal of Experimental Child Psychology, 80,* 44–57.

Patterson, F. G. (1978). The gestures of a gorilla: Language acquisition in another pongid. *Brain and Language*, 5, 72–97.

Pauen, S. (1996). Children's reasoning about the interaction of forces. *Child Development*, 67(6), 2728–2742.

Pauen, S. and Wilkening, F. (1997). Children's analogical reasoning about natural phenomena. *Journal of Experimental Child Psychology*, 67(1), 90–113.

Pears, R. and Bryant, P. (1990). Transitive inferences by young-children about spatial position. *British Journal of Psychology*, 81, 497–510.

Pedersen, N. L., Plomin, R., Nesselroade, J. R. and McClearn, G. E. (1992). A quantitative genetic analysis of cognitive abilities during the second half of the life span. *Psychological Science*, 3, 346–353.

Peña, M., Maki, A., Kovačić, D., Dehaene-Lambertz, G., Koizumi, H., Bouquet, F. and Mehler, J. (2003). Sounds and silence: An optical topography study of language recognition at birth. *Proceedings of the National Academy of Science*, 100(20), 11702–11705.

Penner, D. E. and Klahr, D. (1996). The interaction of domain-specific knowledge and domain-general discovery strategies: A study with sinking objects. *Child Development*, 67(6), 2709–2727.

Pennington, B. F. and Olson, R. K. (2005). Genetics of dyslexia. In M. J. Snowling and C. Hulme (Eds), *The science of reading: A handbook* (pp. 453–472). Malden, MA: Blackwell Publishing.

Pennington, B. F. and Ozonoff, S. (1996). Executive functions and developmental psychopathology. *Journal of Child Psychology and Psychiatry*, 37, 51–87.

Perie, M., Grigg, W. S. and Donahue, P. L. (2005). *The nation's report card: Reading 2005*. Washington, DC: National Center for Educational Statistics.

Perner, J. (1991). *Understanding the representational mind*. Cambridge, MA: MIT Press.

Perner, J. (2000). About + belief + counterfactual. In P. Mitchell and K. J. Riggs (Eds), *Children's reasoning and the mind* (pp. 367–401). Hove: Psychology Press.

Perner, J. and Leekam, S. (2008). The curious incident of the photo that was accused of being false: Issues of domain specificity in development, autism, and brain imaging. *The Quarterly Journal of Experimental Psychology*, 61(1), 76–89.

Perner, J. and Ruffman, T. (1995). Episodic memory and autonoetic conciousness: Developmental evidence and a theory of childhood amnesia. *Journal of Experimental Child Psychology*, 59, 516–548.

Perner, J. and Ruffman, T. (2005). Infants' insight into the mind: How deep? *Science*, 308(5719), 214–216.

Perner, J. and Wimmer, H. (1985). 'John thinks that Mary thinks that …': Attribution of second-order beliefs by 5- to 10-year-old children. *Journal of Experimental Child Psychology*, 39, 437–471.

Perner, J., Aichhorn, M., Kronbichler, M., Staffen, W. and Ladurner, G. (2006). Thinking of mental and other representations: The roles of left and right temporo-parietal junction. *Social Neuroscience*, 1(3–4), 245–258.

Perner, J., Baker, S. and Hutton, D. (1994). Prelief: The conceptual origins of belief and pretence. In C. Lewis and P. Mitchell (Eds), *Children's early understanding of mind* (pp. 261–286). Hove: Lawrence Erlbaum Associates.

Perner, J., Frith, U., Leslie, A. M. and Leekam, S. R. (1989). Exploration of the autistic childs theory of mind – knowledge, belief, and communication. *Child Development*, 60(3), 689–700.

Perner, J., Leekam, S. R. and Wimmer, H. (1987). 2-year-olds difficulty with false belief: The case for a conceptual deficit. *British Journal of Developmental Psychology*, 5, 125–137.

Perrin, E. C. and Gerrity, S. (1981). There's a demon in your belly: Children's understanding of illness. *Pediatrics*, 67(6), 841–849.

Phillips, G. and McNaughton, S. (1990). The practice of storybook reading to preschoolers in mainstream New Zealand families. *Reading Research Quarterly*, 25(3), 196–212.

Piaget, J. (1921). Une forme verbale de la comparaison chez l'enfant. *Archives de Psychologie*, 18, 141–172.

Piaget, J. (1926). *The language and thought of the child*. New York: Harcourt Brace and Co.

Piaget, J. (1932). *The moral judgment of the child*. Glencoe, IL: Free Press.

Piaget, J. (1946/1970). *The child's conception of movement and speed*. New York: Basic Books.

Piaget, J. (1950). *The psychology of intelligence* (M. Piercy and D. E. Berlyne, Trans.). London: Routledge and Kegan Paul. (Original work published 1947).

Piaget, J. (1952a). *The child's conception of number*. London: Routledge and Kegan Paul.

Piaget, J. (1952b). *The origins of intelligence in children*. New York: International University Press.

Piaget, J. (1954). *The construction of reality in the child*. New York: Basic Books.

Piaget, J. (1960). *The psychology of intelligence*. Paterson, NJ: Littlefield, Adams and Co.

Piaget, J. (1962a). The stages of the intellectual development of the child. *Bulletin of the Menninger Clinic*, 26, 120–128.

Piaget, J. (1962b). *Play, dreams and imitation in childhood*. New York: Norton.

Piaget, J. (1967/1971). *Biology and knowledge*. Chicago, IL: Chicago University Press.

Piaget, J. (1968). Quantification, conservation, and nativism. *Science*, 162(3857), 976–979.

Piaget, J. (1969). *The mechanisms of perception*. New York: Basic Books.

Piaget, J. (1970). Piaget's theory. In P. H. Mussen (Ed.), *Carmichael's manual of child psychology* (3rd ed.) (pp. 703–723). New York: Wiley.

Piaget, J. (1985). *The equilibration of cognitive structures: The central problem of intellectual development*. Chicago, IL: University of Chicago Press.

Piaget, J. and Inhelder, B. (1956). *The child's conceptions of space*. London: Routledge and Kegan Paul.

Piaget, J. and Inhelder, B. (1969). *The psychology of the child*. New York: Basic Books.

Piaget, J. and Inhelder, B. (1973). *Memory and intelligence*. New York: Basic Books.

Piaget, J. and Inhelder, B. (1974). *The child's construction of quantities*. London: Routledge and Kegan Paul.

Piaget, J., Montangero, J. and Billeter, J. (1977). La formation des correlats. In J. Piaget (Ed.), *Recherches sur l'abstraction reflechissante I* (pp. 115–129). Paris: Presses Universitaires de France.

Piburn, M. D. (1990). Reasoning about logical propositions and success in science. *Journal of Research in Science Teaching, 27*(9), 887–900.

Pillemer, D. B. and White, S. H. (1989). Childhood events recalled by children and adults. In H. W. Reese (Ed.), *Advances in child development and behavior, Vol. XXI* (pp. 297–340). San Diego, CA: Academic Press.

Pine, J., Lieven, E. and Rowland, C. (1998). Comparing different models of the development of the English verb category. *Linguistics, 36*, 807–830.

Pinker, S. (1984). *Language learnability and language development*. Cambridge, MA: Harvard University Press.

Pinker, S. (1987). The bootstrapping problem in language acquisition. In B. MacWhinney (Ed.), *Mechanisms of language acquisition* (pp. 339–441). Hillsdale, NJ: Lawrence Erlbaum Associates.

Pinker, S. (1989). *Learnability and cognition*. Cambridge, MA: MIT Press.

Pinker, S. (1994). *The language instinct*. Harmondsworth: Allen Lane.

Pinker, S. (1999). *Words and rules*. London: Weidenfield and Nicolson.

Pinker, S. and Jackendoff, R. (2005). The faculty of language: What's special about it? *Cognition, 95*, 201–236.

Pinker, S. and Prince, A. (1988). On language and connectionism: Analysis of a parallel distributed processing model of language acquisition. *Cognition, 28*(1–2), 73–193.

Pinker, S. and Ullman, M. T. (2002). The past and future of the past tense. *Trends in Cognitive Sciences, 6*, 456–463.

Platt, R. D. and Griggs, R. A. (1993). Facilitation in the abstract selection task: The effects of attentional and instructional factors. *Quarterly Journal of Experimental Psychology Section A – Human Experimental Psychology, 46*(4), 591–613.

Plomin, R., DeFries, J. C. and Loehlin, J. C. (1977). Genotype-environment interaction and correlation in the analysis of human behavior. *Psychological Bulletin, 84*, 309–322.

Plomin, R., DeFries, J. C. and McClearn, G. E. (1990). *Behavioral genetics: A primer* (2nd ed.). New York: Freeman.

Plunkett, K. and Marchman, V. (1991). U-shaped learning and frequency effects in a multi-layered perception: Implications for child language acquisition. *Cognition, 38*(1), 43–102.

Polderman, T. J. C., Gosso, M. F., Posthuma, D., Van Beijsterveldt, T. C. E. M., Heutink, P., Verhulst, F. C. and Boomsma, D. I. (2006). A longitudinal twin study on IQ, executive functioning, and attention problems during childhood and early adolescence. *Acta Neurologica Belgica, 106*, 191–207.

Polka, L., Colantonio, C. and Sundara, M. (2001). Cross-language perception of /d - ð/: Evidence for a new developmental pattern. *Journal of the Acoustical Society of America, 109*(5), 2190–2200.

Pons, F., Lewkowicz, D. J., Soto-Faraco, S. and Sebastián-Gallés, N. (2009). Narrowing of intersensory speech perception in infancy. *Proceedings of the National Academy of Sciences, 106*, 10598–10602.

Poulin-Dubois, D., Sodian, B., Metz, U., Tilden, J. and Schoeppner, B. (2007). Out of sight is not out of mind: Developmental changes in infants' understanding of visual perception during the second year. *Journal of Cognition and Development, 8*(4), 401–425.

Premack, D. (1976). Language and intelligence in ape and man. *American Scientist, 64*, 674–683.

Premack, D. and Woodruff, G. (1978). Does the chimpanzee have a theory of mind? *Behavioral and Brain Sciences, 1*(4), 515–526.

Pressley, M. (1982). Elaboration and memory development. *Child Development, 53*(2), 296–309.

Pressley, M. and Levin, J. R. (1977). Developmental differences in subjects' associative-learning strategies and performance: Assessing a hypothesis. *Journal of Experimental Child Psychology, 24*(3), 431–439.

Pretz, J. E. and Sternberg, R. J. (2005). Unifying the field: Cognition and intelligence. In R. J. Sternberg and J. E. Pretz (Eds), *Cognition and intelligence: Identifying the mechanisms of the mind* (pp. 306–318). New York: Cambridge University Press.

Prior, M., Dahlstrom, B. and Squires, T.-L. (1990). Autistic children's knowledge of thinking and feeling states in other people. *Journal of Child Psychology and Psychiatry, 31*(4), 587–601.

Quon, E. and Atance, C. M. (2010). A comparison of preschoolers' memory, knowledge, and anticipation of events. *Journal of Cognition and Development, 11*, 37–60.

Rack, J. P., Snowling, M. J. and Olson, R. K. (1992). The nonword reading deficit in developmental dyslexia: A review. *Reading Research Quarterly*, 27(1), 28–53.

Radford, A. (1990). *Syntactic theory and the acquisition of English syntax: The nature of early child grammars of English*. Oxford: Blackwell.

Raichle, M. E., MacLeod, A. M., Snyder, A. Z., Powers, W. J., Gusnard, D. A. and Shulman, G. L. (2001). A default mode of brain function. *Proceedings of the National Academy of Sciences of the United States of America*, 98(2), 676–682.

Rajendran, G. and Mitchell, P. (2007). Cognitive theories of autism. *Developmental Review*, 27(2), 224–260.

Ramani, G. B. and Siegler, R. S. (2008). Promoting broad and stable improvements in low-income children's numerical knowledge through playing number board games. *Child Development*, 79, 375–394.

Ramey, C. T. and Campbell, F. A. (1984). Preventive education for high-risk children: Cognitive consequences of the Carolina ABC. *American Journal of Mental Deficiency*, 88(5), 515–523.

Ramey, C. T. and Ramey, S. L. (1998). Early intervention and early experience. *American Psychologist*, 53, 109–120.

Ramey, C. T. and Ramey, S. L. (2000). Intelligence and public policy. In R. J. Sternberg (Ed.), *Handbook of intelligence* (pp. 534–548). NY: Cambridge University Press.

Ramey, C. T., Campbell, F. A. and Ramey, S. L. (1999). Early intervention: Successful pathways to improving intellectual development. *Developmental Neuropsychology*, 16, 385–392.

Ramey, S. L. and Ramey, C. T. (1999). Early experience and early intervention for children 'at risk' for developmental delay and mental retardation. *Mental Retardation and Developmental Disabilities Research Reviews*, 5, 1–10.

Ramscar, M. (2002). The role of meaning in inflection: Why the past tense doesn't require a rule. *Cognitive Psychology*, 46, 45–94.

Rasmussen, T. and Milner, B. (1977). The role of early left-brain injury in determining lateralization of cerebral speech functions. *Annals of the New York Academy of Science*, 299, 355–369.

Rattermann, M. J. and Gentner, D. (1998). More evidence for a relational shift in the development of analogy: Children's performance on a causal-mapping task. *Cognitive Development*, 13, 453–478.

Raven, J., Raven, J. C. and Court, J. H. (2000). *Manual for Raven's progressive matrices and vocabulary scales. Section 3: The standard progressive matrices*. San Antonio, TX: Harcourt Assessment.

Recht, D. R. and Leslie, L. (1988). Effect of prior knowledge on good and poor readers' memory of text. *Journal of Educational Psychology*, 80, 16–20.

Redington, M., Chater, N. and Finch, S. (1993). Distributional information and the acquisition of linguistic categories: A statistical approach. *Proceedings of the 15th Annual Conference of the Cognitive Science Society* (pp. 848–853). Hillsdale, NJ: Lawrence Erlbaum Associates.

Reese, H. W. (1962). Verbal mediation as a function of age level. *Psychological Bulletin*, 59, 502–509.

Reese, H. W. (1977). Imagery and associative memory. In R. V. Kail and J. W. Hagen (Eds), *Perspectives on the development of memory and cognition* (pp. 113–175). Hillsdale, NJ: Lawrence Erlbaum Associates.

Reichgelt, H., Shadbolt, N. R., Paskiewicz, T., Wood, D. J. and Wood, H. (1993). EXPLAIN: On implementing more effective tutoring systems. In A. Sloman, D. Hogg, G. Humphreys, D. Partridge and A. Ramsay (Eds), *Prospects for artificial intelligence* (pp. 239–249). Amsterdam: IOS Press.

Repacholi, B. M. and Gopnik, A. (1997). Early reasoning about desires: Evidence from 14- and 18-month-olds. *Developmental Psychology*, 33(1), 12–21.

Rescorla, L. (1980). Overextension in early language development. *Journal of Child Language*, 7, 321–335.

Rice, C. (2009). Prevalence of autism spectrum disorders – autism and developmental disabilities monitoring network, United States, 2006. *Morbidity and Mortality Weekly Report*, 58(SS10), 1–20.

Rigato, S., Farroni, T. and Johnson, M. H. (2010). The shared signal hypothesis and neural responses to expressions and gaze in infants and adults. *Social Cognitive and Affective Neuroscience*, 5, 88–97.

Rimland, B. (1978). Savant capabilities of autistic children and their cognitive implications. In G. Serban (Ed.), *Cognitive defects in the development of mental illness* (pp. 43–65). New York: Brunner/Mazel.

Rispoli, M. (1999). Review of Elman et al. *Rethinking innateness. Journal of Child Language*, 26, 217–225.

Rittle-Johnson, B. and Alibali, M. W. (1999). Conceptual and procedural knowledge of mathematics: Does one lead to the other? *Journal of Educational Psychology*, 91, 1–16.

Rittle-Johnson, B. R. and Siegler, R. S. (1999). Learning to spell: Variability, choice, and change in children's strategy use. *Child Development*, 70, 332–349.

Rivera-Gaxiola, M., Silva-Pereyra, J. and Kuhl, P. K. (2005). Brain potentials to native and non-native speech contrasts in 7- and 11-month-old American infants. *Developmental Science*, 8, 162–172.

Rizzolatti, G. and Craighero, L. (2004). The mirror-neuron system. *Annual Review of Neuroscience*, 27, 169–192.

Rizzolatti, G., Fadiga, L., Gallese, V. and Fogassi, L. (1996). Premotor cortex and the recognition of motor actions. *Cognitive Brain Research*, 3(2), 131–141.

Robinson, E. J. and Mitchell, P. (1995). Masking of children's early understanding of the representational mind: Backwards explanation versus prediction. *Child Development, 66*(4), 1022–1039.

Robinson, K. M. and Dubé, A. K. (2009). Children's understanding of addition and subtraction concepts. *Journal of Experimental Child Psychology, 103*, 532–545.

Rochat, P. (1987). Mouthing and grasping in neonates: Evidence for the early detection of what hard or soft substances afford for action. *Infant Behavior and Development, 10*(4), 435–449.

Roebers, C. M. and Schneider, W. (2001). Individual differences in children's eyewitness recall: The influence of intelligence and shyness. *Applied Developmental Science, 5*, 9–20.

Roebers, C. M. and Schneider, W. (2002). Stability and consistency of children's event recall. *Cognitive Development, 17*(1), 1085–1103.

Roebers, C. M., Moga, N. and Schneider, W. (2001). The role of accuracy motivation on children's and adults' event recall. *Journal of Experimental Child Psychology, 78*, 313–329.

Roediger III, H. L. (1980). Memory metaphors in cognitive psychology. *Memory and Cognition, 8*, 231–246.

Rohde, D. L. T. and Plaut, D. C. (1999). Language acquisition in the absence of explicit negative evidence: How important is starting small? *Cognition, 72*, 67–109.

Ropar, D. and Mitchell, P. (1999). Are individual's with autism and Asperger's Syndrome susceptible to visual illusions? *Journal of Child Psychiatry and Psychology, 40*, 1283–1293.

Ropar, D. and Mitchell, P. (2001). Susceptibility to illusions and performance on visuo-spatial tasks in individuals with autism. *Journal of Child Psychiatry and Psychology, 42*, 539–549.

Rose, J. (2006). *Independent review of the teaching of early reading*. Nottingham: DfES Publications.

Rose, J. (2009). *Identifying and teaching children and young people with dyslexia and literacy difficulties*. Nottingham: DCSF Publications.

Rose, S. A. and Blank, M. (1974). The potency of context in children's cognition: An illustration through conservation. *Child Development, 45*, 499–502.

Rose, S. A. and Feldman, J. F. (1995). Prediction of IQ and specific cognitive abilities at 11 years from infancy measures. *Developmental Psychology, 31*, 685–696.

Rosengren, K. S., Gelman, S. A., Kalish, C. W. and McCormick, M. (1991). As time goes by: Children's early understanding of growth in animals. *Child Development, 62*(6), 1302–1320.

Rosenstein, D. and Oster, H. (1988). Differential facial responses to four basic tastes in newborns. *Child Development, 59*(6), 1555–1568.

Rovee-Collier, C. (1999). The development of infant memory. *Current Directions in Psychological Science, 8*, 80–85.

Rovee-Collier, C., Adler, S. A. and Borza, M. A. (1994). Substituting new details for old? Effects of delaying postevent information on infant memory. *Memory and Cognition, 22*, 644–656.

Rovee-Collier, C., Hartshorn, K. and DiRubbo, M. (1999). Long-term maintenance of infant memory. *Developmental Psychobiology, 35*, 91–102.

Rovee-Collier, C., Sullivan, M. W., Enright, M., Lucas, D. and Fagen, J. W. (1980). Reactivation of infant memory. *Science, 208*(4448), 1159–1161.

Rowe, S. M. and Wertsch, J. V. (2000). Vygotsky's model of cognitive development. In U. Goswami (Ed.), *Blackwell handbook of childhood cognitive development* (pp. 538–554). Oxford: Blackwell.

Rowland, C. (2000). *The grammatical acquisition of wh-questions in early English multi-word speech*. Unpublished doctoral thesis. University of Nottingham.

Rubia, K., Taylor, E., Smith, A., Oksanen, H., Overmeyer, S. and Newman, S. (2001). Neuropsychological analyses of impulsiveness in childhood hyperactivity. *British Journal of Psychiatry, 179*, 138–143.

Ruffman, T., Perner, J., Olson, D. R. and Doherty, M. (1993). Reflecting on scientific thinking: Children's understanding of the hypothesis-evidence relation. *Child Development, 64*(6), 1617–1636.

Ruffman, T., Slade, L., Sandino, J. C. and Fletcher, A. (2005). Are A-not-B errors caused by a belief about object location. *Child Development, 76*(1), 122–136.

Rumbaugh, D. M. (1977). *Language learning by a chimpanzee: The Lana project*. New York: Academic Press.

Rumelhart, D. E. and McClelland, J. L. (1986). On learning the past tenses of English verbs. In J. L. McClelland, D. E. Rumelhart and the PDP Research Group. (Eds), *Parallel distributed processing: Explorations in the microstructure of cognition. Volume II* (pp. 216–271). Cambridge, MA: MIT Press.

Russell, J., Mauthner, N., Sharpe, S. and Tidswell, T. (1991). The 'windows task' as a measure of strategic deception in preschoolers and autistic subjects. *British Journal of Developmental Psychology, 9*, 331–349.

Russell, J., Saltmarsh, R. and Hill, E. (1999). What do executive factors contribute to the failure on false belief tasks by children with autism? *Journal of Child Psychology and Psychiatry and Allied Disciplines, 40*, 859–868.

Rutter, M., Caspi, A., Fergusson, D., Horwood, L. J., Goodman, R., Maughan, B., Moffitt, E., Meltzer, H. and Carroll, J. (2004). Sex differences in developmental reading disability: New findings from four epidemiological studies. *Journal of the American Medical Association, 291*, 2007–2012.

Rutter, M., Kim-Cohen, J. and Maughan, B. (2006). Continuities and discontinuities in psychopathology between childhood and adult life. *Journal of Child Psychology and Psychiatry, 47*(3–4), 276–295.

Sabbagh, M. A. and Gelman, S. A. (2000). Buzzsaws and blueprints: What children need (or don't need) to learn language. *Journal of Child Language, 27*, 715–726.

Sabbagh, M. A., Bowman, L. C., Evraire, L. E. and Ito, J. M. B. (2009). Neurodevelopmental correlates of theory of mind in preschool children. *Child Development, 80*(4), 1147–1162.

Sabbagh, M. A., Moses, L. J. and Shiverick, S. M. (2006). Executive functioning and preschoolers' understanding of false beliefs, false photographs, and false signs. *Child Development, 77*, 1034–1049.

Saffran, J. R. (2003). Statistical language learning: Mechanisms and constraints. *Current Directions in Psychological Science, 12*(4), 110–114.

Saffran, J. R., Aslin, R. N. and Newport, E. L. (1996). Statistical learning by 8-month-old infants. *Science, 274*(5294), 1926–1928.

Salapatek, P. (1975). Pattern perception in early infancy. In L. B. Cohen and P. Salapatek (Eds), *Infant perception: From sensation to cognition Vol. 1: Basic visual processes* (pp. 144–248). New York: Academic Press.

Saloviita, T., Ruusila, L. and Ruusila, U. (2000). Incidence of savant syndrome in Finland. *Perceptual and Motor Skills, 91*, 120–122.

Saltmarsh, R., Mitchell, P. and Robinson, E. (1995). Realism and children's early grasp of mental representation: Belief-based judgments in the state change task. *Cognition, 57*(3), 297–325.

Samarapungavan, A. (1992). Children's judgments in theory choice tasks: Scientific rationality in childhood. *Cognition, 45*(1), 1–32.

Samson, D., Apperly, I. A., Chiavarino, C. and Humphreys, G. W. (2004). The left temporo-parietal junction is necessary for representing someone else's belief. *Nature Neuroscience, 7*(5), 449–500.

Santos, L. (2004). 'Core knowledges': A dissociation between spatiotemporal knowledge and contact-mechanics in a nonhuman primate? *Developmental Science, 7*, 167–174.

Sattler, J. (2008). *Assessment of children: Cognitive applications*. San Diego, CA: Sattler Publishing, Inc.

Savage-Rumbaugh, E. S. (1986). *Ape language: From conditioned response to symbol*. New York: Columbia University Press.

Savage-Rumbaugh, E. S. and Lewin, R. (1994). *Kanzi: At the brink of the human mind*. New York: Wiley.

Savage-Rumbaugh, E. S., McDonald, K., Sevcik, R. A., Hopkins, W. D. and Rupert, E. (1986). Spontaneous symbol acquisition and communicative use by pygmy chimpanzees (Pan paniscus). *Journal of Experimental Psychology: General, 115*, 211–235.

Saxe, R. and Kanwisher, N. (2003). People thinking about thinking people: fMRI investigations of theory of mind. *NeuroImage, 19*, 1835–1842.

Saxe, R. and Powell, L. J. (2006). It's the thought that counts: Specific brain regions for one component of theory of mind. *Psychological Science, 17*, 692–699.

Saxe, R. and Wexler, A. (2005). Making sense of another mind: The role of the right temporo-parietal junction. *Neuropsychologia, 43*, 1391–1399.

Saxe, R., Whitfield-Gabrieli, S., Scholz, J. and Pelphrey, K. A. (2009). Brain regions for perceiving and reasoning about other people in school-aged children. *Child Development, 80*(4), 1197–209.

Saywitz, K. J. and Snyder, L. (1993). Improving children's testimony with preparation. In G. S. Goodman and B. L. Bottoms (Eds), *Child victim, child witnesses: Understanding and improving testimony* (pp. 117–146). New York: The Guilford Press.

Scaife, M. and Bruner, J. S. (1975). Capacity for joint visual attention in the infant. *Nature, 253*(5489), 265–266.

Scarr, S. (1978). From evolution to Larry P., or what shall we do about IQ tests? *Intelligence, 2*, 325–342.

Scarr, S. and McCartney, K. (1983). How people make their own environments: A theory of genotype → environment effects. *Child Development, 54*(2), 424–435.

Schachar, R. J. and Logan, G. D. (1990). Impulsivity and inhibitory control in normal development and childhood psychopathology. *Developmental Psychology, 26*, 710–720.

Schank, R. C. and Abelson, R. P. (1977). *Scripts, plans, goals, and understanding: An inquiry into human knowledge structures*. Hillsdale, NJ: Lawrence Erlbaum Associates.

Schauble, L. (1990). Belief revision in children: The role of prior knowledge and strategies for generating evidence. *Journal of Experimental Child Psychology, 49*(1), 31–57.

Schauble, L. (1996). The development of scientific reasoning in knowledge-rich contexts. *Developmental Psychology, 32*(1), 102–119.

Schauble, L., Klopfer, L. E. and Raghavan, K. (1991). Students transition from an engineering model to a science model of experimentation. *Journal of Research in Science Teaching, 28*(9), 859–882.

Schlagmüller, M. and Schneider, W. (2002). The development of organizational strategies in children: Evidence from a microgenetic longitudinal study. *Journal of Experimental Child Psychology, 81*, 298–319.

Schlesinger, I. M. (1982). *Steps to language*. London: Lawrence Erlbaum Associates.

Schlesinger, I. M. (1988). The origin of relational categories. In Y. Levy, I. M. Schlesinger and M. D. S. Braine (Eds), *Categories and processes in language acquisition* (pp. 121–178). London: Lawrence Erlbaum Associates.

Schmidt, L. R. and Frohling, H. (2000). Lay concepts of health and illness from a developmental perspective. *Psychology and Health*, *15*(2), 229–239.

Schneider, B., Trehub, S. and Bull, D. (1980). High-frequency sensitivity in infants. *Science*, *207*(4434), 1003–1004.

Schneider, B. A., Trehub, S. E., Morrongiello, B. and Thorpe, L. (1986). Auditory sensitivity in preschool children. *Journal of the Acoustical Society of America*, *79*, 447–452.

Schneider, L., Price, H. L., Roberts, K. P. and Hedrick, A. M. (2010). Children's episodic and generic reports of alleged abuse. *Applied Cognitive Psychology*. DOI: 10.1002/acp.1759.

Schneider, W. (1986). The role of conceptual knowledge and metamemory in the development of organizational processes in memory. *Journal of Experimental Child Psychology*, *42*(2), 218–236.

Schneider, W. (2008). The development of metacognitive knowledge in children and adolescents: Major trends and implications for education. *Mind, Brain, and Education*, *2*, 114–121.

Schneider, W. and Bjorklund, D. F. (1998). Memory. In W. Damon, D. Kuhn and R. S. Siegler (Eds), *Handbook of child psychology, Volume 2: Cognition, perception and language* (pp. 467–521). New York: Wiley.

Schneider, W. and Lockl, K. (2002). The development of metacognitive knowledge in children and adolescents. In T. J. Perfect and B. L. Schwartz (Eds), *Applied metacognition* (pp. 224–257). Cambridge: Cambridge University Press.

Schneider, W., Korkel, J. and Weinert, F. E. (1989). Domain-specific knowledge and memory performance: A comparison of high- and low-aptitude children. *Journal of Educational Psychology*, *81*, 306–312.

Schneider, W., Schlagmüller, M. and Visé, M. (1998). The impact of metamemory and domain-specific knowledge on memory performance. *European Journal of Psychology of Education*, *13*, 91–103.

Schneider, W., Visé, M., Lockl, K. and Nelson, T. O. (2000). Developmental trends in children's memory monitoring: Evidence from a judgment-of-learning task. *Cognitive Development*, *15*(2), 115–134.

Scholl, B. J. and Leslie, A. M. (1999). Modularity, development and 'theory of mind'. *Mind and Language*, *14*(1), 131–153.

Scholl, B. J. and Leslie, A. M. (2001). Minds, modules, and meta-analysis. *Child Development*, *72*(3), 696–701.

Schulman-Galambos, C. and Galambos, R. (1979). Brain stem evoked response audiometry in newborn hearing screening. *Archives of Otolaryngology*, *105*(2), 86–90.

Schult, C. A. and Wellman, H. M. (1997). Explaining human movements and actions: Children's understanding of the limits of psychological explanation. *Cognition*, *62*(3), 291–324.

Schwartz, A. N., Campos, J. J. and Baisel, E. J. (1973). The visual cliff: Cardiac and behavioral responses on the deep and shallow sides at five and nine months of age. *Journal of Experimental Child Psychology*, *15*(1), 86–99.

Schwartz, G. M., Izard, C. E. and Ansul, S. E. (1985). The 5-month-old's ability to discriminate facial expressions of emotion. *Infant Behavior and Development*, *8*(1), 65–77.

Scott, L. S., Pascalis, O. and Nelson, C. A. (2007). A domain general theory of the development of perceptual discrimination. *Current Directions in Psychological Science*, *16*(4), 197–201.

Scoville, W. B. and Milner, B. (1957). Loss of recent memory after bilateral hippocampal lesions. *Journal of Neurology, Neurosurgery, and Psychiatry*, *20*, 11–21.

Scribner, S. (1975). Recall of classic syllogisms: A cross-cultural investigation of error on logical problems. In R. J. Falmagne (Ed.), *Reasoning: Representation and process* (pp. 153–173). Hillsdale, NJ: Lawrence Erlbaum and Associates.

Scribner, S. (1977). Modes of thinking and ways of speaking: Culture and logic reconsidered. In P. N. Johnson-Laird and P. C. Wason (Eds), *Thinking* (pp. 483–500). Cambridge: Cambridge University Press.

Seifert, K., Hoffnung, R. and Hoffnung, M. (1997). *Lifespan human development*. Boston, MA: Houghton-Mifflin.

Sen, M. G., Yonas, A. and Knill, D. C. (2001). Development of infants' sensitivity to surface contour information for spatial layout. *Perception*, *30*, 167–176.

Seo, K. H. and Ginsburg, H. P. (2003). 'You've got to carefully read the math sentence …': Classroom context and children's interpretations of the equal sign. In A. J. Baroody and A. Dowker (Eds), *The development of arithmetic concepts and skills: Constructing adaptive expertise* (pp. 161–187). Mahwah, NJ: Lawrence Erlbaum Associates.

Sergeant, J. A., Oosterlaan, J. and van der Meere, J. (1999). Information processing and energetic factors in attention-deficit/hyperactivity disorder. In H. C. Quay and A. E. Hogan (Eds), *Handbook of disruptive behavior disorders* (pp. 75–104). New York: Kluwer Academic.

Serpell, R. (1977). Estimates of intelligence in a rural community of eastern Zambia. In F. M. Okatcha (Ed.), *Modern psychology and cultural adaptation* (pp. 179–216). Nairobi: Swahili Language Consultants and Publishers.

Serpell, R. (1993). *The significance of schooling: Life-journeys in an African society.* Cambridge: Cambridge University Press.

Serpell, R. (2000). Culture and intelligence. In A. Kazdin (Ed.), *Encyclopedia of psychology* (pp. 493–496). Washington, DC and New York: American Psychological Association and Oxford University Press.

Seymour, P. H. K. and Duncan, L. G. (2001). Learning to read in English. *Psychology, 8,* 281–299.

Seymour, P. H. K. and Elder, L. (1986). Beginning reading without phonology. *Cognitive Neuropsychology, 3,* 1–36.

Shah, A. and Frith, U. (1983). An islet of ability in autistic children: A research note. *Journal of Child Psychology and Psychiatry, 24,* 613–620.

Shah, A. and Frith, U. (1993). Why do autistic individuals show superior performance on the block design task? *Journal of Child Psychology and Psychiatry, 34,* 1351–1364.

Shalev, R. S., Manor, O. and Gross-Tsur, V. (1997). Neuropsychological aspects of developmental dyscalculia. *Mathematical Cognition, 3*(2), 105–120.

Shallice, T. and Warrington, E. K. (1974). The dissociation between short term retention of meaningful sounds and verbal material. *Neuropsychologia, 12*(4), 553–555.

Shea, S. L., Fox, R., Aslin, R. N. and Dumais, S. T. (1980). Assessment of stereopsis in human infants. *Investigative Ophthalmology and Visual Science, 19,* 1400–1404.

Sherman, J. and Bisanz, J. (2007). Evidence for use of mathematical inversion by three-year-old children. *Journal of Cognition and Development, 8,* 333–344.

Shields, J. (1962). *Monozygotic twins: Brought up apart and brought up together.* London: Oxford University Press.

Shiffrin, R. M. and Atkinson, R. C. (1969). Storage and retrieval processes in long-term memory. *Psychological Review, 76*(2), 179–193.

Shinohara, T. (1994). Rich classes inferable from positive data: Length-bounded elementary formal systems. *Information and Computation, 108,* 175–186.

Shultz, T. R. (1998). A computational analysis of conservation. *Developmental Science, 1,* 103–126.

Sieg, K. G., Gaffney, G. R., Preston, D. F. and Hellings, J. A. (1995). SPET brain imaging abnormalities in attention deficit hyperactivity disorder. *Clinical Nuclear Medicine, 20,* 55–60.

Siegal, M. (1988). Children's knowledge of contagion and contamination as causes of illness. *Child Development, 59*(5), 1353–1359.

Siegal, M. and Beattie, K. (1991). Where to look first for children's knowledge of false beliefs. *Cognition, 38*(1), 1–12.

Siegal, M. and Peterson, C. C. (1999). Becoming mindful of biology and health: An introduction. In M. Siegal and C. C. Peterson (Eds), *Children's understanding of biology and health* (pp. 1–19). Cambridge: Cambridge University Press.

Siegal, M. and Peterson, C. C. (Eds) (1999). *Children's understanding of biology and health.* Cambridge: Cambridge University Press.

Siegel, L. S. (1992). An evaluation of the discrepancy definition of dyslexia. *Journal of Learning Disabilities, 25,* 618–629.

Siegler, R. S. (1976). Three aspects of cognitive development. *Cognitive Psychology, 8,* 481–520.

Siegler, R. S. (1981). Developmental sequences within and between concepts. *Monographs of the Society for Research in Child Development, 46*(2), 1–84.

Siegler, R. S. (1986). Unities in strategy choices across domains. In M. Perlmutter (Ed.), *Minnesota symposium on child psychology, Vol. 19* (pp. 1–48). Hillsdale, NJ: Lawrence Erlbaum Associates.

Siegler, R. S. (1987). The perils of averaging data over strategies: An example from children's addition. *Journal of Experimental Psychology: General, 116,* 250–264.

Siegler, R. S. (1988). Strategy choice procedures and the development of multiplication skill. *Journal of Experimental Psychology: General, 117,* 258–275.

Siegler, R. S. (1995). How does change occur: A microgenetic study of number conservation. *Cognitive Psychology, 28,* 225–273.

Siegler, R. S. (1996). *Emerging minds: The process of change in children's thinking.* New York: Oxford University Press.

Siegler, R. S. (2009). Improving the numerical understanding of children from low-income families. *Child Development Perspectives, 3,* 118–124.

Siegler, R. S. and Booth, J. L. (2004). Development of numerical estimation in young children. *Child Development, 75,* 428–444.

Siegler, R. S. and Booth, J. L. (2005). Development of numerical estimation: A review. In J. I. D. Campbell (Ed.), *Handbook of mathematical cognition* (pp. 197–212). Boca Ratan, FL: CRC Press.

Siegler, R. S. and Crowley, K. (1991). The microgenetic method: A direct means for studying cognitive development. *American Psychologist, 46,* 606–620.

Siegler, R. S. and Jenkins, E. A. (1989). *How children discover new strategies.* Hillsdale, NJ: Lawrence Erlbaum Associates.

Siegler, R. S. and Lemaire, P. (1997). Older and younger adults' strategy choices in multiplication: Testing predictions of ASCM via the choice/no choice method. *Journal of Experimental Psychology: General, 126,* 71–92.

Siegler, R. S. and Mu, Y. (2008). Chinese children excel on novel mathematics problems even before elementary school. *Psychological Science, 19,* 759–763.

Siegler, R. S. and Opfer, J. E. (2003). The development of numerical estimation: Evidence for multiple representations of numerical quantity. *Psychological Science, 14,* 237–243.

Siegler, R. S. and Ramani, G. B. (2008). Playing linear numerical board games promotes low-income children's numerical development. *Developmental Science, 11,* 655–661.

Siegler, R. S. and Ramani, G. B. (2009). Playing linear number board games – but not circular ones – improves low-income preschoolers' numerical understanding. *Journal of Educational Psychology, 101,* 545–560.

Siegler, R. S. and Robinson, M. (1982). The development of numerical understandings. In H. W. Reese and L. P. Lipsett (Eds), *Advances in child development and behavior: Vol. 16* (pp. 242–312). New York: Academic Press.

Siegler, R. S. and Shipley, C. (1995). Variation, selection and cognitive change. In T. J. Simon and G. S. Halford (Eds), *Developing cognitive competence : New approaches to process modeling* (pp. 31–76). Hillsdale, NJ: LEA.

Siegler, R. S. and Shrager, J. (1984). Strategy choices in addition and subtraction: How do children know what to do? In C. Sophian (Ed.), *The origins of cognitive skills* (pp. 229–293). Hillsdale, NJ: Lawrence Erlbaum Associates.

Sigman, M., Cohen, S. E. and Beckwith, L. (1997). Why does infant attention predict adolescent intelligence? *Infant Behavior And Development, 20*(2), 133–140.

Sigman, M., Cohen, S. E., Beckwith, L., Asarnow, R. and Parmelee, A. H. (1991). Continuity in cognitive abilities from infancy to 12 years of age. *Cognitive Development, 6,* 47–57.

Sigman, M. D., Cohen, S. E., Beckwith, L. and Parmelee, A. H. (1986). Infant attention in relation to intellectual abilities in childhood. *Developmental Psychology, 22*(6), 788–792.

Simcock, G. and Hayne, H. (2002). Breaking the barrier? Children fail to translate their preverbal memories into language. *Psychological Science, 13*(3), 225–231.

Simon, H. A. and Lea, G. (1974). Problem solving and rule induction: A unified view. In L. W. Gregg (Ed.), *Knowledge and cognition* (pp. 105–128). Hillsdale, NJ: Lawrence Erlbaum Associates.

Singer-Freeman, K. E. (2005). Analogical reasoning in 2-year-olds: The development of access and relational inference. *Cognitive Development, 20*(2), 214–234.

Singer-Freeman, K. E. and Bauer, P. J. (2008). The ABCs of analogical abilities: Evidence for formal analogical reasoning abilities in 24-month-olds. *British Journal of Developmental Psychology, 26,* 317–335.

Skinner, B. F. (1957). *Verbal learning.* New York: Appleton-Century-Crofts.

Skinner, B. F. (1974). *About behaviorism.* New York: Alfred A. Knopf.

Slater, A. (1995). Individual differences in infancy and later IQ. *Journal of Child Psychology and Psychiatry and Allied Disciplines, 36,* 69–112.

Slater, A. and Morison, V. (1985). Shape constancy and slant perception at birth. *Perception, 14*(3), 337–344.

Slater, A., Mattock, A. and Brown, E. (1990). Size constancy at birth: Newborn infants' responses to retinal and real size. *Journal of Experimental Child Psychology, 49*(2), 314–322.

Slater, A., Morison, V. and Rose, D. (1983). Locus of habituation in the human newborn. *Perception, 12*(5), 593–598.

Slater, A., Morison, V., Town, C. and Rose, D. (1985). Movement perception and identity constancy in the new-born baby. *British Journal of Developmental Psychology, 3,* 211–220.

Slaughter, V., Jaakkola, R. O. and Carey, S. (1999). Constructing a coherent theory: Children's biological understanding of life and death. In M. Siegal and C. C. Peterson (Eds), *Children's understanding of biology and health* (pp. 71–96). Cambridge: Cambridge University Press.

Slobin, D. I. (1970). Universals of grammatical development in children. In G. B. Flores d'Arcais and W. J. M. Levelt (Eds), *Advances in psycholinguistics* (pp. 174–186). Amsterdam: North-Holland.

Smith, L. (2002). Piaget's model. In U. Goswami (Ed.), *Blackwell handbook of childhood cognitive development* (pp. 515–537). Oxford: Blackwell.

Smith, M. C. (1978). Cognizing the behavior stream: Recognition of intentional action. *Child Development, 49*(3), 736–743.

Snedeker, J., Geren, J. and Shafto, C. L. (in press) Disentangling the effects of cognitive development and linguistic expertise: A longitudinal study of the acquisition of English in internationally-adopted children. *Cognitive Psychology.*

Sneider, C. and Pulos, S. (1983). Children's cosmographies: Understanding the earth's shape and gravity. *Science Education, 67,* 205–221.

Snow, C. E. (1977). Mother's speech research: From input to interaction. In C. E. Snow and C. A. Ferguson (Eds), *Talking to children: Language input and acquisition* (pp. 31–49). Cambridge: Cambridge University Press.

Snow, C. E., Barnes, W. S., Chandler, J., Hemphill, L. and Goodman, I. F. (1991). *Unfulfilled expectations: Home and school influences on literacy.* Cambridge, MA: Harvard University Press.

Snowling, M. and Frith, U. (1986). Comprehension in 'hyperlexic' readers. *Journal of Experimental Child Psychology, 42,* 392–415.

Snowling, M., Goulandris, N., Bowlby, M. and Howell, P. (1986). Segmentation and speech perception in relation to reading skill: A developmental analysis. *Journal of Experimental Child Psychology, 41*, 489–507.

Snowling, M. J. (1981). Phonemic deficits in developmental dyslexia. *Psychological Research, 43*, 219–234.

Snowling, M. J. (2000). *Dyslexia* (2nd ed.). Oxford: Blackwell.

Snowling, M. J. (2008). *State-of-science review: Dyslexia*. London: Government Office for Science.

Sodian, B. (2005). Theory of mind – the case for conceptual development. In W. Schneider, R. Schumann-Hengsteler and B. Sodian (Eds), *Young children's cognitive development* (pp. 95–130). Mahwah, NJ: Lawrence Erlbaum Associates.

Sodian, B. (2011). Theory of mind in infancy. *Child Development Perspectives, 5*, 39–43.

Sodian, B. and Bullock, M. (2008). Scientific reasoning – where are we now? [Special issue]. *Cognitive Development, 23*(4).

Sodian, B. and Frith, U. (1992). Deception and sabotage in autistic, retarded, and normal children. *Journal of Child Psychology and Psychiatry, 33*, 591–606.

Sodian, B. and Thoermer, C. (2008). Precursors to a theory of mind in infancy: Perspectives for research on autism. *Quarterly Journal of Experimental Psychology, 61*(1), 27–39.

Sodian, B. and Wimmer, H. (1987). Children's understanding of inference as a source of knowledge. *Child Development, 58*(2), 424–433.

Sodian, B., Schneider, W. and Perlmutter, M. (1986). Recall, clustering, and metamemory in young children. *Journal of Experimental Child Psychology, 41*(3), 395–410.

Sodian, B., Taylor, C., Harris, P. L. and Perner, J. (1991). Early deception and the child's theory of mind: False trails and genuine markers. *Child Development, 62*, 468–483.

Sodian, B., Zaitchik, D. and Carey, S. (1991). Young children's differentiation of hypothetical beliefs from evidence. *Child Development, 62*(4), 753–766.

Sokol, S. M., Macaruso, P. and Gollan, T. H. (1994). Developmental dyscalculia and cognitive neuropsychology. *Developmental Neuropsychology, 10*(4), 413–441.

Sommer, M., Dohnel, K., Sodian, B., Meinhardt, J., Thoermer, C. and Hajak, G. (2007). Neural correlates of true and false belief reasoning. *NeuroImage, 35*(3), 1378–1384.

Sparling, J. J. and Lewis, I. (1979). *Learningames for the first three years: A guide to parent-child play*. New York: Walker.

Sparling, J. J. and Lewis, I. (1984). *Learningames for threes and fours: A guide to adult and child play*. New York: Walker.

Spearman, C. (1904). 'General intelligence,' objectively determined and measured. *American Journal of Psychology, 15*, 201–293.

Spearman, C. (1927). *The abilities of man, their nature and achievement*. New York: Macmillan.

Spelke, E. S. (1976). Infants' intermodal perception of events. *Cognitive Psychology, 8*, 553–560.

Spelke, E. S. (1985). Perception of unity, persistence, and identity: Thoughts on infants' conceptions of objects. In J. Mehler and R. Fox (Eds), *Neonate cognition* (pp. 89–113). Hillsdale, NJ: Lawrence Erlbaum Associates.

Spelke, E. S. (1990). Principles of object perception. *Cognitive Science, 14*, 29–56.

Spelke, E. S. (1994). Initial knowledge: Six suggestions. *Cognition, 50*, 431–445.

Spelke, E. S. (1998). Nativism, empiricism, and the origins of knowledge. *Infant Behavior and Development, 21*(2), 181–200.

Spelke, E. S. (2000). Core knowledge. *American Psychologist, 55*, 1233–1243.

Spelke, E. S. and Kinzler, K. D. (2007). Core knowledge. *Developmental Science, 10*, 89–96.

Springer, K. and Keil, F. C. (1989). On the development of biologically specific beliefs: The case of inheritance. *Child Development, 60*(3), 637–648.

Stanovich, K. E. (1988). Explaining the differences between the dyslexic and the garden-variety poor reader: The phonological-core variable-difference model. *Journal of Learning Disabilities, 21*, 590–612.

Stanovich, K. E. and Siegel, L. S. (1994). Phenotypic performance profile of children with reading disabilities: A regression-based test of the phonological-core variable-difference model. *Journal of Educational Psychology, 86*, 24–53.

Stanovich, K. E., West, R. F. and Harrison, M. R. (1995). Knowledge growth and maintenance across the life span: The role of print exposure. *Developmental Psychology, 31*, 811–826.

Stattin, H. and Klackenberg-Larsson, I. (1993). Early language and intelligence development and their relationship to future criminal behavior. *Journal of Abnormal Psychology, 102*, 369–378.

Sternberg, R. J. (1985). *Beyond IQ: A triarchic theory of human intelligence*. New York: Cambridge University Press.

Sternberg, R. J. (1986). GENECES: A framework for intellectual abilities and theories of them. *Intelligence, 10*, 239–250.

Sternberg, R. J. (1988). *The triarchic mind: A new theory of human intelligence*. New York: Viking.

Sternberg, R. J. (1997a). The concept of intelligence and its role in lifelong learning and success. *American Psychologist, 52*, 1030–1037.

Sternberg, R. J. (1997b). The triarchic theory of intelligence. In D. P. Flanagan, J. L. Genshaft and P. L. Harrison (Eds), *Contemporary intellectual assessment: Theories, tests, and issues* (pp. 92–104). New York: Guilford Press.

Sternberg, R. J. (2003). Intelligence: The triarchic theory of intelligence. In J. W. Guthrie (Ed.), *Encyclopedia of education* (2nd ed.) (Vol. 4, pp. 1206–1209). New York: Macmillan.

Sternberg, R. J. and Berg, C. A. (1986). Quantitative integration: Definitions of intelligence: A comparison of the 1921 and 1986 symposia. In R. J. Sternberg and D. K. Detterman (Eds), *What is intelligence? Contemporary viewpoints on its nature and definition* (pp. 155–162). Norwood, NJ: Ablex.

Sternberg, R. J. and Davidson, J. E. (1983). Insight in the gifted. *Educational Psychologist, 18*(1), 51–57.

Sternberg, R. J. and Detterman, D. K. (Eds) (1986). *What is intelligence? Contemporary viewpoints on its nature and definition.* Norwood, NJ: Ablex.

Sternberg, R. J. and Downing, C. J. (1982). The development of higher-order reasoning in adolescence. *Child Development, 53*(1), 209–221.

Sternberg, R. J. and Grigorenko, E. L. (2000). Theme-park psychology: A case study regarding human intelligence and its implications for education. *Educational Psychology Review, 12*(2), 247–268.

Sternberg, R. J. and Grigorenko, E. L. (2006). Cultural intelligence and successful intelligence. *Group and Organization Management, 13*(1), 27–39.

Sternberg, R. J. and Nigro, G. (1980). Developmental patterns in the solution of verbal analogies. *Child Development, 51*(1), 27–38.

Sternberg, R. J., Castejón, J. L., Prieto, M. D., Hautamäki, J. and Grigorenko, E. L. (2001). Confirmatory factor analysis of the Sternberg triarchic abilities test in three international samples: An empirical test of the triarchic theory of intelligence. *European Journal of Psychological Assessment, 17*(1), 1–16.

Streeter, L. A. (1976). Language perception of 2-month-old infants shows effects of both innate mechanisms and experience. *Nature, 259*(5538), 39–41.

Stuart, M. and Coltheart, M. (1988). Does reading develop in a sequence of stages? *Cognition, 30*, 139–181.

Sullivan, K. S., Macaruso, P. and Sokol, S. M. (1996). Remediation of Arabic numeral processing in a case of developmental dyscalculia. *Neuropsychological Rehabilitation, 6*, 27–53.

Surian, L. and Leslie, A. M. (1999). Competence and performance in false belief understanding: A comparison of autistic and normal 3-year-old children. *British Journal of Developmental Psychology, 17*, 141–155.

Swan, D. and Goswami, U. (1997). Picture naming deficits in developmental dyslexia: The phonological representations hypothesis. *Brain and Language, 56*, 334–353.

Szpunar, K. K. (2010). Episodic future thought. *Perspectives on Psychological Science, 5*(2), 142–162.

Szpunar, K. K., Watson, J. M. and McDermott, K. B. (2007). Neural substrates of envisioning the future. *Proceedings of the National Academy of Sciences, 104*(2), 642–647.

Tager-Flusberg, H. (1992). Autistic children's talk about psychological states: Deficits in the early acquisition of a theory of mind. *Child Development, 63*, 161–172.

Tager-Flusberg, H. (2007). Evaluating the theory-of-mind hypothesis of autism. *Current Directions in Psychological Science, 16*, 311–315.

Takeuchi, A. H. and Hulse, S. H. (1993). Absolute pitch. *Psychological Bulletin, 113*(2), 345–361.

Tallal, P. (1980). Auditory temporal perception, phonics, and reading disabilities in children. *Brain and Language, 9*, 182–198.

Temple, C. M. (1991). Procedural dyscalculia and number fact dyscalculia: Double dissociation in developmental dyscalculia. *Cognitive Neuropsychology, 8*, 155–176.

Temple, C. M. and Sherwood, S. (2002). Representation and retrieval of arithmetical facts: Developmental difficulties. *Quarterly Journal of Experimental Psychology, 55A*, 733–752.

Terman, L. M. (1916). *The measurement of intelligence: An explanation of and a complete guide for the use of the Stanford revision and extension of the Binet-Simon Intelligence Scale.* Boston: Houghton Mifflin.

Terman, L. M. and Merrill, N. Q. (1972). *Stanford-Binet Intelligence Scale: 1972 Norms Editions.* Boston, MA: Houghton Mifflin.

Theakston, A. L. (2004). The role of entrenchment in children's and adults' performance on grammaticality judgment tasks. *Cognitive Development, 19*(1), 15–34.

Theakston, A. L., Lieven, E. V. M., Pine, J. M. and Rowland, C. F. (2000). The role of performance limitations in the acquisition of 'mixed' verb-argument structure at stage 1. In M. Perkins and S. Howard (Eds), *New directions in language development and disorders* (pp. 119–128). New York: Plenum.

Theakston, A. L., Lieven, E. V. M., Pine, J. M. and Rowland, C. F. (2001). The role of performance limitations in the acquisition of verb-argument structure: An alternative account. *Journal of Child Language, 28*, 127–152.

Thelen, E. and Ulrich, B. D. (1991). Hidden skills: A dynamic systems analysis of treadmill-elicited stepping during the first year. *Monographs of the Society for Research in Child Development, 56*, No. 223.

Thelen, E., Schöner, G., Scheier, C. and Smith, L. B. (2001). The dynamics of embodiment: A field theory of infant perseverative reaching. *Behavioral and Brain Sciences*, 24, 1–86.

Thomas, M. S. C. and Karmiloff-Smith, A. (2002). Modelling typical and atypical cognitive development. In U. Goswami (Eds), *Handbook of childhood development* (pp. 575–599). Oxford: Blackwell.

Thomas, M. S. C. and Karmiloff-Smith, A. (2003). Modeling language acquisition in atypical phenotypes. *Psychological Review*, 110, 647–682.

Thompson, C. A. and Opfer, J. E. (2010). How 15 hundred is like 15 cherries: Effect of progressive alignment on representational changes in numerical cognition. *Child Development*, 81, 1768–1786.

Thompson, C. A. and Siegler, R. S. (2010). Linear numerical magnitude representations aid children's memory for numbers. *Psychological Science*, 21, 1274–1281.

Thompson, S. P. and Newport, E. L. (2007). Statistical learning of syntax: The role of transitional probability. *Language Learning and Development*, 3, 1–42.

Thorndike, R. L., Hagen, E. P. and Sattler, J. M. (1986). *The Stanford-Binet Intelligence Scale: Fourth edition.* Chicago, IL: Riverside.

Thurstone, L. L. (1938). *Primary mental abilities.* Chicago, IL: University of Chicago Press.

Tomasello, M. (1992). *First verbs: A case study of early grammatical development.* Cambridge: Cambridge University Press.

Tomasello, M. (2000). Do young children have adult syntactic competence? *Cognition*, 74(3), 209–253.

Tomasello, M. and Brooks, P. J. (1999). Early syntactic development: A construction grammar approach. In M. Barrett (Ed.), *The development of language* (pp. 161–190). Hove: Psychology Press.

Topal, J., Gergely, G., Miklosi, A., Erdohegyi, A. and Csibra, G. (2008). Infants' perseverative search errors are induced by pragmatic misinterpretation. *Science*, 321(5897), 1831–1834.

Torff, B. and Gardner, H. (1999). The vertical mind – the case for multiple intelligences. In M. Anderson (Ed.), *The development of intelligence* (pp. 139–159). Hove: Psychology Press.

Trabasso, T. (1977). The role of memory as a system in making transitive inferences. In R. V. Kail, J. W. Hagen and J. M. Belmont (Eds), *Perspectives on the development of memory and cognition* (pp. 333–366). Hillsdale, NJ: Lawrence Erlbaum Associates.

Trabasso, T., Riley, C. A. and Wilson, E. G. (1975). The representation of linear order and spatial strategies in reasoning: A developmental study. In R. J. Falmagne (Ed.), *Reasoning: Representation and process in children and adults* (pp. 201–229). Hillsdale, NJ: Lawrence Erlbaum Associates.

Treffert, D. A. (2006). *Savant syndrome: An extraordinary condition – a synopsis: Past, present, future.* Madison, WI: Wisconsin Medical Society.

Treffert, D. A. (2009). The savant syndrome: An extraordinary condition. A synopsis: Past, present, future. *Philosophical Transactions of the Royal Society of London – Series B: Biological Sciences*, 364(1522), 1351–1357.

Trehub, S. E. (1976). The discrimination of foreign speech contrasts by infants and adults. *Child Development*, 47, 466–472.

Trehub, S. E., Schneider, B. and Endman, M. (1980). Developmental changes in infants' sensitivity to octave-band noises. *Journal of Experimental Child Psychology*, 29, 282–293.

Trehub, S. E., Schneider, B. A., Morrongiello, B. A. and Thorpe, L. A. (1988). Auditory sensitivity in school-age children. *Journal of Experimental Child Psychology*, 46, 273–285.

Tschirgi, J. E. (1980). Sensible reasoning: A hypothesis about hypotheses. *Child Development*, 51(1), 1–10.

Tulving, E. (1983). *Elements of episodic memory.* New York: Oxford University Press.

Valian, V. (1986). Syntactic categories in the speech of young children. *Developmental Psychology*, 22, 562–579.

Valian, V. (1990). Null subjects: A problem for parameter-setting models of language acquisition. *Cognition*, 35, 105–122.

Valian, V. (1991). Syntactic subjects in the early speech of American and Italian children. *Cognition*, 40, 21–81.

van Ijzendoorn, M. H. and Bus, A. G. (1994). Meta-analytic confirmation of the nonword reading deficit in developmental dyslexia. *Reading Research Quarterly*, 29, 266–275.

Vargha-Khadem, F., Gadian, D. G., Watkins, K. E., Connelly, A., Van Paesschen, W. and Mishkin, M. (1997). Differential effects of early hippocampal pathology on episodic and semantic memory. *Science*, 277(5324), 376–380.

Vilette, B. (2002). Do young children grasp the inverse relationship between addition and subtraction? Evidence against early arithmetic. *Cognitive Development*, 17, 1365–1383.

Vinden, P. (1999). Children's understanding of mind and emotion: A multi-culture study. *Cognition and Emotion*, 13, 19–48.

von Aster, M. (1994). Developmental dyscalculia in children: Review of the literature and clinical validation. *Acta Paedopsychiatrica*, 56, 169–178.

Von Frisch, K. (1967). *The dance language and orientation of bees.* Ithaca, NY: Cornell University Press.

Von Frisch, K. (1974). Decoding the language of bees. *Science*, 185(4152), 663–668.

Vosniadou, S. and Brewer, W. F. (1992). Mental models of the earth: A study of conceptual change in childhood. *Cognitive Psychology, 24*, 535–585.

Vygotsky, L. S. (1978). *Mind in society*. Cambridge, MA: Harvard University Press.

Walk, R. D. (1966). The development of depth perception in animals and human infants. *Monographs of the Society for Research in Child Development, 31*(5), 82–108.

Walker, C. H. (1987). Relative importance of domain knowledge and overall aptitude on acquisition of domain-related information. *Cognition and Instruction, 4*(1), 25–42.

Walton, G. E., Bower, N. J. A. and Bower, T. G. R. (1992). Recognition of familiar faces by newborns. *Infant Behavior and Development, 15*(2), 265–269.

Wang, S. and Baillargeon, R. (2005). Inducing infants to detect a physical violation in a single trial. *Psychological Science, 16*, 542–549.

Wang, S., Baillargeon, R. and Brueckner, L. (2004). Young infants' reasoning about hidden objects: Evidence from violation-of-expectation tasks with test trials only. *Cognition, 93*, 167–198.

Ward, S. L. and Overton, W. F. (1990). Semantic familiarity, relevance, and the development of deductive reasoning. *Developmental Psychology, 26*(3), 488–493.

Warrington, E. K. and Shallice, T. (1972). Neuropsychological evidence of visual storage in short-term memory tasks. *The Quarterly Journal of Experimental Psychology, 24*, 30–40.

Wason, P. C. (1966). Reasoning. In B. M. Foss (Ed.), *New horizons in psychology, I* (pp. 135–151). Harmondsworth: Penguin.

Wason, P. C. and Johnson-Laird, P. N. (1972). *Psychology of reasoning: Structure and content*. London: Batsford.

Wason, P. C. and Shapiro, D. (1971). Natural and contrived experience in a reasoning problem. *Quarterly Journal of Experimental Psychology, 23*, 63–71.

Waters, H. S. (2000). Memory strategy development: Do we need yet another deficiency? *Child Development, 71*(4), 1004–1012.

Watson, J. B. (1926). What the nursery has to say about instincts. In C. Murchison (Ed.), *Psychologies of 1925* (pp. 1–34). Worcester, MA: Clark University Press.

Wechsler, D. (1967). *Wechsler preschool and primary scale of intelligence*. New York: The Psychological Corporation.

Wechsler, D. (1981). *Wechsler adult intelligence test – revised*. Allen, TX: Psychological Corporation.

Wechsler, D. (1991). *Wechsler intelligence scale for children – third edition: Canadian (WISC-III)*. Toronto: Psychological Corporation.

Wechsler, D. (2002). *Wechsler primary and preschool scale of intelligence, 3rd edition*. San Antonio, TX: Harcourt Assessment.

Wechsler, D. (2003). *Wechsler intelligence scale for children, 4th Edition*. San Antonio, TX: Harcourt Assessment.

Wechsler, D. (2008). *Wechsler adult intelligence scale, 4th Edition*. San Antonio, TX: Pearson.

Wellman, H. M. (1977a). Tip of the tongue and feeling of knowing experiences: A developmental study of memory monitoring. *Child Development, 48*(1), 13–21.

Wellman, H. M. (1977b). Preschoolers' understanding of memory-relevant variables. *Child Development, 48*(4), 1720–1723.

Wellman, H. M. (2002). Understanding the psychological world: Developing a theory of mind. In U. Goswami (Ed.), *Blackwell handbook of childhood cognitive development* (pp. 167–187). Oxford: Blackwell.

Wellman, H. M. and Bartsch, K. (1988). Young children's reasoning about beliefs. *Cognition, 30*(3), 239–277.

Wellman, H. M. and Bartsch, K. (1994). Before belief: Children's early psychological theory. In C. Lewis and P. Mitchell (Eds), *Children's early understanding of mind* (pp. 331–354). Hove: Lawrence Erlbaum Associates.

Wellman, H. M. and Cross, D. (2001). Theory of mind and conceptual change. *Child Development, 72*(3), 702–707.

Wellman, H. M. and Gelman, S. A. (1992). Cognitive development: Foundational theories of core domains. *Annual Review of Psychology, 43*, 337–375.

Wellman, H. M. and Gelman, S. A. (1998). Knowledge acquisition in foundational domains. In D. Kuhn and R. S. Siegler (Eds), *Handbook of child psychology, Vol. 2: Cognition, perception, and language* (pp. 523–573). New York: Wiley.

Wellman, H. M. and Woolley, J. D. (1990). From simple desires to ordinary beliefs: The early development of everyday psychology. *Cognition, 35*(3), 245–275.

Wellman, H. M., Cross, D. and Watson, J. (2001). Meta-analysis of theory-of-mind development: The truth about false belief. *Child Development, 72*(3), 655–684.

Wellman, H. M., Hickling, A. K. and Schult, C. A. (1997). Young children's psychological, physical, and biological explanations. *New Directions for Child Development, 75*, 7–25.

Wells, G. (1981). *Learning through interaction*. Cambridge: Cambridge University Press.

Werker, J. F. and Desjardins, R. N. (1995). Listening to speech in the first year of life: Experiential influences on phoneme perception. *Current Directions in Psychological Sciences, 4*(3), 76–81.

Werker, J. F. and Lalonde, C. E. (1988). Cross-language speech perception: Initial capabilities and developmental change. *Developmental Psychology*, 24(4) 672–683.

Werker, J. F. and Tees, R. C. (2002). Cross-language speech perception: Evidence for perceptual reorganization during the first year of life. *Infant Behavior and Development*, 25(1), 121–133.

Werker, J. F., Shi, R., Desjardins, R., Pegg, J., Polka, L. and Patterson, M. (1998). Three methods for testing infant speech perception. In A. Slater (Ed.), *Perceptual development in infancy* (pp. 389–420). Hove: Psychology Press.

Westermann, G. (1997). A constructivist neural network learns the past tense of English verbs. *Proceedings of the GALA '97 conference on language acquisition*. Edinburgh: HCRC.

Westermann, G. (1998). Emergent modularity and U-shaped learning in a constructivist neural network learning the English past tense. *Proceedings of the 20th annual conference of the Cognitive Science Society*. Hillsdale, NJ: Lawrence Erlbaum Associates.

Wexler, K. (1994). Optional infinitives, head movement and the economy of derivations in child grammar. In D. Lightfoot and N. Hornstein (Eds), *Verb movement* (pp. 305–350). Cambridge: Cambridge University Press.

Wexler, K. (1996). The development of inflection in a biologically based theory of language acquisition. In M. L. Rice (Ed.), *Toward a genetics of language* (pp. 113–144). Hillsdale, NJ: Lawrence Erlbaum Associates.

Wheeler, M. A. (2000). Episodic memory and autonoetic awareness. In E. Tulving and F. I. Craik (Eds), *The Oxford handbook of memory* (pp. 597–608). New York: Oxford University Press.

White, S., Milne, E., Rosen, S., Hansen, P., Swettenham, J., Frith, U. and Ramus, F. (2006). The role of sensorimotor impairments in dyslexia: A multiple case study of dyslexic children. *Developmental Science*, 9(3), 237–269.

Wickelgren, W. A. (1969). Context-sensitive coding in speech recognition, articulation, and development. In K. N. Leibovic (Ed.), *Information processing in the nervous system* (pp. 85–95). New York: Springer-Verlag.

Wilkinson, G. S. (1993). *Wide range achievement test* (3rd ed.). Wilmington, DE: Wide Range.

Willcutt, E. G., Doyle, A. E., Nigg, J. T., Faraone, S. V. and Pennington, B. F. (2005). Validity of the executive function theory of attention-deficit/hyperactivity disorder: A meta-analytic review. *Biological Psychiatry*, 57, 1336–1346.

Williams, J., Waiter, G., Gilchrist, A., Perrett, D., Murray, A. and Whiten, A. (2006). Neural mechanisms of imitation and 'mirror neuron' functioning in autism spectrum disorders. *Neuropsychologia*, 44, 610–621.

Wilson, A. J., Revkin, S. K., Cohen, D., Cohen, L. and Dehaene, S. (2006). An open trial assessment of 'The Number Race', an adaptive computer game for remediation of dyscalculia. *Behavioral and Brain Functions*, 2(20), 1–16.

Wilson, C. and Dupuis, A. (1992). *Poverty and performance. Set: Research information for teachers*. Wellington, New Zealand: New Zealand Council for Educational Research.

Wilson, J. T. L., Scott, J. H. and Power, K. G. (1987). Developmental differences in the span of visual memory for pattern. *British Journal of Developmental Psychology*, 5, 249–255.

Wimmer, H. and Hartl, M. (1991). Against the cartesian view on mind: Young children's difficulty with own false beliefs. *British Journal of Developmental Psychology*, 9, 125–138.

Wimmer, H. and Perner, J. (1983). Beliefs about beliefs: Representation and constraining function of wrong beliefs in young children's understanding of deception. *Cognition*, 13(1), 103–128.

Wimmer, H., Hogrefe, G. J. and Perner, J. (1988). Children's understanding of informational access as source of knowledge. *Child Development*, 59(2), 386–396.

Wimmer, H., Hogrefe, J. and Sodian, B. (1988). A second stage in children's conception of mental life: Understanding informational accesses as origins of knowledge and belief. In J. W. Astington, P. L. Harris and D. R. Olson (Eds), *Developing theories of mind* (pp. 173–192). Cambridge: Cambridge University Press.

Winer, G. A. (1974). A conservation of different quantities among preschool children. *Child Development*, 45, 839–842.

Winer, G. A. and Cottrell, J. E. (1996). Does anything leave the eye when we see? Extramission beliefs of children and adults. *Current Directions in Psychological Science*, 5(5), 137–142.

Wing, L. (1976). *Early childhood autism*. New York: Pergamon Press.

Wing, L. and Gould, J. (1979). Severe impairments of social interaction and associated abnormalities in children: Epidemiology and classification. *Journal of Autism and Developmental Disorders*, 9, 11–29.

Witkin, H., Oltman, P., Raskin, E. and Karp, S. (1971). *A manual for the embedded figures test*. Palo Alto, CA: Consulting Psychologists Press, Inc.

Wober, M. (1974). Towards an understanding of the Kiganda concept of intelligence. In J. W. Berry and P. R. Dasen (Eds), *Culture and cognition: Readings in cross-cultural psychology* (pp. 261–280). London: Methuen.

Wolraich, M. L. *et al.* (1996). Comparison of diagnostic criteria for ADHD in a countrywide sample. *Journal of the America Academy of Child and Adolescent Psychiatry, 35,* 319–324.

Wood, D. (1998). *How children think and learn* (2nd ed.). Oxford: Blackwell Publishing.

Wood, D. and Middleton, D. (1975). A study of assisted problem solving. *British Journal of Psychology, 66,* 181–191.

Wood, D. J., Bruner, J. S. and Ross, G. (1976). The role of tutoring in problem solving. *Journal of Child Psychology and Psychiatry, 17,* 89–100.

Woodward, A. L. and Markman, E. M. (1998). Early word learning. In W. Damon, D. Kuhn and R. S. Siegler (Eds), *Handbook of child psychology, Volume 2: Cognition, perception and language* (pp. 371–420). New York: Wiley.

Woodworth, R. S. and Sells, S. B. (1935). An atmosphere effect in syllogistic reasoning. *Journal of Experimental Psychology, 18,* 451–460.

Wynn, K. (1992a). Addition and subtraction by human infants. *Nature, 358*(6389), 749–750.

Wynn, K. (1992b). Evidence against empiricist accounts of the origins of numerical knowledge. *Mind and Language, 7,* 315–332.

Wynn, K. (1995a). Infants possess a system of numerical knowledge. *Current Directions in Psychological Science, 4,* 172–177.

Wynn, K. (1995b). Origins of numerical knowledge. *Mathematical Cognition, 1,* 35–60.

Wynn, K. (1998). Psychological foundations of number: Numerical competence in human infants. *Trends in Cognitive Sciences, 2,* 296–303.

Yang, S. and Sternberg, R. J. (1997a). Conceptions of intelligence in ancient Chinese philosophy. *Journal of Theoretical and Philosophical Psychology, 17*(2), 101–119.

Yang, S. and Sternberg, R. J. (1997b). Taiwanese Chinese people's conceptions of intelligence. *Intelligence, 25,* 21–36.

Yonas, A. and Granrud, C. E. (2006). Infants' perception of depth from cast shadows. *Perception and Psychophysics, 68,* 154–160.

Yonas, A., Bechtold, A. G., Frankel, D., Gordon, F. R., McRoberts, G., Norcia, A. and Sternfels, S. (1977). Development of sensitivity to information for impending collision. *Perception and Psychophysics, 21*(2), 97–104.

Yonas, A., Granrud, C. E. and Pettersen, L. (1985). Infants' sensitivity to relative size information for distance. *Developmental Psychology, 21,* 161–167.

Yonas, A., Pettersen, L. and Granrud, C. E. (1982). Infants' sensitivity to familiar size as information for distance. *Child Development, 53,* 1285–1290.

Yonas, A., Pettersen, L. and Lockman, J. J. (1979). Young infant's sensitivity to optical information for collision. *Canadian Journal of Psychology, 33*(4), 268–276.

Yopp, H. (1988). The validity and reliability of phonemic awareness tests. *Reading Research Quarterly, 23,* 159–177.

Yu, C. and Smith, L. B. (2007). Rapid word learning under uncertainty via cross-situational statistics. *Psychological Science, 18*(5), 414–420.

Zago, L., Pesenti, M., Mellet, E., Crivello, F., Mazoyer, B. and Tzourio-Mazoyer, N. (2001). Neural correlates of simple and complex mental calculation. *NeuroImage, 13,* 314–327.

Zaitchik, D. (1990). When representations conflict with reality: The preschooler's problem with false beliefs and 'false' photographs. *Cognition, 35,* 41–68.

Zelazo, P. D., Frye, D. and Rapus, T. (1996). An age-related dissociation between knowing rules and using them. *Cognitive Development, 11,* 37–63.

Zhou, X., Huang, J., Wang, Z., Wang, B., Zhao, Z., Yang, L. and Zhengzheng, Y. (2006). Parent-child interaction and children's number learning. *Early Child Development and Care, 176,* 763–775.

Zigler, E. F. and Finn-Stevenson, M. (1999). Applied developmental psychology. In M. H. Bornstein and M. E. Lamb (Eds), *Developmental psychology: An advanced textbook* (4th ed.) (pp. 555–598). Mahwah, NJ: Lawrence Erlbaum Associates.

Zimmerman, C. (2007). The development of scientific thinking skills in elementary and middle school. *Developmental Review, 27*(2), 172–223.

Zimmerman, C. and Glaser, R. (2001). *Testing positive versus negative claims: A preliminary investigation of the role of cover story in the assessment of experimental design skills (Tech. Rep. No. 554).* Los Angeles, CA: UCLA National Center for Research on Evaluation, Standards, and Student Testing (CRESST).

Zimmerman, C., Raghavan, K. and Sartoris, M. L. (2003). The impact of the MARS curriculum on students' ability to coordinate theory and evidence. *International Journal of Science Education, 25*(10), 1247–1271.

Index